Fodor's 2000

Costa Rica

D0004525

The complete guide, thoroughly up-to-date

Packed with details that will make your trip

The must-see sights, off and on the beaten path

What to see, what to skip

Mix-and-match vacation itineraries

City strolls, countryside adventures

Smart lodging and dining options

Essential local do's and taboos

Transportation tips, distances and directions

Key contacts, savvy travel tips

When to go, what to pack

Clear, accurate, easy-to-use maps

Fodor's Travel Publications, Inc. • New York, Toronto, London, Sydney, Auckland
www.fodors.com

Costa Rica 2000

EDITOR: Caragh Matthews Rockwood

Editorial Contributors: Stephanie Adler, Robert Blake, David Dudenhoefer, Richard Garrigues, Justin Henderson, Helayne Schiff

Editorial Production: Melissa Klurman

Maps: David Lindroth, *cartographer*; Steven K. Amsterdam, *map editor*

Design: Fabrizio La Rocca, *creative director*; Guido Caroti, *associate art director*; Jolie Novak, *picture editor*

Production/Manufacturing: Robert B. Shields

Cover Photograph: Buddy Mays/Travel Stock

Copyright

Important Tip

Although all prices, opening times, and other details in this book are
based on information supplied to us at press time, changes occur all
the time in the travel world, and Fodor's cannot accept responsibility
for facts that become outdated or for inadvertent errors or omissions.
So **always confirm information when it matters,** especially if you're making a detour to visit a specific place.

Special Sales

Fodor's Travel Publications are available at special discounts for bulk
purchases for sales promotions or premiums. Special editions, including personalized covers, excerpts of existing guides, and corporate im-
prints, can be created in large quantities for special needs. For more
information, contact your local bookseller or write to Special Markets,
Fodor's Travel Publications, 201 East 50th Street, New York, NY
10022. Inquiries from Canada should be directed to your local Canadian bookseller or sent to Random House of Canada, Ltd., Market-
ing Department, 2775 Matheson Boulevard East, Mississauga, Ontario
L4W 4P7. Inquiries from the United Kingdom should be sent to Fodor's
Travel Publications, 20 Vauxhall Bridge Road, London SW1V 2SA,
England.

CONTENTS

On the Road with Fodor's   vi

About Our Writers *vi*
How to Use This Book *vi*
Don't Forget to Write *vii*

Smart Travel Tips A to Z   xii

1   Destination: Costa Rica   1

Costa Rica: Land of Pleasant Surprises *2*
A Brief History *3*
New and Noteworthy *4*
What's Where *5*
Pleasures and Pastimes *7*
Fodor's Choice *11*

2   San José   13

Exploring San José *15*
Dining *23*
Lodging *28*
Nightlife and the Arts *31*
Outdoor Activities and Sports *32*
Shopping *33*
San José A to Z *34*

3   Central Valley: Around San José   37

Western Central Valley *41*
Eastern Central Valley *51*
Orosi Valley *53*
Turrialba and the Guayabo National Monument *55*
Central Valley: Around San José A to Z *58*

4   Northern Guanacaste and Alajuela   61

Arenal and the Cordillera de Tilarán *66*
Far Northern Guanacaste *78*
Northern Guanacaste and Alajuela A to Z *84*

5   Nicoya Peninsula   87

Puntarenas to Cabo Blanco *93*
Nicoya and the Tempisque River Delta Region *98*
Central Nicoya Beaches: Punta Islita to Nosara *101*
Liberia and the Northern Nicoya Beaches *104*
Nicoya Peninsula A to Z *116*

6 Central Pacific Costa Rica 120

Central Pacific Hinterlands *122*
Coast Near San José *126*
Central Pacific Costa Rica A to Z *134*

7 Southern Pacific Costa Rica 137

General Valley *141*
Osa Peninsula *151*
Southern Pacific Costa Rica A to Z *156*

8 The Atlantic Lowlands
and the Caribbean Coast 160

Braulio Carrillo National Park and the Northern Lowlands *165*
Tortuguero and Barra del Colorado *169*
Coastal Talamanca *173*
The Atlantic Lowlands and the Caribbean Coast A to Z *182*

9 Excursions to Panama and Nicaragua 185

Panama *186*
Chiriquí Province *188*
Bocas del Toro Archipelago *199*
Nicaragua *206*
Southwestern Nicaragua *208*

10 National Parks and Biological Reserves 215

Central Valley: Around San José *218*
Northern Guanacaste and Alajuela *219*
Nicoya Peninsula *221*
Central Pacific Costa Rica *222*
Southern Pacific Costa Rica *223*
Atlantic Lowlands and The Caribbean Coast *225*
Panama *227*
Nicaragua *228*

11 Portraits of Costa Rica 230

A Biological Superpower *231*
Wildlife Glossary *238*
Books and Videos *241*

Index 242

Maps

Costa Rica *viii–ix*
Central America *x–xi*
San José *18*
San José Dining and Lodging *24*
Central Valley: Around San José
  40
Northern Guanacaste
  and Alajuela *65*

Nicoya Peninsula *92*
Central Pacific Costa Rica *123*
Southern Pacific Costa Rica *140*
The Atlantic Lowlands and the
  Caribbean Coast *164*
Chiriquí Province and the Bocas
  del Toro Archipelago *189*
Southwestern Nicaragua *209*

ON THE ROAD WITH FODOR'S

EVERY Y2K TRIP IS A SIGNIFICANT trip. So if there was ever a time you needed excellent travel information, it's now. Acutely aware of that fact, we've pulled out all stops in preparing *Fodor's Costa Rica 2000.* To guide you in putting together your Costa Rican experience, we've created multiday itineraries and neighborhood walks. And to direct you to the places that are truly worth your time and money in this important year, we've rallied the team of endearingly picky know-it-alls we're pleased to call our writers. Having seen all corners of Costa Rica, they're real experts. If you knew them, you'd poll them for tips yourself.

Freelance hack **David Dudenhoefer** has spent the better part of the past decade in Central America. Based in San José, he travels regularly within the isthmus, writing about everything from surfing to presidential summits. His articles have appeared in about two dozen publications in North, Central, and South America. He is a regular Fodor's contributor and is the author of *The Panama Traveler.* When not chained to his computer, he can usually be found wandering through the woods, playing in the waves, or propping up the bar at one of San José's seedier nightspots.

Richard Garrigues has resided in Costa Rica since 1981, and for most of those years he has made a living as a naturalist guide. His touring has taken him to every corner of the country, and given him the fantastic opportunity to get to know its vast and varied flora and fauna, including the creatures listed in the Wildlife Glossary, which he wrote for this edition. He's still hoping to cross paths some day with one of the big cats.

Surfing through Guanacaste every winter and dodging man-eating crocodiles, photogenic turtles, and ill-mannered gringo surfers, **Justin Henderson** still finds time to uncover new territory for Fodor's when not tearing up Costa Rica's epic waves. Back home in Seattle, he writes books and magazine articles on travel, architecture, and design, and lives happily ever after with photographer Donna Day and Paco

the wonder dog, the smartest standard poodle in this sector of the galaxy.

The editor would like to extend warm thanks to Temptress Adventure Cruises and its superb staff for a spectacular journey to the Osa Penisula aboard the *Temptress Explorer.*

How to Use This Book

Organization

Up front is **Smart Travel Tips A to Z,** an easy-to-use section arranged alphabetically by topic. Under each listing you'll find tips and information that will help you accomplish what you need to in Costa Rica. You'll also find addresses and telephone numbers of organizations and companies that offer destination-related services and detailed information and publications.

The first chapter in the guide, Destination: Costa Rica helps get you in the mood for your trip. New and Noteworthy cues you in on trends and happenings, What's Where gets you oriented, Pleasures and Pastimes describes the activities and sights that make Costa Rica unique, and Fodor's Choice showcases our top picks.

The second chapter in *Fodor's Costa Rica 2000* covers San José, with all of the following chapters after Chapter 3 circling counterclockwise around the capital. The San José chapter begins with an Exploring section subdivided by neighborhood; each subsection recommends a walking or driving tour and lists sights in alphabetical order. Each regional chapter is divided by geographical area; within each area, towns are covered in logical geographical order, and attractive stretches of road and minor points of interest between them are indicated by the designation *En Route.* And within town sections, all restaurants and lodgings are grouped.

To help you decide what to visit in the time you have, all chapters begin with our recommended itineraries. The A to Z section that ends all chapters covers getting there and getting around. It also provides helpful contacts and resources. At the end of the book you'll find Portraits, with a won-

derful essay about the biodiversity of
Costa Rica, a useful Wildlife Glossary,
and a Costa Rica book and film primer
called Books and Videos.

Don't Forget to Write

Keeping a travel guide fresh and up-to-date
is a big job. So we love your feedback—
positive and negative—and follow up on
all suggestions. Contact the Costa Rica ed-

itor at editors@fodors.com or c/o Fodor's,
201 East 50th Street, New York, New
York 10022. And have a wonderful trip!

Karen Cure
Editorial Director

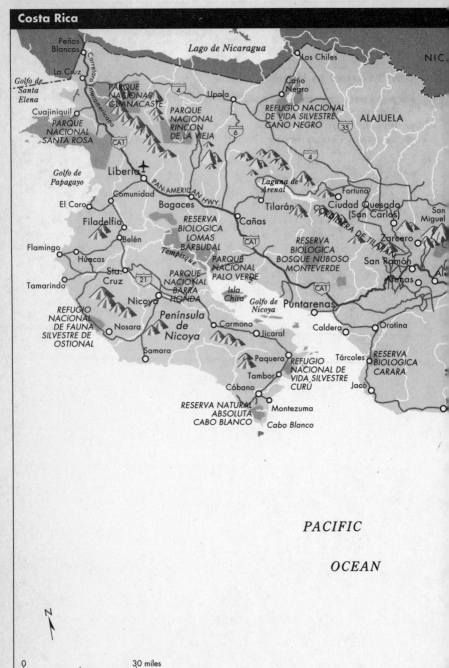

Costa Rica

Peñas Blancas

Lago de Nicaragua

Los Chiles

NIC.

La Cruz

Golfo de Santa Elena

Cuajiniquil

PARQUE NACIONAL GUANACASTE

Carretera Interamericana

4

Upala

Caño Negro

REFUGIO NACIONAL DE VIDA SILVESTRE CAÑO NEGRO

35

ALAJUELA

PARQUE NACIONAL SANTA ROSA

PARQUE NACIONAL RINCON DE LA VIEJA

6

CAT

4

Liberia

Golfo de Papagayo

PAN-AMERICAN HWY

Laguna de Arenal

Fortuna

El Coro

Comunidad

Bagaces

Tilarán

Ciudad Quesada (San Carlos)

San Miguel

Filadelfia

Belén

Cañas

RESERVA BIOLOGICA LOMAS BARBUDAL

CORDILLERA DE TILARÁN

Zarcero

Flamingo

Huacas

Tempisque

CAT

RESERVA BIOLOGICA BOSQUE NUBOSO MONTEVERDE

San Ramón

Tamarindo

Sta. Cruz

21

PARQUE NACIONAL PALO VERDE

Al

PARQUE NACIONAL BARRA HONDA

Isla Chira

CAT

Arenas

Nicoya

Golfo de Nicoya

Puntarenas

REFUGIO NACIONAL DE FAUNA SILVESTRE DE OSTIONAL

Nosara

Península de Nicoya

Carmona

Jicaral

Caldera

Orotina

Samara

Paquera

REFUGIO NACIONAL DE VIDA SILVESTRE CURÚ

Tárcoles

RESERVA BIOLOGICA CARARA

Tambor

Cóbano

Jacó

RESERVA NATURAL ABSOLUTA CABO BLANCO

Montezuma

Cabo Blanco

PACIFIC

OCEAN

N

0   30 miles

0   45 km

ARAGUA

Río San Juan

Río Saraquí

Río Colorado

REFUGIO NACIONAL
DE FAUNA SILVESTRE
BARRA DEL
COLORADO

Tortuguero

Puerto Viejo
de Sarapiquí

Cariari

PARQUE
NACIONAL
TORTUGUERO

La
Virgen

*LA SELVA
RESERVE*

Guápiles

Cinchona

Río Reventazón

PARQUE
NACIONAL
BRAULIO
CARRILLO

4

32

ajuela

Heredia

Siquirres

Río

32

Moín

10

Puerto
Limón

*Caribbean
Sea*

San José

MONUMENTO
NACIONAL
GUAYABO

Cartago

CA2

Pacayas

Turrialba

Cahuita

Puerto Viejo
de Limón

PARQUE
NACIONAL
CHIRRIPÓ

PARQUE
NACIONAL
CAHUITA

Manzanillo

Bribri

Sixaola

San Marcos

Santa
María

CORDILLERA DE TALAMANCA

RESERVA DE
LA BIOSFERA
LA AMISTAD

Parrita

San Isidro
de El General

PANAMA

Quepos

CA2

Ujarrás

PARQUE NACIONAL
MANUEL
ANTONIO

Salitre

Dominical

Buenos
Aires

Uvita

Paso Real

Palmar Norte

Palmar Sur

San
Vito

Carretera Interamericana
(Pan-American Hwy.)

CA2

Río
Claro

Neily

*Drake
Bay*

Rincón

Golfito

*Península
de Osa*

*Golfo
Dulce*

Paso
Canoas

PARQUE NACIONAL
CORCOVADO

Puerto
Jiménez

Zancudo

Carate

Matapalo

Pavones

x

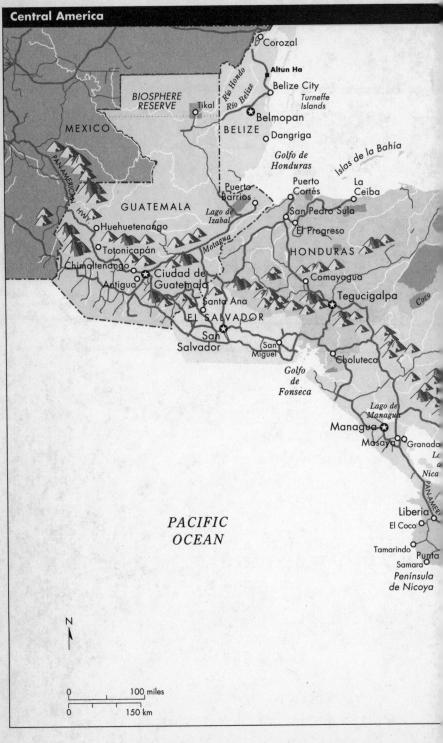

JAMAICA

*Caribbean
Sea*

A

Bluefields

*Bahía
Punta Gorda*

STA
CA

Tortuguero

Chirripó

Puerto
Limón

Heredia
né
Cartago

Changuinolo

Colón

El Porvenir

*Panama
Canal*

Ciudad de
Panama

*Golfo de los
Mosquitos*

Bocas
de Toro

CORDILLERA
TALAMANCA

inical

*Lago
Bayano*

ía de
nado

Golfito

DO N. P.

David

PANAMA

Santiago

*Bahía de
Panamá*

Chuchnaque

*Península
de Osa*

*Golfo de
Chiriqui*

Chitré

*Isla del
Rey*

*Golfo de
Panamá*

Las Tablas

*Isla de
Coiba*

SMART TRAVEL TIPS A TO Z

Basic Information on Traveling in Costa Rica, Panama, and Nicaragua, Savvy Tips to Make Your Trip a Breeze, and Companies and Organizations to Contact

AIR TRAVEL

BOOKING YOUR FLIGHT

When you book **look for nonstop flights** and **remember that "direct" flights stop at least once.** Try to avoid connecting flights, which require a change of plane.

CARRIERS

Given the nations' often difficult driving conditions—what may appear to be a small distance on a map can represent hours of driving time on dirt roads pocked with moon-craters—**consider flying, which, depending on your itinerary, may not cost that much more than renting a car.** Expansion of flights between different regions of Costa Rica means that you can see much of the country by taking domestic flights, which could save days of driving or busing.

Two domestic airlines—Sansa and Travelair—serve Costa Rica, and the Panamanian domestic airline, Aeroperlas, connects major cities within that country and also has five flights a week between Costa Rica and Panama. Sansa is considerably cheaper but its planes sometimes take off late.

➤ MAJOR AIRLINES: **American** (☎ 800/433–7300). **Continental** (☎ 800/231–0856). **Delta** (☎ 800/221–1212). **United** (☎ 800/827–7777). **US Airways** (☎ 800/428–4322).

➤ SMALLER AIRLINES: **Aviateca Guatemala** (☎ 800/327–9832). **Lacsa Costa Rican** (☎ 800/225–2272). **LTU** (☎ 800/888–0200). **Mexicana** (☎ 800/531–7921). **Nica** (☎ 800/831–6422). **TACA Salvadoran** (☎ 800/535–8780).

WITHIN CENTRAL AMERICA

Sansa flies out of Juan Santamaría International Airport, near Alajuela, to the following destinations in Costa Rica: Barra del Colorado, Coto 47, Golfito, La Fortuna, Liberia, Nosara, Palmar Sur, Puerto Jiménez, Punta Islita, Quepos, Samara, Tamarindo, Tambor, and Tortuguero. It also have flights between Quepos and Palmar Sur and between La Fortuna and Tamarindo. One-way fares range from $35 to $55. **Travelair** has daily flights from Tobias Bolaños Airport, in the San José suburb of Pavas, to the following destinations: Carrillo, Golfito/Puerto Jiménez, La Fortuna, Liberia, Palmar Sur, Punta Islita, Quepos, Tamarindo, Tambor, and Tortuguero. More than a dozen flights also go between those destinations, which saves travelers from returning to San José. Prices range from $51 for the one-way hop between San José and Quepos to $93 for a one-way trip to Liberia.

Aeroperlas, Panama's main domestic airline, has five direct flights Monday through Friday between David and San José that connect to direct flights to Bocas del Toro, Changuinola, and Panama City. Aeroperlas also has daily flights between David, Changuinola, Bocas del Toro, and Panama City, from where flights depart to Contadora and the Darien Gap. **Aerotaxi** has daily flights to about a dozen airstrips in the San Blas Islands region.

Grupo Taca offers two flights a day from San José to Managua, Nicaragua, and back. The cost is about $200 per person plus a $20 exit tax at each end. The flights leave San José at 6:30 AM and 2 PM.

➤ AIRLINES: **Aeroperlas** (Costa Rica, ☎ 506/440–0093; 507/269–4555). **Aerotaxi** (Panama, ☎ 507/264–8844). **Grupo Taca** Costa Rica, ☎ 506/296–0909; Panama, ☎ 505/266–3136). **Sansa** (✉ Costa Rica,

☎ 506/221–9414 or 506/441–8035).
Travelair (Pavas, Costa Rica, ☎ 506/
220–3054).

FROM THE U.K.

American Airlines flies from
Heathrow to Miami, from where
flights leave to San José. **British Airways** has a weekly flight from
Gatwick to San José via Puerto Rico.
It's possible to fly London–San José
on **Iberia**, but you have to change
planes in Madrid and Miami. **United
Airlines** flies from Heathrow to Washington, D.C., from where another
flight leaves to Costa Rica via Mexico.
Virgin Atlantic goes from Gatwick to
Miami, from where several airlines
have direct flights to San José.

➤ FROM THE U.K.: **American Airlines**
(☎ 0345/789–789). **British Airways**
(☎ 0345/222–111). **Iberia** (☎
0171/830–0011). **Virgin Atlantic**
(☎ 01293/747–747).

CHARTER FLIGHTS

Several charter companies in San José,
Travelair included, offer charter flights
to places not served by scheduled
flights. The seaplane service Alas
Anfibias offers charters flights to spots
that lie far from airfields, such as
Drake Bay, Lake Arenal, and distant
Cocos Island. Helicópteros de Costa
Rica provides helicopter service.

➤ CHARTER COMPANIES: **Aero Costa
Sol** (☎ 506/440–1444). **Aerolineas
Turisticas** (☎ 506/232–1125). **Aeronaves** (☎ 506/282–4033 in San José,
☎ 506/775–0278 in Golfito). **Helicópteros de Costa Rica** (☎ 506/
232–7534).

CHECK-IN & BOARDING

Airlines ask passengers to **check in
two hours before departure** time for
international flights. If you arrive less
than an hour before your flight is
scheduled to leave, you will not be
allowed to board. When you fly out
of Costa Rica, you have to pay a
$16.50 airport departure tax at Juan
Santamaría Airport (☞ Taxes,
below).

Assuming that not everyone with a
ticket will show up, airlines routinely
overbook planes. When this happens,
airlines ask for volunteers to give up
their seats. In return these volunteers

usually get a certificate for a free flight
and are rebooked on the next flight
out. If there are not enough volunteers, the airline chooses who will be
denied boarding. The first to get
bumped are passengers who checked
in late and those flying on discounted
tickets, so **get to the gate and check in
as early as possible,** especially during
peak periods. Always **bring a government-issued photo ID to the airport.**
You may be asked to show it before
you are allowed to check in.

CUTTING COSTS

The least-expensive airfares must
usually be purchased in advance and
are non-refundable. It's smart to **call
a number of airlines, and when you
are quoted a good price, book it on
the spot**—the same fare may not be
available the next day. Always **check
different routings** and look into using
different airports. Check fares from
your city to San José, as well as fares
from your city to a U.S. gateway city
and from that gateway into San José;
the latter route can be cheaper.

The main tourist season (the dry
season) in Costa Rica, from mid-December to April, coincides with
Thanksgiving, Christmas, and Easter.
Flights are sometimes fully booked
well ahead of time. During the high
season, weekly charter flights (☞
Charter Flights, *above*) run to Costa
Rica from half a dozen United States
and Canadian ports. Some of those
flights land in San José, though most
fly only to Liberia, in the northwest
province of Guanacaste.

Travel agents, especially low-fare
specialists (☞ Discounts & Deals,
below), can be helpful.

Consolidators are another good
source. They buy tickets for scheduled
international flights at reduced rates
from the airlines, then sell them at
prices that beat the best fare available
directly from the airlines, usually
without restrictions. You'll need some
flexibility with travel dates, however.
Sometimes you can even get your
money back if you need to return the
ticket. Carefully read the fine print
detailing penalties for changes and
cancellations, and **confirm your consolidator reservation with the airline.**

THE GOLD GUIDE / SMART TRAVEL TIPS

When you **fly as a courier** you trade your checked-luggage space for a ticket deeply subsidized by a courier service. There are restrictions on when you can book and how long you can stay.

➤ CONSOLIDATORS: **Cheap Tickets** (☎ 800/377–1000). **Discount Airline Ticket Service** (☎ 800/576–1600). **Unitravel** (☎ 800/325–2222). **Up & Away Travel** (☎ 212/889–2345). **World Travel Network** (☎ 800/409–6753).

ENJOYING THE FLIGHT

For more legroom **request an emergency-aisle seat.** Don't sit in the row in front of the emergency aisle or in front of a bulkhead, where seats may not recline. If you have dietary concerns, **ask for special meals when booking.** These can be vegetarian, low-cholesterol, or kosher, for example. On long flights, try to maintain a normal routine, to help fight jetlag. At night **get some sleep.** By day **eat lightly, drink water** (not alcohol), and **move around the cabin** to stretch your legs.

FLYING TIMES

From New York, flights to San José are 5½ hours (via Miami); from Los Angeles, 8½ hours (via Mexico); from Houston, 4½ hours (via Guatemala); and from Miami, 2 hours (direct).

HOW TO COMPLAIN

If your baggage goes astray or your flight goes awry, complain right away. Most carriers require that you **file a claim immediately.**

➤ AIRLINE COMPLAINTS: U.S. Department of Transportation **Aviation Consumer Protection Division** (✉ C-75, Room 4107, Washington, DC 20590, ☎ 202/366–2220). **Federal Aviation Administration Consumer Hotline** (☎ 800/322–7873).

RECONFIRMING

When leaving Costa Rica, Panama, and Nicaragua you must **reconfirm your flight by phone within 72 hours of departure.** Failure to do so may result in your reservation being canceled.

AIRPORTS

➤ AIRPORT INFORMATION: **Aeropuerto Internacional Juan Santamaría** (San José, ☎ 506/443–2682). **Aeropuerto Internacional Daniel Oduber** (San José, ☎ 506/667–0014). **Aeropuerto Internacional Tobías Bolaños** (Pavas, 3 km/2 mi west of San José, ☎ 232–2820).

DUTY-FREE SHOPPING

San José's Aeropuerto Internacional Juan Santamaría has several duty free shops, which sell mostly liquor and perfume.

BIKE TRAVEL

Although much of this region is mountainous, there are also many ideal-for-cycling flatlands in Costa Rica. For a list of bike tour operators, *see* Outdoors & Sports, *below.* Several companies offer organized mountain biking tours, which take you to less-traveled areas, and usually provide lunch and refreshments.

BIKES IN FLIGHT

Most airlines accommodate bikes as luggage provided they are dismantled and boxed. Costa Rica's domestic airlines Sansa and Travelair usually allows disassembled mountain bikes (and 7-ft surfboards) aboard for $15, space provided. For bike boxes, often free at bike shops, you'll pay about $5 (and at least $100 for bike bags) from airlines. International travelers can sometimes substitute a bike for a piece of checked luggage at no charge; otherwise, the cost is about $100. Domestic and Canadian airlines charge $25–$50.

➤ BIKE MAPS: Regional topographical maps sold at the San José department stores called Universal and Lehmann include unpaved roads that are often the perfect mountain biking routes.

➤ BIKE RENTALS: Mountain bikes can be rented in many resort areas and are a great way to simply get around town, or explore off-road trails.

BOAT & FERRY TRAVEL

WITHIN COSTA RICA

Regular passenger and/or car ferries connect Playa Naranjo, Tambor, and Paquera on the south end of the Nicoya Peninsula with Puntarenas. A car and passenger ferry crosses the Río Tempisque, about a one-hour drive northwest from Puntarenas, every 20 minutes from 5 AM to 7 PM. During the holidays and the high season, waits of up to three hours are common for the 15-minute trip. The Arco Iris Passenger Ferry makes daily runs between Golfito and Puerto Jiménez, and the Zancudo ferry makes a daily round-trip to Golfito.

➤ BOAT & FERRY INFORMATION: PUNTARENAS–PLAYA NARANJO FERRY (☎ 506/661–1069).

WITHIN PANAMA

Water taxis travel regularly between Almirante and Bocas del Toro, and make several trips daily between Almirante and Chiriquí Grande. A car ferry also makes one trip daily between Almirante and Chiriquí Grande, stopping at Bocas del Toro twice a week, but water taxis make the same trip in a fraction of the time. Several ferries run daily between Panama City and the Island of Taboga.

WITHIN NICARAGUA

Ferries to Ometepe's Moyogalpa run from San Jorge, near Rivas, six days a week. Boats from Granada and San Jorge run three times a week. Regular weekend hydrofoil service operates from Granada.

➤ BOAT & FERRY INFORMATION: Lake Nicaragua (505/055–22966).

BUSINESS HOURS

BANKS & OFFICES

Most of Costa Rica and Panama's state banks are open weekdays 9 to 3, and many are open on Saturday morning. Several branches of Banco Nacional are open until 6. The growing cadre of private banks tend to keep longer hours, and are usually the best places to change dollars and traveler's checks. Bank hours in Nicaragua are 8:30 to 4:30 week-days and Saturday until noon.

GAS STATIONS

There are 24-hour gas stations near most cities, especially along the Pan-American Highway; most other stations are open from about 7 to 7, and sometimes until midnight.

MUSEUMS

Generalizing about Costa Rican museum opening times is unwise, though most public museums are closed Monday. Most Panamanian and Nicaraguan museums are open 9 to 4 or 5 weekdays.

SHOPS

Most shops in Costa Rica and Panama are open 8 to 6 Monday to Saturday. Shops in Nicaragua are open roughly 9 to 6 weekdays and 9 to 5 Saturday.

BUS TRAVEL

WITHIN COSTA RICA

There is reliable, inexpensive bus service throughout much of the country. A patchwork of private companies operates out of San José from a variety of departure points. For schedules and San José departure points, *see* Getting Around *in* the A to Z sections of individual chapters. On longer routes, buses stop midway at inexpensive restaurants. Tickets are sold at the bus station or on the buses themselves. The only way to reserve a seat is to buy your ticket ahead of time and/or get there early. Near the ends of their runs many nonexpress buses turn into large taxis, dropping passengers off one by one once they reach their destinations. To save time, take a *directo* (express) bus.

➤ BUS COMPANIES: Central Valley: **Empresarios Unidos** (☎ 506/222–0064); **Rapiditos Heredianos** (☎ 506/233–8392); **Sacsa** (☎ 506/233–5350); **Transtusa** (☎ 506/556–0073); **Tuasa** (☎ 506/222–5325). Northern Guanacaste and Alajuela: **Auto Transportes Quesada** (☎ 506/255–4318); **Transportes La Cañera** (☎ 506/222–3006); **Transportes Tilarán** (☎ 506/222–3854). Nicoya Peninsula: **Alfaro Tracopa** (☎ 506/221–4214); **Empresarios Unidos** (☎ 506/222–0064); **Pulmitan** (☎ 506/222–1650). Central Pacific: **Transportes Delio Morales** (☎ 506/223–5567); **Transportes Jacó** (☎ 506/223–1109). Southern Pacific: **Alfaro Tracopa** (☎ 506/221–4214); **Musco** (☎ 506/222–2422); **Transportes Blanco Lobo** (☎ 506/257–4121). Atlantic Lowlands and Pacific Coast: **Autotransportes Sarapiqui** (☎ 506/259–8571);

Empresarios Guapilenos (☎ 506/222–0610); **Transportes Carienos** (☎ 506/256–4248); **Transportes Mepe** (☎ 506/257–8129).

PAYING

Cash only is accepted at bus lines.

RESERVATIONS

During the high season, tickets to most popular beaches should be purchased ahead of time. Reservations aren't taken over the phone—you have to buy a ticket in person.

WITHIN PANAMA

The widespread use of microbuses means that there is very regular service between most Panamanian towns. Buses depart about every 30 minutes between Changuinola and Almirante, and slightly less frequently between Changuinola and the border with Costa Rica. About five buses a day run between Chiriquí Grande and David, from where buses leave every 20 minutes for the Costa Rican border, Volcán and Cerro Punta, and Boquete. Old "Greyhound" buses leave every hour between David and Panama City; it's a seven-hour trip. Direct service also runs daily between Panama City and Chiriquí Grande, departing Panama City at 5 AM, and Chiriquí Grande at 1 PM, when the ferry arrives from Almirante.

Tica Bus buses leave Panama City daily at noon and arrive in San José at 5 AM the next morning, with buses leaving San José for Panama at 10 PM and arriving the following day at 4 PM. Round-trip fare is about $36. **Panaline** has a daily luxury express service that departs from the Hotel Cocorí at 1 PM and arrives in Panama City at 6 AM the next day, returning from Panama City at 1 PM and arriving in San José at 5 AM. The round-trip fare is about $42. **Tracopa** buses leave San José from the Hotel Cocorí daily at 7:30 AM, arriving at David, Panama, at 5:30 PM. From there, buses depart every hour Panama City, seven hours away. The round-trip fare at is around $14. **Bernardo Fumero** runs a daily bus from San José to Changuinola, in northeast Panama, at 10 AM. Leaving from the Hotel Cocorí, the eight-hour trip costs about $6 (each way).

➤ BUS INFORMATION: **Alico** (☎ 507/775–2923, 507/774–9205). **Bernardo Fumero** (Hotel Cocorí, ☞ *above*, ☎ 506/556–1432). **Panaline** (✉ Hotel Cocorí, C. 16 between Avdas. 3 and 5, ☎ 506/255–1205). **Tica Bus** (✉ C. 9 and Avda. 4, San José, ☎ 506/221–8954). **Tracopa** (✉ C. 16 between Avdas. 3 and 5, ☎ 506/221–4214). **Union de Buses Panamericana** (☎ 507/229–6333).

WITHIN NICARAGUA

Nicaragua is served by a network of buses, ranging from low-cost locals—usually recycled American school-buses—to pricier air-conditioned expresses. The transportation hub of southwest Nicaragua is Granada, from where buses regularly leave to the nearby beaches, Lake Nicaragua, Granada, and Managua. Tica runs regular bus service from San José to Managua, with pickup in Liberia.

➤ BUS INFORMATION: **Tica** (☎ 506/221–8954, 506/221–9229, 505/222–6094).

CAMERAS & PHOTOGRAPHY

The *Kodak Guide to Shooting Great Travel Pictures* is an excellent tool and is available in bookstores or from Fodor's Travel Publications.

➤ PHOTO HELP: **Kodak Information Center** (☎ 800/242–2424). *Kodak Guide to Shooting Great Travel Pictures* ($16.50 plus $4 shipping); contact Fodor's Travel Publications (☎ 800/533–6478.

EQUIPMENT PRECAUTIONS

Always **keep your film and tape out of the sun.** Carry an extra supply of batteries, and **be prepared to turn on your camera or camcorder** to prove to security personnel that the device is real. Always **ask for hand inspection of film,** which becomes clouded after successive exposures to airport X-ray machines, and **keep videotapes away from metal detectors.**

FILM & DEVELOPING

Most **film costs at least 20 percent more in Costa Rica** than in the United States, so you'll want to bring enough for your trip. Plenty of places in San José develop film, usually the same day, though they tend to change the chemicals less often than they should, so you risk getting prints of poor quality. Kodachrome slide film can only be developed in the United States.

➤ REPUTABLE LOCAL DEVELOPING LABS: **Dima Color** (✉ 325 m east of U.S. Embassy, Pavas, ☎ 506/231–4130). **Rapi Foto** (✉ C. Central at Avda. 7, San José, ☎ 506/223–7640).

CAR RENTAL

Many travelers shy away from renting a car in Costa Rica, if only for fear of driving on the winding mountain roads. Certainly it's not the ideal place to drive: in San José, traffic is bad and car theft is rampant (look for guarded parking lots or hotels with lots); in rural areas, roads are often unpaved or dotted with potholes. The greatest deterrent, however, should be the fact that rental rates (☞ Rates, *below*) and gas prices (about $1.50/ gallon) are extremely high. Nevertheless, having your own wheels can be quite nice, providing more control over your itinerary and the pace of your trip.

Decide which type of vehicle you want to rent: a *doble-tracción* (four-wheel-drive) vehicle is often essential to reach the more remote parts of Costa Rica, especially during the rainy season. They can cost roughly twice as much as an economy car and should be booked well in advance. Most destinations are easily reached with a standard vehicle. If you plan to rent any kind of vehicle between December 15 and January 3 or during Holy Week, **reserve several months ahead of time.**

Costa Rica has approximately 50 international and local car-rental firms, the larger of which have several offices around San José. At least a dozen rental offices line San José's Paseo Colón, and most large hotels have representatives. Panama and Nicaragua have fewer car-rental companies, but rates are often lower than in Costa Rica. For a complete listing, look in local phone directories under *alquiler de automóviles.*

➤ MAJOR AGENCIES: **Alamo** (☎ 800/522–9696; 0181/759–6200 in the U.K.). **Avis** (☎ 800/331–1084; 800/879–2847 in Canada; 02/9353–9000 in Australia; 09/525–1982 in New Zealand). **Budget** (☎ 800/527–0700; 0144/227–6266 in the U.K.). **Dollar** (☎ 800/800–6000; 0181/897–0811 in the U.K., where it is known as Eurodollar, 02/9223–1444 in Australia). **Hertz** (☎ 800/654–3001; 800/263–0600 in Canada; 0181/897–2072 in the U.K.; 02/9669–2444 in Australia; 03/358–6777 in New Zealand). **National InterRent** (☎ 800/227–3876; 0345/222525 in the U.K., where it is known as Europcar InterRent).

RATES

At press time, rates in San José began at $45 a day and $290 a week (high season) for an economy car with air-conditioning, a manual transmission, unlimited mileage, and obligatory insurance, but rates fluctuate considerably according to demand, season, and company. Rates for a four-wheel-drive-vehicle during high season are $80 a day and $500 per week. When renting a car in San José, **ask if the price includes the mandatory $15 daily fee for collision insurance.**

CUTTING COSTS

To get the best deal **book through a travel agent who shops around.** Payment must be made before you leave home. Ads in *The Tico Times* and other publications often offer discounts.

➤ SAN JOSÉ AGENCIES: **Ada** (☎ 506/233–7733). **Adobe** (☎ 506/233–9937). **Avis** (☎ 506/293–2222). **Budget** (☎ 506/223–3284). **Dollar** (☎ 506/257–1585). **Economy** (☎ 506/232–9130). **Elegante** (☎ 506/257–0026). **Hertz** (☎ 506/221–1818). **Hola** (☎ 506/231–5666). **National InterRent** (☎ 506/290–8787).

➤ PANAMA CITY AGENCIES: **Alamo** (☎ 507/260–0822). **Avis** (☎ 507/264–0722). **Budget** (☎ 507/263–8777). **Dollar** (☎ 507/225–3455). **Hertz** (☎ 507/226–7110). **National InterRent** (☎ 507/264–8277).

➤ MANAGUA AGENCIES: **Budget** (☎ 505/266–6226). **Hertz** (☎ 505/233–1237). **Lugo** (☎ 505/263–2368).

➤ WHOLESALERS: **Auto Europe** (☎ 207/842–2000 or 800/223–5555,

SMART TRAVEL TIPS

THE GOLD GUIDE / SMART TRAVEL TIPS

FAX 800–235–6321). **Kemwel Holiday Autos** (☎ 914/835–3000 or 800/678–0678, FAX 914/835–5126).

INSURANCE

When driving a rented car you are generally responsible for any damage to or loss of the vehicle as well as for any property damage or personal injury that you may cause. Insurance issued by car rental companies in Costa Rica usually has a very large deductible. Before you rent, **see what coverage you already have** under the terms of your personal auto-insurance policy and credit cards. Most American Express cards offer free insurance when used to rent cars.

REQUIREMENTS & RESTRICTIONS

To rent a car in Costa Rica and Panama you need your driver's license, a valid passport, and a credit card. In Nicaragua you need your driver's license and a credit card with at least $500 in credit; you must also be 25 years of age.

SURCHARGES

Before you pick up a car in one city and leave it in another **ask about drop-off charges or one-way service fees,** which can be substantial. Note, too, that some rental agencies charge extra if you return the car before the time specified in your contract. To avoid a hefty refueling fee **fill the tank just before you turn in the car,** but be aware that gas stations near the rental outlet may overcharge.

CAR TRAVEL

Driving in a developing nation may be a bit of a challenge, but it's a great way to explore certain regions, especially in Guanacaste and the Atlantic Lowlands and the Caribbean Coast, apart from Tortuguero and Barra del Colorado. Keep in mind that mountains and poor road conditions make most trips take longer than you would expect. If you want to visit several far-flung areas, domestic flights (☞ Air Travel, *above*) may be a better option.

AUTO CLUBS

➤ IN AUSTRALIA: **Australian Automobile Association** (☎ 02/6247–7311).

➤ IN CANADA: **Canadian Automobile Association** (CAA, ☎ 613/247–0117).

➤ IN NEW ZEALAND: **New Zealand Automobile Association** (☎ 09/377–4660).

➤ IN THE U.K.: **Automobile Association** (AA, ☎ 0990/500–600). **Royal Automobile Club** (RAC, ☎ 0990/722–722 for membership; 0345/121–345 for insurance).

➤ IN THE U.S.: **American Automobile Association** (☎ 800/564–6222).

DRIVING OVER THE BORDER

You can drive over Costa Rica's borders into Panama and Nicaragua, but it must be done in a private vehicle, since a car rented in one country cannot be taken into the next.

EMERGENCY SERVICES

911 is a nationwide number in Costa Rica for accidents. Traffic police are scattered around the country, but Costa Ricans are very good about stopping for people with car trouble. Local car rental companies can provide you with a list of numbers to call in case of accidents or car trouble. In Panama dial 104, and in Nicaragua 119 for police assistance.

GASOLINE

Gas costs about $1.50 per gallon.

PARKING

Car theft is rife in Costa Rica, Panama, and Nicaragua. Be certain to **park overnight in a locked garage or guarded lot, as Central American insurance may hold you liable if your rental car is stolen.** Most hotels, except for the least expensive, therefore offer secure parking with a guard or locked gates.

ROAD CONDITIONS

Road conditions in Costa Rica are lamentable: you'll run into plenty of potholes and many stretches with no pavement at all. Roads are considerably better in Panama and Nicaragua.

RULES OF THE ROAD

There are plenty of would-be Mario Andrettis on Costa Rican and Panamanian highways; **be prepared for**

harebrained passing on blind corners, tailgating, and failures to signal.
Watch out, too, for two-lane roads that feed into one-lane bridges with specified rights of way. And finally, look out for potholes, even in the smoothest sections of the best roads. The highway speed limit in Costa Rica is usually 90 km (54 mi) per hour, which drops to 60 kph (36 mph) in residential areas. Seat belts are obligatory in Panama and Costa Rica. Drunk driving laws tend to be less severe that in other parts of the world. Driving over international borders from Costa Rica is prohibited in a rental car (but permitted in a private car).

CHILDREN IN COSTA RICA

Thanks to the general level of safety and high health standards, Costa Rica is a popular destination for family travel. Most of the health problems one might associate with the tropics are rare or nonexistent in Costa Rica (but not in Nicaragua), and the country's most popular destinations have plenty to offer kids. However, many popular beaches have dangerous rip currents whenever the surf is big.

FLYING

If your children are two or older **ask about children's airfares.** As a general rule, infants under two not occupying a seat fly at greatly reduced fares or even for free. When booking **confirm carry-on allowances** if you're traveling with infants. In general, for babies charged 10% of the adult fare, you are allowed one carry-on bag and a collapsible stroller; if the flight is full the stroller may have to be checked or you may be limited to less.

Experts agree that it's a good idea to use safety seats aloft for children weighing less than 40 pounds. Airlines set their own policies: U.S. carriers usually require that the child be ticketed, even if he or she is young enough to ride free, since the seats must be strapped into regular seats. Do **check your airline's policy about using safety seats during takeoff and landing.** And since safety seats aren't allowed everywhere on the plane, get your seat assignments early.

LODGING

Most hotels in Costa Rica, Panama, and Nicaragua allow children under a certain age to stay in their parents' room at no extra charge, but others charge for them as extra adults; be sure to **find out the cutoff age for children's discounts.**

COMPUTERS ON THE ROAD

Many hotels in Costa Rica have data ports. Batteries are hard to come by. The same with stabilizers, and since the current fluctuates a lot in these countries, a stabilizer is usually necessary. It's best to call ahead for details.

➤ INTERNET CAFÉS: CyberCafe Searchcostarica.com (Avda. 2 between Cs. 1 and 3, ground floor of Las Arcadas building, San José, ☎ 506/233–3310). **Y2K Net Cafe Costa Rica** (200 meters east of Universidad Latina, San Pedro, ☎ 506/283–4829). **Internet Cafe Costa Rica** (50 meters west of the Banco Popular, San Pedro, ☎ 506/283–5375). **Racsa office** (C. 1 at Avda. 5, San José, ☎ 506/287–0087).

CRUISE TRAVEL

Cruises are the most restful way of traveling. The U.S.–Costa Rica cruise season runs September–May, with trips lasting from three days to a week. Your travel agent will be able to give you details of prices, which range from $1,000 to $5,000. Luxury liners equipped with swimming pools and gymnasiums sail from Fort Lauderdale, Florida, to Limón, or through the Panama Canal to Caldera, south of Puntarenas. Some cruises head out of Los Angeles to Caldera, continuing to the canal. Aboard the ship you can sign up for shore excursions and tours. Packages include the cost of flying to the appropriate port in the United States.

➤ CRUISE LINES: Carnival (☎ 800/327–9501). **Crystal Cruises** (☎ 800/446–6645). **Cunard** (☎ 800/221–4770). **Holland America** (☎ 800/426–0327). **Ocean Cruise** (☎ 800/556–8850). **Royal Viking** (☎ 800/422–8000). **Seabourn** (☎ 800/351–9595). **Sitmar Cruise** (☎ 305/523–1219). **Sunline** (☎ 800/872–6400). **Temptress Adventure Cruises** (☎ 800/336–8423).

SMART TRAVEL TIPS / THE GOLD GUIDE

CUSTOMS & DUTIES

When shopping, **keep receipts** for all purchases. Upon reentering the country, **be ready to show customs officials what you've bought.** If you feel a duty is incorrect or object to the way your clearance was handled, note the inspector's badge number and ask to see a supervisor. If the problem isn't resolved, write to the appropriate authorities, beginning with the port director at your point of entry.

IN COSTA RICA, PANAMA, AND NICARAGUA

Visitors entering Costa Rica may bring in 500 milligrams of tobacco, 3 liters of wine or spirits, 2 kilos of sweets and chocolates, and the equivalent of $100 worth of merchandise. Two cameras, six rolls of film, binoculars, and electrical items for personal use only are also allowed. Customs officials at San José's international airport rarely examine tourists' luggage. If you enter by land, however, customs officials will probably look through your bags.

Visitors entering Panama may bring in 500 cigarettes, 3 liters of wine or spirits, two cameras, and personal electronic equipment. Just as in Costa Rica, luggage revision is a rare occurrence with airport arrivals, but standard procedure at land crossings.

Visitors entering Nicaragua may bring 3 cartons of cigarettes, 3 liters of wine or spirits, one camera, and one more piece of personal electronic equipment.

IN AUSTRALIA

Australia residents who are 18 or older may bring home $A400 worth of souvenirs and gifts (including jewelry), 250 cigarettes or 250 grams of tobacco, and 1,125 ml of alcohol (including wine, beer, and spirits). Residents under 18 may bring back $A200 worth of goods. Prohibited items include meat products. Seeds, plants, and fruits need to be declared upon arrival.

➤ INFORMATION: **Australian Customs Service** (Regional Director, ✉ Box 8, Sydney, NSW 2001, ☎ 02/9213–2000, FAX 02/9213–4000).

IN CANADA

Canadian residents who have been out of Canada for at least 7 days may bring home C$500 worth of goods duty-free. If you've been away less than 7 days but more than 48 hours, the duty-free allowance drops to C$200. If your trip lasts 24 to 48 hours, the allowance is C$50. You may not pool allowances with family members. Goods claimed under the C$500 exemption may follow you by mail; those claimed under the lesser exemptions must accompany you. Alcohol and tobacco products may be included in the 7-day and 48-hour exemptions but not in the 24-hour exemption. If you meet the age requirements of the province or territory through which you reenter Canada, you may bring in, duty-free, 1.14 liters (40 imperial ounces) of wine or liquor *or* 24 12-ounce cans or bottles of beer or ale. If you are 16 or older you may bring in, duty-free, 200 cigarettes and 50 cigars. Check ahead of time with Revenue Canada or the Department of Agriculture for policies regarding meat products, seeds, plants, and fruits.

You may send an unlimited number of gifts worth up to C$60 each duty-free to Canada. Label the package UNSOLICITED GIFT—VALUE UNDER $60. Alcohol and tobacco are excluded.

➤ INFORMATION: **Revenue Canada** (✉ 2265 St. Laurent Blvd. S, Ottawa, Ontario K1G 4K3, ☎ 613/993–0534; 800/461–9999 in Canada).

IN NEW ZEALAND

Homeward-bound residents 17 or older may bring back $700 worth of souvenirs and gifts. Your duty-free allowance also includes 4.5 liters of wine or beer; one 1,125-ml bottle of spirits; and either 200 cigarettes, 250 grams of tobacco, 50 cigars, or a combination of the three up to 250 grams. Prohibited items include meat products, seeds, plants, and fruits.

➤ INFORMATION: **New Zealand Customs** (Custom House, ✉ 50 Anzac Ave., Box 29, Auckland, New Zealand, ☎ 09/359–6655, FAX 09/359–6732).

IN THE U.K.

From countries outside the EU, including Costa Rica, Panama, and Nicaragua, you may bring home, duty-free, 200 cigarettes or 50 cigars; 1 liter of spirits or 2 liters of fortified or sparkling wine or liqueurs; 2 liters of still table wine; 60 milliliters of perfume; 250 milliliters of toilet water; plus £136 worth of other goods, including gifts and souvenirs. If returning from outside the EU, prohibited items include meat products, seeds, plants, and fruits.

➤ INFORMATION: **HM Customs and Excise** (✉ Dorset House, Stamford St., Bromley Kent BR1 1XX, ☎ 0171/202–4227).

IN THE U.S.

U.S. residents who have been out of the country for at least 48 hours (and who have not used the $400 allowance or any part of it in the past 30 days) may bring home $400 worth of foreign goods duty-free. U.S. residents 21 and older may bring back 1 liter of alcohol duty-free. In addition, regardless of your age, you are allowed 200 cigarettes and 100 non-Cuban cigars. Antiques, which the U.S. Customs Service define as objects more than 100 years old, enter duty-free, as do original works of art done entirely by hand, including paintings, drawings, and sculptures.

You may also send packages home duty-free: up to $200 worth of goods for personal use, with a limit of one parcel per addressee per day (and no alcohol or tobacco products or perfume worth more than $5); label the package PERSONAL USE and attach a list of its contents and their retail value. Do not label the package UNSOLICITED GIFT or your duty-free exemption drops to $100. Mailed items do not affect your duty-free allowance on your return.

➤ INFORMATION: **U.S. Customs Service** (inquiries, ✉ 1300 Pennsylvania Ave. NW, Washington, DC 20229, ☎ 202/927–6724; complaints, ✉ Office of Regulations and Rulings, 1300 Pennsylvania Ave. NW, Washington, DC 20229; registration of equipment, ✉ Resource Management, 1300 Pennsylvania Ave. NW, Washington, DC 20229, ☎ 202/927–0540).

DINING

Though Costa Rican, Panamanian, and Nicaraguian food don't quite compare with the world's great cuisines, all three of the countries have some interesting local dishes well worth trying. There are also plenty of foreign-owned restaurants offering everything from French and Italian to Cantonese and Peruvian cuisine.

The restaurants we list are the cream of the crop in each price category.

CATEGORY	COST*
$$$$	over $20
$$$	$10–$20
$$	$5–$10
$	under $5

Dining prices are for cost of a dinner entrée and a nonalcoholic beverage.

MEALTIMES

Dining hours in Costa Rica, Panama, and Nicaragua are usually noon–3 and 7–10.

PAYING

Cash is generally the rule at local restaurants. In Costa Rica, 23% is added to all the prices on the menu— 13% for tax and 10% for the service. Because the gratuity is included, there is no need to tip, but if service is good, it's nice to add a little money to the obligatory 10%. Restaurants in Panama do not charge for service on the bill, so a 10% gratuity is expected. The rule of thumb for tips in Nicaragua is 10%, and the tip is often included in the bill.

WINE, BEER & SPIRITS

The country's one brewery puts out half a dozen brands of beer, including the popular Imperial, a dark brew called Steinbrau, and a local version of Heineken. All wine is imported, and the best deals are usually from Chile and Argentina. The country's best rum is Centenario, and the cheaper Nicaraguan rum, Flor de Caño, is just as good, but most Ticos drink a rot-gut rum called *guaro*. All of the above is served at restaurants and bars, and sold at abundant supermarkets and liquor stores.

DISABILITIES & ACCESSIBILITY

Accessibility in Costa Rica, Panama, and Nicaragua is extremely limited. Wheelchair ramps are practically nonexistent, and outside major cities, roads are unpaved, making wheelchair travel difficult. Exploring most of the area's attractions involves walking down cobblestone streets and, sometimes, steep trails and muddy paths, though some attractions require little or no walking. Buses are not equipped to carry wheelchairs, so people using wheelchairs should hire a van to get around and have someone with them to help out. There is a growing awareness of the needs of people with disabilities, and some hotels and attractions in Costa Rica have made the necessary provisions. **Costa Rican Tourist Institute**, known locally as the ICT, has information on accessibility.

➤ LOCAL RESOURCES: **Costa Rican Tourist Institute** (✉ Avda. 4 and Cs. 5 and 7, 11th floor, San José, Costa Rica, ☎ 506/223–1733).

LODGING

For the most extensive facilities meeting the latest legal specifications **opt for newer accommodations.** Unfortunately, very few hotels in Costa Rica are equipped for travelers in wheelchairs. In San Jose, the Hampton Inn and Hacienda El Rodeo, both near the international airport, have some wheelchair accommodations. Wilson Botanical Gardens, in San Vito (Southern Pacific) has one room equipped for a wheelchair.

SIGHTS & ATTRACTIONS

Most Costa Rican attractions are inaccessible for travelers with wheelchairs, as are all of its rare public bathrooms. Poás Volcano National Park is probably the country's most wheelchair-friendly site, with Irazú Volcano being the second runner-up. The Orosi Valley and Sarchi also offer limited wheelchair exploring options, whereas the Rain Forest Aerial Tram is a real challenge, though a possibility for some.

TRANSPORTATION

Costa Rica, Panama, and Nicaragua present serious challenges to travelers with disabilities. Though developed areas, especially San José and the Central Valley, can be managed in a wheelchair, most rural areas are tougher. The tour company **Vaya con Silla de Ruedas** (Go with Wheelchair) provides transportation and guided tours.

➤ TOUR COMPANY: **Vaya con Silla de Ruedas** (Apdo. 1146-2050, San Pedro Montes de Oca, ☎ 506/393–3087, 506/225–8561, FAX 506/253–0931).

ECOTOURISM

Ecotourism, green tourism, environmental tourism: these buzzwords and catch phrases have been flying around Costa Rica for well more than a decade. Many of the tour companies currently operating in Costa Rica and Panama have evolved a high level of environmental awareness in their business practices. **Find out whether or not a tour company you're interested in practices "eco-friendly" policies,** such as hiring and training local people as guides, drivers, managers, and office workers; teaching people as much as possible about the plant and animal life, the geography, and the history they are experiencing; controlling the numbers of people allowed daily onto a given site; restoring watersheds or anything else damaged by trail-building, visitors, or overuse; or discouraging wildlife feeding or any other unnatural or disruptive behavior (i.e., making loud noises to scare birds into flight). All of this can mitigate the effects of intense tourism; and, after all, it is better to have a hundred people walking through a forest than to cut the forest down.

There are numerous environmental organizations in Costa Rica and Panama, and most of them are heavily dependent on private donations and dedicated volunteers. To obtain a list of Costa Rican groups that might need a hand and/or donation, consult the *Directorio de Organizaciones, Instituciones y Consultores en El Sector de Recursos Naturales en Costa Rica,* published in Spanish by the Costa Rican Federation for the Preservation of the Environment (FECON). Also, for locally generated advice about ecotourism, consult the

Sustainable Tourism Newsletter, published by the Eco-Institute of Costa Rica.

IN COSTA RICA

Costa Rica Expeditions has won awards for its commitment to conservation and the quality of its tours. **Horizontes** is an award-winning natural history tour operator with some of the country's best guides. **Sun Tours** has several properties with private nature reserves. **Tikal Tours** specializes in small groups and nature tours. **Temptress Adventure Cruises** offers multi-day natural-history cruises along the Southern Pacific coast aboard the 185-ft *M/V Temptress.*

➤ CONTACTS: **Costa Rica Expeditions** (☎ 506/222–0333, FAX 506/257–1665). **Horizontes** (☎ 506/222–2022, FAX 506/255–4513). **Sun Tours** (☎ 506/255–2011, FAX 506/233–6890). **Tikal Tours** (☎ 506/223–2811, FAX 506/223–1916). **Temptress Adventure Cruises** (☎ 506/232–6672, 800/336–8423 in the U.S.).

➤ COSTA RICAN ENVIRONMENTAL ORGANIZATIONS: **AECO** (☎ 506/233–3013). **ANAI** (☎ 506/224–6090). **APREFLOFAS** (☎ 506/240–6087). **ARBOFILIA** (506/240–7145). **Neotropica Foundation** (☎ 506/253–9462).

IN PANAMA

Ancon Expeditions is owned by Panama's biggest environmental group and has several field stations around the country, including one in Bocas del Toro. It offers a variety of multi-day packages. **Pesántez Tours**, a pioneer in bird-watching tours in Panama, holds trips throughout the country. **Turtle Divers**, in Bocas del Toro, runs tours to dive spots, islands, and indigenous communities, and supports environmental education in local schools. **Río Monte Ecological Tours**, in Boquete, is run by the Collins family, which has been involved in ecotourism since long before the term was coined. **Expediciones Tierras Altas**, in Boquete, is a small operation offering low-budget nature and hiking tours.

➤ CONTACTS: **Ancon Expeditions** (☎ 507/269–9415). **Expediciones Tierras Altas** (☎ 507/720–1342). **Pesántez Tours** (☎ 507/263–8771). **Río Monte Ecological Tours** (☎ 507/720–1327). **Turtle Divers** (☎ FAX 507/757–9594).

ELECTRICITY

The electrical current in Central America is 110 volts (AC), and plugs are the same as in the United States.

EMBASSIES

Most embassies are on the western end of San José, or in nearby suburbs. Citizens of Australia and New Zealand should contact the British Embassy (☞ *below*).

➤ CANADA: (⊠ Sabana Sur, next to tennis club, ☎ 506/296–4146).

➤ UNITED KINGDOM: (⊠ Centro Colón, Paseo Colón between Cs. 38 and 40, ☎ 506/221–5566).

➤ UNITED STATES: ⊠ Pavas, ☎ 506/220–3939).

EMERGENCIES

Local people are usually quick to respond in an emergency. In a hotel or restaurant, the staff would offer immediate help, and in a public area, passersby can be counted to stop and help.

➤ CONTACTS: **Costa Rica**: Emergencies (☎ 911). **Ambulance** (☎ 128). **Police** (☎ 117, 127 outside cities). **Panama**: **Fire** (☎ 103). **Police** (☎ 104). **Nicaragua**: **Fire** (☎ 115). **Police** (☎ 119).

ENGLISH-LANGUAGE MEDIA

English is practically everywhere in Costa Rica, from the cable TV available at most San José hotels to abundant publications.

BOOKS

A good selection of English-language books, used and new, can be found at several San José bookstores, at slightly higher prices that one would expect in the United States. Many large hotels and other shops also sell some English-language books, especially those dealing with tropical flora and fauna.

➤ BOOKSTORES: **7th Street Books** (⊠ C. 7 between Avdas. Central and 1, San José, ☎ 506/256–8251). **Lehmann** (⊠ Avda. Central between

Cs. 1 and 3, San José, ☎ 506/223–1212).

NEWSPAPERS & MAGAZINES

U.S. newspapers and magazines are widely distributed at newsstands and hotels in San José, and available at some resorts outside the capital. The local English-language weekly *The Tico Times,* published every Friday, has local news and information about entertainment and travel.

TELEVISION & RADIO

Most mid- to upper-priced hotels in San José have cable TV in guest rooms with at least a dozen English-language channels. Some hotels outside the capital have satellite disks. Local TV is in Spanish and not that great. There is one English-language radio station that plays rock: 107.5 FM.

ETIQUETTE & BEHAVIOR

On the whole, Costa Ricans are extremely polite people, quick to shake hands and place a soft kiss on the left cheek, as is the local custom. At the same time, an unsettlingly large portion of the men make a habit of ogling or making gratuitous comments when young women pass on the street. Panamanians and Nicaraguans are on the whole a bit less gregarious, but less prone to harassment. In all countries, churches should be visited in a respectful manner.

BUSINESS ETIQUETTE

On the whole, people will find business meetings friendlier and more relaxed in Costa Rica and its neighboring nations than at home. Dress is usually casual, and lateness is a chronic problem.

GAY & LESBIAN TRAVEL

While harassment of gays and lesbians is infrequent in Costa Rica, Panama, and Nicaragua, so are public displays of affection—discretion is advised. As a result of its history of tolerance, Costa Rica has attracted many gays from other Latin American nations and, consequently, has a large gay community. San José and Manuel Antonio are probably Costa Rica's two most gay-friendly towns, with plenty of gay-friendly places and bars.

The beach at the northern end of Playa Espadilla in Manuel Antonio National Park is a small, secluded cove known as a nude gay beach. No anti-gay laws exist in Costa Rica.

Panama and Nicaragua, on the other hand, don't have as extensive a gay population, but gays who practice a little discretion should encounter no problems here.

LOCAL RESOURCES

Associacion Triangulo Rosa, in San José, provides information and support for gay and lesbian travelers. **Costa Rica Human Rights Commission** in San José gives legal advice to gays and lesbians who feel their rights have been violated. **Abraxas** is a gay association that organizes activities every Sunday near Alajuela.

➤ CONTACTS: **Abraxas** (✉ Apartado Postal 1619–4050, Alajuela). **Associacion Triangulo Rosa** (C. 11 at Avenida 2, ☎ 506/234–2411). **Costa Rica Human Rights Commission** (San Pedro, ☎ 506/226–2658 or 506/226–2081).

HEALTH

ENGLISH-SPEAKING DOCTORS

Many of the doctors at San José's Clinica Biblica and Clinica Catolica speak English well; some even studied at U.S. Medical Schools.

➤ LOCAL MEDICAL HELP: **Clinica Biblica** (Avda. 14 at C. 1, San José, ☎ 506/221–3922). **Clinica Catolica** (San Antonio Guadelupe, ☎ 506/283–6616).

FOOD & DRINK

Costa Rican and Panamanian food and water supplies are sanitary for the most part. In rural areas there is a mild risk posed by the contamination of drinking water, fresh fruit, and vegetables by fecal matter, which causes intestinal ailments known variously as Montezuma's Revenge (traveler's diarrhea), and leptospirosis (another disease borne on contaminated food or water that can be treated by antibiotics if detected early). So if you tend to exercise caution with such matters, **watch what you eat.** Avoid ice, uncooked food, and unpasteurized milk and milk products, and **drink bottled water.** Health standards in Nicaragua are lower than in the other two countries, which is why it is best to stick to only bottled water there, and to avoid unpeeled fruits and vegetables. Mild cases of Montezuma's Revenge may respond to Imodium (known generically as loperamide) or Pepto-Bismol (not as strong), both of which can be purchased over the counter. Paregoric is another antidiarrheal agent and requires a doctor's prescription in Costa Rica. Drink plenty of purified water or tea—chamomile is a good folk remedy. In severe cases, rehydrate yourself with a salt-sugar solution (½ teaspoon salt and 4 tablespoons sugar per quart of water).

MEDICAL PLANS

No one plans to get sick while traveling, but it happens, so **consider signing up with a medical-assistance company.** Members get doctor referrals, emergency evacuation or repatriation, hot lines for medical consultation, cash for emergencies, and other assistance.

➤ CONTACTS: **International SOS Assistance** (✉ 8 Neshaminy Interplex, Suite 207, Trevose, PA 19053, ☎ 215/245–4707 or 800/523–6586, FAX 215/244–9617; ✉ 12 Chemin Riantbosson, 1217 Meyrin 1, Geneva, Switzerland, ☎ 4122/785–6464, FAX 4122/785–6424; ✉ 331 N. Bridge Rd., 17-00, Odeon Towers, Singapore 188720, ☎ 65/338–7800, FAX 65/338–7611).

OVER-THE-COUNTER REMEDIES

Most of the drugs one needs a prescription for in the United States are sold over the counter in Central America, and pharmacies, or *farmacias,* as they are locally known, are pretty abundant. Asprin, *aspirina* in Spanish, is sold in most stores. Sunscreen, in a wide range of SPFs, is also pretty easy to find, though it's more expensive than in the States.

PESTS & OTHER HAZARDS

Mild repellents, such as those contained in certain skin softeners, are not adequate for the intense levels of mosquito activity that occur in the hot, humid regions of the Atlantic Lowlands. Also, note that perfume, aftershave, and other body lotions and potions can attract mosquitoes. The CDC recommends chloroquine (analen) as an antimalarial agent; no vaccine exists against dengue.

Poisonous snakes, scorpions, and other pests, pose a small, overrated threat. The greatest danger actually lies off the region's popular beaches—riptides are common everywhere there are waves, and several tourists drown in them every year. If there are waves, ask the locals where it's safe to swim, and if you're uncertain, don't go in any deeper than your waist. If caught in a rip current, swim parallel to the beach until you're well out of it, then swim back to shore.

SHOTS & MEDICATIONS

According to the Centers for Disease Control (CDC), there is a limited risk of malaria, hepatitis A and B, dengue fever, typhoid fever, and rabies in Central America. Travelers in most urban or easily accessible areas need not worry. However, if you plan to visit remote regions or stay for more than six weeks, check with the CDC's International Travelers Hotline (☞ Health Warnings, *below*). In areas with malaria and dengue, both of which are carried by mosquitoes, **take mosquito nets, wear clothing that covers the body, apply repellent containing DEET and use a spray against flying insects in living and sleeping areas.**

Though dengue and malaria are less of a problem in Panama, the threat of infection exists there as well, especially in the country's western and eastern extremes and along the Atlantic coast. The threat of malaria is the worst during the May to mid-December rainy season. Be especially careful in Nicaragua, which suffers a higher incidence of malaria and dengue.

Travelers to Nicaragua should be aware of the risk of contracting dengue fever or malaria in jungle areas. Hepatitis A vaccinations are not necessary, but it is a good precautionary measure. Children traveling to Central America should have current inoculations against measles, mumps, rubella, and polio.

➤ HEALTH WARNINGS: **National Centers for Disease Control** (CDC, National Center for Infectious Diseases, Division of Quarantine, Traveler's Health Section, ✉ 1600 Clifton Rd. NE, M/S E-03, Atlanta, GA 30333, ☎ 888/232–3228, FAX 888/232–3299).

HOLIDAYS

National holidays are known as *feriados*. On these days government offices, banks, and post offices are closed, and public transport is restricted. Religious festivals are characterized by colorful processions. Panama's annual carnival celebrations feature some spectacular costumes.

2000 dates: January 1, New Year's Day; January 9, Day of the Martyrs (Panama only); March 7, Shrove Tuesday; March 7 Carnival Tuesday (Panama); April 21–23, Good Friday–Easter Sunday; April 11, Juan Santamaría Day (Costa Rica); May 1, Labor Day; July 25, Annexation of Guanacaste (Costa Rica); August 2, Virgin of Los Angeles (Costa Rica's patron saint); September 15, Independence Day (Costa Rica); October 12, Columbus Day (Día de la Raza); November 3, Independence from Colombia (Panama); November 10, Call for Independence (Panama); November 28, Independence from Spain (Panama); December 25, Christmas.

INSURANCE

The most useful travel insurance plan is a comprehensive policy that includes coverage for trip cancellation and interruption, default, trip delay, and medical expenses (with a waiver for preexisting conditions).

Without insurance you will lose all or most of your money if you cancel your trip, regardless of the reason. Default insurance covers you if your tour operator, airline, or cruise line goes out of business. Trip-delay covers expenses that arise because of bad weather or mechanical delays. Study the fine print when comparing policies.

If you're traveling internationally, a key component of travel insurance is coverage for medical bills incurred if you get sick on the road. Such expenses are not generally covered by Medicare and by some private policies. U.K. residents can buy a travel-insurance policy valid for most vacations taken during the year in which it's purchased (but check pre-existing-condition coverage). Always **buy travel policies directly from the insurance company**; if you buy it from a cruise line, airline, or tour operator that goes out of business you probably will not be covered for the agency or operator's default, a major risk. Before you make any purchase **review your existing health and homeowner's policies** to find what is covered away from home.

➤ TRAVEL INSURERS: In the U.S. Access America (✉ 6600 W. Broad St., Richmond, VA 23230, ☎ 804/285–3300 or 800/284–8300). **Travel Guard International** (✉ 1145 Clark St., Stevens Point, WI 54481, ☎ 715/345–0505 or 800/826–1300). In Canada **Voyager Insurance** (✉ 44 Peel Center Dr., Brampton, Ontario L6T 4M8, ☎ 905/791–8700; 800/668–4342 in Canada).

➤ INSURANCE INFORMATION: In the U.K. the **Association of British Insurers** (✉ 51–55 Gresham St., London EC2V 7HQ, ☎ 0171/600–3333, FAX 0171/696–8999). In Australia the **Insurance Council of Australia** (☎ 03/9614–1077, FAX 03/9614–7924).

LANGUAGE

Spanish is the official language of Costa Rica, Panama, and Nicaragua, although some people speak English, especially along the Caribbean coast. Your stay in Central America will be much better if you learn some basic Spanish before you go and bring a phrase book with you. At the very least, attempt to **learn the rudiments of polite conversation**—such phrases as *por favor* (please) and *gracias* (thank you) are sure to be appreciated.

LANGUAGE-STUDY PROGRAMS

Thousands of people travel to Costa Rica every year to study Spanish. The country has dozens of schools in and around San José offering professional instruction and home stays, as well as several small schools outside the capital.

➤ PROGRAMS: **Conversa** (✉ Apdo. 17–1007, Centro Colon, San José, ☎ 506/221–7649, 800/354–5036 in U.S. or Canada) also has a school in Santa Ana, west of San José. **ICAI** (✉ Apdo. 10302, San José, ☎ 506/233–8571, 916/432–7690 in U.S.). **ILISA** (✉ Dept. 1420, Box 25216, Miami, FL 33102, ☎ 506/225–2495, 800/454–7248, ext. 3000 in U.S.). **La Escuela D'Amore** (✉ Apdo. 67, Quepos, ☎ 506/777–1143) is located in beautiful Manuel Antonio.

LANGUAGES FOR TRAVELERS

Fodor's Spanish for Travelers, a phrase book and language-tape set, can help get you started.

➤ PHRASE BOOKS & LANGUAGE-TAPE SETS: *Fodor's Spanish for Travelers* (☎ 800/733–3000 in the U.S.; 800/668–4247 in Canada; $7 for phrase-book, $16.95 for audio set).

LODGING

Hotels are going up fast in Costa Rica, to keep pace with the country's growing popularity as a vacation destination. Development is moving more slowly in Panama and Nicaragua, which are still fairly unknown destinations. For Costa Rica's popular beach and mountain resorts, Panama City's best hotels, and the Chiriquí highlands, **reserve well in advance for the dry season** (mid-December–April)—you'll need to give credit card information or send a deposit to confirm the reservation. During the rainy season, May to mid-December, most hotels drop their rates considerably, which sometimes puts them into a lower price category.

Luxury international hotels are found mainly in San José and Panama City. Many visitors prefer the smaller one-of-a-kind hotels in former homes with verdant courtyards found in and around San José. Except for along the most popular Pacific beaches, lodging in outlying areas is usually in smaller, simpler hotels, which often go by the name of *cabinas* (cabins), *cabañas,* as they are called in Panama, and *hospedajes* in Nicaragua. Cabinas range from basic cement boxes with few creature comforts to flashier units with all the modern conveniences. There are also plenty of nature lodges

(often within private biological reserves) in Costa Rica and Panama that cater to naturalist vacationers. Though most of these lodges have only rustic accommodations, a few of the newer ones are luxurious. About half of the national parks have campsites with facilities.

Assume that hotels operate on the European Plan (EP, with no meals) unless we specify that they use the Continental Plan (CP, with a Continental breakfast daily), Modified American Plan (MAP, with breakfast and dinner daily), or are all-inclusive (including all meals and most activities).

The lodgings we list are the cream of the crop in each price category. We always list the facilities that are available—but we don't specify whether they cost extra: when pricing accommodations, always ask what's included and what costs extra.

CATEGORY	COST*
$$$$	over $90
$$$	$50–$90
$$	$25–$50
$	under $25

Lodging prices are for a double room, excluding service and 16.4% tax in Costa Rica, 10% tax in Panama, and 15% tax in Nicaragua.

APARTMENT & VILLA RENTALS

If you want a home base that's roomy enough for a family and comes with cooking facilities **consider a furnished rental.** These can save you money, especially if you're traveling with a group. In Costa Rica the English-language weekly, *The Tico Times,* has local news and information about entertainment and travel. Home-exchange directories sometimes list rentals as well as exchanges. In Costa Rica, Costa Rica Rentals International has rental homes and apartments in the San José area and elsewhere. Tropical Waters arranges short-term rentals in the Dominical area. Pacific Coast Sales and Rentals sets up house and condo rentals in the Playa Flamingo area.

➤ CONTACTS: **Costa Rica Rentals International** (✉ Apdo. 1136–1250, Escazú, ☎ 506/228–6863). **Tropical**

SMART TRAVEL TIPS / THE GOLD GUIDE

Waters (⊠ 3km north of Dominical, ☎ 506/787–0031). **Pacific Coast Realty** (⊠ Suites Presidenciales, Playa Flamingo, Guanacaste, ☎ 506/654–4068). *The Tico Times* (☎ 506/258–1558).

➤ INTERNATIONAL AGENTS: **Europa-Let/Tropical Inn-Let** (⊠ 92 N. Main St., Ashland, OR 97520, ☎ 541/482–5806 or 800/462–4486, ℻ 541/482–0660). **Rent-a-Home International** (⊠ 7200 34th Ave. NW, Seattle, WA 98117, ☎ 206/789–9377, ℻ 206/789–9379). **Vacation Home Rentals Worldwide** (⊠ 235 Kensington Ave., Norwood, NJ 07648, ☎ 201/767–9393 or 800/633–3284, ℻ 201/767–5510). **Villas and Apartments Abroad** (⊠ 420 Madison Ave., Suite 1003, New York, NY 10017, ☎ 212/759–1025 or 800/433–3020, ℻ 212/755–8316). **Villas International** (⊠ 950 Northgate Dr., Suite 206, San Rafael, CA 94903, ☎ 415/499–9490 or 800/221–2260, ℻ 415/499–9491). **Hideaways International** (⊠ 767 Islington St., Portsmouth, NH 03801, ☎ 603/430–4433 or 800/843–4433, ℻ 603/430–4444; membership $99).

B&BS

San José has an overabundance of B&Bs, many set in former homes in the historic Amon and Otoya neighborhoods.

CAMPING

Many, though not all, national parks have camping areas; usually it's best to contact the park rangers for information. Some of the popular beaches, including Manuel Antonio, Jacó, Sámara, Tamarindo, and Puerto Viejo, have private camping areas with bathrooms and showers. If you camp on the beach or in other unguarded areas, **don't leave belongings unattended in your tent.**

HOSTELS

No matter what your age you can **save on lodging costs by staying at hostels.** In Costa Rica, information about and reservations for any of the country's six hostels are available at the Toruma Youth Hostel in San José (☞ Chapter 2). In some 5,000 locations in more than 70 countries around the world, Hostelling International (HI), the umbrella group for a

number of national youth-hostel associations, offers single-sex, dorm-style beds and, at many hostels, couples rooms and family accommodations. Call for membership information.

➤ ORGANIZATIONS: **Hostelling International–American Youth Hostels** (⊠ 733 15th St. NW, Suite 840, Washington, DC 20005, ☎ 202/783–6161, ℻ 202/783–6171). **Hostelling International–Canada** (⊠ 400–205 Catherine St., Ottawa, Ontario K2P 1C3, ☎ 613/237–7884, ℻ 613/237–7868). **Youth Hostel Association of England and Wales** (⊠ Trevelyan House, 8 St. Stephen's Hill, St. Albans, Hertfordshire AL1 2DY, ☎ 01727/855215 or 01727/845047, ℻ 01727/844126). **Australian Youth Hostel Association** (⊠ 10 Mallett St., Camperdown, NSW 2050, ☎ 02/9565–1699, ℻ 02/9565–1325). **Youth Hostels Association of New Zealand** (⊠ Box 436, Christchurch, New Zealand, ☎ 03/379–9970, ℻ 03/365–4476).

HOTELS

There are a few big hotels found on the outskirts of San José and on some of the more popular beaches, but most of them are smaller, offering more personalized service. For a double bed, request a *cama doble*. It is almost impossible to find a hotel room outside of San José from Christmas to the New Year and during Easter Week; reservations must be made one to three months in advance. Most hotels drop their rates during the "green season," from May to December, and from mid-April to July and September to December it is quite feasible to travel without reservations and to haggle over rates, which could bring your hotel budget down to nearly half of what it might be in the high season. All hotels listed have private bath unless otherwise noted.

➤ TOLL-FREE NUMBERS: **Best Western** (☎ 800/528–1234). **Holiday Inn** (☎ 800/465–4329). **Marriott** (☎ 800/228–9290). **Quality Inn** (☎ 800/228–5151). **Radisson** (☎ 800/333–3333).

NATURE LODGES

Since Mother Nature's wonders are Costa Rica's biggest attractions, it should come as no surprise that there is an abundance of nature lodges offering guests an ecologically educational experience.

MAIL & SHIPPING

Mail from the States or Europe can take two to three weeks to arrive in Costa Rica (occasionally it never does); within the country, mail service is even less reliable. Outgoing mail is marginally quicker, especially when sent from the capitals. **Always use airmail for overseas cards and letters**; delivery may take anywhere from five days to two weeks, or more. Mail theft is a chronic problem, so **do not mail checks, money, or anything else of value.**

OVERNIGHT SERVICES

Unfortunately, for anywhere farther than Miami, overnight is usually a misnomer—most U.S. cities take two days, whereas Britain takes three, and Australia and New Zealand can take four or five. If you need to send important documents, checks, or other noncash valuables, you can use one of the courier services, such as Federal Express, DHL, Jetex, or any of the other local courier services, which have offices in the Costa Rican, Panamaian, and Nicaraguan capitals. Look in the yellow pages under "Courier."

POSTAL RATES

Rates are low. Letters sent from Costa Rica to the United States and Canada cost just 70 colones and 55 colones for postcards; to the United Kingdom, 90 colones for letters and 70 for postcards. A letter to New Zealand or Australia costs 100 colones, a postcard 85 colones. Letters sent from Panama to the United States cost 35¢; to Canada 40¢; to the United Kingdom, New Zealand, and Australia 45¢. A letter from Nicaragua to the United States and Canada costs 7.50 cordobas (6.5 to Miami), to the United Kingdom 10 cordobas, and to Australia and New Zealand 12 cordobas.

RECEIVING MAIL

You can have mail sent to your hotel or use poste restante at the post office (Lista de Correos). Most Costa Ri-

cans have to go to the post office to pick up their mail, because of the absence of both street names and any house-to-house service. *Apartado* (abbreviated *apdo.*) means post-office box.

Anyone with an American Express card or traveler's checks can have mail sent to them at the American Express offices in San José, Panama City, and Managua.

A faster and more functional alternative for nonpersonal letters, particularly those confirming reservations and the like, is the fax machine, which is nearly ubiquitous in Costa Rica.

SHIPPING PARCELS

Packages can be mailed from any of the post offices in the three countries, with rates running between $6 and $12 per kilo, according to destination. It can take a week to a month for packages to arrive, depending upon where they're mailed. A quicker, though more expensive alternative is United Postal Service, which has offices in all three countries and charges about 10 times as much as the post offices, but delivers in a matter of days.

MONEY MATTERS

Here is an approximation of what costs what in Costa Rica: bottle of Coca-Cola, 200–300 colones; cup of coffee, 200–300 colones; bottle of beer, 250–500 colones; sandwich, 600–1,000 colones; daily U.S. newspaper, 400–700 colones. Prices throughout this guide are given for adults. Substantially reduced fees are almost always available for children, students, and senior citizens. For information on taxes, *see* Taxes, *below.*

ATMS

ATMs connected to the Plus system are found at offices of the Banco Popular, found in Alajuela, Cartago, Heredia, Limón, Puntarenas, Quepos and half a dozen other cities. In San José, the main office of the Banco Popular is located at Avenida 2 and Calle 1, near the National Theater. Cash advances are also available through the Credomatic office, on

280 Colones to the dollar

Calle Central between Avenidas 3 and 5, or the Banco de San José, across the street, which also has an American Express office on the third floor. All offices of the Banco de San José have ATMs connected to the Cirrus system—Liberia, Puerto Limón, San Isidro, etc.—as well as at more than a dozen locations around San José, including the Centro Omni, one block north of the Gran Hotel Costa Rica.

In Panama, the Banco del Istmo, which has branches in Changuinola and David, gives cash advances on MasterCard and Visa.

You'll find ATMs in Managua, but they are rare outside Nicaragua's cities. ATMs will also give cash advances, but with hefty service charges.

CREDIT CARDS

Major credit cards are accepted at most major hotels and restaurants in all three countries, outside of Panama's Bocas del Toro. As the phone system improves and expands, many budget hotels, restaurants, and other facilities are accepting credit cards. That said, there are still plenty of places that don't accept any credit cards, some of which are in the expensive price categories. **Don't count on using plastic all the time**—it is essential, especially when traveling away from San José, Panama City, and Managua, to **carry enough cash or traveler's checks** for the many businesses without phones or credit-card capabilities. Note that some hotels, restaurants, tour companies, and other businesses add a surcharge (app. 5%) to the bill if you pay with a credit card, while others give you a 5%–10% discount if you pay cash.

Throughout this guide, the following abbreviations are used: **AE**, American Express; **DC**, Diner's Club; **MC**, MasterCard; and **V**, Visa.

➤ REPORTING LOST CARDS: **American Express** (☎ 910/333–3211 collect to U.S.). **Diner's Club** (☎ 702/797–5532 collect to U.S.). **Mastercard** (☎ 0800/011–0184 toll-free to U.S.). **Visa** (☎ 0800/011–0030 toll-free to U.S.).

CURRENCY

All prices are quoted in U.S. dollars, due to the following:

The Costa Rican currency, the colón (plural: colones), is subject to continual, small devaluations; at press time (spring 1999), the colón had topped 280 to the dollar, 451 colones to the pound sterling, 192 colones to the Canadian dollar, 186 to the Australian dollar, and 156 to the New Zealand dollar.

Panama's national currency is the balboa, which has been out of print for decades—they use the U.S. dollar instead, and simply call it a balboa. The Panamanian government mints its own coins, which are the same size as U.S. coins, and circulate together with their American counterparts. Since the dollar is currency, and traveler's checks are accepted by most businesses, there is little need to go to the bank. Carry lots of $10 and $20 bills; the abundance of counterfeit dollars has caused many businesses to stop accepting $50 and $100 bills.

The Nicaraguan unit of currency is the cordoba (plural: cordobas), but U.S. dollars are widely accepted. At press time, 11 cordobas matched the dollar, 7 cordobas the Canadian dollar, and 18 cordobas the pound sterling.

CURRENCY EXCHANGE

For the most favorable rates, **change money through banks.** You won't do as well at the exchange booth in the airport, in hotels, in restaurants, or in stores, although you may find their hours more convenient. **Exchange booths in U.S. airports give extremely low rates,** and since the cabbies at Costa Rica's International Airport accept dollars, and most hotels change them, there is no need to buy colones outside of Costa Rica. Although ATM transaction fees may be higher abroad than at home, ATM rates are excellent because they are based on wholesale rates offered only by major banks.

It's best to **avoid people on the city streets who offer to change money.** The money changers in the streets of San José are notorious for short-changing people and passing counterfeit bills. The guys who change money at the airport aren't quite as shady, though they might not be above shortchanging you, and they don't give a great exchange rate.

➤ EXCHANGE SERVICES: **International Currency Express** (☎ 888/842–0880 on East Coast; 888/278–6628 on West Coast). **Thomas Cook Currency Services** (☎ 800/287–7362 for telephone orders and retail locations).

TRAVELER'S CHECKS

Do you need traveler's checks? It depends on where you're headed. If you're going to rural areas and small towns, go with cash; traveler's checks are best used in cities. Lost or stolen checks can usually be replaced within 24 hours. To ensure a speedy refund, buy your own traveler's checks—don't let someone else pay for them: irregularities like this can cause delays. The person who bought the checks should make the call to request a refund.

Travelers who have an American Express card and money in a U.S. checking account can purchase traveler's checks at the American Express office in San José, or Panama City, and Managua; there's a 1% service charge.

OUTDOORS & SPORTS

BIKING

Although much of this region is mountainous, there are also many ideal-for-cycling flatlands in Costa Rica. A number of Costa Rican companies currently offer mountain-biking tours out of San José; tours range in length from a single day to a week. In La Fortuna de San Carlos, Desafío rents bikes and offers guided tours. You can also rent your own bicycles in most Costa Rican and Panamanian mountain and beach resorts.

➤ BIKE TOUR OPERATORS: **Costaricabike** (San Pedro, ☎ 506/224–0899). **Desafío** (La Fortuna de San Carlos, ☎ 506/479–9464). (☎ 202/647–0518). **Dos Montañas** (San José, ☎ 506/233–6455).

BIRD-WATCHING

➤ BIRD-WATCHING TOUR OPERATORS: **Ancon Expeditions** (☎ 507/269–9415). **Costa Rica Expeditions** (☎ 506/222–0333). **Horizontes** (☎ 506/222–2022). **Pesántez Tours** (☎ 507/263–8771).

WATER SPORTS

Costa Rica and Panama are worth visiting for their water sports alone. Wild rivers provide plenty of white water for rafting, and Costa Rica's Lake Arenal is acclaimed as one of the best places in the world to wind-surf. Skin diving excursions are available out of Costa Rica's Drake Bay, Flamingo, Ocotal, and Playa del Coco, but Costa Rica's best dive spot, Cocos Island, can only be visited on 10-day scuba safaris on the *Okeanos Aggressor* and the *Undersea Hunter.* Panama has even more diving options, with dive centers at several Caribbean and Pacific locations, including three dive operations in Bocas del Toro. Both countries also have excellent surf, especially Costa Rica, where popular surfing beaches include Tamarindo, Jacó, Hermosa and Dominical. Airlines generally allow surfboards on board, and charge the standard weight charge.

➤ DIVE OPERATORS IN COSTA RICA: **Bill Beard's Diving Safaris** (Playa Hermosa, ☎ 506/672–0012). **El Ocotal Diving Safaris** (Playa del Ocotal, ☎ 506/222–4259). *Okeanos Agressor* (Puntarenas; office: Across from Colegio Los Angeles, Sabana Norte, San José, ☎ 506/232–6672). *Undersea Hunter* (Puntarenas; office: Escazú, ☎ 506/228–6535).

➤ DIVE OPERATORS IN PANAMA: **Scuba Panama** (Panama City, ☎ 507/261–3841). **Starfleet Eco Adventures** (Bocas del Toro, ☎ 507/757–9630). **Turtle Divers** (Bocas del Toro, ☎ 507/757–9594).

➤ RAFTING OUTFITTERS: **Aventuras Naturales** (☎ 506/225–3939). **Chiriquí River Rafting** (☎ 507/720–1505). **Costa Rica Expeditions** (☎ 506/222–0333). **Ríos Tropicales** (☎ 506/233–6455).

➤ WINDSURFING OUTFITTERS: **Tilawa** (Lake Arenal, ☎ 506/695–5050).

PACKING

Pack light. Bring comfortable, hand-washable clothing. T-shirts and shorts are acceptable near the beach and in heavily touristed areas. Loose-fitting long-sleeve shirts and pants are good in smaller towns (where immodest attire is frowned upon) and to protect your skin from the ferocious sun and mosquitoes. **Bring a large hat to block the sun from your face and neck.** Pack a light sweater or jacket for cool nights, early mornings, and trips up volcanoes; you'll need even more warm clothes if you plan on descending Chirripó or Barú Volcano, or spend a night in San Gerardo de Dota or La Providencia Lodge. Sturdy sneakers or hiking boots are essential for sightseeing and hiking. Waterproof hiking sandals (such as Tevas) are good for boating, beach walking, fording streams, and light hiking trails.

Insect repellent, sunscreen, sunglasses, and umbrellas (during the rainy season) are musts. Other handy items—especially if you are traveling on your own or camping—include toilet paper, facial tissues, a plastic water bottle, and a flashlight (for occasional power outages or use at campsites). Snorkelers should consider bringing their own equipment unless traveling light is a priority, though gear can be rented at most beach resorts. Some beaches, such as Playa Grande, do not have shade trees, so if you're planning a stay at the beach you might consider investing in a sturdy, shade-making tarpaulin. For long-term stays in remote rural areas, *see* Health, *above*.

In your carry-on luggage **bring an extra pair of eyeglasses or contact lenses** and **enough of any medication you take** to last the entire trip. You may also want your doctor to write a spare prescription using the drug's generic name, since brand names may vary from country to country. In luggage to be checked, **never pack prescription drugs or valuables.** To avoid customs delays, carry medications in their original packaging. And don't forget to copy down and carry addresses of offices that handle refunds of lost traveler's checks.

CHECKING LUGGAGE

How many carry-on bags you can bring with you is up to the airline. Most allow two, but not always, so make sure that everything you carry aboard fits under your seat, and get to the gate early. Note that if you have a seat at the back of the plane, you'll probably board first, while the overhead bins are still empty.

If you are flying internationally, note that baggage allowances may be determined not by piece but by weight—generally 88 pounds (40 kilograms) in first class, 66 pounds (30 kilograms) in business class, and 44 pounds (20 kilograms) in economy.

Airline liability for baggage is limited to $1,250 per person on flights within the United States. On international flights it amounts to $9.07 per pound or $20 per kilogram for checked baggage (roughly $640 per 70-pound bag) and $400 per passenger for unchecked baggage. You can buy additional coverage at check-in for about $10 per $1,000 of coverage, but it excludes a rather extensive list of items, shown on your airline ticket.

Before departure **itemize your bags' contents** and their worth, and label the bags with your name, address, and phone number. (If you use your home address, cover it so that potential thieves can't see it readily.) Inside each bag **pack a copy of your itinerary.** At check-in **make sure that each bag is correctly tagged** with the destination airport's three-letter code. If your bags arrive damaged or fail to arrive at all, file a written report with the airline before leaving the airport.

PASSPORTS & VISAS

When traveling internationally **carry a passport even if you don't need one** (it's always the best form of I.D.), and **make two photocopies of the data page** (one for someone at home and another for you, carried separately from your passport). If you lose your passport promptly call the nearest embassy or consulate and the local police.

ENTERING COSTA RICA, PANAMA, AND NICARAGUA

Although U.S. citizens do not need a valid passport to enter Costa Rica for stays of up to 30 days—you can enter using a Tourist Card if you have a photo ID and a copy of your birth certificate—we recommend that you **bring your passport:** for passage from Costa Rica into Panama, for emergencies, for longer stays, and because it is the most recognizable form of identification for changing money, renting hotel rooms, or any other transaction. U.S. citizens with valid passports are allowed to stay in Costa Rica for 90 days, after which they must leave for at least 72 hours.

A valid passport is needed to visit Panama, either with a visa issued by a Panamanian embassy or consulate (free of charge) or a tourist card that can be purchased at the border, airport, or the tourist board offices in Paso Canoas (cost $5). Travelers who don't have a visa must purchase a $10 stamp at the Banco General and get it stamped at the immigration office in Bocas del Toro or Changuinola. In Costa Rica, you can get a visa free of charge from the Panamanian Consul, 350 North of the Centro Colon in western San José (☎ 202/256–8160); you'll need a round-trip ticket and photocopy of the photo page of your passport; drop it off on a weekday morning, and it will be ready the next workday.

To visit Nicaragua, you need a valid passport with a tourist card (5$), which you can purchase at the airport or border, and a return ticket.

AUSTRALIAN AND NEW ZEALAND CITIZENS

Citizens of Australia and New Zealand need only a valid passport to enter Costa Rica for stays of up to 30 days (once in the country, you can go to the Migracion office in La Uruca and get it extended to 90 days). A 30-day visa for Panama can be purchased for US$10 at a Panamanian consulate (☞ U.S. Citizens, *above*). Tourist cards, also good for 30 days, can be purchased for $5 at the border, airport, Paso Canoas, or Sixaola. To visit Nicaragua, Australian and New Zealand citizens need a valid passport with a tourist card (5$), which can be purchased at the airport or border, and a return ticket.

CANADIANS

You need only a valid passport to enter Costa Rica for stays of up to 90 days. A 30-day visa for Panama can be purchased for $10 U.S. at a Panamanian consulate (☞ U.S. Citizens, *above*). Tourist cards, also good for 30 days, can be purchased for $5 at the airport of Paso Canoas border. To visit Nicaragua, Canadian citizens need a valid passport with a tourist card (5$), which can be purchased at the airport or border, and a return ticket.

U.K. CITIZENS

Citizens of the United Kingdom need only a valid passport to enter Costa Rica for up to 90 days, and to enter Panama for stays of up to 30 days. To visit Nicaragua, citizens from the United Kingdom need a valid passport with a tourist card (5$), which can be purchased at the airport or border, and a return ticket.

PASSPORT OFFICES

The best time to apply for a passport or to renew is during the fall and winter. Before any trip, check your passport's expiration date, and, if necessary, renew it as soon as possible.

➤ AUSTRALIAN CITIZENS: **Australian Passport Office** (☎ 131–232).

➤ CANADIAN CITIZENS: **Passport Office** (☎ 819/994–3500 or 800/ 567–6868).

➤ NEW ZEALAND CITIZENS: **New Zealand Passport Office** (☎ 04/494– 0700 for information on how to apply; 04/474–8000 or 0800/225– 050 in New Zealand for information on applications already submitted).

➤ U.K. CITIZENS: **London Passport Office** (☎ 0990/210–410) for fees and documentation requirements and to request an emergency passport.

➤ U.S. CITIZENS: **National Passport Information Center** (☎ 900/225– 5674; calls are 35¢ per minute for automated service, $1.05 per minute for operator service).

SAFETY

Rural areas tend to be safe, but crime is a problem in capital cities, where caution is advised. The greatest dangers outside of cities are driving on mountain roads and swimming in the ocean, where rip currents pose a serious threat. If there are big waves, don't go in any deeper than your waist, unless you're an experienced ocean swimmer. Some beaches are always dangerous, such as the one at

Tortuguero—ask locals if it's safe to swim. If you get caught in a rip current, swim parallel to shore until you're well out of it, then back to the beach.

LOCAL SCAMS

San José has plenty of scammers and thieves who prey on tourists. Drug addicts tell tales of being a recent robbery victim and ask for a donation; distraction artists squirt you with cream, then try to clean you off while his partner steals your backpack; pickpockets and bag slashers work buses and crowds, while street money changers pass off counterfeit bills. To top it off, car theft is rampant. Beware of anyone who is overly friendly, aggressively helpful, or who invades your personal space.

WOMEN IN COSTA RICA

Latin machismo means young women will have to deal with suggestive comments and ogling by men on the street—common in cities, but rare in the countryside—which local women tend to ignore, avoiding eye contact. Local men are rarely aggressive to a point of being dangerous. Rape is as common in these countries as it is at home, if not more so, which is why standard precautions are advised. That said, hundreds of thousands of women visit these countries every year, many of them traveling alone, and have a great time.

SENIOR-CITIZEN TRAVEL

Older travelers may encounter more mobility challenges than they do at home—especially on those muddy jungle trails—but should otherwise find the area most hospitable.

To qualify for age-related discounts **mention your senior-citizen status up front** when booking hotel reservations (not when checking out) and before you're seated in restaurants (not when paying the bill). When renting a car ask about promotional car-rental discounts, which can be cheaper than senior-citizen rates.

➤ EDUCATIONAL PROGRAMS: **Elderhostel** (⊠ 75 Federal St., 3rd fl., Boston, MA 02110, ☎ 877/426–8056, FAX 877/426–2166). **Interhostel** (⊠ University of New Hampshire, 6 Garrison Ave., Durham, NH 03824, ☎ 603/862–1147 or 800/733–9753, FAX 603/862–1113).

SHOPPING

Costa Rica has few artisans, which is why much of what's sold here is from other countries. The coffee and rum are quite good, and you will find some nice T-shirts, jewelry, leather goods, and wooden handicrafts. Nicaragua has similar products at better prices, as well as interesting ceramics and woven mats that make good wall hangings. Panama's Indians produce some colorful handicrafts, such as the woven bags of the Gaymí and the Kuna's *molas,* or fabric pictures.

STUDENTS IN COSTA RICA

Central America is a fantastic place for students and youths on a budget. Although prices are on the rise in Costa Rica, it is still possible to travel on $25 to $30 a day. There are youth hostels all over Costa Rica, and though Panama and Nicaragua lack hostels, they have their share of inexpensive hotels. One of the cheapest ways to spend the night is camping. As long as you have your own tent, it's easy to set up camp anywhere. (If it looks like you're near someone's home, it's always a good idea to inquire first). Don't ever leave your things unattended.

➤ STUDENT I.D.s & SERVICES: For student travel discounts in Costa Rica, head to OTEC (⊠ C. 3 at Avda. 3, San José, ☎ 506/256–0633. **Council on International Educational Exchange** (CIEE, ⊠ 205 E. 42nd St., 14th fl., New York, NY 10017, ☎ 212/822–2600 or 888/268–6245, FAX 212/822–2699) for mail orders only, in the U.S. Travel Cuts (⊠ 187 College St., Toronto, Ontario M5T 1P7, ☎ 416/979–2406 or 800/667–2887) in Canada.

STUDYING ABROAD

The University of Costa Rica has exchange programs with at least half a dozen American universities, the oldest of which is the University of Kansas program. Many of the private language institutes offer Spanish courses for college credit (☞ Language Study Programs, *above*).

TAXES

When you fly out of Costa Rica, you'll have to pay the $16.50 airport departure tax at Juan Santamaría Airport. Individuals may offer to sell you the exit stamp as you climb out of taxis and buses. Look for properly displayed credentials, and **make sure you get the appropriate stamps in exchange for your dollars or colones.** The Panamanian airport tax is $20, which must be paid at a booth in the Tocumen International Airport, near Panama City.

There is no policy of giving tourists refunds for value-added tax (V.A.T.) paid while in Central American countries. All Costa Rican businesses charge a 13% sales tax, and an extra 4% tourist tax is added to hotel bills. In Panama, sales tax is 5%, and the hotel tax is another 5%. In Nicaragua, sales tax is 15%.

TELEPHONES

The Costa Rican, Panamanian, and Nicaraguan phone systems are very good by Third World standards. Calls within those countries are very cheap, but you pay more if you call from your hotel room. Most hotels also have fax machines.

COUNTRY & AREA CODES

The country code for Costa Rica is 506; for Panama, 507; for Nicaragua, 505. The country code for the United States is 1 for the United States, 61 for Australia, 64 for New Zealand, 44 for the U.K., and it varies for Canada (403 for Alberta; 250 for British Columbia; 204 for Manitoba; 506 for New Brunswick; 709 for Newfoundland; 902 for Nova Scotia; 905 for Ontario; 450 for Quebec; 306 for Saskatchewan; 867 for Yukon).

DIRECTORY & OPERATOR INFORMATION

Call ☎ 113 for domestic directory inquiries and ☎ 110 for domestic collect calls in Costa Rica, ☎ 102 in Panama, and ☎ 112 in Nicaragua.

INTERNATIONAL CALLS

The *guía telefónica* (phone book) contains numbers for various services as well as rates for calling different countries. To call overseas direct, dial 00, then the country code (☞ *above*), the area code, and the number. It is more expensive to phone from your hotel. Calls through the operator are more than twice as expensive, the only advantage being that if the person you need to speak to isn't in, there is no charge even if somebody answers. Discount times for calling the United States and Canada are weekdays 10 PM–7 AM and weekends; for calling the United Kingdom the only discounted time is between Friday at 10 PM and Monday at 7 AM.

LOCAL CALLS

Pay phones are abundant, though there's usually someone using them, and often people waiting. Some phones take change, others require phone cards sold in shops.

LONG-DISTANCE CALLS

International calls made from hotels can be quite expensive. It's cheaper to call from a pay phone using an international calling card, which are also sold in shops. However, if you don't use up your calling card, you lose money, which is why it's often better to call from a telephone office or use an AT&T, MCI, or Sprint calling card (☞ *below*).

LONG-DISTANCE SERVICES

AT&T, MCI, and Sprint access codes make calling long distance relatively convenient, but you may find the local access number blocked in many hotel rooms. First ask the hotel operator to connect you. If the hotel operator balks ask for an international operator, or dial the international operator yourself. One way to improve your odds of getting connected to your long-distance carrier is to travel with more than one company's calling card (a hotel may block Sprint, for example, but not MCI). If all else fails call from a pay phone.

➤ ACCESS CODES: **AT&T Direct** (☎ 0800/011–4114 from Costa Rica, 109 from Panama, and 800/435–0812 for other areas). **MCI World-Phone** (☎ 0800/012–2222 from Costa Rica, 108 from Panama, and 800/444–4141 for other areas). **Sprint International Access** (☎ 0800/013–

0123 from Costa Rica and 800/877–4646 for other areas).

➤ TELEPHONE OFFICES: **Radiográfica Costarricense** (✉ Avda. 5 between Cs. 1 and 3), open daily 7 AM–10 PM, also has phone, fax, and Internet facilities. **Cable & Wireless** (✉ C. Manuel María Icaza, 100 m south of the Vía España), open daily 8 AM–10 PM, is the phone office of choice in Panama City.

PHONE CARDS

Costa Rica has two kinds of phone cards: a domestic card, which have chips in them that record what you spend, and international cards, which have codes you have to punch into the telephone. Both cards are sold in an array of shops.

TIME

Costa Rica and Nicaragua lie in the central standard time zone, but move into the mountain time zone during daylight saving time (April to October). Panama is in the eastern standard time zone, but moves into the central standard time zone during daylight saving time.

TIPPING

In Costa Rican restaurants, a 13% tax and 10% service charge is added to the bill—sometimes tax and service are included in the prices on the menu, sometimes they aren't. Additional gratuity is not expected, especially not in less expensive restaurants, but if the service is good, people often leave something extra. In Panamanian restaurants, only the 5% tax is added, which means you are expected to leave at least 10% gratuity. It is customary to leave a 10% tip in Nicaraguan restaurants; check the bill first, as the tip is often added.

TRAIN TRAVEL

Costa Rica's train system has been defunct for years due to recurring earthquakes.

TRANSPORTATION

The most common form of transportation in these countries is the bus, which is why cities and towns are connected by regular, inexpensive bus service. Buses, however, can be a slow, uncomfortable way to travel, which makes domestic flights a good option in Costa Rica and Panama, where most major destinations are served by daily domestic flights. One way tickets cost $35 to $60 (round-trip is double), but they can get you in one hour where it would take most of the day to reach by land. Renting a car provides the most freedom, but can be expensive, especially in Costa Rica, where rates are the highest, and four wheel drive is often a necessity.

TRAVEL AGENCIES

A good travel agent puts your needs first. Look for an agency that has been in business at least five years, emphasizes customer service, and has someone on staff who specializes in your destination. In addition **make sure the agency belongs to a professional trade organization.** The American Society of Travel Agents (ASTA), with 27,000 agents in some 170 countries, is the largest and most influential in the field. Operating under the motto "Integrity in Travel," it maintains and enforces a strict code of ethics and will step in to help mediate any agent-client disputes if necessary. ASTA also maintains a website that includes a directory of agents. (Note that if a travel agency is also acting as your tour operator, *see* Buyer Beware *in* Tour Operators, *above*.)

➤ LOCAL AGENT REFERRALS: **American Society of Travel Agents** (ASTA, ☎ 800/965–2782 24-hr hot line, FAX 703/684–8319, www.astanet.com). **Association of Canadian Travel Agents** (✉ 1729 Bank St., Suite 201, Ottawa, Ontario K1V 7Z5, ☎ 613/521–0474, FAX 613/521–0805). **Association of British Travel Agents** (✉ 55–57 Newman St., London W1P 4AH, ☎ 0171/637–2444, FAX 0171/637–0713). **Australian Federation of Travel Agents** (✉ Level 3, 309 Pitt St., Sydney 2000, ☎ 02/9264–3299, FAX 02/9264–1085). **Travel Agents' Association of New Zealand** (✉ Box 1888, Wellington 10033, ☎ 04/499–0104, FAX 04/499–0786).

VISITOR INFORMATION

➤ TOURIST INFORMATION: **Costa Rica, Instituto Costarricense de Turismo**

(ICT, C. 5 between Avdas. Central and 2 San José, ☎ 506/222–1090. **Panama** (✉ Avda. 3 de Noviembre and C. A Norte, David, ☎ 507/775–5120). **Nicaragua** C. Arsenal and Avda. Miguel Cervantes, ☎ 505/0552–6858).

➤ COSTA RICA INFORMATION IN THE U.S.: **Costa Rica Tourist Board** (☎ 800/343–6332). **Embassy of Costa Rica** (✉ 2114 S St., NW, Washington, DC 20008, ☎ 202/234–2945). **Brochures nationwide** (☎ 800/343–6332). **Chicago Consulate** (✉ 185 N. Wabash Ave., Ste. 1123, Chicago, IL 60603, ☎ 312/263–2772). **Houston Consulate** (✉ 2901 Wilcrest Dr., Suite 275, Houston, TX 77042, ☎ 713/266–0484). **Los Angeles Consulate** (✉ 3450 Wilshire Blvd., Suite 404, Los Angeles, CA 90010, ☎ 213/380–6031). **Miami Consulate** (✉ 1600 N.W. Le June Rd., Ste 102, Miami, FL 33126, ☎ 305/871–7485, FAX 305/871–0860). **New York City Consulate** (✉ 80 Wall St., New York, NY 10005, ☎ 212/425–2620).

➤ COSTA RICA INFORMATION IN CANADA: **Ottawa Consulate** (✉ 150 Argyle Ave., Suite 115, Ottawa, Ontario K2P 1 B7, ☎ 613/562–2855).

➤ COSTA RICA INFORMATION IN THE U.K.: **Costa Rica Tourist Services** (✉ 47 Causton St., London SW1P 4AT, ☎ 0171/976–5511, FAX 0171/976–6908).

➤ PANAMA INFORMATION IN THE U.S.: **Panamanian Embassy** (✉ 2862 McGill Terr., NW, Washington, DC 20008, ☎ 202/483–1407).

➤ NICARAGUA INFORMATION IN THE U.S.: **Nicaraguan Embassy** (✉ 1627 New Hampshire Ave., NW, Washington, DC 20009, ☎ 202/939–6570).

➤ U.S. GOVERNMENT ADVISORIES: **U.S. Department of State** (✉ Overseas Citizens Services Office, Room 4811 N.S., 2201 C St. NW, Washington, DC 20520; ☎ 202/647–5225 for interactive hot line; 301/946–4400 for computer bulletin board; FAX 202/647–3000 for interactive hot line); enclose a self-addressed, stamped, business-size envelope.

VOLUNTEER & EDUCATIONAL TRAVEL

Some, but not many, Costa Ricans have smartened up of late in realizing the need to preserve the country's precious, eye-opening biodiversity. Volunteer and educational efforts have been created by natives and far-flung environmentalists, and you, too, can have an impact. You do, however, pay for the privilege.

➤ OPERATORS: **CCC** (✉ 4424 Northwest 13th St., Suite A-1, Gainesville, FL 32609, ☎ 800/678–7853, FAX 352/375–2449). **Earthwatch Institute** (✉ 680 Mt. Auburn St., Box 9104, Watertown, MA 02272–9104, ☎ 800/776–0188, FAX 617/926–8532). **ATEC** (✉ Puerto Viejo de Talamanca, Puerto Limón,, ☎ 750–0188).

WEB SITES

Do check out the World Wide Web when you're planning. You'll find everything from up-to-date weather forecasts to virtual tours of famous cities. Fodor's Web site, www.fodors.com, is a great place to start your on-line travels.

➤ WEB SITES: Costa Rica: There are plenty of Web sites, which are best sorted out using one of the following Internet directories: www.info.co.cr and www.cr. For current events, check out www.ticotimes.co.cr. For natural history tours in Costa Rica, check out www.horizontes.com or www.expeditions.co.cr.

For general information on Panama, consult www.ipat.gob.pa. For ecotourism, see www.ecopanama.com. For Bocas del Toro, visit www.bocas.com. For Cerro Punta, see www.losquetzales.com.

WHEN TO GO

The most popular time to visit Costa Rica is during the dry season, which runs from mid-December through April. From mid-December until early February, you have the combined advantages of good weather and lush vegetation. If you want to visit the beach during the rainy season, it is often dry and sunny in the morning and rainy in the afternoon. Much of the region experiences sunnier

SMART TRAVEL TIPS / THE GOLD GUIDE

weather during July, August, and early September, whereas the Caribbean coast around Cahuita and Bocas del Toro tends to enjoy a short dry season during September and October, when the Pacific slope is being drenched by daily storms. Remember that hotels are much more likely to be booked up during the dry season.

Despite the fact that temperatures in Costa Rica vary little from season to season, the dry season (mid-December–April) is referred to as *verano* (summer) and the rainy season (May–mid-December) as *invierno* (winter).

To escape the tourist crowds and prices, visit during the rainy season, which has been promoted in recent years as the "Green" season. Green it is. The vegetation is at its lushest and most gorgeous, but some roads—those without asphalt—are washed out, and thus require four-wheel-drive vehicles. Bear in mind that during a visit in April, some areas, especially Guanacaste, are drier and dustier for lack of enriching rains. Visit during either July and August, when the storms let up a bit, or mid December,

when the rains are tapering off, but the high tourist season has yet to kick in. Keep in mind that during the rainiest months—September and October—some rural hotels simply shut down. The majority stay open, however, and not only are reservations easy to get, even at top establishments, you'll also have the beaches to yourself.

CLIMATE

Central America's climate varies greatly between the lowlands and the mountains. Tropical temperatures generally hover between 70°F and 85°F. The high humidity, especially in the dense jungle of the Caribbean coast, is the true sweat culprit. Guanacaste, on the more arid Pacific coast, is perhaps the hottest region, with dry-season temperatures frequently up in the 90s. Remember to drink plenty of bottled water to avoid dehydration. The following are average daily maximum and minimum temperatures for cities in Costa Rica.

➤ FORECASTS: **Weather Channel Connection** (☎ 900/932–8437), 95¢ per minute from a Touch-Tone phone.

GOLFITO, COSTA RICA

Jan.	91F	33C	May	91F	33C	Sept.	91F	33C
	72	22		73	23		72	22
Feb.	91F	33C	June	90F	32C	Oct.	90F	32C
	72	22		73	23		72	22
Mar.	91F	33C	July	90F	32C	Nov.	91F	32C
	73	23		72	22		72	22
Apr.	91F	33C	Aug.	90F	32C	Dec.	91F	33C
	73	23		72	22		72	22

Golfito, which lies at sea level, has a climate similar to that of most coastal and lowland towns, such as Panama City, David, Manuel Antonio, Jacó, Puntarenas, and the better part of Guanacaste.

SAN JOSÉ, COSTA RICA

Jan.	75F	24C	May	80F	27C	Sept.	79F	26C
	58	14		62	17		61	16
Feb.	76F	24C	June	79F	26C	Oct.	77F	25C
	58	14		62	17		60	16
Mar.	79F	26C	July	77F	25C	Nov.	77F	25C
	59	15		62	17		60	16
Apr.	79F	26C	Aug.	78F	26C	Dec.	75F	24C
	62	17		61	16		58	14

San José's average temperatures are similar to those of other highland towns, such as Monteverde and Panama's Boquete, but are warmer than San Gerardo de Dota and Panama's Cerro Punta.

1 DESTINATION: COSTA RICA

COSTA RICA: LAND OF PLEASANT SURPRISES

IT USED TO BE THAT WHEN YOU asked Americans and Europeans where Costa Rica was, the reply would invariably be, "Um. It's that island in the Caribbean. Right?" Times have certainly changed. Mention Costa Rica to someone today and most likely they'll conjure up visions of rain forests, tropical beaches, and exotic wildlife. The reason perceptions about Costa Rica have changed is simple: the country has become one of the hottest destinations on the map.

You don't need to spend too long contemplating Costa Rica's attractions to understand why it's such a popular place to visit. Tucked away in the Central American isthmus, with Nicaragua to the north and Panama to the south, Costa Rica is about the same size as the state of West Virginia. But packed into this small country are incredible biological diversity, equally varied landscapes, and a seemingly endless selection of outdoor diversions. From its exemplary system of parks and preserves to its sun-drenched Pacific beaches, and from the tropical jungles of the Caribbean coast to the bustling towns of the Central Valley, Costa Rica is full of pleasant surprises.

You might well be astonished by the cleanliness of the country, its raw natural beauty, the panoramic views, colorful mountain towns, and even by the fact that you can drink water straight from the tap. Though more famous for its flora, fauna, and spectacular scenery, Costa Rica has its greatest asset in its people. Ticos, as Costa Ricans call themselves, are fiercely proud of their history, culture, and achievements, but they are also a remarkably polite and accommodating people.

Perhaps what makes Ticos so special is their desire to *"quedar bien"*—"to leave a good impression." Or it could be the exuberant friendliness they express so naturally, with a marked willingness to get to know you and help them where they can. Whatever the reason, one thing is for sure—it is a rare visitor who does not return home impressed with the Ticos' warmth and hospitality.

Costa Rica was never an important part of the Spanish empire, which is one of the reasons why the country developed along lines very different from Spain's other colonies. Largely neglected during the colonial era, Costa Rica experienced most of its growth after independence from Spain. It is consequently a nation of immigrants, who came to work and prospered. Although most Latin American countries remain dominated by families that were granted vast tracts of land by the Spanish Crown, Costa Rica is more of a workingman's republic, and the consequent economic and political democracy results in citizens who believe in their country. This can be seen today in the strong sense of national identity—Ticos pride themselves first on being Costa Ricans rather than Central Americans, or even Latin Americans—and in the fact that the country has largely avoided the political turmoil that has beset so much of the region.

However, it is a fact that the strife and upheaval that rocked Central America during much of the past two decades painted a less-than-rosy picture of the area in the minds of most Americans and Europeans. People not well acquainted with Costa Rica often equate the problems in countries such as El Salvador and Nicaragua with all of Central America. In the midst of political unrest, Costa Rica managed to remain an island of stability and peace. The country has no army, for example—it was abolished in 1949. Costa Rica is also the region's most sturdy democracy, and the country has a deep-rooted respect for human rights.

When visiting, you'll hear a wide variety of superlative statistics, such as "Costa Rica has more teachers than policemen" and "The only thing that doesn't grow is what you don't plant," among others. In education, for example, Costa Rica ranks with many developed countries (the literacy rate is a very respectable 93%). Its telecommunications system is probably the best in the region.

The country's most striking feature, however, is the amazing variety of flora, fauna, landscape, and climate within its frontiers. Its national parks and biological preserves protect a vast array of habitats, covering more than 13% of the national territory, which should ensure the survival of its 850 species of birds, 205 species of mammals, 376 types of reptiles and amphibians, and more than 9,000 different species of flowering plants, among them 1,200 varieties of orchids. That spectacular biological diversity is distributed through an equally impressive array of landscapes, which include cool mountain valleys, sultry mangrove forests, and massive volcanoes draped with lush forests and topped with desolate craters.

The rivers that wind down the country's valleys churn through steep stretches that are popular white-water-rafting routes, whereas others end up as languid jungle waterways appropriate for both animal watching and sportfishing. With mile upon mile of beaches backdropped by coconut palms and thick forest, the Caribbean and Pacific coasts are ideal for shell collectors and sun worshipers, and when the sun goes down, many beaches are visited by nesting sea turtles. The oceans that hug those coasts hold intricate coral formations, rugged islands, colorful schools of fish, and plentiful waves, which provide the perfect playground for skin divers, anglers, surfers, and sea kayakers. What more could you want?

A BRIEF HISTORY

First Encounters with the Old World

In mid-September 1502, on his fourth and last voyage to the New World, Christopher Columbus was sailing along the Caribbean coast of Central America when his ships were caught in a violent tropical storm. Seeking shelter, he found sanctuary in a bay protected by a small island; ashore, he encountered natives wearing heavy gold disks and gold bird-shape figures who spoke of great amounts of gold in the area. Sailing farther south, Columbus encountered more natives, also wearing pendants and jewelry fashioned in gold. He was convinced that he had discovered a land of great wealth to be claimed for the Spanish empire. The land itself was a vision of lush greenery; popular legend has it that, on the basis of what he saw and encountered, Columbus named the land Costa Rica, the rich coast.

The Spanish Colonial Era

The first Spaniard to attempt conquest of Costa Rica was Diego de Nicuesa in 1506. But he found serious difficulties due to sickness, hunger, and Indian raids. Similar hardships were encountered by other Spaniards who visited the region. The first successful expedition to the country was made by Gil González de Ávila in 1522. Exploring the Pacific coast, he converted more than 6,000 Indians of the Chorotega tribe to Catholicism. A year later he returned to his home port in Panama with the equivalent of $600,000 in gold, but more than 1,000 of his men had died on the exhausting journey. Many other Spanish expeditions were undertaken, but all were less than successful, often because of rivalries between various expeditions. By 1560, almost 60 years after its discovery, no permanent Spanish settlement existed in Costa Rica (this name was then in general use, although it incorporated an area far larger than its present-day boundaries), and the natives had not been subdued.

Costa Rica remained the smallest and poorest of Spain's Central American colonies, producing little wealth for the empire. It tended to be largely ignored in terms of the conquest and instead began to receive a wholly different type of settler—hardy, self-sufficient individuals who had to work to maintain themselves. The population stayed at less than 20,000 for centuries (even with considerable growth in the 18th century) and was mainly confined to small, isolated farms in the highland Central Valley and the Pacific lowlands. Intermixing with the native Indians was not a common practice, and the population remained largely European.

By the end of the 18th century, however, Costa Rica had begun to emerge from isolation. Some trade with neighboring Spanish colonies was carried out—in spite of constant harassment by English pirates, both at sea and on land—and the population had begun to expand across the Central Valley.

Seeds of political discord, which were soon to affect the colony, had been planted in Spain when Napoléon defeated and removed King Charles IV in 1808 and installed his brother Joseph on the Spanish throne. Costa Rica pledged support for the old regime, even sending troops to Nicaragua in 1811 to help suppress a rebellion against Spain. By 1821, though, sentiment favoring independence from Spain was prevalent throughout Central America, and Costa Rica supported the declaration of independence issued in Guatemala on September 15 of that year. Costa Rica did not become a fully independent sovereign nation until 1836, after annexation to the Mexican empire and 14 years as part of the United Provinces of Central America. The only major threat to that sovereignty took place in 1857 when the mercenary army of U.S. adventurer William Walker invaded the country from Nicaragua, which it had conquered the year before. Walker's plan to turn the Central American nations into slave states was cut short by Costa Rican president Juan Rafael Mora, who raised a volunteer army and repelled the invaders, pursuing them into Nicaragua and joining troops from various Central American nations to defeat the mercenaries.

Foundations of Democracy

The 19th century saw dramatic economic and political changes in Costa Rica. For the major part of that century, the country was ruled by a succession of wealthy families whose grip was partially broken only toward the end of the century. The development of agriculture included the introduction of coffee in the 1820s and bananas in the 1870s, both of which became the country's major sources of foreign exchange.

In 1889 the first free popular election was held, characterized by full freedom of the press, frank debates by rival candidates, an honest tabulation of the vote, and the first peaceful transition of power from a ruling group to the opposition. This event provided the foundation of political stability that Costa Rica enjoys to this day.

During the early 20th century each successive president fostered the growth of democratic liberties and continued to expand the free public school system, started during the presidency of Bernardo Soto in the late 1880s. By the 1940s economic growth was healthy due to agricultural exports, but the clouds of discontent were again gathering. In 1948 the president, Rafael Angel Calderón Guardia, refused

to hand over power after losing the election; the result was a civil uprising by outraged citizens, led by the still-revered José Figueres Ferrer. In a few short weeks the rebellion succeeded and an interim government was inaugurated.

New Beginnings

On May 8, 1948, Figueres accepted the position of president of the Founding Junta of the Second Republic of Costa Rica. One of his first acts was to disband the army, creating in its stead a national police force.

Significant changes took place during the 1950s and 1960s, including the introduction of new social-welfare policies, greater expansion of the public school system, and greater involvement by the state in economic affairs. The early 1970s saw further growth, but then an economic crisis introduced Costa Ricans to hyperinflation. By the mid-1980s, Costa Rica had begun pulling out of its economic slump, in part thanks to efforts to diversify the economy, which had long been dominated by coffee and bananas. Still, the country's currency continues to be devalued on a regular basis.

Today the challenge facing Costa Rica is how best to cope with its booming tourism industry, which has surpassed coffee and banana exports as the country's top moneymaker. Although tourism provides a much-needed injection of foreign exchange into the economy, it has yet to be fully decided which direction it should take. The buzzwords now are "ecotourism" and "sustainable development," and with so much in the way of natural beauty to protect, it is hoped that Costa Rica will find it possible to continue down these roads rather than opt for something akin to the Acapulco or Cancún style of development.

NEW AND NOTEWORTHY

A slow but steady increase in flights to Costa Rica is making the country easier to reach and, in some cases, less expensive to visit. An "open-skies" agreement signed by Costa Rica and the United States has lead to the addition of new routes, and, during high season, there are more charter flights available. Most of the new charter flights land only at the Aeropuerto Internacional Daniel Oduber, near the Guanacaste city of Liberia, which is a four-hour drive from San José, but just 20 to 40 minutes from some of the country's nicest beaches. Liberia also lies just an hour from Nicaragua, making it a convenient base for excursions into that neighboring nation (☞ Chapter 9). Five direct flights a week between San José and the Panamanian provinces of Chiriquí and Bocas del Toro make it easy to visit Costa Rica's southern neighbor as well.

Costa Rica has recently experienced a bit of a golf boom, with several new courses open on the Pacific coast and several more either under construction or in planning. Golf resorts in the Parque Nacional Marino Las Baulas's backyard, behind Playa Grande's turtle preserve, and Playa Conchal—replete with two golf courses, 310 luxury hotel rooms, and the "largest swimming pool in Central America"—are finished, and other courses are on the way.

The new lodge, El Albergue, in Parque Nacional Chirripó (☞ Chapter 7) is making it easier to visit that cold, remote spot. The park's extensive lodge includes 15 rooms holding a total of 60 beds, and the park also rents such amenities as blankets and gas stoves. The showers, however, still have icy water.

Parque Nacional Isla del Coco was recently declared a World Heritage Site by the United Nations, ranking it among the planet's greatest natural and cultural treasures. Nevertheless, the remote island, located more than 530 km (330 mi) from the Costa Rican mainland, can still only be visited on a cruise, such as the 10-day scuba trips that depart from Puntarenas twice a month.

WHAT'S WHERE

Costa Rica can be divided into several distinct territories, each of which possesses its own unique qualities and defining characteristics. San José, for example, is a bustling, cosmopolitan city with a population of more than a million; it is the political, social, historical, and cultural center of the entire country. Each of the other regions has its own special features as well, from the northwest with its rolling plains to the cool mountains of the Central Valley and the humid jungles of the Atlantic lowlands.

Our coverage of Panama concentrates on two regions, each of which makes for an easy excursion from Costa Rica: the Bocas del Toro Archipelago, where spectacular coral reefs and deserted beaches are complemented by laid-back island towns, and Chiriquí Province, a largely undiscovered area that is home to raging rivers, verdant highland valleys, and protected cloud forests.

Another alluring excursion is to continue north from Guanacaste into the southwest corner of Nicaragua, where an interesting mix of attractions lies relatively close to Costa Rica. Timeless, charming Granada has more Colonial architecture than any town in Costa Rica, and the artisans of nearby Masaya are some of Central America's best. Natural wonders such as the massive Volcán Concepción, towering over Isla Ometepe, in Lake Nicaragua, and the beaches of San Juan del Sur complement the country's rich cultural heritage.

San José

The capital of Costa Rica has several good museums, a varied cultural calendar, and many of the country's best hotels and restaurants. Located in the approximate center of the country, and sitting more than 3,000 ft above sea level in the Meseta Central, or Central Valley, San José offers a surprisingly pleasant climate for the capital of a tropical country. From almost any location within the city, you can catch a glimpse of the green hills and volcanoes that surround it—and that hold tranquil agricultural communities and natural attractions that can be visited on a variety of day trips. And since it is the transportation hub of a conveniently compact country, many of Costa Rica's other destinations lie just a short drive, flight, or bus ride from the capital.

Central Valley: Around San José

The Meseta Central, or Central Valley, is a broad bowl planted with neat rows of coffee, dotted with traditional towns, and surrounded by a ring of stunning volcanoes and mountains. Its altitude of more than 3,000 ft above sea level assures a pleasant mixture of warm days and cool nights, whereas the upper slopes can often become quite cold. The mountains hold some of the valley's great attractions, such as active volcanic craters, luxuriant cloud forests, and hotels and restaurants with unforgettable vistas. Costa Rica's most accessible volcanoes—Poás and Irazú—define the valley's northern edge. The Central Valley also has some interesting small cities and towns, such as Cartago, Escazú, Heredia, and San Ramón, with their handsome churches and provincial charm. To the east lies the smaller Orosí Valley, which holds two historical monuments and lovely scenery, and the agricultural community of Turrialba, near which is the country's most important archaeological site, the Monumento Nacional Guayabo.

Northern Guanacaste and Alajuela

This northwest sector encompasses the mountainous chain of volcanoes of the Cordillera de Guanacaste and the northern portion of the Cordillera di Tilaran. Also within its radius are the hot, dry, cattle-grazing plains to the west of the mountains and the upland and lowland jungles, forests, and plains to the east. At the heart of the northern Guanacaste zone lies the perfect cone of the Volcán Arenal, the country's most active. Laguna de Arenal's powerful winds create conditions for some of the best windsurfing in all the Americas. South of Arenal are the magnificent cloud forests of Monteverde and the other preserves. The Caño Negro Wildlife Refuge in the far north is a bird-watchers' delight, for it lies in the migratory flyway of hundreds of thousands of birds. In the far west, the national parks of Rincón de la Vieja and Guanacaste offer uncrowded miles of cloud forest, rain-forest mountain trails for hiking and bird-watching, as well as close-up views of geothermal activity.

Nicoya Peninsula

The country's driest region, the Nicoya Peninsula is a land of contrast where dry cattle ranches give way to lush river deltas. Along the northwest coast lie most of Costa Rica's most popular beaches, made so by the reliably rain-free dry season. The fine weather and beautiful settings have also turned the northwest's beaches into a "Gold Coast," and so it is here that development of overscale resorts most threatens the country's tranquil way of life and magnificent scenery. But, there are still miles of desolate beach, and the national parks—some remote and little visited—are endowed with an abundance of flora and fauna. There are party towns like Montezuma, Coco, and Tamarindo, but it's easy to get away and find a secret place, an uncrowded shore where the only footprints are the trucklike tracks of the leatherback turtles, who come ashore to lay their eggs on a beach at the end of a trail through a forest full of howler monkeys and raccoonlike coatis.

Central Pacific Costa Rica

Though a relatively small region, the Central Pacific packs in many of the interests that have made Costa Rica famous. Two of the country's most popular beaches—Jacó and Manuel Antonio—are found here, but there is more to the region than surf and sand. Although Jacó is a surfer's mecca with an array of accommodations, it lies very close to the Reserva Biológica Carara, where bird-watchers can spot such striking bird species as the scarlet macaw and roseate spoonbill. Manuel Antonio features beaches and rain forest side by side in the national park, plus diversions such as sportfishing charters and horseback-riding trips into the mountains. If you want to stray from the crowd, the Central Pacific is also home to secluded luxury resorts and nature lodges.

Southern Pacific Costa Rica

The southwest corner of Costa Rica is a wild and varied region containing an array of ecosystems that ranges from the cloud forests of the Cordillera de Talamanca to the lowland rain forests of the Osa Peninsula. It comprises some of the country's more pristine, less accessible regions—which happen to be some of its most beautiful—but many of its enticements are actually quite easy to reach. Amateur naturalists head there to look for such rare creatures as the tapir, resplendent quetzal, scarlet macaw, and Central American squirrel monkey or to wander the paths of one of the best botanical gardens in Latin America. Active travelers are drawn to this region by its world-class conditions for fishing, hiking, bird-watching, skin diving, white-water rafting, and surfing. And to top it off, many of these natural wonders are complemented by first-class accommodations, some surrounded by rain forest and overlooking the blue Pacific.

Atlantic Lowlands and the Caribbean Coast

Costa Rica's Atlantic lowlands region is a world apart, separated from the rest of the country by towering mountains and volcanoes. Long isolated from the rest of Costa Rica, the residents of the Atlantic lowlands have turned in other directions to find commonality: most of the blacks of the region claim Jamaica as their ancestral home, while the Indians that live here have more in common with the peoples of western Panama. Their language partakes of both English and Spanish, with a little spice provided by regional Indian dialects. The lifestyle is slower and more laid-back, reflecting the reality of a hot, wet climate, for this is a land dominated by the intense heat of a tropical sun interspersed with frequent bouts of torrential rain. Closer to San José, you'll find rivers for rafting with rapids in every category and the jungle preserves of La Selva and Rara Avis amidst the farmlands and banana plantations of the region.

Excursions to Panama and Nicaragua

The archipelago of Bocas del Toro, off the northwest coast of Panama, is among the most remote places in the Americas. It is quickly becoming another hot spot on the international vagabond circuit because it has much to offer: great beaches, jungle-covered islands, friendly indigenous peoples, low-priced hotels, and, best of all, an abundance of pristine coral reefs for skin divers to explore. The most popular snorkeling area is around the Zapatilla Cays, which are protected within the confines of the Parque Nacional Marina Isla Bastimentos, but there are at least a dozen other dive spots in the area, each of which has its own marine life. And for those who have no interest in skin diving, there are plenty of untouched beaches, trails through the rain forest, Indian villages, and the laid-back towns of Bocas and Bastimentos.

The Panamanian province of Chiriquí boasts impressive landscapes, tranquil mountain towns, traditional cultures, and the flora and fauna of the cloud forest. The upper reaches of the Cordillera de Talamanca, which stretch southeast out of Costa Rica, are largely covered with pristine forest, home to everything from jaguars to quetzals. The mountains' lower slopes and valleys contain tranquil agricultural communities, Guaymí Indian villages, and pleasant pastoral scenery. The mountain forests are the perfect playground for hikers and birders, and the rivers that flow from them are exciting whitewater-rafting routes. But probably the best thing about western Panama is the fact that it is still relatively undiscovered, so you won't have to share it with crowds of tourists.

With one of the world's largest freshwater lakes, active and inactive volcanoes, miles of sparkling beaches, and an array of cultural attractions, the southwest corner of Nicaragua packs in a lively mix. The beautiful city of Granada—its cobbled streets lined with adobe homes and Colonial churches—holds more historic buildings than you'll find in all of Costa Rica. The nearby town of Masaya is the place to head for handicrafts, whereas muddy Lake Nicaragua, which lies to the southeast, has freshwater sharks and sawfish swimming in its murky depths. Isla Ometepe, from where mighty Concepción Volcano towers over the lake and region, provides a rural, rustic overnight option. The Pacific surf and shimmering strands of San Juan del Sur, on the other hand, give an idea of what Costa Rican beaches were like decades ago.

PLEASURES AND PASTIMES

Archaeological Treasures

Though Costa Rica was never part of the Maya empire and has nothing to compare with the ruins of Guatemala and Mexico, it was home to some sophisticated cultures prior to the arrival of Christopher Columbus. Those people may never have erected temples to rival those of Tikal and Palenque, but they left behind a treasure trove of gold, jade, ceramics, and stonework that can be admired at several San José museums. Pre-Columbian Costa Rica was home to some incredibly talented artisans, and thanks to good laws prohibiting the export of their works, museums such as the Museo de Jade and the Museo de Oro house collections that could be envied by the nations of the former Maya realm. Though the country's most impressive pre-Columbian heritage is found in the museums, there is one noteworthy archaeological site: Monumento Nacional Guayabo, a partially excavated city of 20,000 surrounded by protected rain forest.

Dining

Costa Rica is a veritable garden of fresh vegetables and fruit, which means that most cooking is flavorful regardless of the recipe. Just don't expect anything spicy, since the local fare tends to be mild. Typical Costa Rican food is available from the ubiquitous and inexpensive *sodas* (small cafés). In San José, a string of higher-priced restaurants serve an international cornucopia of dishes—Italian, French, Spanish, Chinese, Peruvian, you name it. Panamanian food is similar, though a bit greasy, and that country boasts an even greater selection of international cuisine than Costa Rica. Nicaraguan food also bears comparison to Costa Rican, favoring fresh fruits and fish, but with less of an international influence.

The typical Costa Rican main course is called a *casado,* which consists of rice, black beans, a shredded raw cabbage and tomato salad, meat or fish, and sometimes fresh cheese, a fried egg, and *plátanos* (fried plantains); this is standard fare at most sodas and small restaurants. The national breakfast dish is *gallo pinto* (fried rice and beans), usually served with a fried or scrambled egg, sour cream, and tortillas. Panamanians tend to eat eggs or meat for breakfast, often served with a deep-fried, unleavened bread called *ojaldre.* In Nicaragua, you can get your eggs with bread or tortillas. Maize is a popular staple in all nearby countries, especially for snacks: options include *guiso de maíz* (corn stew), empanadas (corn turnovers filled with beans, cheese, potatoes, and meat), *gallos* (meat, beans, or cheese in a sandwich of tortillas or maize pancakes), and *elote* (corn on the cob), served *asado* (roasted) or *cocinado* (boiled). Delicious seviche is made from raw fish, or other seafood, cured in lime juice with onions, peppers, and coriander; the acid in the lime juice actually cooks the fish. In Costa Rica, chicken is often roasted using coffee wood.

Panamanians tend to eat chicken *guisado* (served in a red sauce), or in a soup called *sancocho.* A favorite Nicaraguan dish—not for the faint of heart—is *mondongo,* tripe or beef stomach cooked with beef knuckles. You can find good-quality *lomito* (beef tenderloin) at amazingly low prices in all three countries. Popular fish include dorado, mahimahi, and corvina, which are sautéed or panfried. Small corvina fish are often deep-fried whole and served as *pescado entero* (whole fish).

Fried plátanos, *yuca* (cassava), and boiled *pejibaye* (palm fruit that tastes like a cross between avocado, chestnut, and pumpkin) are also popular and often eaten on their own. Common fruits are mango, papaya, *piña* (pineapple), and banana. Lesser-known and therefore more exciting options include the *marañon* (the fruit of the cashew tree), *granadilla* (passion fruit), *guanabana* (soursop), *mamón chino* (similar to a litchi with a spiky red skin), and *carambola* (star fruit). You can get many of these in the form of delicious juices, called *refrescos,* made with either water or milk. Recommended desserts include *tres leches* (a Nicaraguan specialty made of treacle sponge and three kinds of milk); *arroz con leche* (rice pudding); *queque seco* (dry cake, like pound cake); and *flan de coco* (a sweet coconut flan).

Flora and Fauna

Costa Rica and Panama possess an almost unfathomable wealth of natural treasures, with more species of plants and animals than scientists have been able to count, and a variety of scenery that ranges from barren mountain peaks to luxuriant lowland forests. Because Costa Rica is such a small country, it is easy to visit many different ecosystems, and see some of the plants and animals that are contained in them, in a short period of time. Costa Rica has made a concerted effort to preserve its natural heritage, and it has paid off: more than 13% of Costa Rica's national territory is under the aegis of the parks system, which contains nearly all the country's ecosystems. The most pristine of those protected areas lie in remote locations, which can take some time and effort to reach, but whether you hike in, take a four-wheel-drive vehicle, or board a boat or small plane, the trip there is often half the adventure. There are also a growing number of private nature reserves, many of which are just as wild and beautiful as the national parks and which often have better facilities and easier access. Western Panama holds the larger half of the binational Parque Internacional La Amistad, best visited from the highland community of Cerro Punta, and the abundant marine life of the Parque Nacional Marina Isla Bastimentos. Nicaragua's southwest offers a major national park, Parque Nacional Volcán Masaya, with its own active volcano, an enormous visitor-center complex, and several hiking trails.

Horseback Riding

Because horses remain one of the most common forms of transportation in Costa Rica, you can ride just about everywhere in that country. Experienced equestrians should be pleased with the frisky spirit of some of the horses in Costa Rica, but even if you can't remember when you were last in the saddle, exploring a bit of the countryside on horseback is recommended. Horses are available for rent at most of the popular beach towns and mountain resorts, and guided trail rides often head to waterfalls, scenic overlooks, and other landmarks that you might otherwise never visit. The most interesting places to ride are the many farms and ranches that have been converted to nature lodges, several of which border national parks. There are also dozens of day trips available out of San José, which usually take you up into the mountains for a morning of trail riding followed by a typical Costa Rican lunch.

Lodging

Costa Rica and neighboring nations offer accommodations to fit every taste and budget, from modern resorts complete with golf courses to rustic nature lodges surrounded by jungle. Costa Rica has a few big resort hotels—near San José and on Pacific beaches—and a growing number of boutique hotels offer comparable comfort and cuisine on a much smaller scale. For travelers on tighter budgets, there are plenty of B&Bs scattered around the region that probably provide more comfort for the dollar. Nature lodges tend to be a bit more expensive, due to the extra costs their isolation implies, but many of them offer first-class food and amenities, as well as expert guides who introduce guests to the complexities of tropical nature.

Snorkeling and Scuba Diving

The options for observing the marine life range from simple snorkeling sessions off the beach near your hotel to a full-fledged scuba-diving safari. Coastal reefs submerged off Costa Rica's southern Caribbean coast are home to colorful coral gardens and hundreds of species of fish and invertebrates. The country's most extensive reef is protected within the Parque Nacional Cahuita, but there are several other good diving spots spread between Puerto Viejo and Manzanillo. The Pacific coast has less coral diversity, but more big animals, such as manta rays, sea turtles, and even whale sharks. The northwest is a popular diving area, with dozens of diving spots in sheltered Bahía Culebra (Snake Bay) and around Santa Catalina and the Islas Murcielagos (Bat Islands), all of which can be visited from the area's beach resorts. The snorkeling is good at such popular beaches as Montezuma and Manuel Antonio, but the best diving spot along the Pacific coast is Isla del Caño, in the southwest. Even better diving, however, is found at distant Isla del Coco, some 530 km (330 mi) southwest of the mainland. Two commercial boats offer 10-day trips to Cocos, which feature three daily dives and the opportunity to swim with hammerhead sharks, dolphins, and occasional whales.

In the Parque Nacional Marina Isla Bastimentos, near the faded town of Bocas del Toro in northeast Panama, the tropical fish are bountiful, and there are at least 25 different kinds of coral to gawk at, not to mention an even greater diversity of sponges. Much of the water is shallow, precluding the need for the complications of scuba equipment (although here, as in any good diving area, a regulator and a set of tanks open up a whole new world), and it is fairly easy to book a ride to the best snorkeling sites. Several dive shops in the town of Bocas del Toro rent scuba and snorkeling equipment and run regular excursions to the Cayos Zapatillas and half a dozen other interesting spots.

Sportfishing

Anglers have long flocked to Costa Rica, drawn by phenomenal offshore fishing all along its Pacific coast and the abundance of snook and tarpon in the rivers and coastal canals of the northern

Caribbean. The Pacific charter fleet is scattered along the ports and beach towns from Playa del Coco, in the northwest, to Zancudo, deep within the Golfo Dulce, making sportfishing possible from almost every resort on the west coast. Those fully equipped boats usually head a few miles out to troll for marlin and sailfish, but they also catch plenty of tuna, dolphin, wahoo, and roosterfish. Though the Pacific fishing is good year-round, it drops off a bit during the rainiest months (September–November). The balmy Caribbean offers a more languid type of angling—casting into the murky waters of canals and rivers, where silvery snook and tarpon lurk, waiting to burst into the air when hooked. Several lodges in the northeast specialize in fishing packages. The best months for tarpon are January to August, whereas the snook fishing is best from September to February.

Surfing

Both Costa Rica's east and west coasts are dotted with innumerable surfing spots, from the radical, experts-only reef break at Puerto Viejo, on the Atlantic Coast, to the mellower waves off the town of Tamarindo in northern Guanacaste. Together with Jacó, Tamarindo is one of the country's most popular surfer hangouts, and thanks to boards for rent and manageable waves, both are good spots for people who have been away from the sport for a while. More consistent and less populated breaks are found nearby those two towns, such as Hermosa, a short drive south of Jacó. There are about a dozen surf spots scattered along the coast to the south of Tamarindo, among them Langosta, Avellanas, and Negra, and two isolated breaks hidden within Parque Nacional Santa Rosa, to the north. Polluted, but mightily long, are the waves at Boca Barranca, just south of Puntarenas. Manuel Antonio often has surf, but the waves are usually bigger at Dominical, farther to the south. And those willing to make the long journey to Pavones and Matapalo, in the extreme southwest, will get to ride some of the longest waves in the world. Though Costa Rica's short Atlantic coast has few surf spots, Puerto Viejo's Salsa Brava is one of the best breaks in the country. The islands of Bocas del Toro, just over the border in Panama, offer similar waves.

Volcanoes

Volcanic activity was one of the principal forces in the geological process that created Costa Rica, Panama, and Nicaragua and volcanoes remain a predominant part of the landscape in these countries. They range from sleeping giants, such as Panama's extinct Volcán Barú, to hyperactive Arenal, which towers over the lake of the same name. The easiest ones to visit are Irazú and Poás, both of which have paved roads leading up to the edges of their craters, each just a 90-minute drive from San José. Irazú's crater bears the scars of an active period that ended three decades ago, whereas the active crater of Poás regularly emits a plume of sulfuric smoke. Volcanoes that can only be ascended on foot or horseback include nearby Barva and Turrialba; Rincón de la Vieja, in Guanacaste province; and Panama's Barú. Only lunatics try to scale Arenal, Costa Rica's most active volcano, which regularly spews lava and incandescent boulders into the air—an incendiary performance most spectacular when viewed by night.

White-Water Rafting

Costa Rica and western Panama together constitute a rafter's paradise. It is no coincidence that several Olympic kayaking teams include Costa Rican rivers as part of their winter training schedule. Nevertheless, the warm weather (water temperatures average about 70°F), spectacular river scenery, and the wide variety of runs make these countries worthy destinations for neophytes and experts. Costa Rica's most popular rafting river is the Reventazón, on the country's Atlantic side, which has an excellent first-time run and intense class IV and V sections that are fit for experts only. The Pacuare, which runs parallel to it, is one of the most beautiful rafting rivers in the world, with a breathtaking mix of rain forest, waterfalls, rocky gorges, and lively class III and IV rapids. It is usually run in one day, but two- and three-day trips, with camp-out or lodge overnights by the riverbank, are highly recommended. Less navigated rivers include the Parrita, near Manuel Antonio; the more beautiful Sarapiquí, near La Fortuna; the Peñas Blancas, with class II and III trips available out of the La Fortuna area; and the Corobicí, in Guanacaste, which is a mellow river enlivened with an abundance of very visible animal life. Panama's western province of Chiriquí has two rafting rivers, both of which carry the name of the province and offer exciting whitewater action year-round.

Windsurfing

Although there are a limited number of spots to practice the sport, windsurfing has reached legendary proportions in Costa Rica. A combination of natural and man-made events have conspired to produce one of the best freshwater windsurfing sites in the western hemisphere at Laguna de Arenal. It was ICE, Costa Rica's national electric institute, that in the 1970s created Laguna de Arenal—a large, electricity-producing reservoir—and it is nature, in the form of trade winds passing through a conveniently located gap in the mountains, that produces the 32- to 80-kph (20- to 50-mph) winds that rip across the lake's northwest end. This northern end of Laguna de Arenal has been compared with such windsurfing meccas as the Columbia River Gorge and Italy's Lago di Garda. (The wind is so consistent that wind generators run by windmills have been placed on the hills above the north end of the lake.) If the timing is right, you can watch distant Volcán Arenal erupt while you're tacking across the lake. You'll find serious windsurfers here from December to April, when the winds are too strong for beginners, whereas it becomes a good spot to learn the sport during the rest of the year. There's a well-supplied rental shop run by the Hotel Tilawa on the shore, near a convenient launch site. Although fanatics head straight for Laguna de Arenal, a less demanding windsurfing area is Playa Hermosa, where rental equipment and windsurfing tours are available.

FODOR'S CHOICE

Archaeological Site

★ **Monumento Nacional Guayabo.** This ancient city, once home to 20,000 inhabitants, was abandoned in the 1400s and wasn't rediscovered until 1968.

Restaurants

★ **Ambrosia, San José.** Fifteen minutes from downtown San José, this eclectic restaurant has long been popular among local epicureans, thanks to its menu of delicious culinary inventions such as *sopa Neptuna* (Neptune soup). *$$$*

★ **The Garden, Puerto Viejo de Limón.** Chef and owner Vera Mabon's Indian-Canadian-Trinidadian background provides inspiration for Costa Rican fusion cooking at its most inventive. This charming restaurant, tucked in a garden a few blocks from the waterfront, offers the most sophisticated menu on Costa Rica's east coast. Don't miss it if you're in the area. *$$–$$$*

★ **Nogui's (Sunrise Café), Tamarindo.** Most of the expatriate restaurateurs and hoteliers who call Tamarindo home swear by Nogui's, a scruffy little restaurant just off the circle near the south end of Tamarindo. They say Nogui's *langostino* (lobster) is the best in Guanacaste. Hearty American-style breakfasts are also served. *$$–$$$*

★ **Café Mundo, San José.** Set in a lovely old wooden house in historic Barrio Amón, this popular spot offers an inventive selection of pastas, salads, meat, and seafood dishes at very reasonable prices. Save room for dessert—the pastries are to die for. *$$*

★ **Chubascos Restaurant, Poás Volcano.** Whether you prefer the brisk mountain air, the delicious refrescos, the green surroundings, or the platters packed with traditional Costa Rican taste treats, this spot on the road to Volcán Poás offers a winning combination. *$$*

★ **Edith Soda y Restaurant, Cahuita.** Ticos and outsiders alike flock to this restaurant for the outrageous Caribbean menu, which includes a variety of vegetarian dishes and herbal teas that owner Miss Edith claims will remedy whatever ails you. *$$*

Hotels

★ **Hotel Punta Islita, Guanacaste, Nicoya Peninsula.** This isolated luxury resort spread over a hill overlooking the Pacific features comfortable rooms, splendid views, good food, and an abundance of peace and quiet. *$$$$*

★ **La Mariposa, Manuel Antonio.** This elegant, white Spanish-style villa and series of private bungalows set high on a promontory offer luxury and tranquility complemented by the best view in Manuel Antonio. *$$$$*

⭐ **Lapa Ríos, Cabo Matapalo.** Perched on a ridge in a private rain-forest reserve, with views of the surrounding jungle and ocean beyond, Lapa Rios is a small luxury hotel that provides close contact with tropical nature without ever skimping on the amenities. *$$$$*

⭐ **Villa Caletas, Tárcoles.** Each of these exquisite bungalows scattered over a forested promontory seems to enjoy a better view than the rest. Though isolation and natural beauty jockey for position as the hotel's strongest selling points, the architecture, interior decorating, and cuisine are equally stupendous. *$$$$*

⭐ **Xandari, Alajuela.** Whether you admire the original design of its spacious villas, contemplate the view—lovely by both day and night—or observe the birds and butterflies that frequent the surrounding tropical gardens, its hard not to be enchanted by this unique inn. *$$$$*

⭐ **Grano de Oro, San José.** Built at the turn of the century, this pink, wooden house has been transformed into one of the capital's finest hotels, with interior gardens, a sundeck, and a first-class restaurant. *$$$–$$$$*

⭐ **Hotel Capitán Suiz, Tamarindo.** Many consider this Swiss-run gem to be the finest beachfront hotel in Guanacaste, since its lush gardens provide a wonderful sense of seclusion, yet Tamarindo's resort-town amusements and gorgeous beach are close at hand. Birds, monkeys, and flowers adorn the serene landscaped grounds surrounding the pool. *$$$–$$$$*

⭐ **Sueño del Mar, Playa Langosta.** Susan Money's sweet little Mexican-style B&B has Balinese outdoor showers, fantastic breakfasts, charming gardens, and a perfect beach for a front yard. With just three rooms and a casita, the level of intimacy is high, but you won't mind—Susan's a high-energy charmer. Rent the whole place for a family reunion or a gathering of friends. *$$$–$$$$*

⭐ **Fonda Vela, Monteverde.** Spacious rooms crafted using local hardwoods have plenty of windows for enjoying the surrounding forest and distant Gulf of Nicoya, and the restaurant features great food to match the view. *$$$*

⭐ **Le Bergerac, San José.** The deluxe rooms and extensive gardens have long kept this friendly hotel in a quiet neighborhood a notch above the competition, and the recent addition of L'Ile de France, one of the city's best restaurants for the past two decades, simply makes Le Bergerac that much more alluring. *$$$*

⭐ **Pacific Edge, Dominical.** These four simple cabins perched on a ridge high in the hills south of town feature great views and close contact with nature. *$$–$$$*

⭐ **Hotel Aranjuez, San José.** Lush gardens, abundant common areas, hearty breakfasts, and low rates make this little B&B in the quiet neighborhood of Barrio Aranjuez a real bargain. *$$*

Natural Wonders

⭐ **Arenal Volcano erupting at night.** If you have never seen an active volcano, then this will be a spectacular first—the perfectly conical profile dominates the southern end of Laguna de Arenal, where it thrills viewers with regular incendiary performances.

⭐ **Jungle rivers.** Many Costa Rican and Panamanian rivers are actually excellent routes into the rain forest, and the river trips available range from an invigorating, heart-stopping paddle down the hair-raising rapids of the Pacuare to the lazy navigation of Costa Rica's Caribbean canals or Pacific coast estuaries. With any luck, in the estuaries like the Tamarindo you'll spot the regal roseate spoonbill, the quirky purple gallinule, and hundreds of other birds, howler monkeys, and possibly an American crocodile or caiman.

⭐ **Pacific sunsets.** The suggestion that sunsets are more beautiful on the Pacific coasts of Costa Rica than in other parts of the world may seem ridiculous, but there is something about the cloud formations, colors, and venues that makes them exemplary crepuscular productions. Frequently, flocks of frolicking, diving pelicans, scarfing up sardines and other treats, add a layer of foreground action to the dramatic backdrops.

2 SAN JOSÉ

Most visits to Costa Rica begin and end in San José, the capital, home to excellent museums and cultural attractions and some of the country's best hotels, restaurants, and nightlife. You can use San José as a base for exploring the Central Valley and points beyond: drive to the top of one of the nearby volcanoes, raft white-water rapids, or take a day tour to a Pacific island.

DOWNTOWN SAN JOSÉ IS A BUSY grid-plan metropolis with more than its share of potholes and insipid architecture, but it is not without its at-

Updated by
David
Dudenhoefer

tributes. The city's shady parks, quiet museums, and cobbled pedestrian mall offer needed respite from the traffic jams and gray office blocks that dominate downtown, and the side streets of its older neighborhoods and more affluent suburbs can be downright charming. San José is home for somewhere between 300,000 and 1 million Ticos (as Costa Ricans call themselves), depending on how many suburbs you include. It boasts such big-city pleasures as fine dining and nightlife, but also suffers such urban problems as crime and clouds of automobile exhaust. Nevertheless, downtown San José lies a mere 40-minute drive from verdant, tranquil countryside.

San José's best assets are its location and climate. The city stands in a broad, fertile bowl at an altitude of more than 3,000 ft, bordered to the southwest by the jagged Cerros de Escazú (Escazú Hills), to the north by Volcán Barva (Barva Volcano), and to the east by lofty Volcán Irazú. In the dry season, these green uplands are almost never out of sight, and during rainy-season afternoons, they are usually enveloped in cloudy mantles. Temperatures ranging from 15°C to 26°C (59°F to 79°F) create cool nights and pleasant days. The rainy season lasts from May to December, although mornings during this time are often sunny and brilliantly clear.

The city was founded in 1737 and replaced nearby Cartago as the country's capital in 1823, shortly after independence from Spain. San José grew relatively slowly during the following century, as revenues from the coffee and banana industries financed the construction of stately homes, theaters, and a trolley system that was later abandoned. The city mushroomed after World War II, when many older buildings were razed to make room for cement monstrosities and an ever-growing urban sprawl eventually connecting it with nearby cities. Today, San José truly dominates national life, and nearly one-third of the country's population lives within its metropolitan area. The national government, diplomats, industry, and agribusiness have their headquarters here, and all the institutions required of a capital city—good hospitals, schools, the main university, theaters, restaurants, and nightclubs—flourish within its limits.

Pleasures and Pastimes

Day Tripping

San José's central position in the Central Valley and relative proximity to both the Pacific coast and the mountains allow you to make easy day trips—you can be out in the countryside in just 20 to 30 minutes. The Central Valley is a boon for quick outdoor adventures, among them horseback tours on private ranches, mountain hikes, and white-knuckle rafting excursions down the Reventazón and Pacuare rivers. Most tours—several of which head out to the Central Valley—will pick you up and return you to your San José hotel the same day (☞ Guided Tours *in* San José A to Z, *below*).

Dining

Costa Rican specialties include *arroz con pollo* (chicken with rice), *ensalada de palmito* (heart-of-palm salad), *sopa negra* (black bean soup), *gallo pinto* (rice and black beans), and *casados* (plates of rice, beans, fried plantains, salad, cheese, and fish or meat). Take advantage of the cheap lunch special *plato del día* (plate of the day), which often includes or red-light district, it is frequented by hard-luck whores, drunks, and other delinquents. It's best avoided, unless you're headed to one of the bus companies there, in which case you should take a taxi. Much of the city's southern half—south of Avenida 4 between Calles Central and 14—is equally undesirable. If you follow Avenida Central west to where it becomes Paseo Colón, you'll enter a nice area, with plenty of restaurants, cinemas, and hotels. The farther west you head, the more exclusive the neighborhoods become. Escazú, in the hills west of San José, is a traditional town with relaxed ambience and numerous small inns and good restaurants.

Most museums, shops, and restaurants are located within walking distance. If you're headed for one of the more far-flung spots, or need to get from one end of the city to another, grab a taxi, which are abundant and inexpensive ($2–$3 for most trips).

On the whole, San José is a relatively safe city, but the influx of tourists has resulted in an increase in the number of thieves that prey on them, such as bag and backpack slitters, pickpockets, and distraction artists who usually work in pairs—one person molests you, or sprays something on you then helps you clean it off, while his or her partner gets your purse, wallet, backpack, camera, etc. Make sure you always have a copy of your passport and a list of credit card numbers stored in your luggage. Don't leave anything in an unguarded car.

Numbers in the text correspond to numbers in the margin and on the San José map.

Great Itineraries

San José is home to several interesting museums and theaters, more shops than you can shake a credit card at, and such urban amenities as newsstands and ice-cream vendors, which makes it a comfortable base for day trips into the surrounding countryside. If you are visiting San José during the rainy months, head into the countryside in the morning and return to the city to shop and visit museums during the afternoon.

IF YOU HAVE 3 DAYS

On day one you'll definitely want to explore San José and visit at least one or two of its many museums. Wander down the Avenida Central mall, pop into the Teatro Nacional and the Catedral Metropolitana, and visit either the Museo Nacional, Museo de Oro, or Museo de Jade. In the morning of day two, you may want to horseback ride in the mountains above town, visit a butterfly farm, or tour the Café Britt (☞ Chapter 3) coffee plantation in Heredia, saving the afternoon for another museum. On day three you'll no doubt want to head up a volcano or, if it's cloudy, explore the Orosí Valley southeast of San José.

IF YOU HAVE 5 DAYS

San José really deserves two days' exploration, since it has excellent museums, plentiful shopping, and an enticing enough nightlife to make you want to sleep in. Take the walking tour below, being sure to visit either the Museo Nacional, Museo de Oro, or Museo de Jade on the first day. Save one museum and spots such as the Serpentario or Jardín de Mariposas Spyrogyra for day two. On day three you'll definitely want to climb either the Poás or Irazú volcanoes, stopping in at the nearby towns of Alajuela and Cartago. Head to the Orosí Valley on day four, spending the morning in Parque Nacional Tapantí and the afternoon touring the valley. On day five, take a white-water rafting trip down the Río Pacuare on the class III and IV rapids (thrilling but not heart-attack inducing); swimmable warm water and spectacular scenery make this a must for the moderately adventurous traveler.

a main course, *fresco natural* (fresh fruit drink), and
dessert. Tico food, however, is often mild, but luckily the
to a smorgasbord of international restaurants. To comple
selection, you can also choose from restaurants in Esc
ter 3), a town dotted with coffee crops just 5 km (3 mi

Festivals

Every other year for two weeks in late March an arts fe
Internacional de las Artes, brings performances by da
groups, and musicians from Costa Rica and other natio
venues in San José. There's a December dance festiva
Coreógrafos, and each July and August the Festival Interna
sica (International Music Festival) is held. A carnival
down Avenida 2 every December 26, and a horse parade ge
December 27. During Semana Universitaria (University W
held in April, students at the Universidad de Costa Rica (I
Costa Rica) put their studies on hold to spend the week d
dancing. The Día de la Virgen de Los Angeles honors Cost
tron saint every August 2 with processions and a well-atte
On the night before, nuns, athletes, families, and friends walk
a 22-km (14-mi) trek along the highway from San José to

Lodging

San José offers every type of accommodation, from luxury
cessity. You'll find massive hotels with all the modern conver
amenities, historic buildings with more atmosphere but few
comforts, and smaller establishments with the kind of sim
preciated by backpackers. Dozens of former residences in the
neighborhoods, such as Barrio Amón and Barrio Otoya, have
verted to bed-and-breakfasts (B&Bs), most in the middle pr

EXPLORING SAN JOSÉ

The Costa Rican capital is laid out on a grid: *avenidas* (aver
east and west; *calles* (streets), north and south. Avenidas nor
Avenida Central have odd numbers, and those to the south h
ones. On the western end of the city, Avenida Central becom
Colón; on the eastern end, at about Calle 31, it becomes an
busy, though nameless, four-lane boulevard. Calles to the east
Central have odd numbers; those to the west are even. Sounds s
forward, doesn't it? It would be, but Costa Ricans do not us
addresses. Instead, Ticos use an archaic system of directions tha
perfect sense to them but tends to confuse foreigners. A typic
address could be 200 m north and 50 m east east of the Correc
Office). The key to interpreting such directions is to keep track
and west, and remember that a city block is 100 meters long.

Beyond the block and street level, downtown San José is divide
numerous barrios (neighborhoods), which are also commonly u
directions. Some of those barrios are worth exploring, others you'l
to avoid. Northeast of the town center, Barrio Amón and Barrio
are two of the oldest parts of the city and are consequently ho
plenty of historic buildings, many being transformed into charmin
tels. Los Yoses and Barrio Escalante, east of downtown, are basi
residential neighborhoods that include some nice restaurants and a
B&Bs. San Pedro, another pleasant area even farther east, is the h
of the University of Costa Rica and numerous bars and restaurants c
ing to students.

The northwest quarter of the city (everything west of Calle Central
north of Avenida 3) is a much different story; called the Zona R

Spend day one getting acquainted with the city and visit at least one museum. On day two, hit one or two museums and either the Serpentarium, Parque Zoológico Simón Bolívar, or Jardín de Mariposas Spyrogyra, the butterfly garden. On day three, try a horseback riding trip or coffee plantation tour in the morning and return to San José in the afternoon for a museum or another sight. On day four, visit the Orosí Valley. By day five, you'll be ready to head to the top of either Poás or Irazú. Though only hikers can reach the summit of Volcán Barva, you can drive along its green slopes and visit historic Heredia. Dedicate day six to a far-flung excursion, either white-water rafting or taking a cruise to to Isla Tortuga. The Guápiles Highway enters Parque Nacional Braulio Carrillo (☞ Chapters 8 and 10), a short drive north from San José, which makes an excellent day trip for day seven that can easily be combined with the Rain Forest Aerial Tram (☞ Chapter 8).

Downtown San José

A Good Walk

Start at the eastern end of the **Plaza de la Cultura** ①, where wide stairs lead down to the **Museo de Oro** ②, with a gold collection that deserves an hour or two of perusing. Pop into the Instituto Costarricense de Turismo, the tourist information office, next to the Museo entrance, for a free map, bus schedule, and brochures. After wandering around the bustling plaza, slip into the **Teatro Nacional** ③ for a look at the elegant interior and maybe a cup of coffee in the lobby café. When you leave the theater, you will be facing west; the city's main eastbound corridor, Avenida 2, will be to your left. Walk 1½ blocks west along Avenida 2 to the **Parque Central** ④ and the **Catedral Metropolitana** ⑤. Cross Avenida 2 and head north one block on Calle Central to Avenida Central, where you should turn left and follow the pedestrian zone to the small plaza next to the **Banco Central** ⑥. Continue west along the pedestrian zone to the **Mercado Central** ⑦, where you can do a bit of shopping or browsing. After exploring the market, head back east two blocks on the Avenida Central pedestrian zone; then turn left on Calle 2 and walk one block north to the green-and-gray stuccoed **Correos** ⑧, the central post office. From there, return to Avenida Central and walk east along the mall back to the Plaza de la Cultura.

From the eastern end of the Plaza de la Cultura, near the Museo de Oro, walk two blocks east on Avenida Central, turn left onto Calle 9, walk one block north, turn right, and slither halfway down the block to the **Serpentario** ⑨, home to an interesting collection of creepy crawlers. Turn left when you leave and head 1½ blocks west on Avenida 1 and one block north to **Parque Morazán** ⑩. Walk across the park—be careful crossing busy Avenida 3—and walk along the yellow metal school building to shady **Parque España** ⑪. On the north side of the park, on Avenida 7, is the modern Instituto Nacional de Seguros (INS) building and its 11th-floor **Museo de Jade** ⑫, with an extensive American jade collection and great city vistas.

From the INS building, continue east on Avenida 7 two blocks, passing the Cancilleria, or Foreign Ministry, and the Embajada de México, the Mexican Embassy, on your left; then turn right on Calle 15 and walk a block south to the corner of **Parque Nacional** ⑬. Take a look at the Monumento Nacional at the center of the park, and then head two blocks south to the entrance of the **Museo Nacional** ⑭, housed in the old Bellavista Fortress, on the west side of which lies the terraced **Plaza de la Democracia** ⑮. From here you can walk west down Avenida Central to return to the Plaza de la Cultura, five blocks away.

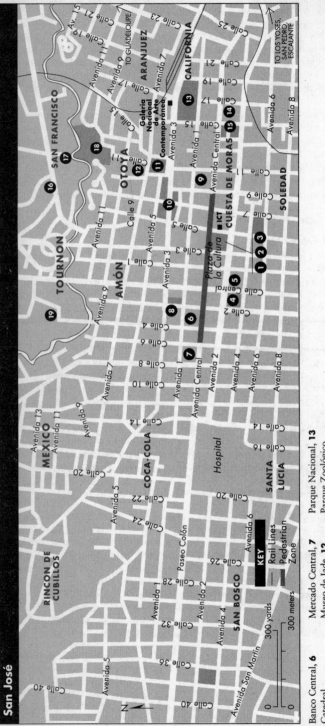

San José

Banco Central, **6**
Catedral
Metropolitana, **5**
Centro Comercial El
Pueblo, **16**
Correos, **8**
Jardín de Mariposas
Spyrogyra, **17**

Mercado Central, **7**
Museo de Jade, **12**
Museo de Oro, **2**
Museo del Niño, **19**
Museo Nacional, **14**
Parque Central, **4**
Parque España, **11**
Parque Morazán, **10**

Parque Nacional, **13**
Parque Zoológico
Simón Bolívar, **18**
Plaza de la Cultura, **1**
Plaza de la
Democracia, **15**
Serpentario, **9**
Teatro Nacional, **3**

KEY

Rail Lines
Pedestrian
Zone

It could take an entire day to walk this tour if you spend a little time exploring each museum and monument and stop to shop here and there. You could, however, easily split the tour in half: see all the sights west of the Plaza de la Cultura (bullets ①–⑧) one day, and the remaining places (bullets ⑨–⑮) on another. Every stop on this tour is open Tuesday to Friday; if you're visiting on Monday or a weekend, check the hours listed below to make sure the sights you want to see will be open.

Sights to See

❻ Banco Central (Central Bank). Outside of the western end of the country's unattractive, modern federal reserve bank are 10 sculpted figures of bedraggled *campesinos* (peasants). The small, shady plaza south of the bank is popular with hawkers, money changers, and retired men and can be a good spot to get a shoe shine and listen to street musicians. Beware: the money changers here are notorious for circulating counterfeit bills and using doctored calculators to shortchange customers. ⊠ *Between Avdas. Central and 1 and Cs. 2 and 4.*

❺ Catedral Metropolitana (Metropolitan Cathedral). To the east of the park stands this mostly uninteresting 1871 neoclassical exterior and corrugated tin dome; inside, however, the cathedral interior has patterned floor tiles and framed polychrome bas-reliefs. The interior of the small chapel on the north side of the cathedral is much more ornate than that of the main building, but it is usually closed. ⊠ *Between Avdas. 4 and 2 and Cs. Central and 1,* ☎ 221–3820. ☉ *Daily 8–8.*

❽ Correos (Central Post Office). The ornate, handsome exterior of the this building, dating from 1917, is hard to miss amid the insipid architecture surrounding it. Upstairs is a display of first-day stamp issues. Also, here's your opportunity to watch the loading of *apartados* (post office boxes) going on below: Ticos covet having one of these hard-to-come-by boxes, since the city's lack of street addresses makes mail delivery quite a challenge. Opposite the post office is a small park shaded by massive fig trees, behind which stands the marble facade of the exclusive, members-only Club Unión. The large building behind the Correos is the Banco Nacional, one of the country's state-run banks. ⊠ *C. 2 between Avdas. 1 and 3.* ☉ *Weekdays 8–6:30, Sat. 8–noon.*

Instituto Costarricense de Turismo (Costa Rican Institute of Tourism, ICT). Got some questions? Head for the country's main tourist office, next door to the **Museo de Oro** (☞ *below*). The people who work here are usually friendly and informative and have maps, bus schedules, and assorted brochures. ⊠ *C. 5 between Avdas. Central and 2,* ☎ 222–1090. ☉ *Weekdays 9–5.*

❼ Mercado Central (Central Market). San José's block-long melting pot is a warren of dark, narrow passages flanked by stalls packed with exotic spices (some purported to have medicinal value), fish, fruit, flowers, pets, and wood and leather crafts. You'll also find dozens of cheap restaurants and food stalls, including the country's first ice-cream vendor. Be warned: the concentration of shoppers here makes this a hot spot for pickpockets, purse snatchers, and backpack slitters. ⊠ *Avdas. Central and 1 and Cs. 6 and 8.* ☉ *Mon.–Sat. 6–6.*

★ **⓬ Museo de Jade** (Jade Museum). Nearly all the items exhibited at this museum—the world's largest collection of American jade—were produced in pre-Columbian times, and most of the jade dates from between 300 BC to AD 700, before the local Indians learned goldsmithing. In the spectacular **Jade Room**, pieces are illuminated from behind so you can appreciate the jade's translucency. A series of drawings explains how this extremely hard stone was cut using string saws with quartz and sand abrasive. Although jade was used to create a variety of jewelry, it was most often carved into oblong pendants, evidently to represent ears of corn, that also doubled as knives. The museum also contains other pre-Columbian artifacts, such as polychrome vases and three-legged metates (low tables for grinding corn). The final room on the tour displays a startling array of ceramic fertility symbols. ⊠ *11th floor of INS building, Avda. 7 between Cs. 9 and 11,* ☎ *223–5800, ext. 2584.* ☞ *$2.* ⊘ *Weekdays 8:30–4:30.*

★ ❷ **Museo de Oro** (Gold Museum). The dazzling, modern museum of gold, in a three-story underground building, contains the largest collection of pre-Columbian gold jewelry in Central America—20,000 troy ounces in more than 1,600 individual pieces—all owned by the Banco Central. Many pieces are in the form of frogs and eagles, two animals perceived by the region's pre-Columbian cultures to have great spiritual significance. Most spectacular are the varied shamans, representing man's connection to animal deities. ⊠ *Eastern end of Plaza de la Cultura,* ☎ *223–0528.* ☞ *$5.* ⊘ *Tues.–Sun. 10–4:30.*

⓮ **Museo Nacional** (National Museum). In the whitewashed colonial interior of the **Bellavista Fortress,** dating from 1870, the National Museum gives you a quick and insightful lesson in Costa Rican culture from pre-Columbian times to the present. Rooms display pre-Columbian artifacts, period dress, colonial furniture, and photos of Costa Rican life through the ages. Outside is a veranda and a pleasant manicured courtyard garden. A former army headquarters, this now-tranquil building saw fierce fighting during the 1948 revolution, as the bullet holes pocking its turrets attest. ⊠ *C. 17 between Avdas. Central and 2,* ☎ *257–1433.* ☞ *$2.* ⊘ *Tues.–Sun. 8:30–4:30.*

❹ **Parque Central** (Central Park). Technically the city's nucleus, this simple tree-planted square has a gurgling fountain and cement benches. In the center of the park is a spiderlike, avocado-color gazebo donated by former Nicaraguan dictator Anastasio Somoza. Several years ago, a referendum was held to decide whether to demolish the despot's gift, and the citizens voted to preserve the bandstand for posterity. Across Avenida 2, to the north, stands the **Teatro Melico Salazar,** San José's second leading venue after the Teatro Nacional. The venerable **Soda Palace,** a restaurant and black-market exchange, is on the western end of that block. The fast-food outlet sitting between the two was once one of the city's main movie theaters, the Cinema Palace. ⊠ *Between Avdas. 2 and 4 and Cs. 2 and Central.*

⓫ **Parque España.** This shady little park is one of the capital's most pleasant spots. A bronze statue of a conquistador overlooks an elevated fountain on its southwest corner; the opposite corner has a lovely tiled guardhouse. A bust of Queen Isabella of Castille stares at the yellow compound to the east of the park that was a government liquor factory until 1994 and then converted into the **Centro Nacional de la Cultura** (National Center of Culture). Covering a double block, the complex includes offices of the Ministerio de Cultura (Ministry of Culture), two theaters, and the extensive **Museo de Arte y Diseño Contemporáneo** (Museum of Contemporary Art and Design), which hosts temporary exhibits of work by artists and designers from Costa Rica and Latin America. To the west of the park is a two-story, metal-sided school made in Belgium and shipped to Costa Rica in pieces more than a century ago. The yellow colonial-style building to the east of the INS building is called the **Casa Amarilla;** it houses the country's Cancilleria, or Foreign Ministry. The massive kapok tree in front, planted by the presidents of all the Central American nations in 1963, gives you an idea of how quickly things grow in the tropics. A few doors to the east is the elegant Mexican Embassy, a former private home. ⊠ *Between Avdas. 7 and 3 and Cs. 11 and 17.*

⑩ **Parque Morazán.** Centered on a neoclassical bandstand, downtown San José's largest park is slightly barren and dull—though the tabebuia trees on its northwest corner brighten things up when they bloom in the dry months. Avoid it late at night, when prostitutes, drunks, and occasional muggers hang out. Along the park's southern edge are a public school and two lovely old mansions, both with beautiful facades (one is a private residence, the other a prostitute pickup bar). A park annex with a large fountain is to the northeast, across busy Avenida 3, in front of the metal school building. ⊠ *Avda. 3 between Cs. 5 and 9.*

★ ⑬ **Parque Nacional** (National Park). A large and leafy downtown park, the Nacional is centered on a monument commemorating the nation's battle against American invader William Walker (1824–60) in 1856. It's a pleasant downtown block of greenery dominated by tall trees that often have colorful parakeets high in their branches. An enjoyable spot to relax in by day, it gets very dark at night, when it is sometimes the haunt of muggers, and therefore best avoided. The massive red building to the west of the park houses the **Registro Público** (National Registry) and the **Tribunal Supremo Electoral** (Electoral Tribunal), which keep track of voters and oversee elections. The modern building to the north is the **Biblioteca Nacional** (National Library), beneath which, on the western side, is the **Galería Nacional de Arte Contemporánea**. That small gallery houses exhibits by contemporary artists, mostly Costa Rican. The quality varies, but since admission is free, it's always worth taking a peek. The walled complex to the northwest is the Centro Nacional de Cultura (☞ Parque España, *above*). Across from the park's southwest end is the Moorish **Asamblea Legislativa** (Legislative Assembly), home to Costa Rica's congress. Next door is the **Casa Rosada**, a colonial-era residence now home to bureaucrats, and behind it is a more modern onetime home now used by the government for parties and special events. One block to the northeast of the park is the old train station for journeys to the Atlantic coast. ⊠ *Between Avdas. 1 and 3 and Cs. 15 and 19.*

★ ❶ **Plaza de la Cultura.** This large cement square surrounded by shops and fast-food restaurants is somewhat sterile, but it is a pleasant spot to feed the pigeons and buy some souvenirs. It is also a favored performance spot for local marimba bands, clowns, jugglers, and colorfully dressed South Americans playing Andean music. The stately **Teatro Nacional** (☞ *below*) dominates the plaza's southern half, and its western edge is defined by the venerable **Gran Hotel Costa Rica**, (☞ Lodging, *below*) with the 24-hour **Café Parisienne**. ⊠ *Between Avdas. Central and 2 and Cs. 3 and 5.*

⑮ **Plaza de la Democracia.** President Oscar Arias built this terraced open space, to the west of the Museo Nacional, to mark 100 years of democracy and to receive visiting dignitaries during the 1989 hemispheric summit. The view west toward the dark green Cerros de Escazú is nice in the morning, and it's a great spot from which to enjoy a sunset. The monument that dominates the plaza is dedicated to three-time president and leader of the 1948 revolution José Figueres. Along the western edge of the plaza are a number of stalls where vendors sell jewelry, T-shirts, and varied crafts from Costa Rica, Guatemala, and South America. ⊠ *Between Avdas. Central and 2 and Cs. 13 and 15.*

⟳ ❾ **Serpentario** (Serpentarium). Don't be alarmed by the absence of motion within the display cases here—all the snakes and lizards are very much alive. Most notorious is the terciopelo, responsible for more than half the poisonous snakebites in Costa Rica. The menagerie also features boa constrictors, Jesus Christ lizards, poison dart frogs, iguanas, and an aquarium full of deadly sea snakes. There are also such exotic creatures as king cobras and Burmese pythons. ⊠ *Avda. 1 between Cs. 9 and 11,* ☎ *255–4210.* ⊠ *$5.* ☉ *Weekdays 9–6, weekends 10–5.*

★ ❸ **Teatro Nacional** (National Theater). Easily Costa Rica's most enchanting building, the National Theater stands at the southwest corner of the Plaza de la Cultura. Chagrined that touring prima donna Adelina Patti bypassed San José in 1890, wealthy coffee merchants raised export taxes in order to hire Belgian architects to design a building lavish with cast iron and Italian marble. The sandstone exterior is decorated with Italianate arched windows, marble columns with bronze capitals, and statues of odd bedfellows Ludwig van Beethoven (1770–1827) and 17th-century Spanish golden-age playwright Calderón de la Barca. The Muses of Dance, Music, and Fame are silhouetted in front of a maroon iron cupola. Given the provenance of the building funds, it's not surprising that frescoes on the stairway inside depict coffee and banana production. The theater was inaugurated in 1894 with a performance of Gounod's *Faust,* starring an international cast. The sumptuous Baroque interior sparkles owing to an extensive restoration project undertaken after the theater was damaged in a 1991 earthquake. Tickets are remarkably inexpensive. The theater closes occasionally for rehearsals. The stunning Belle Epoque **Café Ruiseñor,** just off the vestibule, serves exotic coffees, good sandwiches, and exquisite pastries. ⊠ *Plaza de la Cultura,* ☎ *233–4488.* ⊠ *Entry $2.50, performance tickets $4–$40 ($10 average).* ☉ *Mon.–Sat. 9–5, Sun. 10–5.*

North of Downtown

A Good Tour
The first two of these destinations are north of the city center, very close to each other. Take a taxi to the **Centro Comercial El Pueblo** ⑯, in the northern neighborhood of Barrio Tournón. One block east and half a block south of El Pueblo is the **Jardín de Mariposas Spyrogyra** ⑰, a butterfly garden that overlooks the greenery of the country's zoo, the **Parque Zoológico Simón Bolívar** ⑱. The best way to reach the zoo, however, is to walk north from the bandstand in the Parque Morazán (☞ *above*) along Calle 7 to the bottom of the hill, then turn right. The **Museo del Niño** ⑲, a Children's Museum housed in an old jail, lies several blocks to the west and is surrounded by bad neighborhoods, so you'll want to take a taxi there.

TIMING
You can visit all four sights in one morning. Allow a half hour to see the Centro Comercial El Pueblo, an hour or two for the Jardín de Mariposas Spyrogyra, an hour to see the Parque Zoológico Simón Bolívar, and an hour for the Museo del Niño. All sights are open daily, except the Museo del Niño, which is closed Monday.

Sights to See
⑯ **Centro Comercial El Pueblo** (El Pueblo Shopping Center). This shopping center was built to resemble the kind of colonial village that Costa Rica lacks. "Pueblo" is the Spanish term for town, and the cobbled passages, adobe walls, and tiny plazas are surprisingly convincing. Most of the locales are occupied by bars, restaurants, and discos—El Pueblo gets very busy at night, especially on weekends—but there are also a few shops worth checking out. ⊠ *Barrio Tournón, Avda. 0.* ☉ *Daily 24 hrs.*

★ ♻ ⑰ **Jardín de Mariposas Spyrogyra** (Butterfly Garden). An hour or two spent at this magical garden will prove entertaining and educational for travelers of all ages. Self-guided tours provide information about butterfly ecology and a chance to observe the winged creatures close up. Visitors watch a 15-minute video, then guide themselves through screened-in gardens following a numbered trail. Some 30 species of colorful butterflies flutter around the gardens, together with several types of hummingbirds. Visit when it's sunny, since that's when butterflies are most active. Though the garden abuts the northern edge of the Parque Zoológico Simón Bolívar (☞ *below*), its entrance is on the outskirts of Barrio Tournón, near the El Pueblo shopping center. *55 yards west and 164 yards south of brick church of San Francisco, Guadelupe* ☎ *222–2937.* ⌚ *$6.* ☉ *Daily 8–3.*

⑲ Museo del Niño. The Children's Museum is housed in a former jail, and big kids may want to check it out just to marvel at the architecture and the old cells that have been preserved in an exhibit about prison life. The exhibits, which range in subject from local ecology to outer space, are all in Spanish, but since most of them are interactive, language doesn't tend to be as much of a problem as it would be in a museum for adults. Two exhibition halls are usually occupied by the work of Costa Rican artists, for which no admission is charged. ✉ *North end of C. 4,* ☎ *257–8595.* ⌚ *$2.50.* ☉ *Tues.–Sun. 8–5.*

🦆 ⑱ Parque Zoológico Simón Bolívar. Bearing in mind the country's mind-boggling diversity of wildlife, San José's zoo is rather modest in scope. It does, however, provide an introduction to some of the animals that you may see in the jungle. The park is set in a forested ravine in historical Barrio Amón and provides soothing green space in the heart of the city. ✉ *Avda. 11 and C. 11, Barrio Amón,* ☎ *233–6701.* ⌚ *$1.50.* ☉ *Weekdays 8–3:30, weekends 9–4:30.*

DINING

Wherever you eat—whether it be a small *soda* (café) or a sophisticated city restaurant—in San José, dress is casual. Meals tend to be taken earlier here than in many Latin American countries, and so few restaurants serve past 10 PM. Also note that 23% is added to all the prices on the menu—13% for tax and 10% for the service. Because the gratuity is included, there is no need to tip, but if service is good, it's nice to add a little money to the obligatory 10%. Except for those in hotels, most restaurants close between Christmas and New Year's and during Holy Week (Palm Sunday to Easter Sunday), and those that do stay open aren't allowed to sell alcohol from Thursday to Easter Sunday.

Downtown San José
CHINESE

$–$$ ✗ Fulusu. Some like it hot: this Chinese place around the corner from the pink Hotel Presidente is one of the very few restaurants in the country where you can get a spicy food fix. The decor is mundane, with red-and-white tablecloths and Chinese prints, but the food is authentic and delicious. Start off with some *empanadas chinas* (dumplings similar to pot stickers); then head on to something like *vainicas con cerdo* (green beans with pork) or *pollo estilo sichuan* (Szechuan chicken). Note that one entrée and two orders of rice are usually enough food to satisfy two people. ✉ *C. 7 between Avdas. Central and 2,* ☎ *223–7568. Reservations not accepted. AE, MC, V. Closed Sun., around Easter, and last wk in Dec.*

COSTA RICAN

$$–$$$ ✗ La Cocina de Leña. In the charming Centro Comercial El Pueblo,
★ La Cocina serves up traditional Costa Rican fare surrounded by white walls hung with old tools and straw bags to make you feel like you're

24

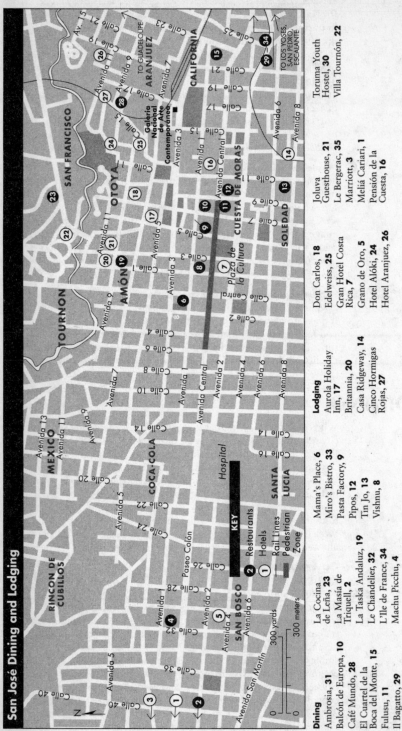

San José Dining and Lodging

KEY

2 Restaurants
1 Hotels
Rail Lines
Pedestrian Zone

Dining
Ambrosia, **31**
Balcón de Europa, **10**
Café Mundo, **28**
El Cuarrel de la Boca del Monte, **15**
Fulusu, **11**
Il Bagatto, **29**
La Cocina de Leña, **23**
La Masia de Triquell, **2**
La Taska Andaluz, **19**
Le Chandelier, **32**
L'Ile de France, **34**
Machu Picchu, **4**
Mama's Place, **6**
Miro's Bistro, **33**
Pasta Factory, **9**
Pipos, **12**
Tin Jo, **13**
Vishnu, **8**

Lodging
Aurola Holiday Inn, **17**
Britannia, **20**
Casa Ridgeway, **14**
Cinco Hormigas Rojas, **27**
Don Carlos, **18**
Edelweiss, **25**
Gran Hotel Costa Rica, **7**
Grano de Oro, **5**
Hotel Alóki, **24**
Hotel Aranjuez, **26**
Joluva Guesthouse, **21**
Le Bergerac, **35**
Marriott, **3**
Meliá Cariari, **1**
Pensión de la Cuesta, **16**
Toruma Youth Hostel, **30**
Villa Tournón, **22**

down on the farm. Popular Tico dishes such as black bean soup, seviche, tamales, oxtail with yucca, and plantains cost more here than in the Mercado Central, but the quality and hygiene are more in keeping with the standards of the North American palate and stomach. The restaurant presents folk dancing and music several nights a week during the high season. This is one of the few places that don't close during Holy Week. ⊠ *Centro Comercial El Pueblo, Barrio Tournón,* ☎ *223–3704. AE, MC, V.*

$$ ✕ **El Cuartel de la Boca del Monte.** One of the city's more popular late-night spots, El Cuartel in Barrio California is actually a nice place to have a meal. If you dine here on a weekend, head for the more private room to the left, which is decorated with original art. The menu is filled with such Tico standards as *lomito encebollado* (tenderloin grilled with onions), sopa negra, and gallo pinto, though you have to order the eggs separately. They also have plates of *bocas* (snacks), such as the *plato de gallos,* (corn tortillas topped with beef, potatoes, and other fillings), or *piononos* (sweet plantains stuffed with cheese or beans and served with sour cream). ⊠ *Avda. 1 between Cs. 21 and 23,* ☎ *221–0327. AE, MC, V. Closed around Easter and last wk in Dec. No lunch weekends.*

$–$$ ✕ **Mama's Place.** Mama's is a Costa Rican restaurant with a difference, the difference being that the owners are Italian, so in addition to such Tico standards as arroz con pollo and corvina *al ajillo* (sautéed with garlic), they serve homemade minestrone, an array of pastas, and meat dishes with delicate wine sauces. The brightly decorated coffee shop opens onto busy Avenida 1; the more subdued restaurant is upstairs. At lunchtime, it is usually packed with business types drawn to the delicious and inexpensive daily specials. ⊠ *Avda. 1 between Cs. Central and 2,* ☎ *223– 2270. AE, MC, V. Closed Sun., around Easter, and last wk in Dec.*

$ ✕ **Pipos.** This is a narrow establishment—two floors packed with small tables and chairs—and during weekday lunch hours it's usually full of businesspeople enjoying the inexpensive lunch special, the plato del día. Snapshots of local scenery decorate the walls, and there's usually rock on the radio and sports on TV. You can fill up on such Tico standards as arroz con pollo and *olla de carne* (tropical beef stew with cassava and plantains). The *plato vegetariano* (vegetarian plate) pairs an ample salad and a fried fish fillet. Breakfast is also served. ⊠ *Avda. Central between Cs. 9 and 11,* ☎ *233–4623. AE, DC, MC, V. Closed Sun., around Easter, and last wk in Dec.*

ECLECTIC

$$$ ✕ **Ambrosia.** A navy-blue canopy of an open-air shopping mall her-
★ alds this chic restaurant in San Pedro serving innovative international dishes. From among the choices of inventive salads, soups, pasta, and fish dishes, start with the *sopa Neptuna* (a creamy fish soup with tomato and bacon); follow with either the light fettuccine ambrosia (a rich cream sauce with ham and oregano) or corvina *troyana* (covered with a shrimp and tarragon sauce). The atmosphere is relaxed and informal, and the decor matches the adventurous cooking: watercolors, wood and cane chairs, and plants. ⊠ *Centro Comercial de la Calle Real, San Pedro,* ☎ *253–8012. AE, DC, MC, V. Closed around Easter and last wk in Dec. No dinner Sun.*

$$ ✕ **Café Mundo.** You could easily walk by this corner restaurant with-
★ out noticing it behind the foliage or seeing its small sign. Step through the entrance and up the stairs, however, and you'll discover an elegant little restaurant that serves some excellent food. Seating is available on the porch, garden patios, or in any of several dining rooms. The menu includes an inventive array of salads, pastas, pizzas, hot and cold sandwiches at lunch, and grill dishes at dinner. Start off with the soup of the day and some fresh baked bread, and then move on to penne pasta

in a shrimp and vegetable cream sauce or *lomito en salsa de vino tinto* (tenderlion in a red-wine sauce). Save room for dessert—the pastries are to die for. ⊠ *C. 15 and Avda. 9, Barrio Otoya,* ☎ *222–6190. AE, MC, V. Closed Sun. and around Easter.*

$$ ✕ **Miro's Bistro.** Hidden in a little brick building by the railroad tracks,
★ Miro's has long been popular with locals. Croatian-born Miro spent most of his life in Italy, and the menu reflects the mix: goulash, eggplant Parmesan, and various types of tortellini. You might see Miro greeting guests, taking orders, and cooking. The decor is very red, with a few watercolors on the walls and simple pine tables and chairs. It's a bit cramped, especially at the three-stool bar tucked away in the corner, but the terrific food and reasonable prices make it well worth your while. *Barrio Escalante, 333 yds north of Pulpería de la Luz, around the corner of brick building,* ☎ *253–4242. MC, V. Closed Sun, around Easter, and last wk in Dec.*

FRENCH

$$$$ ✕ **Le Chandelier.** In terms of decor, ambience, and cooking, this is San José's classiest restaurant, with wicker chairs, tile floor, original paintings, and formal service. The Swiss chef, Claude Dubuis, creates such unique dishes as corvina in a *pejibaye* (peach palm) sauce or the more familiar *pato a la naranja* (duck with orange sauce). ⊠ *San Pedro, from ICE, 1 block west and 1 block south,* ☎ *225–3980. AE, MC, V. Closed Sun. and last wk in Dec. No lunch Sat.*

$$$$ ✕ **L'Ile de France.** Long one of San José's most popular restaurants,
★ L'Ile de France recently moved from a downtown location to the Hotel Le Bergerac (☞ Lodging, *below*) in Los Yoses, where guests can dine in the tropical garden courtyard. Chef and proprietor Jean-Claude Fromont offers a fairly traditional French menu with some interesting innovations. Start off with the classic onion soup, or *pâté de lapin* (rabbit liver pâté); then sink your teeth into a pepper steak or corvina in a spinach sauce. Save room for the profiteroles (pastry puffs filled with vanilla ice cream and smothered in chocolate sauce). Reservations are recommended. ⊠ *C. 35 between Avdas. Central and 2, first entrance to Los Yoses,* ☎ *283–5812. AE, DC, MC, V. Closed Sun. No lunch.*

ITALIAN

$$–$$$ ✕ **Balcón de Europa.** In existence since 1909, this restaurant was long owned and managed by chef Franco Piatti, who died in 1996. His widow now runs it with the same staff, and so little has changed. The ambience has always been half the attraction, with hardwood floors and walls, old sepia photos of Costa Rica, and a strolling guitarist. Pasta dishes like the *plato mixto* (mixed plate with lasagna, tortellini, and ravioli) are the house specialties, but they also serve some quality Costa Rican fare, such as heart-of-palm salad or sautéed corvina. ⊠ *Avda. Central and C. 9,* ☎ *221–4841. AE, MC, V. Closed Sat. and Holy Week.*

$$–$$$ ✕ **Il Bagatto.** Ask one of Costa Rica's many Italian expatriates what
★ their favorite San José restaurant is, and they'll almost certain to answer "Il Bagatto!" You don't have to be a Roman, though, to appreciate these fresh pastas and top-heavy pizzas. Set in an old wooden house on the outskirts of town, and marked by a giant, rotating sign, Il Bagatto has little in the way of decoration other than colorful tablecloths and some modern art on the walls. But it's the food that packs them in, such as the *gnocchi alla Gorgonzola* (pasta dumplings with Gorgonzola cheese), homemade tagliatelle with any of a dozen sauces, or *lomito Il Bagatto* (tenderloin in a mushroom sauce). Choose from more than a dozen pizzas, or invent your own combination. Reservations are recommended. ⊠ *Across from Registro Nacional,* ☎ *224–5297. AE, MC, V. Closed Mon., Easter wk, and Dec. 20–Jan. 10.*

$$–$$$ ✕ **Pasta Factory.** The Italian food at this place is so authentic, it's hard to believe the owner is French. In addition to an ample selection of pastas, they make some of the best pizza in town: a dozen different combinations include an excellent vegetarian pie, and *quattro stagioni* (ham, mushrooms, olives, and onions). The restaurant is on a busy corner, with lots of windows, two seating levels, and brightly colored walls. Start off with some focaccia and perhaps some mushrooms *al ajillo* (sautéed with garlic). ⊠ *C. 7 and Avda. 1,* ☎ *222–4642. AE, MC, V. Closed Sun., around Easter, and Dec. 25–Jan. 2.*

PAN-ASIAN

$$ ✕ **Tin Jo.** There are two other Chinese restaurants on this block, but
★ thanks to its food, Tin Jo stands apart from them and from the vast majority of the city's other Asian eateries. Set in a former home, the restaurant achieves an elegant ambience with hardwoods, pastel tablecloths, and flowers on every table. The menu includes Cantonese, Szechuan, Thai, and Indian dishes, among which are such treats as *kaeng* (Thai shrimp and pineapple curry in coconut milk), *mu shu* (a beef, chicken, or veggie stir-fry with crepes), and *samosas* (stuffed Indian pastries). ⊠ *C. 11 between Avdas. 6 and 8,* ☎ *221–7605. AE, MC, V.*

PERUVIAN

$$–$$$ ✕ **Machu Picchu.** On a quiet street just north of Paseo Colón, this small
★ restaurant set in a converted house is *the* place for excellent Peruvian cuisine or just a good pisco sour, a cocktail made with lime juice, egg whites, and pisco brandy. A few travel posters and a fishnet holding crab and lobster shells are about the only concessions the management makes to decor—but no matter: the food is anything but plain and the seafood is excellent. The *pique especial de mariscos* (special seafood platter), big enough for two people, has shrimp, conch, and squid cooked four ways. The seviche here is quite different, and better, than that served in the rest of the country. A blazing Peruvian hot sauce served on the side adds zip to any dish, but be careful—apply it by the drop. *C. 32, 150 yards north of Kentucky Fried Chicken, Paseo Colón,* ☎ *222–7384. AE, DC, MC, V. Closed Sun.*

SPANISH

$$$–$$$$ ✕ **La Masía de Triquell.** San José's most authentic Spanish restaurant is appropriately housed in the Casa España, a Spanish cultural center. The dining room follows the theme with a tile floor; wood beams; red, green, and yellow walls; white tablecloths; and leather-and-wood Castilian-style chairs. Start with *champiñones al ajillo* (mushrooms sautéed with garlic and parsley), and, as a main course, try the *camarones Catalana* (shrimp in a tomato and garlic cream sauce). The wine list is long and strongest in the Spanish and French departments. Reservations are a good idea. *Sabana Norte, 50 yards west and 150 yards north of Burger King,* ☎ *296–3528. AE, DC, MC, V. Closed Sun., last wk in Dec., and around Easter.*

$$–$$$ ✕ **La Taska Andaluz.** From the flamenco music usually playing on the tape deck to the mantillas hung on the wall, this place is unmistakably Spanish. In this former home in Barrio Amón, you'll dine in one of the several eclectic rooms or during the dry season on a small terrace out front. Iberian favorites include paella, *conejo a la parrilla* (grilled rabbit), and corvina *a la andaluza* (sautéed with garlic and parsley). If you're not too hungry, you may opt for a drink and something from the *tapa* menu, with small portions of Spanish standards such as *tortilla española* (egg and potato pie). ⊠ *C. 3 near Avda. 9,* ☎ *257–6556. Reservations not accepted. AE, DC, MC, V. Closed daily 2:30–5 and Sun. off-season.*

VEGETARIAN

$ ✕ **Vishnu.** Though a restaurant named after a Hindu god may seem a bit out of place, Vishnu has become a bit of an institution in San José. Even the ambience is institutional—sterile Formica booths and posters of fruit hanging on the wall—but the attraction is the inexpensive vegetarian food. The best bet is usually the plato del día, which includes soup, beverage, and dessert, but they also serve soy burgers, salads, fresh fruit juices, and a yogurt smoothie called *morir soñando* (literally, die dreaming). Vishnu is open long hours. ⊠ *Avda. 1, just west of C. 3,* ☎ *222–2549. Reservations not accepted. No credit cards.*

LODGING

Downtown San José

$$$$ 🏨 **Aurola Holiday Inn.** The upper floors of this 17-story mirrored-glass building, three blocks north of the Plaza de la Cultura, have the best views in town. If ignoring the view, however, you could easily imagine you're in Ohio, so devoid of local influence is their decoration. The high-ceiling lobby is modern and airy, with lots of shiny marble. The good restaurant and casino on the top floor have the best views in the house. ⊠ *Avda. 5 and C. 5, Apdo. 7802–1000,* ☎ *233–7233, 800/ 465–4329 in the U.S.,* FAX *255–1036. 188 rooms with bath, 12 suites. Restaurant, bar, cafeteria, indoor pool, hot tub, sauna, exercise room, casino. AE, DC, MC, V.*

$$$–$$$$ 🏨 **Britannia.** On a busy corner in Barrio Amón, this pink house with a tiled porch has changed very little since its construction in 1910, except for a row of newer rooms; the old cellar, too, has been converted into an intimate restaurant. Rooms in the newer wing are slightly small, with carpeting and hardwood furniture. Deluxe rooms and junior suites in the old house are spacious, with high ceilings and windows on the street side—they're worth the extra money but are close enough to the street that noise could be a problem if you're a light sleeper. The cellar restaurant, overlooking the interior gardens that separate the old and new wings, serves dishes such as cream of pejibaye soup and tenderloin with béarnaise sauce. ⊠ *C. 3 and Avda. 11, Apdo. 3742– 1000,* ☎ *223–6667,* FAX *223–6411. 19 rooms with bath, 5 junior suites. Restaurant. AE, MC, V.*

$$$–$$$$ 🏨 **Grano de Oro.** This turn-of-the-century wooden house, on a quiet
★ side street on the western edge of San José, is one of the city's most charming inns. The former house was expanded with new rooms, a restaurant, and indoor gardens. The older rooms are the nicest, especially the Garden Suite, with its hardwood floors, high ceilings, and private garden. The standard rooms are a bit small but tasteful. The restaurant overlooks an interior patio, and the kitchen is run by a French chef. The hotel's sundeck has a spiffy view of both the city and the far-off volcanoes. ⊠ *C. 30 between Avdas. 2 and 4,* ☎ *255–3322,* FAX *221– 2782;* ⊠ *Box 025216, SJO 36, Miami, FL 33102-5216. 31 rooms with bath, 3 suites. Restaurant, hot tub. MC, V.*

$$$–$$$$ 🏨 **Hotel Alóki.** In a quiet, upscale residential neighborhood five blocks
★ from the city center, Hotel Alóki inhabits an elegant, turn-of-the-century manor house. Guest rooms surround a covered central courtyard restaurant, with wicker furniture and potted tropical plants spilling onto multicolor glazed tiles. The antique furniture, gilt mirrors, and old prints in the rooms make this small, quiet place one of the city's most tasteful. The Presidential Suite has a large drawing room. Breakfast is included. ⊠ *C. 13 between Avdas. 9 and 11,* ☎ *222–6702,* FAX *221–2533. 7 rooms with bath, 1 suite. Restaurant, bar. MC, V.*

$$$ 🏨 **Don Carlos.** A rambling, multilevel gray villa was one of this city's
★ first guesthouses and has been in the same family for four generations.

Most rooms are in new additions, with ceiling fans, big windows, and lots of paintings on the walls. Those in the Colonial Wing have a bit more personality, and several newer rooms on the third floor feature volcano views. Abundant public areas are adorned with orchids, pre-Columbian statues, and original art depicting scenes of Costa Rican life. The on-site crafts shop probably has the city's best selection. Complimentary breakfast is served on the garden patio; the small restaurant serves lunch, dinner, and drinks. ✉ *C. 9 and Avda. 9,* ☎ *221–6707,* ℻ *255–0828;* ✉ *Box 025216, Dept. 1686, Miami, FL 33102-5216. 20 rooms with bath, 13 suites. Restaurant, hot tub, travel services. AE, MC, V.*

$$$ 🏨 **Le Bergerac.** Set in the quiet, residential, eastern neighborhood of
★ Los Yoses, Le Bergerac is the cream of a growing crop of small upscale San José hotels. French owned and managed, it occupies two former private homes and is furnished with antiques and surrounded by extensive green areas. Guest rooms have custom-made stone-and-wood dressers and writing tables. Deluxe rooms have private garden terraces or balconies and large bathrooms. The hotel's restaurant, L'Ile de France (☞ *Dining, above*), is one of the city's best, which is why dinner reservations are necessary, even for guests. Complimentary breakfast is served on a garden patio. ✉ *C. 35, first entrance to Los Yoses, Apdo. 1107–1002,* ☎ *234–7850,* ℻ *225–9103. 18 rooms with bath. Restaurant, meeting room, travel services. AE, MC, V.*

$$$ 🏨 **Villa Tournón.** North of downtown, just two blocks from El Pueblo shopping center, the Tournón is a popular place with traveling businesspeople, who head here for the peace, security, and reasonable rates. Sloping wooden ceilings and bare, redbrick walls may recall a ski chalet, but the kidney-shape pool out back is surrounded by tropical foliage. The carpeted rooms are snug and tastefully decorated, with pastel shades and prints. The restaurant has a very good reputation, and the buffet breakfast is big enough to make you skip lunch. ✉ *Barrio Tournón, Apdo. 6606–1000,* ☎ *233–6622,* ℻ *222–5211. 80 rooms with bath. Restaurant, pool. AE, MC, V.*

$$–$$$ 🏨 **Edelweiss.** The name may seem out of place—one of the owners is Austrian—and the interior may look more European than Latin American, but this elegant little hotel offers comfortable rooms in a charming corner of the city, near the Parque España, and at very reasonable prices. Rooms have carved doors, custom-made furniture, small baths, and ceiling fans. Most have hardwood window frames and floors; several have bathtubs. Complimentary breakfast is served in a garden courtyard, which doubles as a bar. ✉ *Avda. 9 and C. 15, Barrio Otoya,* ☎ *221–9702,* ℻ *222–1241. 16 rooms with bath. Bar. AE, MC, V.*

$$–$$$ 🏨 **Gran Hotel Costa Rica.** Opened in 1930, the dowager of San José hotels remains a focal point of the city and is consequently the choice of travelers who want to be where the action is. It's a good deal for the money, but the flow of nonguests who frequent the 24-hour casino, Café Parisienne, restaurant, and bar reduces the intimacy quotient to zero. Rooms are large, with small windows, ceiling fans, and tubs in the tiled baths. Most overlook the Plaza de la Cultura, which can be a bit noisy, and the quieter interior rooms are pretty dark. There have been complaints about the lack of air-conditioning. ✉ *Avda. 2 and C. 3, Apdo. 527–1000,* ☎ *221–4000,* ℻ *221–3501. 106 rooms with bath, 4 suites. Restaurant, bar, café, casino. AE, DC, MC, V.*

$$ 🏨 **Cinco Hormigas Rojas.** The name of this colorful little lodge translates as "Five Red Ants." The interior is full of original art and is wildly decorated—from the bright colors on the walls right down to the toilet seats. What can we say, the owner's an artist. Owner Mayra Güell, who lives here, turned the house she inherited from her grandmother into San José's most original B&B–cum–art gallery. It's in the historic Barrio Otoya, one of San José's few pleasant neighborhoods. A hearty

breakfast is included in the rate. ⊠ *C. 15 between Avdas. 9 and 11,* ☎ 🅵🅰🆇 *257–8581. 6 rooms, 1 with bath. Free parking. AE, MC, V.*

$$ 🏨 **Hotel Aranjuez.** Hidden in the quiet residential neighborhood of Bar-
★   rio Aranjuez, a short walk from most San José attractions, this family-
run B&B occupies several old houses complete with extensive gardens
and cozy common areas. Every room is comfortable but different—it pays
to check out a few, if you can—as some have private gardens or little
sitting rooms. Not only is it an ecologically friendly hotel, but they offer
such perks as free E-mail access, cable TV, and a discount tour service.
The complimentary breakfast buffet is hearty enough to make lunch un-
thinkable. Reserve well in advance during the high season. ⊠ *C. 19 be-
tween Avdas. 11 and 13,* ☎ *256–1825,* 🅵🅰🆇 *223–3528. 30 rooms, 22 with
bath. Breakfast room, travel services, free parking. MC, V.*

$$ 🏨 **Joluva Guesthouse.** This small B&B caters primarily to a gay clientele, but the accommodations and price make it appealing to every-
one. Housed in a white cement building, on one of the quieter streets
of Barrio Amón, the Joluva is marked by only a small sign. A narrow
entrance, flanked by white columns detailed in gold, leads to a high-
ceiling common area with a lovely tile floor, couches, and armchairs.
Rooms have hardwood floors, rugs, and small baths; the two cheapest rooms share a bath. Complimentary Continental breakfast is served.
⊠ *C. 3 Bis between Avdas. 9 and 11, Apdo. 1998–1002,* ☎ *223–7961,
619/224–2418 in the U.S.,* 🅵🅰🆇 *257–7668. 8 rooms, 6 with bath. Breakfast room. AE, MC, V.*

$$ 🏨 **Pensión de la Cuesta.** The rooms of this laid-back, centrally located
wooden villa on Cuesta de Nuñez have hardwood floors, brightly
painted walls, and original art. Rooms in back are quieter, but those
in front are brighter. You can lounge and read in the sunken sitting area
(also used as the breakfast room), which has a high ceiling, wall of win-
dows, and cable TV. Breakfast is included in the price, and you are wel-
come to use the kitchen at other times. The nine rooms share four baths.
A furnished apartment is also for rent. ⊠ *Avda. 1 between Cs. 11 and
15, Apdo. 1332,* ☎ 🅵🅰🆇 *255–2896. 9 rooms without bath, 1 apartment.
Breakfast room. AE, DC, MC, V.*

$ 🏨 **Casa Ridgeway.** Affiliated with the Quaker Peace Center next door,
★   Casa Ridgeway is the budget option for itinerants concerned with
peace, the environment, and social issues in general. In an old villa on
a quiet street, the bright, clean premises include a planted terrace, lend-
ing reference library, and kitchen where you can cook your own food.
There are three rooms with two bunkbeds each, two rooms with sin-
gle beds, and one with a double bed, all of which share three bathrooms.
⊠ *Avda. 6 Bis and C. 15, Apdo. 1507–1000,* ☎ 🅵🅰🆇 *233–6168. 6 rooms
without bath. Library, meeting room. No credit cards.*

$ 🏨 **Toruma Youth Hostel.** The headquarters of Costa Rica's expanding
hostel network is housed in an elegant colonial bungalow, built around
1900, in the suburb of Los Yoses, east of downtown. The tiled lobby
and veranda are ideal spots for backpackers to hang out and exchange
travel tips. Beds on the ground floor are in little compartments with
doors, and the second-floor rooms have standard bunks. There are also
two private rooms available for couples. An on-site information cen-
ter offers discounts on tours. ⊠ *Avda. Central between Cs. 29 and 31,
Apdo. 1355–1002,* ☎ 🅵🅰🆇 *224–4085. 2 rooms without baths, 80 beds.
Dining room. MC, V.*

Northwest of San José

$$$$ 🏨 **Marriott.** Towering over a coffee plantation west of San José, the
★   stately building evokes an unusual colonial splendor. The thick columns,
wide arches, and central courtyard are straight out of the 17th cen-
tury, and hand-painted tiles and abundant antiques complete the his-

toric ambience. Guest rooms have a more contemporary decor, though they're elegant enough, with hardwood furniture—including a cabinet that holds the TV set—and sliding glass doors that open onto tiny "Juliet" balconies. ✉ *San Antonio de Belén,* ☎ *298–0000, 800/228–9290 in the U.S.,* 📠 *298–0044. 245 rooms with bath, 7 suites. 2 restaurants, café, lobby lounge, 2 pools, beauty salon, driving range, putting green, 3 tennis courts, health club, business services, meeting rooms, travel services, car rental. AE, DC, MC, V.*

$$$$ 🏨 **Meliá Cariari.** The low-rise Meliá Cariari was San José's original luxury hotel, and it remains popular because of a wide range of facilities and its out-of-town location. Set down from the busy General Cañas Highway, about halfway between San José and the international airport, the Cariari is surrounded by thick vegetation that buffers it from traffic noise. Spacious, carpeted guest rooms in back overlook the pool area. The relaxed poolside bar, with cane chairs and mustard tablecloths, and nearby casino are popular spots. ✉ *Autopista General Cañas, Apdo. 737–1007, just east of intersection for San Antonio de Belén,* ☎ *239–0022, 800/227–4274 in the U.S.,* 📠 *239–2803. 220 rooms with bath. 2 restaurants, bar, cafeteria, pool, hot tub, golf privileges, 4 tennis courts, exercise room, casino. AE, DC, MC, V.*

NIGHTLIFE AND THE ARTS

The Arts

Film

Dubbing is rare in Costa Rica, so moviegoers can see films in their original language, usually English, and brush up on their Spanish by reading the subtitles. The film scene is dominated by U.S. movies, which reach San José from one to several months after their release in the United States. Movie theaters are all over downtown San José, as well as in the malls that surround the city. Check the local paper *La Nación* or the *Tico Times* for current listings. **Sala Garbo and Laurence Olivier** (✉ Avda. 2 and C. 28, ☎ 222–1034) shows more artsy films, though they're often in languages other than English. **Cine Variedades** (✉ C. 5 between Avdas. Central and 1, ☎ 222–6108) is San José's other art cinema.

Theater and Music

The baroque **Teatro Nacional** (✉ Plaza de la Cultura, ☎ 221–1329 tickets and info) hosts performances of the excellent National Symphony Orchestra, whose season runs from April to December, with concerts on Friday evening and Sunday morning. The Teatro Nacional also stages performances from visiting musical groups and dance troupes. San José's second main theater is the **Teatro Melico Salazar** (✉ Avda. 2 between Cs. Central and 2, ☎ 221–4952 tickets and info). There are also frequent dance performances and concerts in the **Teatro Fanal** and the **Teatro 1887,** both of which are inside the **Centro Nacional de la Cultura** (✉ C. 13 between Avdas. 3 and 5, ☎ 257–5524 tickets and info; ☞ Exploring San José, *above*). Dozens of theater groups, including one that performs in English, put on shows at smaller theaters around town; check the English-language *Tico Times* for information about upcoming performances.

Nightlife

Bars

No one could accuse San José of having too few watering holes, but outside of the hotels, there aren't too many places to have a quiet drink—Tico bars tend to be on the lively side. For a little taste of Mexico in Costa Rica, head to **La Esmeralda** (✉ Avda. 2 between Cs. 5 and 7), a popular late-night spot where the locals gather to enjoy live mariachi music until the wee hours. If you want to watch a game, and hang out with the gringos, you can try the bar in the **Hotel del Rey** (⊠ Avda. 1 between Cs. 9 and 11), which is a major pickup spot for San José's thriving prostitution trade. The second floor of the **Casino Colonial** (☞ Casinos, *below*) is a quieter, less racy spot to watch a game.

A trendy place to see and be seen is **El Cuartel de la Boca del Monte** (⊠ Avda. 1 between Cs. 21 and 23), a large, low-ceiling bar, where young artists and professionals gather to sip San José's fanciest cocktails and share plates of tasty bocas (appetizers or snacks). It has live music on Monday and Wednesday night. **Río** (⊠ Avda. Central between Cs. 41 and 43), in the eastern suburb of Los Yoses, is usually rocking and crowded with young Ticos. The Spanish village–themed shopping arcade **Centro Comercial El Pueblo** (☞ Exploring San José, *above*) features a bar for every taste, from quiet pubs to thumping discos (☞ *below*). Several of the bars have live music on weekends, so it's best to wander around and see what sounds good. **Café Mundo** (☞ Dining, San José, *above*) is a quieter spot frequented by gay men at night. **El Bochinche** (⊠ C. 11 between Avdas. 10 and 12) and **Kashbah** (⊠ C. Central between Avdas. 7 and 9) are two more of the city's many gay bars.

Casinos

The 24-hour **Casino Colonial** (⊠ Avda. 1 between Cs. 9 and 11, ☎ 258–2827) has a complete casino, cable TV, bar, restaurant, and a betting service for major U.S. sporting events. Most of the country's larger hotels also have casinos, including the Aurola Holiday Inn (the view from the casino is breathtaking), Meliá Cariari, and Gran Hotel Costa Rica (☞ Lodging, *above*).

Discos

Coyote, in the basement of the San Pedro Mall, the massive building overlooking the San Pedro Rotunda, is a popular discotheque that plays a wide variety of music. **Planet Mall,** on the top floor of the San Pedro Mall, is one of the city's newest and most expensive dance bars. The **Centro Comercial El Pueblo** (☞ *above*) has two full-fledged discos: for dancing to Latin music head to **Cocoloco; Infinito** has two dance floors, one of which plays mostly techno, pop, and funk, and another which plays only Latin music. Across the parking lot from the Centro Comercial El Pueblo is **Plaza,** a larger, slightly more upscale disco that plays a good mix of northern and Latin music.

Déjà Vu (⊠ C. 2 between Avdas. 14 and 16A) is a mostly gay, techno-heavy disco with two dance floors. Gay and lesbian travelers may also want to check out **La Avispa** (⊠ C. 1 between Avdas. 8 and 10), which has two dance floors and a quieter upstairs bar.

OUTDOOR ACTIVITIES AND SPORTS

Participant Sports

Fitness Centers

Luxury hotels like the Aurola Holiday Inn, Marriott, and the Meliá Cariari (☞ Lodging, *above*) have modern gyms attached, available to guests only. **Gimnasio Perfect Line** (⊠ C. 1 and Avda. Central, 6th floor) is a full gym offering inexpensive one-month memberships. For a complete listing, look under "Gimnasios" in the *Páginas Amarillas* (Yellow Pages).

Horseback Riding

Most of the city's travel agencies can arrange one-day horseback tours, which take you to farms in the surrounding Central Valley. Several Central Valley hotels also run their own horseback tours, one of the best of which is offered by **La Providencia Lodge** (☎ 380–6315; ☞ Chapter 3), near the top of Volcán Poás. The horseback tour at the **Sacramento Lodge** (⊠ Just above Sacramento, ☎ 237–2116, FAX 237–2976), on the upper slopes of Volcán Barva, includes round-trip transportation, breakfast, lunch, and great views. A cheaper option is to get yourself to the **Centro Equestre Valle de Yos-Oy** (⊠ 1 km/½ mi south on road to Salitral, ☎ 282–6934), outside the western town of Santa Ana, where they simply charge by the hour for guided trail rides.

Running
Once the airport but now a eucalyptus-shaded park, **Parque La Sabana,** at the end of the Paseo Colón, is the best place to run in San José, with 5-km (3-mi) routes along cement paths.

White-Water Rafting
White-water trips down the Reventazón, Pacuare, Sarapiquí, and General rivers all leave from San José (☞ *below*). Nearly half a dozen licensed tour companies out of San José operate similar rafting and kayaking trips of varying length and grade. The Reventazón's class III and IV–V runs are both day trips. The General (class III–IV) is descended in a three-day camping trip. The Pacuare (class III–IV) can be run in one, two, or three days.

Accommodations for overnight trips on the General or Pacuare Rivers are usually in a tent; however, both Aventuras Naturales and Riós Tropicales have comfortable lodges on the Pacuare, which make them the most popular outfitters for overnight trips on that river. The cost is around $70 to $90 for one day, according to which river. Two- and three-day packages with overnight stays are considerably more expensive. Try **Costa Rica Expeditions** (⊠ Avda. 3 and C. Central, San José, ☎ 257–0766, FAX 255–4354), **Ríos Tropicales** (⊠ 50 yards south of Centro Colón, San José, ☎ 233–6455, FAX 255–4354), **Aventuras Naturales** (⊠ Behind Banco Nacional, San Pedro, ☎ 225–3939 and 224–0505, FAX 253–6934), and **Pioneer Raft** (2 blocks north of Bar La Luz, ☎ 225–8117 or 225–4735, FAX 253–4687).

Spectator Sport

Soccer
Professional soccer matches are usually played on Sunday mornings or Wednesday nights in either of two San José stadiums: the **Estadio Nacional,** on the western end of La Sabana park, and the **Estadio Ricardo Saprissa,** in the northern suburb of Tibás. Consult the Spanish-language daily *La Nación,* or ask the receptionist at your hotel about where and when the next game will be held.

SHOPPING

Specialty Items

Antiques
Antigüedades Gobelino (⊠ Avda. 9 between Cs. 3 and 5, ☎ 223–9552) sells antique paintings, ceramics, jewelry, and other smaller items. **Antigüedades Chavo** (⊠ C. Central between Avdas. Central and 1, ☎ 258–3966) sells mostly furniture but has some smaller antiques.

Books and Maps
7th Street Books (⊠ C. 7 between Avdas. Central and 1, ☎ 256–8251) has an excellent selection of new and used books in English, especially those concerning Latin America and tropical ecology. **Lehmann** (⊠ Avda.

Central between Cs. 1 and 3, ☎ 223–1212) has some books in English, as well as a stock of large-scale topographical maps.

Coffee and Liquor

Coffee can be purchased in souvenir shops and supermarkets. The best brand is Café Rey Tarrazú; the second best is Café Britt. You can also buy good, fresh-roasted coffee at **La Esquina del Café** (⊠ Avda. 9 at C. 3 Bis, ☎ 257–9868). The country's best rum is the aged Centenario, and you can pick up a bottle for about $5. There are also several brands of coffee liqueurs, the oldest of which is Café Rica, but the best of which is Britt. These national liquors can be purchased at any of the city's abundant supermarkets and liquor stores.

SAN JOSÉ A TO Z

Arriving and Departing

By Bus

A handful of private companies operates from San José, providing reliable, inexpensive bus service throughout much of the country from a variety of departure points, as San José has no central bus station. For bus stops and companies, *see* Chapter 3.

By Car

San José is the hub of the national road system. Paved roads fan out from Paseo Colón south to Escazú, or north to the airport and Heredia. For the Pacific coast, Guanacaste, and Nicaragua, take the Carretera Interamericana (Pan-American Highway, CA1). Calle 3 runs east into the highway to Guápiles, Limón, and the Atlantic coast. If you follow Avenidas Central or 2 east through San Pedro, you'll enter the Pan-American Highway (CA2) south, which has a turnoff for Cartago, Volcán Irazú, and Turrialba, before heading over the mountains to the southwest and Panama.

By Plane

AIRPORTS

All international and some domestic flights to San José arrive at **Aeropuerto Internacional Juan Santamaría** (☎ 441–0744), 16 km (10 mi) northwest of downtown San José. Some domestic flights depart from **Aeropuerto Internacional Tobías Bolaños** (☎ 232–2820) in the suburb of Pavas, 3 km (2 mi) west of downtown San José.

BETWEEN THE AIRPORT AND DOWNTOWN

Taxis from the airport to downtown cost around $10; drivers do not expect tips. Beware of taxi drivers eager to take you to a hotel they know, which no doubt pays them a hefty commission. Far cheaper (about 40¢), and almost as quick, is the bus marked RUTA 200 SAN JOSÉ, which will drop you at the west end of Avenida 2, close to the city's heart. The other option is to rent a vehicle from one of the car-rental offices (☞ Car Rentals, *below*). Driving time is about 20 minutes, but allow 40 to be safe. Note that some hotels provide a free shuttle service—inquire when you book.

Getting Around

By Bus

Bus service within San José is absurdly cheap (15¢–20¢) and easy to use. For Paseo Colón and La Sabana take buses marked SABANA-CEMENTERIO from stops on the southern side of the Parque Morazán, or on Avenida 3 next to the Correos building. For the suburbs of Los Yoses and San Pedro near the university, take one marked SAN PEDRO, CUR-RIDABAT, or LOURDES from Avenida Central, between Calles 9 and 11.

By Car

Almost all the streets in downtown San José are one-way. Traffic gets surprisingly congested at peak hours, when it's ill-advised to drive. There are parking lots scattered all over the city, which charge around $1 an hour. It is possible to park on the street outside of the center of town, but make sure someone guards your vehicle if you plan to leave it for a while.

By Taxi

Taxis are a good deal in the capital. You can hail them—all taxis are red—in the street or call a taxi company directly. It's best to get a Tico to call a cab for you, since cabbies only speak Spanish and addresses are complicated. A 3-km (2-mi) ride costs around $1; tipping is not usually done here. Taxis parked in front of expensive hotels charge about twice the normal rate. By law, all cabbies must use their meters, and if one refuses, negotiate a price before going anywhere. Cab companies include **San Jorge** (☎ 221–3434), **Coopetaxi** (☎ 235–9966), and, if you need to go to the airport, **Taxis Unidos** (☎ 221–6865).

Contacts and Resources

Car Rentals

ADA (✉ Avda. 18 between Cs. 11 and 13, ☎ 233–7733 and 800/570–0671). **Budget** (✉ Paseo Colón and Calle 30, ☎ 223–3284 and 800/527–0700). **Dollar** (✉ Paseo Colón and Calle 32, ☎ 257–1585 and 800/800–4000). **Hertz** (✉ Paseo Colón and Calle 38, ☎ 221–1818 and 800/654–3001). **National** (✉ 1 km/½ mi north of Hotel Best Western Irazú, ☎ 290–8787 and 800/227–3876). Note: it is practically impossible to rent a car in Costa Rica from December 20 to January 3; try to book far in advance. Any other time of year, shop around for the best rate.

Doctors and Dentists

Your embassy can provide you with a list of recommended doctors and dentists. Hospitals open to foreigners include the following: **Clínica Bíblica** (✉ Avda. 14 between Cs. Central and 1, ☎ 257–0466 emergencies, 221–3922 appointments) and **Clínica Católica** (✉ Guadalupe, attached to San Antonio Church on C. Esquivel Bonilla St., ☎ 283–6616).

Embassies

Canada (✉ Sabana Sur, next to tennis club, ☎ 296–4146). **U.K.** (✉ Centro Colón, Paseo Colón between Cs. 38 and 40, ☎ 221–5566). **U.S.** (✉ C. 120 and Avda. 0, Pavas, Apdo. 920-1200, ☎ 220–3939).

Emergencies

In just about any **emergency** you can dial ☎ 911, but here are some additional useful numbers: **Fire** (☎ 118). **Ambulance** (☎ 128). **Police** (☎ 117; 127 outside cities). **Traffic Police** (☎ 222–9330).

English-Language Bookstores

See Shopping, *above*, for English-language bookstores.

Guided Tours

ADVENTURE

Costa Rica Eco Adventure Services (Apdo. 1244-1000, San José, ☎ 283–9152, pager 224–2400, www.ecoguides.com) will customize natural history and adventure tours run by expert guides to anywhere in Costa Rica; activities include tropical rain-forest and cloud forest hikes, kayaking, diving, snorkeling, and horseback riding. **Aventuras Naturales** (✉ Behind Banco Nacional, San Pedro, ☎ 225–3939, FAX 253–6934) leads rafting and mountain-biking tours. **Costa Rica Expeditions**

(✉ Avda. 3 at C. Central, San José, ☎ 222–0333, FAX 257–1665) is one of the country's most experienced rafting outfitters. **Rios Tropicales** (✉ 50 yards south of Centro Colón, San José, ☎ 233–6455, FAX 255–4354) offers rafting, sea-kayaking, and mountain-biking tours. **Rain Forest Aerial Tram** (✉ Avda. 7 between Cs. 5 and 7, ☎ 257–5961) takes visitors floating through the treetops on a modified ski lift. **Tropical Bungee** (✉ Sabana Sur, 100 yards west and 200 yards south of Controlaría, Sabana, ☎ 232–3956) runs bungee jumps near San José on weekends.

DAY TRIPS

Bay Island Cruises (✉ 125 yards north of Toyota Paseo Colón, ☎ 258–3536, FAX 258–1189) and **Calypso** (✉ Arcadas building, 3rd floor, next to Gran Hotel Costa Rica, Apdo. 6941–1000, ☎ 256–2727, FAX 256–6767) run cruises to Isla Tortuga. Hail, coffee lovers: the popular coffee tour run by **Café Britt** (✉ 900 yards north and 400 yards west of the Comandancia, Heredia, ☎ 260–2748, FAX 238–1848), in Heredia, presents the history of coffee via skits, a tour of a coffee farm, and a coffee tasting.

NATURAL HISTORY

Although everyone is setting up ecological tours, there are a few companies that have more experience than the majority, among them the following: **Costa Rica Eco Adventure Services** (☞ Adventure, *above*); **Costa Rica Expeditions** (✉ Avda. 3 at C. Central, San José, ☎ 222–0333, FAX 257–1665); **Costa Rica Sun Tours** (✉ 200 yards south of Toyota Paseo Colón, ☎ 255–2011, FAX 255–4410); **Horizontes** (✉ 150 yards north of Pizza Hut Paseo Colón, ☎ 222–2022, FAX 255–4513); **Tikal Tours** (✉ Avda. 2 between Cs. 7 and 9, ☎ 223–2811, FAX 223–1916).

WHITE-WATER RAFTING

See Outdoor Activities and Sports, *above*.

Late-Night Pharmacies

The Clínica Bíblica (☞ Doctors and Dentists, *above*) operates a 24-hour pharmacy.

Travel Agencies

Galaxy (✉ C. 3 between Avdas. 5 and 7, ☎ 233–3240). **Aviatica** (✉ Avda. 1 and C. 1, ☎ 222–5630). **Intertur** (✉ Avda. Central between Cs. 31 and 33, ☎ 253–7503).

Visitor Information

The **Instituto Costarricense de Turismo** (ICT, C. 5 between Avdas. Central and 2, ☎ 222–1090) has a tourist information office beneath the Plaza de la Cultura, next to the Museo de Oro. The people who work there will answer questions and provide free maps, bus schedules, and brochures. The office is open weekdays 9–5.

3 CENTRAL VALLEY: AROUND SAN JOSÉ

A ring of spectacular volcanoes defines the Central Valley. This agricultural area is densely planted with neat rows of coffee bushes and dotted with colorful farm towns and small cities. In its center is San José, a convenient base for exciting excursions. Peer into the crater of a volcano, wander amidst radiant orchids, or visit colonial-era towns that prosper thanks to the grano de oro (golden bean).

By David
Dudenhoefer
and Justin
Henderson

HOVERING MORE THAN 3,000 FT ABOVE SEA LEVEL, the Meseta Central, or Central Valley, is Costa Rica's approximate geographic center. The valley is sandwiched among hulking mountain chains—the foothills of the Cordillera de Talamanca define the southern edge of the valley and the Cordillera Central sweeps across the northern border. The fuming volcanoes marching along these chains, their summits protected within national parks, are within easy reach of San José: Volcán Irazú, Costa Rica's highest, towers to the east of San José; Poás, whose active crater often spews a plume of sulfuric smoke, stands to the northwest; the older Volcán Barva looms between the two. Dramatic craters and thick cloud forests envelop these sleeping giants, while the slopes in their shadows host a variety of coffee communities and charming agricultural hamlets.

The plateau is the nation's cultural cradle, with San José and other important historical cities among its inhabitants—not to mention a population of 1.5 million. Though most of the region's colonial architecture has been destroyed by earthquakes and the ravages of time, several smaller cities preserve a bit more history than does San José. The central squares of Alajuela, Escazú, and Heredia, for example, are surrounded by an architectural mixture of old and new. Cartago, the country's first capital, has scattered historical structures and the impressive Basílica de Los Angeles. Beyond those small cities lie dozens of tiny farming communities, where you can discover lovely churches and adobe farmhouses with coffee growing in the backyard. The Central Valley's varied attractions can easily be experienced on a series of half- or full-day excursions from San José, but the abundance of excellent accommodations and restaurants in the valley's other cities and towns means lodging in San José is by no means obligatory.

Pleasures and Pastimes

Dining
This region's dining options run the gamut, from the rustic mountain lodges, where hearty meals are enhanced by the beauty of the natural surroundings, to the exceptional restaurants in the hills above Escazú—fine dining with a backdrop of San José's city lights. Since Escazú lies so close to San José, consider venturing to this bedroom community for a meal or two.

Festivals
The Día de la Virgen de Los Angeles, which honors Costa Rica's patron saint, is celebrated in Cartago on August 2 with processions and a well-attended mass. The night before, tens of thousands of faithful worshippers walk *la romaría*, a 22-km (14-mi) trek east down the highway from San José to Cartago. April 11 is Día de Juan Santamaría in Alajuela, when a loud parade and other fun gets underway. The Festival de los Mangos (Festival of Mangoes), also in Alajuela, involves nine days of music, parades, markets, and general merrymaking in July. The second Sunday in March marks the Día del Boyero (Oxcart Driver Day), when a colorful procession of carts parades through San Antonio de Escazú.

Lodging
The accommodations scattered across this area range from rustic *cabinas* (cottages) to elegant suites. Most travelers tend to stay in San José, since its convenient position makes it possible to visit all of the Central Valley's attractions on day trips. The city has an ample selection of hotels and restaurants, but it also has the crime, noise, and pollu-

tion that accompany crowds and traffic, which can make lodging in one of the surrounding communities a more attractive option.

Volcanoes

Some of Costa Rica's most accessible volcanoes stand along the northern edge of the Central Valley, two of which, Poás and Irazú, have paved roads right to their summits. Volcán Poás is very popular, since it packs in an extensive visitor center, an impressive active crater, a luxuriant forest, and a jewel-like, blue-green lake. Volcán Irazú, the country's highest, is topped by a desolate but impressive landscape—the result of violent eruptions in the early 1960s—but on a clear day the view is unparalleled. Barva, in the southern section of Parque Nacional Braulio Carrillo north of San José, is cloaked in an extensive cloud forest resounding with the songs of colorful birds such as the emerald toucanet and resplendent quetzal. You can visit all three volcanoes on day trips from San José; Poás and Irazú require only a morning, whereas you'll need a full day to hike the summit of Barva.

Exploring the Central Valley: Around San José

The Central Valley has an extensive network of paved roads, many of which are in relatively good shape. The Pan-American Highway runs east–west through the valley—through the center of San José—and turns south at Cartago. Dozens of roads head off of this well-marked highway, but if you stray from the main tourists routes, you may encounter a lack of road signs. If you do, don't despair—the locals are always happy to point you in the right direction.

Numbers in the text correspond to numbers in the margin and on the Central Valley: Around San José map.

Great Itineraries

Most of the Central Valley's towns stand in the shadows of volcanoes, so you should include stops at one or two towns on your way down from the summit of any volcano you visit. To reach Volcán Poás, for example, you have to drive through Alajuela. Heredia lies on the road to Volcán Barva, and Cartago sits at the foot of Irazú. From Irazú, you can take the serpentine roads eastward to Volcán Turrialba, Turrialba, and the Monumento Nacional Guayabo, the country's most important archaeological site. Paraíso, just southeast of Cartago, is the gateway to the Valle de Orosi (Orosi Valley) southeast of San José.

IF YOU HAVE 2 DAYS

Start by ascending ⛰ **Volcán Poás** ⑤ by car; you can settle in for a night near the summit or simply enjoy a good lunch before returning to warmer ⛰ **Alajuela** ④ or San José. The next day, explore the Orosi Valley, stopping at the fascinating **Jardín Lankester** ⑪ on the way.

IF YOU HAVE 4 DAYS

On day one, head north to ⛰ **Heredia** ② and the adjacent coffee communities, continuing up the slopes of **Volcán Barva** ③ for a picnic or gourmet lunch in the cool mountain air. If an energetic traveler, you may want to spend a day to hiking up to the crater lakes atop the volcano or to a high-altitude horseback jaunt. Head northeast and spend the next day exploring **Cartago** ⑨ and the Orosi Valley, starting off in the **Parque Nacional Tapantí** ⑭; overnight in the valley. Early the next morning drive up to the summit of **Volcán Irazú** ⑩, and then wind your way down its slopes to ⛰ **Turrialba** ⑮, stopping at **Monumento Nacional Guayabo** ⑯ on the way. If you spend the night in Turrialba, on the fourth day you could go rafting or return to the western Central Valley and spend the day at ⛰ **Volcán Poás** ⑤, visiting the towns of ⛰ **Grecia** ⑥ and **Sarchí** ⑦ in the afternoon.

Central Valley: Around San José

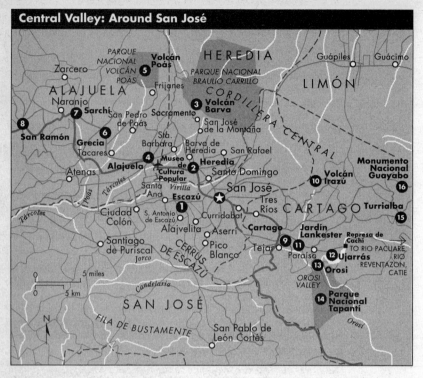

Start by exploring the community of ⊞ **Escazú** ①; then spend the afternoon in ⊞ **Sarchí** ⑦ and ⊞ **Grecia** ⑥. On day two, visit the summit of ⊞ **Volcán Poás** ⑤, stopping at ⊞ **Alajuela** ④ and Zoo Ave, the bird zoo, afterward. Dedicate day three to horseback riding or hiking in the mountains above ⊞ **Heredia** ② or exploring this historic city and the surrounding towns. Head for the Orosi Valley the following day, where you should start by visiting the **Parque Nacional Tapantí** ⑭. The fifth day should begin with a trip up **Volcán Irazú** ⑩, after which you can wander through **Cartago** ⑨ and the **Jardín Lankester** ⑪, continuing east to ⊞ **Turrialba** ⑮. On day six explore **Monumento Nacional Guayabo** ⑯ and the CATIE or go white-water rafting on either the Río Reventazón or Río Pacuare.

When to Tour the Central Valley

From January to May it tends to be sunny and breezy on an almost daily basis in the Central Valley. Nights in January and February can get quite cold on the upper slopes of the volcanoes. Regular afternoon downpours are consistent starting in mid-May, dropping off a bit between mid-July and mid-September. From mid-September to December, the precipitation becomes more copious. But don't rule out travel to Costa Rica during the rainy season—days here and there are spared rain, and when it does rain, it's usually for a few hours in the afternoon when you can break for siesta. Few tourists visit during this period, so you probably won't need reservations. The area is swathed in green after the rainy months, but come January the sun begins to beat down, and by April the countryside is parched. Costa Ricans generally take their vacations the week preceding Easter and the last two weeks of the year; it is essential to reserve cars and hotel rooms ahead during these periods.

WESTERN CENTRAL VALLEY

As you drive north or west out of San José, the suburbs and industrial zones of the city quickly give way to arable land, most of which is dedicated to vast coffee plantations. Coffee has come to symbolize the prosperity of both the Central Valley and the nation as a whole; as such, this all-important cash crop has developed a certain amount of cultural mystique and folklore. Costa Rican artists, for example, have long venerated coffee workers, and the painted oxcart, once used to transport coffee to the coast, has become a national symbol.

Within Costa Rica's coffee heartland, you'll find plenty of tranquil agricultural towns and two provincial capitals, Alajuela and Heredia, each of which holds a few rare architectural treasures. Those two cities owe their relative prosperity to the coffee beans cultivated on the fertile lower slopes of Poás and Barva volcanoes that tower to the north. The upper slopes of both these volcanoes are too cold for coffee crops and have thus been dedicated to dairy cattle, strawberries, ferns, and flowers, making for markedly different, though thoroughly enchanting, landscapes.

This area deserves at least two days: one for Alajuela, Grecia, Sarchí, and Volcán Poás northwest of San José, and one for Heredia and Volcán Barva to the north. Escazú lies close enough to San José to be visited in a matter of hours, or it can serve as your base in the Central Valley. Since there are some excellent lodging options hidden in the hills above these towns, rural overnights are a wonderful way to stretch out your exploration of this compact area.

Escazú

❶ *5 km (3 mi) southwest of San José.*

A quick drive to the west of San José takes you to Escazú, a traditional coffee-farming town and now a bedroom community of the capital at the foot of a small mountain range. Local lore has coined it "the city of witches," as it is known as a popular spot among those spell-casting women. An ancient church faces a small plaza, and plenty of adobe homes nearby have weathered the years. Scattered amidst the coffee fields that cover the steep slopes above town are well-tended farmhouses, often painted blue and white, with tidy gardens and the occasional oxcart parked in the yard—just the kind of scenes that have captured the attention of many Costa Rican painters over the past century. There are also plenty of fancy homes between the humble farmhouses, since Escazú has long been home to wealthy foreigners and Ticos.

High in the hills above Escazú stands the tiny community of **San Antonio de Escazú,** famous for its annual oxcart festival held the second Sunday of March. The view of the Central Valley—nearby San José and distant volcanoes—is impressive from San Antonio, both by day and night, but for even greater drama, head higher: practically vertical roads wind up into the mountains, toward **Pico Blanco,** the highest point in the Escazú Cordillera.

Dining and Lodging

$$$$ ✕ **Le Monastere.** The view from here is one of Escazú's best—a 270-degree panorama of ominous volcanoes. The interior of the restaurant, a former chapel dressed up with antiques, is equally impressive. But Le Monastere would be popular regardless of its charm since the Belgian owner has stayed true to his homeland's outstanding culinary tradition, offering classic French dishes and some interesting original Costa Rican items, such as iguana sautéed with vegetables. The restaurant only serves dinner, from 7 PM to 11 PM. Reservations are recommended. *San Rafael de Escazú, take old road to Santa Ana, turn left 4 streets after U.S. ambassador's residence, and follow signs,* ☎ 289–4404. *AE, DC, MC, V. Closed Sun. No lunch.*

$$$ ✕ **Hostaría Cerutti.** This little Italian restaurant on a busy intersection in Escazú is the diva of San José's Italian eateries. It occupies a lovely adobe house that's more than 100 years old, its whitewashed walls adorned with antique prints. The seafood-friendly menu is extensive: start off with octopus and asparagus in pesto, or ravioli with mushrooms in a truffle sauce; then sink your teeth into some grilled tuna or *cordero al horno,* rack of lamb roasted with vegetables. Reservations are recommended. ⊠ *Cruce de San Rafael de Escazú,* ☎ 228–4511. *AE, MC, V. Closed Tues.*

$$$$ ▣ **Alta.** This restaurant is lofty in location, appearance, *and* price. Its design evokes colonial Spain with its barrel-tile roofs, ocher mixed into the stucco on the walls, and hand-painted bathroom tiles. A high-ceilinged foyer leads into a sloping stairway lined with tall columns and palm trees, reminiscent of a narrow street in some ancient Iberian city. Arranged above the guest rooms' red-tile floors are earth tones on the fabrics and walls, colonial-style furniture, and a couple of paintings. Rooms on floors two through five have small balconies, and ground-floor rooms have garden terraces and direct pool access. The culinary creations of the Californian chef have made the restaurant popular among residents. ⊠ *Old road to Santa Ana, Escazú,* ☎ 282–4160, ℻ 282–4162; ⊠ *Interlink 964, Box 02–5635, Miami, FL 33102,* ☎ 888/388–2582. *19 rooms with bath, 4 suites. Restaurant, pool, sauna. AE, DC, MC, V.*

$$$$ ▣ **Tara Resort Hotel.** Scarlett never had it so good. Modeled after the
★ house of the same name in *Gone with the Wind* and decorated in antebellum style, this hotel near the top of Pico Blanco is a luxurious little inn. Hardwood floors throughout the three-story, white-and-green building are covered with patterned area rugs. Guest rooms are decorated with floral spreads and lace curtains; French doors open onto the veranda. At the Atlanta Dining Gallery, try the beef tenderloin in green-peppercorn sauce and chicken Tara in a mango-avocado sauce. ⊠ *Apdo. 1459–1250, Escazú, from central church head south and follow signs,* ☎ 228–6992, ℻ 228–9651. *12 rooms with bath, 1 suite, 1 bungalow. Restaurant, pool, hot tub, massage, spa. AE, MC, V.*

$$$ ▣ **Costa Verde Inn.** Rooms at this B&B on the outskirts of Escazú make nice use of local hardwoods in the furniture and trim and display traditional Peruvian art on white walls. South American art adorns the main building, where a large sitting area has comfortable chairs and a fireplace. The inn is surrounded by gardens, and at night you can see the lights of San José twinkling to the east. Complimentary breakfast is served on the shady patio. ⊠ *From the southeast corner of the Parque Central, 654 yards west and 109 yards north,* ☎ 228–4080, ℻ 289–8591; ⊠ *SJO 1313, Box 025216, Miami, FL 33102-5216. 15 rooms with bath. Pool, hot tub, tennis court. AE, MC, V.*

$$$ ▣ **Posada El Quijote.** At this friendly, family-run bed-and-breakfast—perched on a hill in the neighborhood of Bello Horizonte on the San José side of Escazú—you'll find the best vantage point from the sundeck. The living room has big windows, a couch, fireplace, and lots of modern art. Deluxe rooms also have city views, and superior rooms overlook the gardens. All rooms have queen-size beds, ceiling fans, and cable TV; complimentary breakfast is served on a covered interior patio. ⊠ *Bello Horizonte de Escazú,* ☎ 289–8401, ℻ 289–8729; ⊠ *Dept. 239–SJO, Box 025216, Miami, FL 33102-5216. 9 rooms with bath, 2 apartments. Breakfast room, travel services. AE, MC, V.*

Heredia

②   *15 km (9 mi) north of Escazú, 9 km (6 mi) north of San José.*

With a population of around 30,000, Heredia is the capital of one of the country's most important coffee-producing provinces. Perhaps Costa Rica's best-preserved colonial town, Heredia bears witness to just how little that means in an earthquake-prone country: it has lost nearly all its colonial structures. Nevertheless, a fair number of old adobe buildings are still scattered throughout the city, and you can see even more in the nearby towns of Barva de Heredia, Santo Domingo, and San Rafael.

The **Parque Central** does retain a bit of its colonial charm. At its eastern end stands the impressive stone **Catedral de Heredia,** dating back to 1797, whose thick walls, small windows, and squat buttresses have kept it standing through countless quakes and tremors. Unfortunately, the church's stained-glass work has not fared as well as the walls. The park itself is sparsely landscaped with a simple kiosk and a cast-iron fountain imported from England in 1897. *Parque Central,* ☎ 237–0779. ☉ *Daily 6–6.*

Surrounding the park are some interesting buildings, such as the barrel-tile-roofed **Casa de la Cultura,** which often houses art exhibits, and the brick **Municipalidad** (Municipal building), behind which stands a strange, decorative tower called the *fortín,* or small fort.

Between Heredia and Barva is the **Museo de Cultura Popular** (Museum of Popular Culture), a turn-of-the-century farmhouse constructed with an adobe-like technique called *bahareque.* Run by the Universidad Nacional, the museum has been furnished with antiques and is surrounded by a small garden and coffee fields. An inexpensive, open-air, lunch-only restaurant serves authentic Costa Rican cuisine; it can be a lively spot on weekends, when a more extensive menu is sometimes paired with marimba music and folk dancing. ⊠ *Between Heredia and Barva, follow signs for right turn,* ☎ 260–1619. 🎫 *$1.50.* ☉ *Daily 9–2, restaurant 11–2. No credit cards.*

Costa Rica's most popular export-quality coffee, **Café Britt,** welcomes visitors at its working coffee plantation. A tour highlights the history of coffee cultivation in Costa Rica and includes a theatrical presentation, a short walk through the coffee farm and processing plant, and a coffee-tasting session. ⊠ *900 yards north and 400 yards west of the Comandancia, Heredia,* ☎ 260–2748, 📠 238–1848. 🎫 *$15, $20 with transport from San José.* ☉ *Dec.–May, tours daily 9, 11, and 3; June–Nov., open daily 9–11.*

Just to the northeast (about 2 km/1 mi) of Heredia lies **San Rafael,** a quiet, mildly affluent coffee town with a large church notable for its stained-glass windows and bright interior. The road north from the church winds its way up the slopes of Volcán Barva to the Hotel Chalet Tirol (☞ Lodging *in* Volcán Barva, *below*) and the Monte de la Cruz. **Santo Domingo,** to the southeast of Heredia, is another attractive agricultural community with two churches, an abundance of adobe houses, and some traditional coffee farms on its outskirts.

The small community of **Barva de Heredia,** just to the north of Heredia proper (about 2 km/1 mi), has a wonderful Parque Central surrounded by old Spanish-tiled adobe houses on three sides and a white stucco church to the east. That stout, handsome church flanked by royal palms dates from the late 18th century; behind it is a lovely little garden shrine to the Virgin Mary. On a clear day you can see verdant Volcán Barva towering to the north, and if you follow the road that runs in front of the church, veering to the right, you'll reach the village of

COSTA RICA'S GOLDEN BEAN

WHEN COSTA RICA'S FIRST elected president, Juan Mora Fernandez, began encouraging his compatriots to cultivate coffee back in 1830, he could hardly have imagined how profound an impact the crop would have on his country. During the last century, coffee has transformed Costa Rica from a colonial backwater into a relatively affluent and cosmopolitan republic.

The "golden bean" financed the construction of most of the nation's landmarks. Founding families owned the biggest plantations, creating a coffee oligarchy from which the majority of Costa Rican presidents have come. The bean also provided an economic incentive for tens of thousands of immigrant families, who, during the 1800s and early 1900s, were given land if they would cut down the forest and plant coffee. These farmers formed the backbone of a middle-class majority that has long distinguished Costa Rica from most of Latin America. Whether you credit the power of caffeine, or the socioeconomic factors surrounding the crop, the tidy homes, colorful gardens, and orderly farms of the Central Valley make Costa Ricans look like the original coffee achievers.

Thanks to its altitude and mineral-rich volcanic soil, the Central Valley is ideal for growing coffee, and the crop covers nearly every arable acre of that region. Considering its domination of the Central Valley's physical and cultural landscape, it may come as a surprise that coffee isn't native to Costa Rica. Biologists claim the plant evolved in the mountains of Ethiopia. Arab nations were sipping the aromatic beverage as early as the 7th century—its scientific name is *Coffea arabica*—but it didn't gain popularity in Europe until the 1600s. Coffee plants first arrived in Costa Rica from the Caribbean, probably in the early 1820s.

The coffee-growing cycle begins in May, when the arrival of annual rains makes the dark green bushes explode into a flurry of white blossoms—as close as it comes to snowing in Costa Rica. By November, the fruit starts to ripen, turning from green to red, and the busy harvest begins as farmers race to get picked "cherries" to *beneficios*, processing plants where the beans—two per fruit—are removed, washed, dried by machine, and packed in burlap sacks for export. Costa Rica's crop is consistently among the world's best, and most of the high-grade exports wind up in Europe and the United States.

Traditionally, coffee bushes are grown in the shade of trees, such as citrus or nitrogen-fixing members of the bean family. Recently, however, many farmers have switched to sun-resistant varieties, cutting down shade trees to pack more coffee bushes into every acre. Shade farms provide habitats for migratory birds and other animals, but the new shadeless farms are practically biological deserts, which is why environmentalists are promoting a return to the old system, labeling shade coffee ECO-OK.

TICOS ARE FUELED BY AN inordinate amount of coffee, which they filter through cloth bags, a method that makes for a stronger cup of José than your average American brew. The mean bean is even used for a favorite local dish, chicken roasted with coffee wood. Sadly, Ticos drink the low-grade stuff, often mixed with molasses, peanuts, or corn for bulk and roasted too long. You are thus best off buying such reliable brands as Café Rey's Tarrazú, Café Britt, Américo, Volio, or Montaña.

Sacramento. Here the road turns into a steep, dirt track leading to the Barva sector of Parque Nacional Braulio Carrillo.

Lodging

$$$$ 🏨 **Finca Rosa Blanca Country Inn.** There's nothing common about
★ this bed-and-breakfast overlooking the coffee farms west of Barva de Heredia; you need merely step through the front door of the Gaudiesque main building and marvel at the soaring ceiling, white stucco arches, columns, and polished wood. Each guest room is different, all with original art, local hardwoods, colorful fabrics, and paintings. The spacious, two-story suite is out of a fairy tale, with its spiral staircase leading up to a window-lined tower bedroom. On the grounds—nicely planted with tropical flowers and shaded by massive fig trees—are two villas, each with two bedrooms. Four-course dinners are optional. ⊠ *Barrio Jesus, 6 km (4 mi) west of Barva de Heredia,* ☎ *269–9392,* ℻ *269–9555;* ⊠ *SJO 1201, Box 025216, Miami, FL 33102-5216. 6 rooms with bath, 2 villas. Dining room, pool, horseback riding, airport shuttle. AE, MC, V.*

$$$ 🏨 **Hotel Bougainvillea.** Here you'll easily forget that you're just 15 min-
★ utes from San José. Set amidst the coffee farms of Santo Domingo de Heredia, the hotel has extensive areas dominated by tall trees and brightened by plentiful flowers. Spacious, carpeted rooms feature local hardwoods; tiled baths come with tub and hair dryer. Decorating the lobby and excellent restaurant are paintings by local artists and pre-Columbian pieces. ⊠ *Apdo. 69–2120, San José, from San José take Guápiles Hwy. to Tibas exit, then road to Santo Domingo, and follow signs,* ☎ *244–1414,* ℻ *244–1313. 80 rooms with bath, 4 suites. Restaurant, bar, pool, sauna, tennis court. AE, MC, V.*

Volcán Barva

❸ *20 km (12 mi) north of Heredia, 30 km (19 mi) north of San José.*

North of Barva de Heredia the road becomes narrow and steep as it winds its way up the verdant slopes of Volcán Barva (Barva Volcano), the 9,500-ft summit of which is the highest point in **Parque Nacional Braulio Carrillo** (☞ Chapter 8). To the east a similar road climbs up the volcano from San Rafael de Heredia, ending atop **Monte de la Cruz,** which borders the national park. Long extinct, Barva is massive in size: its lower slopes are almost completely planted with coffee fields and host about a dozen small towns. The upper slopes consist of pastures divided by exotic pines and the occasional native oak and cedar that give way to the botanical diversity of the cloud forest near the top. The air is usually cool at the peak. Coupled with the pines and pastures, the atmosphere here will surprise you if you expect only rain forest, bananas, and coffee beans to grow in Costa Rica.

Any vehicle can make the trip above San Rafael to the Monte de la Cruz, and even buses follow the loop above Barva via **San José de la Montaña,** but it's rough going if you want to get much higher than this. Expect a four-hour hike from San José de la Montaña to the crater; but a four-wheel-drive vehicle will get you to the park entrance during the dry months.

The misty, luxuriant summit is the only part of the park where camping is allowed and is a good place to see the rare resplendent quetzal if you camp or arrive in the early morning. Because of the difficulty in accessing it, Barva receives a mere fraction of the visitors that flock to the summits of Poás and Irazú. A 30-minute hike in from the ranger station takes you to the main crater, which is about 200 yards across. Its almost vertical sides are covered in poor man's umbrellas, a plant that thrives in the highlands, and oak trees laden with epiphytes. At the bottom of the crater is a dark lake; farther down the track into the forest lies another crater lake. Bring rain gear, boots, and a warm shirt, and stay on the trails—even experienced hikers who know the area have lost their way up here. ☎ *National Parks Service information: 192 and 290–8202.* ☜ *$6.* ⊙ *Tues.–Sun. 7–4.*

Lodging

$$$$ ⊡ **Hotel Occidental La Condesa.** In keeping with the highland climate and scenery of Barva Volcano, the interior of this resort hotel evokes lodges of more northern latitudes. A stone fireplace surrounded by couches, armchairs, and a small bar dominates the lobby. The central courtyard is topped by a giant skylight and is occupied by one of the hotel's three restaurants. A similarly enclosed pool area also holds a tropical garden. Guest rooms are carpeted and tastefully furnished, with picture windows. Junior suites have bedroom lofts, sitting areas, and some of the best views. ⊠ *San Rafael de Heredia, 10 km (6 mi) north of Heredia,* ☎ *267–6000,* ℻ *267–6200. 60 rooms with bath, 36 suites. 3 restaurants, bar, pool, hot tub, health club, horseback riding, squash, meeting rooms, travel services, car rental. AE, DC, MC, V.*

$$$ ⊡ **Hotel Chalet Tirol.** Amazingly enough, this place's Austrian archi-
★ tectural style doesn't seem out of place amidst the pines, pastures, and cool air of Volcán Barva's upper slopes. The replica of a cobbled Tirolean town square—complete with fountain and church—may be a bit much, but the cozy, bright, two-story wooden chalets are quite charming, as is the restaurant, with its ivy, wooden ceiling, and elegant murals. Quality French cuisine makes it a popular weekend destination for Costa Ricans, and the hotel hosts occasional classical music concerts. The newer suites offer more privacy and fireplaces. Breakfast is complimentary. ⊠ *San Rafael de Heredia, 10 km (6 mi) north of Heredia,* ☎ *267–6222,* ℻ *267–6229. 13 suites, 10 chalets. Restaurant, bar, 2 tennis courts. AE, DC, MC, V.*

Outdoor Activities and Sports

HIKING

The upper slopes of Volcán Barva provide excellent hiking conditions, thanks to cool air, vistas, and plentiful birds. The crater lakes that top the volcano can only be reached by hikers, and if you haven't got a four-wheel-drive vehicle, you'll have to hike from Sacramento up to the entrance of Parque Nacional Braulio Carrillo. **Hotel Chalet Tirol** (☞ Lodging, *above*) runs an early morning walking tour down a 4-km (2½-mi) trail through the cloud forest—an excellent trip for bird-watchers.

HORSEBACK RIDING

Horseback riding tours along the upper slopes of Volcán Barva, near the Parque Nacional Braulio Carrillo (☞ Chapter 8), combine views of the Central Valley with close exposure to the cloud forest and resident bird life. You can book them through the **Hotel Chalet Tirol** (☞ Lodging, *above*), **Hotel Occidental La Condesa** (☞ Lodging, *above*), the **Sacramento Lodge** (☎ 237–2116, ℻ 237–2976), just above Sacramento, in the mountains due north of Barva de Heredia, or most San José travel agents (☞ Contacts and Resources *in* San José A to Z, *in* Chapter 2).

Alajuela

❹ *20 km (13 mi) northwest of San José.*

Although it is Costa Rica's second-largest city (population 50,000) and only a 30-minute bus ride from the capital, Alajuela has a decidedly provincial feel. Architecturally it differs little from the bulk of Costa Rican towns with its low-rise grid plan with structures painted in primary colors. Alajuela's picturesque **Parque Central** is dominated by royal palms and mango trees, a lovely fountain imported from Glasgow, and cement benches where locals gather to chat. Surrounding the plaza is an odd mix of charming old buildings and insipid cement boxes. The large, neoclassical **Cathedral,** badly damaged by a 1990 earthquake, has interesting capitals decorated with local agricultural motifs and a striking red dome. Although spacious, the interior is rather plain except for the ornate dome over the altar. *C. Central between Avdas. 1 and Central,* ☎ *441–0769.* ⊙ *Daily 8–6.*

To the north of the park stands the **old jail,** which now houses the local offices of the Ministry of Education—an appropriate metaphor for a country that claims to have more teachers than police.

Alajuela was the birthplace of Juan Santamaría, the national hero who lost his life in a battle against the mercenary army of U.S. adventurer William Walker (1824–60), who invaded Costa Rica in 1856 (☞ Parque Nacional Santa Rosa *in* Chapter 4). A statue of Santamaría has been erected in the **Parque Juan Santamaría,** one block south of the Parque Central, and his deeds are celebrated in the **Museo Juan Santamaría,** one block north of the Parque Central. The museum contains maps, compasses, weapons, and paintings, including one of Walker's men filing past to lay down their weapons. The colonial building that houses it is more interesting than the displays, however. ⊠ *Corner of C. 2 and Avda. 3,* ☎ *441–4775.* ☎ *Free.* ⊙ *Tues.–Sun. 10–6.*

☾ Spread over the lush grounds of **Zoo Ave** (Bird Zoo) is a collection of large cages holding macaws, toucans, hawks, and parrots, as well as crocodiles, monkeys, and other interesting critters. The zoo is running a breeding project for rare and endangered birds, which are eventually destined for release. Head west from the center of Alajuela past the cemetery; then turn left after the stone church in Barrio San José. ⊠ *La Garita de Alajuela,* ☎ *433–8989.* ☎ *$8.* ⊙ *Daily 9–5.*

☾ The **Finca de Mariposas** (Butterfly Farm) in La Guácima, Alajuela, has a presentation about the ecology of these delicate insects and gives you a chance to observe and photograph them up close. The farm contains a variety of habitats holding 40 rare species of butterflies and an apiary exhibit. It's best to visit the farm when it is sunny, when butterflies are most active. You can make lunch of the excursion at the restaurant here. The farm will provide transportation for $6. ⊠ *From San José, turn south (left) at the intersection just past Cariari Hotel, then right at church of San Antonio de Belén, then left, and then follow the butterfly signs,* ☎ *438–0115.* ☎ *$14.* ⊙ *Daily 9–4.*

Lodging

$$$$ 🏠 **Xandari.** Along a ridge about 5 km (3 mi) north of Alajuela, in the
★ middle of a coffee plantation and well-tended gardens, the tranquil Xandari is a strikingly original inn. This brainchild of a talented couple—he's an architect, she's an artist—exhibits aesthetic sensibility in everything from the design of the villas to the contemporary furniture and bold, colorful artwork that fill them. They are all spacious, with plenty of windows, large terraces, and secluded lanai sunbathing patios. Ultra villas are independent; two prima villas share one building. The attractive restaurant serves low-fat food, many ingredients grown on the grounds. A trail through the hotel's forest reserve winds past five waterfalls. ⊠ *Apdo. 1485–4050, Alajuela,* ☎ *443–2020,* ⅢX *442–4847. 16 villas. Restaurant, bar, 2 pools, hot tub, horseback riding. AE, MC, V.*

$$$ 🏠 **Orquídeas Inn.** Shaded by tall trees and surrounded by colorful tropical blossoms, the Orquídeas Inn was once the home of a coffee farmer. The Spanish-style residence, complete with arches and a barrel-tile roof, now houses a couple of suites; a third suite sits under a geodesic dome. Pastel-color standard rooms have red tile floors, Guatemalan bedspreads, and paintings by Central American artists. The Marilyn Monroe bar displays an impressive collection of posters and photos of Norma Jean and is a popular watering hole for American expatriates. Pet toucans, parrots, and macaws inhabit the wooded grounds, which means there's lots of squawking by the light of day. ✉ *Apdo. 394, Alajuela, 5 km (3 mi) west of the cemetery,* ☎ *433–9346,* 𝔽𝔸𝕏 *433–9740. 20 rooms with bath, 3 suites. Restaurant, bar, pool. AE, MC, V.*

Volcán Poás

❺ *37 km (23 mi) north of Alajuela, 57 km (35 mi) north of San José.*

Volcán Paós' main crater, at nearly 1½ km (1 mi) across and 1,000 ft deep, is one of the largest active craters in the world. The sight of this vast, multicolored pit, gurgling with smoking fumaroles and a greenish-turquoise sulfurous lake at its bottom, is simply breathtaking. All sense of scale is absent here because of the lack of vegetation within the crater. One of the reasons so many people visit this park is that a paved road leads all the way to the top of the 8,800-ft summit. The road up from Alajuela winds past coffee fields, pastures, screened-in fern plantations, and, near the summit, thick cloud forest. The summit is frequently enshrouded in mist, and many who come up see little beyond the lip of the crater. But wait a while, especially if there is some wind, because the clouds can disappear quickly. The earlier in the day you go, the better chance of less haze. If you're lucky, you will see the famous geyser in action, spewing a column of gray mud high into the air. Poás last had a major eruption in 1953 and is thought to be approaching another active phase; at any sign of danger, the park is closed to visitors. It can be very cold and wet at the summit, so dress accordingly. If you come ill-equipped, you can duck under the poor man's umbrella plant. It is forbidden to venture onto the edge of the crater.

The 57-sq-km (22-sq-mi) **Parque Nacional Volcán Poás** (Poás Volcano National Park) protects the epiphyte-laden cloud forest on the volcano's slopes and dwarf shrubs near the summit. One trail, which leads some 15 minutes off to the right of the main crater trail, winds through shrubs and dwarfed trees toward the large and eerie **Laguna Botos,** which occupies an extinct crater. The other trail, **Sendero Escalonia,** leads through a taller stretch of cloud forest from the picnic area back to the parking lot; boards along the way feature sentimental eco-poetry. Mammals are rare in the area, but you should see various birds, including insect-size hummingbirds and larger sooty robins. On occasion, quetzals have also been spotted in the park. A last note of warning: this is a popular sight, and because of the crowds, especially on Sunday, it is not a good choice if you seek solitude. ✉ *From San José, take Pan-American Highway to Alajuela, Rte. 130 to Poás, and follow signs.* ☎ *National Parks Service information: 192 and 290–8202.* 💲 *$6.* ☉ *Daily 7–4.*

Dining and Lodging

$$
★ ✕ **Chubascos Restaurant.** Set amidst tall pines and colorful flowers on the upper slopes of Poás Volcano, this popular restaurant has a limited menu of traditional Tico dishes and delicious daily specials. Pick from the full selection of *casados* (plates of white rice, beans, fried plantains, salad, cheese, and meat) and platters of *gallos,* a variety of fillings served on homemade tortillas. The *refrescos* (fresh fruit drinks) are top-drawer, especially the ones made from locally grown *fresas* (strawberries) and *moras* (blackberries), served in milk. Reservations are recommended. ✉ *West side of road to Poás Volcano National Park, between Fraijanes and Poásito,* ☎ *482–2069. AE, MC, V.*

$$ 🏨 **La Providencia Lodge.** If you're looking for outdoor adventure,
★ tranquility, and close contact with nature, this rustic, remote lodge
perched on the northern edge of Poás Volcano National Park is just
the place if you have a four-wheel-drive vehicle. Cabins scattered along
the hillside have red cement floors, colorful quilts, and hot water. The
walls in the restaurant are mostly of glass. Hiking trails wind through
the lodge's 500-acre forest reserve, where you may spot quetzals and
dozens of other birds. The three horseback tours are among the coun-
try's best. It can get very cold at night, so bring warm clothes and rain
gear. ✉ *Apdo. 10240–1000, San José, on left after entering Poás Vol-
cano National Park,* ☎ *380–6315,* 🖷 *290–0289. 6 cabins with bath.
Restaurant, hiking, horseback riding. No credit cards.*

Outdoor Activities and Sports

HIKING

Although the footpaths in Poás Volcano National Park are rather
short, the nearby **La Providencia Lodge** (☞ Dining and Lodging, *above*)
has more extensive trails for exploring the cloud forest.

HORSEBACK RIDING

La Providencia Lodge (☞ Dining and Lodging, *above*) offers three dif-
ferent horseback tours, one of which leads around Volcán Poás to view
waterfalls and charred forests. You don't need to be a guest to take
the tours, but you'll have to call the day before to reserve horses.

Shopping

A number of roadside stands on the way up Poás sell strawberry jam,
cajeta (a pale fudge), and corn crackers called *biscoche*. The **Neotrópica
Foundation** has a store in the visitor center of Poás Volcano National
Park (☞ *above*) that sells a variety of T-shirts, cards, and posters with
nature themes, and a portion of the profits is spent on conservation
projects.

Grecia

❻   *26 km (16 mi) northwest of Alajuela, 46 km (29 mi) northwest of San
José.*

Grecia's brick-red, prefabricated iron **Gothic church** overlooks a small
Parque Central, where you might spot one of the resident sloths in the
trees. The church was one of two buildings in the country imported
from Belgium in the 1890s—the second is the metal schoolhouse next
to San José's Parque Morazán—when some prominent Costa Ricans
became convinced that metal structures would better withstand the pe-
riodic earthquakes that have taken their toll on the country's archi-
tecture. The pieces of metal were shipped from Antwerp to Limón, then
transported by train to Alajuela—from there, the church was carried,
appropriately, by oxcarts.

An interesting collection of mounted insects from Costa Rica and
other tropical countries is on display half a block from the park. The
☯ **Joyas del Bosque Húmedo** (Jewels of the Rain Forest) exhibit was do-
nated to a local foundation by biologist Richard Whitten, who trav-
eled the world collecting and mounting the colorful creepy crawlers.
✉ *Half a block north of Parque Central's western end,* ☎ *494–5620.
💲 $3. ☉ Mon.–Sat. 9–noon and 1–5.

☯ At the **Mundo de las Serpientes** (World of Snakes), serpents are kept
in large outdoor cages—ask if you want to take the snakes out for pet-
ting or photographing. ✉ *3 km (2 mi) east of Grecia, on road to Ala-
juela,* ☎ *494–3700.* 💲 *$11. ☉ Daily 8–4.*

Lodging

$$$$ 🏨 **Posada las Palomas.** This lovely little B&B on an orange and cof-
★   fee plantation outside Grecia overlooks the Río Grande canyon. Optional three-course dinners—the menu changes daily—are served in the
main house, where you can relax in the spacious living room. Guest
rooms in the house are comfortable, but the cottages are much nicer
and well worth the extra money. The Tea House is the biggest, but the
others have nicer views. They have virtually no interior decoration—
in the Japanese tradition—with simple wooden furniture and French
doors opening onto small porches. The hotel has a forest reserve in
the canyon, with a trail leading down to a waterfall. Complimentary
breakfast is served by the pool. ⊠ *Apdo. 1485–4050, Alajuela, on highway 1 km (½ mi) west of Grecia, first right after bridge, follow signs,*
☎ *450–0800,* 𝖥𝖠𝖷 *451–1165. 2 rooms with bath, 8 cottages. Dining
room, pool. No credit cards.*

Sarchí

❼   *8 km (5 mi) west of Grecia, 53 km (33 mi) northwest of San José.*

Tranquil little Sarchí is spread over a collection of hills surrounded by
coffee plantations. Though plenty of its inhabitants are farmers, it is
also one of the country's principal carpentry and crafts centers. People from other Central Valley communities drive here to shop for furniture, and caravans of tour buses regularly descend upon the souvenir
shops outside of town. Local artisans work native hardwoods into bowls,
boxes, toys, platters, and even jewelry, but the area's most famous products are its brightly colored oxcarts—replicas of the carts traditionally
used to transport coffee. Trucks and tractors have replaced oxcarts on
the farm, but the little wagons retain their place in the local folklore
and can be spotted everywhere from small-town parades to postcards.

The vast majority of people who visit Sarchí spend all their time wandering down the aisles of one of the crafts bazaars, but this traditional
community is well worth poking around. The **church** dates only from
the 1950s and is much less elaborate than some of the region's other
temples, but it is a colorful structure with several statues of angels alighted
on its facade and a simple interior revealing some nice woodwork. It
is flanked by small gardens and faces a multilevel park with a brightly
decorated oxcart displayed beneath a roof. If you turn right when you
leave the church, walk two blocks north, turn right again, and walk
another block and a half, you'll come upon the town's only real oxcart factory, on your left. **Taller Eloy Alfaro e Hijos** was founded in 1923,
and its carpentry methods have changed little since then. The two-story
wooden building housing the wood shop is surrounded by trees and
flowers—usually orchids—and all the machinery on the ground floor
is powered by a waterwheel at the back of the shop. Carts are painted
in back, and though the factory's main product is a genuine oxcart—
which sells for about $2,000—they make some smaller mementos that
can be shipped home. ⊠ *2 blocks north, 1½ blocks east of church,* ☎
no phone. 🎫 *Donation.* ◷ *Weekdays 8–4.*

Shopping

Sarchí is the best place in the country to purchase miniature oxcarts,
the larger of which are designed to serve as patio bars and can be broken down for easy transport or shipped to your home. Another popular item is a locally produced rocking chair with leather seat and back.
One store is just north of town, and several larger complexes are to
the south. The nicest is the **Chaverri Factory,** a little over a mile south
of town on the main road, with workshops in back that you can wander through and watch people work. These shops are good places to

buy wood crafts, but coffee, T-shirts, and most other nonwood products are cheaper in San José. The street behind the shop, Taller Eloy Alfaro e Hijos (☞ *above*), comes alive on Friday, when the local **farmers' market** is held.

San Ramón

❽ *23 km (14 mi) west of Sarchí, 59 km (36 mi) northwest of San José.*

San Ramón is known locally as the City of Poets due to the fact that it has produced a number of minor bards, and you may well be tempted to wax poetic as you admire the facade of its church or stroll through its tidy Parque Central. As pleasant a little town as it may be, San Ramón has its real attractions in the countryside to the north, on the road to La Fortuna, where comfortable nature lodges offer access to their private nature preserves. Aside from the poets, the massive **Iglesia de San Ramón** is the city's claim to fame, as it should be, since the great gray cement structure that mixes Romanesque and Gothic styles took a quarter of a century to complete—construction began in 1925 and lasted until 1954. It stands in place of a smaller adobe church that was destroyed by an earthquake in 1924. To ensure that the second church would be earthquake proof, the cement was poured around a steel frame that was designed and forged in Germany (by Krupp). Step past its formidable facade, and you'll discover a bright, elegant interior. ⊠ *Across from Parque Central,* ☎ *455–5592.* ۞ *Daily 8–6.*

Lodging

$$$–$$$$ 🏨 **Villablanca.** Owned by former Costa Rican president Rodrigo Carazo, who is often around, this charming hotel is on a working dairy and coffee farm. The farmhouse now houses the reception, bar, and restaurant. Down the hill are lovely cottages called *casitas,* Spanish for "little houses," that are tiny replicas of traditional adobe farmhouses, complete with whitewashed walls, tile floors, cane ceilings, and fireplaces. Resident guides lead nature walks through the adjacent cloud-forest reserve, which also holds a pulse-quickening canopy tour. Horses are available for exploring the rest of the farm. ⊠ *Apdo. 1485–4050 Alajuela, 20 km (12 mi) north of San Ramón on road to La Fortuna,* ☎ *228–4603,* 𝔽𝔸𝕏 *228–4004. 48 casitas. Dining room, horseback riding. AE, DC, MC, V.*

$$$ 🏨 **Valle Escondido.** "Hidden Valley" lies within an ornamental plant farm in a long valley at the edge of a 618-acre forest preserve. Nature lovers could spend days exploring the 20 km (12 mi) of trails, which wind through the forest past waterfalls and giant trees. Spacious, carpeted rooms have ceiling fans and covered porches with jungle views. The restaurant serves good Italian food, and even if you just stop here for lunch, you can hike in the preserve for free. ⊠ *32 km (19 mi) north of San Ramón,* ☎ *231–0906 or 460–1227,* 𝔽𝔸𝕏 *232–9591. 28 rooms with bath. Restaurant, pool, hot tub, hiking, horseback riding. AE, MC, V.*

EASTERN CENTRAL VALLEY

East of San José you'll find Costa Rica's highest volcano and the remains of both the country's most important archaeological site and its oldest church. There are several interesting churches in the area, two of which are in the scenic Orosi Valley, as well as the ecological attractions of a botanical garden and a protected cloud forest. Cartago, the country's first capital, has scattered historical structures and the impressive Basílica de Los Angeles. You could explore this area in two days but only if you want to be on the road from dawn till dusk. For a more leisurely pace, dedicate at least three days to this end of the valley, visiting Volcán Irazú and Cartago one day, tackling the Orosi Valley on another, and ending up in the Turrialba area the last day.

Cartago

9 *22 km (14 mi) southeast of San José.*

Costa Rica's original capital is much older than San José, but earthquakes have destroyed most of its colonial structures, leaving just a few interesting buildings standing amidst the concrete boxes. The country's capital for almost three centuries, Cartago became Costa Rica's second city in 1923, when the seat of government was switched to San José. A major quake in 1910 was one of the reasons the capital was moved. The quake also prevented completion of the central Romanesque cathedral. **Las Ruinas** (the ruins) now stand in a pleasant central park planted with tall pines and bright bougainvillea. You'll spot some attractive old buildings as you head through town, most of which were erected after the 1910 quake. The majority of the city's architecture, however, is bland, with one exception: Cartago's most impressive landmark, the gaudy Basílica, on the eastern edge of town.

The spectacular **Basílica de Nuestra Señora de Los Angeles** (Basilica of Our Lady of the Angels) at the edge of Cartago, 10 blocks east of the central square, is a hodgepodge of architectural styles from Baroque to Byzantine with a dash of Gothic. The church's interior is even more imposing, with a colorful tile floor, intricately decorated wood columns, and lots of stained glass. It is also the focus of an amazing annual pilgrimage: during the night of August 1 and well into the early morning hours of the 2nd, the road from San José clogs with people on their way to celebrate the 1635 appearance of La Negrita (the Black Virgin), Costa Rica's patron saint. The faithful come here to fill bottles at a spring behind the church that is believed to have curative waters. Miraculous healing powers are attributed to the saint, and the devoted have placed thousands of symbolic crutches, ears, eyes, and legs next to her diminutive statue in recognition of her gifts. The constant arrival of tour buses and school groups, along with shops selling candles and bottles of holy water in the shape of the saint, add a bit of a circus atmosphere to the scene. La Negrita has twice been stolen, most recently in 1950 by José León Sánchez, now one of Costa Rica's best-known novelists, who spent 20 years on the prison island of San Lucas for the purloined Madonna. ⊠ *C. 16 between Avdas. 2 and 4,* ☎ *551–0465.* ☉ *Daily 8–6.*

En Route Bear left where Irazú is signposted, 4 km (2½ mi) short of Cartago, to bypass the city. Driving time from San José to the summit is just short of 1½ hours.

Volcán Irazú

10 *31 km (19 mi) northeast of Cartago, 50 km (31 mi) east of San José.*

Volcán Irazú is Costa Rica's highest volcano, at 11,260 ft, and its summit has long been protected as a national park (☞ Chapter 10). The mountain looms to the north of Cartago, and its eruptions have dumped a considerable amount of ash over the city over the centuries. The most recent eruptive period lasted from 1963 to 1965, beginning on the day that John F. Kennedy arrived in Costa Rica for a presidential visit. Boulders and mud rained down on the countryside, damming rivers and causing serious flooding. Although farmers who cultivate Irazú's slopes live in fear of the next eruption, they are also grateful for the soil's richness, a direct result of the volcanic deposits.

The road up to the summit climbs past vegetable fields, pastures, and native oak forests. You'll pass through the villages of Potrero Cerrado and San Juan de Chicoá, both with lookout points, before reaching the bleak, gaping **crater** at the summit. Although Irazú is currently dormant, the gases and steam that billow out from fumaroles on the northwestern slope are sometimes visible from the peak above the crater lookouts. The gray, moonscape summit of Irazú is one of the few places from which you can see both the Pacific Ocean and the Caribbean Sea, although clouds frequently obscure both from view. The **Area Recreativa de Prusia** (Prusia Recreation Area), halfway down, has hiking trails through oak and pine forest. Picnic areas are available if you want to bring your own supplies. Warm, waterproof clothing is advisable for the summit. Leave San José very early in the day so as not to be thwarted by low clouds. ☎ *National Parks Service information: 192 and 290–8202.* ▦ *$6.* ⊙ *Daily 8–3:30.*

Jardín Lankester

⑪ *7 km (4½ mi) east of Cartago, 57 km (35 mi) southeast of San José.*

If you are interested in plants, especially orchids, you'll definitely want to visit Jardín Lankester (Lankester Botanical Garden). Created in the 1950s by the English naturalist Charles Lankester to help preserve the local flora, it is now under the auspices of the University of Costa Rica. The lush garden and greenhouses contain one of the world's largest orchid collections, more than 800 native and introduced species. Orchids, by the way, are mostly epiphytes, meaning they use other plants for support without damaging them in the process. Bromeliads, heliconias, and aroids also abound, along with 80 species of trees, including rare palms, bamboo, torch ginger, and other ornamentals. The diversity of plants attracts a wide variety of birds. The best time to visit is January through April, when the most orchids are in bloom. To reach the gardens, drive through the center of Cartago, turn right at the Basílica, then left on the busy road to Paraíso and Orosi. After 6 km (4 mi), an orange sign on the right marks the short dirt road that leads to Jardín Lankester. ✉ *Dulce Nombre, Cartago,* ☎ *552–3151.* ▦ *$2.50.* ⊙ *Daily 9–3:30.*

Shopping
The gift shop in Jardín Lankester (☞ *above*) is one of the few places in Costa Rica where you can buy orchids that you can bring home legally. Along with the endangered plants comes a CITES certificate—a sort of orchid passport—that permits you to take them across international borders without any customs problems.

OROSI VALLEY

The Orosi Valley, an area of breathtaking views and verdant landscapes 30 km (19 mi) south of San José, contains remnants of the colonial era and of the tropical forest that covered the country when the Spanish first arrived. The valley was one of the earliest parts of Costa Rica to be settled by Spanish colonists, in the 17th century, as ruins and a colonial church attest. The rich soil and proximity to San José have combined to make it an important agricultural area, with extensive plantations of coffee, chayote, and other vegetables. The valley is fed in the west by the confluence of the Navarro and Orosi rivers and drained in the east by the ferocious Reventazón. A dam built in the 1970s to create one of the country's first hydroelectric projects formed the Lago de Cachí, or Cachí Reservoir.

Two roads descend into the valley from Paraíso, an unattractive town 8 km (5 mi) east of Cartago, both of which lead to a loop around the reservoir, past the tidy patchworks of cultivated crops, small towns, and the Represa de Cachí (Cachí Dam). The roads are reached by turning right just before Paraíso's shady Parque Central. If you turn left at the *bomberos* (fire station), which houses some splendid old-style fire engines, you'll be on your way to Ujarrás. If you go straight, the road will lead you toward the town of Orosi and the Parque Nacional Tapantí. Whichever route you choose, you'll eventually end up back at the same intersection, since both roads lead into a loop around the valley floor. As you snake down into the valley, past coffee plantations, pastures, and patches of forest, keep your eyes open for the mirador.

Ujarrás

⑫ *10 km (6 mi) southeast of Paraíso, 18 km (11 mi) southeast of Cartago.*

The ruins of the country's oldest church, **Iglesia de Ujarrás,** stand in a small park at the site of the former town of Ujarrás, on the floor of the Orosi Valley, just down the hill from Paraíso. Built between 1681 and 1693 in honor of the Virgin of Ujarrás, the church, together with the surrounding village, was abandoned in 1833 after a series of earthquakes and floods. An unlikely victory in 1666 by the Spaniards over a superior force of invading British pirates was attributed to a prayer stop here. Today it is a pleasant monument surrounded by well-kept gardens and large trees that often attract flocks of parakeets and parrots. ⊠ *Ujarrás.* ⊙ *Daily 8–5.*

Dining

$$$ ✕ **La Casona del Cafetal.** Set in a coffee plantation overlooking the Cachí
★   Reservoir, this restaurant is the best lunch stop in the valley. It's housed in a spacious brick building with a high, barrel-tile roof and has seating both inside and on a tiled portico on the lake side. Inventive twists on the local fare include *arroz tucurrique* (baked rice with palm heart and cheese) and corvina *jacaranda* (stuffed with shrimp), as well as a variety of casados. Reservations are recommended. ⊠ *2 km (1 mi) southwest of Cachí Dam,* ☎ *533–3280. AE, DC, MC, V. Closed Mon.*

Shopping

In the Orosi Valley, 1 km (½ mi) south of the Cachí Dam, stands the unique **Casa del Soñador** (House of the Dreamer), which was built by local wood sculptor Macedonio Quesada. Though Macedonio died several years ago, his son and a former apprentice are still there, carving interesting little statues out of coffee wood.

Orosi

⑬ *7 km (4 mi) south of Paraíso, 35 km (22 mi) southeast of San José.*

The town of Orosi, in the heart of the valley, has but one tourist attraction: a beautifully restored **colonial church.** Built in 1743, the structure has a low-slung, whitewashed facade. The roof is made of cane overlaid with terra-cotta barrel tiles. Inside are an antique wooden altar and ancient paintings of the stations of the cross and the Virgin of Guadelupe, all brought to Costa Rica from Mexico. The **museum** in the cloister annex houses a small collection of old religious regalia, multicolored wood carvings, and colonial furniture. ⊠ *Across from soccer field,* ☎ *533–3297.* 🖾 *Museum 50¢.* ⊙ *Church daily 9–5; museum hrs fluctuate (ask around for someone to open it up).*

South of town, some **thermal pools** fed by a hot spring are open to the public for a nominal fee.

En Route From Orosi, veer right at the fork in the road for Tapantí. The road becomes rougher as you near the park but is in decent shape once you enter it.

Parque Nacional Tapantí

(14) *12 km (7 mi) south of Orosi, 28 km (17 mi) southeast of Cartago.*

Tucked into a steep valley to the south of Orosi, Parque Nacional Tapantí (Tapantí National Park, ☞ Chapter 10) encompasses a 47-sq-km (18-sq-mi) cloud-forest preserve teeming with birds. This extremely lush forest, drained by countless streams, provides refuge for more than 200 bird species, including the graceful, shy, and endangered resplendent quetzal. Quetzals are most visible during the dry season, when they mate; ask the park rangers where to look for them. The rough, 10-km (6-mi) track to Tapantí follows the course of the Río Orosi past coffee plantations, elegant *fincas* (farmhouses), and seasonal barracks for coffee pickers before being hemmed in by the steep slopes of thick jungle. The large rangers' office and visitor center, on the right upon entering the park, is where you stop to pay the entry fee. The road continues deep into the reserve; you can leave your vehicle at the start of the various trails, the first of which leads to some small swimming holes in the chilly Rió Orosi. Since the park tends to cloud up in the afternoon, it's best to get an early start. Taxis carrying up to six people will make trips to the reserve from the soccer field in Orosi. ☎ *National Parks Service information 192; Amistad Atlántico branch of the National Parks Service 758–3996.* ▨ *$6.* ☉ *Daily 7–4.*

Lodging

$$ 🄴 **Complejo Kiri.** Less than 1 km (½ mi) from the entrance to Tapantí,
★ this small lodge has its own forest preserve, covering 173 acres, with more miles of hiking trails than the nearby national park. Guest rooms are in two cement buildings, the covered porches of which overlook flower beds frequented by legions of hummingbirds, beyond which stand forested hillsides. Those in the upper building are a bit cramped. Complimentary breakfast is served in the lodge's bright restaurant. ⊠ *Purisil, 11 km (6 mi) south of Orosi on road to Tapantí,* ☎ *284–2024. 6 rooms with bath. Restaurant, hiking, horseback riding. AE, MC, V.*

TURRIALBA AND THE GUAYABO NATIONAL MONUMENT

The tranquil town of Turrialba and the nearby Guayabo ruins lie considerably lower than the rest of the Central Valley and consequently enjoy more tropical climates. There are two ways to reach this area, both of which will take you past spectacular scenery. The more direct route, which is reached by heading straight through both Cartago and Paraíso, winds through coffee and sugar plantations before abruptly descending into Turrialba. For the second route, turn off the road between Cartago and the summit of Irazú near the town of Cot. That narrow route twists its way along the slopes of Irazú and Turrialba volcanoes, passing some stunning scenery—pollarded trees line the road to form formal avenues, and white girdered bridges cross crashing streams. From Santa Cruz a track leads up to within hiking distance of the 10,900-ft summit of Volcán Turrialba. As you begin the descent to Turrialba, the temperature rises and neatly farmed coffee crops blanket the slopes.

Turrialba

15 *58 km (36 mi) east of San José.*

The relatively well-to-do agricultural center of Turrialba (population 30,000) suffered when the main San José–Puerto Limón route was diverted through Guápiles. The demise of the famous Jungle Train that connected San José and Puerto Limón was an additional blow to the town. Although pleasant enough, the town of Turrialba itself doesn't have much to offer, but the surrounding countryside holds some spectacular scenery, patches of rain forest, and a few excellent lodges. It also lies near two of the country's best white-water rivers—the Pacuare and Reventazón—which is why kayakers and rafters flock here (☞ Outdoor Activities and Sports, *below*). Serious enthusiasts, including the white-water Olympic kayaking teams from a handful of countries, stay all winter.

OFF THE
BEATEN PATH

CATIE – Just outside of Turrialba, on the road to Siquirres, is the Centro Agronómico Tropical de Investigación y Enseñanza (Center for Tropical Agricultural Research and Education), known by its Spanish acronym CATIE. It is one of the world's leading tropical research centers and draws students and experts from all over the Americas. The 8-sq-km (3-sq-mi) property includes modern labs and offices, landscaped grounds, seed conservation chambers, greenhouses, orchards, experimental agricultural projects, a large swath of rain forest, and lodging for students and teachers. A muddy trail leads down into the forest behind the administration building, where there is a view of some of the biggest rapids on the Reventazón River. CATIE is also a good bird-watching spot; in fact, you might catch sight of the yellow-winged jacana or purple gallinule in the lagoon near the main building. Call ahead to reserve a free tour. ☎ 556–6431 or 556–0169, ℻ 556–1533. ☺ Daily 7–4.

Lodging

$$$$ 🏨 **Casa Turrire.** This timeless hotel at the edge of a sugar plantation looks like a manor house that has survived from the turn of the century miraculously intact, but it is the much more recent product of creative imaginations and attention to detail. From the royal palms that line the driveway to the tall columns and tile floors, Casa Turrire is an exercise in elegance. High-ceilinged rooms feature tropical hardwoods, small balconies, and bright bathrooms with tubs. The central courtyard, complete with potted palms and marble-topped tables, and many sitting rooms are excellent spots to relax after a day's adventure. ✉ *9 km (5½ mi) southeast of Turrialba, Apdo. 303–7150, Turrialba,* ☎ ℻ *267–7138,* ☎ *531–1111,* ℻ *531–1075. 12 rooms with bath, 4 suites. Restaurant, bar, pool, hot tub, tennis court, horseback riding. AE, MC, V.*

$$$$ 🏨 **Rancho Naturalista.** Set inside a 125-acre private nature reserve, Rancho Naturalista specializes in guided horseback and bird-watching tours. Three hundred species of birds and thousands of different types of moths and butterflies live on the reserve, and a resident naturalist guide helps you see and learn as much as you want to. The two-story lodge is rustically decorated throughout, as are two separate cabins. Good home cooking is served in both the indoor and outdoor dining rooms. The hotel provides free transportation from San José. The management requires a two-day minimum stay. ✉ *Southeast of Turrialba, 2½ km (1½ mi) up a dirt track from Tuís,* ☎ ℻ *267–7138, 531–1516;* ✉ *Dept. 1425, Box 025216, Miami, FL 33102-5216. 9 rooms with bath. Dining room. No credit cards.*

$$–$$$ 🏨 **Albergue Volcán Turrialba.** In the foothills of the volcano and reachable only by four-wheel-drive vehicle (the lodge will arrange transport for a fee), the Volcán has comfortable rooms. You'll eat well, too: the proprietors serve healthy, Costa Rican–style meals cooked up on a wood-burning stove (all meals are included). More compelling are the tours offered: one goes deep into the Turrialba crater; a second visits the fumaroles and thermal waters of Volcán Irazú. Mountain biking, horseback riding, and a 10-hour trek from the Volcán Turrialba to Guápiles via Parque Nacional Braulio Carrillo can also be arranged. ⊠ *Apdo. 1632–2050, San José, 20 km (12 mi) east of Cot, turn right from road to Irazú,* ☎ FAX *273–4335. 12 rooms with bath. Bar, dining room. MC, V.*

$$ 🏨 **Turrialtico.** Eight kilometers (5 mi) out of Turrialba on the Limón road, a hedged drive winds its way up to this dramatically positioned, open-sided hotel. The second-floor rooms, handsomely designed with wood floors and Guatemalan spreads on firm beds, could be the country's best bargain. Try to get a room on the west side for a dazzling view toward Turrialba and, if you're in luck, Volcán Irazú. The restaurant serves a small selection of authentic Costa Rican cuisine cooked on a wood stove. A possible minus is that the place is a breakfast stopover for tour/rafting buses. ⊠ *Apdo. 121, Turrialba, take Highway 10 toward Limón 8 km (5 mi),* ☎ *556–1111. 12 rooms with bath. Restaurant. AE, MC, V.*

Outdoor Activities and Sports

RAFTING AND KAYAKING

It's no coincidence that half a dozen Olympic kayaking teams use Turrialba as their winter training ground: it lies conveniently close to two excellent white-water rivers, the Reventazón and the Pacuare. But despite their appeal among the experts, these rivers offer options for neophytes. The **Río Reventazón** flows right by Turrialba and has several navigable stretches, below and above the city. The most popular stretch of the Reventazón, the Tucurrique section (class III), was unfortunately cut short by the construction of a dam. The Pascua section (class IV–V), below Turrialba, is one of the country's wildest stretches of white water—a liquid roller coaster requiring previous rafting experience.

Just to the southeast is the **Río Pacuare,** Costa Rica's most spectacular white-water route, which provides rafters with an unforgettable, exhilarating, adrenaline-pumping experience. The 32-km (20-mi) Pacuare run includes a series of class III and IV rapids with evocative nicknames such as Double Drop, Burial Grounds, and Magnetic Rock. The trip takes you past some astoundingly beautiful scenery that includes lush canyons where waterfalls plummet into the river and vast expanses of rain forest—stretches of the Pacuare stood in for Africa in the otherwise eminently forgettable 1995 film *Congo.* That riverine landscape is inhabited by an array of birds—toucans, kingfishers, aracaris, and *oropéndolas* (golden orioles) among them—along with blue morpho butterflies, the odd river otter, and other interesting critters. The rafting outfitters Aventuras Naturales and Ríos Tropicales have their own lodges on the river, which make them the best options for highly recommended two- and three-day trips that include jungle hikes.

Contact **Aventuras Naturales** (☎ 225–3939 and 224–0505, FAX 253–6934), **Costa Rica Whitewater** (☎ 257–0766, FAX 255–4354), **Ríos Tropicales** (☎ 233–6455, FAX 255–4354), **Ticos River Adventures** (☎ FAX 556–1231), and **Instinct** (☎ 556–2598). **Serendipity Tours** (⊠ Next to Servicio Super, ☎ 566–2592) has hot-air balloon flights, in addition to white-water rafting.

Monumento Nacional Guayabo

🔟 *19 km (12 mi) north of Turrialba, 72 km (45 mi) east of San José.*

Nestled on the slopes of the Volcán Turrialba is the Monumento Nacional Guayabo (Guayabo National Monument), Costa Rica's most significant archaeological site. In 1968 a local landowner was out walking her dogs when she discovered what she thought was a tomb. A friend, archaeologist Carlos Piedra, began excavating the site and unearthed the base wall of the chief's house in what eventually turned out to be the ruins of a large city (around 20,000 inhabitants) covering 49 acres. The city was abandoned in AD 1400, probably due to disease or starvation. A guided tour (in Spanish only) takes you through the rain forest to a mirador from where you can see the layout of the excavated circular buildings. Only the raised foundations survive, since the conical houses themselves were built of wood. As you descend into the city ruins, observe the well-engineered surface and covered aqueducts leading to a drinking-water trough still functioning today. Next you'll pass the end of an 8-km (5-mi) paved walkway used to transport the massive building stones. Abstract patterns carved on the stones continue to baffle archaeologists, although some clearly depict jaguars, which were revered by Indians as deities. The hillside jungle setting is captivating, and the trip is further enhanced by the bird-watching possibilities. Sacklike nests of oropéndolas hang from many of the trees. The last few miles of the road are in such bad shape that you'll need a four-wheel-drive vehicle to get here. ☎ *National Parks Service information: 192 and 290–8202.* ✉ *$6.* ☉ *Tues.–Sun. 8–4.*

CENTRAL VALLEY: AROUND SAN JOSÉ A TO Z

Arriving and Departing

By Bus

WESTERN CENTRAL VALLEY

Departures for Escazú from San José, from Avenida 6 between Calles 12 and 14, are every 20 minutes. Departures for Heredia, from Calle 1 between Avenidas 7 and 9, are every 10 minutes (25-min ride). For Volcán Barva, take Paso Llano bus from Heredia (**Rapidos Heredianos,** C. 1 and Avdas. 7 and 9, ☎ 233–8392) get off at Sacramento crossroads; the first bus is at 6:30 AM. (Note: some go only as far as San José de la Montaña, adding an hour to the hike; check first.) Departures for Alajuela are from Avenida 2 between Calles 12 and 14 (**TUASA,** ☎ 222–5325) daily every 10 minutes 6 AM–7 PM; every 40 minutes 7 PM–midnight; every hour midnight–6 AM (20-min ride). An excursion bus for Volcán Poás departs San José daily at 8:30 AM from Calle 12 between Avenidas 2 and 4 (90-min ride) and returns at 2:30 PM. Departures for Grecia, from the Coca-Cola station, Calle 16 at Avenida 1, are every 30 minutes (40-min ride). For Sarchí, first take the bus to Naranjo (50-min ride), which departs from San José's Coca-Cola station (C. 16 between Avdas. 1 and 3) every 40 minutes 6 AM–6 PM; buses to Sarchí (15-min ride) leave from Naranjo every half hour. Buses for the 60-min ride to San Ramón (**Empresarios Unidos,** C. 16 at Avda. 12, ☎ 222–0064) leave from the Puntarenas bus station, at Calle 16 between Avenidas 10 and 12, departing every hour 6 AM to 7 PM.

EASTERN CENTRAL VALLEY

Departures to Cartago from Calle 5 and Avenida 18 (**SACSA,** ☎ 233–5350) are daily every 10 minutes (45-min ride); however, it is more convenient to catch it on Calle 9 at Avenida Central. An excursion bus departs San José for Irazú every Saturday and Sunday at 8 AM from Avenida 2 between Calles 1 and 3, across from the Gran Hotel Costa Rica (**Metropoli,** ☎ 272–0651), and returns at 1 PM (2-hr ride).

TURRIALBA AND THE MONUMENTO NACIONAL GUAYABO

Departures to Turrialba from Calle 13 between Avenidas 6 and 8 (**TRANSTUASA,** ☎ 556–0073) are every hour 8–8 (2-hr ride).

By Car

WESTERN CENTRAL VALLEY

To reach Escazú from San José, turn left at the western end of Paseo Colón, take the first right, get off the highway at the first exit, and turn right at the traffic light. Turn right at the bottom of the hill for San Rafael and the old road to Santa Ana. The Paseo Colón ends at La Sabana park, on the west end of San José; turn right here for Alajuela and Heredia. For Heredia, turn right off the highway just before it heads up an overpass, where the Hotel Irazú stands on the right; turn left when you reach the Universidad Nacional to reach the center of Heredia, or continue straight for the town and volcano of Barva. The route to Volcán Barva heads north out of Heredia through the communities of Barva, San José de la Montaña, Paso Llano, and Sacramento. At Sacramento the paved road turns to dirt, growing worse as it nears the ranger station. A four-wheel-drive vehicle can make it all the way to the ranger station during the dry season. For Alajuela, take the highway all the way out to the airport, where you turn right. You can reach Grecia by continuing west on the highway past the airport—the turnoff is on the right—or by turning left just before the Alajuela cemetery. For Sarchí, take the highway well past the airport to the turnoff for Naranjo; then veer right just as you enter Naranjo. San Ramón is on the Pan-American Highway west of Grecia. Head straight through town and follow the signs to reach the hotels to the north.

EASTERN CENTRAL VALLEY

All of the eastern Central Valley's attractions are reached from San José by first driving east on Avenida 2 through San Pedro; a traffic light shortly before Cartago marks the beginning of the road up Irazú, with traffic to Cartago veering right. For the Jardín Lankester head straight through Cartago (entrance on right), turning right at the Basílica and left after two blocks.

OROSI VALLEY

For the Orosi Valley head straight through Cartago, turning right at Paraíso's central plaza. A few blocks to the east, at the fire station, you can either turn left for Ujarrás or continue straight for Orosi and Tapantí National Park; either way takes you into the same loop around the valley.

TURRIALBA AND THE MONUMENTO NACIONAL GUAYABO

The road through Cartago and Paraíso continues east to Turrialba, where you pick up another road that leads north to the monument, heading out of Turrialba a few blocks east of that town's central plaza.

By Plane

The **Aeropuerto Internacional Juan Santamaría** (☎ 441–0744) is 16 km (10 mi) northwest of downtown San José.

BETWEEN THE AIRPORT AND CENTRAL VALLEY

There is taxi service to and from the airport to anywhere in the Central Valley (price ranges from $5 to $50). Buses travel between the airport and Alajuela from every five minutes to on the half hour. From here, you can catch buses to Grecia, Sarchí, and San Ramón. There is less frequent service (every 20 minutes to one hour) to Heredia. For trips from the airport and Escazú, Cartago, or Turrialba you must change buses in San José.

Getting Around

By Bus

WESTERN CENTRAL VALLEY

Buses travel between Alajuela and Heredia's main bus stations every half hour. To reach Zoo Ave take the bus to La Garita, which departs every hour from the main bus station in Alajuela. Direct buses to Sarchí depart from Alajuela (C. 8 between Avda. 1) every 30 minutes 6 AM–9 PM (90-min ride). Buses traveling between San José and Grecia or San Ramón pick up passengers on the southern edge of Alajuela. Departures for Grecia leave from Naranjo hourly 6 AM–7 PM.

EASTERN CENTRAL VALLEY

To visit Jardín Lankester, take the Paraíso bus, which departs from the south side of the Parque Central in Cartago daily every 15 minutes.

OROSI VALLEY

Hourly buses (☎ 551–6810) departing from Cartago's southern side of Las Ruinas do a loop around the Orosi Valley, stopping at Orosi and Ujarrás. To reach Tapantí, you'll have to hire a taxi in Orosi.

TURRIALBA AND THE MONUMENTO NACIONAL GUAYABO

The bus to Guayabo National Monument departs once a day from one block south of the bus station in Turrialba, Monday to Saturday at 11 AM and Sunday at 9:30 AM (50-min ride).

By Taxi

Taxis parked near the central plazas of Alajuela, Cartago, and Heredia can take you to up Poás, Irazú, and Barva volcanoes, respectively, but the trips will be quite expensive (about $50) unless you can get a small group together. If you don't have a car, the only way to get to Tapantí National Park is to take a taxi from Orosi. Taxis parked near San Ramón's Central Plaza likewise can take you to the nature lodges north of town.

Contacts and Resources

Car Rentals

See Car Rentals *in* San José A to Z, *in* Chapter 2.

Emergencies

Emergencies (☎ 911). **Fire** (☎ 118). **Police** (☎ 117). **Traffic Police** (☎ 222–9330).

Guided Tours

FROM SAN JOSÉ

Costa Rica Eco Adventure Services (Apdo. 1244–1000, San José, ☎ 283–9152, www.ecoguides.com) provides expert adventure and natural history guided tours in the Central Valley and beyond. Most San José tour offices can set you up with guided tours to such spots as Poás and Irazú volcanoes or the Orosi Valley. **Swiss Travel** (✉ Meliá Corobicí Hotel lobby, San José, ☎ 231–4055) is one of oldest operators in the country. For information about white-water rafting tours, *see* Outdoor Activities and Sports *in* Turrialba, *above*.

Visitor Information

See Visitor Information *in* San José A to Z, *in* Chapter 2.

4 NORTHERN GUANACASTE AND ALAJUELA

From Caño Negro's remote, bird-filled waters to the windsurfing mecca of Laguna de Arenal, Costa Rica's northernmost reaches contain wonders to endlessly beguile: astonishingly green Monteverde cloud forests; sparkling Pacific coast beaches; dusty, deforested uplands with cowboys and grazing cattle; exotic jungles alive with birds, monkeys, and butterflies; and a ragged row of fiercely beautiful volcanoes.

Updated by
Justin
Henderson

ITH ONLY 65 INCHES OF RAINFALL per year, Costa Rica's <u>northwest</u> is the country's driest region. The northwest is also home to countless natural wonders: large expanses of wet and dry forest, river deltas and estuaries overflowing with animal life, and miles of sundrenched beaches. The northwest offers you far more than the myriad ecosystems of the dry coastal plain; the territory contains the cloud and rain forests of Monteverde and other mountain preserves as well as the volcanoes and peaks of the Cordillera de Guanacaste, the Cordillera de Tilarán, and sections of the Cordillera Central. East of Guanacaste are the northern uplands and lowland plains of Alajuela, from the wildlife-filled wetlands of Caño Negro Wildlife Refuge in the far north, down to the green farmlands and foothills around La Fortuna and Ciudad Quesada, east of Volcán Arenal.

Costa Rica's northwesternmost province, <u>Guanacaste</u> is bordered by Nicaragua and the Pacific Ocean. The province derives its name from the broad ear-pod trees that shade the lounging white Brahman cattle so prevalent in the region. An independent province of Spain's colonial empire until 1787, when it was ceded to Nicaragua, Guanacaste became part of Costa Rica in 1814. After independence in 1821, both Nicaragua and Costa Rica claimed Guanacaste for their own. The Guanacastecos themselves were divided: The provincial capital, Liberia, wanted to return to Nicaragua, while rival city Nicoya favored Costa Rica. Nicoya got its way, helped by the fact that at the time the vote was taken, Nicaragua was embroiled in a civil war.

Guanacaste's far northwestern coastline, still unblemished for the most part, offers everything the Nicoya Peninsula does and more: the dry forests and pristine sands of Parque Nacional Santa Rosa, the bird sanctuary of Isla Bolaños, the endless beaches of the Golfo de Santa Elena, and breezy Bahia Salinas. But tourist-driven development is not limited to the Nicoya: a pair of new beachfront resort hotels have opened in Bahia Salinas, and others are in the works. Time will tell if this relatively untraveled stretch of Costa Rican turf near the town of La Cruz and the Nicaraguan border finds itself home to the unnatural green of fairways and aqua-blue swimming pools.

East of the Carretera Interamericana (Pan-American Highway), Guanacaste's dry plains and forests slope upward into volcano country. Marching northwest to southeast in a rough but formidable line, the volcanoes of the Cordillera de Guanacaste include Orosí, Rincón de la Vieja and its nearby sister Santa Maria, Miravalles, Tenorio, and Arenal, looming over the southeast end of Laguna de Arenal. The most northerly peak in the Cordillera de Tilarán, <u>Arenal ranks</u> as one of the <u>most active volcanoes in the</u> world. Below and between these active and not-so-active craters and calderas, the terrain ranges from dry forest to impassable jungle, from agricultural plain to roadless swamp.

A few of the parks and destinations in this region are relatively accessible from San José, even for day trips. Others require grueling hours of driving over pothole-scarred roads. As you contemplate spending time in this region—or anywhere in Costa Rica, for that matter—be sure to allow plenty of time for <u>excruciatingly slow driving when</u> and <u>where necessary</u>. That brief hop from the smooth pavement of the Pan-American Highway up to the famously lush cloud forests of Monteverde, for example, looks like 30 minutes behind the wheel when measured on the map. In reality, it's two hours of bone-jarring road, barely passable without high clearance or a four-wheel-drive vehicle.

Pleasures and Pastimes

Dining

Guanacaste's traditional foods derive from dishes prepared by pre-Columbian Chorotegan Indians. Typical dishes include *frito guanacasteco* (a dish of beans, rice, vegetables, and meat), *pedre* (a mixture of carob beans, pork, chicken, onions, sweet peppers, salt, and mint), *sopa de albóndigas* (meatball soup with chopped eggs and spices), and *arroz de maíz* (a kind of corn stew, sometimes made *con pollo,* with chicken). More prevalent at breakfast are eggs and *gallo pinto* ("spotted rooster," a mix of beans and rice); at lunch and dinner you can always depend on a *casado,* the *tipico* Costa Rican meal of rice and beans served with meat, chicken, or fish. Seafood here is plentiful: *camarones* (shrimp), sautéed in garlic and butter and served with fries and salad; *langostinos* (a kind of lobster); and a fine variety of fish are available in most restaurants at reasonable prices, although langostino dinners can get costly. Meat lovers, rejoice: the northwest, whose plains are covered with cattle ranches, produces the country's best steak.

Lodging

East and west of the mountains, Costa Rica's far northern zone offers a good mix of quality hotels, nature lodges, and more basic *cabinas* (cottages). In the areas of Monteverde and La Fortuna, a range of low- and mid-priced hotels, cabinas, and resorts appear to be filling the demand generated by visitors to Volcán Arenal and the cloud forest. If you're headed to the coast it is wise to book ahead during the dry season (December–April), especially for weekends, when Ticos flock to the beach.

Volcanoes

The sheer mass and power of Volcán Arenal, often ringed with an ominous haze, dominates Lake Arenal. It reiterates its presence at night, when you can see red-hot molten lava oozing from the cone, a flirtatious dance with disaster. Arenal can be easily reached from the Pan-American Highway—watch for the turnoff at the town of Cañas—or from the east through La Fortuna. You may have to spend more than one day here, as the cone can be covered by clouds. Farther northwest, experienced hikers can trek to the lip of the steaming Rincón de la Vieja crater on trails through the namesake national park; less-active travelers can check out Las Pailas, a cluster of miniature volcanoes, fumaroles, and mud pots encircled by a relatively easy trail on the lower mountain slopes. Among the other (inactive) volcanoes are Orosí, which lies within the borders of Parque Nacional Guanacaste, and Tenorio, now boasting its own national park. Parque Nacional Guanacaste is minimally developed for tourism, and Tenorio as yet has no infrastructure whatsoever.

Windsurfing

When winter settles in up north, serious American windsurfers look to the south. These days many of head to Lake Arenal, which many world-champion windsurfers have called "one of the world's top five windsurfing spots." From December through April, trade winds from the Caribbean sneak through a pass in the Cordillera Central, crank up to 80 kph (50 mph) or more, and blow from the east toward the northwest end of the lake, creating perfect conditions for high-wind freshwater sailing. The scenery here, too, is unmatched: watch the frequent volcanic eruptions while you glide across the lake. The lake is somewhat choppy due to its narrow shape, but strong winds, fresh water, and hassle-free rigging and launch sites on both shores make it worthwhile.

Exploring Northern Guanacaste and Alajuela

Northern Guanacaste and Alajuela encompass the volcanic mountains of the Cordillera de Guanacaste, the northern section of the Cordillera de Tilaran, and the plains stretching west to the sea and north to the Nicaraguan border. Most of the destinations on the west side of the mountains, including the coastal beaches, national parks, and the northwestern end of Laguna de Arenal (Lake Arenal), lie within easy reach of the Pan-American Highway. To reach La Fortuna, Volcán Arenal, the east end of Lake Arenal, and points farther east, including Caño Negro and Upala, the easiest drive is by way of Zarcero and Ciudad Quesada. You will find several roads that pass through the mountains, linking these two distinct zones.

Though they are paved for the most part, these roads—one follows the northern bank of Lake Arenal and the other skirts the volcanoes along the northern edge of the country—still have unpaved stretches and can be subject to washouts and other difficulties. Always try to get a report on road conditions before setting out on any long trips.

Numbers in the text correspond to numbers in the margin and on the Northern Guanacaste and Alajuela map.

Great Itineraries

As you consider these assorted itineraries, know in advance that a fair amount of your time—more, perhaps, than you had realized or hoped as you planned this trip—will be spent on the road. That is simply the reality of travel in Costa Rica and in this spread-out region.

IF YOU HAVE 3 DAYS

Head northeast out of San José and through the mountains around **Zarcero** ①, en route to 🖬 **Ciudad Quesada** ② or 🖬 **La Fortuna** ③. The next day, hike to the La Fortuna waterfall; drive to 🖬 **Volcán Arenal** ⑤, checking out the Tabacón Resort's hot springs; or take a rafting trip on the Río Peñas Blancas, the Río Sarapiqui, or the Río Toro. Stay the night in an area hotel or continue north by northwest around Lake Arenal, with a stop at 🖬 **Tilarán** ⑦ or one of the lake-view hotels for a day or two of windsurfing, hiking, mountain biking, or volcano viewing.

IF YOU HAVE 5 DAYS TO SEE PARKS

Start from San José with a predawn drive to the 🖬 **Reserva Biológica Bosque Nuboso Monteverde** ⑧ and spend a day hiking in the cloud forest. If Monteverde is too crowded, the compelling but smaller Reserva Santa Elena is just down the road (north). After overnighting in the area, another crack-of-dawn drive will take you to 🖬 **Tilarán** ⑦ by way of the mountain track (four-wheel-drive vehicle only) or the Pan-American Highway for an active day on Lake Arenal. Stay in Tilarán or in one of the lodges at the lake's northwesterly end. Early the next day return to the highway and drive north and then inland again for a day hike in 🖬 **Parque Nacional Rincón de la Vieja** ⑨. Stay at the mountain lodge, or return to the highway and head farther north for a night and a day at Hacienda Los Inocentes, the 100-year-old hacienda lodge on the northern border of 🖬 **Parque Nacional Guanacaste** ⑫. Stay a second night in the lodge, or late in the day head down to **Parque Nacional Santa Rosa** ⑩, being sure to tour the historically important La Casona Hacienda. For a break from parks, your four-wheel-drive vehicle will safely deliver you to Playa Naranjo for a day at the beach.

IF YOU HAVE 5 DAYS FOR PARKS AND THE BEACH

After a pass through **Zarcero** ①, spend a day and night in the Lake Arenal area—🖬 **La Fortuna** ③, 🖬 **Nuevo Arenal** ⑥, or 🖬 **Tilarán** ⑦—and see the volcano (and its nocturnal performance), lake, Tabacón Resort,

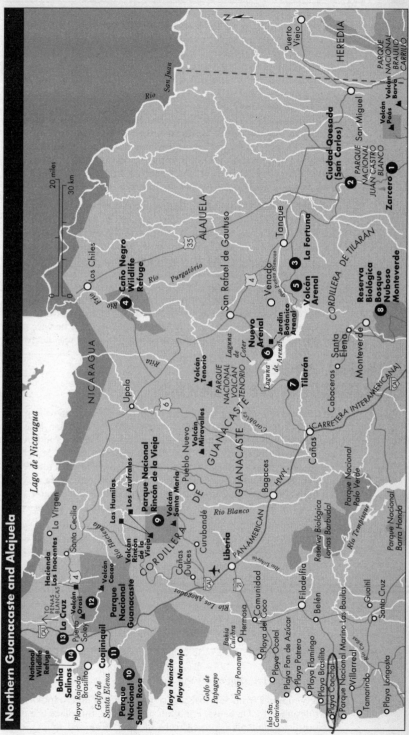

Northern Guanacaste and Alajuela

65

and/or the La Fortuna waterfall. From La Fortuna, head north to spend a day touring the **Caño Negro Wildlife Refuge** ④. Then take the road northwest that leads through the San Rafael de Guatuso area and continues around the Volcán Orosí. Stop for a mind-expanding look at Lago de Nicaragua from the mirador (lookout) at La Virgen, near Santa Cecilia, and then continue down the west slope of the mountains. Spend a night at Hacienda Los Inocentes, near ☷ **Parque Nacional Guanacaste** ⑫, then a day hiking or horseback riding before continuing on to ☷ **La Cruz** ⑬ and the new resorts on the south shore of the half-moon-shape ☷ **Bahia Salinas** ⑭. After a night (or two) here, work your way down to **Parque Nacional Santa Rosa** ⑩ for a day at the beach or take a day hike in the mixed environments of **Parque Nacional Rincón de la Vieja** ⑨. Either camp in the park or, more comfortably, tuck yourself into one of the nearby lodges or hotels.

When to Tour Northern Guanacaste and Alajuela

The areas in Guanacaste west of the Cordillera de Guanacaste are best toured in the dry season, from December to March. However, during the rainy season, rain generally falls on this coastal plain for just an hour or two each day, so beyond the effect on the roads, problems with traveling are minimal. Farther inland, the northern uplands and lowlands offer a mixed climactic bag—the more easterly lowlands share the humid Caribbean weather of the east coast, while the uplands partake of the drier, cooler mountain clime. Given the larger numbers of tourists that visit Volcán Arenal and especially Monteverde, it might be wise to try an off-season, or edge-of-season, trip to avoid the high-season crowds.

ARENAL AND THE CORDILLERA DE TILARÁN

Dense green cloud forests cloak the rugged mountains and rolling hills of the Cordillera de Tilarán extending northwest from San José. On the east side of the hills and on the plains below, logging and farming contend with tourism for dominance of the local economy. Still, there are great swaths of primary forest and jungle, including the marvelous cluster of forest reserves that straddle the continental divide at Monteverde. Farther north and west, Lake Arenal and the rolling green hills around the lake pay homage to the dark heart of this region—fiery, magnificent Volcán Arenal.

Lake Arenal has two distinct personalities: the northwest end is windsurf central—a row of power-generating windmills, with blades awhirl on the ridge above the Hotel Tilawa, signals another use for the relentless, powerful wind. The more sheltered southeast end, closer to the dam, is popular for other water sports, especially fishing for guapote. The southeast is also a marvelous place from which to view the volcano. If you took away the volcanoes, you might mistake the countryside of green, rolling hills for the English Lake District.

Zarcero

❶ *70 km (43 mi) northwest of San José.*

Ninety minutes from San José, the small town of Zarcero looks like it was designed by Dr. Seuss. For a fan of topiaries, this place is a must: Evangelisto Blanco's cypress shrubs in fanciful animal shapes—motorcycle-riding monkeys, a light-bulb-eyed elephant—enliven the park in front of the town church. The church interior is covered with elaborate pastel stencils and detailed religious paintings by Misael Solis, a local old-timer.

Shopping

Zarcero is renowned for its peach preserves and mild white cheese, both of which are sold in stores around town and along the highway.

SOUVENIRS

Stop at **El Tiesto Souvenir Shop** (☎ 463–3196), across from the park, and talk politics with owner Rafael, a native Tico who lived in New Jersey for a while. He knows everything about the area and can arrange day trips to nearby waterfalls. At the tiny café-store **Super Dos,** on the main road opposite the church in Zarcero, you can get a coffee and empanada *de piña* (of pineapple) while you mull over buying some of the excellent local peach preserves.

En Route   Passing through Sarchí (☞ Chapter 3) and Naranjo on your way to Zarcero, you'll wind upward through miles of coffee plantations, with spectacular views of the mountains, and come down the other side to the city of Ciudad Quesada. There are some hair-raising roadside chasms, particularly on the east slope of the mountains, but the road is paved all the way. The drive should take roughly 2½ to three hours.

Ciudad Quesada

❷ *115 km (71 mi) northwest of San José.*

This lively, if not particularly picturesque, mountain market town (also known as San Carlos) is worth a stop for a soak in the soothing thermal waters of the El Tucano Resort and Spa (☞ Lodging, *below*). The new **Parque Nacional Juan Castro Blanco** (☞ Chapter 10) can also be found nearby, although presently there are no facilities in the park.

Lodging

$$$$ 🏨 **Hotel El Tucano Resort and Spa.** You come to El Tucano for the waters: the hotel abuts a river of hot, healing, marvelously invigorating natural springs. Two large outdoor hot tubs, the Olympic-size pool, natural steam room, and cool plunge are all fed by the Río Aguas Caliente, the cascading river that flows through the property. The hotel itself is somewhat overscale, and its public spaces suffer from the impersonality of any hotel subject to tour-group bookings. Still, the complex is surrounded by primary-growth forest, and the rooms are a study in understated luxury: simple, elegant, and comfortable, with oversize showers and tubs. ⊠ *8 km (5 mi) east of Ciudad Quesada, Apdo. 114–1017, San José,* ☎ *460–3141,* 🖷 *460–1692, 221–9095 reservations office in San José. 81 rooms with bath, 9 suites. Restaurant, bar, pool, spa, steam room, 2 tennis courts, horseback riding, bicycles. AE, MC, V.*

La Fortuna

❸ *40 km (27 mi) east of Volcán Arenal, 125 km (80 mi) northwest of San José.*

At the foot of towering, overpowering Volcán Arenal, the small farming community of La Fortuna de San Carlos (commonly called La Fortuna) attracts volcano watchers from around the world. The town overflows with restaurants, hotels, and tour operators. La Fortuna is also the number one place to arrange tours to the Caño Negro refuge (☞ *below*). Tours vary in price and quality, so ask around, but whoever you choose will provide an easier alternative than busing up north to Los Chiles and hiring a boat to take you down through the rain forest on Río Frío.

Besides offering access to a multitude of outdoor adventures, La Fortuna also provides you with the opportunity for some serious pampering.

Where else can you lounge in a natural hot-springs waterfall with a volcano spitting fireballs overhead? Kick back at the **Tabacón Resort,** 12 km (7 mi) northwest of La Fortuna on the highway toward Nuevo Arenal. This heavily touristed day spa and hotel (23 cabinas, $$$$) is a highly recommended stop in spite of the crowds and the slightly tacky Spanish-colonial design. An inspired medley of tropical gardens, waterfalls, swimming pools, swim-up bars, and dining facilities mingles in a florid Latin interpretation of grand European baths. ☎ 222–1072 or 233–0780, FAX 221–3075. ✉ *Entry: $14, $13 after 6 PM; 45-min massage $26, mud-pack facial $9.* ☉ *Daily 10–10.*

A pleasant day hike from La Fortuna takes you to the 164-ft-high **La Fortuna waterfall.** The 6-km (4-mi) walk begins off the main road toward the volcano; look for the yellow sign marking the entrance (☞ Outdoor Activities and Sports, *below*). If you don't feel like walking, several operators in La Fortuna will take you on horseback or in a four-wheel-drive vehicle. If you've got your own wheels, use them: standard cars can also navigate the rocky road, but take it very slowly— and double-check passability in the rainy season.

OFF THE
BEATEN PATH

VENADO CAVES – In 1945 a farmer in the mountain hamlet of Venado fell in a hole, and thus were discovered the Venado Caves. The limestone caves, 45 minutes (about 35 km/21 mi) north of La Fortuna and 15 km (9 mi) southeast of San Rafael, comprise a series of eight rooms with an assortment of stalactites, stalagmites, underground streams, and other unusual subterranean formations. Sunset Tours runs trips from La Fortuna (☞ Outdoor Activities and Sports, *below*). Note that at press time the caves were closed due to heavy rains. ☎ *479–9415 Sunset Tours.* ✉ *Tours $25.* ☉ *Daily 9–5.*

En Route   A newly paved road (Highway 4) leads northwest from Tanque, 10 km (6 mi) east of La Fortuna, passing through San Rafael de Guatuso and Upala as well as several hamlets tucked in among forest preserves, farmland, and the reserves of the indigenous Guatuso peoples. The road winds west, roughly paralleling Costa Rica's northern border, and offers smooth, pothole-free driving except for one short, nasty stretch just east of Santa Cecilia. As you head through remote rural territory, you'll see the eastern slopes of Guanacaste's volcanoes on the left and rolling farmland to the right. The dwellings visible here and there along the road are small and ramshackle, many lacking electricity. From Santa Cecilia, a short trip north on a dirt track leads to La Virgen, noteworthy for a nearby mirador with a spectacular view north across Lago de Nicaragua and the volcanoes beyond. From Santa Cecilia, the road descends toward the coast, skirting the northern edge of Parque Nacional Guanacaste. After passing citrus groves and the splendid **Hacienda Los Inocentes** (☞ Parque Nacional Guanacaste, *below*), the road terminates at the Pan-American Highway a few miles south of La Cruz. An alternative route south from Upala traverses the saddle between the Tenorio and Miravalles volcanoes, arriving at the Pan-American Highway just north of Cañas.

Dining and Lodging

$–$$ ✕ **La Vaca Muca.** It isn't a posh place, but the food is good and the servings generous. This restaurant is draped with foliage outside and, inside, has turquoise paneling and bamboo aplenty. Try the casado heaped with chicken or fish, rice, beans, fried egg, fried banana, cabbage salad, and a meat course—easily enough for two. *1 km (½ mi) west of town,* ☎ 479–9186. *MC, V.*

$–$$ ✕ **Rancho la Cascada.** Perhaps the best thing about La Cascada is its center-of-town location, making it a great place to grab breakfast before heading out on a rafting or riding trip. You can phone home, too: a bank of public telephones (get phone cards at Sunset Tours) waits just outside the restaurant's high, palm-thatch-covered roof. A pool hall should be open upstairs by mid-1999, and downstairs, the invitingly spacious dining room serves basic, mid-priced Costa Rican fare, including a range of hearty, American-style breakfasts and casados. By the bar toward the back, a color TV offers soccer and other diversions. *Across from northeast corner of Parque Central,* ☎ *479–9145. AE, MC, V.*

$$$ ⊞ **Chachagua Rain Forest Lodge.** At this working ranch intersected by a sweetly babbling brook, you can see caballeros at work, ride into the rain forest, and watch toucans in the open-air restaurant, which serves beef, milk, and cheese produced on the premises. Each cabina features a pair of double beds and a deck with a picnic table for alfresco dining. Large, reflective windows enclosing each cabina's shower serve a marvelous purpose: birds gather outside your window to watch their own reflections while you bathe and watch them. Downstream from the Children's Eternal Rainforest, San Ramon, and Monteverde reserves, the lodge is 3 km (2 mi) up a rough track—four-wheel drive is recommended in rainy season—on the road headed south from La Fortuna to La Tigra. ⊠ *Apdo. 476–4005, Ciudad Cariari, San José,* ☎ *239–1164,* ℻ *239–4206. 23 cabinas. Restaurant, pool, horseback riding, meeting room. AE, MC, V.*

$$$ ⊞ **Las Cabañitas Resort.** This group of red-roof cabinas set on landscaped grounds has terraces that face the volcano and rocking chairs from which to enjoy the view. The wood-panel cabins with bath have solid wood furnishings and quilted bedspreads. ⊠ *1 km (½ mi) east of La Fortuna, Apdo. 5–4417, La Fortuna, San Carlos,* ☎ *479–9000,* ℻ *479–9408. 30 cabins. Restaurant, bar, room service, pool, car rental. AE, MC, V.*

$$$ ⊞ **Tilajari Hotel Resort.** As a comfortable, upscale base, this elegantly landscaped, 40-acre resort can't be beat. "Papaya on a stick" feeders hang just outside the open-air dining room, attracting a raucous array of toucans and parrots while you sip your morning coffee. Though set in relative isolation, this place is a tour group haven. The cozy guest quarters have river-view balconies, satellite TV, and excellent bedside reading lights. The hotel organizes horseback or tractor tours through its own rain-forest preserve plus area tours. *San Carlos Valley just outside Muelle (follow signs), about 25 km (15 mi) from La Fortuna,* ⊠ *Apdo. 81, Ciudad Quesada, San Carlos,* ☎ *469–9091,* ℻ *469–9095. 56 rooms with bath, 4 suites. Restaurant, bar, air-conditioning, 2 pools, saunas, 4 tennis courts, basketball, horseback riding, racquetball, meeting room. AE, MC, V.*

$$–$$$ ⊞ **Hotel San Bosco.** The owners have added a two-story hotel covered
★ in blue-tile mosaics to complement the string of small, inexpensive cabinas. Two kitchen-equipped cabinas (which sleep 8 or 12) are a good deal for families. The spotlessly clean, white rooms have polished wood furniture and firm beds and are linked by a long veranda lined with benches and potted plants. You pay a little more for air-conditioning. ⊠ *La Fortuna de San Carlos, 220 yards north of La Fortuna's gas station,* ☎ *479–9050,* ℻ *479–9109. 18 rooms with bath, 11 cabinas. Restaurant, air-conditioning, pool, hot tub, laundry service. AE, MC, V.*

$$ ⊞ **La Pradera.** A building containing 10 comfortable cabinas has been put up next to La Pradera, a moderate-priced roadside restaurant beneath a high *rancho* on the route from La Fortuna to Arenal. Five rooms have air-conditioning, two have hot tubs, and all have verandas. Beef lovers should try the restaurant's steak with jalapeño sauce—a fine, spicy dish. *About 5 km (3 mi) west of La Fortuna de San Carlos* *toward Arenal,* ✉ *Alajuela,* ☎ ℻ *479–9167. 10 rooms with bath. Restaurant, air-conditioning, hot tubs. AE, MC, V.*

$$ 🏨 **Montana de Fuego Inn.** These cabinas are set on a grassy roadside knoll a few miles west of La Fortuna with utterly spectacular views of Volcán Arenal. The spacious, well-made hardwood structures are notable for their large porches. All rooms have ceiling fans, hot-water baths, and rustic decor. Plans are afoot for a restaurant, but meanwhile a host of good, low-priced eateries are to be found in nearby La Fortuna. The management can arrange area tours. *6 km (4 mi) west of La Fortuna,* ☎ *382–0759,* ℻ *479–9579. 18 cabinas. MC, V.*

Outdoor Activities and Sports

FISHING

The eastern side of Lake Arenal has the best freshwater fishing in Costa Rica, with guapote aplenty, although it is difficult to fish from the shore. Arenal Lodge (☞ Dining and Lodging *in* Nuevo Arenal, *below*) is one of many hotels and tour companies in the area offering boats and guides.

HIKING

To take the 6-km (4-mi) day hike from La Fortuna to the **La Fortuna waterfall,** look for the yellow entrance sign off the main road toward the volcano. After walking 1½ km (1 mi) and passing two bridges, turn right and continue hiking straight until you reach the river turnoff. You'll go 10 or 15 minutes down a steep but very well constructed step trail that has a few vertiginous spots along the way. Swimming in the pool under the waterfall is fairly safe. You can work your way around into the cavelike area behind the cataract for an unusual rear view, but you'll have to swim in turbulent waters and/or hike over slippery rocks. A $1.50 entrance fee is collected at the head of the trail.

HORSEBACK RIDING

If you are interested in getting up to Monteverde from the Arenal–La Fortuna area without taking the grinding four-hour drive, there's an alternative: the ever-ingenious Suresh Krishnan, a transplant from California, offers a wonderfully appealing adventure out of his tour agency, **Desafio** (✉ Apdo. 37–4417, La Fortuna SC, ☎ 479–9464, ℻ 479–9178)—a 4½-hour guided horseback trip around Volcán Arenal and up to Monteverde. They'll take your luggage and drive your car up there if need be. Suresh claims there are spots along the route that allow you to look down into Volcán Arenal. Several other agencies now offer the same trip, but Desafio discovered this trip; it deserves the business. You leave La Fortuna at 7 AM, arrive in Monteverde at 1 PM. It's $65 per person, plus $20 for a pack horse and car shuttle.

RAFTING

Desafio (☞ *above*) and several other La Fortuna operators offer class III and IV white-water trips on the Río Toro, Río Sarapiquí, and the Río Peñas Blancas, whose headwaters in the Monteverde–Santa Elena region assure the pristine quality of the waters. The narrow shapes of the Peñas Blancas and Toro rivers require the use of special, streamlined U.S.-made boats that seat just four and go very fast. Fees range from $37 per person for half-day Peñas Blancas and Toro trips to longer trips on the Sarapiquí ($65–$80).

SPELUNKING

Sunset Tours (✉ La Fortuna de San Carlos, across from Desafio, ☎ 479–9415, ℻ 479–9099) will take you to the Venado Caves for $25, including guide, entrance fee, boots, and a lantern. Prepare to get wet and muddy.

Caño Negro Wildlife Refuge

❹ *91 km (57 mi) north of La Fortuna.*

The 38½-sq-mi Caño Negro Wildlife Refuge (Refugio Nacional de Vida Silvestre Caño Negro) in the far northern reaches of Alajuela might be miles off your itinerary, but the vast Lago di Caño Negro is an excellent place for watching such waterfowl as the roseate spoonbill, jabiru stork, and anhinga, as well as for observing a host of resident exotic animals (☞ also Chapter 10). In the dry season you can rent horses; in the rainy season you are better off renting a boat. Camp or stay in basic lodging for around $8, including meals. Approach via Upala—a bus from there takes 45 minutes. ☎ *$6.* ⊙ *Daily 7–4.*

A popular tour down the Río Frío is run by **Esteban Cruz** (☎ 471–1032). The tour starts in Los Chiles, north of the Caño Negro reserve on Highway 35. **Sunset Tours** (☎ 479–9415) is one of the best of the many operators in La Fortuna, running daylong tours down the Río Frío to Caño Negro. Bring your jungle juice: the mosquitoes are voracious.

Volcán Arenal

❺ *17 km (11 mi) west of La Fortuna, 128 km (80 mi) northwest of San José.*

If you have never seen an active volcano, Arenal makes a spectacular first—its perfect conical profile dominates the southern end of Lake Arenal. Night is the best time for observing it, when you can clearly see rocks spewing skyward and red-hot molten lava enveloping the top of the cone. Phases of inactivity do occur, however, so it is wise to check just before you go to judge whether your trip will be worthwhile. The volcano is also frequently hidden in cloud cover, so you may have to stay more than one day to get in a good volcano-viewing session.

Arenal lay dormant until 1968. On July 29 of that year an earthquake shook the area, and 12 hours later Arenal blew. Pueblo Nuevo to the west bore the brunt of the shock waves, poisonous gases, and falling rocks; 80 people perished in all. Since then, Arenal has been in a constant state of activity—eruptions, accompanied by thunderous grumbling sounds, are sometimes as frequent as one per hour. An enormous eruption in May 1998 put the fear back into the local community and led to closure of Route 42 and the evacuation of several nearby hotels. This earth-shaking event reminded everyone in the area what it really means to coexist with an active volcano.

Hiking is possible on the volcano's lower slopes, but definitely not higher up; in 1988 two people were killed when they attempted to climb it. Ask at the **Smithsonian Institute's Observatory** (Arenal Observatory Lodge, ☎ 695–5033) near the base of the volcano, or at any one of the dozens of tour operators, such as Desafio (☞ Outdoor Activities and Sports *in* La Fortuna, *above*), working out of La Fortuna. They'll let you know how close you can safely approach. Beyond that, you should attempt exploration only with a guide.

Nuevo Arenal

❻ *40 km (25 mi) west of La Fortuna.*

There's little reason to stop in Nuevo Arenal itself. Off the main road, the pleasant if nondescript little town was created in 1973 to replace the original Arenal, flooded when the lake was created. If you're staying overnight in the area make sure you find a hotel with a view of the volcano. On the north shore, between the dam and the town of Nuevo

Arenal, there is one short stretch of road still unpaved, potholed, and at times quite dangerous; beware of deep, tire-wrecking washouts at all times. Be careful! A carload of American tourists went out of control on this road in 1998, resulting in one death and several severe injuries. This stretch adds a bone-jarring hour to an otherwise lovely drive with spectacular lake and volcano views all the way.

Five kilometers (3 mi) east of Nuevo Arenal, the **Jardín Botánico Arenal** (Arenal Botanical Gardens) exhibits more than 2,000 plant species from around the world in a single, elegantly organized sight. Countless orchids, bromeliads, heliconias, and roses; varieties of ferns; and a Japanese garden with a waterfall are among the many floral splendors laid out along well-marked trails. An accompanying brochure describes everything in delightful detail; well-placed benches and a fruit and juice stand provide resting places along the paths. ☎ 694–4273. ✉ $4. ☉ Daily 9–5.

Lodging

$$$$ 🛏 **Hotel Joya Surena.** In the midst of a working coffee plantation about 1½ km (1 mi) down a rocky road that leads north out of Nuevo Arenal, this property and its variously sized suites occupy a rather imposing three-story hacienda-style building surrounded by tropical gardens. The style is fairly luxurious for up-country Costa Rica. Extensive trails in and around the place bring a rich diversity of plant, animal, and bird life to view. ✉ Nuevo Arenal, Guanacaste, ☎ 694–4057, FAX 694–4059. 28 rooms with bath. Restaurant, pool, hot tub, massage, sauna, health club, hiking, horseback riding, boating, fishing. AE, MC, V.

$$$ 🛏 **Lake Coter Eco-Lodge.** This ruggedly handsome mountain hideaway is tucked into cloud forest, 3 km (2 mi) up a rough track off the north shore of Lake Arenal. The lodge is associated with a tour company and tends to fill up with oversize groups, but hit it on a nontour day and you'll have a choice of comfortable ridge-top cabinas. Clean, basic rooms are attached to the main brick-and-hardwood reception building, which has a friendly bar, dining facilities, fireplace, and pool table. The lodge offers canopy tours; hikes on 29 km (18 mi) of trails; kayaking, sailing, and beginning windsurfing on Laguna de Coter; and an extensive stable for trail rides through the cloud forest. ✉ Apdo. 85570–1000, San José, ☎ 257–5075, FAX 257–7065. 23 rooms with bath, 14 cabinas. Restaurant, bar, hiking, horseback riding, boating. AE, MC, V.

$$–$$$ 🛏 **Arenal Lodge.** This modern white bungalow is surrounded by macadamia trees and rain forest, high above the Lake Arenal Dam and midway between Nuevo Arenal and La Fortuna. A four-wheel-drive vehicle is needed to negotiate the steep 2-km (1-mi) drive, but the hotel will ferry you from the bottom for a small fee. The bedroom suites, some in a newer annex, are pleasantly furnished, and there are also cheaper, smaller, and darker rooms without volcano views. The interiors are finished in natural wood, with walls of louvered windows. The lodge's perks include an extensive library, a small snooker table, breakfast with the price of a room, and manicured gardens. ✉ Posada Arenal, Apdo. 1139–1250, Escazú 1250, San José, ☎ 383–3957, FAX 289–6798 reservations office in San José. 6 rooms with bath, 9 suites. Dining room, hiking, fishing, library. AE, MC, V.

$$ 🛏 **Arenal Observatory Lodge.** On your way to the observatory, the closest lodge to Arenal's base, you cross three large rivers whose bridges are regularly washed away, restricting access to those with four-wheel-drive vehicles. Built in 1987 for researchers, the lodge is rustic but comfortable; some bedrooms are dorms and some are doubles. The dining room has great views in both directions and serves hearty food included in the price of the room. 3 km (2 mi) east of dam on Lake Arenal; at intersection turn right and continue for 9 km (5½ mi), ☎ FAX 695–5033,

☎ 257–9489, FAX 257–4220 *reservations office in San José;* ✉ *John Aspinall, Arenal Observatory Lodge, Box 025216–1660, Miami, FL 33102-5216. 23 rooms with bath, 5 rooms and 1 cabina without bath. Restaurant, bar. AE, MC, V.*

Shopping

Toad Hall, along the road between Nuevo Arenal and La Fortuna (☎ 470–9178), an eclectic store-café, is open daily from 8:30 to 5 and sells everything from indigenous art to maps to recycled paper. The store is also a terrific information center—the owners can give you the low-down on every tour and tour operator in the area. There's also a deli-café with tables on a veranda featuring stunning views of the lake and volcano.

Tilarán

❼ *22 km (14 mi) southwest of Nuevo Arenal, 62 km (38 mi) west of La Fortuna.*

Heading west around Lake Arenal, you'll pass a couple of small villages and several charming hotels ranging from the Cretan-inspired fantasy Hotel Tilawa to the rustic Rock River Lodge (☞ Lodging, *below*). The quiet whitewashed town of Tilarán, on the southwest side of Lake Arenal, is used as a base by bronzed windsurfers.

Lodging

$$$–$$$$ 🏨 **Hotel Tilawa.** Eight kilometers (5 mi) north of Tilarán, this unique-
★ looking hotel sits on a bluff overlooking the windy western end of Lake Arenal. It's a knockoff of the Palace of Knossos on Crete, and with its neoclassical murals, columns, and arches draped with flowering plants, scarily enough, it works. Spacious, comfortable rooms feature two queen-size beds with bright Guatemalan bedspreads beneath natural wooden ceilings; the hot water–equipped bathrooms are especially spacious. Owned and operated by serious windsurfers, Tilawa now offers a host of activities such as sailing tours in a 36-ft catamaran. The hotel runs a windsurfing school and shop on the lake; packages include the use of windsurfing gear. ✉ *Apdo. 92–5710, Tilarán,* ☎ *695–5050,* FAX *695–5766. 28 rooms with bath. Restaurant, bar, pool, hiking, horseback riding, windsurfing, boating, mountain bikes. AE, MC, V.*

$$–$$$ 🏨 **Rock River Lodge.** This handsome hotel perches on a grassy hill above the road leading from Tilarán to Nuevo Arenal. A long building houses half a dozen rustic wooden cabinas sharing a shaded front porch. Eight Santa Fe–style cabinas are farther up the hill. The restaurant, bar, and lobby occupy another wooden building a bit closer to the road, with plenty of porch space and lounging sofas, an open kitchen, a welcoming fireplace, and cafeteria-style dining tables. The owner, Norman List, is a dedicated windsurfer and rents gear; his is the launching site across the lake from the Hotel Tilawa's (☞ *above*). He also organizes tours for inner tubing on the Sarapiquí and bird-watching. The restaurant serves well-made food at reasonable prices. ✉ *Apdo. 95, Tilarán,* ☎ FAX *695–5644. 6 rooms with bath, 8 cabinas. Restaurant, bar, horseback riding, windsurfing, fishing, mountain bikes. No credit cards.*

$$–$$$ 🏨 **Xiloe Lodge and Equus Bar/Full Moon Disco.** On the road between Tilarán and Nuevo Arenal, the Xiloe stands out among the plethora of low-budget cabinas, hotels, and inns for its lovely setting, sheltered from the wind on a rise in the trees not far from the northwesternmost end of the lake. Xiloe offers three spacious wooden cabinas, each with three double bedrooms and kitchenette, plus two smaller two-bedroom cabinas (without kitchenettes) that sleep up to four; all have hot-water bath. The barbecue at Equus restaurant fires up excellent carnivorous fare—grilled beef and smoked chicken. And during weekends and full moons, the Full Moon disco, a multilevel, stone-floored, open-air extravaganza behind the restaurant, is one of the hottest dance floors in Costa Rica. ✉ *Apdo. 35, Tilarán,* ☎ *259–9806,* FAX *259–9882. 5 cabinas. Restaurant, dance club. No credit cards.*

$ 🏠 **Cabinas El Sueño.** Upstairs on a street just off Tilarán's central plaza, "The Dream" is probably the best low-priced deal in town—and for you budget-minded wind riders, it's a few scant miles from the pricier Hotel Tilawa's (☞ *above*) waterfront windsurf center. The quiet rooms with hot-water bath surround a serene central courtyard with a fountain and a hammock for lounging. Downstairs, the hotel's Restaurant El Parque specializes in seafood dishes. ✉ *Off Parque Central, Tilarán,* ☎ *695–5347. 12 rooms with bath. Restaurant. No credit cards.*

Outdoor Activities and Sports

HORSEBACK RIDING

Hotel Tilawa (☞ Lodging, *above*) and nearly every reputable hotel in the area offer access to guided and unguided horseback rentals. The Lake Coter Eco-Lodge (☞ Lodging *in* Nuevo Arenal, *above*) has 25 horses in its own stable. Uncounted miles of good trails for horses and bikes cover a marvelous mix of terrain.

MOUNTAIN BIKING

For those days when the windsurfers get "skunked" (the wind fails to blow), the **Hotel Tilawa** (☞ Lodging, *above*) rents mountain bikes for riding a network of roads and trails in the area at the north end of Lake Arenal.

WINDSURFING

Several hotels, including the Rock River Lodge (☞ Lodging, *above*), have equipment for rent for windsurfing on Lake Arenal, but the best selection can be found at **Tilawa Viento Surf** (☎ 695–5008), the lakefront shop associated with the Hotel Tilawa (☞ Lodging, *above*).

Reserva Biológica Bosque Nuboso Monteverde and Environs

★ ⑧ *35 km (22 mi) southeast of Tilarán, 167 km (104 mi) northwest of San José.*

In close proximity to several fine hotels, the Reserva Biológica Bosque Nuboso Monteverde (Monteverde Cloud Forest Biological Reserve) is one of the country's best-kept reserves, with well-marked trails, lush vegetation, and a cool climate. The area's first residents were a handful of Costa Rican families fleeing the rough-and-ready life of nearby gold-mining fields during the 1940s. They were joined in the 1950s by Quakers from Alabama who came in search of peace, tranquillity, and good grazing, but the cloud forest that lay above their dairy farms was soon to attract the attention of ecologists.

The collision of moist winds with the continental divide here creates a constant mist whose particles provide nutrients for plants growing at the upper layers of the forest. Giant trees are enshrouded in a cascade of orchids, bromeliads, mosses, and ferns, and, in those patches where sunlight penetrates, brilliantly colored flowers flourish. The sheer size of everything, especially the leaves of the trees, is striking. No less astounding is the variety: 2,500 plant species, 400 species of birds, 500 types of butterflies, and more than 100 different mammals have so far been cataloged at Monteverde. A damp and exotic mixture of shades, smells, and sounds, the cloud forest is also famous for its population of resplendent quetzals, which can be spotted feeding on the *aguacatillo* (like an avocado) trees; best viewing times are early mornings from January until September, and especially during the mating season of April and May. Other forest-dwelling inhabitants include hummingbirds and multicolored frogs. For those who don't have a lucky eye, a short-stay aquarium is in the field station; captives here stay only a week before being released back into the wild. Although the reserve limits visitors to 100 people at a time, Monteverde is one of the country's most popular destinations and gets very busy, so get here early and allow a generous slice of time for leisurely hiking to see the forest's flora and fauna; longer hikes are made possible by some strategically placed overnight refuges along the way. At the entrance to the reserve you can buy self-guide pamphlets and rent gum boots; a map is provided when you pay the entrance fee. ☎ 645–5122, FAX 645–5034. ✉ *Reserve $8, guide $15.* ☉ *Daily 7–4.*

If your bones can take it, a very rough track leads from Tilarán via Cabeceras to Santa Elena, near Monteverde, doing away with the need to cut across to the Pan-American Highway. You may well need a four-wheel-drive vehicle—inquire locally (in Tilaran if you're heading up, in Monteverde if you're heading down) about the present condition of the road—but the views of Nicoya Peninsula, Lake Arenal, and Volcán Arenal reward those willing to bump around a bit. Consider also the fact that you don't really save much time—it takes about 2½ hours as opposed to the three required via Cañas and Río Lagarto on the highway.

To reach Monteverde from San José, travel north approximately 125 km (78 mi) on the Pan-American Highway to the Río Lagarto turnoff. From here, an unpaved 30-km (19-mi) track to the reserve snakes dramatically up through hilly farming country; it takes 1½ to two hours to negotiate it, less by four-wheel-drive vehicle. (If you aren't renting a four-wheel-drive vehicle, at least get a car with high clearance—you'll be glad you did.) Those inclined to complain about the road should contemplate how busy the already-crowded Monteverde area would be if the road were smooth. At the junction for Santa Elena, bear right for the reserve. The Monteverde settlement has no real nucleus; houses and hotels flank a 5-km (3-mi) road at intervals until you arrive at the reserve's entrance.

The Monteverde cloud forest can be visited from high in the air courtesy of **Canopy Tours,** which has five platforms up in the trees that you arrive at using a cable-and-harness traversing system, and another which you climb 40 ft inside a strangler fig to reach. The tours last 2½ hours. Tours leave from the Canopy Tour Basecamp in Santa Elena at 7:30 and 10:30 AM and 2:30 PM. ✉ *Apdo. 80–5655, Santa Elena de Monteverde,* ☎ *645–5243, 226–1315 reservations office in San José,* FAX *645–5022, 255–3573 in San José.* ✉ *$45.* ☉ *Tours 7:30 and 10:30 AM and 2:30 PM.*

Introducing a new twist on the canopy tour, **Valverde's Puentes Colgantes** lets you hike between treetops, up to a height of 126 ft, by way of five hanging bridges connected from tree to tree. ☎ 645–5238. ✉ *$5.* ☉ *Daily 7–4.*

At the **Serpentario Monteverde,** you can check out an exhibition of live Costa Rican reptiles. ☎ 645–5238. ✉ *$3.* ☉ *Daily 9–4.*

Several conservation areas that have sprung up near Monteverde make attractive day trips for reserve visitors, particularly if the Monteverde reserve is too busy. The **Reserva Santa Elena,** an almost 1½-sq-mi forest, just west of Monteverde, has a series of trails that can be walked alone or with a guide. *5 km (3 mi) north of the town of Santa Elena,* ☎ *645–5014.* ✉ *$5.* ☉ *Daily 7–4.*

With tours operating out of the El Sapo Dorado Hotel (☞ Dining and Lodging, *below*), the **Reserva Sendero Tranquilo** offers you a chance to hike 200 acres containing four different stages of cloud forest, including one area illustrating the results of cloud-forest devastation. ☎ *645–5010.* ☞ *$20, 2-person minimum.*

🌀 The **Jardín Mariposa** (Butterfly Garden), near the Pensión Monteverde Inn, displays tropical butterflies in three enclosed botanical gardens from which there are stunning views of the Golfo de Nicoya. A guided tour helps you understand the stages of a butterfly's life. The private **bird farm** next door has several trails through secondary forest. More than 90 bird species have been sighted here, from the crowned motmot to the resplendent quetzal. ☎ *645–5512.* ☞ *$6.* ☉ *Daily 9:30–4.*

Dining and Lodging

$ ✕ **Stella's Bakery.** This shop serves everything from chocolate brownies to hearty breakfasts in a warm, wood-panel room decorated with Stella's oil paintings and her daughter Meg's stained-glass windows. You can also sip coffee on the backyard patio. *On main road halfway between Santa Elena and Monteverde,* ☎ *645–5560. No credit cards. No lunch or dinner.*

$$$ ✕ **El Sapo Dorado.** Having started its life as a nightclub, El Sapo Do-
★ rado (The Golden Toad) became a popular restaurant and graduated into a very pleasant hotel. Geovanny Arguedas's family arrived here to farm 10 years before the Quakers did, and he and his wife, Hannah Lowther, have built secluded hillside cabins with polished paneling, tables, open fires, and rocking chairs. The restaurant is renowned for its pasta, pizza, vegetarian dishes, and fresh sailfish from Puntarenas; the dance floor is still put to use with live music on weekends. The 6-km (4-mi) distance from the park entrance isn't a problem if you enjoy hiking or have a car. ☒ *Apdo. 09–5655, Monteverde,* ☎ FAX *645–5010 or 645–5181,* FAX *645–5180. 20 rooms with bath. Restaurant, bar, massage, bicycles, dance club. No credit cards.*

$$$ **Fonda Vela.** The most innovatively designed of Monteverde's ho-
★ tels is also one of the closest to the reserve entrance. Owned by the Smith brothers, whose family were among the first American arrivals in the 1950s, these steep-roofed chalets have large bedrooms with white stucco walls, wooden floors, and huge windows. Some have markedly better views of the wooded grounds, so specify when booking. Local and international recipes, prepared with flair, are served in the dining room or on the veranda. ☒ *Apdo. 70060–1000, San José, 1½ km (1 mi) northwest of Monteverde entrance,* ☎ *645–5125,* FAX *645–5119,* ☎ FAX *257–1413 reservations office in San José. 28 rooms with bath. Restaurant, bar, horseback riding. AE, DC, MC, V.*

$$$ **Hotel Belmar.** Built into the hillside, Hotel Belmar resembles two tall
★ Swiss chalets and commands extensive views of the Golfo de Nicoya and the hilly peninsula. The amiable Chilean owners have designed both elegant and rustic rooms, paneled with polished wood; duvets cover the beds, and most rooms have balconies. In the dining room, you can count on adventurous and delicious *platos del día* (daily specials). *4 km (2½ mi) north of Monteverde,* ☒ *Puntarenas,* ☎ *645–5201,* FAX *645–5135. 34 rooms with bath. Restaurant, bar, basketball. No credit cards.*

$–$$ **El Bosque.** Convenient to the Bajo Tigre nature trail and Meg's Stables (☞ Outdoor Activities and Sports, *below*), El Bosque is a popular shady diner with a veranda; the paneled dining room has a tile floor and wood tables. A bridge from the veranda crosses a stream; a track from there leads to the hotel. The hotel features quiet, simple rooms with private baths grouped around a central camping area with a volleyball court. For $60 the hotel will deliver two people to the Monteverde reserve entrance and pay entry fees. ☒ *Apdo. 5655, Santa Elena,*

EYES AFLIGHT IN COSTA RICA

F YOU VISIT A COSTA RICAN CLOUD forest, you'll probably have your eyes peeled for the emerald toucanet or the three-wattled bellbird, but if you're here between October and April, you'll actually be just as likely to see a Kentucky warbler. Experienced birders shouldn't be surprised to see that some of their feathered friends from home made similar vacation plans, but many people probably don't realize that when northern birds fly south for the winter, they don't all head to Miami.

Seasonal visitors are just part—about a quarter—of the amazing avian panorama in Costa Rica. Nearly 850 bird species have been identified here, more than the United States and Canada have between them—all in an area about half the size of Kentucky. The country is consequently a mecca for amateur ornithologists, who flock here by the thousands. Though the big attractions tend to be such spectacular species as the keel-billed toucan and resplendent quetzal, it is the diversity of shape, size, coloration, and behavior that makes bird-watching in Costa Rica so fascinating.

The country's avian inhabitants range in size from the scintillant hummingbird, standing a mere 2½ inches tall and weighing just over 2 grams, to the long-legged jabiru stork, which reaches a height of more than 4 ft and a weight of 14 pounds. The diversity of form and color varies from such striking creatures as the showy scarlet macaw and the quirky purple gallinule to the relatively inconspicuous, and seemingly ubiquitous, clay-colored robin, which is, surprisingly enough, Costa Rica's national bird. These robins may look a bit plain, but their song is a melodious one, and since the males sing almost constantly toward the end of the dry season—the beginning of their mating season—local legend has it they call the rains, which play a vital role in a nation so dependent on agriculture.

Foreigners tend to ooh and aah at the sight of those birds associated with the tropics: parrots, parakeets, and macaws; toucans and toucanets; and the elusive but legendary resplendent quetzal. But there are many other equally impressive species flitting around, such as the motmots, with their distinctive racket tails; oropéndolas (golden orioles), which build remarkable hanging nests; and an amazing array of hawks, kites, and falcons.

On the color scale, the country's tanagers, euphonias, manakins, cotingas, and trogons are some of its loveliest plumed creatures, but none of them match the iridescence of the hummingbirds and their hyperactive cousins. Costa Rica hosts 51 members of the hummingbird family, compared to the just one species for all of the United States east of the Rocky Mountains. A bit of time spent near a hummingbird feeder will treat you to an unforgettable display of accelerated aerial antics and general pugnacity.

YOU JUST MIGHT FIND THAT THE more you observe Costa Rica's birds, the more interesting they get. Bird-watching can be done everywhere in the country—all you need is a pair of binoculars and a copy of A Guide to the Birds of Costa Rica, the excellent field guide by Stiles and Skutch. Wake up early, get out into the woods or the garden, focus those binoculars, and you'll quickly be enchanted by the beauty on the wing. For more information about Costa Rican birds, see the Wildlife Glossary in Chapter 11.

☎ 645–5221 or 645–5158, ⅀ 645–5129. 21 rooms with bath. Restaurant, volleyball. AE, MC, V. Closed Oct.

$ 🖭 **Pensión Monteverde Inn.** Situated on a 28-acre private preserve, the cheapest inn in Monteverde is quite far—about 5 km (3 mi)—from the park entrance. The bedrooms are basic, but they have stunning views of the Golfo de Nicoya and contain hardwood floors, firm beds, and powerful, hot showers. Home cooking is served by the chatty David Savage and family. Their dog, Bambi, warms up to guests soon enough. ✉ Monteverde, next to Butterfly Garden, Puntarenas, ☎ 645–5156. 10 rooms, 8 with bath. Dining room. No credit cards.

Outdoor Activities and Sports

HIKING

The Monteverde Conservation League's **Bajo del Tigre trail** (follow signs along the highway to Monteverde) makes for a pleasant, 1½-km (1-mi) hike through secondary forest. Admission to the trail is $5.

HORSEBACK RIDING

Next door to Stella's Bakery (☞ Dining and Lodging, above), **Meg's Stables** (☎ 645–5052) offers horseback riding for everyone from toddlers to seasoned experts. Guided rides through the Monteverde area cost around $10 an hour, with prices dropping for longer rides. Reservations are a good idea in high season.

Shopping

In Monteverde, the **Cooperative de Artesanas Santa Elena y Monteverde** (CASEM, ☎ 645–5190), an artisans' cooperative open next door to the El Bosque hotel-restaurant (☞ Dining and Lodging, above), sells locally made crafts. The **Hummingbird Gallery,** near the reserve entrance, sells prints, slides, books, gifts, T-shirts, and great Costa Rican coffee. Farther down on the right is the **Cheese Factory** (☎ 645–5029, ⅀ free, ☉ Mon.–Sat. 7:30–4, Sun. 7:30–12:30), established by the Quakers in the 1950s and now one of the largest dairy producers in Costa Rica. Watch the art of cheese making through a window in the sales room—you'll surely be lured into buying some.

FAR NORTHERN GUANACASTE

This area encompasses the mountains, plains, and Pacific coastline north of Liberia up to the border of Nicaragua. The primary town in the area, Liberia (☞ Chapter 5), serves as the capital of Guanacaste and home to Costa Rica's second-largest airport. You will most likely pass through Liberia on your way to the beaches west of the city and on the Nicoya Peninsula (☞ Chapter 5), or up north to the national parks of Rincón de la Vieja, Guanacaste, or Santa Rosa. Volcán Rincón, an active volcano that last erupted in 1991, is pocked with eerie wonders such as boiling creeks, bubbling mud pools, and vapor-emitting streams—look, but don't touch!

West of Rincón de la Vieja, on the coast, Parque Nacional Santa Rosa is a former cattle ranch where Costa Ricans defeated the invading mercenary army of American William Walker in 1857. Santa Rosa is also home to Playas Naranjo and Nancite, where hundreds of thousands of olive ridley turtles lay their eggs between June and November. Closer still to the Nicaraguan border are the Parque Nacional Guanacaste and the town of La Cruz, overlooking the pristine beaches and new resorts of the lovely Golfo de Santa Elena and Bahía Salinas.

En Route   From Liberia, access to Parque Nacional Rincón de la Vieja is on 27 km (17 mi) of unpaved road. The road begins 6 km (4 mi) north of Liberia off the Pan-American Highway (follow signs for Albergue

Guachipelín) or 25 km (15 mi) along the Colonia Blanca route north-east from Liberia, which follows the course of the Río Liberia to the Santa María park headquarters. A four-wheel-drive vehicle is recommended, though not essential, for either of these bone-rattling one- to 1½-hour rides.

Parque Nacional Rincón de la Vieja

⑨ *27 km (17 mi) north of Liberia.*

Some compare the geysers, mud pots, and hot springs of Parque Nacional Rincón de la Vieja (Rincón de la Vieja National Park) to those of Yellowstone National Park in the United States. The park's more than 177 sq km (54 sq mi) of protected land is primarily dry forest, much of which has been regenerated since the park's inception in 1973. The wildlife here is tremendously diverse: 200 species of birds, including keel-billed toucans and blue-crowned motmots, plus mammals such as brocket deer, tapirs, coatis, jaguars, sloths, armadillos, and raccoons. Needless to say, hiking here is fantastic, but it's wise to do some planning to know where to head. Trail maps and hiking information are available at the park headquarters by the entrance gate; alternatively, head to Rincón de la Vieja Mountain Lodge (☞ Lodging, *below*), which has guides for foot or horseback hiking available; call ahead to check availability. ☎ 695–5598. ✉ $6. ☉ *Daily 8–4.*

The composite mass of **Volcán Rincón de la Vieja,** often enveloped in a mixture of sulfurous gases and cloud, dominates the scenery to the right of the Pan-American Highway as you head north. The volcano complex has two peaks: **Santa María** (6,284 ft) and **Rincón de la Vieja** (6,225 ft), to the northeast. The latter is vegetationless and has two craters. Rincón de la Vieja is thought unlikely to erupt violently due to the profusion of fumaroles through which it can constantly let off steam. The last violent eruptions were between 1966 and 1970. If you want to explore the slopes of the volcano, it is advisable to go with a guide; the abundant hot springs and geysers have given unsuspecting visitors some very nasty burns in the past. **Las Hornillas** ("the Kitchen Stoves"), on the southern slope of the Rincón de la Vieja crater, is a 124-acre medley of mud cones, hot-water pools, bubbling mud pots, and vent holes most active during the rainy season. To the east, **Los Azufrales** are hot sulfur springs in which you can bathe; be careful not to get sulfur in your eyes.

Lodging

$$ ★ **Rincón de la Vieja Mountain Lodge.** Resting on the slopes of Rincón de la Vieja, this lodge has paneled cabins, small doubles, and comfy bunk dormitory-style rooms. The sitting room has a terra-cotta floor, local maps, and cases of butterflies and some intimidatingly oversize insects. The food is good: meat, fish, and vegetarian entrées, and much of the produce is homegrown. The affable staff of the owner, Alvaro, can take you to explore the park and volcano on foot or on horseback through the woods. Trails lead to a hot-water, sulfur bathing pool and a blue lake and waterfall. Canopy tours are run by Treetop Trails (☞ Outdoor Activities and Sports, *below*). ✉ *Apdo. 114–5000, Liberia,* ☎ FAX *695–5553. 27 rooms without bath. Dining room, pool. AE, MC, V.*

Outdoor Activities and Sports

From the Rincón de la Vieja Mountain Lodge (☞ Lodging, *above*), **Treetop Trails** runs four-hour canopy tours (✉ $49.50) that include a forest-floor hike and canopy observation from 16 cable-linked treetop platforms. A more elaborate seven-hour tour (✉ $77) also includes horseback riding to the park's blue lake and waterfall.

Parque Nacional Santa Rosa

⑩ *48 km (30 mi) south of the Nicaraguan border, west of the Pan-American Highway at Km 269.*

Parque Nacional Santa Rosa (Santa Rosa National Park) was established in 1971 to protect **La Casona Hacienda,** scene of the famous 1856 battle in which a ragged force of ill-equipped Costa Ricans routed the superior army of William Walker. A U.S. filibuster from Tennessee, Walker had established himself as chief of staff of the Nicaraguan army as part of his Manifest Destiny–influenced scheme to create a slave empire in the region. In 1857, the hostilities having continued onto Nicaraguan soil, Juan Santamaría, a drummer boy from Alajuela, threw burning wood into the building where Walker and his henchmen were gathered, so ending the war and thereby winning undying national fame for himself. (Walker was later turned over to Honduras and shot by a firing squad.) The rambling colonial-style farmstead of La Casona stands as a monument to this national triumph and contains an interesting museum, with maps, weapons, uniforms, and furniture. The start of a short explanatory nature trail is visible just out front. Keep an eye out for the numbers of large green parrots inhabiting the trees around the farmstead. ☎ 695–5598. ⌧ $6. ☉ *Museum daily 8–4:30.*

For ecologists, Santa Rosa has a more important role—protecting and regenerating 495 sq km (191 sq mi) of forest land, both moist, basal belt transition and deciduous, tropical dry forests. The central administrative area is a hive of scientific activity. Much of the research here has been into forest propagation, the fruits of which are evident in former cattle pastures where windblown seeds have been allowed to establish themselves. Bush fires are a constant hazard in the dry season, making firebreaks a necessity. Typical dry-forest vegetation includes oak, wild cherry, mahogany, calabash, bullhorn acacia, hibiscus, and gumbo-limbo, with its distinctive reddish-brown bark. Because of its less luxuriant foliage, the park is a good one for viewing wildlife, especially if you station yourself next to water holes during the dry season. Inhabitants include spider, white-faced, and howler monkeys, as well as deer, armadillos, coyotes, tapirs, coatis, and ocelots. Ocelots, commonly known as *manigordos* ("fat paws") on account of their large feet, are striped wildcats that have been brought back from the brink of extinction by the park's conservation methods. These wildlands also define the southernmost distribution of many North American species such as the Virginia opossum and the *cantil* moccasin. Throughout the park it is wise to carry your own water, since water holes are none too clean. From the entrance gate, 7 km (4½ mi) of paved road leads to the park headquarters. ☎ 695–5598. ⌧ *Park $6.* ☉ *Daily 7–5.*

Thirteen kilometers (8 mi) west of the administrative area—a two- to three-hour hike or one hour by four-wheel-drive vehicle—is the white-sand **Playa Naranjo,** popular for beachcombing thanks to its pretty shells and for surfing because of its near-perfect break. The campsite here has washing facilities, but bring your own drinking water. The lookout at the northern tip of the beach has views over the entire park.

Turtle *arribadas*—the phenomenon of turtles arriving on a beach to nest—do take place on Naranjo, but the big ones occur at a point reached by a two-hour walk north to **Playa Nancite,** also accessible by four-wheel-drive vehicle. It is estimated that 200,000 of the 500,000 turtles that nest each year in Costa Rica choose Nancite. Backed by dense hibiscus and button mangroves, the gray-sand beach is penned in by steep, tawny, brush-covered hills. Previously a difficult point to get to, it is now the only totally protected olive-ridley turtle arribada in the world. The busy time is August to December, peaking in September and October. Olive ridleys are the smallest of the sea turtles (average carapace, or hardback shell, is 21–29 inches) and the least shy. The majority arrive at night, plowing the sand as they move up the beach and sniffing for the high-tide line, beyond which they use their hind flippers to dig holes into which they will lay their eggs. They spend an average of one hour on the beach before scurrying back to the sea. Hatching also takes place at night. The phototropic baby turtles naturally know to head for the sea, which is vital for their continued survival, since the brightest light is that of the shimmering ocean. Many of the nests are churned up during subsequent arribadas, and predators such as coatis, ghost crabs, raccoons, and coyotes lie in wait; hence just 0.2% of eggs reach the sea as young turtles. Permits are needed to stay at Nancite; ask at the headquarters.

Camping

$ ⚠ **La Casona.** Campers enjoy the rugged terrain and isolated feel of Santa Rosa National Park. The campsite, overhung by giant strangler figs, has no set sites—allowing you a choice of where to set up—and provides washing facilities and picnic tables. Be careful of snakes. Between Playas Naranjo and Nancite, another campground at Estero Real is available with tables only. ✉ *Parque Nacional Santa Rosa,* ☎ 695–5598, 🖷 *no fax. Bathrooms, picnic tables. No credit cards.*

Cuajiniquil

⓫ *10 km (6 mi) north of Santa Rosa National Park.*

North from Santa Rosa on the Pan-American Highway is the left turn to Cuajiniquil, famous for its waterfalls. If you have time and a four-wheel-drive vehicle, Cuajiniquil has lovely views. The **Golfo de Santa Elena** is renowned for its calm waters, which is why it is now threatened by tourist development. **Playa Blanca** in the extreme west has smooth white sand, as its name implies. The rough track there passes through a valley of uneven width caused, according to geologists, by the diverse granulation of the sediments formerly deposited here. To the south rise the rocky **Santa Elena hills** (2,332 ft), bare except for a few chigua and nancite shrubs.

Parque Nacional Guanacaste

⓬ *32 km (20 mi) north of Liberia.*

To the east of the Pan-American Highway is Parque Nacional Guanacaste (Guanacaste National Park, ☎ 695–5598), created in 1989 to preserve rain forests around **Volcán Cacao** (5,443 ft) and **Volcán Orosí** (4,877 ft), which are seasonally inhabited by migrants from Santa Rosa. Much of the park's territory is cattle pasture, which it is hoped will regenerate into forest. Three biological stations within the park have places for visitors to stay. The **Mengo Biological Station** (☎ no phone) lies on the slopes of Volcán Cacao at an altitude of 3,609 ft; accommodation is in rustic wooden dormitories with bedding provided, but bring a towel. From Mengo one trail leads up Volcán Cacao, and another heads north to the modern **Maritza Station** (☎ no phone), a three-hour hike away at the base of Orosí, with more lodging available. You can also reach Maritza by four-wheel-drive vehicle. From Maritza you can trek two hours to **Llano de los Indios,** a cattle pasture dotted with volcanic petroglyphs. Farther north and a little east is rustic **Pitilla Station,** and despite its lower elevation, it has views of the coast and Lago de Nicaragua.

Lodging

$$–$$$ 🏨 **Hacienda Los Inocentes.** Built more than 100 years ago by the great-grandfather of Violeta Chamorra, the president of Nicaragua, this handsome, exquisitely maintained hardwood hacienda is in a private reserve along the northern border of Guanacaste National Park. A 14-km (8½-mi) drive on a smoothly paved road east from the Pan-American Highway takes you to the entrance of the working ranch, with its horses, cattle, and numerous birds. The hardwood-finished rooms are rustic but comfortable, with hot showers in bathrooms (some shared by two rooms) across the halls. Meals are included in most packages. Experienced ranch-hand guides, friendly horses, and miles of trails get you into the forests. ✉ *Apdo. 228–3000, Heredia,* ☎ FAX *679–9190,* ☎ *265–5484 reservations office in San José, 888/613–2532 in the U.S.;* FAX *265–4385. 11 rooms without bath. Dining room, pool. AE, MC, V.*

La Cruz

⓭   *56 km (35 mi) north of Liberia, 20 km (12 mi) south of the Nicaraguan border.*

Farther north on the west side of the highway is a turnoff to La Cruz, noteworthy for the stunning views of Bahía Salinas (☞ *below*) from the restaurants and hotels along the bluff. It also serves as a gateway to the resorts and beaches on the south shore of Bahia Salinas (☞ *below*), the hamlet of Puerto Soley, and the Golfo de Santa Elena.

Dining and Lodging

$$ ✕ **El Mirador Ehecatl.** You don't want to pass up a chance to have a drink at this two-story restaurant and bar with a cliffside promenade overlooking Bahia Salinas, Isla Bolaños, and the Nicaraguan coastline. Even better, the food is delicious: try anything with seafood—the seviche is especially well prepared—or one of the many cheap, rice-based combination plates. The chef has a surprisingly refined hand. Ehecatl, by the way, means "god of the wind" in the old Chorotegan language, and the name suits, for Bahia Salinas is a very windy place. To find the restaurant, turn left and go around the La Cruz town square; at the "end" of the road veer slightly left rather than taking the steep downhill road that leads to Bahia Salinas. ☎ *No phone. V.*

$$ 🏨 **Amalia's Inn.** The late Lester Bounds, an American artist, and his Costa Rican wife, Amalia, created this breezy little inn on the cliff overlooking Bahia Salinas. Amalia now runs the inn with help from her brother. Bounds is also survived by his art, colorful modern paintings and prints that decorate the place and rooms. On the left or south side of the road as you head into town, the inn features spacious rooms with private baths and balconies. The surrounding forest preserve was given to the town of La Cruz by Amalia's sister, who lives in and owns the magnificent Hacienda Quebrada de Agua, visible in the valley below La Cruz. Amalia's is a fine budget alternative to the pricier new resorts on the bay's south shore. ✉ *La Cruz, Guanacaste,* ☎ FAX *679–9181. 8 rooms with bath. Pool. No credit cards.*

$$ 🏨 **Colinas del Norte.** Nicaragua-bound adventurers will appreciate this outpost. On the Pan-American Highway halfway between La Cruz and the Nicaraguan border, 20 km (12 mi) north at Peñas Blancas, this rugged two-story hardwood hotel bills itself as a touring base for the surrounding dry tropical forest, but its most appealing feature appears to be its large pool, surrounded by shady palms. At the outdoor disco you can dance till you drop, then hop into the pool. The indoor-outdoor restaurant specializes in pizza and Italian food. Modest but comfortable upstairs rooms come with private hot water baths and terraces. ✉ *Pan-American Highway, about 10 km (6 mi) north of La Cruz, Apdo. 10493–*

1000, San José, ☎ Ⓕ🅐🅧 *679–9132, 289–7318 reservations office in San José. 24 rooms with bath. Restaurant, pool. AE, MC, V.*

Bahia Salinas

⑭ *7 km (4½ mi) west of La Cruz.*

Several dirt and rock roads dead end on different beaches along Bahia Salinas, the pretty little half-moon bay that lies at the very top of Costa Rica's Pacific coast—just turn right off the "main" road to the resorts. You'll probably end up on or near the beach, or in the hamlet of **Puerto Soley,** a tiny town tucked in off the bay—look for the salt flats to find the town, which is roughly 5–6 very slow-going km (3–4 mi) from La Cruz. There is public beach access along the bay, so if you have your own windsurfing equipment there's no need to utilize the resorts, which have inevitably crept up on the bay.

The wind usually blows year-round, except in September and October, the height of the rainy season, so windsurfing here is supreme. Winds here are generally not as powerful as at Lake Arenal, but there is enough to make this a viable alternative (stay on the south side for stronger winds), or accompaniment, to the Arenal experience. Ranking among the most beautiful beaches in all of Costa Rica are a couple of secluded, wind-sheltered strands, including the gorgeous, pristine **Playa Rajada,** with fine swimming and snorkeling. Just offshore is **Isla Bolaños,** a bird refuge and nesting site for thousands of endangered frigate birds as well as brown pelicans. The Bolaños Bay Resort (☞ Lodging, *below*) has a motor launch for Isla Bolaños tours, but don't try to land—it is against the law.

Lodging

$$$–$$$$ 🏨 **Ecoplaya Beach Resort.** On the same stretch of Bahia Salinas as the Bolaños Bay Resort (☞ *below*), the Ecoplaya emphasizes upscale luxury amenities. Every well-made room has a small but fully equipped kitchen, satellite TV, air-conditioning, phones, hot water, and custom hardwood furniture. The nearly 1-km-long (½-mi-long) beach fronting the hotel is flanked by bird- and wildlife-filled estuaries. Be warned, nonsailors: the wind blows hard here, much of the time. ✉ *Plaza Colonial, Escazú, No. 4, San José,* ☎ *679–9380, 289–8920 reservations office in San José;* Ⓕ🅐🅧 *679–9460, 289–4536 in San José. 16 suites. Restaurant, bar, air-conditioning, pool. AE, MC, V.*

$$$ 🏨 **Bolaños Bay Resort.** Take the dirt road down the steep hill from La Cruz, follow the signs for about 15 km (9 mi), and you'll soon spot the high double *rancho* that shelters the resort's reception area, bar, and restaurant. Given the winds that rocket across the bay, the resort's emphasis on windsurfing comes as no surprise. For windsurfing widows, a sheltered pool with a swim-up bar provides a diversion. The Belgium-based Three Corners Company runs its hotels European style, with high-quality meals—especially hearty breakfasts—and modest rooms built into multiunit low-rise cabinas neatly arrayed across grassy lawns. ✉ *325 oeste de la Rodonda de la Bandera Oficentro Holland House, No. 4, San José,* ☎ *679–9444, 283–8901 reservations office in San José;* Ⓕ🅐🅧 *679–9654, 283–8870 in San José. 36 rooms with bath. Restaurant, bar, pool, hot tub, windsurfing. AE, MC, V.*

Outdoor Activities and Sports

WATER SPORTS

The windsurfing **Pro Center** (☎ 679–9444) at Bolaños Bay Resort (☞ Lodging, *above*) is run by friendly, knowledgeable Bjorn Voigt. Charlie at La Cruz–based **Iyok Trips** (☎ 679–9444 at Bolaños Bay Resort, ☞ *above*) offers boat trips around Isla Bolaños, and snorkeling, fishing, and waterskiing trips to Playa Cuajiniquil and other spots in the Golfo de Santa Elena. Charlie promises sightings of nurse sharks, manta rays, and lots of large fish. Iyok's guides also lead horseback riding and mountain-biking tours of the area and know where the monkeys hang out in the woods.

NORTHERN GUANACASTE AND ALAJUELA A TO Z

Arriving and Departing

By Bus

ARENAL AND THE CORDILLERA DE TILARÁN

Buses (**Auto Transportes Ciudad Quesada,** ☎ 255–4318) for Ciudad Quesada leave San José from Calle 16 between Avenidas 1 and 3 daily, every hour from 5 AM to 7:30 PM (3-hr trip). You can continue from Ciudad Quesada to Arenal and Tilarán. Buses (**Transportes Tilaran,** ☎ 222–3854) for Tilarán leave from Calle 14 between Avenidas 9 and 11 daily at 7:30 AM, 9:30 AM, 12:45 PM, 3:45 PM, and 6:30 PM (4-hr trip). You can continue to Nuevo Arenal and Volcán Arenal from Tilarán. Buses (**Transportes Tilaran,** ☎ 222–3854) for Monteverde depart from Calle 12 between Avenidas 7 and 11 weekdays at 6:30 AM and 2:30 PM (4-hr trip).

Buses (**Auto Transportes,** ☎ 460–5032) for Los Chiles (Caño Negro) depart from Calle 12, Avenida 9, daily at 5:30 AM and 3:30 PM. Buses (**Transportes La Canera,** ☎ 221–0953) for Cañas, and the turnoff for Tilarán and Arenal, run daily at 8:30 AM, 10:30 AM, 12:30 PM, 1:20 PM, 2:30 PM, and 4:30 PM from Calle 16, between Avenidas 3 and 5.

FAR NORTHERN GUANACASTE

Buses (**Pulmitan,** ☎ 222–1650) to Liberia (4-hr ride) leave from Calle 14, Avenidas 3 and 4, daily every hour from 6 AM to 8 PM, with direct buses at 3 PM and 5 PM. Friday they leave every hour from 1 PM to 8 PM, and Saturday they leave at 6, 7, 9, 10, and 11:30 AM. Buses (**Transportes La Canera,** ☎ 222–3006) to La Cruz and Peñas Blancas (6-hr trip, passing through Liberia) leave daily at 5 AM, 1:20 PM, and 4:10 PM. Express buses (4½-hr trip) leave from Calle 16, Avenidas 3 and 5, at 4:30 AM and 7 AM. The La Cruz buses pass the Santa Rosa National Park entrance about five hours after leaving San José.

By Car

ARENAL AND THE CORDILLERA DE TILARÁN

Road access to the northwest is by way of the paved two-lane Pan-American Highway (Carretera Interamericana, CA1), which starts from the top of Paseo Colón in San José and runs northwest through Cañas and Liberia and to Peñas Blancas (Nicaraguan Border). The drive to Liberia takes about three to four hours. Turnoffs to Monteverde, Arenal, and other destinations are often poorly marked—drivers must keep their eyes open. The Monteverde turnoff is at Lagarto, about 125 km (78 mi) northwest of San José. The turnoff for Tilarán and the northwestern end of Lake Arenal lies in the town of Cañas. At Liberia, Highway 21 west leads to the beaches of the northern Nicoya Peninsula (☞ Chapter 5). To reach Ciudad Quesada, La Fortuna, and Caño Negro, a picturesque drive (Highway 35) takes you up through the coffee plantations and over the Cordillera Central by way of Sarchí and Zarcero.

FAR NORTHERN GUANACASTE

On the Pan-American Highway (CA1) north of Liberia, the first turn for Rincón de la Vieja is easy to miss. Look for the Guardia Rural station on the right around 5 km (3 mi) north of town; turn inland and head for Curubande. Turnoffs for Parque Nacional Santa Rosa and La Cruz on CA1 are well marked.

By Plane

At press time, various charter companies were flying into Liberia on changing schedules. If your destination lies in Guanacaste, make sure your travel agent investigates the possibility of flying into Liberia instead of San José—you'll save some serious hours on the road. Locally, **Sansa** (⌧ C. 24 between Avdas. Central and 1, San José, ☎ 506/221–9414 or 506/441–8035, ℻ 506/255–2176) and **Travelair** (⌧ Aeropuerto Internacional Tobías Bolaños, Apdo. 8–4920, ☎ 506/220–3054 or 506/232–7883, ℻ 506/220–0413) fly to Liberia from San José daily.

Getting Around

By Bus

ARENAL AND THE CORDILLERA DE TILARÁN

Buses to Ciudad Quesada continue to Tilarán and Arenal (☞ Arriving and Departing, *above*).

FAR NORTHERN GUANACASTE

Buses do not serve Rincón de la Vieja and Guanacaste national parks.

By Car

Four-wheel-drive vehicles are recommended, but not essential, for most roads. The most important thing to know is that short drives can take a long time when the road is potholed or torn up. Plan accordingly. Most minor roads are unpaved and either muddy in rainy season or dusty in dry season. Once you get off the main highways, the pavement holds out only so far, and then dirt, dust, mud, potholes, and other impediments interfere with driving conditions and prolong hours spent behind the wheel. Take a four-wheel-drive vehicle if possible.

ARENAL AND THE CORDILLERA DE TILARÁN

From this easterly zone (La Fortuna), you can head west by way of the road around Lake Arenal. For the newly paved road (Highway 4) that parallels the Nicaraguan border and loops west all the way to La Cruz, follow the signs out of Tanque (east of La Fortuna) northwest to San Rafael de Guatuso, Upala, and Santa Cecilia.

FAR NORTHERN GUANACASTE

The Pan-American Highway (CA1) and other paved roads run to the Nicaraguan border; paved roads run west to the small towns like Filadelfia and La Cruz. The roads into Rincón de la Vieja are unpaved and very slow; figure on an hour from the highway, and be prepared to walk the last half a mile to the Las Pailas entrance. The road into Santa Rosa National Park is smooth going as far as La Casona. Beyond that, it gets dicey and very steep in places. The national park service encourages you to walk, rather than drive, to the beach. A couple of dirt roads lead into various sections of Guanacaste National Park. A four-wheel-drive vehicle is recommended for all of them.

Contacts and Resources

Car Rentals

A few of the high-end resorts on the beach will arrange car rentals. Otherwise, *see* Contacts and Resources *in* San José A to Z *in* Chapter 2 and Nicoya Peninsula A to Z *in* Chapter 5.

Emergencies

Emergencies (☎ 911). **Ambulance** (☎ 221–5818). **Fire** (☎ 118). **Police** (☎ 117 in towns, 127 in rural areas). **Traffic Police** (☎ 227–8030).

Guided Tours

DAY TRIPS

Guanacaste Tours (☎ 666–0306) is recommended for day trips from within the northwest to Santa Rosa and Arenal; you can get transportation from large hotels in the area.

SPECIAL-INTEREST TOURS

Tikal Tours (✉ Avda. 2 between Cs. 7 and 9, Apdo. 6398–1000, San José, ☎ 223–2811) runs highly informative weeklong ecoadventure tours in Carara, Manuel Antonio, Lomas Barbudal reserve, Playa Grande (☞ Chapter 5), Santa Rosa, and Arenal. The excellent **Horizontes** (✉ 150 yards north of Pizza Hut, Paseo Colón, San José, ☎ 222–2022) specializes in more independent tours with as few as eight people, including transport by four-wheel-drive vehicle, naturalist guides, and guest lectures. **Geotur** (☎ 234–1867) operates a three-day horseback exploratory tour of the dry forests around Hacienda Los Inocentes, near Parque Nacional Guanacaste.

Visitor Information

The tourist office in San José (☞ Visitor Information *in* San José A to Z, *in* Chapter 2) has information covering the northwest.

In Liberia, the **Casa de la Cultura** (✉ 3 blocks from Central Plaza, ☎ 666–1606, ☉ Mon.–Sat. 8–4) has local tourist information.

5 NICOYA PENINSULA

On the sun-drenched Nicoya Peninsula, expatriate California surfers wander endless golden beaches, coatimundis caper, monkeys howl in the dry tropical forests, and turtles ride in on the night high tide to lay their eggs on the beaches. All these natural wonders, coupled with a burgeoning number of high-end resorts with golf courses and convention centers, make the Nicoya Peninsula a microcosm of Costa Rica.

Updated by
Justin
Henderson

LIMESTONE CAVERNS, BIRD-FILLED RIVER DELTAS, tracts of wet and dry forest, and miles of palm-flanked beaches are just some of the natural wonders found in the Nicoya Peninsula. Separated from the mainland by the Golfo de Nicoya, the Peninsula de Nicoya, or Nicoya Peninsula, is a roughly thumb-shaped protrusion comprising the southwestern section of Guanacaste, Costa Rica's northwesternmost province. The southern end of the Nicoya Peninsula lies within the Puntarenas province. Averaging just 65 inches of rain per year, the Nicoya Peninsula and much of Guanacaste constitute the country's driest zone.

The Guanacastecos, descendants of the Chorotegan Indians and early Spanish settlers, started many of the traditions that are now referred to as typically Costa Rican, and a strong folkloric character is evident in the region. As you travel through the region, you might notice traditional costumes, folk dancing, music, and recipes handed down from colonial times.

As a travel destination, the Nicoya Peninsula—especially the coastal areas—seems somewhat confused at present: on one hand, politically correct ecotourists and their backpack- and surfboard-toting younger cousins still come in search of environmental enlightenment or good waves; on the other hand, sun- and golf-seekers, content to admire caged toucans in plush hotel lobbies, are lured by azure pools and manicured putting greens bathed in tropical sun. As a result, the area has experienced huge amounts of investment and development, so along with the endless miles of untracked beaches and thousands of acres of unexplored territory, expect some sparkling strands to be backed by sprawling all-inclusive monoliths that come with such opportunism.

Pleasures and Pastimes

Beaches

Although you'll find graceful palms and elegant tamarindo trees lining most beaches, the shrubby dry-forest vegetation of the northwest Guanacaste coast contrasts sharply with the tropical beach backdrops you'll encounter farther south along the peninsula in the Puntarenas province. The great advantage to the peninsula is the climate, which is far drier than the more inland regions and the Caribbean coast during the rainy season. Swimmers, however, should be careful of riptides, which are most frequent at beaches with high waves such as the surfing area at Playa Grande. As a general rule, where you see surfers, beware of riptides.

A couple of strands near Coco, which itself is rather dirty, are worth checking out: Playa Ocotal, in a cove with snorkeling potential and good views, and Playa Hermosa—a curving gray-sand beach hemmed in by rocky outcrops. Playa Pan de Azúcar offers good snorkeling and is deserted, but it's rather stony in the rainy season. Despite a few half-built condos and the Flamingo Beach Hotel, Playa Flamingo is still relatively low-key, and the beach is white and handsome. Playa Brasilito allows you to observe the goings-on of fishing-village life. Playa Conchal is famous for its tiny shells. Playa Grande, a restricted-access (at night) turtle-nesting beach stretching north from Tamarindo for 5 km (3 mi), is safest for swimming, except in the surfing area near the Hotel Las Tortugas. Tamarindo, with a long white strand interrupted by the occasional rock formation, shelters a fleet of fishing and sailing boats on the lee side of Isla Capitán, a few hundred yards offshore. There are several good local beachfront bars in Tamarindo.

Playa Langosta, adjacent to a bird sanctuary, has good surfing waves, nesting turtles at night, and few people. Playa Avellanes offers a half mile of pristine sand, eight good surfing spots, and both a river estuary and a mangrove swamp close at hand for bird-watching. Playa Negra is a mix of short sandy stretches and rocky outcroppings and has some of the best surfing waves in Costa Rica. Playa Junquillal features an un-interrupted 3-km (2-mi) stretch of grayish-white sand with low shore-break waves and very few buildings. Playa Pelada is a perfect jewel of a beach hemmed in by rocks on both sides, great for snorkeling. Nosara has a long beach backed by dense jungle where you might see wildlife. The long, clean, and smooth Playa Guiones has a good beach-break surf-ing wave and a coral reef suitable for snorkeling. Playa Sámara offers some lively stretches near the Sámara community and quieter stretches farther down the beach. Playa Carrillo is on a very picturesque and de-serted half-moon bay. Playa Cabo Blanco, on the southwestern tip of the Nicoya Peninsula, is a pristine jewel reached only by hiking through the Reserva Natural Absoluta Cabo Blanco. Montezuma has several col-orful, shell-strewn beaches, some of them long and some short. Tam-bor, in Bahía Ballena, edges calm swimming waters.

Dining

Seafood is plentiful on the peninsula: *camarones* (shrimp), *langostinos* (a kind of lobster), and a fine variety of fish are available in most restau-rants at reasonable prices, although langostino dinners can get costly. Most of the places serve international as well as local dishes such as the ubiquitous, moderate-priced *casados* (plates of white rice, beans, fried plantains, salad, cheese, and meat), so you can take your pick.

Festivals

Santa Cruz celebrates its patron-saint day on January 15 with marimba music, folk dances, and bullfights. On July 16 you can see a colorful regatta and carnival in Puntarenas in honor of its patron saint. The annexation of Guanacaste is celebrated July 17–25 with folk dances, bullfights, and rodeos in Liberia. The festival of La Yeguita in Nicoya on December 12 features a solemn procession, dancing, fireworks, and bullfights. Almost every small town in Guanacaste has a rodeo fiesta once a year, complete with carnival rides, gaming, and the Costa Rican rodeo version of bullfighting. It's wild! Guanacasteco cowboys ride the bulls, American-rodeo style, while troupes of young men race around the ring, distracting the bulls after they throw the riders, and a couple of cowboys with lariats stand by on horseback to lasso the beasts should they get too ornery. If you're in Guanacaste, be sure to take one in— if you're not too squeamish. Be warned the men do torment the bulls to get them riled up, and that riders get thrown violently and are oc-casionally stomped or gored. Ask around or check posters and you'll probably find one to attend.

Lodging

A good mix of quality hotels, nature lodges, and more basic *cabinas* (cottages) can be found on the Nicoya Peninsula. It is wise to book ahead during the dry season (December–April), especially for week-ends, when Ticos can fill beach hotels to bursting. A number of lux-ury hotels ranging in size have opened along the coast, catering to an upscale clientele.

Spelunking

For the modern-day spelunker, the caves in Parque Nacional Barra Honda offer the opportunity to take a serious plunge into the underworld. Ter-ciopelo Cave, in particular, contains a vast assortment of oddly shaped rock formations; some stretches of the cave system are reputedly un-explored to this day.

Surfing

Costa Rica was "discovered" in the 1960s surf film classic, *The End-less Summer* and revisited in the sequel. But with its miles of coastline punctuated with innumerable points, rock reefs, river-mouth sandbars, and other wave-shaping geological configurations, it comes as no sur-prise that the Nicoya Peninsula is a surfer's paradise of warm water, beautiful beaches, cheap beer, and relatively uncrowded waves. What more could a California boy or girl ask for?

Boca Barranca near Puntarenas—a somewhat dingy mainland town you might check out while waiting for the ferry to the Nicoya Penin-sula's south end—has one of the world's longest lefts, but the water is dangerously polluted with sewage runoff from the nearby river. Tamarindo is a good base for a couple of decent sandbar and rock-reef breaks, a superb low-tide river-mouth break, and the consistently high quality, if at times overcrowded, Playa Grande beach break 5 km (3 mi) up the beach. The best waves at Playa Grande can be found just south of the Hotel Las Tortugas. Inquire at Iguana Surf, the surfboard shop in Tamarindo, to find out where the waves are breaking. Sámara, Giuones, and Nosara have decent beach breaks. Avellanes features a total of eight different surf spots, ranging from beach breaks to rock-reef breaks to river-mouth sandbar breaks. Witches Rock, in the Par-que Nacional Santa Rosa (☞ Chapters 4 and 10), accessible by car only in summer (you can also get there by a 1½-hour boat trip, informally chartered at Playa del Coco or other beaches along the Guanacaste coast), has a right river-mouth, and Ollie's Point, a bit farther north and also reachable primarily by boat, offers excellent right point-break waves. For well-heeled wave riders, there's a good break directly in front of the Hotel Tango Mar. Playa Negra, about a 45-minute dirt-road drive south from Tamarindo, is also gnarly, and its excellent right rock-reef break was showcased in *The Endless Summer II*. Playa Langosta, just south of Tamarindo, has a good river-mouth wave. Malpais, just above Cabo Blanco, is home to some of the largest waves in Costa Rica. At all these spots you should be careful of riptides.

Turtle-Watching

The Nicoya Peninsula provides wonderful opportunities for viewing the nesting rituals of several varieties of sea turtles. The nesting sea-son of the olive ridley turtle runs year-round but peaks from July to October. Leatherbacks arrive from October through April, though nesting is largely over by mid-February. Occasionally, you can see Pa-cific green turtles. Difficult to reach but worth the effort are Playa Nancite in Parque Nacional Santa Rosa (☞ Chapters 4 and 10, *and* Close Up: Tico Turtles *in* Chapter 8) and the Ostional National Wildlife Refuge near Nosara. Both are prime for watching the mass *arribadas,* or nest-ings, of thousands of olive ridley turtles. More accessible are Playas Langosta and Grande—they book-end the resort town of Tamarindo to the south and north, respectively—which provide wonderful op-portunities for viewing the nesting rituals of the enormous, ponder-ous, and yet exquisitely dignified leatherback turtles, who arrive with high tide to dig holes and deposit their eggs. They also show up at Jun-quillal and other beaches.

Word of mouth has it that locals at Junquillal and possibly Langosta are still stealing the eggs like there's an endless supply. You can go on your own to find the Langosta turtles at night from Tamarindo, but you've got to get across the Río San Francisco estuary—not something you should attempt at high tide. On the other hand, Playa Grande's turtle tours, now run by officially sanctioned guides drawn from the local populace, have become very well organized.

In case you want to see the world.

At American Express, we're here to make your journey a smooth one. So we have over 1,700 travel service locations in over 130 countries ready to help. What else would you expect from the world's largest travel agency?

do more

Travel

In case you want to be welcomed there.

We're here to see that you're always welcomed at establishments everywhere. That's why millions of people carry the American Express® Card – for peace of mind, confidence, and security, around the world or just around the corner.

do more **AMERICAN EXPRESS**

Cards

In case you're running low.

We're here to help with more than 190,000 Express Cash locations around the world. In order to enroll, just call American Express at 1 800 CASH-NOW before you start your vacation.

do more

Express Cash

And in case you'd rather be safe than sorry.

We're here with American Express® Travelers Cheques. They're the safe way to carry money on your vacation, because if they're ever lost or stolen you can get a refund, practically anywhere or anytime. To find the nearest place to buy Travelers Cheques, call 1 800 495-1153. Another way we help you do more.

do more AMERICAN EXPRESS

Travelers Cheques

It can get crowded (though the guides at the Playa Grande park entrance take people out in groups, and recent rule changes may severely limit the nightly numbers), and you have to stay up very late, but many find the arrival and egg-laying ritual of the leatherback mothers a singularly moving event. Others find the appearance of the babies, or hatchlings, even more interesting, and you can see them during the day. Just walk down Playa Grande at dawn, two to three months after the commencement of the egg-laying season, and the hatchlings just might be making their amazing emergence from the sand. If you're like most ecotourists, you'll want to spend some time with them, shepherding the tiny creatures on their arduous, dangerous journey from the nest to the sea. If you don't perform this protective function, chances are you'll be watching a less pleasant slice of life in the natural world, as a predatory frigate bird scoops your hatchling from the sand and eats it for breakfast.

If you do want to watch the turtles, do it with a legitimate guide, and follow the rules. It may be frustrating to experience this natural phenomenon while governed by such unnatural rules, but they are critical for the health of the turtles. You'd be better off not trying to watch the turtles the week between Christmas and New Year's, when the crowds get very heavy.

Exploring the Nicoya Peninsula

Bear in mind that aside from the Carretera Interamericana (Pan-American Highway, CA1), many of the roads in the region are of the pitted, pocked, and rock-and-dirt variety, with the occasional river rushing over, rather than under, the pavement. As a result, covering seemingly short distances can require long hours behind the wheel, and a four-wheel-drive vehicle is often essential. For this reason, we highly recommend flying, when possible and affordable, if any of the beach resorts you plan to visit have nearby airstrips, such as Tamarindo, Carrillo, and Tambor. Many northern beach resorts can be most easily reached from Liberia, where an international airport has been operational for a couple of years.

Numbers in the text correspond to numbers in the margin and on the Nicoya Peninsula map.

Great Itineraries

The ideal Nicoya Peninsula itinerary can be comfortably divided between spending lazy days on the beach, swimming in the surf, and hiking and leisurely exploring a number of appealing and unusual sights—caverns, forests, rivers, and estuaries. The beach towns and resorts can be clustered into three loose geographical groups based, in part, on location and, in part, on the routes you must take to reach them: those on the south end of the Nicoya Peninsula, accessible by ferry from Puntarenas or by plane to Tambor; areas in the central Nicoya Peninsula, reachable by plane to Punta Islita, Carrillo, and Nosara, or by car via the Tempisque Ferry and the roads through Carmona, Curime, and Nicoya; and towns in the northern Nicoya Peninsula, accessible by plane to Tamarindo or Liberia, or by car through Liberia and Comunidad. These three loose clusters of beach towns have a lot in common, but there are distinct differences as well: if your time is limited and you have to make a choice, consider whether you want, for example, lively surf or calm waters; turtle-watching options at night; an isolated resort or a more active beach town.

IF YOU HAVE 3–5 DAYS
Fly to ✈ **Tambor** ④, ✈ **Punta Islita** ⑫, ✈ **Playa Carrillo** ⑬, ✈ **Nosara** ⑯, or ✈ **Tamarindo** ㉘ for a three-night stay at one of the dozens of beach

Nicoya Peninsula

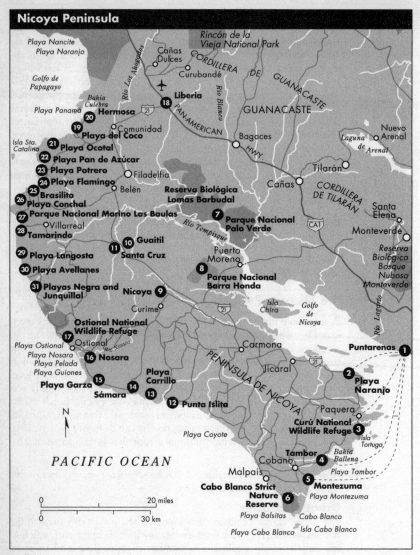

Playa Nancite
Playa Naranjo

Golfo de
Papagayo

Bahía
Culebra
Playa Panama

20 Hermosa

19 Playa del Coco   Comunidad

Isla Sta.
Catalina   **21 Playa Ocotal**

22 Playa Pan de Azúcar

23 Playa Potrero

24 Playa Flamingo   Filadelfia

25 Brasilito   Belén

26 Playa Conchal

27 Parque Nacional Marino Las Baulas

28 Tamarindo   Villarreal

29 Playa Langosta

30 Playa Avellanes

31 Playas Negra and   **Nicoya 9**
Junquillal

Ostional National
Wildlife Refuge   **17**   Ostional   Curime
Playa Ostional
Playa Nosara   **16 Nosara**
Playa Pelada
Playa Guiones

Playa Garza   **15**
Sámara   **14**

Playa
Carrillo   **13**

12 Punta Islita

N

PACIFIC OCEAN

0   20 miles
0   30 km

Cañas
Dulces
Curubandé

Rincón de la
Vieja National Park

CORDILLERA   DE   GUANACASTE

18 Liberia

GUANACASTE

Bagaces

Nuevo
Arenal

Laguna
de Arenal

Tilarán

Cañas

CORDILLERA
DE TILARÁN

Santa
Elena

Monteverde

Reserva
Biológica
Bosque
Nuboso
Monteverde

Reserva Biológica
Lomas Barbudal

7 Parque Nacional
Palo Verde

Puerto
Moreno

8 Parque Nacional
Barra Honda

Isla
Chira

Golfo
de
Nicoya

10 Guaitil

11 Santa Cruz

Carmona

PENINSULA DE NICOYA

Jicaral

Puntarenas 1

2
Playa
Naranjo

Paquera

Curú National
Wildlife Refuge 3

Isla
Tortuga

Tambor 4   Bahía
Ballena   Playa Tambor

Malpais
Cobano   **5 Montezuma**
Playa Montezuma

Cabo Blanco Strict
Nature   **6**
Reserve

Playa Balsitas   Cabo Blanco

Playa Cabo Blanco   Isla Cabo Blanco

Playa Coyote

resorts on the Nicoya Peninsula. If you stay in Tambor or ⊞ **Montezuma** ⑤, a short drive will take you to Cabo Blanco, where you can
hike the trail through the **Cabo Blanco Strict Nature Reserve** ⑥ to deserted Playa Cabo Blanco, diving and frolicking grounds of hundreds
of pelicans. You can also visit the ⊞ **Curú National Wildlife Refuge** ③.
Surfers can hit the waves at Tango Mar Hotel (if you are a hotel guest)
or at Malpais, just north of Cabo Blanco, which reputedly has the largest
surfing waves in Costa Rica. To extend this itinerary to five days, head
to ⊞ **Playa Naranjo** ②, near Naranjo, and book a two- or three-day
sea-kayaking adventure at the Hotel Oasis del Pacific or just settle into
a hotel for a couple days of relaxation.

If you choose one of the central Nicoya beaches as a base, from the
Nosara area you can spend a day hiking, bird-watching, or spelunking at **Parque Nacional Palo Verde** ⑦ or **Parque Nacional Barra Honda** ⑧; on your second day visit **Guaitil** ⑩ and **Santa Cruz** ⑪ for pottery
shopping. If lounging on the sand isn't enough, if it's the right season

(July–October) you can stay up late to watch the arribada of the olive ridley turtles at **Ostional National Wildlife Refuge** ⑰.

A third option for a short visit to Nicoya is to come from Liberia, the hub to the north; spend anywhere from three to five nights at one or more of the beaches between ⌖ **Tamarindo** ㉘ and ⌖ **Hermosa** ⑳. In season, you can also watch the leatherback turtles come in at night at **Parque Nacional Marino Las Baulas** ㉗. For dedicated surfers, ⌖ **Playa Negra** ㉛ and ⌖ **Playa Avellanes** ㉚ offer great access to excellent surfing waves and many other recreational activities—just pick your spots.

IF YOU HAVE 7 DAYS

Take the ferry from ⌖ **Puntarenas** ① to ⌖ **Playa Naranjo** ② and head to ⌖ **Curú National Wildlife Refuge** ③, spending the nights in ⌖ **Tambor** ④ or ⌖ **Montezuma** ⑤. During the day, you can take hikes, bird- and animal-watch, and swim in the lazy, sheltered waters of the southern Nicoya Peninsula. Alternatively, stay in ⌖ **Playa Naranjo** ② and spend a day or even two sea kayaking among the many ruggedly beautiful islands in the Golfo de Nicoya. Then take Highway 21 north and swing east to Puerto Moreno to catch the Río Tempisque ferry and do some bird-watching on the river or in **Parque Nacional Palo Verde** ⑦; then spend a day hiking and spelunking in **Parque Nacional Barra Honda** ⑧. Continue on through **Nicoya** ⑨ and **Santa Cruz** ⑪ and overnight in ⌖ **Tamarindo** ㉘ or at one of the beach resorts to the north. Spend several days relaxing on the beach or exploring the Tamarindo and Río San Francisco estuaries north and south of Tamarindo, with nights watching turtles at **Parque Nacional Marino Las Baulas** ㉗ (in season only); then head back to the highway via ⌖ **Liberia** ⑱.

When to Tour the Nicoya Peninsula

Although the dry season from December to April is considered the best time to visit Costa Rica, the northwest, especially the Nicoya Peninsula, is actually most appealing in the rainy season (except for the *really* wet months of September and October). The Guanacastecos have renamed the rainy season the "green" season, and that it is: the countryside—tending toward brown and arid in the dry season—blooms lush and green from a couple of hours of rain each day (it's warm and sunny before and after the rain). The roads are muddy, but there are far fewer tourists, and prices go down everywhere. For turtle-watching, you have to go during the dry season, but for most other activities in the northwest, you can go at almost any time of year. A good bet would be to travel in November or April to May, around the edges of the dry season.

PUNTARENAS TO CABO BLANCO

Catch a ferry from Puntarenas to the southern tip of the Nicoya Peninsula and you'll be strokes away from gorgeous beaches—including Cocal, Cocalito, and Quizales—with waterfalls and tidal pools galore. The region contains two well-preserved and undervisited national parks where you can explore caves and pristine forests, or travel by boat or sea kayak to remote islands and wildlife preserves for bird-watching, snorkeling, diving, and camping. Not too remote, and thus at times somewhat overcrowded, is Isla Tortuga, ringed by some of the most beautiful beaches in all of Costa Rica. If you like to mix nightlife with your outdoor experiences, the town of Montezuma and its nearby beaches are frequently jammed with an international cast of hippies, mystics, musicians, and misfits of all sorts, from German boys in leather pants to Swedish girls in nothing at all. (One wise guy has called it a gathering place for the "toxic youth of Europe.")

Puntarenas

❶ *95 km (59 mi) west of San José.*

Five kilometers (3 mi) beyond Esparza, a popular truck stop about 90 km (56 mi) northwest of San José on the Pan-American Highway, is the turnoff to Puntarenas. As its name implies, this erstwhile coffee-shipping port is on a narrow spit of sand protruding into the Gulf of Nicoya with splendid views across to the peninsula. Most tourists stop here only on the way by ferry to Playa Naranjo, Paquera, and Montezuma (pedestrians only) on the Nicoya Peninsula. The boardwalk is pleasant in a honky-tonk kind of way, but this downtrodden town suffers from rising crime and polluted water and is not worth a special trip. Grid-plan streets are lined with restaurants and markets, and the southern palm-lined promenade is popular with day-trippers from San José, although the Ministry of Health warns against swimming here. On Saturday night the massive influx of weekenders from San José presents a golden opportunity to watch the Costa Rican middle class at play. In summer the series of theater, music, and dance performances at the **Casa de la Cultura** (✉ 3 blocks from Parque Central, ☏ 666–1606) can be fun.

The murky estuary to the north is fringed with mangroves; at its western end pelicans cast a watchful eye from the treetops over the Nicoya ferries, really the sole purpose of making your way through this run-down port town that doesn't warrant an overnight. **Caldera,** 10 km (6 mi) southeast, has a modern harbor where cruise ships dock.

OFF THE
BEATEN PATH

ISLA TORTUGA – Soft, bleached sand and casually leaning palms fringe Isla Tortuga, an island of tropical dry forest that makes for a perfect day trip from Puntarenas, Montezuma, and other beach towns. Though state-owned, the island is leased and inhabited by a Costa Rican family that privately funded efforts to reintroduce such species such as deer and wild pig to the island some years ago. A 40-minute hiking trail wanders past monkey ladders, strangler figs, bromeliads, orchids, and the fruit-bearing *guanabana* (soursop) and *marañón* (cashew) trees, and goes up to a lookout point with tantalizing vistas. A short canopy tour has been set up on the beach. For information on getting to the island, *see* Guided Tours *in* Nicoya Peninsula A to Z, *below*). ✏ *Hike $5; canopy tour $10.*

Dining and Lodging

$$–$$$ ✕ **La Caravelle.** The red-patterned tablecloths and dark blue walls adorned with antique musical instruments create a chic ambience in this unexpectedly elegant French restaurant opposite the sea. The cooking concentrates on sauces: try the corvina *al gratin con hongos* (with a white wine sauce and mushrooms) or fillet *con salsa oporto y hongos* (with port and mushroom sauce). If you want to accompany this with claret, prepare to dig deep into your pocket. ✉ *Paseo de los Turistas,* ☏ 661–2262. *MC, V. Closed Mon.–Tues.*

$$–$$$ ☷ **Hotel Las Brisas.** A white, two-story, motel-style building wraps around the pool of this hotel in the west end of town, where the views of the sun setting over the Nicoya Peninsula are terrific. The hotel is across the street from the beach and not far from the ferry docks. The restaurant serves decent Greek-influenced seafood and meats. The fluorescent lighting in the open-air dining room could be improved. ✉ *Paseo de los Turistas, Puntarenas,* ☏ 661–4040, 🖷 661–2120. *19 rooms with bath. Restaurant, pool. MC, V.*

$$ ☷ **Hotel Porto Bello.** Porto Bello's main asset is its thickly planted garden next to the wide estuary north of town. Bedrooms are housed in

white stucco bungalow units with tile floors, zanily patterned bedspreads, air-conditioning, TVs, and verandas. ☒ *Apdo. 108, Puntarenas, 2 km (1½ mi) from downtown, 1 block north of main road,* ☎ *661–1322,* FAX *661–0036. 35 rooms with bath. Restaurant, bar, air-conditioning, pool. AE, MC, V.*

$$ ☷ **Hotel Tioga.** The blue-and-white courtyard in this central hotel has
★ the look of an ocean liner. The best guest rooms are upstairs overlooking the gulf, have air-conditioning, tile floors, quilted pink bedspreads, floral pastel curtains, and functional 1970s furniture. There is a tiny pool in the courtyard with a palm tree growing from the islet in its center. ☒ *Paseo de los Turistas, Apdo. 96, Puntarenas,* ☎ *661–0271,* FAX *661–0127. 46 rooms with bath. Bar, cafeteria, air-conditioning, pool. AE, MC, V.*

Playa Naranjo

❷ *1½–2 hrs by ferry southwest of Puntarenas.*

Accessible by ferry from Puntarenas or by car from Nicoya, Playa Naranjo has a reputation as a kind of nowheresville en route from Puntarenas to Montezuma and points west that is undeserved. This is the best access point to the islands in the Golfo de Nicoya. There is also wonderful hiking, mountain biking, and sea kayaking in the area.

En Route If you're driving on the tip of the peninsula, be prepared to spend some hours at the wheel. The road to the southern tip of the peninsula is partly paved, partly gravel, and it winds up and down and around various bays. Much of the countryside is still wild and wooded, although some has been turned into fruit farms or cattle pasture. Paquera, 45 minutes southeast of Playa Naranjo, is the closest town with shops and bars and is also linked to Puntarenas by ferry. Heading north toward Nicoya, the road from Playa Naranjo (Highway 21) is paved though rather badly potholed almost all the way.

Lodging

$$–$$$ ☷ **Hotel Oasis del Pacific.** The enticing pier and coconut palms of the Oasis del Pacific's 12 roomy acres of waterfront are in the last cove on the left as you approach the Playa Naranjo ferry dock. Run by former ship's captain Lucky Wilhelm and his wife, Aggie, the hotel itself is a tad run-down and frayed around the edges, but it won't matter when you're lazing in your hammock, catching the afternoon breeze off the gulf. The indoor-outdoor restaurant-bar does a fine job with all three meals (not included in price). Fishing charters, sailing, horseback riding, and hiking trips can be arranged. The hotel also offers sea-kayaking trips along the coast and among the islands in the Golfo de Nicoya. ☒ *Apdo. 200–5400, Puntarenas,* ☎ FAX *661–1555;* ☒ *P.l. Wilhelm 1552, Box 025216, Miami, FL 33102-5216. 36 rooms with bath. Restaurant, bar, pool, beach, dock, boating. AE, MC, V.*

Outdoor Activities and Sports

Ranging in length from one day up to seven or more, sea-kayaking trips from a base near the ferry dock at Playa Naranjo can take you along the coast and among the islands of the Golfo de Nicoya. These outings offer kayakers of every level of experience a chance to visit wild islands, remote fishing villages, wildlife reserves, national parks, and more. Some of the more pristine islands include San Lucas, with its fascinating history as a penal island; and Negritos, Guayabo, Venado, and Chira islands, home to isolated fishing villages or wildlife refuges. You can book kayak trips through the Hotel Oasis del Pacific (☞ *above*).

Curú National Wildlife Refuge

❸ *7 km (4½ mi) south of Paquera.*

South of the ferry dock at Paquera is the private Curú National Wildlife Refuge (Refugio Nacional de Vida Silvestre Curú), established by Federico Schutt in 1933 and given an indigenous name for the *pochote* and *guanacaste* trees, both native species. Trails lead through the forest and high salinity mangroves, where you'll find hordes of phantom crabs on the beach, howler and white-faced monkeys readily visible in the banana trees, and plenty of bird-watching for hummingbirds, kingfishers, woodpeckers, trogons, and manakins (including the coveted long-tailed), to name a few. The refuge is working to reintroduce spider monkeys and scarlet macaws back into the wild. Some very basic accommodations, originally designed for students and researchers, are available by the beach. Call ahead to arrange lodging, guides, and early bird-watching walks. Take a passenger boat or ferry from Puntarenas to Paquera, where you can catch a bus to the refuge. *Schutt family, Curú, Paquera, 5370 Puntarenas,* ☎ *710–8097.* ✉ *$5; lodging $25 per person, including 3 meals and admission.* ☉ *Daily 7–4.*

Tambor

❹ *20 km (14 mi) south of Curú National Wildlife Refuge, 27 km (17 mi) south of Paquera.*

The next village you reach after Curú is Tambor, nestled in the back of the large half-moon Bahía Ballena. This area is undergoing a land-sale frenzy similar to that at Tamarindo. A golf course and housing development are visible from the road, and signs of further development are everywhere. You can hike from Tambor around the Piedra Amarilla point to Tango Mar resort (☞ Lodging, *below*), about an 8-km (5-mi) trek. The trees nearby resound with the throaty utterings of male howler monkeys. Tambor can also be reached by plane from San José.

Lodging

$$$$
★   **Tambor Tropical.** This collection of five cabinas, with two units per building, surrounds a pool in the palm trees off Playa Tambor in Bahía Ballena. The place is remarkable for the buildings themselves: using local hardwoods, the builders have outdone themselves with exquisitely wrought details. Each comfortable and spacious 1,000-sq-ft unit contains a living room, bedroom, hot-water bathroom, and a fully equipped kitchen. ✉ *Follow main street of Tambor toward water; hotel fronts beach,* ☎ *683–0011,* 🅵🅰🆇 *683–0013;* ✉ *867 Liberty St. NE (P.O. Box 12945), Salem, OR 97301,* ☎ *503/365–2872,* 🅵🅰🆇 *503/371–2471. 10 cabinas. Restaurant, bar, kitchenettes, pool, hot tub. AE, MC, V.*

$$$$
★ **Tango Mar.** At this fine resort, choose between rustic palm-thatch cabins on stilts or rooms in the main hotel. The former are much more interesting; some have fully equipped kitchens, and all are wood-paneled and come with fans and air-conditioning. Those in the main hotel are luxurious by conventional standards but largely uninspired, and all have balconies and excellent sea views. The restaurant serves international cuisine. On the grounds are a spring-fed pool sculpted from rock and an immaculate nine-hole golf course. A good surfing wave fronts the hotel. ✉ *Apdo. 3877–1000, San José, 2 km (1 mi) west of Tambor,* ☎ *683–0002 or 222–3503 reservations office in San José,* 🅵🅰🆇 *683–0003. 6 villas with bath, 20 rooms with bath, 12 suites. Restaurant, 2 bars, air-conditioning, pool, 9-hole golf course, 2 tennis courts, hiking, horseback riding, surfing, boating, waterskiing, fishing. AE, DC, MC, V.*

En Route   As you continue past the turn to Tango Mar resort, Cobano is the next real village, a collection of wooden bungalows straddling a crossroads and offering the conveniences of a bank, gas station, and a group of cabinas for rent. The road to Malpais and the other remote southern Nicoya beaches runs west from here. Or turn left (heading southeast) toward Montezuma and Cabo Blanco, and bear in mind that the final unpaved hill down to Montezuma is extremely steep and shouldn't be attempted in a non-four-wheel-drive vehicle if the hill is wet.

Montezuma

❺ *7 km (4½ mi) southeast of Cobano, 45 km (28 mi) south of Paquera.*

Montezuma is beautifully positioned on a sandy bay, hemmed in by a precipitous wooded bank. At the bottom of the hill, the grubby but quaintly colorful town "center" consists of an oft-muddy crossroads with several shops, restaurants, bars, and hotels offering their assorted diversions. Postpunk hipsters and other wannabe bohemians seem to make this their first destination after touching down in San José, and if you don't mind entering the odd conversation on such Mother Jones–related subjects as yogurt and cheap deals, this is an entertaining place to be. But Montezuma is on the international vagabond circuit these days, and its hippy dippy aura has taken on a distinctly seedy quality, although the beaches remain gorgeous. In 1995, hotel owners in Montezuma banded together to form the **Cámara de Turismo de Montezuma** (CATUMA), an organization dedicated to cleaning up and improving the area. Meanwhile, the atmosphere feels ripe for intrigue, and the swinging bars resound—often, unfortunately, late into the night—with tunes from '60s to the early '80s. Just over a bridge 900 ft south, a path leads upstream to a 100-ft **waterfall**, a good swimming spot but overcrowded at times.

Lodging

$$$ **🏨 Cabinas El Sano Banano.** The restaurant at this bungalow colony
★ serves creative dishes and is a good place to get acquainted with the town's vaguely hippie atmosphere. The owners have built several cabinas and some funky domed bungalows (sleeping four) in the woods near the beach about a 10-minute walk from town. Some bungalows have kitchen facilities. If you don't care to cook, stop by the unpretentious vegetarian restaurant for the eggplant Parmesan with mashed potatoes. ⊠ *Montezuma, main road,* ☎ ℻ *642–0068. 3 rooms with bath, 8 bungalows. Restaurant. AE, MC, V.*

$$–$$$ **🏨 Hotel Amor de Mar.** Take the time to walk 10 minutes out of "town"
★ to find this ruggedly handsome, two-story natural wood hotel surrounded by trees and a grassy lawn stretching to the sea. Great breakfasts, a natural sea-fed pool, and immediate access to the waterfall hike make this perhaps the finest little hotel in Montezuma. Rooms are comfortable and simply furnished, with wood paneling. The dining room serves breakfast and lunch only. ⊠ *South of town on beach road,* ☎ *642–0262. 11 rooms without bath. Dining room, pool. MC, V.*

$$ **🏨 Cabinas Mar y Cielo.** The advantage of this pleasant old two-story wooden house is its quiet location—still on the beach, but far from the boisterous bars. The rooms are rather small but clean and cozy. The restaurant serves basic budget fare—casados and the like—with an emphasis on fresh seafood. Book ahead. ⊠ *Puntarenas, 43 yards from town center,* ☎ ℻ *642–0036. 6 rooms with bath. Restaurant, bar. AE, MC, V.*

En Route   The 40- to 60-minute drive from Montezuma to Cabo Blanco is on a rough road that fords two streams on the way. If traveling in the rainy season, take a four-wheel-drive vehicle.

Cabo Blanco Strict Nature Reserve

❻ *10 km (6 mi) southwest of Montezuma, 55 km (43 mi) south of Paquera.*

Conquistadors named this area Cabo Blanco on account of its white earth and cliffs, but it was a more benevolent pair of foreigners who bestowed the other half of Cabo Blanco's name. The Cabo Blanco Strict Nature Reserve (Reserva Natural Absoluta Cabo Blanco) covers 12 sq km (4½ sq mi) in all and was created by the pioneering efforts of Nils Olof Wessberg and his wife, Karen, who arrived here from Sweden in 1950. Appalled by the first clear-cut in the Cabo Blanco area in 1960, they launched an international appeal to save the forest. In time their efforts and those of their supporters not only led to the creation of the reserve in 1963 but also to the founding of Costa Rica's national parks service. Olof Wessberg was murdered on the Osa Peninsula in 1975 while researching the area's potential as a national park.

The Cabo Blanco reserve receives more rainfall than other parts of the peninsula, and hence the vegetation is properly described as tropical moist forest; there are more evergreen species here than in the sparsely vegetated Santa Rosa (☞ Chapters 4 and 10), and it is generally lusher. The most abundant trees are strawberry, *apamate*, brazilwood, cow tree, *capulen, pochote*, and *sapodilla*. Sapodillas produce a white latex used to make gum; you will often see V-shape scars where they have been cut to allow the latex to run into containers placed at the base. The wildlife is quite diverse considering the comparatively small size of the reserve. Olof Wessberg cataloged a full array of animals here: porcupine, hog-nosed skunk, spotted skunk, gray fox, anteater, cougar, and jaguar. Resident birds include coastal pelicans, white-throated magpies, toucans, cattle egrets, green herons, parrots, and turquoise-browed motmots. A fairly strenuous 4-km (2½-mi) hike follows a trail from the reserve entrance to **Playa Cabo Blanco** and takes two hours in each direction. The beach is magnificent, with hundreds of pelicans flying in formation, dive-bombing for fish, and paddling in the calm waters offshore. You can wade right in and join them. Trickling down a cliff behind the beach is a stream of potable water. Off the tip of the cape is the 7,511-sq-ft **Isla Cabo Blanco,** with pelicans, frigate birds, brown boobies, and an abandoned lighthouse. As a strict reserve, Cabo Blanco has no tourist facilities, although rangers will act as guides if you turn up. ▨ *$6.* ⊘ *Daily 8–4.*

NICOYA AND THE TEMPISQUE RIVER DELTA REGION

This northerneastern corner of the peninsula encompasses the parks in and around the Río Tempisque basin—prime spots for viewing birds and other wildlife—and Nicoya, the commercial and political hub of the northern Nicoya Peninsula. Besides providing the best access to the central Nicoya beach towns, Nicoya is also linked by a smooth, well-paved road to the artisan communities of Santa Cruz and Guaitil, to the northern Nicoya beach towns, and to Playa Naranjo and the southern Nicoya Peninsula by way of Carmona.

Parque Nacional Palo Verde and Reserva Biológica Lomas Barbudal

❼ *Palo Verde: 28 km (17 mi) southwest of Bagaces; Lomas Barbudal: 20 km (12 mi) southwest of Bagaces.*

Bordered in the west by the meandering Río Tempisque, the territories in Parque Nacional Palo Verde (Palo Verde National Park) and

Reserva Biológica Lomas Barbudal (Lomas Barbudal Biological Reserve) extend over 95 sq km (36½ sq mi) of mainly flat terrain (☞ also Chapter 10). Migrating herons, egrets, ducks, and grebes rest up on the Tempisque's abandoned oxbow lakes and lagoons. Camping is allowed in both parks; meals and lodging are available by request at Palo Verde. ☎ 671–1062. ✉ $6 each park. ◷ Daily 8–4.

Lodging is also available at the **Organization for Tropical Studies** station (☎ 240–6696, ℻ 240–6783 reservations office in San José).

From Puerto Moreno, you can hire a motorboat to take you north up the river into the Palo Verde National Park. This way you'll get a closer look at **Isla Pajaros** (Bird Island), home to thousands of birds from January to March. Boats are to the right of the ferry dock as you disembark. The trip takes roughly 45 to 60 minutes. The price is negotiable but will probably be high, in the range of $50. However, along with spotting the birds on the island, you may see alligators, howler monkeys, and other wildlife on the way. Bring something soft to put on your plank seat and something waterproof to wear—these are small fishing boats, not tour boats, and the river ride can be windy, bumpy, and wet.

There are two ways to reach the parks near the Río Tempisque: on the Río Tempisque passenger and car ferry or by car from farther north. For the ferry, heading north from San José on the Pan-American Highway, turn left about 48 km (30 mi) north of the Puntarenas turnoff and drive 25 km (16 mi) to the ferry, which takes you across to Puerto Moreno. Note that the ferry gets extremely crowded during high season, and a wait of several hours is possible. The second option is to continue north another 42 km (26 mi) on the Pan-American Highway and make a left at the gas station in Bagaces, 15 km (9 mi) north of Cañas, which will lead you after 15 km (9 mi) to the Reserva Biológica Lomas Barbudal and after 35 km (22 mi) to the adjacent Palo Verde National Park.

Outdoor Activities and Sports

CATA Tours (☎ 221–5455 or 690–1203) offers wildlife and bird-watching boating adventures down the Río Bebedero into Palo Verde from a starting point on the Pan-American Highway north of Cañas. **Safaris Corobicí**'s (☎ ℻ 669–1091) low-action adventure trips on the Río Corobicí cover some of the same wildlife-rich territory not far from Palo Verde and Lomas Barbudal (follow signs from highway).

Parque Nacional Barra Honda

8   *6 km (4 mi) west of Puerto Moreno.*

Parque Nacional Barra Honda (Barra Honda National Park; ☞ also Chapter 10) covers almost 23 sq km (9 sq mi) north of the road that runs between the Nicoya–Carmona highway and Tempisque ferry. The limestone ridge that rises from the surrounding savanna was once thought to be a volcano but was later found to contain an intricate network of caves, formed as a result of erosion once the ridge had emerged from beneath the sea. Some caves remain unexplored, and surprisingly abundant animal life exists in them, including bats, birds, blindfish, salamanders, snails, and rats. ☎ 671–1062 or 233–5284. ✉ $6. ◷ Daily 8–4.

In the dry season, with a week's notice, rangers will take you down a 60-ft steel ladder to the **Terciopelo Cave,** which shelters unusual formations shaped like fried eggs, popcorn, and shark's teeth, and sonorous columns collectively known as the organ. Travel companies no longer take tourists or speleologists deeper underground, but local groups reportedly have organized tours into the caves. Check with park guards to verify safety standards before taking a trip, and don't attempt to visit the caves on your own unless accompanied by a park guard.

Barra Honda peak (1,082 ft) can be climbed from the northwest (the southern wall is almost vertical): follow in sequence the Ojoche, Trampa, and Terciopelo trails. From the summit plateau there are fantastic views over the islet-studded Golfo de Nicoya; the plateau surface is pocked with orifices and white rocks eroded into odd shapes, and some of the ground feels dangerously hollow. Surface wildlife includes howler monkeys, skunks, coatis, parakeets, and iguanas. The relatively open, deciduous-forest vegetation makes viewing the fauna easy. The park has camping facilities.

Nicoya

❾ *30 km (19 mi) west of Puerto Moreno.*

Nicoya, although often referred to as Guanacaste's colonial capital, is a typical provincial town, not really worth visiting unless you want a taste of everyday life. The Chorotegan chief Nicoya greeted the Spanish conquistadors upon their arrival here in 1523, and many of his people were converted to Catholicism. These days the culture and traditions of the Chorotegans are being emphatically revived. A Chinese population, descendants of 19th-century railroad workers, gives the place a certain cosmopolitan feel, as evidenced by the numerous Chinese restaurants in town. Its only colonial landmark is the whitewashed 16th-century **San Blas** church in the central square; a museum displays silver, bronze, and copper objects dating from pre-Columbian times.

Lodging

$ 🏨 **Hotel Jenny.** If you do need to stay in Nicoya, choose this hotel— it's a bit sterile, but adequate. The rooms have white walls, wooden beds, tile floors, and reasonable rates. ⊠ *South of main square,* ☎ *685–5050,* 🅵🅰🆇 *686–6874. 24 rooms with bath. No credit cards.*

Guaitil

❿ *24 km (15 mi) north of Nicoya.*

Near the town of Santa Bárbara (look for the left-hand turn just south of Santa Cruz) is the sleepy country village of Guaitil. Artists here, most of them women in this matriarchal indigenous culture, have rescued a vanishing tradition by producing clay pottery handmade in the manner of pre-Columbian Chorotegans. The town square is a soccer field, and almost every house facing the square has a pottery shop in the front and a round, wood-fired kiln in the back. The designs range from imitation Mexican to inspired Picasso-like abstractions. Every artisan's style is different, so take the time to wander from shop to shop. The prices are very reasonable, and though the pieces are rumored to crack rather too easily, if you get one home in one piece it'll be a wonderful keepsake or gift.

Santa Cruz

⓫ *14 km (9 mi) west of Guatil, 20 km (13 mi) north of Nicoya.*

The National Folklore City of Santa Cruz is dedicated to preserving Guanacaste's rich traditions and customs. Music and dance programs are still held in town despite a fire that destroyed much of the town's center and the popular Casa de la Cultura. From a resort-oriented point of view, Santa Cruz isn't very exciting, but it's a lively town with a bustling commercial center where you can get a feeling for the daily life of the Guanacastecans.

Dining

$–$$ ✕ **Coope-Tortillas.** Founded by a local women's cooperative to help create jobs, Coope-Tortillas has enjoyed resounding success. Watch tortillas baked the old-fashioned way—on thick, round plates on an open fire—by chatty women in pink uniforms. Family-style meals are served at a picnic table in a long, high-ceilinged corrugated metal building that once served as an electricity-generating plant. This is one of the few places around that still serves traditional Guanacasteco foods: try the absolutely delicious *arroz de maíz* (a kind of corn stew). This place isn't that easy to find; go straight through the business district, past the plaza, and look for the peaked-roof metal structure. ✉ *Near the central plaza,* ☎ *no phone.* ◷ *Daily 5* AM–7 PM. *No credit cards.*

CENTRAL NICOYA BEACHES: PUNTA ISLITA TO NOSARA

Strung along the coast of the Nicoya Peninsula are sparkling sand beaches lined with laid-back fishing communities along with hotels and resorts in every price category. Don't be in a rush to get anywhere; take life one hour at a time, and you'll soon be as mellow as the locals. Bus service connects the larger cities to each other and to the more popular beaches, but forget about catching a bus from beach to beach; you'll have to backtrack to the inland hubs of Nicoya, Carmona, or Santa Cruz. The road that leads southwest from Nicoya via Curime continues to Sámara, Nosara, Carrillo, Guiones, Punta Islita, and Ostional; it's smoothly paved all the way to the beach at Sámara, except for a 100-yard stretch near Curime. However, the dirt roads between the beach towns are subject to washouts and are often passable only by four-wheel-drive vehicle. You literally have to drive through two rivers, for example, to get from Sámara north to Garza and Nosara (consider renting a four-wheel drive vehicle, especially for Nosara). There are airstrips at Carrillo and Nosara, so flying in from San José is worth considering.

Punta Islita

⓬ *8 km (5 mi) south of Carrillo.*

Hidden in a slender cove, Islita beach is rather rocky, but there is good snorkeling near the point. The only hotel in the area, the intimate, luxurious Hotel Punta Islita, has a private dry-forest nature preserve threaded with well-made trails.

Lodging

$$$$ 🏨 **Hotel Punta Islita.** This secluded inn overlooking the Pacific south
★ of Carrillo and Sámara may be Guanacaste's best. Adobe-style bungalows with barrel-tile roofs and clay-color walls surround the main building, where a massive thatched dome rises over the open-air restaurant. The hotel's French chef turns fresh seafood into inventive daily specials, and both the bar and restaurant open onto a blue-tile pool. The rustic bungalows have private porches and are complete with hammock, big windows, red-tile floors, and rough-hewn wooden bedposts (plus TVs and hair dryers). Suites have private hot tubs and interior gardens. Boat tours to nearby beaches are available. Since the "road" to the hotel is passable only by a four-wheel-drive vehicle, most guests fly in and are picked up at the airstrip by the hotel staff. ✉ *Just below Playa Camaronal, a couple of mi south of Playa Carrillo;* ☎

231–6122 reservations office in San José, FAX 232–2183 in San José; ⊠ SJO 2505, Box 0255216, Miami, FL 33131-5216. 22 rooms with bath, 2 suites. Restaurant, bar, minibars, pool, driving range, tennis court, exercise room, horseback riding, boating, fishing, mountain bikes, laundry service. AE, DC, MC, V.

Playa Carrillo

🔞 *6 km (4 mi) south of Sámara.*

A long, reef-protected beach backed by an elegant line of swaying palms and sheltering cliffs, Carrillo is good for swimming, snorkeling, walking, and lounging. Camping is allowed here, too. This is one of the most beautiful and undeveloped beaches in Costa Rica—fly in and land at the airstrip, or head south on the dirt road from Sámara.

Lodging

$$$$ ⊞ **Hotel La Guanamar.** Beautifully positioned above the southern end
★   of Playa Carrillo, this used to be a private fishing club, and as a hotel it continues its tradition as a sportfishing mecca, with two boats of its own for use by guests. It occupies several levels, connected by wooden terraces and steps, thus bringing to mind a luxury cruise liner. The white bedrooms have elaborate headboards, patterned bedcovers, olive-green carpets, and amazing views. *Apdo. 71880, San José, ☎ 656–0054, 239–2000 reservations office in San José, FAX 656–0051, 239–2405 in San José; ⊠ Costa Sol International, 2490 Coral Way, Suite 301, Miami, FL 33145, ☎ 800/245–8420. 41 rooms with bath. Restaurant, bar, pool, horseback riding. AE, MC, V.*

Sámara

🔞 *29 km (18 mi) south of Nicoya.*

When you reach Sámara, you'll see a sign proclaiming it the BEST BEACH IN AMERICA. Maybe this is a slight overstatement, but not much. Two forest-covered hills jut out on either side of a clean, white-sand beach, forming one giant cove ideal for swimming. The coral reef 1½ km (1 mi) from shore is a snorkeler's nirvana. With a smooth road paved all the way from Nicoya, Sámara is flourishing these days, and the numerous hotels springing up around town cater to both Ticos and foreigners—and thankfully Tico spirit, not tourist spirit, still dominates.

Lodging

$$$$ ⊞ **Hotel Villas Playa Sámara.** This secluded hotel well down the beach from the town of Sámara has rooms set up in 57 freestanding, Spanish-style white bungalows with red-tile roofs. The bungalows range in size from one bedroom to three, and they are nicely dispersed among gardens, a pool, and the beachfront. Each unit has a kitchen along with living room, bedroom(s), and bathroom, so you can cook your own meals if desired. The hotel runs tours to most nearby destinations. You can rent or book equipment for every water sport, from waterskiing to snorkeling (there's a small reef-surrounded island a few hundred yards offshore). Windsurfing equipment is free of charge. ⊠ ☎ 256–8228, FAX 221–7222. 88 rooms with bath. Restaurant, bar, kitchenettes, pool, hot tub, horseback riding, snorkeling, windsurfing, waterskiing. AE, MC, V.

Playa Garza

🔞 *16 km (10 mi) north of Playa Sámara.*

Playa Garza occupies a short and serene horseshoe-shape bay 16 km (10 mi) north of Sámara. The rustic fishing village of Garza is front and center, its fleet of fishing boats anchored offshore. Driving here is tough at times, as coming from either direction you'll be driving on badly maintained dirt roads, and your vehicle will have to ford a river or two. These rivers are manageable in the dry season with two-wheel drive, but don't try it without four-wheel drive in the rainy season.

Lodging

$$$–$$$$ ⊞ **Hotel Villagio La Guaria Morada.** Don't be confused by the rustic thatch: this is a luxury complex whose elegant, white freestanding guest rooms form an arc around a landscaped tropical garden. Kitchenettes have been installed in the cabinas, as plans are afoot to transform the property into a time-share resort. Meanwhile, the restaurant serves inspired pasta and seafood dishes in a new open-air dining area. Poolside lounging is top-notch, and there's a wide-screen satellite TV for sports-starved gringos. ⊠ *Apdo. 860–1007, Centro Colón, San José,* ☎ *680–0784 or 233–2476,* 🖷 *222–4073 reservations office in San José. 30 rooms with bath. Restaurant, bar, pool, horseback riding, volleyball, snorkeling, waterskiing, fishing. MC, V.*

Nosara

16 *10 km (6 mi) northeast of Garza.*

Set a bit inland, the minor and not very exciting town of Nosara is a good base from which to explore Playa Nosara and neighboring beaches as well as the nearby Ostional National Wildlife Refuge (☞ *below*), a haven for nesting turtles. This whole area of Guanacaste is currently being subdivided and settled by Europeans and Americans at a fairly rapid pace. If you're looking to buy land in Costa Rica and you want the security of other expatriates nearby, try Nosara. To approach from the north, you'll need to ford the Río Nosara; from the south, you're coming from Garza and will have already done your river crossings.

Dining and Lodging

$–$$ ✕ **Olga's Bar.** Directly behind Playa Pelada, Olga's place serves local food at local prices. The open-air eatery has some rough wooden chairs and oilcloth covered tables, a dirt floor, and a great beach right in front. This is a great place to eat fresh seafood after a day on one of the area's prettiest beaches. ⊠ *Playa Pelada,* ☎ *no phone. No credit cards.*

$$$ ⊞ **Hotel Rancho Suizo Lodge.** The proximity to tiny Playa Pelada, just 300 yards away by forest trail, makes this one of the most attractive small hotels in the Nosara area. Monkeys are partial to the property's shady ambience. The Swiss operators are renowned for their hearty breakfasts, included in the price of a room, and they also barbecue on the beach occasionally. Turtle tours are run during the arribadas. ⊠ *Apdo. 14, Bocas de Nosara 5233,* ☎ *682–0057,* 🖷 *682–0055. 10 bungalows. Restaurant, 2 bars, hot tub. No credit cards.*

$$$ ⊞ **Hotel Villas Taype.** Roughly 100 yards back from the long, lovely Playa Guiones, the Villas Taype's 18 cabinas are set in a low-rise building that forms a U shape around a pair of pools set in a garden; five freestanding bungalows with refrigerators offer more privacy. A breakfast buffet comes with the price of a room. Dinner is offered in a separate restaurant with its own street entrance. The German owners rent out surfboards, boogie boards, and snorkeling gear as well as bicycles and tennis racquets for the night-lit tennis court. They can also arrange all the local tours. ⊠ *Apdo. 8–5233, Nosara,* ☎ *682–0188,* 🖷 *682–0187. 18 cabinas, 5 bungalows. Restaurant, 2 bars, breakfast room, air-conditioning, 2 pools, tennis court, Ping-Pong, beach, laundry service. AE, MC, V.*

$$$ ⚅ **Lagarta Lodge.** Named for the alligators that live in the delta of the Ríos Nosara and Montaña, which is visible from the hotel's bird- and beach-watching lobby area, this property has a magnificent promontory setting offering views of the Ostional National Wildlife Refuge (☞ *below*). The rooms, with private balconies, are in a separate building. A 125-acre private nature reserve flanks the banks of the Río Nosara; stairs lead to boats and riverside trails. Tours to neighboring Ostional can be arranged, and a 10-minute walk through a monkey-filled forest takes you out onto beautiful Playa Guiones. ✉ *Apdo. 18, Nosara,* ☎ *682–0035,* FAX *682–0135. 7 rooms with bath. Restaurant, pool. V.*

Ostional National Wildlife Refuge

⑰ *7 km (4½ mi) north of Nosara.*

Apart from sun and sand, the main reason to travel to the central Nicoya is to visit the Ostional National Wildlife Refuge (Refugio Nacional de Fauna Silvestre de Ostional), with its wonderful opportunities for turtle-watching. During the rainy season you will probably need a four-wheel-drive vehicle to ford the river just north of Nosara; a four-wheel-drive-vehicle track then leads through shrubs to the reserve, which protects one of Costa Rica's major breeding grounds for olive ridley turtles. Local people run the reserve on a cooperative basis. During the first 36 hours of the arribadas, they harvest the eggs on the premise that eggs laid during this time would as likely as not be destroyed by subsequent waves of mother turtles. These eggs, believed by some to be powerful aphrodisiacs, are sold to be eaten raw in bars. Members of the cooperative take turns guarding the beach from poachers, but they are happy to let you view the turtles. Turtle arrivals at this and most other nesting sites are dependent on the moon and tides as well as the time of year; nesting peaks October through April. Before you go to watch the turtles, be sure to consult with local people to get a feel for the conditions and a sense of when, if ever, the turtles will arrive. (For further information, *see* Close Up: Tico Turtles *in* Chapter 8, and Parque Nacional Santa Rosa *in* Chapters 4 and 10.)

LIBERIA AND THE NORTHERN NICOYA BEACHES

Highway 21, from Liberia south toward Nicoya, starts opposite Liberia's Hotel Bramadero on the Pan-American Highway. It runs through cattle country sporadically shaded by guanacaste and tabebuia trees. Just past the village of Comunidad is the turnoff to Playas Hermosa, del Coco, and Ocotal. Continue on toward Belén, and 5 km (3 mi) past Filadelfia you'll hit the Belén junction, where you turn right to get to the surfing hot spots of Tamarindo and Playa Grande. Some roads leading to the coast are intermittently paved, depending on which beach you head for. As you work your way toward the coast, pay close attention to the assorted hotel signs at intersections—they may be the only indicators of which road to take.

Liberia

⑱ *234 km (145 mi) northwest of San José.*

North of San José on the Pan-American Highway, Liberia is a low-rise, grid-plan, cattle-market town with a huge central square dominated by an ugly modern church. It is the capital of Guanacaste province and acts as the gateway to a northern route that encompasses Volcán Rincón de la Vieja (☞ Chapters 4 and 10), several spectacular and biologically important national parks, and a turtle-nesting site on the Pacific coast (☞ Chapter 4). Liberia's Daniel Oduber International Airport jet runway can service national and international flights; if and when San José and Liberia sort out their differences on the economically volatile issue of air traffic, Liberia's proximity to the resort-oriented beaches of Guanacaste will make it the arrival point of choice for even more travelers. Though it's a pleasant and prosperous city, Liberia doesn't offer much to see or do. If you do have the time, visit the museum and get tourist information at the **Casa de Cultura.** ⊠ *3 blocks south of Parque Central,* ☎ *666–1606.* ☉ *Mon.–Sat. 8–4.*

Dining and Lodging

$$ ✕ **Pókopí.** In Costa Rica's cattle capital, Pókopí eclipses rival steak houses amidst white walls with ranching memorabilia, wooden chairs and tables, and a Latin cowboy atmosphere. Try the delicious chateaubriand with *salsa Barnesa* (béarnaise sauce, fresh vegetables, and a stuffed tomato). And it ain't all beef: dig into the *dorado* (sea bass) in white sauce with mushrooms, onions, green pepper, and white wine. ⊠ *500 yards down road to Nicoya, on the right, 75 yards west of gas station,* ☎ *666–1036. AE, MC, V.*

$$$ 🏨 **Hotel El Sitio.** If you're overnighting in Liberia, El Sitio is worth considering for its spacious, modern rooms with TVs, as well as for the on-premises Italian restaurant, casino, volleyball court, pools, car rental agency, tour planning, and walking trails. It's basically a nondescript roadside motel, but a fine choice for its modern conveniences. ⊠ *Apdo. 134–5000,* ☎ *666–1211,* FAX *666–2054. 52 rooms with bath. Restaurant, air-conditioning, 2 pools, spa, horseback riding, volleyball, mountain bikes, casino, meeting rooms, car rental. AE, MC, V.*

$$ 🏨 **Hotel La Siesta.** The advantage of this modern hotel is its quiet location three blocks south of the central plaza. The rooms, surrounding a landscaped patio with a pool, have narrow, firm beds, white walls, and functional bathrooms that are beginning to show signs of age. The upstairs rooms are slightly larger and quieter. ⊠ *Apdo. 15–5000,* ☎ *666–0678,* FAX *666–2532. 24 rooms with bath. Restaurant, bar, air-conditioning, pool. AE, MC, V.*

Nightlife and the Arts

In late July, Liberia hosts an annexation-secession-from-Nicaragua celebration called Guanacaste Day, with folk dances, bullfights, and rodeos. Semana Cultural, or Cultural Week, brings many arts events to Liberia in the first week of September. Year-round, the Fiestas Bravas at the **Hacienda la Cueva Liberia** (☎ 666–0450) will appeal to the John Wayne—or the kitschy tourist—in you. Hollering, whooping cowboys on horseback accompany the last stretch of your bus ride as you pull up to the working ranch and 1824 adobe farmhouse. Music, lasso shows, bull-riding, dancing, and a Guanacaste specialty dinner all follow.

Playa del Coco

⑲ *35 km (22 mi) southwest of Liberia.*

Playa del Coco is a slightly seedy beachfront town for those who want noise, discos, and bustle. As perhaps the most accessible beach in Guanacaste, Playa del Coco serves as a playground for Costa Rica's college kids, who like many of their American and European peers are unfortunately not terribly environmentally aware. The beaches can get littered with garbage, and the holiday season is impossibly crowded. But Coco's scruffy pier, slightly down-at-the-heels ambience, and open-air trinket and souvenir stands are actually rather appealing, especially if you like your resorts colorful.

Dining and Lodging

$–$$ ✕ **Mariscos La Guajira.** Try seviche for starters at this informal open-sided beachfront restaurant with wooden tables, a cement floor, and potted plants. As main courses, dorado served with salad and fried bananas, camarones, and *langosta al ajillo* (lobster in garlic) are all recommended. ✉ *West along beach, look for round, palm-thatch shades,* ☎ *670–0107. Reservations not accepted. AE, MC, V.*

$–$$ ✕ **San Francisco Treats.** The friendly, long-haired former San Francisco corporate lawyer who, with his wife, started this wonderful tiny open-air eatery on the main road into Coco has put it up for sale, but plans to pass on the recipes. So, the great American-style sandwiches, home-baked bread, lasagna—both vegetarian and *con carne* (with meat)—and the fantastic desserts should still be available when someone does buy the place out. *Right side of main road into Playa del Coco,* ☎ *no phone. No credit cards.*

$$–$$$ ⌂ **Villa Flores.** Weight-lifting, scuba-diving Italians run the Villa Flores, on the same street—paralleling the beach—as Cabinas Chale. Their bed-and-breakfast and dive center specializes in scuba trips. In the handsome, two-story hardwood building are fan-cooled downstairs rooms, two upstairs rooms with air-conditioning, and one—Room 9—that contains an amazingly commodious bathtub. The hotel features a well-equipped gym and a large pool, and the beach is a minute away. Italian dishes are served in the three-meal restaurant. ✉ *Apdo. 2,* ☎ FAX *670–0269. 10 rooms with bath. Restaurant, air-conditioning, pool, exercise room. AE, MC, V.*

$$ ⌂ **Cabinas Chale.** To find Chale, turn right at San Francisco Treats (☞ *above*) and head down the road. Bedrooms are bright and large, containing up to five beds, a refrigerator, table and chairs, tile floor, and overhead fans. They are spotlessly clean and have modern bathrooms. Take a 50-yard stroll to the beach straight ahead, and walk west 500 yards to town. ☎ *670–0036,* FAX *670–0303. 25 rooms with bath. Pool, badminton, basketball. V.*

$$ ⌂ **Villa del Sol.** The French-Canadian operators of the Villa del Sol offer seven quiet, spacious, light-filled rooms in a contemporary B&B with a pool out front. Well away from Coco's main drag, the Villa del Sol lies just 100 yards from the quieter part of Playa del Coco, which is visible from the upstairs balconies. The owners will organize the usual area tours and activities. ☎ FAX *670–0085. 7 rooms, 5 with bath. Breakfast room, pool. AE, MC, V.*

Hermosa

㉒   *13 km (8 mi) east of Playa del Coco.*

Hermosa has a relaxed village atmosphere, reminiscent of a Mexican beach town. Although several large hotels have opened here in recent years, the full length of the village beach is occupied by buildings—hotels, restaurants, and private houses—and so the newer, larger hotels and other developments have been forced to set up shop off the beach or on other beaches in the area. Hermosa's crescent of grayish sand fronts a line of trees that provide a welcome respite from the heat of the sun. At the north end of the beach, low tide creates wide, rock-lined tidal pools for exploring.

Dining and Lodging

$–$$ ✕ **Aqua Sport.** This beachfront hotel complex (6 rooms with bath, 1 suite) has a gift shop, minimarket, and water-sports equipment rentals, but the main draw is a casual open-air restaurant decorated with tree trunks. The seafood platter of lobster, shrimp, calamari, and oysters is highly recommended. ✉ *Apdo. 100–5019, Playa del Coco,* ☎ FAX *672–0050. AE, MC, V.*

$$$$ 🏨 **Blue Bay Village Papagayo.** Encompassing 78 hilly beachfront acres, this resort is on the south shore of Bahía Culebra, a bit north of Hermosa. Freestanding villas each house two guest rooms with private baths, marble floors, in-room satellite TV, and direct-dial phones. The Blue Bay package is all-inclusive, with meals and use of all facilities in the per-couple price. All water sports and tours can be arranged. ✉ *Playa Arenilla, Golfo de Papagayo,* ☎ *672–0131, 233–8566 reservations office in San José;* FAX *672–0138, 221–0739 in San José. 80 bungalows. 2 restaurants, 3 bars, 2 snack bars, 2 pools, hot tub, tennis court, health club, theater, meeting rooms. AE, DC, MC, V.*

$$$$ 🏨 **Costa Smeralda.** The grand scale of the Costa Smeralda—an all-inclusive resort with air-conditioned, satellite-TV-equipped guest rooms—is evident from the size of the Mediterranean-style lobby-reception building, with its large entry, enormous open-air buffet dining area, casino, and upstairs conference rooms. But the guest rooms counterpoint the overscale quality, as they are carefully distributed down a long, gently sloping site from the main building to a sliver of beach, with gardens, lawns, and an appealing, amoeba-shape pool. The restaurant's dishes reflect the resort's Italian ownership. Guests choose from a wide range of extracurricular activities. ✉ *Playa Panamá,* ☎ *672–0042, 672–0070, or 672–0041,* FAX *672–0079. 120 rooms with bath. Restaurant, snack bar, air-conditioning, pool, beach, casino, meeting rooms. AE, MC, V.*

$$$–$$$$ 🏨 **Sula Sula.** Pleasantly set in a shady forest behind quiet Playa Panamá, just north of Hermosa, Sula Sula's yellow cabinas with red-tile roofs have telephones, air-conditioning, minibars, satellite TV, hair dryers, good reading lights, and comfortable furnishings. A formal restaurant serves international cuisine; three bars and a large pool enhance the cool provided by the shade trees. A stone wall encloses the entire property and separates it from a popular campground at the south end of the beach. ✉ *Playa Panamá,* ☎ *670–0000,* FAX *670–0492. 24 cabinas. Restaurant, 3 bars, air-conditioning, pool. AE, MC, V.*

$$$ 🏨 **El Velero Hotel.** The elegant, two-story Velero has large, white rooms with arched doorways. The Canadian owners have a boutique, a satellite-equipped TV room upstairs, and resident caged toucans. Along with the use of Jet Skis, sea kayaks, and a sailboat, the hotel offers sunset cruises and all-day snorkeling trips. The sailboat also serves as a spare guest room on occasion—don't be afraid to ask if you like sleeping on board. David and Jessica Anne Trogler, from Baltimore, anchor their 44-ft sailing yacht, the *Jessica Anne,* just offshore and offer three-day sailing charters. At the restaurant, sample the jumbo shrimp with rice and vegetables, or anything with mashed potatoes—a rare treat in Costa Rica. ✉ *Playa Hermosa,* ☎ *672–0016,* ☎ FAX *672–0036. 13 rooms with bath. Restaurant, bar, pool, snorkeling, boating, jet skiing. AE, MC, V.*

$$ 🏨 **Hotel Cabinas Playa Hermosa.** Monkeys, coatis, and birds once frolicked outside these peaceful white cabinas, which sleep five with bath, on the quiet south end of the beach. Now two caged coatis seem to be the only sign of wildlife. Nevertheless, this hotel is still a good deal. The restaurant serves pasta, steak, and seafood. ✉ *Apdo. 112, Liberia,* ☎ FAX *672–0046. 22 cabinas. Restaurant. V.*

Outdoor Activities and Sports

SCUBA DIVING

Just off the beach at the Hotel Sol Playa Hermosa (at the north end of Playa Hermosa), **Bill Beard's Diving Safaris** (☎ FAX 672–0012 or 670–0495, 800/779–0055 in the U.S., FAX 954/351–9740 in the U.S.) offers a complete range of scuba activities, from beginner training to open-

water certification courses and even multitank dives at more than 20
tantalizing sites off the coast of Guanacaste, alive with rays, sharks,
fish, and turtles. His guides and trainers know underwater Guanacaste
as well as anyone. Prices range from $40 for a one-tank afternoon dive
to $375 for a PADI (Professional Association of Diving Instructors)
open-water certification course. On the beach below the dive shop, an
independent **kiosk** rents boogie boards, plastic kayaks, Jet Skis, and
other water toys.

Playa Ocotal

㉑ *3 km (2 mi) west of Playa del Coco.*

In spite of its proximity to college-kid-thronged Coco, Playa Ocotal is
a serene spot, with a lilliputian crescent of beach sheltered by rocks.
At the entrance to the Golfo de Papagayo, it's a good spot for sportfishing enthusiasts to hole up between excursions. Good diving can be
found at Las Corridas, just 1 km (½ mi) away.

Lodging

$$$–$$$$ ☒ **El Ocotal Beach Resort.** Three kilometers (2 mi) west of Playa del
★   Coco down a paved road, this luxury hotel with a sportfishing fleet
and dive shop is situated above secluded Ocotal Bay. From the upper
rooms you look north to the Peninsula Santa Elena and northwest to
Rincón de la Vieja. Air-conditioned rooms have blue carpets, pat-
terned bedspreads, white walls, watercolors, overhead fans, TVs, and
huge French windows. Freestanding units down the hill are bigger and
triangular in shape with polished wood floors. ☒ *Apdo. 1, Playa del
Coco,* ☎ *670–0321,* ℻ *670–0083. 40 rooms with bath, 3 suites, 6
bungalows. Restaurant, bar, air-conditioning, pool, tennis court, horse-
back riding, boating, dive shop. AE, DC, MC, V.*

$$$ ☒ **Villa Casa Blanca.** Surely one of the finest B&Bs in Costa Rica, the
★   Casa Blanca lives in a hillside Mediterranean-style building buried in
a bower of tropical plantings. The intimate, junglelike setting attracts
numerous colorful, talkative birds. Victorian-influenced rooms comfort you with air-conditioning, pleasant wood details and artwork, spacious showers, and canopy beds. Secluded, romantic, and with a pool,
the Casa Blanca also turns out Guanacaste's heartiest breakfasts. For
dinner, you can have specialties from an area restaurant delivered if
you wish. ☒ *Apdo. 176–5019, Playa Ocotal,* ☎ ℻ *670–0448. 13 rooms
with bath. Breakfast room, air-conditioning, pool. AE, MC, V.*

Playa Pan de Azúcar

㉒ *8 km (5 mi) north of Playa Flamingo.*

Pan de Azúcar's beach, at the end of a hilly dirt road, lends its only
hotel one quality that is not always easy to come by in this area—privacy. There are good islands for snorkeling just offshore.

Lodging

$$$$ ☒ **Hotel Sugar Beach.** Reached via a dirt track 8 km (5 mi) north of
★   Flamingo, this hotel overlooks a thin, curving white-sand beach. The
nicely varied, air-conditioned rooms and suites frame idyllic views. A
beach house with two bedrooms (or take the upstairs as well and
make it three) can be rented by the day or week. You can snorkel at
either edge of the bay, but expect to pay dearly for the use of snorkeling (and other sports) equipment at the hotel since it has virtually no
competition. The open-sided rotunda restaurant serves good seafood
dishes. Management offers a full complement of activities and area tours,
from boat trips to surfing at Witches Rock to golf, horseback riding,
and volcano tours. ☒ *Apdo. 90, Santa Cruz,* ☎ *654–4242,* ℻ *654–*

4239. 29 rooms with bath, 1 beach house. Restaurant, bar, air-conditioning, pool, horseback riding, snorkeling. AE, MC, V.

Playa Potrero

㉓ *1 km (½ mi) north of Flamingo.*

Although Potrero previously has been known mostly for its views of nearby Flamingo, it has its own charm, primarily due to its wide, white-sand beach. There's excellent swimming at an island nearby, and the bird refuge **Isla Santa Catalina** is 10 km (6 mi) offshore.

Lodging

$$$$ 🏨 **Bahía Potrero Beach and Fishing Resort.** At this squat, white bungalow fishing and water sports are the major activities. Rustic rooms have air-conditioning and refrigerators; deluxe rooms have private patios. A shady, open-air restaurant serves seafood, pizza, and pasta concoctions. The beach is ideal for young children because the sea is shallow and safe. ✉ *Apdo. 45, Santa Cruz,* ☎ *654–4183,* FAX *654–4093. 14 rooms with bath. Restaurant, bar, air-conditioning, pool, fishing. AE, MC, V.*

$$$ 🏨 **Hotel El Sitio Cielomar.** The simple and secluded (but slightly overpriced) Cielomar sits just a few feet back from the picturesque beach just north of Potrero called Playa Penca. It's a sister hotel of the well-run El Sitio in Liberia. This place is a charming hideaway: the white-sand beach and green lawn behind it are well shaded, and islets a few hundred yards offshore offer good snorkeling. If you want action, the Flamingo resorts are 5 minutes away by car, 20 on foot. The three-meal restaurant is for guests only. Breakfast is included with the price of a room. ✉ ☎ *666–1211 or 654–4194,* FAX *666–2059. 11 rooms with bath. Restaurant, snorkeling. MC, V.*

$$ 🏨 **Casa Sunset.** Five minutes away on foot from the village of Potrero,
★ on the inland side of the dirt road to Hotel Sugar Beach, the American-run Casa Sunset offers wonderful views of the sunset from cabinas stacked up the steep hillside above the road. Each cabina contains four single beds, ceiling fans, and a bath with warm, not hot, showers. A sunbathing patio surrounds a pool near the top of the property, and a community kitchen allows some on-site cooking. Secluded Playas Penca and Prieta are also within walking distance, as is the hustle and bustle of Flamingo Beach, about a half hour away. ✉ *Apdo. 5111, Playa Potrero, Santa Cruz,* ☎ FAX *654–4265. 7 cabinas. Pool, horseback riding, surfing, boating, fishing. No credit cards.*

Playa Flamingo

㉔ *39 km (24 mi) west of Filadelfia.*

Flamingo was one of the first of the northern Nicoya beaches to experience the wonders of overscale resort development, witnessed in the huge Aurola Flamingo Beach Resort that dominates the landscape. The beach is still a welcome oasis. If you like large, characterless hotels with your beach—and some do, strictly for their anonymity—this is a good place for you. A half-finished, abandoned condo project adds an unfortunate sour note to the south end of an otherwise beautiful stretch of sand.

Dining and Lodging

$$ ✕ **Marie's Restaurant.** Friendly Marie and her fresh food make this
★ place well worth a detour. Shortly after the road bends toward the north end of Flamingo, look for Marie's veranda furnished with sliced tree-trunk tables and settle back for a rewarding meal of generous helpings of fresh seafood at very reasonable rates. The seviche is delightful, as is the house specialty, *plato de mariscos* (shrimp, lobster, and oysters served with garlic butter, potatoes, and salad), but be sure to save room

for pudding—the *tres leches,* topped with the cream of three different milks, is superb. ⊠ *Main road near north end of Flamingo,* ☎ 654–4136. *Reservations not accepted.* V.

$$$–$$$$ 🏨 **Aurola Flamingo Beach Resort.** The elegant if somewhat overscale building features a very large pool with a swim-up bar, a poolside snack bar, and a pricey restaurant. The interiors of the lobby and restaurant are coolly contemporary and very appealing in a somewhat impersonal fashion. It works well as a luxe international-style resort; and if that's what you're looking for in Costa Rica, this is the place for you. Reality check: stay here and you could easily forget that you are in Costa Rica; you might, instead, think yourself to be in Miami, Cancún, or Palm Springs. ⊠ *Apdo. 692–4050, Alajuela,* ☎ 654–4011, 𝔽𝔸𝕏 654–4060. 136 *rooms with bath, 36 condominiums. 2 restaurants, 4 bars, air-conditioning, 3 pools, tennis court, health club, casino, travel services.* AE, DC, MC, V.

$$$ 🏨 **Mariner Inn.** Near the marina, this white, two-story building is the least-expensive hotel in Flamingo. Rooms are tiny, but they do have ceiling fans, air-conditioning, and firm beds. ⊠ *Apdo. 65, Santa Cruz,* ☎ 654–4081, 𝔽𝔸𝕏 654–4024. 11 *rooms with bath, 1 suite. Restaurant, bar, air-conditioning, pool.* AE, MC, V.

Brasilito

㉕ *35 km (22 mi) west of Filadelfia.*

Around this fishing village's town square, which doubles as the soccer field, huddles a ramshackle row of houses. Boats waiting for high tide line up just offshore of a white-sand beach that is the equal of Flamingo, but without the megahotels. The presence of the nearby Meliá Playa Conchal hotel (☞ Dining and Lodging, *below*), however, has begun to wear on the charm and has infused Brasilito with a tacky resort energy, with new shops and at least one gas-station market, strung along the road through town, now selling overpriced sunglasses, T-shirts, and water toys.

Dining and Lodging

$–$$ ✕ **El Camerón Dorado.** This bar-restaurant derives much of its appeal from the shaded setting on Brasilito's beautiful beach, and no less from the small-vessel fishing fleet anchored offshore that assures you of the freshness of seafood available. The chef has a way with preparing the variety of fresh-caught fish, from deep fried to grilled, and creates savory sauces to accompany. The westernmost tables are right on the beach, and the surf crashes just yards away as you dine beneath the stars. Due to its spectacular sunset views, this is a popular place for an early evening drink. ⊠ 220 *yards north of Brasilito Plaza,* ☎ 654–4244. AE, DC, MC, V.

$$ 🏨 **Hotel Brasilito.** This appealing, intimately scaled German-run establishment has a high-ceilinged dining room just off the beach. A wooden, open-air restaurant with tables and chairs arrayed beneath lazily turning ceiling fans fronts the sea. The sparely furnished but comfortable rooms occupy both floors of the old, two-story wooden building behind the restaurant; ask for one of the few rooms with unobstructed sea views. ⊠ *Next to square and soccer field,* ☎ 654–4237, 𝔽𝔸𝕏 654–4247. 17 *rooms with bath. Restaurant.* V.

Playa Conchal

㉖ *Immediately south of Playa Brasilito.*

Playa Conchal, one of Guanacaste's finest and most secluded beaches, is aptly named, as it is sprinkled with shells that offer themselves up for easy collecting. The sprawling Meliá Playa Conchal Resort (☞ Lodging, *below*) dominates the scene here.

Lodging

$$$$ ☷ **Meliá Playa Conchal Beach & Golf Resort.** For the golfing traveler in search of luxury in a remote destination, this resort is ideal. Standing in the enormous, open-air, marble-floored reception lobby, you'll see the massive resort spreading out over almost 4 sq km (1½ sq mi) of manicured golf courses, bungalows, tennis courts, and distant beach. The rooms (four per bungalow), set in low-slung buildings, are large and luxurious, air-conditioned, and satellite-TV equipped. The restaurants serve a range of international fare. ✉ *Entrance less than 1 km (½ mi) south of Brasilito*, ☎ *654–4123, 800/336–3542 in the U.S.*, FAX *654–4181. 308 bungalows. 5 restaurants, air-conditioning, 2 bars, pool, 2 18-hole golf courses, 4 tennis courts, meeting rooms. AE, MC, V.*

En Route   To get to the Parque Nacional Marino Las Baulas, take the Pan-American Highway north to Liberia and from there head south to Santa Cruz, then west to the coast.

Parque Nacional Marino Las Baulas

➋ *37 km (23 mi) west of Filadelfia, 3 km (2 mi) north of Tamarindo.*

Just north of Tamarindo, across an estuary, the Parque Nacional Marino Las Baulas (Las Baulas Marine National Park) protects the long **Playa Grande,** an important nesting site of the leatherback sea turtle (☞ Chapter 10). It's a great surf spot as well. The owners of the Hotel Las Tortugas (☞ Lodging, *below*), Louis Wilson and Marianela Pastor, struggled for a decade to get the national park established and have a real understanding of the importance of balancing the oft-conflicting needs of locals, tourists, and turtles. An evening spent discussing ecotourism, ecopolitics, and related matters with them is a real education.

The resort boom in Guanacaste can be witnessed at this bucolic spot—a couple of small hotels have opened not far from Hotel Las Tortugas, and a golf and country club is offering property for sale behind the adjacent estuary.

Lodging

$$$ ☷ **Hotel Las Tortugas.** This hotel stands at the edge of Las Baulas Marine National Park, proximate to the turtle-nesting beach. Rooms are comfortable, with good beds and air-conditioning as well as stone floors and stucco walls. Owners Louis Wilson and Marianela Pastor—he American, she Costa Rican—offer a number of long-term rentals, including the apartments they call Greek 1, 2, and 3. The restaurant serves healthful, high-quality food. Beware: the beach surf break sometimes has dangerous rip currents, at which time you can retreat to the turtle-shape pool. Local guides escort you along the beach at night, and the hotel also offers canoe trips in the nearby Tamarindo Wildlife Refuge (Refugio Vida Silvestre de Tamarindo). ✉ *Apdo. 164, Santa Cruz de Guanacaste,* ☎ *653–0423,* ☎ FAX *653–0458. 11 rooms with bath. Restaurant, air-conditioning, pool, boating. V.*

Tamarindo

➋ *37 km (23 mi) west of Filadelfia.*

Tamarindo is a lively town with a great variety of restaurants, cabins, bars, and hotels at all price levels. Developmental hustle is everywhere evident in the presence of condo projects and mini-strip malls. Still, Tamarindo remains appealing because it's a virtually complete self-contained Costa Rican destination: its beaches are great for snorkeling, boating, kayaking, diving, surfing, and just plain swimming; there are estuaries north and south of town for bird- and animal-watching; and two turtle-nesting beaches—Langosta to the south and Grande to the north—are nearby. With an airstrip just outside town, Tamarindo is also a convenient base from which to explore all of Guanacaste. The road is in dire need of being paved—although some sections through the middle of town were paved in 1998, most of it remains unpaved and very dusty in the dry season.

Dining and Lodging

$$–$$$ ✕ **Nogui's.** Local gringos swear by this scruffy near-beachfront restau-
★ rant. Also known as the Sunrise Café, Nogui's is considered by afi-cionados to have the freshest, best, and most reasonably priced seafood in all of Tamarindo. A dirt road separates Nogui's alfresco plastic ta-bles and chairs from the beach. When it gets crowded, some stand in the parking area eating on their feet rather than waiting for a table. The langostino is highly recommended, as is the swimsuit selection in the adjacent Nogui's shop. ✉ *Just south of Zullymar on the Tamarindo circle,* ☎ 653–0029. V.

$–$$ ✕ **Bakery de Paris/Restaurant Cocodril.** The owners of this bakery, for-
★ merly Johann's, on the right side of the road near the entrance to town, own the adjacent Cocodril Restaurant and Disco 24. At dining tables nicely distributed on a shady, off-road patio you can enjoy all three meals of the day, especially the great morning European pastries. Have a closer (not too close) look at the pond behind the adjacent tire-re-pair shop: you may be rewarded with a sighting of the rather fat crocodile that lives there, feeding, they say, on roast chickens from the Cocodril. ✉ *On right side of the main road just as you enter town,* ☎ 653–0255. AE, MC, V.

$–$$ ✕ **Fruitas Tropicales.** The friendly waiters hose down the road to
★ dampen the dust that would otherwise smother this busy street-side eatery. The white plastic tables and chairs stay full for a reason—the restaurant does a great job, dishing out Costa Rican food at Costa Rican prices to tourists of every shape and description. The food is nothing fancy, but the casados and other dishes are tasty and substantial. There are plenty of American-style items on the menu as well and great *fruitas tropicales* (tropical fruit drinks). ✉ *Main road, toward north end of town,* ☎ 653–0041. AE, MC, V.

$–$$ ✕ **Iguana Grill.** Beneath the Iguana Surf's high Rancho, Nancy Money's Iguana Grill (her mother owns the Sueño del Mar in nearby Playa Lan-gosta, ☞ *below*) offers hearty, Nuevo Mexican–American breakfasts—burritos, *huevos rancheros* (egg tortillas), and other less-northern delights as well as lunch. A ground-floor shop dispenses bathing suits and stylish surf gear along with hundreds of surfboards. Take a seat at one of the tables reserved for customers. Don't miss the great cof-fee drinks from the best espresso machine in Tamarindo and the trop-ical smoothies. This is a good place for a break from the casado routine. ✉ *Below Iguana Surf,* ☎ FAX 653–0148. MC, V.

$$$$ ⌂ **El Jardín del Eden.** The only disadvantage suffered by the Jardín is
★ that it is not directly on the beach—and that's not really much of a disadvantage in the dust of the dry season. The three-tier mauve hotel, set among lush gardens (hence the name) on a hill, has rooms with green interiors and elegantly styled bathrooms. All rooms have ocean views, air-conditioning, refrigerators, and fans. A thatched-roof restaurant pre-pares French and Italian food and outstanding steaks. Fishing pack-ages are available. ✉ *Apdo. 1094–2050, San Pedro,* ☎ 653–0137, FAX 653–0111. 18 rooms with bath, 2 apartments. Restaurant, 2 bars, air-conditioning, 2 pools, hot tub. AE, MC, V.

$$$$ ☷ **Hotel Capitán Suiz.** The "Swiss Captain" is Ruedi Schmid, and he and his partner, Ursula Schmid, have created an elegant accommodation at the south end of Tamarindo. The bungalows are set in a lushly landscaped garden around a pool, steps from a relatively quiet stretch of Tamarindo's gorgeous beach. The rather pricey restaurant serves international cuisine. They will arrange horseback riding, kayaking, sportfishing, and diving trips. A lot of monkeys hang around the Swiss Captain's place as well, so you get your "wildlife" with the price of a room. *On right side of road toward Playa Langosta (veer left before circle),* ☎ *653–0075,* FAX *653–0292. 22 rooms with bath, 8 bungalows. Restaurant, pool. AE, MC, V.*

$$$$ ☷ **Hotel Tamarindo Diría.** The shady tropical garden next to the beach eliminates the need to stray far from Tamarindo's first high-end hotel, still a very posh spot. The contemporary three-story building has striking white-painted furnishings with aqua trim and matching ceilings; rooms have tile floors and modern furniture, and each has a spacious balcony looking onto treetops. The thatched rotunda bar and restaurant overlook a large rectangular pool. ✉ *Apdo. 676–1000, San José,* ☎ *653–0031, 293–4340 reservations office in San José,* FAX *289–8727 in San José. 80 rooms with bath. Restaurant, bar, pool. AE, DC, MC, V.*

$$$–$$$$ ☷ **Casa Cook.** Two one-bedroom, hardwood-detailed cabinas posi-
★ tioned just off Tamarindo's beach are owned by a retired American couple, Chuck and Ruthann Cook. Each has a full kitchen, an individual hot-water heater, a queen-size sofa bed in the living room, a queen-size bed in the bedroom, ceiling fans, and screened doors and windows. The second story of the main house is the "villa," a 1,500-sq-ft, two-bedroom apartment with private baths, a kitchen, dining area, living room, and large deck. *On road to Playa Langosta, north of the Swiss Captain Hotel (☞ above),* ☎ FAX *653–0125;* ✉ *4269 Chapman Way, Pleasanton, CA 94588,* ☎ *500/675–0421 or 510/846–0784,* FAX *500/677–1781 or 510/426–1141. 2 cabinas, 1 villa. Pool. AE, MC, V.*

$$–$$$ ☷ **Cabinas Marielos.** In high season few decent bargain rooms are to be had in Tamarindo. Across the main dirt road from the beach, in what is more or less town center, rooms at Cabinas Marielos are among the best of them. The cabinas are housed in two wings, flanking a courtyard set well back from the noise and dust of the road. The atmosphere is surprisingly serene. Note the water doesn't get too, too hot. *Near the north of town, follow signs,* ☎ FAX *653–0141. 16 cabinas. V.*

$$ ☷ **Hotel Pasatiempo.** Steps from the beach and just off the dirt road to Playa Langosta, the Pasatiempo is one of the better bargains in Tamarindo. The cabinas, each named after a Guanacaste beach, are placed amidst nicely landscaped grounds and around a pool; each has a hand-painted mural over the bed and ceiling fans (two have air-conditioning). The bar frequently hires live music—"grown-up rock-and-roll," according to owner Ron Stewart—and a wide-screen satellite TV provides American sports fans with their necessary fix. ✉ *200 yards from beach behind the Tamarindo circle,* ☎ *653–0096,* FAX *653–0275. 10 cabinas. Restaurant, bar, air-conditioning. AE, MC, V.*

$ ☷ **Arco Iris Restaurant & Cabinas.** A pair of spirited Italian sisters, Laura
★ and Simona Fillipini, run a wonderful Italian vegetarian restaurant and hotel set up on the hill behind the Tamarindo circle (follow signs). Dishes don't run more than $5, and the food is healthful and lovingly prepared. Four bright, cheery cabinas are painted in primary colors and decorated with distinct themes, and one has two bedrooms and a kitchen. *Follow signs past Hotel Pasatiempo (☞ above) and up hill to the right,* ☎ *653–0330. 4 cabinas. Restaurant. No credit cards.*

Outdoor Activities and Sports

BOATING, SURFING, AND KAYAKING

Iguana Surf (☎ FAX 653–0148, www.tamarindo.com/iguana) rents surfboards and also offers guided kayak tours into the bird-watching paradises of the nearby Ríos San Francisco and Tamarindo estuaries. The San Francisco seems to have more birds, and a nature walk up-river might include an encounter with a troop of howler monkeys. The larger Tamarindo is a more exotic, overgrown, junglelike estuary, with *African Queen*–like ambience deep in the mangrove jungle.

SPORTFISHING

For saltwater anglers, a number of fishing charters operate in Tamarindo. Probably the best among them is **Tamarindo Sportfishing** (☎ 653–0090), run by Randy Wilson, who has led the way in developing new fish-saving catch-and-release techniques that go as easily as possible on the fish. Wilson has roamed and fished the Guanacaste waters for 25 years now, and he knows where the big ones lurk. His boat, the *Talking Fish*, is equipped with a marlin chair and a cabin with a shower. Full days run $875, half days $550.

Playa Langosta

🕗 *2 km (1 mi) south of Tamarindo.*

Playa Langosta, a leatherback turtle nesting beach, is less protected than the beach at Tamarindo. Informal viewings with private guides are a lot cheaper than the more organized Playa Grande turtle tours, but eggs are stolen in huge quantities, and the whole arrangement will most likely be formalized in the near future. Big, well-shaped river-mouth waves near the north end of the beach make it popular with surfers. An over-size casino-condo-hotel complex is going up on the bluff overlooking the river mouth.

Lodging

$$$–$$$$ 🏠 **Sueño del Mar.** Gather a group of friends and take over American
★   Susan Money's gorgeous dream of a B&B for a week—you'll love every minute. The complex has swinging hammocks, lovely gardens, a pool, and intimate patios and is adorned throughout with hand-painted frescoes and colorful antique tiles. The adobe-style buildings house three double rooms with overhead fans, and Balinese-style showers open to the sky. A casita with its own kitchen and veranda sleeps four. Upstairs, the matrimonial suite offers even greater privacy. Gourmet breakfast is served in the "community" room, where three-course dinners are offered a couple of times a week. The lively Ms. Money and her part-ner-husband, surfing forester Greg Mullins, will help arrange trips. ⊠ *Playa Tamarindo, Santa Cruz,* ☎ FAX 653–0284; ⊠ *Susan Money, 4 Mountainview Ct., Burlington, VT 05401,* ☎ FAX 802/658–8041. *3 rooms with bath, 1 suite, 1 casita. Dining room, pool, horseback rid-ing, snorkeling, surfing, boating, fishing, bicycles. No credit cards.*

En Route   To reach Playa Avellanes, Negra, and Junquillal from the highway, take the turn south toward Tamarindo at the Huacas junction; then when you reach the village of Villarreal continue south 14 km (8½ mi) rather than turning right toward Tamarindo. The road is in fairly good shape ex-cept for a few spots. At the T junction, turn right for Paraiso and Jun-quillal (left heads on to Santa Cruz). From the junction, it's about 12 km (7 mi) to Paraiso along a decent mixed dirt and paved road. The dirt road north from Paraiso to Playa Negra (6 km/4 mi) is funky but pass-able; the road south from Paraiso, 2 km (1 mi) to the north end of Jun-quillal, is in better shape. To reach Playa Avellanes, take the road past Villareal via Hernandez and follow signs to Cabinas Las Olas (☞ *below*).

Playa Avellanes

30 *20 km (12 mi) south of Tamarindo.*

Avellanes is a beautiful half-mile stretch of pale golden sand with rocky outcroppings, a river mouth, and a mangrove swamp estuary. Locals claim there are eight surf spots when the swell is strong.

Lodging

$$–$$$ **Cabinas Las Olas.** Frequented primarily by surfers on holiday surf-tour packages from Brazil and Argentina, these spacious freestanding cabinas in an airy forest behind Playa Avellanes should also appeal to bird-watchers, animal lovers, and all manner of naturalists. Monkeys and other critters often lurk around this isolated spot. An elevated boardwalk leads from the cabinas through a protected mangrove estuary to the beach. The three-meal restaurant, with an adjacent outdoor video bar, serves reasonably priced food. ✉ *Apdo. 1404–1250, Escazú,* ☎ *233–4455,* FAX *222–8685. 10 cabinas. Restaurant, bar, laundry service. AE, MC, V.*

En Route From Playa Avellanes, questionably passable roads lead south to Playa Negra—sage drivers will only attempt it with four-wheel-drive vehicles. It's better to double back to the T-junction on the main road from Villarreal and head south again. After 21 km (12½ mi) you'll come to a junction with a left turn to Santa Cruz (a terribly potholed road) and a right to Paraiso and Junquillal. Turn right, and another 15 km (8 mi) of decent mixed dirt and paved road gets you to the hamlet of Paraiso. From here it's about 6 km (4 mi) north on a funky but passable dirt road to Playa Negra, and 2 km (1 mi) south on a better road to the north end of Junquillal, which stretches south uninterrupted for about 3 km (2 mi).

Playas Negra and Junquillal

31 *44 km (27 mi) south of Playa Langosta.*

Americans—surfers at least—got their first look at Playa Negra in *The Endless Summer II,* which featured some dynamite sessions at this spectacular rock-reef point break. Surfing cognoscenti will dig the waves—almost all rights, and most beautifully shaped. Junquillal (pronounced hoon-key-*yall*), to the south, is a long stretch of uninterrupted beach with calm surf and only one hotel on the beach side of the road. This is one of the quieter beaches in Guanacaste, and a real find for tranquility seekers.

Lodging

$$$ ★ **Hotel Antumalal.** Set back off the beach at the south end of Junquillal, the resort of Atumalal is perhaps a bit too slick for its location. On the other hand, why not play tennis, slide into the pool, have an Italian dinner, then disco the night away close to a perfect beach in the middle of nowhere? The grounds are pleasant, and the views of the sea from the main dining room behind the reception area are splendid. Breakfast is included in the price of a room. ✉ *Apdo. 49, Santa Cruz,* ☎ FAX *653–0425. 23 rooms. Restaurant, 3 bars, refrigerators, pool, tennis court, dance club. AE, MC, V.*

$$$ ★ **Hotel Playa Negra.** For years, surfers and other adventurers have roughed it at assorted motley lodges and cabinas in the area. All that changed with the 1996 opening of Lito Pedro Fernandez's hotel. Behind the restaurant-bar facing the sea, a collection of round thatched-roof cabinas sits among lawns and plantings. Cooled by ceiling fans, the cabinas are all bright pastels outside and built-in sofas and beautiful tile bathrooms inside. The ocean is good for swimming and snorkeling, with rock reefs providing shelter, tidal pools, and swim-

ming holes. And for surfers, with a good swell running, this is paradise found. The restaurant serves Latin and European dishes deftly prepared by the French and Costa Rican chefs. ⊠ *Go north on the dirt road out of Paraiso, follow signs carefully at forks in the road,* ☎ 🅵🅰🆇 *382–1301, 293–0332 reservations office in San José. 10 cabinas. Restaurant, bar, pool, tennis court, horseback riding, volleyball. AE, MC, V.*

$$–$$$ 🏨 **Guacamaya Lodge.** Up on the hill a few hundred yards off Playa Jun-
★ quillal (follow signs), the secluded Guacamaya offers expansive views and ideal bird-watching. Swiss brother and sister Alice and Bernie Etene have established a delightful compound, with flocks of visiting parrots in the morning and a multitude of cranes visible in the estuary below. The three-meal restaurant is very reasonably priced. ⊠ *Apdo. 6, Santa Cruz,* ☎ 🅵🅰🆇 *653–0431. 6 cabinas. Restaurant, bar, pool. No credit cards.*

$$–$$$ 🏨 **Hotel Iguanazul.** Spread out along the bluff at the north end of Playa
★ Junquillal, the Iguanazul is an isolated beachfront resort that has it all: cabinas, a pool, a three-meal restaurant and bar, and 3 km (2 mi) of beach stretching south from the hotel. The hotel management will arrange an endless array of tours and offers karaoke nights and trips to local fiestas. The fabulous surf of Playa Negra is 10 minutes away. Ask for air-conditioning. ⊠ *Apdo. 130–5150, Santa Cruz,* ☎ *653–0124,* 🅵🅰🆇 *653–0123. 24 cabinas. Restaurant, bar, air-conditioning, pool, volleyball. AE, MC, V.*

$$–$$$ 🏨 **Mono Congo Lodge.** "Mono Congo" translates as howler monkey, and the noisy but endearing creatures are plentiful at this hotel on the road to Playa Negra. The hard-working American owners have trans-
formed 10 acres of barren cattle pasture into a little gem, with exten-
sive plantings surrounding a handsome three-story hardwood structure housing a restaurant, comfortable seating areas, and four guest rooms. A separate cabina rents for slightly more. If the waves go flat, take a ride: the owners guide horseback tours. Good food, good waves, boards for rent, and rustic, comfortable accommodations are available on demand: a perfect spot for a surfer's dream holiday. ⊠ *Apdo. 177–5150, Santa Cruz,* ☎ *382–6926,* 🅵🅰🆇 *680–0208. 4 rooms with bath, 1 cabina. Restaurant, pool, horseback riding. No credit cards.*

$ 🏨 **Hotel Playa Junquillal.** Highly recommended for low-budget wan-
★ derers in search of a secret spot, the Hotel Playa Junquillal is an old-
fashioned, funky little resort, short on amenities but long on charm. After all, with a 3-km (2-mi) stretch of beach in your front yard, you can do without amenities. The only hotel on the beach proper, it is run by a shifting cast of American partners, all very friendly and happy to share stories over cold beers. The restaurant sits on one side of the quasi-
landscaped courtyard, and the sparely furnished cabinas sit on the other. ⊠ *Apdo. 22, Santa Cruz,* ☎ 🅵🅰🆇 *653–0432;* ⊠ *May–Sept. contact Robin and Mike Lake, Box 67, Kyburz, CA 95720,* ☎ *916/659–0714. 4 cabinas. Restaurant. No credit cards.*

NICOYA PENINSULA A TO Z

Arriving and Departing

By Boat
See Getting Around, *below.*

By Bus
PUNTARENAS TO CABO BLANCO
Buses (**Empresarios Unidos,** ☎ 222–0064) run from San José (C. 12 between Avdas. 7 and 9) to Puntarenas daily, every 30 minutes 6 AM–7 PM (2-hr trip). Ferries (**Asociacion de Desarrollo Integral Paquera,**

☎ 661–2830) connect Puntarenas with Playa Naranjo and Paquera, with continuing bus service to Montezuma.

NICOYA AND THE TEMPISQUE RIVER DELTA REGION

Buses (**Empresa Alfaro,** ☎ 222–2666) run from San José (C. 14 between Avdas. 3 and 5) daily to Nicoya (includes Río Tempisque ferry) at 6 AM, 8 AM, and 2 PM. Buses run to Liberia at 6:30 and 10 AM and 1:30, 3, and 5 PM, same location. Daily buses (**Tralapa,** ☎ 221–7202) to Santa Cruz leave from San José's Calle 14 between Avenidas 1 and 3 every hour from 7 AM to 1 PM and at 2, 4, and 6 PM.

CENTRAL NICOYA BEACHES: PUNTA ISLITA TO NOSARA

Buses (**Empresa Alfaro,** ☎ 222–2666) leave San José (C. 14 between Avdas. 3 and 5) daily at 6 AM for the six-hour trip to Nosara. Buses (**Empresa Alfaro,** ☎ 222–2750) leave from Calle 14 between Avenidas 3 and 5 for Sámara daily at 12:30 PM (4½ hrs).

LIBERIA AND THE NORTHERN NICOYA BEACHES

Buses (**Pulmitan,** ☎ 222–1650) leave hourly (6 AM–8 PM) from San José's Calle 14 between Avenidas 1 and 3 for Liberia (4 hrs). For Playa del Coco, a bus runs daily at 8 AM and 2 PM from Calle 14 between Avenidas 1 and 3 (5 hrs). For Hermosa and Playa Panamá, a bus (**Empresa Esquivel,** ☎ 666–1249) departs daily at 3:20 PM (5 hrs) from Calle 12 between Avenidas 5 and 7. Buses (**Tralapa,** ☎ 221–7202) for Brasilito, Flamingo, and Potrero leave daily from Calle 20 between Avenidas 3 and 5 at 8 and 10 AM and 3:30 PM (6 hrs). For Tamarindo, a bus (**Empresa Alfaro,** ☎ 222–2666) leaves daily at 3:30 PM from Calle 14 between Avenidas 3 and 5 (5½ hrs). A bus (**Tralapa,** ☎ 221–7202) bound for Junquillal leaves every day at 2 PM from Calle 20 between Avenidas 3 and 5.

By Car

Road access to the northwest is by way of the paved two-lane Pan-American Highway (CA1), which starts from the top of Paseo Colón in San José.

By Plane

Sansa (✉ C. 42 between Avdas. 3 and 5, San José, ☎ 221–9414, FAX 255–2176) and **Travelair** (✉ Aeropuerto Internacional Tobías Bolaños, Apdo. 8–4920, ☎ 220–3054, FAX 220–0413) fly to San José, Liberia, Tamarindo, Carrillo, Nosara, Punta Islita, and Tambor.

Getting Around

By Boat

Note that these schedules are subject to change, especially as relates to the high and low seasons. If possible call ahead to verify schedules.

PUNTARENAS TO CABO BLANCO

The Puntarenas–Playa Naranjo **car ferry** (☎ 661–1069) takes 1½ hours and departs daily at 3:15, 7, and 10:30 AM and 2:50 and 7 PM. The 1½-hour Puntarenas–Paquera ferry features six departures daily between 6 AM and 7: 15 PM, with an equal number of return trips. Two competing companies run this service, so don't be fooled by the signs with only three departures listed. The Tambor ferry departs from Puntarenas daily at 4:15 AM, 8:45 AM, 12:30 PM, and 5:30 PM. A passenger-only ferry leaves Puntarenas daily at 6 AM, returning at 2:30 PM. Bus links and cabs are available at the Nicoya ends of the ferry lines. Pedestrian-only ferry service from Montezuma to Paquera and Puntarenas is also available; just ask around in town. Expect long waits in high season and holiday weekends on all car ferries.

NICOYA AND THE TEMPISQUE RIVER DELTA REGION

The Tempisque car ferry crosses continuously and takes 20 minutes; lines can get very long in the dry season.

By Bus

PUNTARENAS TO CABO BLANCO

Buses run to Montezuma from Paquera daily at 8 AM and 5 PM, returning at 5:30 AM and 2 PM. There may be schedule changes and added routes since press time: the best place to check for the latest routes and times is the tourist office in San José.

CENTRAL NICOYA BEACHES: PUNTA ISLITA TO NOSARA

Buses (**Empresa Rojas,** ☎ 685–5352) leave Nicoya for Nosara, Garza, and Guiones daily at 10 AM and 2 PM; the same line offers service from Nicoya to Samara, Monday to Friday at 8 and 10 AM, noon, 3 and 4:15 PM, and to Carrillo leaving Nicoya at 3 PM.

LIBERIA AND THE NORTHERN NICOYA BEACHES

Buses (☎ 666–1249) from Liberia leave daily for Hermosa and Panama at 7:30 and 11:30 AM and 3:30, 5:30, and 7 PM. A bus from Santa Cruz to Junquillal departs daily at 6: 30 PM.

By Car

Paved roads run down the spine of the Nicoya Peninsula all the way to Playa Naranjo, with just a few unpaved stretches. Once you get off the main highway, the pavement holds out only so far, and then dirt, dust, mud, potholes, and other factors come into play. The roads to Playa Sámara and Playa del Coco are paved all the way; every other destination requires some dirt-road maneuvering. If you're headed down to the coast via unpaved roads, be sure to get as much information as possible, in advance, regarding the condition of the roads you plan to travel. Take a four-wheel-drive vehicle if possible.

Contacts and Resources

Car Rentals

It's always best to contact the main rental offices in San José. **ADA** (Avda. 18 between Cs. 11 and 13, San José, ☎ 233–7733, 800/CAR–RENT) offers pickup and car delivery in Liberia. **Sol Rentacar** (✉ In front of Hotel El Bramadero, San José, ☎ 666–2222). **Budget** (10 km/6 mi west of airport, ☎ 223–3284 San José office). **Economy** (Sabana Norte, ☎ 232–9130) now offers cars in Tamarindo. **Elegante** (C. 10 between Avdas. 13 and 15, ☎ 221–0066) also offers cars in Tamarindo.

Emergencies

In case of **emergency,** dial ☎ 911. **Ambulance** (☎ 221–5818). **Fire** (☎ 118). **Police** (☎ 117 in towns, 127 in rural areas). **Traffic Police** (☎ 227–8030).

Guided Tours

ADVENTURE

The **Hotel Oasis del Pacific** (✉ Apdo. 200–5400, Puntarenas, ☎ FAX 661–1555) in Playa Naranjo serves as a base for riveting sea-kayaking trips along the coast and among the islands of the Golfo de Nicoya.

DAY TRIPS

Day trips to the idyllic Isla Tortuga in the Golfo de Nicoya are very popular, and **Calypso Tours** (✉ Arcadas building, 3rd floor, Apdo. 6941–1000, San José, ☎ 233–3617, FAX 256–6767) has been doing them the longest. **Guanacaste Tours** (☎ 666–0306) is recommended for day trips from within the northwest to Santa Rosa, Palo Verde, Playa Ostional, Playa Grande by night (to see turtles), and Arenal (☞ Chapter 4); guides pick up tour participants from large hotels in the area.

SPECIAL-INTEREST TOURS

Tikal Tours (⌧ Avda. 2, between Cs. 7 and 9, Apdo. 6398–1000, San José, ☎ 223–2811) runs highly informative weeklong tours that take in Parque Nacional Carara, Parque Nacional Manuel Antonio, the Lomas Barbudal reserve, Playa Grande, Parque Nacional Santa Rosa, and Arenal (☞ Chapter 4). The excellent **Horizontes** (⌧ 150 yards north of Pizza Hut Paseo Colón, San José, ☎ 222–2022) specializes in more independent tours with as few as eight people, including transport by four-wheel-drive vehicle, naturalist guides, and guest lecturers.

Visitor Information

The tourist office in San José (☞ Visitor Information *in* San José A to Z, *in* Chapter 2) has information covering Guanacaste. In Liberia, the **Casa de la Cultura** (⌧ 3 blocks from Central Plaza, ☎ 666–1606) has local tourist information. It is open Monday–Saturday 8–4.

6 CENTRAL PACIFIC COSTA RICA

This may be one of Costa Rica's smallest regions, but it is endowed with disproportionate natural assets. Playas Jacó, Hermosa, and Manuel Antonio promise sparkling surf and sun-baked sand, while the Reserva Biológica Carara and Parque Nacional Manuel Antonio hold rare, beautiful species. And since it's so close to San José, it is the perfect destination if you are in a hurry to start your rest and recreation.

Updated by
David
Dudenhoefer

SMALL BUT VARIED, the region southwest of San José packs in most of the attractions that would draw you to Costa Rica: lush tropical forests, palm-lined beaches, and varied terrain for an array of outdoor activities. The region—its Reserva Biológica Carara in particular—is a transition zone between the tropical dry forest of the northwest and the wet forests of the nearby southern Pacific coast. However, since most of its woodlands were cut years ago, the central Pacific landscape is dominated by steep coffee farms, vast oil palm plantations, and rolling green pastures that provide the perfect setting for horseback riding. Parque Nacional Manuel Antonio protects an indented stretch of coastal rain forest and idyllic white-sand beaches. Despite the fact that the region's protected areas are among the smallest in the country, they are vibrant habitats alive with an amazing variety of flora and fauna, including such endangered species as the scarlet macaw and the Central American squirrel monkey. Decent snorkeling and world-class sportfishing are paramount in Playas Jacó and Manuel Antonio thanks to abundant marine life. Ideal conditions for surfing, sea kayaking, horseback riding, rafting, hiking, and bird-watching also abound in this region, within just 160 km (100 mi) of San José.

Pleasures and Pastimes

Dining

Since the central Pacific zone is one of the most-visited parts of Costa Rica, it is only natural that it should have some excellent dining options. Manuel Antonio and Jacó have restaurants with some of the best food in the country, but by no means do they have the dining market cornered—some of the region's isolated lodges also serve delicious and tasty local food. Given the area's world-class fishing, it's no surprise that seafood—from fresh caught dorado and mahimahi to crustaceans—is the forte among the area's best chefs.

Lodging

The central Pacific's accommodations are as varied as its scenery; you can choose from beachside cement boxes to luxury hotels—the country's premier establishments among them—perched on verdant hillsides. Manuel Antonio hosts some of the country's most expensive accommodations, charging more than $150 for a double during high season, but nearby Quepos has rates to please backpackers, and there are plenty of inns that fall between the extremes. As a rule, prices drop 20% to 30% during low season.

Outdoor Adventures

There is no shortage of outdoor diversions to choose from in this corner of the country. Several white-water rivers—Ríos Parrita, Naranjo, and the less accessible Savegre—flow down from the Cordillera de Talamanca chain to the northeast. Horseback riding can be done just about everywhere, and two working ranches near Orotina that double as hotels have enough trails to keep you in the saddle for a week. Skin diving is good in the Manuel Antonio area, and the offshore sportfishing is among the best in the world. The region also has great surfing, sea kayaking, and ocean excursions ranging from wave-runner tours to dolphin-watching sunset cruises.

Exploring Central Pacific Costa Rica

This region's attractions lie conveniently close to each other, which makes it easy to combine beach time with forest exploration or country living with marine diversions. Every one of its destinations lies between two and four hours from San José by road. A winding mountain road passes through Atenas on the way to Orotina, from where the coastal highway, or Costanera, heads southeast to Tárcoles, Jacó, Playa Hermosa, and Quepos. The flight from San José to Quepos is speedy, a mere half hour.

Numbers in the text correspond to numbers in the margin and on the central Pacific Costa Rica map.

Great Itineraries

IF YOU HAVE 3 DAYS

Fly directly to ☒ **Quepos** ⑧ and hit the beach at ☒ **Manuel Antonio** ⑨. If you are driving, be sure to stop at **Reserva Biológica Carara** ③ on your way to Manuel Antonio. Get up early the next day and explore **Parque Nacional Manuel Antonio** ⑩. Spend the afternoon either horseback riding or relaxing on the beach. Dedicate the third morning to river rafting, skin diving, or going on another tour; then catch an afternoon flight back to San José.

IF YOU HAVE 6 DAYS

Spend the first two nights at one of the ranches near ☒ **Orotina** ②, enjoying horseback riding, rafting, and bird-watching, and from there explore the **Reserva Biológica Carara** ③. On the third morning, head to either the ☒ **Tárcoles** ④, ☒ **Jacó** ⑤, or ☒ **Playa Hermosa** ⑥ to get your beach and surfing fix. On day four go south to ☒ **Manuel Antonio** ⑨, spending the day fishing, skin diving, rafting, horseback riding, or lounging on the beach. Visit **Parque Nacional Manuel Antonio** ⑩ early on day five; then drive back into the mountains to spend the last night in **Atenas** ①, which lies just 40 minutes from the international airport. Since Quepos and Manuel Antonio have so much to offer, an alternative would be to fly straight there, and dedicate all five days to that diverse beach resort. If you crave more remote conditions, spend two days in the Manuel Antonio area and head south to the Osa Peninsula (☞ Chapter 7) for the last three days, catching a flight from Golfito back to San José.

When to Tour Central Pacific Costa Rica

The weather in the central Pacific region follows the same dry- and rainy-season weather patterns common to the rest of the Pacific slope, which means lots of sun from December to May and frequent rain from September to November. Since you'll have to share the area with plenty of tourists during the dry months, consider touring the region during the low season. The weather actually tends to be perfect in July and August, with lots of sunny days and occasional light rain.

CENTRAL PACIFIC HINTERLANDS

Beaches may be this region's biggest draw, but the countryside hosts vast haciendas interspersed with patches of tropical wilderness where you might encounter an array of interesting critters ranging from capuchin monkeys to collared aracaris, and estuaries where crocodiles lurk amidst the mangroves. Because it is an ecological transition zone, the region is host to extreme biological diversity, making it great for bird-watchers and other nature enthusiasts.

Atenas

❶ *42 km (26 mi) west of San José.*

National Geographic magazine once listed Atenas as one of the 12 places with the best climates in the world, which is pretty much this little town's

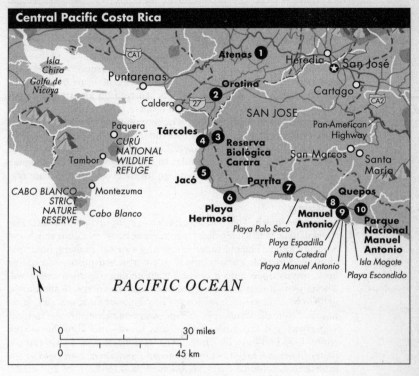

Central Pacific Costa Rica

Atenas **1**
Héredia
San José
Isla Chira
Golfo de Nicoya
Puntarenas
CA1
Orotina **2**
Cartago
CA2
Caldera
27
SAN JOSE
Paquera
Tárcoles
4 **3**
Reserva Biológica Carara
Pan-American Highway
San Marcos
Santa María
CURÚ NATIONAL WILDLIFE REFUGE
Tambor
Montezuma
Jacó **5**
Parrita **7**
Quepos
CABO BLANCO STRICT NATURE RESERVE
Cabo Blanco
6
Playa Hermosa
Playa Palo Seco
8
Manuel Antonio
9 **10**
Parque Nacional Manuel Antonio
Playa Espadilla
Punta Catedral
Playa Manuel Antonio
Isla Mogote
Playa Escondido

N

PACIFIC OCEAN

0   30 miles
0   45 km

only claim to fame. In addition to having spectacular weather, Atenas is a pleasantly quiet, traditional community that few foreigners visit, despite the fact that it lies on the main route to the central Pacific beaches. Some well-kept wooden and adobe houses are scattered around a small church and central plaza, and surrounding the town are coffee farms, cattle ranches, and patches of forest. Just to the west of Atenas, the road to Orotina winds its way down the mountains past breathtaking views.

Lodging

$$$ 🏨 **El Cafetal Inn.** The friendly owners of this B&B—a Salvadorean-Colombian couple—go out of their way to make you comfortable and to help with travel plans. Their small two-story cement lodge is set on a hill amidst a coffee farm. The larger tower rooms have curved windows for panoramic views. Complimentary breakfast is usually served on the patio out back. Trails through the surrounding countryside are the perfect routes for hiking or horseback riding tours. This place is halfway between Grecia and Atenas and is as close to the airport as San José. ⊠ *Apdo. 105, Atenas, on highway 1 km (½ mi) west of Grecia, left just before bridge, follow signs,* ☎ 446–5785, FAX 446–7028. *10 rooms with bath. Restaurant, pool. AE, MC, V.*

$$ 🏨 **Ana's Place.** Though it's just a few blocks from Atenas center, this cozy B&B may give you the impression you're in the countryside, thanks to its large garden inhabited by squawking macaws and parrots. Rooms in the main house are slightly brighter, but those in separate buildings overlooking the garden offer more privacy. Breakfast and dinner are served on the main house's back porch. ⊠ *3 blocks east of church,* ☎ 446–5019, FAX 446–6975. *10 rooms with bath. Pool. MC, V.*

Orotina

② *24 km (15 mi) southwest of Atenas, 66 km (41 mi) southwest of San José.*

One of the central Pacific's oldest communities, Orotina is a laid-back commercial center and transportation hub in the heart of an important agricultural region. The town is centered on an attractive park shaded by tall tropical trees, with a modern church towering over its eastern end. The town market, a rickety building near the park, is a good place to pick up some of the fruits, such as mangoes, grown in the area. The main agricultural endeavor around Orotina, however, is cattle ranching; the two haciendas to the west of town (☞ Lodging, *below*) that have been converted into lovely hotels are the main reasons to stop here.

Lodging

$$$ 🏨 **Dundee Ranch.** This 850-acre hacienda right up the road from Hacienda Doña Marta (☞ *below*) is something between a dude ranch and a nature lodge. The old ranch house and a newer building hold spacious, comfortable guest rooms with colorful bedspreads and ceiling fans; rooms open onto a portico surrounding a garden courtyard. Though you'll hear chittering wildlife from the rooms, in the Cañón del Río Machuca (Machuca River Canyon), monkeys, macaws, iguanas, and toucans abound; in a shallow lagoon nearby are the resident waterfowl and crocodile. Two dozen tours—including horseback trips—keep you busy. ✉ *Apdo. 7812–1000, San José, 16 km (10 mi) west of Orotina, take Costanera toward Puntarenas, turn right at 3rd intersection, look for ABOPAC factory,* ☎ *428–8776 or 267–6222,* FAX *267–6229. 25 rooms with bath. Restaurant, air-conditioning, pool, horseback riding. AE, MC, V.*

$$$ 🏨 **Hacienda Doña Marta.** Part cattle ranch, part romantic hideaway, ★ this little complex of wooden *cabinas* surrounding a tiny pool shaded by *marañón* (cashew fruit) and coconut trees is a real find. Fine hardwoods and bamboo ceilings, cool tile floors, expansive bathrooms and showers, and sweet country-style appointments characterize the rooms—each one different and prettier than the next. The no-funnybusiness kitchen crew cooks stellar traditional meals, served in the handsome wood-beamed dining room, where you'll find handmade pottery for sale. Horseback riding among acres of woods, cattle pastures, and mango trees is a must, as is early morning bird-watching. ✉ *Apdo. 463–1000, San José, (for directions, ☞ Dundee Ranch, above),* ☎ *253–6514 or 428–8126,* FAX *234–0958. 6 cabinas, 2 rooms. Dining room, pool, horseback riding. No credit cards.*

Reserva Biológica Carara

③ *21 km (13 mi) southwest of Orotina, 83 km (51 mi) southwest of San José.*

Situated between Costa Rica's drier northwest and the more humid south, Reserva Biológica Carara (Carara Biological Reserve, ☞ also Chapter 10) is part of an ecological transition zone and consequently contains a great diversity of flora and fauna. Much of the 47-sq-km (18-sq-mi) reserve is covered in primary forest growing on steep slopes, the massive trees laden with vines and epiphytes. The relatively sparse undergrowth makes wildlife easier to see here than in many other parks—though animals are always tough to spot in the tropics. If you're lucky, you might catch a glimpse of armadillos, baslisk lizards, blue-crowned motmots, scarlet macaws, iguanas, coatis, and various kinds of monkeys.

You'll find the first trail on the left shortly after the bridge that spans the Río Tárcoles. It leads to a horseshoe lagoon, which was abandoned as an oxbow lake by the meandering Tárcoles. It is now almost entirely covered with water hyacinths and is home to water birds such as the northern jacana and boat-billed heron, as well as river turtles and crocodiles. The main ranger station is several miles farther south, and next to it another trail heads into the forest. Remember that the earlier in the morning you get here, the more likely you are to see the animals. *CA1 to Atenas turnoff, turn left and follow signs for Jacó; on left after crossing Río Tárcoles.* ☎ *$6.* ☉ *Daily 8–4.*

Tárcoles

❹ *90 km (56 mi) southwest of San José.*

Although the town of Tárcoles doesn't warrant a stop, it is the departure point for a crocodile-watching boat tour up the Río Tárcoles. Two exceptional hotels are nearby (☞ Lodging, *below*), as is a spectacular waterfall set in a private nature reserve. If you pull over just after crossing the **Río Tárcoles bridge,** you can often spot such elegant birds as roseate spoonbills, great egrets, and baby blue herons strutting through the shallows as well as massive crocodiles lounging along the banks (bring your binoculars). The entrance to Tárcoles is on the west side of the road, just south of the Reserva Biológica Carara (☞ *above*); across the highway is a dirt road that leads to the Hotel Villa Lapas (☞ Lodging, *below*) and the waterfall reserve.

The **Manantial de Agua Viva** is a 600-ft waterfall in the heart of a private reserve across from Tárcoles. The waterfall flows into 10 natural pools, perfect for a refreshing dip after the hike into the reserve. The forest surrounding the waterfall is home to parrots, monkeys, scarlet macaws, and most of the other animals found in the adjacent Reserva Biológica Carara (☞ *above*). A 2½-km (1½-mi) trail makes a loop through the woods, passing the waterfall and pools; it can take from 40 minutes to two hours to hike, depending on how much bird-watching you do. The entrance is 5 km (3 mi) from the coastal highway, up the same dirt road that leads to the Hotel Villa Lapas (☞ Lodging, *below*). ☎ *$7.* ☉ *Daily 8–5.*

Lodging

$$$$ 🏨 **Villa Caletas.** Set amidst the rain forest atop a promontory, this elegant collection of villas built along lush slopes may seem remote, but
★ it is only minutes from Jacó and Carara. Although the architecture is reminiscent of Southeast Asia, guest rooms are decorated in the French style, with fine antiques and art, black furniture, and sweeping draperies. French is also the predominant influence in the cuisine, served in an attractive open-air restaurant. The cleverly designed pool appears to blend into the horizon. The entrance is on the west side of the road between Tárcoles and Jacó. ✉ *Apdo. 12358–1000, San José,* ☎ *257–3653 or 382–5794,* 🖷 *222–2059. 8 rooms with bath, 6 suites, 11 villas. Restaurant, bar, pool. AE, MC, V.*

$$$–$$$$ 🏨 **Hotel Villa Lapas.** The grounds of this hotel, just a short drive from Carara and the waterfall reserve (☞ *above*), are shaded by tall trees with a stream flowing by, making it a great spot for bird-watching. A trail heads up the valley into the hotel's patch of protected forest. White bungalows with barrel-tile roofs and small porches hold two rooms each; those closest to the restaurant have views of the stream and forest. Three meals and all beverages are included in the price. Reservations are handled by Alegro Resorts. ✉ *Apdo. 171–5400, Puntarenas,* ☎ *663–0811,* 🖷 *663–1516. 46 rooms with bath. Restaurant, bar, pool. AE, MC, V.*

Outdoor Activities and Sports

BOAT TRIPS

After hiking the trails of Carara, the most popular activity in the area is the river trip up the muddy Río Tárcoles to see ferocious crocodiles and colorful birds. **Victor Pineda** (☎ 637–0426), out of Tárcoles, runs a boat tour that guarantees close encounters of the crocodilian kind. Jacó's **Fantasy Tours** (✉ Best Western lobby, ☎ 643–3032) runs its own boat trip on the Río Tárcoles.

COAST NEAR SAN JOSÉ

Along this short stretch of Pacific coast are some of Costa Rica's most accessible beaches and the popular Parque Nacional Manuel Antonio. Since its attractions lie just a few hours' drive from San José, it is a region where, if you are short on time, you can get a quick overview of Costa Rica's rich natural splendor.

Jacó

❺ *18 km (11 mi) south of Tárcoles, 108 km (67 mi) southwest of San José.*

The relative proximity to San José, coupled with the attractiveness of its wide sandy bay, has lead to Jacó's development into a major resort during the last two decades. More than 50 hotels and cabinas reside behind its long gray-sand beach, and the cluttered appearance of the town's main drag makes it look distinctly overdeveloped. But stroll along that beach, and you'll find that the development is hidden behind the palms and that it's big enough to allow you to escape from the package tours and surfer dudes, except during the major holidays. If you do want fun in the sun and nightlife, this is the closest beach resort to the capital. Aside from sunbathing and surfing, you can rent bicycles, go horseback riding, or take a tour to the nearby Reserva Biológica Carara or the Río Tárcoles.

The gray sand of Jacó's long, palm-lined **Playa Jacó** can burn the soles of your feet on a sunny afternoon. It's a popular spot with surfers due to the consistency of its waves, but riptides make the sea hazardous for swimmers when the waves are big. If you're traveling with children, you might want to hit the **miniature golf** course on the town's main drag.

Dining and Lodging

$$ ✗ **Chatty Cathy's.** This small, second-floor restaurant in the heart of Jacó is the place to go for breakfast. The friendly Canadian owners serve an array of fast-breaking favorites—banana pancakes, bacon, hash browns, cinnamon buns—as well as some tasty inventions of their own and a small lunch menu. The name's no joke; she'll happily talk your ear off if you let her. *Across from Rayo Azul supermarket, ☎ no phone. No credit cards. Closed Mon.–Tues. and Apr. No dinner.*

$$ ✗ **El Recreo.** This place has Jacó's most extensive seafood menu: if it swims in the sea, they probably serve it, with the possible exception of surfers and tourists. Sure, they have a few meat and vegetable dishes, but the menu is dominated by tuna, lobster, shrimp, and mahimahi, all prepared in a variety of ways. Seating is beneath a big thatched roof overlooking Jacó's main street; a colorful marine mural covers the only wall. *Across from Rayo Azul supermarket, ☎ 643–1172. AE, MC, V.*

$$ ✗ **Rioasis.** This colorful, open-air restaurant just off Jacó's main street is the reincarnation of Killer Munchies, which used to be one of this town's most popular eateries. Seating is on the front patio or under a high roof hung with ceiling fans and backed by a long bar. The menu is eclectic—burritos and other Tex-Mex treats, a few pastas, and sal-

ads—but the big draw is the pizza, with more than two dozen different pies baked in a wood-burning oven. *Just north of the Banco Nacional,* ☎ 643–3354. V.

$$$–$$$$ 🏨 **Hotel Club del Mar.** It's easy to forget you're in busy Jacó when you
★ stay at this secluded spot on the southern extreme of the beach. Bungalows are shaded by giant trees, and iguanas lounge on the lawn. Handsome superior rooms have green tile floors, high ceilings, and wooden shutters that open onto porches or balconies. Smaller standard rooms in back have kitchenettes, sitting areas, and balconies. Budget rooms are a bit cramped. The restaurant is not only one of the few in Jacó with an ocean view, but it also serves some of the best food in town. ✉ *Apdo. 107–4023, follow Costanera south past main entrances, turn right at first street after service station,* ☎ FAX *643–3194. 18 rooms with bath. Restaurant, bar, pool. AE, MC, V.*

$$$ 🏨 **Tangerí Chalets.** The first six rooms in these two-story cement buildings have ocean views, whereas the remaining eight overlook the hotel's lawn and two pools. All rooms have tile floors, high ceilings, two double beds, and small balconies or porches. Each eccentrically designed bungalow has a kitchen, covered patio, and eight beds, perfect for a family or small group. ✉ *Apdo. 622–4050, Alajuela, on main street, between Jacó center and Best Western,* ☎ *643–3001,* FAX *643–3636. 14 rooms with bath, 10 bungalows. Restaurant, air-conditioning, pool, basketball. AE, MC, V.*

$$–$$$ 🏨 **Aparthotel Flamboyant.** This small, quiet oceanfront hotel is a good
★ deal, especially if you take advantage of the cooking facilities. All the rooms have kitchenettes, breakfast bars, tile floors, ceiling fans, and a double and single bed. Small terraces with chairs overlook the verdant pool area, where there's a grill for your use. It's all just a few steps from the beach and Jacó's busy main strip. ✉ *Jacó center, behind Flamboyant Restaurant, Apdo. 018, Puntarenas,* ☎ *643–3146,* FAX *643–1068. 9 rooms with bath. Kitchenettes, pool. AE, MC, V.*

$$ 🏨 **Mar de Luz.** It may be a couple of blocks from the beach, and it doesn't look like much from the street, but Mar de Luz is a surprisingly pleasant place. The Dutch owners are dedicated to cleanliness and details, such as the grill next to the pool, well-stocked kitchenettes, and cable TV. Pastel older rooms have two queen-size beds and small porches. Split-level newer rooms are a bit larger, with attractive stone walls, white tile floors, and windows overlooking the gardens. *50 yards east of main road, across from Tangerí Chalets,* ☎ FAX *643–3259. 27 rooms with bath. Kitchenettes, air-conditioning, pool. No credit cards.*

$–$$ 🏨 **Cabinas Alice.** Spread along a narrow oceanfront property, these cabinas are one of the best deals in town. Rooms open onto a lawn that doubles as a parking lot. Those closest to the beach are slightly bigger and brighter; they also have several with kitchenettes, which cost a bit more. The modern, open-air restaurant serves good seafood and Costa Rican standards. ✉ *Jacó, end of the first street south of Red Cross building,* ☎ FAX *643–3061. 22 rooms with bath. Restaurant, kitchenettes, pool. AE, MC, V.*

Nightlife and the Arts

During the high season, Jacó gets lively when the sun goes down. Cut loose at the popular disco **La Central** (☎ 643–3076), on the beach opposite Tienda La Flor. You can also dance at **Los Tucanes** (☎ 643–3226), next door to La Central. If you prefer to have a seat and watch a game, you should hit the **sports bar** by the Copacabana Hotel's pool.

Outdoor Activities and Sports

SURFING

Jacó has several excellent beach breaks, which are best around high tide. The town's reputation as a surfer's paradise has spread far and wide, and you'll consequently see dozens of surfboard-toting tourists. Several places rent surfboards, such as **Chosita del Surf** (☎ no phone), which also repairs them; it's on the main street just north of the Hacienda Restaurant. If you're going to spend more than a week surfing, it might be cheaper to buy a used board and sell it before you leave. **Mother of Fear** (☎ 643–2001), on the main street south of Tangerí Chalets (☞ Dining and Lodging, *above*), has the best selection of used surfboards in the country.

Playa Hermosa

❻ *5 km (3 mi) south of Jacó, 113 km (70 mi) southwest of San José.*

Just over the rocky ridge that defines the southern end of Jacó is Playa Hermosa, a swath of gray sand stretching off to the southeast as far as the eye can see. The northern end of Playa Hermosa is a popular spot with surfers; because of the beach's angle, it often has waves when Jacó and other spots are flat. But you don't have to be a surfer to enjoy Hermosa, a quiet alternative to Jacó. If you want to swim, keep in mind that dangerous rip currents are common when the waves are big.

Lodging

$$$ 🏨 **Fuego del Sol.** A colorful tropical garden surrounds the pool area of this modern beachfront hotel. There's a small, open-air sports bar by the pool, next to which is a simple restaurant with an ocean view. Rooms are in a two-story cement building; all have tile floors, ceiling fans, and rain-forest wall paintings. Those upstairs have high wooden ceilings and balconies overlooking either the pool area or beach, and those downstairs have small terraces. *North end of beach,* ☎ 643–3737, FAX 643–3736. 20 rooms with bath. Restaurant, bar, air-conditioning, pool, exercise room. AE, MC, V.

$$ 🏨 **Ola Bonita.** Just a few steps from the surf break, this two-story building with a barrel-tile roof is a nicer alternative to Hermosa's other low-budget hotels. Rooms have red-tile floors, white-stucco walls, simple kitchenettes, fans, and one bunk and one double bed. There's a tiny pool out front for a quick dip after the ocean. ⊠ *Playa Hermosa,* ☎ FAX 643–3990. 5 rooms with bath. Kitchenettes, pool. No credit cards.

Outdoor Activities and Sports

HORSEBACK RIDING

If you tire of the surf and sand, **Hermosa Stables** (☎ 643–3808) runs a nice horseback tour into the nearby rain forest.

SURFING

Most people who stay at Playa Hermosa are here for one thing. Because of the beach's angle, it almost always has waves, even when most other breaks are flat. The surf is best at high tide. Boards can be rented, purchased, and repaired at nearby Jacó (☞ *above*).

Parrita

❼ *45 km (28 mi) south of Jacó, 150 km (93 mi) southwest of San José.*

Set in the heart of an African palm plantation, Parrita is a dusty town of painted wooden bungalows. First planted in 1945 by the United Fruit Company after its banana plantations were decimated by Panama disease, the palms are cultivated for their fruit, from which oil is extracted for margarine, cooking oil, scent, and soap. Though the town has little to offer travelers, a dirt road that heads west from the Costanera just south of town leads to **Playa Palo Seco,** an endless beach backed by palms and mangrove swamps.

Quepos

8 *23 km (14 mi) south of Parrita, 174 km (108 mi) southwest of San José.*

With around 12,000 inhabitants, Quepos is the largest and most important town in this corner of the country. The town owes its name to the Indian tribe that inhabited the area when the first Spaniard, Juan Vásquez de Coronado, rode through the region in 1563. Though there is some controversy as to whether those Indians were called Quepos or Quepoa, it is known that they lived by a combination of farming, hunting, and fishing, until the violence and disease that accompanied the Spanish conquest wiped them out.

For centuries following the conquest, Quepos hardly existed, but in the 1930s, the United Fruit Company put it on the map, building a banana port here and bringing in workers from other parts of Central America to populate the area. The town thrived for a decade, but when Panama disease decimated the banana plantations around 1945, the fruit company switched to the less lucrative oil palms, and the area slipped into a prolonged depression. Only during the past decade have tourism revenues lifted the town out of the extended slump. The town owes this renaissance to the natural beauty of the nearby beach and Parque Nacional Manuel Antonio (☞ *below*).

En Route   If you're traveling with children, or have a keen interest in wildlife, you may want to visit the **Jardín Gaia,** a small zoo that rehabilitates former pets and injured animals and releases them back into the wild. The zoo holds mostly parrots and macaws that were confiscated by government wildlife officials, as well as monkeys that were electrocuted while playing on power lines. *Left side of road to Manuel Antonio, 2½ km (1½ mi) from Quepos,* ☎ *777–0535.* 🎟 *$5.* ☉ *Thurs.–Tues. 2–5.*

Dining and Lodging

$$–$$$ ✕ **El Gran Escape.** On a corner on Quepos's waterfront street, with
★   seating scattered among an old wooden building, patio, and second-floor bar, this is the place to go for seafood and is a favorite spot with sportfishermen—they've got a "you hook 'em, we cook 'em" policy. The menu ranges from broiled shrimp with a tropical sauce to the catch of the day prepared in any of a half dozen ways. An impressive array of appetizers includes crab cakes, unusual in Costa Rica, and a good selection of burgers and Tex-Mex standards. ⊠ *Waterfront,* ☎ *777–0395. V. Closed Tues. and 2 wks in June.*

$–$$ 🏨 **Hotel Malinche.** One block west of the Quepos bus terminal, this small hotel has two types of rooms, all of which are a bargain. Newer air-conditioned ones are carpeted and have large tile baths with hot-water showers. Rooms cooled by ceiling fans cost about half as much. Those on the ground floor are nicer, with white tile floors and baths; those on the second floor have wooden floors and are slightly smaller. ⊠ *Avda. Central, ½ block south of bus station,* ☎ 🖷 *777–0093. 29 rooms with bath. MC, V.*

Nightlife and the Arts

American expatriates gather beneath the ceiling fans of **El Banco** (☎ 777–0478), on Avenida Central, to watch U.S. sports on the TV or to listen to live rock and roll. A popular watering hole with younger travelers is **La Bodeguita** (☎ no phone), upstairs behind the bus station, where wild murals cover the walls and reggae is usually blasting on the stereo. The popular disco **El Arco Iris** (☎ 777–0449), built out over the estuary just north of the bridge, gets packed on weekends and holidays. The late-night dance scene is at large, glitzy **Maracas** (☎ 777–

0707), south of town, next to the docks. There is a small casino in the ground floor of the **Hotel Kamuk** (☎ 777–0379) in Quepos.

Outdoor Activities and Sports

HORSEBACK RIDING

Lynch Travel (✉ Quepos, ☎ 777–1170) has two horseback tours, a three-hour ride to a scenic overlook, and an all-day trip to the Catarata de Nara, a waterfall that pours into a natural swimming pool. **Rain Maker** (✉ Next to Si Como No hotel, Manuel Antonio, ☎ 777–0850) offers a more exclusive horseback excursion through the pristine rain forest of a private reserve in the nearby mountains.

SPORTFISHING

The Southwest's waters have some of the country's finest deep-sea fishing, and Quepos is one of the best ports from which to head out. There are fewer boats trolling those waters than off Guanacaste, and they usually catch plenty of sailfish, marlin, wahoo, mahimahi, roosterfish, and yellowfin tuna. The following are some of the sportfishing operations in Quepos: **Costa Rican Dreams** (☎ 777–0593), **Sportfishing Karahé** (☎ 777—0170), **Sportfishing Costa Rica** (☎ 257–3553 or 800/862–1003), and **Lynch Travel** (☞ Horseback Riding, *above*).

WHITE-WATER RAFTING

There are three white-water rivers near Quepos, but unfortunately, they have rather limited seasons. The Parrita is a mellow (class II–III) route that is perfect for a first rafting trip; it can be run in rafts from May till January, when it drops so low that it is only navigable in two-person inflatable "duckies." The Naranjo (class III–IV) requires some experience and can only be run from June to December. The Savegre (class II–III) is a fun river that flows past plenty of rain forest and wildlife and can be navigated from June to March, but landslides sometimes limit access. **Iguana Tours** (☎ 777–1262), the oldest rafting outfitter in Quepos, also offers sea-kayaking tours. **Amigos del Río** (☎ 777–0082) operates trips down all the area's rivers.

Manuel Antonio

⑨ *3 km (2 mi) south of Quepos, 179 km (111 mi) southwest of San José.*

It doesn't take long to figure out why Manuel Antonio has become one of Costa Rica's most famous destinations; you need merely contemplate one of its many views of beaches, jungle, and the shimmering Pacific dotted with rocky islets. Spread over the hill that separates Quepos (☞ *above*) from Parque Nacional Manuel Antonio (☞ *below*), the town of Manuel Antonio is surrounded by dozens of hotels and restaurants that are scattered along the road between Quepos and the park. The best of those hotels are near the top of the hill, where the views are most spectacular. Since there is nearly as much rain forest around those hotels as in the nearby national park, most of the wildlife found in the park can also be seen near the hotels.

As the road approaches the national park, it skirts the lovely, palm-lined strand of **Playa Espadilla**, which stretches north from the rocky outcropping that defines the park's border. That long, palm-lined beach is popular with sunbathers, surfers, volleyball players, and vacationing Ticos, but beware of deadly rip currents when the waves are big.

Dining and Lodging

$$$–$$$$ ✕ **Jardín Gourmet.** Though seafood reigns here, as it does all over town, this open-air restaurant at the top of the hill stands apart from the crowd thanks to its Mediterranean kitchen. The extensive menu combines Italian and French influences with dishes such as *tagliatelle ai frutti di mare*

(mixed seafood pasta), and *poisson en papillote* (whole red snapper baked in parchment). The decoration is also a bit Mediterranean, with a red tile floor and white-stucco walls and pillars. *Next to Hotel Casitas Eclipse,* ☎ *777–1728. AE, DC, MC, V. Closed Wed.*

$$$ ✕ **Karolas.** Nestled in the forest just below the Barba Roja (☞ *below*), with tables on two simple patios surrounded by greenery, Karolas makes up for its lack of ocean view with the quality of its cuisine. And at night, it is easily Manuel Antonio's most attractive, intimate restaurant. The menu features such varied choices as grilled tuna and chicken caribe. Fresh fish and shrimp dishes are the specialties, as are homemade desserts—leave room for a piece of macadamia pie. Reservations are recommended. *Manuel Antonio,* ☎ *777–1557. V.*

$$–$$$ ✕ **Barba Roja.** Perched near the top of the hill, with sweeping views of the Manuel Antonio shoreline, the Barba Roja is one of this town's oldest and most popular restaurants. The dining room is furnished with dark hardwoods and decorated with colorful prints. Food takes a close second to atmosphere; try the daily fish specials and excellent sandwiches at lunchtime. Desserts are delicious, and breakfasting is quite popular, but the view is never more impressive than at sunset. *Manuel Antonio,* ☎ *777–0331. V. No lunch Mon.*

$$$$ 🏨 **La Mariposa.** Set high on a promontory, Manuel Antonio's classi-
★ est hotel has the best view in town, perhaps in the country: a sweeping panorama of verdant hills, pale beaches, rocky islands, and shimmering Pacific. The main building is a white Spanish-style villa with an open-air dining room and pool area below. Older, split-level units are perched along the edge of the ridge and have sitting rooms, balcony bedrooms, and conservatory bathrooms alive with plants. Newer one-level suites and deluxe rooms have hot tubs and cost slightly less. There are also a few rooms above the restaurant, which are smaller and less private. *Top of the hill,* ☎ *777–0355,* 🅵🅰🆇 *777–0050. 6 rooms, 12 suites, 4 villas. Restaurant, bar, pool. MC, V.*

$$$$ 🏨 **Makanda by the Sea.** Small and secluded Makanda has just half a
★ dozen unique villas scattered around the rain forest, with ocean views through the trees. The surrounding forest is popular with troops of monkeys and colorful birds, and a footpath winds through it to the hotel's small beach, a good snorkeling spot. All villas have high roofs, ceiling fans, hammocks, couches, and kitchenettes. The larger Villa 1 is completely open on the ocean side; the three "studios" below it are smaller and less expensive. The poolside restaurant serves some of the best food in town and is open to nonguests, if you reserve in time. *1 km (½ mi) west of La Mariposa,* ☎ *777–0442,* 🅵🅰🆇 *777–1032. 6 villas, 3 studios. Restaurant, kitchenettes, pool, beach. AE, MC, V.*

$$$$ 🏨 **Si Como No.** This eco-friendly place uses solar power, energy-efficient air-conditioning systems, and very little hardwoods and was designed to damage as little of the forest as possible. The result is an attractive inn surrounded by jungle that is frequented by fearless monkeys and varied birds. Tasteful rooms have pastels and stained-glass windows in the bathrooms; suites have small kitchens and balconies. Two suites join to make a villa, a good deal for two couples or a family. The blue-tiled pool has an artificial cascade, water slide, and swim-up bar. The hotel has a poolside grill, a formal Costa Rican restaurant, and a small movie theater. *Top of the hill,* ☎ *777–1250, 800/237–8201 in the U.S.;* 🅵🅰🆇 *777–1093. 6 rooms with bath, 32 suites. 2 restaurants, 2 bars, air-conditioning, pool, cinema. AE, MC, V.*

$$$$ 🏨 **Tulemar Bungalows.** The scenery surrounding these octagonal bungalows is impressive, and since the walls are almost completely made of windows, the rooms take good advantage of it. Spacious bungalows each have a small kitchen, sitting area with hideaway bed, and large bath with tub. A paved road winds down past the pool and grill and through the forest to a small private beach complete with a rustic bar and kayaks. The hotel provides transportation to and from the beach, but a walk down early in the morning makes for the perfect bird-watching expedition. *South of soccer field,* ☎ 777–0580, FAX 777–1579. *14 bungalows. Bar, kitchenettes, pool, beach, boating. AE, MC, V.*

$$$–$$$$ ★ ⌂ **Costa Verde.** The builders of this place located near the end of the road to Manuel Antonio were careful to damage the forest as little as possible. The hotel is therefore surrounded by lush foliage, where you might spot squirrel monkeys, sloths, and iguanas outside your room. Two types of rooms are spread through five buildings: smaller efficiencies, short on privacy, and spacious studios, with tile floors, larger beds, tables, chairs, and kitchenettes. All have ceiling fans, lots of screened windows, and large balconies shared between two rooms. An open-air restaurant serves good seafood and killer tropical drinks. ⊠ *Southern slope of hill, near park,* ☎ 777–0584, FAX 777–0560. *44 rooms with bath. Restaurant, bar, kitchenettes, 2 pools. AE, DC, MC, V.*

$$$–$$$$ ⌂ **Villas El Parque.** These wooden apartments are stacked along the southern slope of the hill that separates Quepos from Manuel Antonio, offering breathtaking views of the national park and adjacent coastline. Rooms are bright and spacious, with large seaward balconies complete with chairs and hammocks. Two rooms can be connected to form a villa, a good deal for a family or two couples. A small pool below the rooms, next to the restaurant, is surrounded by the rain forest. ⊠ *South side of hill,* ☎ 777–0096, FAX 777–0538. *34 rooms with bath. Restaurant, bar, pool. AE, MC, V.*

$$$ ⌂ **Hotel Verde Mar.** Also known as La Casa del Sol, this attractive little hotel sits inside the rain forest just back from the beach. Rooms are all in one long cement building, with colorfully decorated interiors and windows on each end, outside of which the foliage proliferates. A small pool lies in back, from where a wooden catwalk leads through the woods to the nearby beach. ⊠ *½ km (¼ mi) north of park,* ☎ 777–0481, FAX 777–1311. *20 rooms with bath. Kitchenettes, pool. AE, MC, V.*

$$$ ★ ⌂ **Villas Nicolas.** The more elevated of these attractive tiered apartments—Mediterranean white with barrel-tile roofs—have wonderful views over the Pacific. The more private rooms at the bottom look out at the jungle, where there's usually some interesting creature stirring. Half the units have well-equipped kitchens; all have terra-cotta floors and large balconies furnished with wooden chairs and hammocks. Some interconnect to form larger units. Waterfalls unite separate pools. It's a tasteful, friendly place that has very competitive rates during the low season. ⊠ *Top of the hill,* ☎ 777–0481, FAX 777–0451. *18 rooms with bath. Restaurant, pool. V.*

$$–$$$ ⌂ **Hotel Playa Espadilla.** This small hotel a short walk from the beach and national park entrance has its own forest reserve. The owners' land was declared part of the park decades ago, but they were never paid for it, so they petitioned the government to create a private preserve. Two cement buildings hold simple but spacious rooms with tile floors and kitchenettes. There's a blue-tile pool and small bar under a barrel-tile roof in back, and the surrounding lawn is bordered by the reserve's thick foliage. They also have some smaller, less-expensive cabinas across the street. *1 block east of beach,* ⊠ *Apdo. 195,* ☎ FAX 777–0903. *16 rooms with bath, 16 cabins. Bar, kitchenettes, air-conditioning, pool. AE, MC, V.*

$$–$$$ ⌂ **Hotel Vela Bar.** Set just a hundred yards back from Playa Espadilla on a paved road, this small, low-key hotel has a variety of rooms, all of which have white stucco walls decorated with framed tapestries, terra-cotta floors, and ceiling fans. The bungalow (which sleeps four) is a good value for small groups. The open-air restaurant set beneath a high, circular roof is a popular spot with nonguests, since it serves a good selection of vegetarian, meat, and fresh seafood dishes. ✉ *Next to Hotel Playa Espadilla (☞ above),* ☎ *777–0413,* FAX *777–1071. 9 rooms with bath, 2 bungalows. Restaurant, bar. AE, MC, V.*

$$–$$$ 🖬 **La Colina.** The new cement tower of this small B&B on the Quepos side of the Manuel Antonio hill holds the nicest rooms, with tile floors, ceiling fans, big windows, and balconies; two have air-conditioning. Smaller rooms without views are less expensive; there are also two cozy apartments. Next to the small split-level pool is the thatch-roof, open-air restaurant, where you can enjoy the complimentary breakfast, a light lunch menu, and nightly dinner specials. The friendly American owners are happy to book tours and help you with travel arrangements. *North side of hill,* ☎ *777–0231,* FAX *777–1553. 11 rooms with bath, 2 apartments. Restaurant, bar, pool. AE, MC, V.*

$ 🖬 **Hotel Manuel Antonio.** One of Manuel Antonio's oldest hotels, this small, wooden building is also one of its least expensive. Simple rooms with fans, windows, and private baths are upstairs, and the ground floor holds a large restaurant. The location couldn't be better: a short walk from the beach and national park. ✉ *End of the road,* ☎ *777–1237. 6 rooms with bath. Restaurant. No credit cards.*

Nightlife and the Arts

Most of Manuel Antonio's nightlife is found in Quepos (☞ *above*), which has several bars and two full-fledged discotheques. **Mar y Sombra** (☎ 777–0468), the restaurant on the beach, becomes an open-air disco on weekend nights. The **Barba Roja** (☞ *above*) has a bit of a bar scene to complement the dining. There is a casino in the **Hotel Divisamar** (☎ 777–0371), across from the Barba Roja.

Outdoor Activities and Sports

HORSEBACK RIDING

Horses can be rented in Manuel Antonio from **Malboro Stables** (☎ 777–1108), which has a two-hour guided tour through the forest. **Equus** (☎ 777–0001) can provide mounts and a guide to lead you through the forest and beach.

SEA KAYAKING

Iguana Tours (☎ 777–1262) runs sea-kayaking adventures to the islands of Parque Nacional Manuel Antonio (☞ *below*), which requires a bit of experience when seas are high, and a mellower paddle to the mangrove estuary of Isla Damas, where you might see monkeys, crocodiles, and plenty of birds.

SKIN DIVING

Playa Manuel Antonio, inside the national park, is a good snorkeling spot, as is Playa Biesanz, near the **Hotel Parador.** During the high season, **Lynch Travel** (☎ 777–1170) offers scuba diving for experienced divers only around the islands in the national park.

SWIMMING

Manuel Antonio's safest swimming area is the sheltered second beach in the national park, Playa Manuel Antonio, which also has great snorkeling conditions. When the surf gets big, rip currents are a dangerous problem on Playa Espadilla, the long beach north of the park. Riptides are characterized by a strong current running out to sea. The important thing to remember if you become caught in one of these currents is not to struggle against it but instead to swim parallel to shore. If you can't swim out of it, the current will simply take you out just past the breakers, where its power dissipates. If you conserve your strength, you can then swim parallel to shore a bit, and back into the beach. The best policy, however, is not to go in deeper than your waist if the waves are big.

Shopping

There is no shortage of shopping opportunities in this town, from the T-shirt vendors lining the road near the national park to the boutiques in the big hotels. There is little in the way of local handicrafts, so you'll find much the same things you would in San José, at slightly elevated prices. **La Buena Nota** (☎ 777–0345) is one of the oldest souvenir shops in town, on the right on the southern slope of the hill.

Parque Nacional Manuel Antonio

⑩ *5 km (3 mi) south of Quepos, 181 km (112 mi) southwest of San José.*

The white-sand beaches, turquoise waters, and verdant coastal forest of Parque Nacional Manuel Antonio (Manuel Antonio National Park, ☞ also Chapter 10) have made it one of the most popular protected areas in Costa Rica. Though small—only 6½ sq km (2½ sq mi)—the park protects a remarkable stretch of coast comprising three idyllic beaches and luxuriant rain forest where massive ficus, cow, kapok, and gumbo limbo trees tower over hiking trails. Mangrove swamps, marshland, and coral reefs contribute further to the park's biodiversity. Manuel Antonio is home to endangered Central American squirrel monkeys, as well as two- and three-toed sloths, green and black iguanas, capuchin monkeys, agoutis (which are large jungle rodents), and nearly 200 species of birds.

To enter the park, you'll need to cross a narrow estuary at the end of the road, waist-deep at high tide, ankle-deep at low tide. The first beach after the ranger station, **Playa Espadilla Sur,** is the longest and least crowded, since it can be rougher than the second beach. At its southern end is a tombolo (isthmus formed from sedimentation and accumulated debris) leading to a steep forested path that makes a loop over **Punta Catedral.** That trail passes an overlook from where you can gaze over the blue Pacific at some of the park's 12 islands, such as **Isla Mogote,** which was the site of pre-Columbian Quepos Indian burials. The lovely, white-sand strand east of the tombolo is **Playa Manuel Antonio,** a small, relatively safe swimming beach. At low tide you can see the remains of a Quepos Indian turtle trap on the right— the Indians stuck poles in the semicircular rock formation, which would trap turtles as the tide receded. This deep bay is a good snorkeling area, with coral formations a mere shell's toss from the beach. Walking even farther east, you arrive at the rockier, more secluded **Playa Escondido.**

Be careful of the manzanillo trees (indicated by warning signs)—the leaves, bark, and apple-like fruit secrete a gooey substance that irritates the skin. Also, do not feed or touch the monkeys, who have seen so many tourists that they sometimes walk right up to them and have bitten several overfriendly visitors. Because it's so popular, you'll want to get here as early as possible, especially during the dry season. There is a limit on the number of people allowed in it on any given day; it is closed Monday. ☎ 777–0644. ⊠ $6. ⊙ Tues.–Sun. 7–4.

CENTRAL PACIFIC COSTA RICA A TO Z

Arriving and Departing

By Bus

CENTRAL PACIFIC HINTERLANDS

Coopetransatenas (Coca-Cola bus station, C. 16 between Avdas. 1 and 3, ☎ 446–5767) buses to Atenas leave every 40 minutes daily. Buses to Orotina also leave the Coca-Cola bus station daily at 8, 9:30, and

11:15 AM and 12:30, 1:45, 2:45, and 4 PM. All buses heading toward San José can drop you off at the airport, but you need to ask the driver ahead of time. Buses to Jacó and Quepos (☞ Getting Around, *below*) can drop you off at Reserva Biológica Carara.

COAST NEAR SAN JOSÉ

Transporte Jacó (Coca-Cola bus station, ☎ 223–1109) buses from San José to Jacó leave from the Coca-Cola bus station daily at 7:15 AM, 10:30 AM, and 3:30 PM (2½-hr trip), returning at 5 AM, 11 AM, and 3 PM, with more frequent direct buses on weekends. **Fantasy Tours** (☎ 220–2126) has a quick, comfortable, though expensive, shuttle to Jacó leaving from the Best Western Irazú in San José daily at 9:30 AM (2-hr trip) and returning at 2 PM. **Transportes Delio Morales** (Coca-Cola bus station, ☎ 223–5567) express buses depart from San José's Coca-Cola bus station for Quepos and Parque Nacional Manuel Antonio at 6 AM, noon, and 6 PM (3½-hr trip), returning at 6 AM, noon, and 5 PM. To explore the southern Pacific region (☞ Chapter 7), buses leave Quepos for Dominical daily at 9 AM and 1:30, 4:30, and 6:30 PM, returning at 6 AM, 2 PM, and 2:45 PM (2½ hrs).

By Car

The quickest way to reach the central Pacific is to take the Carretera Inter-Americana (Pan-American Highway, CA1) west past the airport to the turnoff for Atenas, turning left (south) and driving through Atenas to Orotina. The coastal highway, or Costanera, heads southeast from Orotina to Tárcoles, Jacó, Hermosa, and Quepos and is well marked and paved most of the way. A paved road connects Quepos to Manuel Antonio National Park.

By Plane

Most travelers find the 30-minute flight between San José and Quepos preferable to the three-hour drive or 3½-hour bus trip. During the high season, **Sansa** (☎ 221–9414, 777–0683 in Quepos) has five flights daily between San José and Quepos. It also has one flight daily between Quepos and Palmar Sur (☞ Chapter 7). **Travelair** (☎ 220–3054, 777–1170 in Quepos) has four flights daily between San José and Quepos and one flight daily between Quepos and Palmar Sur (☞ Chapter 7).

Getting Around

By Bus

CENTRAL PACIFIC HINTERLANDS

All buses traveling between San José and either Jacó or Quepos can drop you off at Orotina.

COAST NEAR SAN JOSÉ

The short stretch of road between Quepos and Manuel Antonio is serviced by buses that leave Quepos every half hour from dawn till dusk, with a few more runs after dark. Buses leave Puntarenas for Quepos daily at 5 AM and 2:30 PM, returning at 10:30 AM and 3 PM (3 hrs); they stop at Hermosa and on the outskirts of Jacó. Buses to Quepos and Parque Nacional Manuel Antonio (☞ Arriving and Departing, *above*) can drop you off at Jacó or Playa Hermosa.

By Car

The Costanera connects Orotina with the Reserva Biológica Carara, Tárcoles, Jacó, Playa Hermosa, and Quepos. It is well marked and was in the process of being repaired at press time. The road between Quepos and Manuel Antonio National Park takes about 15 minutes by car.

Contacts and Resources

Car Rentals

Elegante (☎ 643–3224 in Jacó, 777–0115 in Quepos). **Economy** (☎ 643–3280 in Jacó).

Emergencies

Emergency (☎ 911). **Ambulance** (☎ 221–5818). **Fire** (☎ 118). **Police** (☎ 911, 117 in towns, 127 in rural areas). **Traffic Police** (☎ 227–8030).

Guided Tours

FROM SAN JOSÉ

Temptress Adventure Cruises (✉ 351 N.W. LeJeune Rd., Penthouse 6, Miami, FL 33126, ☎ 305/643–4040, FAX 305/643–6438) runs four- and seven-day natural-history and adventure cruises that visit spots along the central and southern Pacific coast, including Parque Nacional Manuel Antonio. Transfers to and from San José are provided from Puntarenas (7-day cruise) and Golfito (3- and 4-day cruises). Contact Temptress direct or **Cruceros del Sur** (✉ Across from Colegio Los Angeles, Sabana Norte, San José, ☎ 232–6672, FAX 220–2103), which also offers 10-day scuba safaris to distant Cocos Island, one of the world's top 10 dive spots. The **Undersea Hunter** (✉ San Rafael de Escazú, 600 yards north and 50 yards west of Rosti Pollos, ☎ 228–6535, FAX 289–7334) also offers 10-day dive trips to Cocos Island.

Many tours can be arranged out of San José: **Costa Rica Eco Adventure Services** (✉ Apdo. 1244-1000, San José, ☎ 283–9152, pager 224–2400, www.ecoguides.com), **Cosmos Tours** (✉ 50 yards north and 50 yards east of Centro Cultural Norteamericano Coastarricense, ☎ 234–0607, FAX 253–4707), **Costa Rica Expeditions** (✉ Avda. 3 and C. Central, San José, ☎ 222–0333, FAX 257–1665), and **Horizontes** (150 yards north of Pizza Hut Paseo Colón, ☎ 222–2022, FAX 255–4513).

COAST NEAR SAN JOSÉ

An array of tours are offered out of Jacó by **Fantasy Tours** (✉ Best Western Jacó Beach Hotel, ☎ 643–3032), among them hiking in the Reserva Biológica Carara, going on a boat trip on the Río Tárcoles, horseback riding, kayaking, and taking a cruise to Isla Tortuga. In Tárcoles, **Victor Pineda** (☎ 637–0426) leads an unforgettable crocodile tour.

In Quepos, **Lynch Travel** (✉ Behind bus station, ☎ 777–1170) offers a wildlife-watching boat trip to the Isla Damas Estuary, guided tours of the national park, several horseback trips, river rafting, sportfishing, and more. **Iguana Tours** (✉ Across from soccer field, Quepos, ☎ 777–1262) specializes in sea kayaking and white-water rafting. The **Eco-Era Foundation** (✉ Manuel Antonio, ☎ 777–1661) runs an invigorating jungle hike to a waterfall in its private reserve and a less strenuous bird-watching and conservation tour. **Rain Maker** (✉ Next to Si Como No Hotel, Manuel Antonio, ☎ 777–0850) offers horseback riding, hiking, and canopy touring in its private reserve.

Visitor Information

The tourist office in San José (☞ Visitor Information *in* San José A to Z, *in* Chapter 2) has information on the central Pacific. In Quepos, **Lynch Travel** (☞ *above*) provides information and arranges tours.

7 SOUTHERN PACIFIC COSTA RICA

Diverse and wild, the southern Pacific zone is marked by the cloud forests of the Cordillera de Talamanca and remote Osa Peninsula beaches. Isolated national parks, private biological preserves, comfortably rustic nature lodges, and one of the finest botanical gardens in Latin America, plus sublime surfing, fishing, hiking, bird-watching, skin diving, and horseback riding, make this region seventh heaven for outdoor enthusiasts.

Updated by
David
Dudenhoefer

IF TRAVELING TO THE SOUTHERN PACIFIC ZONE, you will discover what most of Costa Rica was like decades, or even centuries, ago. Since it was the last part of the country to be settled—a road into the region from San José wasn't completed until the 1950s—the southern Pacific retains a disproportionate percentage of its original wilderness. Much of that nature lies within several of the country's largest national parks, and other patches are protected within private reserves. From the surprising highland scenery of the Cordillera de Talamanca, Costa Rica's highest mountain range, to the pristine beaches and coastal rain forest of the Osa Peninsula, the southern Pacific holds some of the most dramatic and diverse scenery and wildlife in Costa Rica.

At Parque Nacional Chirripó you can climb Costa Rica's highest mountain and explore remote wilderness ranging from rugged forest to glacial lakes. On the Osa Peninsula, the creation of Parque Nacional Corcovado put something of a halt to the furious logging and gold mining that was destroying the rain forest. Corcovado contains a wide range of habitats, including large areas of swamp, deserted beaches, cloud forest, and luxuriant lowland rain forest, which provide habitat for most of the country's endangered species.

Excellent conditions for practicing a variety of outdoor sports abound. Some of Costa Rica's best surfing breaks, as well as its second-best skin diving area, are found here. Anglers can fish the renowned Pacific waters. Rafters can take on the rambunctious Río General. Trekkers can climb Costa Rica's highest peak, Cerro Chirripó. Bird-watchers who head to the right spots are almost guaranteed glimpses of the country's two most spectacular birds: the resplendent quetzal and scarlet macaw. Botany lovers, too, will go gaga here, especially at the Wilson Botanical Garden near San Vito, with its spectacular displays of local and imported plant life.

Pleasures and Pastimes

Dining

The southern Pacific zone may not be renowned for its gourmet cooking, but you can actually enjoy some tasty meals here. Thanks to the prime fishing off the coast, seafood is a dining staple. Apples, peaches, and plums are grown in profusion in the upper reaches of the Cordillera de Talamanca, and the lowlands are the source of those thirst-quenching pineapples. If you're here between June and August, try rambutans, locally called *mamones chinos,* with red spiky shells protecting a succulent white fruit very similar to a litchi.

Lodging

The southern Pacific zone's accommodations are as diverse as its terrain. There are simple, low-budget oceanside *cabinas* (cottages), tranquil mountain retreats, and luxury hotels set amidst the greenery of the rain forest. Be aware that nature lodges may appear to be more expensive than they are in reality, since the price of rooms includes three hearty meals a day.

Outdoor Adventures

The southwest could be called an outdoor person's nirvana. Horseback riding is done along spectacular beaches and forest trails. This is hiking territory—hikes range from one-day jaunts through private reserves to more demanding multi-day treks up Chirripó or into the Corcovado jungles. The water surrounding Isla del Caño is a lively habitat offering some of Costa Rica's best skin diving, and prime sportfishing is enjoyed off the entire southern Pacific coast. The surf here whips up into a half dozen breaks, and in the more tranquil waters of Golfo Dulce you can take sea-kayaking excursions.

Private Nature Preserves

In addition to the southern Pacific zone's celebrated national parks, there are a growing number of private nature preserves, some of which run their own lodges. Dominical's Hacienda Barú, a 700-acre reserve, offers a number of ways to experience the rain forest, as does Lapa Ríos, on the southern tip of the Osa Peninsula, with its extensive protected rain forest. Cabinas Chacón, in San Gerardo de Dota, has a large cloud-forest reserve crisscrossed by footpaths.

Exploring Southern Pacific Costa Rica

The southern Pacific zone comprises the western slope of the Cordillera de Talamanca, the Valle de El General, and the Osa Peninsula. There are two routes into the region: the Costanera (Route 34), or coastal highway, and the Carretera Interamericana (Pan-American Highway, CA2). To take the Costanera, drive west from San José, turn off the highway at the road to Atenas, and after Orotina, turn south toward Jacó and Quepos. This road is unpaved and pretty rough south of Quepos. To get to the Valle de El General from the Pan-American Highway, drive east out of San José and turn south outside Cartago. The CA2 heads high over the Cordillera de Talamanca and then descends down to and across the rolling hills of the Valle de El General all the way to Panama. The Costanera runs into the CA2 at Palmar Norte, to the south of which is the turnoff for Puerto Jiménez. Though a faithful translation from the Spanish, "highway" is really a misnomer for these neglected two-lane roads.

The good news is that between the country's two domestic airlines, there are regular flights from San José to the southern Pacific zone's most important destinations (Golfito, Palmar Sur, Puerto Jiménez, Pavones, Drake Bay, and Coto 47) and charter service to many of its more isolated spots. The great distance that separates the Osa Peninsula, Golfito, and San Vito from San José makes flying even more attractive, since a one-hour flight and short trip by land or water can save you six to eight hours behind the wheel or in a bus seat.

Numbers in the text correspond to numbers in the margin and on the Southern Pacific Costa Rica map.

Great Itineraries

IF YOU HAVE 3 DAYS

Fly straight to the Golfo Dulce–Osa Peninsula area, where comfortable nature lodges are in or near pristine wilderness in three distinct areas. You can fly direct to ⊡ **Playa Pavones** ⑩ on a charter arranged by the Tiskita Jungle Lodge. Or, fly to ⊡ **Puerto Jiménez** ⑪, a short drive from the nature lodges of ⊡ **Cabo Matapalo** ⑬ and the Tent Camp at the edge of ⊡ **Parque Nacional Corcovado** ⑫. The third option is to fly to Palmar Sur, where the taxi and boat trip to ⊡ **Bahía Drake** ⑭ begins.

IF YOU HAVE 5 DAYS

In five days you can extend the 3-day itinerary (☞ *above*) or explore the region's inland areas. Drive south on the Pan-American Highway (CA2) into the cool mountain air and cloud forests of ⊡ **San Gerardo de Dota** ①, the perfect place for hiking and bird-watching. On day two, you may want to make the drive up and the hike down the Cerro de la Muerte, or simply explore the Dota Valley. On day three, head down out of the mountains to the coastal enclave of ⊡ **Dominical** ④

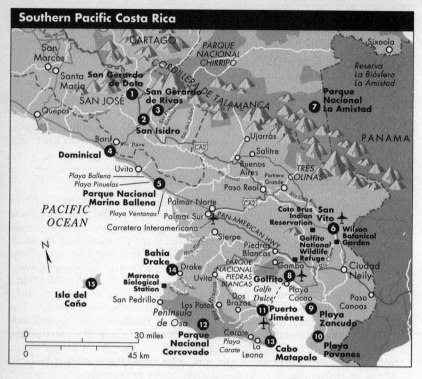

Southern Pacific Costa Rica

or the nearby ▥ **Parque Nacional Marino Ballena** ⑤. Spend day four and the morning of day five enjoying the area's waterfalls, nature reserves, and beaches before heading up the coast to the central Pacific zone (☞ Chapter 6) and/or San José.

IF YOU HAVE 8 DAYS

Head south on the CA2 to ▥ **San Gerardo de Dota** ① for quetzal-watching and hiking. On the second afternoon, work your way down to ▥ **Dominical** ④, which deserves at least two nights. On the morning of day four, drive to either ▥ **Golfito** ⑧ or ▥ **San Vito** ⑥, and from here you can continue on to **Parque Nacional La Amistad** ⑦, ▥ **Playa Zancudo** ⑨, or ▥ **Playa Pavones** ⑩ the following day. If you are so inclined, you can slip across the border into Panama for three days to explore Chiriquí Province (☞ Chapter 9). Another alternative is to go from Dominical on day four straight out to the rain forests and isolated beaches of the Osa Peninsula for three nights. Drive or bus to ▥ **Puerto Jiménez** ⑪ and ▥ **Cabo Matapalo** ⑬ or park in Sierpe and take a boat to ▥ **Bahía Drake** ⑭.

When to Tour Southern Pacific Costa Rica

You'll experience the same wet- and dry-season weather patterns here as in the rest of the Pacific. It rains considerably more here than in the northwest during the rainy months, but during July and August you may catch a week without any serious precipitation. The Osa Peninsula and Talamanca highlands are especially susceptible to downpours, making the region the last place you want to visit during the October–November deluge, when you'd have to be amphibian to be comfortable.

GENERAL VALLEY

The Valle de El General (General Valley) is bounded to the north by the massive Cordillera de Talamanca and to the south by the Golfo Dulce, or Sweet Gulf. This region comprises vast expanses of highland wilderness on the upper slopes of the Cordillera de Talamanca and the high-altitude *páramo* (shrubby ecosystem) of the Parque Nacional Chirripó, as well as isolated beaches and the lowland rain forest in the Dominical and Golfito areas.

San Gerardo de Dota

❶ *80 km (50 mi) southeast of San José.*

Cloud forests, cool mountain air, pastoral imagery, and excellent bird-watching make San Gerardo de Dota one of Costa Rica's great overlooked destinations. You'll find San Gerardo in a narrow valley of the Río Savegre, 9 km (5½ mi) down a twisting track that descends abruptly to the west from the Pan-American Highway. This tranquil and beautiful spot more closely resembles the Rocky Mountains than something you would expect to see in Central America. Hike down the waterfall trail (☞ Outdoor Activities and Sports, *below*), however, and the vegetation quickly becomes tropical again. The trail is steep and vigorous but is well worth the effort if you're in shape. Other activities include tours on horseback and trout fishing, but you might just be content to wander around the pastures and forests, marveling at the valley's varied avian inhabitants.

The damp, epiphyte-laden forest of giant oak trees, now broken up by bare, stump-strewn patches, is renowned for its high count of quetzals, for many the most beautiful bird in the New World. Males are the more spectacular, with metallic green feathers, bright crimson stomachs, helmetlike crests, and long tail streamers especially dramatic in flight. Quetzals commonly feed on *aguacatillos* (small avocado-like fruits) in the tall trees scattered around the valley's forests and pastures. The people who run your hotel can usually point you in the direction of where the quetzals have been hanging out. Early morning is the best time to spot them.

Lodging

$$$–$$$$ 🏨 **Cabinas Chacón.** Nearly 30 years ago, Efrain Chacón and his brother bushwhacked their way through the mountains to homestead in San Gerardo. With hard work and business acumen, they built a successful dairy farm. Now a hotelier and staunch conservationist, Efrain aids researchers and runs tours on his extensive farm for quetzal-spotting. Also called the Albergue de Montaña Savegre, after the river that runs by it, Chacón's hotel consists of comfortable and clean cabinas and a main building that houses the restaurant and a bar with a fireplace and a veranda. Meals are included. They will pick you up from the turnoff on the Pan-American Highway or anywhere in the country for a fee. ✉ *Apdo. 482, Cartago,* ☎ FAX *771–1732. 20 cabinas. Restaurant, bar, hiking, horseback riding. AE, MC, V.*

$$$–$$$$ 🏨 **Trogon Lodge.** A collection of green cabins nestled in a secluded part
★ of an enchanting valley, the Trogon Lodge overlooks the cloud forest and boulder-strewn Río Savegre. Each cabin has two rooms with hardwood floors, colorful quilts, big windows, white-tile baths with hot showers, and small electric heaters for those chilly mountain nights. Meals are served in a small dining hall and can be taken separately or as part of a package. The lodge can also provide a guide and/or transportation from San José. ✉ *Apdo. 10980–1000, San José,* ☎ *222–2421 or 771–1266,* FAX *223–5463. 10 rooms with bath. Restaurant. AE, DC, MC, V.*

Outdoor Activities and Sports

HIKING

The network of trails and country roads around San Gerardo de Dota can keep you hiking for days. A short trail heads through the forest above the Trogon Lodge (☞ Lodging, *above*), ending in a pasture, and Cabinas Chacón (☞ Lodging, *above*) has miles of trails winding through its forest reserve. The best trail in the valley is the one that follows the Río Savegre down to a **waterfall.** Follow the main road past Cabinas Chacón to a fork, where you veer left, cross a bridge, and head over the hill to a pasture that narrows to a footpath. The path becomes steep near the bottom, and the hike takes about three hours each way. A longer, guided hike is offered by Cabinas Chacón: you'll drive you up to the páramo near **Cerro de la Muerte,** from where you spend all day hiking back down through the forest into the valley.

San Isidro

❷ *54 km (34 mi) south of San Gerardo de Dota, 205 km (127 mi) northwest of Golfito.*

San Isidro has no attractions of its own, but it's not a bad place to get stuck spending a night, since it has friendly inhabitants and a fairly agreeable climate. The second-largest town in the province of San José, San Isidro has a bustling market and colorful, grid-plan streets. The large central square is the town's hub, with a modern church towering to the east. A couple of blocks south is the market, where buses depart for San Gerardo de Rivas (☞ *below*), the starting point of the trail into Parque Nacional Chirripó. The regional office of the **National Parks Service** (Across from Camara de Cañeros, ☎ 771–3155) can provide information about Chirripó and reserve space in the park's cabins. Buses to the nearby beach town of Dominical (☞ *below*) leave from near the fire station.

OFF THE BEATEN PATH
CENTRO BIOLÓGICO LAS QUEBRADAS – In a lush valley 7 km (4 mi) north of San Isidro is a community-managed nature reserve that protects 1,853 acres of dense forest where elegant tree ferns grow in the shadows of massive trees and where colorful tanagers and euphonias flit about the foliage. A 3-km (2-mi) trail winds through the forest and along the Río Quebradas, which is the water supply for San Isidro and surrounding communities. The Centro Biológico is 2 km (1 mi) north of the town of Las Quebradas and can be reached by private vehicle or taxi from San Isidro. ✉ Apdo. 73–8257, San Isidro, Perez Zeledon, ☎ 771–4131. ✆ $4. ☉ Tues.–Sun. 8–2.

Lodging

$$ ⊞ **Hotel del Sur.** The extensive grounds of this rambling complex, 6 km (4 mi) south of town on the Pan-American Highway, include a pool and tennis court. Rooms are spacious with large windows and tile floors. Bungalows in back are good for families and offer an escape from the drone of the highway; they have kitchenettes, bunks, and separate bedrooms. ✉ Apdo. 4–8000, San Isidro, Perez Zeledon, ☎ 771–3033, FAX 771–0527. 48 rooms with bath, 12 bungalows. Restaurant, bar, pool, sauna, tennis court, basketball. AE, MC, V.

$$ ⊞ **Talari.** A 10-minute drive northeast from San Isidro on the road to San Gerardo di Rivas takes you to this family-run lodge on a small farm, where the gurgling of the Río General lulls you to sleep and dozens of bird songs awaken you. Simple rooms with big windows, tile floors, and porches are set in two cement buildings, near which lies a small pool. The surrounding fruit trees and forest patches make for good bird-watching, and the owners can arrange guided trips into Chirripó Na-

tional Park. Turn left off of the Pan-American Highway after second bridge south of San Isidro. ✉ *Apdo. 517–8000, San Isidro, Perez Zeledon,* ☎ FAX *771–0341. 8 rooms with bath. Restaurant, pool. AE, MC, V.*

Outdoor Activities and Sports

WHITE-WATER RAFTING

With the country's longest white-water run, the Río General makes for a fun rafting or kayaking trip. The white water begins to the south of San Isidro, flowing through predominantly agricultural land before winding its way through a rocky canyon. Three-day camping expeditions on the Río General, a class III–IV river, are offered by the major rafting companies in San José (☞ Chapter 2) during the wettest months (September to November). Based in San Isidro, **Brunca Tours** (✉ 75 yards south of ICE, 1st floor, San Isidro, ☎ 771–3100, 771–0008) offers one- to three-day rafting trips on the Río General and nearby Río Coto Brus from May to January. Brunca Tours also offers guided trips to Chirripó National Park and Reserva La Biósfera La Amistad, the hot springs near San Gerardo de Rivas, and Wilson Botanical Gardens (☞ *below*).

San Gerardo de Rivas

❸ *20 km (12 mi) northeast of San Isidro.*

The trail up to **Parque Nacional Chirripó** (Chirripó National Park, ☞ Chapter 10), home of Costa Rica's highest peak, begins above this scenic agricultural community. It's a grueling climb up to the park—6 to 10 hours, depending on your physical condition—so you should head out of San Gerardo with the first light of day. Even if you aren't up for the hike into Chirripó National Park, San Gerardo de Rivas is a great place to spend a day or two. Spread over steep terrain at the end of the narrow valley of the boulder-strewn Río Chirripó, San Gerardo offers a cool climate, good bird-watching, spectacular views, and outdoor options that include hiking and horseback riding to waterfalls. A favorite stop is the **Aguas Termales,** small hot springs on a farm above the road to Herradura, about 1½ km (1 mi) after the ranger station.

Lodging

$–$$ 🏠 **El Pelicano.** This wooden lodge perched on a ridge south of town has an odd name for a mountain hotel—it refers to a chunk of wood that resembles a pelican—and that's not the only unusual thing about it. Dozens of strange wooden statues, created by the owner, decorate the restaurant, which also features a gorgeous view of the valley below San Gerardo. All of the upstairs rooms have windows, lots of wood, and share several clean, tiled bathrooms. ✉ *Apdo. 932–8000, San Gerardo de Rivas, Perez Zeledon,* ☎ *382–3000. 10 rooms without bath. Restaurant, horseback riding. No credit cards.*

Dominical

❹ *22 km (14 mi) southwest of San Isidro.*

Fifty minutes to the southwest of San Isidro, Dominical, once a sleepy fishing village, is slowly being discovered. It still has a mere fraction of the tourists found at beaches like Tamarindo and Manuel Antonio, but it certainly isn't for lack of natural attractions. Dominical's magic lies in its combination of terrestrial and marine wonders: the rain forest grows right up to the beach at some points, and the sea offers world-class surfing. The beaches here are long, practically empty, and perfect for strolling and shell collecting, but beware of rip currents when the waves are big.

There is also plenty to see and do on land at Dominical. The area's steep hillsides are covered with lush forest, much of which is protected within private nature reserves. Several of those reserves are trying to finance preservation of the rain forest through ecotourism by offering hiking and horseback tours. Two private reserves border the spectacular **Cataratas de Nauyaca** (Nauyaca Waterfalls), a massive double cascade that is simply one of the country's most spectacular sights. The **Pozo Azul** is a considerably smaller waterfall in the jungle about 5 km (3 mi) south of town. Both are accessible by foot or on horseback (☞ Outdoor Activities and Sports, *below*).

Dining and Lodging

$$ ✕ **La Campanna.** A little slice of Italy near the beach, La Campanna
★ is the most popular restaurant with Dominical's many resident foreigners. Burlap sacks and palm fronds are about the only concessions the Italian owners have made to decor, but the food is first rate. In addition to pizzas, they offer minestrone, marinated eggplant, baked squid stuffed with vegetables and Parmesan cheese, and a variety of fresh pasta dishes. ⊠ *Main road,* ☎ 787–0072. *No credit cards. Closed Mon.*

$$ ✕ **San Clemente Restaurant.** This is the local surfer hangout, most crowded whenever it's too dark or too flat to catch a wave. Dozens of broken surfboards ply the ceiling and photos of the sport's early years hang on the walls. Seating is in wooden booths inside next to the pool table or out in the garden. The menu is dominated by fresh seafood (grilled outdoors at dinner), sandwiches, and such Tex-Mex standards as burritos and nachos. They also serve inventive breakfast items. Satellite TV is tuned into U.S. sporting events and news, and next door are the local post office, surf shop, and laundromat all rolled into one. ⊠ *Halfway along the main road,* ☎ FAX 787–0055. *AE, MC, V.*

$$$ 🏨 **Villas Río Mar.** Upriver from the beach, this hotel on landscaped grounds is the fanciest in town. The adobe-style bungalows have thatched roofs, white-tile floors, and cane ceilings. The rooms and baths are on the small side, but each has a porch with a hammock, wet bar with refrigerators, and mosquito-net curtains. The restaurant, with lots of plants and elegant table settings, sits beneath a giant thatched roof. ⊠ *Apdo. 1350–2050, San José,* ☎ 787–0052 or 257–1138, FAX 787–0054. *40 rooms with bath. Restaurant, bar, pool, tennis court, exercise room. AE, DC, MC, V.*

$$–$$$ 🏨 **Hacienda Barú.** These bungalows are part of a large private reserve, which makes it the ideal place from which to explore the rain forest. Bungalows are basic, with red cement floors, bare white walls, small kitchens, sitting rooms, and either two or three bedrooms (perfect for three or four people). You can spend an hour on a platform in the rain-forest canopy or overnight at a shelter in the heart of the forest. ⊠ *Selva Mar, 1,000 yards north of Dominical, Apdo. 215–8000, San Isidro, Perez Zeledon,* ☎ 771–4582 or 771–4579, FAX 771–1903; ⊠ *AAA Express Mail, 1641 N.W. 79th Ave., Miami, FL 33126-1105. 8 bungalows. Restaurant, kitchenettes, hiking, horseback riding. AE, MC, V.*

$$–$$$ 🏨 **Pacific Edge.** The forest grows right up to this small lodge on a
★ mountain ridge south of town. The grounds are planted with flowers and fruit trees visited by many a bird and butterfly, and the four rustic but comfortable bungalows are surrounded with screened windows and have large, hammock-strung porches. Each one has a simple kitchen, which costs $5 a day to use, but the lodge's small restaurant, set under a thatched roof, serves great breakfasts and dinners, including some Thai dishes. The road up to Pacific Edge leaves the coastal highway 4 km (2½ mi) south of Dominical and requires a four-wheel-drive vehicle, but the hotel will pick you up in town. ⊠ *Apdo. 531–800, Dominical,* ☎ FAX 787–0031 or 771–4582. *4 bungalows. Restaurant. AE, MC, V.*

$–$$ 🏨 **Cabinas San Clemente.** With a great location, just across the road from the beach, and a wide selection of accommodations, San Clemente has something for just about everyone. A two-story building overlooking a tropical garden holds the best rooms, which are spacious, bright, nicely decorated, and well ventilated. They have lots of screened windows, ceiling fans, and small baths; several also have air-conditioning. Rooms in the building next door are smaller, darker, and warmer, but are much cheaper. They also rent several houses and have dorm-style accommodations. ⊠ *Across from the beach,* ☎ *787–0026,* FAX *787–0055. 18 rooms with bath. Air-conditioning. AE, MC, V.*

$ 🛏 **Posada del Sol.** This small place offers simple, clean accommodations in a tranquil atmosphere and at very reasonable rates. Rooms are on the ground floor of a cement building and open onto a narrow porch with chairs and tables. There is also a little garden in back with a cement table and an area for washing clothes. The Costa Rican owners are friendly and helpful. ⊠ *Main road,* ☎ *787–0085. 4 rooms with bath. No credit cards.*

Outdoor Activities and Sports

ECOTOURISM

Hacienda Barú (☞ Dining and Lodging, *above*) is definitely the best-organized ecotourism operation in Dominical, offering such unusual tours as a trip into the rain-forest canopy, which entails being hoisted up to a platform in the crown of a giant tree, and a night spent in a shelter in the woods.

INNER TUBING

A popular excursion is an inner-tube trip down green **Río Barú,** which flows into the Pacific south of town. Trips can be arranged through your hotel or at the San Clemente Restaurant (☞ Dining and Lodging, *above*).

SPORTFISHING

Angling options range from expensive sportfishing charters to a trip in a small boat with a local fisherman. The people at **Tropical Waters** (⊠ 3½ km/2 mi north of Dominical on road to San Isidro, ☎ 787–0031) or the San Clemente Restaurant (☞ Dining and Lodging, *above*) can arrange trips.

SURFING

Surfers have long been flocking to Dominical, which has one of the country's most consistent beach breaks. Boards can be rented, purchased, and repaired at the surf shop next to the San Clemente Restaurant (☞ Dining and Lodging, *above*).

WATERFALLS

The easiest way to get to Nauyaca Waterfalls is with **Don Lulo** (☎ 771–3187), 12 km (8 mi) north of town. He offers horseback trips to the falls that include swimming in the natural pools below the cascades and enjoying a hearty, typical Costa Rican lunch. Book through your hotel, Tropical Waters (☞ above), or the San Clemente Restaurant (☞ Dining and Lodging, *above*). The other option is through the private reserve of the **Bella Vista Lodge** (☎ 771–1903), which entails a longer horseback trek but takes you through much more rain forest. To hike to **Pozo Azul,** head up the road toward the Bella Vista lodges, and when it begins to climb the hill, look for a trail down to the river on your right.

Parque Nacional Marino Ballena

❺ *20 km (12 mi) southeast of Dominical.*

One of Costa Rica's few marine parks, Parque Nacional Marino Ballena (Ballena Marine National Park) protects several beaches, a small mangrove estuary, and a vast swath of ocean with rocky isles and islets.

At the park's northern end, **Playa Uvita** stretches out into Punta Uvita, a long swath of sand, or tombolo, that connects a former island to the coast. **Playa Ballena,** to the southeast, is an even lovelier strand, backed by lush vegetation, and tiny **Playa Pinuelas** is set in a deep cove that serves as the local port. **Playa Ventanas,** just south of the park, is another beautiful beach that is a popular spot for sea kayaking. The mountains that rise up behind all these beaches hold rain forest, waterfalls, and lots of wildlife. This is one of the only parks where they don't charge an admission fee, since there are so many places to enter it.

Lodging

$$$ ⊞ **Villas Gaia.** Far from the beaten track, this tasteful lodge provides
★   access to beaches and wilderness that few foreigners see. The hotel consists of a collection of colorful villas spread around the jungle on a ridge behind Playa Tortuga, just south of Playa Ventanas. Villas, with pastel colors and local hardwoods throughout, have sliding windows and doors and small balconies overlooking forested ravines. The blue-tile pool has an ocean view and an open-air bar. The restaurant serves some of the best food in the region. The Dutch owners rent mountain bikes and arrange horseback, mangrove, and sea-kayaking tours as well trips to Caño Island and Parque Nacional Corcovado. ⊠ *Playa Tortuga,* ☎ FAX *256–9996,* ☎ *223–2240. 12 cabinas. Restaurant, pool. AE, MC, V.*

San Vito

➏ *139 km (86 mi) southeast of San Isidro, 93 km (58 mi) northeast of Golfito.*

The little town of San Vito lies at an altitude of 3,150 ft and close to the Panama border. It owes its founding in 1952 to a government scheme whereby 200 Italian families were given grants to convert the rain forest into coffee, fruit, and cattle farms. It is now a busy, modern agricultural center with little to offer visitors beyond the nearby botanical garden. Since it is close to the **Coto Brus Indian Reservation,** San Vito is one of the few towns in Costa Rica where you might see Ngwobe, or Guaymí, Indians, who are easy to spot thanks to the colorful dresses worn by the women.

Six kilometers (4 mi) south of San Vito is the extensive and enchanting **Wilson Botanical Garden.** These 25 hillside acres were converted from a coffee plantation in 1961 by U.S. landscapers Robert and Catherine Wilson. They planted a huge collection of tropical species, including palms—an amazing 700 species—orchids, aroids, ferns, bromeliads, heliconias, and marantas, all linked by a series of neat grass paths. Today the gardens hold around 3,000 native and 4,000 exotic species. The property was transferred to the Organization for Tropical Studies (OTS) in 1973 and in 1983 became part of the **Reserva La Biósfera La Amistad** (☞ *below*). The garden functions mainly as a research and educational center, but visitors and overnight guests (☞ Dining and Lodging, *below*) are welcome. Spending a night at the garden is recommended, though it costs considerably less to sleep in San Vito. ⊠ *Apdo. 73–8257, San Vito,* ☎ *773–4004,* FAX *773–3665.* 🎫 *$8 full day, $5 half day.* ☉ *Daily 8–4.*

OFF THE   **CIUDAD NEILY –** The 33 km (21 mi) of road that connects San Vito and
BEATEN PATH   Ciudad Neily is twisting and spectacular, with views over the Coto Colorado plain to the Golfo Dulce and Osa Peninsula beyond. Much of this steep terrain is covered with tropical forest, which makes it an ideal route for bird-watching and picture-taking.

Dining and Lodging

$ ✕ **Pizzeria Liliana.** A simple, small-town restaurant near San Vito's central square, the Liliana serves large portions of good food at remarkably low prices. The decor is basic, with wooden tables and a bar at one end, but the pastas and pizzas are delicious. Go for the baked chicken or the steak with mushroom sauce if you aren't up for Italian. ⊠ *1½ blocks west of central square,* ☎ *773–3080. V.*

$$$–$$$$ 🏨 **Wilson Botanical Garden.** A row of 12 rooms with hardwood floors,
★   high ceilings, and large balconies lines a ridge in the heart of the pretty garden. Four cabins have small sitting rooms and more windows but a less-panoramic view. Room rates include three hearty, home-style meals and 24-hour access to the garden. Staying overnight is the easiest way to see the garden at dusk and dawn, a highly recommended experience. ⊠ *OTS, Apdo. 676–2050, San Pedro,* ☎ *240–6696 or 773–4004,* FAX *240–6783. 16 cabinas. Restaurant. AE, MC, V.*

$–$$ 🏨 **Hotel El Ceibo.** The hotel's owner, Antonio Papili, arrived here from Italy at age two, and he has some interesting stories about his early days in San Vito. The modern bedrooms are pleasant and clean—foam-rubber mattresses are their only drawback. This is really quite a deal. Rooms in the back of the two-story buildings overlook a forested ravine. The airy restaurant, with its sloping wood ceiling, arched windows, and wine trolley, serves a solidly good mix of Italian and Costa Rican fare. ⊠ *San Vito, behind the Municipalidad,* ☎ FAX *773–3025. 40 rooms with bath. Restaurant, bar. MC, V.*

Shopping

An old farmhouse on the east side of the road between San Vito and the botanical garden houses a shop called **Cántaros** (3 km/2 mi south of San Vito, ☎ 773–3760), which features crafts by local indigenous artisans as well as ceramics from San José artists. Profits help support the adjacent children's library.

Parque Nacional La Amistad

❼ *40 km (25 mi) northwest of San Vito.*

The Parque Nacional La Amistad (La Amistad National Park), at more than 1,980 sq km (765 sq mi), is by far the largest park in the country, but it is actually a mere portion of the vast **Reserva La Biósfera La Amistad** (Amistad Biosphere Reserve)—a collection of protected areas that stretches from southern Costa Rica into western Panama. The park itself covers altitudes ranging from 700 to 11,600 ft and has an array of ecosystems that hold two-thirds of the country's vertebrate species. Unfortunately, the national park is practically inaccessible, but is a worthwhile excursion for the adventurous. The easiest part of the park to visit is the **Tres Colinas** sector, 23 km (14 mi) north of Potrero Grande, a small town just north of Paso Real, which is where the road to San Vito leaves the Pan-American Highway. There is a ranger station in Potrero Grande, from where a four-wheel-drive-vehicle-only road winds its bumpy way up into the mountains. Camping is allowed here; reserve space at the regional office in San Isidro (☎ 771–3155).

Golfito

❽ *339 km (211 mi) southeast of San José.*

Beautifully situated overlooking a small gulf (hence its name), and hemmed in by a steep bank of forest, Golfito has a great location but little else beyond that. The town itself consists of a pleasant older section and a long and ugly strip of newer buildings, dilapidated former workers' quarters, and overabundant seedy bars. For several decades,

Golfito was a thriving banana port—the United Fruit arrived in 1938—and a center of activity, with a dock that could handle 4,000 boxes of bananas per hour and elegant housing for its plantation managers. On the northwestern end of town is the so-called **American Zone,** full of stilted wooden houses where the expatriate managers lived, courtesy of United Fruit, and which were bought by Costa Ricans when United Fruit departed. With a golf course nearby, and several swimming pools, life here must have been more than bearable for the privileged few.

The fruit company pulled out in 1985 in response to labor disputes and rising export taxes, and Golfito promptly slipped into a state of poverty and neglect from which it has yet to recover completely. To inject new life into the town, the government declared it a duty-free port in 1990. The handful of shops called the **Depósito Libre** (Duty-free Zone) is located in the former American Zone, within a fenced compound. It does much of its business during the month preceding Christmas, when it can be very difficult to find a room in Golfito.

Although Golfito doesn't have a beach itself, **Playa Cacao** lies across the bay from town—just a five-minute boat ride. The beach has several restaurants and lodges, which make it a convenient option when the hotels in Golfito fill up.

The hills behind Golfito are covered with the lush forest of the **Golfito National Wildlife Refuge** (Refugio Nacional de Vida Silvestre Golfito). Adjacent is the **Parque Nacional Piedras Blancas** (Piedras Blancas National Park), which makes the Golfito area great for bird-watching. Follow the main road northwest through the old American Zone, past the airstrip and a housing project, and where a dirt road heads into the rain forest is the best area to see birds. If you have a four-wheel-drive vehicle, you can follow that dirt track through the heart of Piedras Blancas National Park to the community of **La Gamba,** the Esquinas Rain Forest Lodge, and Villa Briceño, on the Pan-American Highway. This back route can cut miles off a trip to or from the north, and it passes through a gorgeous patch of wilderness.

Farther into the Golfo Dulce, accessible by boat, is **Casa Orquideas** (✉ Apdo. 69, Golfito), a menagerie of ornamental plants, palms, bromeliads, heliconias, cycads, orchids, and flowering gingers tended to with care by the American owners Ron and Trudy MacAllister. A two-hour tour (Saturday through Thursday at 8:30 AM) includes touching, tasting, and smelling, plus spotting toucans and hummingbirds. A cabin ($$$$) for rent is on the grounds. Transport from Golfito is included.

Lodging

$$$$ 🖬 **Caña Blanca Beach and Rain Forest Lodge.** Don't be put off by the resident scarlet macaw's habit of swooping close to your head, as it's harmless. Spread out on an utterly idyllic beach and in the lush Caña Blanca private reserve are three open-air cabins and a lodge-bar owned by ex–Bay Area folks Earl and Carol Crews. The cabins are made entirely of fine wood and have double or single beds, built-in benches, and lights covered with wicker Asian-style paper, and the occasional shell. The package includes transport from Puerto Jiménez or Golfito, all drinks, three gourmet meals, and a daily tour through the reserve, which is a verdant primary and secondary forest with cocoa and breadfruit trees and birds and mammals aplenty. You can arrange a day hike (about $5, $25 with transport). *30 mins by boat from Golfito in Golfo Dulce,* ✉ *Puerto Jiménez, Península de Osa,* ☎ *735–5062, 383–5707,* FAX *735–5043. 3 cabins. Dining room, bar, hiking, boating. Subject to close and book up; call far in advance.*

CRUISING THE PACIFIC COAST

" **A** WOODPECKER," WHISPERED Max, binoculars trained on a
tree wrapped with strangler figs and bromeliads. Cicadas
chanted a hypnotic mantra, broken by the throaty call of
the three-wattled bellbird and the crashing of waves. A morpho butterfly floated by, winking atomic blue. "No, it's a branch,"
Max sheepishly sighed, eliciting a collective chuckle.

The group of 12, along with a naturalist guide, had been sped to
the beach by dinghy at 6 AM for a hike through Caña Blanca (☞
above), a privately owned patch of lush tropical jungle. They were
part of an eco-adventure tour aboard the 185-ft *Temptress Explorer*,
which nudged right up to the Pacific Coast's pristine islands, funky
towns, and rain forests, some too remote for roads. Excellent rain
forest hikes, horseback riding, bird-watching, snorkeling, sea kayaking, and a visit to a luxuriant botanical garden were all easily accessible.

On the trails, friendly Tico guides pointed out fascinating organisms in the forest—a cavalcade of leaf-cutter ants, the coveted treasure of a cacao tree—and such critters as the scarlet macaw and
white-faced Capuchin monkey. At sunset, drinks sprouting paper
umbrellas were shared at the top-deck bar amid lively chatter and
Max, happy that other branch wasn't a poisonous snake. For more
information, *see* **Temptress Adventure Cruises** *in* Southern Pacific
Costa Rica A to Z, *below*, and Cruise Travel *in* Smart Travel Tips
A to Z.

$$–$$$ 🏨 **Hotel Las Gaviotas.** Just south of town on the water's edge, this hotel
has wonderful views over the inner gulf. Rooms have terra-cotta floors,
teak furniture, fans, air-conditioning, and cable TV. Outside each one
is a small veranda with two chairs, which overlook the well-tended tropical gardens and the shimmering ocean beyond. An open-air restaurant looks onto the pool, which has a terrace that is barely divided from
the sea. ☒ *Playa Tortuga, Apdo. 12, Golfito,* ☎ 775–0062, FAX 775–
0544. 18 rooms with bath, 3 suites. Restaurant, bar, air-conditioning,
pool. AE, DC, MC, V.

$ 🏨 **Jardin Alamedas.** This property's popular restaurant occupies the
ground floor of a former administrator's house in what was once the
banana company's American Zone. Guest quarters are in a newer cement building next door. The rooms are simple but clean, with tile floors,
small baths, and too many beds. The restaurant's good food ranges
from fried rice dishes to fresh seafood and several kinds of pastas. ☒
110 yards south of airstrip, Apdo. 9 Golfito, ☎ 775–0126. 6 rooms
with bath. Restaurant. AE, MC, V.

Outdoor Activities and Sports

SPORTFISHING

There is great fishing in the waters off Golfito, either in the Golfo Dulce or out in the open ocean. The open ocean holds plenty of sailfish, marlin, and roosterfish during the dry months, as well as dolphin, tuna, and wahoo during the rainy season; excellent bottom fishing can be had any time of year. Contact **Roy Ventura** (☞ Outdoor Activities and Sports *in* Playa Zancudo, *below*).

Shopping

Duty-free bargains on such imported items as TV sets, stereos, linens, and tires are what draw most visitors to Golfito. You can shop in the **Depósito Libre,** but you won't find things that much cheaper than they are at home. To buy things in the Depósito you have to spend the night, which means you register in the afternoon, with your passport, and shop the next morning. Shopping here is sheer madness in December.

Playa Zancudo

⑨ *32 km (20 mi) south of Golfito.*

Playa Zancudo, a long, palm-lined beach fronting the tiny fishing village of Zancudo, can be reached either by driving or by hiring a boat at the municipal dock in Golfito. Zancudo has a good surf break, but it is nothing compared with Playa Pavones. There are also some good swimming areas, and if you get tired of playing in the surf and sand, you can arrange a boat trip to the nearby mangrove estuary to see birds and crocodiles. Zancudo is also home to the area's best sportfishing operation.

Lodging

$$–$$$ 🏨 **Roy's Zancudo Lodge.** Most of the people who stay at Roy's are anglers on all-inclusive sportfishing packages, but the hotel is a good option even if you've never caught anything more exciting than a cold. It's on the beach, with ample, verdant grounds surrounding a pool and open-air restaurant, where buffet breakfasts and dinners are served. Rooms have hardwood floors, firm beds, ceiling fans, air-conditioning, and ocean views. They can be rented on their own, or with the three meals and open bar included. ⊠ *Playa Zancudo, Apdo. 41, Zancudo,* ☎ *776–0008,* ℻ *776–0011. 14 cabinas. Restaurant, bar, air-conditioning, pool. V.*

$$ 🏨 **Cabinas Sol y Mar.** This group of beachside cabins is a 20-minute walk south of where the boat from Golfito drops you off. Rooms were designed and built to look like polyhedral space modules, with elegant charcoal-clay tiles, wooden beds, and white canvas sofas. Boat transportation can be arranged from the dock if you call ahead. ⊠ *Playa Zancudo, Apdo. 87, Golfito,* ☎ *776–0014,* ℻ *776–0015. 4 cabinas, 1 house. Restaurant, bar. V.*

Outdoor Activities and Sports

SPORTFISHING

If you've got your own gear, you can do some good shore fishing from the beach or the mouth of the mangrove estuary, or hire one of the local boats to take you out into the gulf. **Roy Ventura** (☞ Lodging, *above*) runs the best charter operation in the area, with 10 boats ranging in length from 22 to 32 ft. Packages include room, food, and drink, and you can get pick-up service in Golfito or Puerto Jiménez.

Playa Pavones

⑩ *45 km (28 mi) south of Golfito.*

On the southern edge of the Golfo Dulce's mouth stands Pavones, a windswept beach town at the end of a dirt road. Famous among surfers for having one of the longest waves in the world, the town also has pristine beaches and virgin rain forest in its favor. It's far from everything, but the rain forest, beaches, horseback-riding opportunities, and a small arboretum make the trip worthwhile for for adventurous travelers.

Lodging

$$$$ 🏨 **Tiskita Jungle Lodge.** Peter Aspinall has planted 100 different fruit trees from all over the world as a kind of research exercise into alternative exports. For you he has built wooden cabins on stilts, surrounded by screens and lush vegetation and equipped with rustic furniture and open bathrooms from which you can observe wildlife. Trails allow you to explore the jungle and the wide variety of wildlife lured by the fruit trees' fine pickings. Most people fly into the lodge, but you can reach it with a four-wheel-drive vehicle. ✉ *Costa Rica Sun Tours, 4 km (2½ mi) north of Pavones, Apdo. 1195–1250, Escazú,* ☎ *255–2011,* 📠 *233–6890. 16 cabinas. Dining room, pool, hiking, horseback riding, snorkeling. AE, DC, MC, V. Closed Sept.–Oct.*

OSA PENINSULA

Some of Costa Rica's most spectacular scenery and striking wildlife thrives on the Osa Peninsula, one-third of which is covered by Parque Nacional Corcovado. A paradise for backpackers, who can hike into the park on any of three routes, Corcovado can also be visited on day trips from nearby nature lodges, most of which lie within private preserves that are home for much of the same wildlife you might see in the park. And to complement the peninsula's lush forests and pristine beaches, the sea that surrounds it holds great sportfishing and skin diving.

En Route If you're driving from San José, you've got an eight-hour trip; take the Pan-American Highway (CA2) south to Piedras Blancas, where you turn right for the rough road into the Osa Peninsula.

Puerto Jiménez

⑪ *127 km (79 mi) west of Golfito, 364 km (226 mi) southeast of San José.*

There isn't much to write home about in Puerto Jiménez, but it can be a convenient base for exploring some of the nearby wilderness. Its claim to fame is that it's the biggest town on the Osa Peninsula. You won't be dodging any pigeons in this urban center, but you are likely to see scarlet macaws flying noisily over the rooftops or perched in the Indian almond trees. Most people spend a night here either before or after visiting the Parque Nacional Corcovado (☞ *below*), as Puerto Jiménez has the best access to the park's two main trailheads. Puerto Jiménez also lies just 40 minutes by car from spectacular Cabo Matapalo (☞ *below*), where virgin rain forest meets the sea at a rocky point.

The headquarters of the **National Parks Service** (☎ 735–5036) are at the southern end of town, opposite the Texaco gas station. This is where you check in before entering Corcovado or when you want to ask about hiking routes and present trail conditions. During the dry season, you'll want to reserve camping space, meals, or accommodations at the **Sirena ranger station** well ahead of time by calling the above number. You may be asked to deposit money into an account in the Banco Nacional to reserve space.

Dining and Lodging

$ ✕ **Restaurante Carolina.** It may not look like much, but this simple
★ restaurant in the heart of Puerto Jiménez is known to serve the best food in town, especially fresh seafood. The restaurant also has five small rooms in back, making it a good spot for backpackers on their way in or out of Corcovado. Rooms are your basic cement boxes, with private bathrooms and cold running water, but they are clean and convenient. The truck to Carate leaves daily from in front of the restaurant. ⊠ *Center of town, two blocks south of soccer field,* ☎ *735–5007. No credit cards.*

$–$$ ⌷ **Cabinas Los Manglares.** Although fairly basic, this small lodge provides the most comfortable accommodations in Puerto Jiménez proper, and you can see an amazing amount of wildlife in the surrounding mangrove forest. Cabins have tile floors, white walls, fans, and simple wooden furniture. Five of them stand by the parking lot, and five are scattered around a lawn on the other side of the mangroves, which are crossed by a catwalk. The thatched-roof restaurant serves an unexciting selection of meat and seafood dishes. ⊠ *Puerto Jiménez, across from the airport,* ☎ FAX *735–5002. 10 cabinas. Restaurant, bar. No credit cards.*

Outdoor Activities and Sports

HIKING

A truck that carries hikers to **Carate** and its nearby beach leaves from the Mini Mercado El Tigre every morning at 6 AM (☞ Outdoor Activities and Sports *in* Parque Nacional Corcovado, *below*). If you have a four-wheel-drive vehicle, it's just a 30-minute drive to **Dos Brazos,** and the Tigre sector of the park, which few hikers explore.

RAFTING AND SEA KAYAKING

Taxis in town can be hired to take you to the **Río Rincón,** near Los Patos. Puerto Jiménez is a good base for boat or sea-kayaking trips on the **Golfo Dulce** or to one of the nearby mangrove estuaries and rivers.

Parque Nacional Corcovado

⑫   *From Puerto Jiménez: 1-hr four-wheel drive to Carate plus 20-min walk to La Leona; 20-minute drive to the Río Rincón plus 2- to 3-hr hike to Los Patos.*

Comprising 435 sq km (168 sq mi), Parque Nacional Corcovado (Corcovado National Park, ☞ Chapter 10) is one of the largest and wildest protected areas in the country. Much of the park is covered with virgin rain forest, where massive *espavel* and *nazareno* trees tower over the trails, thick lianas hang from their branches, and animals such as toucans, spider monkeys, scarlet macaws, and poison dart frogs abound. There are three entrances to Corcovado: San Pedrillo to the north, Los Patos to the east, and La Leona to the south. There are no roads in the park, and the ones that approach it are dirt tracks that require four-wheel-drive vehicles most of the year. Visitors to Corcovado often arrive by boat on day trips from the nature lodges in Bahía Drake (☞ *below*), but the best way to explore the park is to sling on a backpack and hike into the wilderness.

Camping

$$$ **Corcovado Lodge Tent Camp.** Costa Rica Expeditions owns this rus-
★ tic lodge and the surrounding 400-acre forest reserve. The 20 tents, with two single beds each, are pitched on wooden platforms just off the beach. There are communal bathrooms and a bar-restaurant serving family-style meals. Resident naturalist guides will lead you through

the jungle and hoist you into the forest canopy to a 100-ft-high platform. Bring a flashlight—there's electricity only a few hours each day—and insect repellent. Charter planes depart from San José to Carate, a 20-minute walk away, several times a week, but it's cheaper to fly to Puerto Jiménez and hire a taxi to Carate. ⊠ *Apdo. 6941–1000, San José,* ☎ *222–0333,* ℻ *257–1665. 20 tents without bath. Restaurant, bar. AE, MC, V.*

Outdoor Activities and Sports

HIKING

Three hiking routes go into Corcovado, two of which begin near Puerto Jiménez, the other in Bahía Drake, which follows the coast down to San Pedrillo. You can hire a taxi in Puerto Jiménez to go to the Los Patos trailhead, or at least to the first crossing of the Río Rincón (from where you hike a couple of miles upriver to the trailhead). The beach route, via La Leona, starts in Carate, about 37 km (23 mi) southwest of Puerto Jiménez. A four-wheel-drive truck carries hikers to Carate every day, departing Puerto Jiménez at 6 AM and returning at 7:30 PM; for information call the **Mini Mercado El Tigre** (☎ 735–5075).

Cabo Matapalo

⓭ *16 km (10 mi) south of Puerto Jiménez.*

The southern tip of the Osa Peninsula possesses the kind of natural beauty that people are happy to travel halfway across the country to experience. Its ridges afford views of the blue Pacific, where schools of dolphin and whales may sometimes be spotted in the distance. The forest is tall and dense, its giant trees draped with thick lianas, branches covered with aerial gardens of bromeliads and orchids. The translation of Cabo Matapalo is "Strangler Fig Cape," a reference to the fig trees that germinate in the branches of other trees and eventually grow to smother them with their roots and branches. Strangler figs are common to the area, as they are nearly everywhere else in the country, but Matapalo's greatest attractions are its rarer species such as the brilliant scarlet macaw and the *gallinazo* tree, which bursts into yellow blossom as the rainy season draws to an end.

A forested ridge extends east from Corcovado down to Matapalo, where the foliage clings to almost vertical slopes and waves crash against the black rocks below. This continuous forest corridor is protected within a series of private preserves, which means that Cabo Matapalo has most of the same wildlife as the national park—even the big cats. Most of the point itself lies within the private reserves of the area's two main hotels, and that forest is crisscrossed by footpaths, some of which head to tranquil beaches or to waterfalls that pour into small pools.

Lodging

$$$$ 🏨 **Bosque del Cabo.** The tip of Capo Matapalo lies within the 200-
★ acre grounds of this nature lodge, more than half nestled in primary forest and home to all kinds of wild critters. Comfortably rustic bungalows are scattered along the edge of a wide lawn, from where you enjoy breathtaking views of the ocean through the foliage. Each bungalow is slightly different, but they all have wood floors, private baths, solar energy, and porches with hammocks. Delicious meals are served family style in a simple, open-air restaurant. Trails wind down through the forest to two secluded beaches and a waterfall with a natural swimming pool. Additional distractions include sportfishing, sea kayaking, bird-watching, and horseback riding. ⊠ *Matapalo, Apdo. 15, Puerto Jiménez,* ☎ ℻ *735–5206. 8 bungalows with bath. Restaurant, pool. V.*

$$$$ 🖼 **Lapa Rios.** More than just one of Costa Rica's finest hotels, Lapa
★   Ríos—spread along a ridge in the jungle and a 4-sq-km (1½-sq-mi) nature reserve—is part of an innovative conservation project by owners
Karen and John Lewis to preserve endangered wildlife. You can explore the pristine wilderness on foot or horseback, accompanied by one
of several resident naturalist guides, but you are quite likely to spot
toucans, sloths, iguanas, and other animals from the restaurant and
bungalows. Spacious and airy villas constructed with local hardwoods,
with thatched roofs, four-poster beds draped with mosquito nets, and
large balconies, look like how Tarzan might live on Bill Gates' budget. The hotel's restaurant is excellent. ⊠ *Apdo. 100, Puerto Jiménez,*
☏ *735–5130,* 🖷 *735–5179;* ⊠ *Box 025216, SJO 706, Miami, FL*
33102-5216. 14 bungalows with bath. Restaurant, bar, pool, hiking,
horseback riding. AE, MC, V.

Outdoor Activities and Sports

WATER SPORTS

On the eastern side of the point, the waves break over a platform that
creates a perfect right that draws surfers from far away. The area also
has excellent sea kayaking, and both Lapa Ríos and Bosque del Cabo
(☞ Lodging, *above*) can arrange horseback excursions, guided tours
to Corcovado, or deep-sea fishing trips.

Bahía Drake

⑭ *10 km (6 mi) north of Corcovado, 40 km (25 mi) southwest of Pal-*
mar Sur.

Bahía Drake (Drake Bay) was named after Sir Francis Drake (1540 or
1543–1596), the British explorer who, legend has it, anchored here more
than four centuries ago. The rugged coast that stretches south from
the mouth of the Río Sierpe to Corcovado probably doesn't look much
different than it did in Drake's day: small beaches backed by thick jungle, cropped by rocky points and overlooking dark, igneous islets. The
tiny villages and nature lodges scattered along the coast are hemmed
in by the rain forest, which is home for troops of monkeys, inconspicuous
sloths, striking scarlet macaws, and hundreds of other birds species.

A trip here is a true tropical adventure, with plenty of hiking and some
rough boat rides. Most people reach this isolated area by boat via the
Río Sierpe, though direct flights are now available, and backpackers
occasionally hike north out of Corcovado (two hours from Marenco,
four from Drake Bay). Another option is to visit the area on **Temptress**
Adventure Cruises, whose 185-ft Costa Rican ship runs three-, four-,
and seven-night nature cruises that include Drake Bay, Corcovado, and
Isla del Caño (☞ Southern Pacific Costa Rica A to Z, *below* and
Close-Up: Cruising the Pacific Coast, *above*); a four-day cruise sails
from Golfito (☞ *above*).

The town of **Drake,** which is scattered along the bay, has the cheapest
accommodations in the area, and there are several nature lodges near
the Río Agujitas (Drake Bay Wilderness Camp, Aguila de Osa, and La
Paloma Lodge, ☞ *below*), on the bay's southern end, which offer
comprehensive packages that include trips to Corcovado and Isla de
Caño. They also offer horseback touring, scuba diving, and deep-sea
fishing. Nature lodges farther to the south (Marenco Biological Station, Punta Marenco, and Casa Corcovado, ☞ *below*), near Corcovado, offer the same excursions from even wilder settings.

Lodging

All places listed below have packages that include round-trip transportation from San José.

Finally, a travel companion that doesn't snore on the plane or eat all your peanuts.

When traveling, your MCI WorldCom Card is the best way to keep in touch. Our operators speak your language, so they'll be able to connect you back home—no matter where your travels take you. Plus, your MCI WorldCom Card is easy to use, and even earns you frequent flyer miles every time you use it. When you add in our great rates, you get something even more valuable: peace-of-mind. So go ahead. Travel the world. MCI WorldCom just brought it a whole lot closer.

You can even sign up today at www.mci.com/worldphone or ask your operator to make a collect call to 1-410-314-2938.

EASY TO CALL WORLDWIDE

1 Just dial the WorldPhone access number of the country you're calling from.
2 Dial or give the operator your MCI WorldCom Card number.
3 Dial or give the number you're calling.

Australia ◆	
To call using OPTUS	1-800-551-111
To call using TELSTRA	1-800-881-100
Bahamas/Bermuda	1-800-888-8000
British Virgin Islands	1-800-888-8000
Costa Rica ◆	0-800-012-2222
Denmark	8001-0022
Norway ◆	800 -19912
India	000-127
For collect access	000-126
United States/Canada	1-800-888-8000

For your complete WorldPhone calling guide, dial the WorldPhone access number for the country you're in and ask the operator for Customer Service. In the U.S. call 1-800-431-5402.

◆ Public phones may require deposit of coin or phone card for dial tone.

EARN FREQUENT FLYER MILES

MCI WorldCom, its logo and the names of the products referred to herein are proprietary marks of MCI WorldCom, Inc. All airline names and logos are proprietary marks of the respective airlines. All airline program rules and conditions apply.

The first thing you need overseas is the one thing you forget to pack.

FOREIGN CURRENCY DELIVERED OVERNIGHT

Chase Currency To Go® delivers foreign currency to your home by the next business day*

It's easy—before you travel, call 1-888-CHASE84 for delivery of any of 75 currencies

Delivery is free with orders of $500 or more

Competitive rates— without exchange fees

You don't have to be a Chase customer—you can pay by Visa® or MasterCard®

CHASE

THE RIGHT RELATIONSHIP IS EVERYTHING.®

1•888•CHASE84
www.chase.com

$$$$ ⊞ **Aguila de Osa Inn.** Just because you're out in the woods doesn't mean you have to rough it, and in the tradition of great fishing lodges, this inn offers plenty of comfort and good food. Sportfishing is the specialty here—the inn has a four-boat fleet and extensive tackle room—but scuba diving and the area's standard excursions can be arranged. Spacious rooms set in a series of cement buildings are spread along a ridge, with views of Drake Bay through the bamboo, and details such as hand-carved doors and large tile baths set them apart. Meals centered on fish, maybe what you caught that day, are served family style in the handsome thatched-roof restaurant. ⊠ *Apdo. 10486–1000, San José,* ☎ *232–7722,* FAX *296–2190. 14 rooms with bath. Restaurant, horseback riding, fishing. No credit cards. Closed Oct.*

$$$$ ⊞ **Casa Corcovado.** This place's advantage is the fact that it borders Corcovado National Park; since a trail leads right into the park from here, you can often explore its forests hours before anyone else arrives. Rooms are spread around a garden surrounded by the rain forest, into which trails lead, and a sunset bar is set up down the hill. Modern cement rooms have bright tile floors, large baths, screened walls, and ceiling fans. There's plenty of room for relaxation: you can navigate a tropical cocktail at the second bar overlooking the jungle and a small pool, or contemplate your next endeavor from one of the hammocks or chairs on the beach below. ⊠ *Apdo. 1482-1250, Escazú, northern border of Corcovado,* ☎ *256–3181,* FAX *256–7409. 10 rooms with bath. 2 bars, dining room, pool, hiking, horseback riding, beach, snorkeling, boating. AE, MC, V. Closed Sept.–mid-Nov.*

$$$$ ⊞ **La Paloma Lodge.** The sweeping views and sense of jungle seclu-
★ sion enjoyed at La Paloma make its deluxe bungalows the area's best. Airy, wooden villas, scattered along a forested hill south of Drake Bay, have bedroom lofts and large porches complete with hammocks. Smaller standard rooms, not nearly as nice, are farther up the hill. The lodge's tiled pool, overlooking forest and ocean, is another important plus. The hotel offers skin diving and trips to Corcovado and Isla del Caño. ⊠ *Apdo. 97–4005, San Antonio de Belen, Heredia,* ☎ *239–2801,* FAX *239–0954. 4 rooms with bath, 5 bungalows. Restaurant, pool, horseback riding, fishing. MC, V.*

$$$$ ⊞ **Marenco Biological Station.** Bordering a wildlife refuge that protects
★ almost 52 sq km (20 sq mi) of rain forest along the coast between Drake Bay and Corcovado National Park, Marenco was one of the country's first ecotourism enterprises. Resident biologist guides interpret the wonders of tropical nature on a series of well-marked trails that wind through the forest. Breezy, wooden bungalows with large balconies; smaller-size rooms; and an open-air dining hall overlook the forest and ocean from a high ridge. It's a bit rustic—no hot water—but the contact with nature can't be topped. Excursions to Corcovado and Isla del Caño are part of all-inclusive package tours. ⊠ *Apdo. 4025–1000, San José, 11 km (7 mi) southwest of Drake Bay,* ☎ *258–1919,* FAX *255–1346. 25 rooms with bath. Dining room, hiking, horseback riding, beach, snorkeling. MC, V.*

$$$–$$$$ ⊞ **Drake Bay Wilderness Camp.** Spread over a grassy point between the Río Agujitas and the ocean, at the southern end of the bay, the Wilderness Camp is this area's second-oldest lodge and one of its best deals, especially if you stay long. Rooms in cement buildings with tile floors, ceiling fans, and small porches are scattered around manicured grounds. Tent cabins (big tents set on cement platforms) with beds share baths and are a bit cramped, but they are considerably less expensive and have great ocean views. Most of the people who stay here come to see the rain forest, but scuba diving and sportfishing are also available, as well as horseback touring, canoeing, and sea kayaking. Charter flights direct to Drake Bay make this lodge the quickest, easiest place to reach. ⊠ *Apdo. 98–8150, Palmar Norte,* ☎ FAX *771–2436 or 256–7394. 20 rooms with bath, 5 tent cabins without bath. Restaurant, bar, horseback riding, boating, fishing. MC, V.*

$$$–$$$$ 📺 **Punta Marenco.** Perched right next to Marenco Biological Station (☞ *above*), and belonging to one of the brothers of the same family that owns the station, Punta Marenco offers equal access to the adjacent wildlife refuge. Its guides may not be biologists, but Punta Marenco is much smaller, if less organized, and offers the same excursions. The airy, thatched-roof bungalows are even nicer than Marenco's, with gorgeous views, and their prices are considerably lower. ⊠ *11 km (7 mi) southwest of Drake Bay,* ☎ *268–6770,* FAX *268–7743. 8 bungalows. Dining room, hiking, horseback riding, beach, snorkeling. MC, V.*

Isla del Caño

⑮   *19 km (12 mi) off the Osa Peninsula, due west of Drake Bay.*

Most of the more than 2½ sq km (1 sq mi) of the uninhabited island of Isla del Caño and its Reserva Biológica (Biological Reserve) are covered in evergreen forest containing fig, locust, and rubber trees. Coastal Indians used it as a burial ground, and the numerous bits and pieces unearthed here have prompted archaeologists to speculate about pre-Columbian long-distance maritime trade. The island's big attraction, however, is the surrounding ocean, which offers superb conditions for scuba diving and snorkeling. The snorkeling is excellent around the rocky points that flank the island's main beach, and if a certified diver, you will want to explore such nearby dive spots as Bajo del Diablo and Paraiso, where you are guaranteed to encounter thousands of big fish. Lodges in Drake Bay (☞ *above*) offer day trips to Isla del Caño.

SOUTHERN PACIFIC COSTA RICA A TO Z

Arriving and Departing

By Boat
Drake Bay is usually reached by boat from Sierpe, south of Palmar Norte, but it is also possible to arrange direct boat trips from Dominical (contact Tropical Waters, ☎ 232–6672) or from **Villas Gaia,** near Parque Nacional Marino Ballena.

By Bus
GENERAL VALLEY

Musoc (C. 16 and Avdas. 1 and 3, ☎ 222–2422) buses from San José to San Isidro depart hourly between 5:30 AM and 5 PM (3-hr trip), returning at the same times. Buses from San José to Dominical (**Transporte Delio Morales,** ☎ 223–5567) and Parque Nacional Marino Ballena via Quepos leave from the Coca-Cola Station daily at 5:30 AM and 3 PM (6-hr trip), returning at 5:30 AM and 2 PM.

Tracopa-Alfaro buses from San José to Golfito depart from Calle 14 between Avenidas 3 and 5 daily at 7 AM and 3 PM (8-hr trip), returning at 5 AM and 1 PM. **Tracopa** buses from San José to San Vito depart from Calle 14 between Avenidas 3 and 5 daily at 5:45 AM, 8:15 AM, 11:30 AM, and 2:45 PM (7-hr trip).

Transportes Blanco-Lobo (☎ 257–4121) buses from San José to Puerto Jiménez leave from Calle 12 between Avenidas 7 and 9 at 6 AM and noon (8-hr trip), returning at 5 AM and 11 AM. **Tracopa Alfaro** buses from San José to Palmar Norte depart from Calle 14 between Avenidas 5 and 7 daily at 5, 7, and 10 AM and 1 and 2:30 PM (6-hr trip); buses to Golfito, Puerto Jiménez, and San Vito also stop here. In Palmar Norte, you can hire a taxi to Sierpe, the port for boats to Drake Bay.

By Car

The quickest way to reach the coastal highway, or Costanera, which leads past Jacó and Quepos (☞ Chapter 6) to Dominical and the rest of the southern Pacific zone, is to take the Carretera Interamericana (Pan-American Highway, CA1) west past the airport to the turnoff for Atenas, turning left and driving through Atenas to Orotina, where you head south on the coastal highway. The southern Pacific region can also be reached by taking the Pan-American Highway south (CA2), past Cartago and over the Cerro de la Muerte—where the turnoff for San Gerardo de Dota is located—to San Isidro, Valle de El General, and the Osa Peninsula. Foggy conditions atop Cerro de la Muerte make it best to cross the mountains as early in the day as possible.

By Plane

Sansa (✉ C. 42 between Avdas. 3 and 5, San José, ☎ 506/221–9414 or 506/441–8035, FAX 506/255–2176) has several flights daily from San José to Golfito and daily flights to Palmar Sur (for Drake Bay), Puerto Jiménez, and Coto 47 (for Panama). **Travelair** (✉ Aeropuerto Tobias Bolaños, Pavas, ☎ 220–3054, FAX 506/220–0413) has daily flights to Golfito, Palmar Sur, and Puerto Jiménez. Both airlines also have daily flights from Quepos to Palmar Sur, which is the quickest way to move between the central (☞ Chapter 6) and southern Pacific zones. **Costa Rica Expeditions** (☎ 222–0333, FAX 257–1665) runs several charter flights per week to Carate, a 40-minute hike from its Corcovado Tent Camp. **Drake Bay Wilderness Camp** (☎ FAX 771–2436 or 256–7394) has daily charter flights directly from Bahía Drake.

Getting Around

By Boat

A small ferry crosses the Golfo Dulce, leaving Puerto Jiménez daily at 6 AM and returning from Golfito at 11:30 AM. Boat transportation to Zancudo or the more distant Pavones can be arranged through the **Coconut Cafe** (✉ Golfito, ☎ 775–0518). Drake Bay is usually reached by boat from Sierpe, south of Palmar Norte. Travel among the Drake Bay lodges, Corcovado, and Caño Island is in small boats owned by those lodges listed above.

By Bus

Transportes Blanco (771–2550) buses leave San Isidro for Dominical daily at 5:30 and 7 AM and 1:30 and 3 PM (1-hr trip); for San Gerardo de Rivas, the trailhead for Chirripó, at 5 AM and 2 PM.

From San Isidro, buses leave for Puerto Jiménez at 9 AM and 3 PM (5-hr trip). A truck for hikers leaves Puerto Jiménez daily at 6 AM for Carate, returning at 7:30 AM.

By Car

The coastal highway is a bit rough south of Dominical, but it can take you all the way to Palmar Sur on the Pan-American Highway (CA2).

The Pan-American Highway also has some rough, potholed spots, but is predominantly paved. From San Isidro, good roads head northeast to San Gerardo de Rivas and west to Dominical. The Pan-American Highway continues southeast from San Isidro to the turnoffs for San Vito, Puerto Jiménez, and Golfito before reaching Paso Canoas and the border of Panama. The turnoff for the back road to Golfito (four-wheel-drive vehicle only) is on the right at Villa Briceño; look for signs to La Gamba and the Esquinas lodge. The road from the Pan-American Highway into the Osa Peninsula was in rough shape at press time (four-wheel-drive vehicle recommended).

By Plane

Aeronaves (☎ 775–0278), based in Golfito, offers a wide array of charter destinations. **Aerotaxi Alfa Romeo** (☎ 735–5178, FAX 735–5112) offers charter flights to Carate, Drake Bay, Puerto Jiménez, Sirena ranger station (☞ Puerto Jiménez, *above*), Tiskita Jungle Lodge (☞ Playa Pavones, *above*), and anywhere else you want to go. You have to charter the whole plane, which is expensive, so it's best to fill it with the maximum capacity of five.

Contacts and Resources

Car Rentals

See Contacts and Resources *in* San José A to Z, *in* Chapter 2.

Emergencies

Ambulance (☎ 221–5818). **Fire** (☎ 118). **Police** (☎ 911; 117 in towns; 127 in rural areas). **Traffic Police** (☎ 227–8030).

Guided Tours

CRUISES

Temptress Adventure Cruises (⊠ 351 N.W. LeJeune Rd., Penthouse 6, Miami, FL 33126, ☎ 305/643–4040, FAX 305/643–6438) runs three-, four-, and seven-day adventure cruises on the *Temptress Explorer* that visit Corcovado National Park, Drake Bay, Isla del Caño, and Parque Nacional Manuel Antonio (☞ Chapter 6). Activities include hiking through national parks and refuges, bird-watching, nature walks, snorkeling, horseback riding, fishing, and diving accompanied by excellent naturalist guides (☞ Close-Up: Cruising the Pacific Coast, *above*). The ship sails from Puntarenas (three- or seven-day cruises) and Golfito (four-day cruises), with transport to the airport in San José. Contact Temptress direct or **Cruceros del Sur** (⊠ Across from Colegio Los Angeles, Sabana Norte, San José, ☎ 232–6672, FAX 220–2103), which also offers 10-day skin-diving expeditions to distant Isla del Coco on the *Okeanos Agressor*. The **Undersea Hunter** (☎ 228–6535, FAX 298–7334) is a smaller vessel that runs similar dive trips to Isla del Coco.

HIKING TOURS

Brunca Tours (☎ 771–3100) offers hiking and nature tours to Chirripó and other areas. In Dominical, **Hacienda Barú** (1 km/½ mi north of Dominical, ☎ 771–4582) has a number of guided hikes through the rain forest. **Ecole Travel** (⊠ C. 7 between Avdas. Central and 1, San José, ☎ 223–2240, FAX 223–4128) offers inexpensive guided hiking tours into Chirripó and Corcovado national parks.

NATURE LODGES

Out of San José, **Costa Rica Sun Tours** (⊠ C. 36 at Avda. 4, San José, ☎ 255–2011, FAX 233–6890) runs tours to its remote Tiskita Jungle Lodge. **Costa Rica Expeditions** (⊠ Avda. 3 at C. Central, San José, ☎ 222–0333, FAX 257–1665) runs guided tours to its Corcovado Tent Camp (☞ Parque Nacional Corcovado, *above*).

SEA-KAYAKING TOURS

In Puerto Jiménez, **Rainforest Trex** (⊠ Restaurante Carolina, Puerto Jiménez, ☎ 735–5210) organizes sea-kayaking tours that range from a sunset paddle to a one-week trip that explores the entire Golfo Dulce.

Visitor Information

The tourist office in San José (☞ Visitor Information *in* San José A to Z, *in* Chapter 2) can assist with information about the southern Pacific zone. In Dominical contact **Tropical Waters** (3½ km/2 mi north of Dominical on road to San Isidro, ☎ 787–0031).

8 THE ATLANTIC LOWLANDS AND THE CARIBBEAN COAST

Inhabited by African-Caribbean, Spanish, and indigenous peoples, the Atlantic lowlands contains wild outposts, banana and cacao plantations, and dense primary jungle. Too hot and humid to be anything but laid back, it's a world unto itself. Come pioneer the turbulent rivers, verdant national parks, and the easygoing villages and coral-fringed beaches of the Caribbean Coast.

Updated by
Justin
Henderson

DOMINATED BY CLOUD FORESTS, sprawling banana plantations, and thick tropical jungle, the Atlantic lowlands lie in the provinces of Heredia and Limó adjacent to the Caribbean Sea. The widespread, largely untamed region stretches from the eastern slope of the Cordillera Central up to the Sarapiquí area northeast of San José, home to the private Rara Avis and La Selva reserves, east through banana-growing country, and down to the pristine beaches at Cahuita and Puerto Viejo de Limón on the southern Caribbean Sea. The region also stretches north to the Nicaraguan border, encompassing the coastal jungles and canals of the Parque Nacional Tortuguero and Barra del Colorado Wildlife Refuge. Turtles arrive by the thousands to lay their eggs on these northern beaches. The occasional caiman can be spotted here, sunning on a bank or drifting like a log down a jungle waterway. And farther north still, sportfishing fans will find tarpon and snook aplenty to detain them off the shores of Barra del Colorado.

Roughly a third of Limón province's population are Afro-Caribbeans, descendants of early 1800s turtle fishermen and the West Indians who arrived in the late-19th century to construct the Atlantic Railroad and then remained to work on banana and cacao plantations. Some 4,000 Jamaicans are reputed to have died of yellow fever, malaria, and snakebites during the construction of the first 40 km (25 mi) of railroad to San José. They were paid relatively well, however, and gradually their lot improved. By the 1930s many had obtained their own small plots of land, and when the price of cacao rose in the 1950s, they emerged as comfortable landowners employing migrant, landless Hispanics. However, until the Civil War of 1948, Afro-Caribbeans were forbidden from crossing into the Central Valley for fear of upsetting the country's racial balance, and they were thus prevented from following work when, in the 1930s, United Fruit abandoned many of its blight-ridden plantations for green-field sites on the Pacific plain. Although Jamaicans brought some aspects of British colonial culture along with them, such as the maypole dance and cricket, these habits have long since given way to reggae and salsa, soccer and baseball. Many of the Atlantic-coast Ticos are bilingual, speaking fluent English and Spanish, and to the south, around Puerto Viejo de Limón, you'll even hear some phrases that derive from the language of the indigenous peoples, among them the Kekoldi, the Bribri, and the Cabecar.

A note on crime: During the 1990s some of the cocaine flowing from Latin America into the United States spilled into the Puerto Viejo de Limón and Cahuita area, resulting in a drug-related crime problem. In the far north, close to the Nicaraguan border, Nicaraguan refugees have become rather aggressive in their efforts at squatting on and claiming land, some belonging to American and European investors. One does not wish to overemphasize difficulties in a country far safer than most, but they are real: two kidnappings of Europeans occurred in 1996. (Ransoms were paid, and no one suffered harm in the end.) If you are eager to experience Costa Rica's Caribbean beaches and jungles but wish to avoid the possibly more dangerous towns, head by boat or plane directly to Tortuguero or Barra del Colorado, or drive south through Puerto Viejo de Limón to savor the seaside jungle experience while being holed up in one of the many lodges, hotels, and tent camps that have opened along the road between Puerto Viejo de Limón and Manzanillo.

Pleasures and Pastimes

Dining

The number of upscale hotels, lodges, and restaurants opening in recent years has introduced a more varied international cuisine to the region. Yet much of the cooking along the Caribbean coast finds its roots in old Jamaican recipes. *Rondon,* for example, is a traditional Jamaican stew that requires hours of preparation. Rice and beans are flavored with coconut; meat is fried with hot spices to make *paties* (pies); and fish or meat, yams, plantains, breadfruit, peppers, and spices are boiled in coconut milk. Johnnycakes and *panbón* (a heavy, spicy fruit bread) are popular baked goods. Various medicinal herbal teas are ubiquitous in the lowlands. Seafood is, of course, readily available, as is a wide variety of fresh fruit.

Fishing

World-class tarpon and snook attract serious sportfishermen to the northern Caribbean shore in and offshore of the national parks of Tortuguero and Barra del Colorado. January through May is the best time for tarpon, August through November for snook.

Hiking and Jungle Boating

From the beach hikes of Parque Nacional Cahuita to the more leisurely jungle-boat cruises arranged by the lodges near Parque Nacional Tortuguero, the opportunities for plunging into tropical jungle and rain forest abound in the Atlantic lowlands. Farther inland on the eastern slope of the mountains, Braulio Carrillo's cloud- and rain-forested mountains offer scenic trails, and the private lowland reserves of La Selva and Rara Avis provide excellent jungle exploring. In the southeast, the remote and little-touristed Reserva Biológica Hitoy Cerere contains a mix of difficult and easy hiking trails as the jungle climbs into the hills of the Talamanca range. Look for waterfalls, swimming holes, and an encyclopedic variety of Costa Rican flora and fauna.

Lodging

The Atlantic lowlands have little in the way of luxury hotels, although in recent years a number of relatively upscale, self-proclaimed ecotourist lodges and other pricier accommodations have opened along the highway south of Puerto Limón and (especially) on the beach road south of Puerto Viejo de Limón. Nonetheless, most of the places to stay are either rustic *cabinas* (cottages) or nature lodges. Often isolated in the jungle and reached only by boat or strenuous hike, some of the lodges are rough, bare-essentials kinds of places and a few verge on the luxurious. Given the difficulty inherent in getting supplies in to these luxe lodges, you will find that you'll have to pay a hefty price for the comforts of a hot shower and a cold beer in the jungle.

Snorkeling and Scuba Diving

Cahuita has Costa Rica's largest coral reef, and although it has been severely damaged by pollution, there is plenty still to admire. Other dive spots include the coral reef at Isla Uvita off Puerto Limón, the many reefs off the beaches of the Gandoca-Manzanillo Wildlife Refuge, and the sea caverns off Puerto Viejo de Limón. The water is clearest during the dry season. In and around Parque Nacional Marina Isla Bastimentos near Bocas del Toro (☞ Chapter 9) in Panama, the snorkeling and diving are magnificent.

Surfing

Although some point breaks were badly affected by coastal uplift in 1991, other new ones were created—a left at Punta Cocles and a right at Punta Uva. Puerto Viejo de Limón's famous and formidable Salsa Brava is still ridable, but its spectacular waves are really only for the experienced, fearless surfer. Less hairy spots include Playa Negra, Cahuita, Beach Break just south of Puerto Viejo, Playa Bonita north of Puerto Viejo de Limón, and Isla Uvita, 20 minutes from Puerto Limón by boat. You must always beware of riptides. December to March and June to August are the best times to surf this coast.

Turtle-Watching

The Caribbean coast is one of the few places in the world where the green sea turtle nests. Great groups of them descend on Parque Nacional Tortuguero from July to October each year. Three other turtle species—the hawksbill, loggerhead, and giant leatherback—also nest in the park (☞ Close-Up: Tico Turtles, *below*).

Exploring the Atlantic Lowlands and the Caribbean Coast

Below the cloud- and rain-forested mountains and foothills of the Cordillera Central and the Cordillera de Talamanca lie fertile plains and dense tracts of primary tropical jungle. Much of the land has been cleared and given over to farming and ranching, but vast expanses of this region are still inaccessible by car. No roads lead to Barra del Colorado and Tortuguero. You must fly from San José or take a jungle boat in from Móin, an alluring prospect if you crave solitude. Coastal Talamanca, the region to the south, however, is accessible by car and the Carretera Guápiles (Guápiles Highway).

Keep in mind that there are two towns called Puerto Viejo on the Atlantic side of Costa Rica. One, Puerto Viejo de Sarapiquí, is a former river port that lies in the more northerly, inland section of the lowlands; the other, Puerto Viejo de Limón, is on the coast not far from the border with Panama. Keeping these towns straight can be confusing, since locals often refer to both of them merely as "Puerto Viejo" without the clarifying "de Sarapiquí" and "de Limón." To add to the confusion, plain Puerto Limón, often called Limón, is north along the coast from Puerto Viejo de Limón.

Numbers in the text correspond to numbers in the margin and on the Atlantic Lowlands and the Caribbean Coast map.

Great Itineraries

You need at least a week to cover this territory, but even three days are enough to sample the charms of Costa Rica's Caribbean side if you plan your time judiciously. In addition to the difficulties of getting around, it should be emphasized that the Atlantic lowlands offers a wide selection of activities requiring different levels of physical endurance and commitment, ranging from seashore lounging to rain-forest trekking. If your time, energy, and willingness to put up with discomfort—mud, mosquitoes, and rain, for starters—are limited, you'll have to make choices. Another consideration is travel time. The Rara Avis preserve, for example, is a wonderful place to visit, but the difficulty in getting there—a two- to four-hour tractor haul into the park—explains the two-night minimum-stay requirement. Note that many lodges require reservations.

IF YOU HAVE 3 OR 4 DAYS AND LOVE THE BEACH

Hop on an early flight from San José to ⊞ **Tortuguero** ⑥ or ⊞ **Barra del Colorado** ⑦ for a jungle-boat tour, turtle-watching session, or fishing trip. The next morning take the boat down to **Móin** ⑩ and then head to **Puerto Limón** ⑨. Take a bus or drive south to ⊞ **Cahuita** ⑪ and/or ⊞ **Puerto Viejo de Limón** ⑬. Relax on the beach or spend the day playing in the surf, snorkeling, and hiking through the Parque Nacional Cahuita. Camp at Puerto Vargas or stay a couple of nights in Cahuita, Puerto Viejo de Limón, Punta Uva, or farther south along the beach

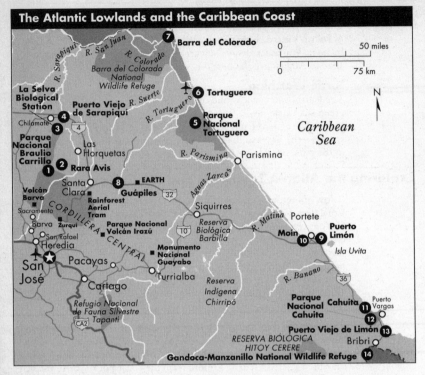

The Atlantic Lowlands and the Caribbean Coast

road that terminates at the bird-filled jungles and deserted beaches of the **Gandoca-Manzanillo National Wildlife Refuge** ⑭.

IF YOU HAVE 3 DAYS AND LOVE THE RAIN FOREST

Wake early in San José and drive or take a bus over the Guápiles Highway to hike in **Parque Nacional Braulio Carrillo** ① or ride the **Rain Forest Aerial Tram**—get there early, since the people in the first gondolas into the forest will see the most wildlife. Then drive or take a bus to 🏠 **La Selva Biological Station** ③ (it's a 2-km/1-mi walk from the road to the La Selva entrance, so pack lightly if you're taking public transportation) and spend the afternoon hiking its network of trails. Spend a night there and then move to one of the lodges in the 🏠 **Puerto Viejo de Sarapiquí** ④ area, most of which offer horseback excursions into the jungle, hiking, rafting, and kayaking. Or after a night at La Selva you can leave early the next morning and bus or drive back to Las Horquetas to meet the 9 AM tractor, which will take you into 🏠 **Rara Avis** ② for two days and nights.

IF YOU HAVE 7 DAYS

Consider some variations: add an overnight rafting trip down the Río Pacuare, near Turrialba (☞ Chapter 3), or take a multi-day fishing trip out of **Barra del Colorado** ⑦ or **Tortuguero** ⑥. You might want to arrange to visit the Bribri, Cabecar, or Kekoldi Indian reservations in the hills west of **Puerto Viejo de Limón** ⑬ or hike into the remote Reserva Biológica Hitoy Cerere. Finally, if you love snorkeling amidst pristine coral reefs, block out two or three days to visit Bocas del Toro and Bastimentos Island National Marine Park in Panama (☞ Chapter 9). From Changuinola, two hours by water taxi and bus gets you to Bocas, and an eight-hour bus ride gets you back to San José.

When to Tour the Atlantic Lowlands and the Caribbean Coast

In three words: when it's dry. This realm absorbs 200 or more inches of rain a year, so unless you are planning to view the turtles laying eggs on the beach (each species has its own schedule), you'll want to avoid the worst of it. Chances are you'll be rained on no matter when you go, but your best bets for good weather are the Atlantic Coast's two short "dry" seasons—September and October and March and April—which unfortunately do not correspond to the dry season or the high tourist season in the rest of the country. If you don't mind the rain, go in the rainy season: you may be waterlogged your entire visit, but at least you'll find lower prices and few tourists.

BRAULIO CARRILLO NATIONAL PARK AND THE NORTHERN LOWLANDS

The immense Parque Nacional Braulio Carrillo northeast of San José protects virgin rain forest on either side of the highway to Guápiles. You can get some idea of it as you pass through on the highway, but inside is another world. Everywhere you look, green things sprout, twist, and bloom. Bromeliads and orchids cling to arching trees while white-faced monkeys and blue morpho butterflies creep, climb, and flutter. Adjacent to the park is a private reserve with the Rain Forest Aerial Tram, where you can explore the flora and fauna of the rain-forest canopy from gondolas.

After threading through Braulio Carrillo, the Guápiles Highway branches at Santa Clara, having completed its descent onto the Caribbean plain. The Guápiles Highway continues southeast to Puerto Limón and the Caribbean coast. If you take a left and head north, the smoothly paved road (Highway 4) leads through flat, deforested pasture and pockets of old-growth forest toward two preserves, Rara Avis and La Selva. Just north are the old river-port town of Puerto Viejo de Sarapiquí and the forest-clad hills of the eastern slope of the Cordillera Central.

Parque Nacional Braulio Carrillo

❶ *30 km (19 mi) north of San José.*

In a country where deforestation is still rife, Parque Nacional Braulio Carrillo (Braulio Carrillo National Park, ☞ Chapter 10) provides a rare opportunity to witness dense primary tropical cloud forest as far as the eye can see. The park owes its foundation to the public outcry provoked by the construction of the highway through the region in the late 1970s, when the government bowed to pressure from environmentalists. Thanks to the highway running through it, the park is the most accessible for travelers from the San José area. Covering 443 sq km (171 sq mi), the park's extremely diverse terrain extends from 100 to more than 9,500 ft above sea level. The park reaches from the central volcanic range down the Atlantic slope to the La Selva research station near Puerto Viejo de Sarapiquí. Six thousand tree species, 500 different birds, and 135 types of mammals have been cataloged here.

Braulio Carrillo's **Zurquí ranger station** is to the right of the road, a ½ km (¼ mi) before the Zurquí tunnel. Hikes start here and are steep, so the trails inevitably involve a lot of ups and downs. Note that you should wear hiking boots on the trails to protect yourself from the mud and possible snakes. The main 1½-km-long (1-mi-long) trail through primary forest culminates in a mirador, but, unfortunately, the highway mars the view. Monkeys, tapirs, jaguars, kinkajous, sloths, raccoons, margays, and porcupines all live in this forest, and resident birds include the quetzal and the eagle. Orchids, bromeliads, heliconias, fungi, and mushrooms are less likely to hide from you and can be seen throughout. From the **Carrillo ranger station,** 22 km (14 mi) northeast along the highway from Zurquí, the trails are less steep and make for easier hiking. For access to the 9,500-ft **Volcán Barva,** you need to start from Sacramento, north of Heredia. The walk to the crater takes two to three hours, but your efforts will be rewarded by great views provided you've started early, preferably before 8 AM, to avoid the mist that sometimes obscures views of the summit. ☎ *283–8004 for Sistemas de Areas de Conservación in San José; 192 for National Parks toll-free hot line.* ☎ *$6.* ☉ *Daily 7–4.*

Rain Forest Aerial Tram

Adjacent to Braulio Carrillo National Park, a 4-sq-km (1½-sq-mi) preserve houses the Rain Forest Aerial Tram, a privately owned and operated engineering marvel consisting of a series of gondolas strung together in a modified ski-lift pulley system. (To lessen the impact on the jungle, the support pylons were flown into place by helicopter, with the chopper and pilot rented from neighboring Nicaragua's Sandinista Army.) The tram provides students, researchers, and you with a new way of seeing the rain forest canopy and its spectacular array of epiphyte plant life and birds from close above, otherwise possible only if you climbed the trees yourself. The founder, Dr. Donald Perry, developed a more primitive system of canopy touring at nearby Rara Avis. Of the two, this is the easier-to-use, commercialized version. Though purists might complain that it treats the rain forest like an amusement park ride, this is an entertaining and educational way to become enlightened about the beauty and value of rain forest ecology.

The 21 gondolas hold five people each, including a bilingual guide who is also a biologist. The guides are equipped with walkie-talkies so they can request brief stops for viewing or photographing. The 2½-km (1½-mi) ride takes between 1 and 1½ hours, depending on the number of stops. There are simple day accommodations for researchers and students and a breakfast and lunch café on site. The price includes a biologist-guided walk through the area for ground-level orientation before the tram ride. The walk starts at 6 AM (after 9 on Monday) and the tram ride begin at 8 AM. San José pickups can be arranged, and there is regular bus service (on the Guápiles line) every half hour. ☎ *257–5961,* FAX *257–6053 for reservations.* ☎ *Guided walk and tram $47.50. AE, MC, V.* ☉ *Mon. 9–2, Tues.–Sun. 6–2.*

Rara Avis

❷ *Las Horquetas: 17 km (11 mi) north of Santa Clara, 100 km (62 mi) north of San José.*

Toucans, sloths, green macaws, howler and spider monkeys, vested anteaters, and tapirs may be on hand to greet you when you arrive at Rara Avis, one of Costa Rica's most popular private reserves. Ecologist Amos Bien founded Rara Avis with the intent of combining research, tourism, and the sustainable extraction of forest products. Bilingual guides take you along the muddy trails and canopy observation platforms and help spot wildlife. Bring a camera: the reserve's lacy double waterfall is one of Costa Rica's most-photographed sights. It's open only to overnight guests (☞ *Lodging, below*).

The town of **Las Horquetas** is the jumping-off point for the 13-sq-km (5-sq-mi) private reserve. The 16-km (10-mi) trip from Horquetas to the reserve is accomplished in three hours on horseback, two to three hours by tractor (leaves daily at 8:30 AM), or one hour by four-wheel-drive vehicle, plus a rough 3-km (2-mi) hike up to the lodge proper. The trails are steep and rugged, but the flora and fauna along the way are remarkable. One note: some readers have complained that although the reserve itself is lovely, the guides and services were considerably less than what they had expected. From Braulio Carrillo, turn left at signs for Puerto Viejo de Sarapiquí and go 17 km (10½ mi) to Las Horquetas.

Lodging

$$$$ 🏨 **Rara Avis.** You can stay in one of two lodges in the reserve. The Waterfall Lodge was named for the 180-ft waterfall nearby and contains hardwood-paneled rooms with chairs, firm beds, balconies, and hammocks. Despite the property's price range, these are rustic accommodations with minimal amenities. El Plástico Lodge used to be a prison and has more rustic coed bunk rooms and reductions for International Youth Hostel Federation members, students, and scientists. All rates include transport from Horquetas, guides, and three meals daily. Management requires a two-night minimum stay. ✉ *Las Horquetas, Apdo. 8105–1000, San José,* ☎ *710–6872, 253–0844, or 764–3131;* 📠 *253–0844, 764–4187 reservations office in San José. 13 rooms, 8 with bath. Dining room. AE, MC, V.*

La Selva Biological Station

❸ *14 km (9 mi) north of Rara Avis, 79 km (49 mi) northeast of San José.*

La Selva is a biologist's paradise, a 15-sq-km (5¾-sq-mi) reserve at the confluence of the Ríos Puerto Viejo and Sarapiquí, not far from the Rara Avis preserve. La Selva is home to about 420 bird species, 330 different kinds of trees, and 500 butterfly species. It's an excellent place to see animals, such as the spider monkey, poison dart frog, agouti, collared peccary, and dozens of other rare creatures. La Selva is a much more agreeable locale than Rara Avis if you prefer to see wildlife without having to rough it. This **OTS (Organization for Tropical Studies)** biological research station is designed for scientists but welcomes visitors in the daytime and also offers basic lodging in the beautiful Selva Verde Lodge (☞ Lodging, *below*). Extensive and well-marked trails and swing bridges connect habitats as varied as tropical wet forest, swamps, creeks, rivers, secondary regenerating forests, and pasture. Exploring with the reserve's guides, who run informative 3½-hour nature walks and are some of the best in the country, is compulsory. You should reserve a walk and lunch (additional $5) ahead of time. The OTS van can transport you here from San José, or you can take a public bus. ✉ *OTS, Apdo. 676–2050, San Pedro, look for sign for La Selva Biological Station, west side of road,* ☎ *766–6565, 240–6696 reservations office in San José,* 📠 *766–6535.* 🍴 *Nature walk $20, lunch $5.* ☉ *Walks 8 AM and 1:30 PM.*

Lodging

$$$–$$$$ 🏨 **La Selva Verde Lodge.** Other lodges offer more comfort for the money, but none can match La Selva's tropical nature experience. Dorm-style rooms have large bunk beds, ceiling fans, tile floors, and lots of screened windows. The restaurant, something like a school cafeteria, serves decent food but has a very limited schedule (reserve ahead). Lodging for $65 per person for a double ($80 per person for single) includes three meals and a guided nature walk. ✉ *OTS, Apdo. 676–2050, San Pedro,* ☎ *766–6565, 240–6696 reservations office in San José,* 📠 *240–6783. Restaurant, hiking. AE, MC, V.*

Puerto Viejo de Sarapiquí

4 *6½ km (4 mi) north of La Selva.*

During the last century Puerto Viejo de Sarapiquí was a thriving river port and the only link with the Barra del Colorado National Wildlife Refuge and Parque Nacional Tortuguero. Fortunes nose-dived with the construction of the coastal canal from the town of Moín, and today Puerto Viejo has a slightly run-down air. The activities of the Contras also made this a dangerous zone during the 1980s, but with the political situation now improved, boats once again ply the old route up the Río Sarapiquí to the Río San Juan on the Nicaraguan frontier; from the border you can travel downstream to Barra del Colorado or Tortuguero. There's really not much here to grab your attention, although a couple of companies such as Desafio and Sunset Tours (☞ Guided Tours *in* Atlantic Lowlands and the Caribbean Coast A to Z, *below*) now offer river tours, with up to class III rapids, plus plenty of wildlife can be spotted in the area.

Lodging

$$$ ⊞ **El Gavilán Lodge.** The lodge, the erstwhile hub of a fruit and cattle
★ farm, is two stories high and fronted by a veranda. Comfortable bedrooms have white walls, terra-cotta floors, fans, and decorative *artesanía* (crafts). Beautiful manicured gardens run down to the river, and colorful tanagers and three types of toucan feast in the citrus trees. The food, *comida típica* (typical Costa Rican fare), earns its good reputation. As do most, you can come here as part of a tour, with pickup in San José, for horseback jungle treks and boat trips up the Río Sarapiquí. ✉ *Apdo. 445–2010, Zapote, San José, 2 mi southeast of Puerto Viejo; watch for the sign on the road southeast of Puerto Viejo de Sarapiquí,* ☎ *234–9507,* ℻ *253–6556. 13 rooms with bath. Dining room, hot tub, horseback riding, fishing. AE, MC, V.*

$$$ ⊞ **Rancho Leona.** This roadside ranch has small, rustic dormitories with shared bath built by owners Ken and Leona Upcraft mostly to accommodate package kayaking tours. The restaurant, open to the public, serves very cheap, tasty dishes; the menu offers such Italian specialties as eggplant parmigiana and chicken cacciatore and numerous vegetarian dishes. Dazzling works of stained glass are made in the adjacent studio. Activities include kayaking on the Sarapiquí, hiking to a beautiful 30-ft waterfall, and river swimming. ✉ *La Virgen de Sarapiquí, Heredia, 17 km (10½ mi) southwest of Puerto Viejo,* ☎ ℻ *761–1019. 5 rooms without bath. Restaurant, boating, hiking, library. No credit cards.*

$$$ ⊞ **Selva Verde Lodge.** This expanding rancho-style complex in Chilamate is on the edge (across the Río Sarapiquí) of a 2-sq-km (¾-sq-mi) private reserve of tropical rain forest and caters primarily to natural history tours. The river lodge stands on stilts over the Río Sarapiquí. The buildings have wide verandas strung with hammocks, and bedrooms come with polished wood paneling, fans, and mosquito blinds. Activities include guided walks, boat trips, canoeing, rafting, and mountain biking. The rates include three meals per day in the restaurant. ✉ *Apdo. 55, Chilamate, Heredia, 7 km (4½ mi) west of Puerto Viejo de Sarapiquí,* ☎ *766–6800,* ℻ *766–6011. 54 rooms, 47 with bath. Restaurant, horseback riding, boating, fishing, library. MC, V.*

$$–$$$ ⊞ **Islas del Rió.** A reasonable option for Río Sarapiquí travelers, this little lodge about 10 km (6 mi) west of Puerto Viejo has rooms in the main building or in cement cabinas. A spacious open-air restaurant offers basic fare. The greatest feature is the Río Sarapiquí, rushing past in the "backyard." Hikes, horseback riding, and meals are included in the price of a room. ✉ *Bajos de Chilamate, on the road between*

Puerto Viejo de Sarapiquí and Las Virgen, ☎ *710–6898,* ℻ *233–9671,* ☎ ℻ *710–6890. 12 rooms, 9 with bath. Restaurant, hiking, horseback riding. No credit cards.*

$$ 🖭 **Hotel Bambu.** Unlike most of the region's isolated properties, this hotel is right in the heart of Puerto Viejo de Sarapiquí. The upstairs rooms are nothing special, simple but comfortable, with private baths and TVs. A dense cluster of tall bamboo stalks climbs like Jack's beanstalk out of the hotel's garden, providing shade for a new bar and restaurant serving Costa Rican–influenced Chinese food at reasonable prices. ✉ *Apdo. 151–A–2100, Guadeloupe, on main street across from the town square/soccer field,* ☎ *766–6005,* ℻ *766–6132. 11 rooms with bath. Restaurant, bar. MC, V.*

TORTUGUERO AND BARRA DEL COLORADO

Tortuguero means "turtle region," and this area, tucked into northeastern Costa Rica, remains one of the world's prime spots for viewing the awesome life cycle of sea turtles. The stretch of beach between the Colorado and Matina rivers was first mentioned as a nesting ground for sea turtles in 1592 in a Dutch chronicle, and due to the area's isolation—there isn't a road here to this day—the turtles were able to get on with their nesting virtually undisturbed for centuries. By the mid-1900s, however, the harvesting of eggs and catching of turtles had increased to such an extent that the turtles faced extinction. In 1963 an executive decree regulated the hunting of turtles and the gathering of eggs, and in 1970 the government established the Parque Nacional Tortuguero (☞ Chapter 10). The area is also home to watery Barra del Colorado Wildlife Refuge.

Parque Nacional Tortuguero

❺ *50 km (31 mi) northwest (3 hrs by boat) of Puerto Limón.*

Tortuguero National Park's claim to fame is its turtle nesting. At various times of the year, green, hawksbill, loggerhead, and giant leatherback turtles lumber up the beaches here and deposit their eggs for safe keeping—a fascinating natural ritual (☞ Close Up: Tico Turtles, *below*). Freshwater turtles inhabit the rivers at Tortuguero, as do crocodiles, which are most prevalent in the Río Agua Fría, and the endangered *vacas marinas,* or manatees. Manatees consume huge quantities of aquatic plants and are endangered mainly because their lack of speed renders them easy prey for hunters. You might catch glimpses of tapirs (watch for these in the jolillo groves), jaguars, anteaters, ocelots, howler monkeys, collared and white-lipped peccaries, raccoons, otters, skunks, and coatis. Some 350 species of birds and countless butterflies—the iridescent blue morpho one of them—inhabit the area. Deep in the Tortuguero jungle, the **Canadian Organization for Tropical Education and Rainforest Conservation** has set up a small station, where a couple of volunteers are running a butterfly farm, cataloging plants and animals, and exploring sustainable forest practices.

Tortuguero

❻ *There are no roads to Tortuguero; flying time from San José airport 30 mins; 3 hrs by boat from Moín.*

To the north of Tortuguero National Park, the hamlet of Tortuguero, with its 600 inhabitants, two churches, three bars, and two souvenir shops, is a pleasant little place to spend an hour or two. Be sure to get

TICO TURTLES

COSTA RICA'S TURTLE VISITATIONS are renowned in the world of ecotourism. On both the Pacific and Atlantic-Caribbean coasts, an array of species make their predictable but no-less-amazing annual visits to beaches, many set aside to protect them. Nesting turtles come ashore at night, plowing an uneven furrow with their flippers to propel themselves to the high-tide line, beyond which they use their hind flippers to scoop out a hole in which to lay their eggs. A couple of months later, the hatchlings struggle out of the nests and make their perilous journey to the sea.

In spite of this protection, the endangered classifications, and the earnest ecologists and well-meaning people looking after them, turtle populations remain seriously threatened: poachers have for generations harvested the eggs—a rumored aphrodisiac—and the meat and shells; beachfront development, with bright lights, can disorient the turtles; and longline fishermen's hooks and lines entangle the turtles, causing them to drown.

On the east coast, four species of turtles nest at Tortuguero National Park: the green turtle, hawksbill, loggerhead, and giant leatherback. Green turtles reproduce in large groups from July to October. A green turtle lays eggs on average every two to three years and produces two or three clutches each time. In between, they feed as far afield as Florida and Venezuela. Small in comparison with their peers, hawksbills are threatened by hunters because of their shells, a transparent brown hide much sought after to make jewelry in countries like Japan. Loggerheads, as their name implies, have outsized heads and shorter fins and make rare appearances at Tortuguero. The giant leatherback is the largest of all turtle species. Individuals grow up to 6½ ft long and can weigh in at up to 1,000 pounds. They have a tough outer skin instead of a shell, hence the name. From mid-February through April, leatherbacks nest mainly in the southern sector of Tortuguero.

Olive ridleys are the smallest of the sea turtles—the average carapace, or hard-back shell, is 21 to 29 inches—and the least shy. During mass nestings, or arribadas, thousands of olive ridley turtles take to the Pacific shores at night, plowing the sand as they move up the beach sniffing for the high-tide line. It is estimated that 200,000 of the 500,000 turtles that nest each year in Costa Rica choose Playa Nancite, a gray-sand beach in Guanacaste's Parque Nacional Santa Rosa, backed by dense hibiscus and button mangroves. It is the world's only totally protected olive-ridley-turtle arribada.

EASIER TO REACH IS THE OSTIONAL National Wildlife Refuge, near Nosara on the Nicoya Peninsula. Locals harvest the eggs in the early stages of the arribada—visits run from August to December and peak in September and October—for the later arrivals invariably destroy the earlier nests. More accessible is Playa Grande, on Nicoya, stamping ground of the mammoth, ponderous, and yet exquisitely dignified leatherback turtles from November to April. Parque Nacional Marino Las Baulas was created specifically to protect the leatherbacks, who also show up in smaller numbers at Playas Langosta and Junquillal.

To help save these gentle giants, you can volunteer with turtle research and protection at such organizations as ATEC (☞ The Atlantic Lowlands and the Caribbean Coast A to Z, *below*).

information about the park, turtles, and wildlife at the kiosk in the town center. You can also take a stroll along the 32 km (20 mi) of beach—although swimming here is not recommended due to strong riptides and the presence (although, according to locals, no one has ever actually been attacked) of large numbers of bull sharks and barracuda.

The **Caribbean Conservation Corporation** (CCC) opened a visitor's center and museum in Tortuguero in late 1994. Actor Cliff Robertson narrates the video history of the area, and exhibits include excellent animal photos as well as detailed discussions of what's going on in the area, ecologically speaking, and what you can do to help. There's a souvenir shop next door, and at least one other store in Tortuguero sells local crafts. ☒ *Apdo. 246–2050, Tortuguero, San Pedro, from beach walk north along path and watch for sign,* ☎ *710–0547 or 224–9215 reservations office in San José.* ⊙ *Daily 10–noon and 2–5:30.*

For the committed ecotourist, the **Casa Verde Green Turtle Research Station** (By the airport, across the canal from Tortuga Lodge, ☎ 352/373–6441 in the U.S.) has camping areas as well as dormitory-style quarters with a communal kitchen. If you're interested in a deeper involvement in the life of the turtles, you can arrange a stay through the CCC (☞ *above*).

OFF THE BEATEN PATH	**COASTAL CANALS –** The jungle life seen during a three-hour boat trip through the combination of natural and man-made canals between Tortuguero and Moín is awesome, a kind of real-life Indiana Jones adventure. As you swoop through the sinuous turns of the natural waterways, your driver-guide will spot monkeys, snakes, caiman, mud turtles, sloths, and dozens of different birds, including flocks of bright and noisy parrots, kingfishers, aracaris, and assorted herons. The densely layered greenery is highlighted by brilliantly colored flowers, and the visual impact is doubled by the jungle's reflection in the mirror-smooth surface of the water.

Lodging

$$$$ 🏠 **Jungle Tarpon Lodge.** Nestled in 100 acres at the Parsimina River lagoon, this intimate lodge specializes in sportfishing packages—it has a sister program in Alaska's Lake Clark National Park—and also arranges eco-adventure activities, turtle-watching, and custom tours. The small lodge is a deluxe affair, crafted in fine wood with big rooms, modern tiled bathrooms, and beamed ceilings. Savory local cuisine, heavy on fish, of course, is served in the dining room; some meals are enjoyed riverside. Transfers to San José, meals, and charters are included. *May–mid-Oct.: Great Alaska, 33881, Sterling Hwy., Sterling, AK 99672,* ☎ *800/544–2261, 907/262–4515,* ⻗ *907/262–8797; mid-Oct.–mid-Apr.: Great Alaska Box 2670, Poulsbo, WA 98370,* ☎ *360/697–6454,* ⻗ *360/697–7850. 3 rooms with bath. Dining room, hiking, boating, fishing. AE, MC, V.*

$$$$ 🏠 **Mawamba Lodge.** This lodge is the perfect place to kick back and relax. Once whisked from Moín in a fast launch (2½ hrs), you stay in comfortable rustic cabinas with hot-water baths, garden views, and fans and dine in the spacious dining room. Packages include all meals, transfers, and guided tours of the jungle, canals, and turtle-laying beaches. ☒ *Apdo. 10980–1000, San José, 1 km (½ mi) north of Tortuguero on ocean side of canal,* ☎ *710–7282, 223–2421 reservations office in San José,* ⻗ *222–5463. 36 cabinas. Dining room, pool, conference room. MC, V.*

$$$ 🏠 **Tortuga Lodge.** Costa Rica Expeditions owns this thatched riverside
★ lodge surrounded by lush lawns, orchids, and tropical trees and renowned for its tarpon and snook fishing packages. The second-largest tarpon ever caught in Costa Rica, weighing 182 pounds, was

reeled in here in 1987. The bedrooms are comfortable, with fans and mosquito blinds. The mosquitoes can be voracious; wear repellent and long sleeves on the hiking trails. Considering most of the restaurant ingredients are flown in, the chefs do an excellent job producing voluminous quantities of hearty, well-prepared food. The lodge is across the river from the airstrip, 2 km (1 mi) from Tortuguero. ✉ *Apdo. 6941–1000, San José, 20 mins north by boat from Tortuguero National Park or 35 mins by plane from San José,* ☎ FAX *710–6861;* ☎ *257–0766, 222–0333 reservations office in San José;* FAX *257–1665. 25 rooms with bath. Bar, dining room, hiking, fishing. AE, MC, V.*

$$ ▦ **El Manatí.** The friendly owners, Fernando and Lilia Figuls, adopted the indigenous rough-hewn wood-and-cane architectural style when they carved this comfortable lodge out of the jungle. The sparkling-clean, wood-paneled rooms have firm beds, mosquito screens, and fans. The terraces look across a narrow lawn to the river, where you can kayak and canoe. Chestnut-beaked toucans, poison arrow frogs, and three types of monkey hang out in the jungle looming behind the rooms. ✉ *Across river, about 1 km (½ mi) north of Tortuguero,* FAX *239–0911. 8 rooms with bath. Dining room, Ping-Pong, boating. No credit cards.*

Barra del Colorado

❼ *25 km (16 mi) northwest of Tortuguero.*

Farther up the coast is the ramshackle hamlet of Barra del Colorado, a sportfishing paradise characterized by stilted plain wooden houses, dirt paths, and no motorized land vehicles, although some locals have added outboard motors to their hand-hewn canoes. Bordered in the north by the Río San Juan and the frontier with Nicaragua is the vast, 905-sq-km (350-sq-mi) **Barra del Colorado Wildlife Refuge** (Refugio Nacional de Fauna Silvestre Barra del Colorado, ☞ Chapter 10), really the only area attraction for nonanglers. Approach is by air or boat from San José or Tortuguero. Transport once you get here is almost exclusively waterborne, as there are virtually no paths in this swampy terrain. Apart from the route via Tortuguero, you can come from Puerto Viejo de Sarapiquí up the Ríos Sarapiquí and San Juan. The list of species that you are likely to see from your boat is virtually the same as that for Tortuguero; the main difference here is the feeling of being further off the beaten track.

Lodging

$$$$ ▦ *Rain Goddess.* Dining, lodging, and everything else is self-contained on Dr. Alfredo López's 65-ft-long *Rain Goddess,* a small floating luxury hotel that sleeps 12 in six staterooms and travels up the Río San Juan and around the Barra del Colorado area. You can nature cruise and deep-sea fish—there are two seaworthy fishing and excursion boats in tow—depending on your own preferences. The emphasis is on fishing, but the amenities include first-class food, hot showers, air-conditioning, handcrafted furnishings, color TV with a video library, and covered decks. Five- to seven-day packages include van pickup in San José and boat transfer. Note that if you use a credit card, you are charged a 7% fee. ✉ *Apdo. 850–1250, San José,* ☎ *231–4299 reservations office in San José, 800/308–3394 in the U.S.,* FAX *231–3816. 6 rooms with bath. Dining room, boating, air-conditioning. AE, MC, V.*

$$$$ ▦ **Río Colorado Lodge.** This jungle lodge caters almost exclusively to sportfishing folk on its modern fleet of 16- and 23-ft sportfishing vessels. Lodge bedrooms have twin beds with patterned bedspreads, paneled ceilings, white curtains, and basket lamp shades. Expensive all-inclusive tours include the flight here from San José, all meals, and fishing. The lodge also

offers fly-in, boat-out nature tour packages, including Tortuguero National Park tours at lower prices. ⊠ *Apdo. 5094–1000, San José, 35-min flight from San José via Travelair,* ☎ *710–6879, 232–8610 reservations office in San José, 800/243–9777 in the U.S.;* ℻ *231–5987. 18 rooms with bath. Restaurant, bar, fishing. AE, MC, V.*

COASTAL TALAMANCA

The quickest route from San José to the Atlantic coast runs through the magnificent cloud forest of Braulio Carrillo National Park before reaching the Caribbean Sea and the lively and sometimes dangerous port town of Puerto Limón. The 160-km (100-mi) trip along the Guápiles Highway to the coast takes about 2½ hours, with all going well—the highway is carved out of mountainous jungle and is susceptible to landslides. Make sure it's not blocked before heading out. As the highway descends and straightens toward Guápiles, you will enter the Limón province, where cloud forest gives way to banana plantations and partially deforested pastureland. Be warned that the highway gives way to potholes, some big enough to swallow an entire wheel and ruin your car's suspension. This region is also home to farms producing cocoa, exotic export plants, and macadamia nuts. Many of the crystal-clear green rivers running through the area have bathing pools. After passing through villages with names like Bristol, Stratford, and Liverpool, you arrive in the provincial capital, Puerto Limón.

Guápiles

⑧ *60 km (38 mi) east of San José.*

There may not seem to be many reasons to stop in the Guápiles area—the town itself is off the main road—other than weariness or the need for a fast gas and food fix. However, this farm and forest area, home to several major biological research facilities as well as commercial tropical plant producers, might be worth another look. It is a kind of crossroads: more or less equidistant are the palm beaches of the Caribbean shore, the jungles to the north, and the rain-forested mountains looming in the west. For this reason it isn't a bad place to linger for a day or two, day-tripping in any of three directions.

Dining and Lodging

$$ ✕ **The Ponderosa.** This lively restaurant features—you guessed it—a variety of steak dishes and noncarnivorous entrées. Although the grill chef tends to oversalt the meat, the range of beefy selections for $5–$10 is impressive: filet mignon, sirloin, T-bone, and sirloin tips with jalapeños are but a few. There's a full bar, souvenir shop, and live music on weekends. With photographs of Ben Cartwright and the boys, maps of the Ponderosa, and other Bonanza memorabilia, '60s TV buffs should feel right at home. ⊠ *Guápiles Highway, about 5 km (3 mi) east of turnoff for Los Horquetas and northern zone,* ☎ *710–7144. MC, V.*

$$–$$$ ▥ **Hotel Rio Palmas.** Call it a hacienda motel. Proximate to EARTH (☞ *below*), the Rio Palmas grabs your eye as you're speeding by on the Guápiles Highway thanks to the red-tiled roof topping its open-air restaurant. Behind an arched, whitewashed entry gate, one-story whitewashed cabinas with tile roofs wrap around a central courtyard with a fountain and plants. Rooms with bath have TVs. Exotic plantings abound (the hotel is on an ornamental plant farm). The management can arrange hikes, farm and jungle tours, and horseback rides to private waterfalls. ⊠ *Guápiles Highway,* ☎ *760–0305,* ℻ *760–0296. 32 rooms, 24 with bath. Restaurant, pool, hiking, horseback riding. AE, MC, V.*

EARTH

15 km (9 mi) east of Guápiles.

Agriculture and ecology buffs will want to check out EARTH (Escuela de Agricultura de la Region Tropical Humeda), a nonprofit research center emphasizing hands-on involvement in the study and production of less pesticide-dependent bananas and other forms of sustainable agriculture as well as medicinal plants. (You'll find EARTH's elegant collection of stationery and other paper products made from banana stems in many tourist shops.) A banana plantation and a forest reserve with nature trails are on the property, which is on the Guápiles Highway a couple of miles east of Guápiles. You are welcome to stay in the university's 50-person lodging facility, replete with private baths, hot water, and ceiling fans, for $20 to $30, which includes the use of a swimming pool and exercise equipment. **Costa Rica Expeditions** (☎ 222–0333, ℻ 257–1665) offers a one-day guided-tour package for $69. ☎ 255–2000, ℻ 255–2726.

En Route If you are bypassing Puerto Limón entirely, and heading south to Cahuita and Puerto Viejo de Limón, a right turn via Moín 3 km (2 mi) shy of Puerto Limón will take you on an alternate route—a smooth road that weaves through the hills. Look for the white road sign that indicates a right turn to Sixaola and other points south.

Puerto Limón

⑨ *130 km (81 mi) southeast of Braulio Carrillo National Park, 100 km (62 mi) southeast of Guápiles.*

Puerto Limón's promontory setting, overlooking the Caribbean, is inherited from an ancient Indian village, Cariari, which lay close to the Isla Uvita, where Christopher Columbus lay anchor on his final voyage in 1502. The colorful Afro-Caribbean flavor of Costa Rica's most important port (population 50,000) is the first sign of life on Costa Rica's east coast for seafaring visitors. Puerto Limón is a lively if shabby town with a 24-hour street life. The wooden houses are brightly painted, but the grid-plan streets bear a somewhat worn appearance, largely due to the damage caused by the 1991 earthquake. Street crime including pick-pocketing and night muggings is common in this port town, and staying overnight is not recommended. However, several appealing hotels can be found at Portete just north of Limón town, providing easy access to the docks at Moín.

On the left of the highway as you enter Puerto Limón is a large **Chinese cemetery.** Chinese made up a large part of the ill-starred railroad construction team that worked here. Follow the railroad as far as the palm-lined **promenade** that runs around the Parque Vargas. From the promenade you can see the raised dead coral left stranded by the quake. Nine or so hoffman's two-toed sloths live in the trees of **Parque Vargas**; ask a passerby to point them out, as sighting them requires a trained eye. From the park, find the lively **market** on Avenida 2, between Calles 3 and 4, where you can buy fruit for the road ahead.

Dining and Lodging

$–$$ ✕ **Springfield.** Protected from the street by a leafy conservatory, this Caribbean kitchen whips up tasty rice and bean dishes. Decor consists of wood paneling, red tablecloths, and a white-tile floor. Bring your dancing shoes: the huge dance floor out back creaks to the beat of soca, salsa, and reggae on weekends. ✉ *On road north from Puerto Limón to Portete, left opposite hospital,* ☎ 758–1203. AE, MC, V.

$$$ ★ ⊡ **Hotel Maribú Caribe.** Perched on a cliff overlooking the Caribbean Sea between Puerto Limón and Portete these white conical thatched huts have great views, air-conditioning, and hot water. Green lawns, shrubs, palm trees, and a large, kidney-shape pool dominate the lovely gardens. The poolside bar does away with the need for any added exertion. ⊠ *Apdo. 623–7300, San José, Guápiles Highway to Portete,* ☎ *758–4010,* 𝖥𝖠𝖷 *758–3541. 52 rooms with bath. Restaurant, bar, air-conditioning, snack bar, pool. AE, MC, V.*

$$$ ⊡ **Hotel Matama.** If you're coming from San José and planning to catch an early boat north out of Moín, this is a great spot to get your first taste of the Caribbean. The property is across the street from the beach and 2 km (1 mi) up the road from the Maribú Caribe (☞ *above*). A new pool has been installed by the bar, and the grounds are gorgeously landscaped with botanical trails. The open-air restaurant offers lovely views of the gardens. Rooms have phones, air-conditioning, and TVs. ⊠ *Apdo. 606, Limón,* ☎ *758–1123, 758–4409, or 758–1797;* 𝖥𝖠𝖷 *758–4499. 12 rooms with bath. Restaurant, bar, air-conditioning, pool, meeting room. AE, MC, V.*

Moín

❿ *5 km (3 mi) north of Puerto Limón.*

The docks at Moín are a logical next stop after neighboring Puerto Limón, especially if you want to take a boat north to explore the Caribbean coast. You can most likely negotiate a waterway and national park tour with a local guide, and if you're lucky or made a call in advance you'll find the man considered the best guide on the Caribbean coast. His name is Modesto Watson (☞ Guided Tours *in* The Atlantic Lowlands and the Caribbean Coast A to Z, *below*), and he is legendary for his bird- and animal-spotting skills as well as his howler monkey calls.

En Route As you head south from Puerto Limón, the Caribbean character of the Atlantic lowlands becomes powerfully evident, in the surf rolling shoreward on your left; in the hot, humid stir of the Caribbean trade winds; in the laid-back pace of the people you meet. This is tropical Central America, and it feels like another country, its slow, somewhat sultry atmosphere far removed from the business and bustle of San José. The coast is lined with gorgeous black- and white-sand beaches fringed with palm trees. You can see white-water breaks way offshore where the waves crash over coral reefs. Watch carefully for the left turn to Cahuita about 44 km (27 mi) out of Puerto Limón. Turn right at the end of the first of three entrance roads to get to Cahuita's main drag.

Cahuita

⓫ *44 km (27 mi) southeast of Puerto Limón.*

Dusty Cahuita, its main dirt street flanked by wooden-slat cabins, is a backpackers' holiday town with something of a druggy reputation, a hippie hangout with a dash of Afro-Caribbean spice tossed in. The town's image as a dangerous drug haven is only partially deserved. Like Puerto Viejo de Limón, Cahuita has its share of junkies, but they are not perceived as a threat by the locals. Nor should they be by you. From the turquoise **Salón Vaz** bar blasts lively reggae, soca, and samba 24 hours a day; the assemblage of dogs dozing on its veranda sums up the laid-back pace of life here. Turn left at the main intersection for the **Turistica Cahuita** information center (☎ 755–0071). Here, Joaquin Fuentes can set you up with a variety of adventures, including tours to the canals, Indian reservations, and mountains; river rafting and kayaking; and bike and snorkeling-equipment rentals. He can also reconfirm flights and make reservations. At the southern end of Cahuita's main street is the start of **Parque Nacional Cahuita** (☞ *below,* and Chapter 10).

Dining and Lodging

$$ ✕ **Edith Soda y Restaurant.** Miss Edith is revered for her outrageous
★ Caribbean cooking, vegetarian meals, and herbal teas for whatever ails you. Don't expect to get anything in a hurry; most of her dishes are made to order. But her rondon and smoked chicken are worth the wait. Her restaurant is on an easy-to-miss side street at the north end of town, near the *guardia rural* (police station). ✉ *From bus station, follow main road north, turn right at police station,* ☎ *no phone. No credit cards. Closed Tues. No lunch Sun.*

$$ ✕ **Vista del Mar.** The main attraction of this open-air, aluminum-roof eatery is its proximity to Parque Nacional Cahuita. After a hard day of sunbathing, you need walk only about 10 steps past the park exit to sample the Vista's intriguing selection of Chinese-influenced Costa Rican *casados* (plates of white rice, beans, fried plantains, salad, cheese, and meat) and seafood dishes. The *pescado en salsa* (fish in sauce) is always fresh and delicious. ✉ *South of bus stop, next to park entrance,* ☎ *755–0008. AE, MC, V.*

$$$ ▥ **Aviarios del Caribe.** Luís and Judy Arroyo built this lodge and bird-
★ watching sanctuary from the rubble of the 1991 earthquake. More than 285 species of bird have been spotted here, many with the help of the telescope on the wide second-floor deck. Spacious guest rooms have white walls, blue-tile floors, and fresh flowers. Buttercup, the resident three-toed sloth (and our cover girl), oversees the proceedings in the upstairs open-air dining room. For $3 you can hike the wildlife refuge, and $30 will get you an unforgettable 3½-hour riverboat tour with Luís as your guide. ✉ *Apdo. 569–7300, Puerto Limón, head from south of city and follow hotel signs on Río Estrella delta, 9 km (5 mi) north of Cahuita,* ☎ *710–8101 (cell),* ☎ FAX *382–1335. 6 rooms with bath, 16 beds in 2 dormitories. Breakfast room, hiking. MC, V.*

$$$ ▥ **Hotel Jaguar.** This hotel on Playa Negra provides the roomiest digs
★ and some of the fanciest cooking around. White cabinas have high ceilings, queen-size wooden beds, mosquito blinds, solar-heated water, and terra-cotta floors. You'll be delighted by the fruit trees and the virtual menagerie of exotic birds on the 17-acre grounds. With goodies from their herb garden, the owners turn out their most popular recipe, *dorada en salsa de hierbas* (dorado fish in an herb sauce). Call ahead for possible transportation from Puerto Limón. ✉ *Apdo. 7046–1000, San José, from football field, 326 yards to the north, across from Playa Negra,* ☎ *755–0238, 226–3775 reservations office in San José,* FAX *226–4693 in San José. 45 cabinas. Restaurant, bar, pool, hiking. MC, V.*

$$$ ▥ **Magellan Inn.** The owners sailed the seas for 20 years before land-
★ ing here around 1990 to build this group of bungalows, perhaps the most elegant around. Graced with tile-floored terraces facing a pool and gardens growing atop an ancient coral reef, the white-walled rooms have original artwork, custom-made wooden furniture, and ceiling fans. Feast on intensely flavored French and Creole seafood specialties in the Casa Creole, a freestanding coral-pink concoction with an outdoor dining room. Don't miss the house pâté or the homemade ice creams. The hotel's enticing open-air bar rocks to great blues and jazz recordings in the evenings and mellows with classical music at breakfast. ✉ *Apdo. 1132, Puerto Limón, 2 km (1 mi) north of Cahuita at far end of Playa Negra,* ☎ FAX *755–0035. 6 rooms with bath. Restaurant, bar, pool. AE, DC, MC, V.*

$$–$$$ ▥ **Atlántida Lodge.** Atlántida's main assets are its attractively landscaped grounds, the beach across the road, and its large pool. The rooms have

tile floors, beds with headboards and night tables, and terraces with chairs. The guest rooms encircle a thatched restaurant, where you enjoy breakfast with the price of the room. You can also cook your own food. The managers cultivate a younger and trendier ambience than neighboring Jaguar's (☞ *above*). ⊠ *Next to soccer field at Playa Negra,* ☎ *758–0115,* ☎ FAX *755–0213. 30 rooms with bath. Restaurant, pool, hot tub, massage, meeting rooms. AE, MC, V.*

$$ 🏠 **El Encanto B&B.** Just north of town on the beach road, this place consists of three tastefully designed, comfortable bungalows set in a lovely garden. Amenities include queen-size beds, ceiling fans, hot water, and secure parking. The California-born owners, Mike and Karen Russell, offer a hearty vegetarian breakfast with the price of a room. ⊠ *Apdo. 1234, Limón,* ☎ FAX *755–0113. 3 bungalows. MC, V.*

$$ 🏠 **Kelly Creek Hotel-Restaurante.** Andres and Marie-Claude de Alcala from Madrid have created a wonderful budget lodging option in Kelly Creek Hotel-Restaurante. The handsome wooden hotel sits on the creek bank across a short pedestrian bridge from the park entrance. Four spacious hardwood-finished guest rooms feature beds big enough to sleep a small army. Señor de Alcala barbecues meat and fresh fish on an open-air grill and also serves paella and other Spanish specialties. Caiman come to the creek bank seeking snacks, and the monkeys, parrots, jungles, and beaches of the national park are just a few yards away—as is the lively little center of Cahuita. ⊠ *Next to the national park entrance, Cahuita,* ☎ *755–0007. 4 rooms with bath. Restaurant. AE, MC, V.*

Parque Nacional Cahuita

⑫ *Puerto Vargas 5 km (3 mi) south of Cahuita.*

Parque Nacional Cahuita (Cahuita National Park) starts at the southern edge of Cahuita. Lush rain forest extends to the edge of the completely undeveloped, curving white-sand beach that stretches for 3 km (2 mi). A 7-km (4½-mi) trail follows the coastline within the forest to Cahuita point, encircled by a 2½-sq-km (1-sq-mi) coral reef. Blue parrot fish and angelfish weave their way among the various equally colorful species of coral and sponge. The reef escaped the 1991 earthquake with little damage, but biologists are worried that the coral has stopped growing due to silt and plastic bags washed down the Río Estrella from banana plantations upstream. Take a glass-bottom-boat tour operating out of Cahuita to visit this aquatic garden. Visibility is best in September and October. To snorkel independently, swim out from the beach on the Puerto Vargas side. Five kilometers (3 mi) south of Cahuita on the left is the road to Puerto Vargas, the park's main headquarters with the ranger station and the camping area, where campsites carved out of the jungle dot the beach. ✉ *Donation requested at Cahuita entrance, $6 at Puerto Vargas entrance.*

Outdoor Activities and Sports

BICYCLING

You can bike through the national park, but the trail gets pretty muddy at times, and you'll encounter logs, river estuaries, and other obstacles. Nevertheless, mountain bikes are a good way to get around on the dirt roads and trails surrounding Cahuita and Puerto Viejo de Limón. They can be rented at a number of different places in the region, such as **Turística Cahuita** in Cahuita. Near the convergence of the two beach roads, this friendly storefront tourist info and travel office makes reservations; rents surfboards, bicycles, and snorkeling gear; and arranges horseback riding and other tours. ATEC (☞ Outdoor Activities and Sports *in* Puerto Viejo de Limón, *below*) does the same and more down the road in Puerto Viejo de Limó.

HIKING

A hiking trail extends as far as Puerto Vargas. If you stay in Cahuita, you can take a bus or catch a ride into Puerto Vargas and hike back around the point in the course of a day. If you camp at Puerto Vargas, you can also hike south along the beach to Puerto Viejo de Limón and bus or taxi it back to the park. Be sure to bring plenty of water, food, and sunscreen. Along the trail, you might spot howler and white-faced monkeys, coatis, armadillos, and raccoons. Some stretches of beach have much worse currents than others; ask the rangers at Puerto Vargas for advice.

SNORKELING

Parque Nacional Cahuita's reefs are just one of several high-quality dive spots in the area. Snorkeling gear can be rented in Cahuita or Puerto Viejo de Limón or through your hotel. Most hotels will organize dive trips. Or contact the ATEC office (☞ Outdoor Activities and Sports *in* Puerto Viejo de Limón, *below*) in the middle of Puerto Viejo de Limón or Aquamor in Manzanillo (☞ *below*) to make arrangements. It's a good idea to work with a guide because the number of good dive spots is limited, and they are not necessarily easily accessible.

En Route Watch for the left turn for Puerto Viejo de Limón 8 km (5 mi) before Bribri. Beyond Puerto Viejo, the road south to Punta Cocles and Punta Uva is of deeply pocked dirt; it ends a mile or so south of Manzanillo.

Puerto Viejo de Limón

⑬ *16 km (10 mi) south of Cahuita.*

Puerto Viejo de Limón was once quieter than Cahuita, but no more—it's turned into one of the hot spots on the international surfpunk circuit. The muddy, colorful little town is swarming with surfers, New Age hippies, beaded and spangled punks, would-be Rastafarians of all colors and descriptions, and wheelers and dealers both pleasant and otherwise. It used to be that most of the kids came here with only one thing on their mind: surfing. Today, a lot of them seem to be looking for a party, with or without surf. (Nevertheless, the waves are at their best between December and April and again in June and July.) Some locals bemoan the loss of their town's innocence, as the ravages of crack cocaine and other evils have surfaced, but only in small doses: this is still a fun town to visit, with a great variety of hotels, cabinas, and restaurants in every price range. Heading south from Puerto Viejo de Limón to Punta Cocles and Punta Uva, you'll find some of the region's first luxurious tourism developments and interesting ecotourist lodges, new in the last few years. Things move slowly in Talamanca, and numerous hotels in the area are still negotiating phone lines and credit-card contracts; telephone numbers and credit cards accepted are subject to change.

Dining and Lodging

$$–$$$ ✕ **Salsa Brava** The café at Salsa Brava—with sublime surf vistas—has taken on the famed surfing spot's name. Counter service is very casual, or grab a seat at the funky roadside tables for breakfast from 6 AM to noon and barbecued fresh fish and meat dinners from 6:30 to 10 PM. ✉ *Salsa Brava,* ☎ *no phone. No credit cards.*

$$–$$$ ✕ **The Garden.** Transplanted to Costa Rica from Trinidad by way of
★ Toronto, the Garden's owner-chef, Vera Maron, incorporates her Indian heritage into her beautifully prepared and presented Asian-Caribbean food. Colorful decor—candlelight, linen, and flowers—complements the pleasant, competent staff and the round, wood- and thatched-roof open-air building buried in a flowering gar-

den. The Cabinas Jacaranda, on the same property, also belong to Vera Maron. ⊠ *Near the beach, follow signs,* ☎ *750–0069. AE, MC, V.*

$–$$ ✗ **Bambú.** This funky little waterfront bar serves cocktails with a view of the world-class surf of Salsa Brava, which is visible beyond a quarter-mile expanse of Caribbean laced with wicked-looking reefs and treacherous crosscurrents. ⊠ *Outside of town on ocean road,* ☎ *no phone. No credit cards.*

$ ✗ **Elena Brown Soda y Restaurant.** Unpretentious and shaded, Elena's place serves up simple wonders made from locally caught seafood. The dark, cool interior is not as peaceful as it used to be thanks to the blasting TV in the room, but the wooden tables and chairs still charm with handmade, rustic appeal, and the cooking remains top-notch. ⊠ *Along road from Puerto Viejo de Limón to Punta Uva,* ☎ *750–0265. No credit cards.*

$$$ 🏨 **Almonds & Corals.** Buried in a dark, densely atmospheric beachfront jungle within the Gandoca-Manzanillo Wildlife Refuge near the end of the road that runs south from Puerto Viejo to Manzanillo, Almonds & Corals takes tent camping to a new level. The "campsites" are freestanding platforms raised on stilts and linked by boardwalks illuminated by kerosene lamps. Each is protected by a peaked roof, enclosed by mosquito netting, and equipped with electric lamps, fans, beds, hammocks, and a private (cold water) bath. A fine, three-meal restaurant is tucked into the greenery halfway to an exquisite, secluded beach. Your wake-up call will be provided by howler monkeys and gossiping parrots. ⊠ *Apdo. 681–2300,* ☎ *272–2024 or 272–4175,* ℻ *272–2220. 20 tent cabins with bath. Restaurant, beach. AE, MC, V.*

$$$ 🏨 **Shawandha Lodge.** Shawandha's refined, beautifully designed, and
★ spacious bungalows nestle in remote jungle settings well back from the road through Punta Uva. Every bathroom, replete with gorgeous tile work, has been designed by French ceramicist Filou Pascal. Bungalows feature elegant hardwoods, custom-designed furniture, and large verandas with hammocks. In the kitchen of the open-air restaurant, a well-known local chef, Madame Oui Oui, lovingly crafts her distinctive French-Caribbean cuisine; a hearty breakfast is included in the price. A white-sand beach protected by a coral reef lies 200 yards away. The hotel offers all regional tours and activities. ⊠ *On the road to Manzanillo, follow signs,* ☎ *750–0018,* ℻ *750–0037. 12 bungalows. Restaurant, hiking, horseback riding, snorkeling, surfing, boating. No credit cards.*

$$$ 🏨 **Villas del Caribe.** Right on the beach north of Punta Uva, the Del
★ Caribe's multiroom villas are commodious and comfortable, if somewhat pedestrian in design. Each contains a blue-tile kitchen with stove and refrigerator, a small sitting room with low-slung couches, a plant-filled bathroom, and a patio. Upstairs are one or two spacious bedrooms with a wooden deck. Although coffee is served at the reception counter, the nearest restaurant is several hundred yards away—that may not seem far, but when it rains it pours, and the road is unlit and full of potholes. If you bring your own edibles, however, you're set, since the hotel rents all kinds of water-sports equipment and will arrange any kind of tour. ⊠ *Puerto Viejo, Limón,* ☎ *233–2200,* ℻ *221–2801. 12 villas. Kitchenettes. AE, DC, MC, V.*

$$$ 🏨 **Yaré.** The sound of the jungle is overpowering, especially at night, as you relax in your brightly painted cabina. The cabinas have fans, hot water, and private baths. The restaurant is open for breakfast, lunch, and dinner. The owner organizes all kinds of tours. ⊠ *4 km (2½ mi) on right side of road to Manzanillo,* ☎ ℻ *750–0106 or 284–5921,* ☎ *232–7866 reservations office in San José. 10 rooms with bath, 8 cabinas. Restaurant, horseback riding, fishing. AE, MC, V.*

$$–$$$ 🏨 **Cariblue Bed & Breakfast.** Cariblue's finely crafted all-wooden bungalows are spaciously arrayed on the edge of the jungle across the road from the splendid black- and white-sand beaches of Punta Cocles. Paths meandering through a gently sloping lawn shaded with several enormous trees link the cabinas with the main rancho-style building, where the youthful Italian owners serve Continental breakfast, included in the price of the room. Expansive verandas and beautiful bathroom tile work await you. *Across road from beach, south of Puerto Viejo on the road to Manzanillo,* ☎ ℻ *750–0057. 6 cabinas. Breakfast room. No credit cards.*

$$–$$$ 🏨 **El Pizote Lodge.** El Pizote observes local architectural mores while
★   offering more than most in the way of amenities. Rooms have polished wood paneling, reading lamps, mirrors, mats, firm beds, and fans. A two-room bungalow accommodates six people, and four luxe rooms are air-conditioned. The restaurant serves breakfast, dinner, and drinks all day. Guanabana and papaya grow on the grounds; hiking trails lead off into the jungle. ✉ *Apdo. 230–2200, on right side of road into Puerto Viejo,* ☎ *750–0227, 221–5915 reservations office in San José,* ℻ *750–0226, 223–8838 in San José. 8 rooms, 4 with bath, 6 bungalows, 1 cabana. Restaurant, bar, pool, volleyball. MC, V.*

$$–$$$ 🏨 **Hotel La Perla Negra.** The owners' previous experience as designers is evident in the fine construction of this handsome, two-story wooden structure across a tiny dirt road from Playa Negra. The three-meal restaurant features grilled meats and fish. A spacious, inviting pool lies between the building and the beach. ✉ *North of Puerto Viejo on Playa Negra,* ☎ *750–0111,* ℻ *750–0114. 24 rooms with bath. Restaurant, pool. No credit cards.*

$$–$$$ 🏨 **Miraflores Lodge.** It's not difficult to tell that this was a flower farm before a hotel was built on the property in 1990. The collection of bromeliads and heliconias and the intricate landscaping are a dead giveaway. The buildings, designed in the indigenous style, with peaked thatched roofs and cane walls, make you feel as if you're off the tourist trail, while proprietor Pamela Carpenter makes you feel like you're right at home. ✉ *Playa Chiquita, Puerto Viejo, Limón,* ☎ *750–0038, 233–2822 reservations office in San José. 10 rooms, 5 with bath. Breakfast room. No credit cards.*

$$ 🏨 **Casa Verde.** This German-run collection of cabinas is one of the finest moderately priced properties in Puerto Viejo itself. Set back a few blocks from the waterfront hustle, the comfortable cabinas offer handsomely furnished porches sporting hammocks, hardwood finishes, and ceiling fans. Lush plantings screen the cabinas from the street and enhance the jungly atmosphere. Look for the signs as you mosey down "main" street along Puerto Viejo's waterfront. No restaurant is on the premises, but half a dozen are within a five-minute walk. ✉ *Apdo. 1115, Puerto Limón,* ☎ *750–0015,* ℻ *750–0047. 14 rooms, 6 with bath. Laundry service. AE, MC, V.*

$$ 🏨 **Playa Chiquita Lodge.** Elevated a few feet above the damp jungle floor and 100 yards back from the beautiful, secluded Chiquita beach near Punta Uva, these wooden cabinas are tastefully furnished, with spacious verandas. The property is run by German-born Wolf Bissinger and his talented Talamancan-born partner, Wanda Patterson-Bissinger. ✉ *10 km (6 mi) from Puerto Viejo on left side of road,* ☎ *233–6613,* ℻ *223–7479,* ☎℻ *750–0062. 11 cabinas. Restaurant, bar. No credit cards.*

Outdoor Activities and Sports

ECOTOURISM

Founded in 1990, **ATEC** (Talamanca Association for Ecotourism and Conservation) operates out of a small office in the middle of Puerto

Viejo di Limón. ATEC plays an increasingly important role in the eco-tourism movement in Talamanca. The agency's office also serves as a fax and phone center, a post office, and a general information center for the town and the region. Under ATEC's auspices the following tours and activities can be pursued: Afro-Caribbean or indigenous culture and nature walks; rain-forest hikes; coral reef snorkeling or fishing trips; bird-watching and night walks; and adventure treks. ATEC is also an excellent source for information on volunteer vacations in the region. Of the money collected for tours booked through ATEC, 15%–20% goes to local organizations and wildlife refuges. ⊠ *ATEC, Puerto Viejo de Talamanca, Limón,* ☎ *750–0158.* ⊙ *Daily 8–8, except when closes for lunch (hrs vary).*

SURFING

Surfing is the name of the game in Puerto Viejo. There are a number of breaks here, the most famous being Salsa Brava. Salsa Brava breaks rather far offshore. and there are some tricky currents and reefs to maneuver just to get out there. It's a hollow, primarily right-breaking wave over a shallow reef; when it gets big, it is one gnarly wave. If Salsa Brava is too big, or not big enough, check out the breaks at Punta Uva, Punta Cocles, or Playa Chiquita. For a wave conditions forecast, call ☎ 220–2026 all over the country. The operators claim about an 80% success rate, which isn't too bad; the cost is about 50¢ per minute. Boogie boarders and bodysurfers will also dig the beach-break waves to be found at various spots along this tantalizingly beautiful coast.

Gandoca-Manzanillo National Wildlife Refuge

⑭ *15 km (9 mi) south of Puerto Viejo de Limón.*

The Gandoca-Manzanillo National Wildlife Refuge (Refugio Nacional de Vida Silvestre Gandoca-Manzanillo, also ☞ Chapter 10) protects orey and jolillo swamps, 10 km (6 mi) of beach where four species of turtle lay their eggs, and almost 3 sq km (1¼ sq mi) of cativo forest and coral reef. The Gandoca estuary is a nursery for tarpon and a wallowing spot for crocodiles and caimans. The administrators of the park, Benson and Florentino Grenald, can tell you more and recommend a local guide. If you ask when you enter Manzanillo village, residents will point you toward them. From the frontier with Panama, retrace your steps to the main road and head southwest through Bribri to Sixaola, the border town. Indian reserves in the area protect the domains of the Bribri, Cabecar, and Kekoldi Indians.

Dining

$–$$$ ✗ **Restaurant Maxie's.** Cooled by sea breezes and shaded by tall, stately palms, the two-story, brightly painted wooden Maxie's offers weary travelers great seafood at unbeatable prices, cold beer, and potent cocktails after a day's hike in the wildlife refuge. Locals and expatriates alike—and even chefs from the fancier restaurants in Puerto Viejo—come here for their lobster fix, and the fresh fish is wonderful too. Locals tend to congregate in the rowdy but pleasant downstairs bar, where reggae throbs forth seemingly 24 hours a day. *On main town road, Manzanillo,* ☎ *no phone. No credit cards.*

Outdoor Activities and Sports

WATER SPORTS

For surfing; sea, river, and estuary kayaking; and especially snorkeling and scuba-diving trips out of Manzanillo, **Aquamor** (☎ 750–0093 or 228–9513) is the place to go. The Manzanillo-based business, run by Katrina Larkin and her family, will also transport and guide snorkelers and divers down to the magnificent reefs of Bocas del Toro in Panama.

OFF THE
BEATEN PATH

RESERVA BIOLÓGICA HITOY CERERE – The remote, 90-sq-km (35-sq-mi) Hitoy Cerere National Park occupies the head of the Valle de la Estrella. The park's limited infrastructure was badly damaged by the 1991 quake, whose epicenter was precisely here. Paths that do exist are very overgrown due to their limited use—visitors scarcely ever get here. Jaguars, tapirs, peccaries, porcupines, anteaters, and armadillos all live in the forest, along with more than 115 species of birds. Watch for Jesus Christ lizards, which walk on water. The moss-flanked rivers have clear bathing pools and spectacular waterfalls. Take a Valle de la Estrella bus from Puerto Limón and get off at Finca Seis; rent a four-wheel-drive vehicle and you'll be able to get within 1 km (½ mi) of the reserve for $5. Check beforehand with the park service in San José if you want to stay overnight. ☎ *283–8004.*

THE ATLANTIC LOWLANDS AND THE CARIBBEAN COAST A TO Z

Arriving and Departing

By Bus

PARQUE NACIONAL BRAULIO CARRILLO AND THE NORTHERN
LOWLANDS

Buses (**Empresarios Guapilenos,** ☎ 222–0610) from San José to Guápiles will drop you off in Braulio Carrillo National Park; they depart every half hour between 7:30 AM and 7 PM and at 8 and 10 PM from the Gran Terminal del Caribe on Calle Central next to the Kamakiri Restaurant (1-hr trip). Buses (**Autotransportes Sarapiqui,** ☎ 259–8571) go to Río Frío and Puerto Viejo de Sarapiquí (stopping at Rara Avis and La Selva) via Braulio Carrillo from Avenida 9 and Calle 12; they depart daily at 8, 10, and 11:30 AM and 1:30, 3:30, and 4:30 PM (2-hr trip). Alternately, from the same location to the same destination, buses go via Vera Blanca—not passing through Braulio Carrillo—at 8 AM, noon, and 3 PM (4-hr trip).

COASTAL TALAMANCA

Bus service to the Atlantic lowlands from San José includes daily direct service to Puerto Limón from the Gran Terminal del Caribe on Calle Central (**Coopelimon,** ☎ 223–7811) every half hour between 5 AM and 7 PM (2½-hr trip). A second, non-direct bus line (☎ 256–4248) offers service from San José to Puerto Limon with stops in the towns of Siquerres and Guapiles. Service to Cahuita and Sixaola runs from the Gran Terminal del Caribe (**Transportes Mepe,** ☎ 257–8129) daily at 6 AM, 1:30 PM, and 3:30 PM (4-hr trip). Alternatively, the direct bus runs at 10 AM and 4 PM from the same location. Buses (**Transportes Mepe,** ☎ 257–8129) to Puerto Viejo de Limón, Punta Uva, Manzanillo, and Punta Cocles depart daily at 10 AM and 4 PM and Sunday at 8 AM from Calle 1 and Avenida 11 (4½-hr trip).

By Car

PARQUE NACIONAL BRAULIO CARRILLO AND THE NORTHERN LOWLANDS

The Carretera Guápiles (Guápiles Highway) passes the Zurquí and Quebrada González sectors of the **Braulio Carrillo National Park,** whereas the Barva sector lies to the north of Heredia. The roads in the Sarapiquí area of the Atlantic lowlands are mostly paved, with the usual rained-out dirt and rock sections—road quality depends on the time of year, the last pass of the infrequent road crews, or the amount of rain dumped by the latest tropical storm.

COASTAL TALAMANCA

The paved two-lane Guápiles Highway runs from Calle 3 in San José to Puerto Limón, a distance of about 160 km (100 mi).

By Plane

TORTUGUERO AND BARRA DEL COLORADO

Travelair (✉ Aeropuerto Internacional Tobías Bolaños, Apdo. 8–4920, ☎ 506/220–3054 or 506/232–7883, FAX 506/220–0413) flies from San José to Tortuguero and Barra del Colorado daily, with flights departing at 6 AM. **Sansa** (✉ C. 24s between Avda. Central and 1, San José, ☎ 506/221–9414 or 506/441–8035, FAX 506/255–2176) flies to Barra del Colorado on Tuesday and Thursday through Saturday at 6 AM. Several tour companies, such as **Costa Rica Expeditions** (☎ 222–0333, FAX 257–0766), offer regular or charter flights into Tortuguero and/or Barra del Colorado in conjunction with stays in their lodges in the area.

COASTAL TALAMANCA

Currently neither of the two domestic airlines flies to Puerto Limón on a scheduled basis, although a charter is possible because there is a good landing strip just south of town.

Getting Around

By Boat

From Puerto Viejo de Sarapiquí, boats ply the old route up the Río Sarapiquí to the Río San Juan on the Nicaraguan frontier; from here you can travel downstream to Barra del Colorado or Tortuguero, but departure times vary—contact El Gavilán Lodge (☞ Puerto Viejo de Sarapiquí, *above*) or negotiate your own deal dockside. Many private operators will take you from the docks at Moín, just outside of Puerto Limón, to Tortuguero, but there is no scheduled public transportation. Modesto Watson (☞ Guided Tours, *below*), an eagle-eye Miskito Indian guide, will take you upstream if he has room on his boat. You can hire boats to travel between Tortuguero and Barra del Colorado, but prices are quite high.

By Bus

Buses (**Transportes Mepe,** ☎ 758–1572) leave from in front of Distribuidora Tropigas Victor Chin on the west side of Calzado Mary in Puerto Limón for Cahuita, Puerto Vargas, Puerto Viejo de Limón, and Sixaola daily at 5, 8, and 10 AM and 1, 4, and 6 PM (1 hr to Cahuita, 1½ hrs to Puerto Viejo de Limón).

By Car

TORTUGUERO AND BARRA DEL COLORADO

There are no roads to Tortuguero (☞ By Boat, *above,* and Arriving and Departing, By Plane, *above*).

COASTAL TALAMANCA

South of Puerto Limón, a paved road goes for about 40 km (25 mi) to Cahuita, then past the Cahuita turnoff, and proceeds for roughly 16 km (10 mi) toward Puerto Viejo de Limón, passing Bribri and Sixaola, and remains navigable as far as Punta Uva year-round (and Manzanillo during the dry season). A four-wheel-drive vehicle is always preferable, but for the most part the major roads in this region are passable by any kind of car. Watch out for potholes and unpaved sections—they can appear on any road, at any time, without marking or warning.

Contacts and Resources

Car Rentals

See Contacts and Resources *in* San José A to Z, *in* Chapter 2.

Emergencies

Emergencies (☎ 911). **Ambulance** (Cruz Roja, ☎ 128). **Fire** (☎ 118). **Police** (☎ 117 in towns; 127 in rural areas). **Traffic Police** (☎ 227–8030).

Guided Tours

PARQUE NACIONAL BRAULIO CARRILLO AND THE NORTHERN LOWLANDS

Both **Desafio** (✉ Apdo. 37–4417, La Fortuna, ☎ 479–9464, FAX 479–9178) and **Sunset Tours** (La Fortuna, ☎ 479–9415, FAX 479–9099), based in La Fortuna (☞ Chapter 4), run tours to Puerto Viejo de Sarapiquí.

PARQUE NACIONAL TORTUGUERO

Tortuguero National Park tours are usually packaged with one- or two-night stays in local lodges. **Cotur's** (✉ Paseo Colón and Cs. 34 and 36, San José, ☎ 233–0155) offers three-day, two-night tours, including bus and boat transport from San José to the Jungle Lodge in Tortuguero for about $230. **Mawamba** (✉ San José, ☎ 223–2421) offers a slightly more expensive version of the same tour, with the nights spent at the Mawamba Lodge, or a less expensive version with nights at Cabinas Sabina. **Costa Rica Expeditions** (✉ C. Central and Avda. 3, San José, ☎ 222–0333, FAX 257–1665) flies you directly to its rustically charming Tortuga Lodge for three days, two nights, for about $300. **Fran and Modesto Watson** (☎ FAX 226–0986) are experts on the history and ecology of the area. Among other tours, they offer a two-day, one-night tour on their *Riverboat Francesca*, with overnight at Laguna or Manati Lodge (about $144–$157, including meals and transfers).

PUERTO VIEJO DE LIMÓN

ATEC office (✉ Across from Soda Tamara, Puerto Viejo de Limón, ☎ 750–0158) offers such special-interest tours as "Sustainable Logging," "Yorkin Indigenous Tour," and assorted bird-watching, turtle-watching, indigenous culture, and other ecologically oriented trips. **Atlántico Tours** (contact ATEC; ☞ *above*), based in Puerto Viejo, offers tours to Tortuguero and Barra del Colorado as well as more local tours of Parque Nacional Cahuita, Reserva Biológica Hitoy Cerere, and Gandoca-Manzanillo Wildlife Refuge. They also rent surfboards, bicycles, kites, and snorkeling gear.

Visitor Information

The **tourist office** in San José has information covering the Atlantic lowlands (☞ Visitor Information *in* San José A to Z, *in* Chapter 2). The **ATEC** (☎ FAX 750–0158) office in Puerto Viejo de Limón is a great source of information on local tours, guides, and interesting activities.

9 EXCURSIONS TO PANAMA AND NICARAGUA

In the verdant valleys and mountains of Panama's Chiriquí Province, you can explore lush cloud forests, run raging rivers, or climb Volcán Barú. On the islands of Bocas del Toro you'll find stunning coral reefs, palm-lined beaches, and a tumbledown provincial capital. Slip across the border from Guanacaste into southwestern Nicaragua, with its vast fresh-water lake, active and inactive volcanoes, miles of pristine beaches, and the colonial jewel of Granada.

PANAMA

Updated by
David
Dudenhoefer
and Justin
Henderson

THE AMERICAN VISION OF PANAMA is usually restricted to the canal Teddy Roosevelt dug here, a dictator named Manuel Noriega, and the invasion George Bush launched to put Noriega behind U.S. bars. Are we myopic or merely uninformed? Probably a bit of both. If we just look beyond that controversial canal, we'll discover vast expanses of jungle that hold amazing biological diversity, proud and colorful indigenous cultures that preserve centuries-old traditions, idyllic islands ringed with coral reefs, and exuberant mountain forests filled with colorful birds and other interesting creatures. And since Panama has only just started to receive the attention it deserves, you won't have to share its attractions with hordes of tourists.

The western half of the country offers several destinations well worth visiting. Tranquil Chiriquí Province, for example, has two small agricultural communities set in lush valleys surrounded by dense cloud forests with a massive, extinct volcano towering over them. The isolated islands of the Bocas del Toro archipelago, on the other hand, feature long, deserted beaches lined with coconut palms and washed by aquamarine waters that hold an incredible diversity of marine life.

Pleasures and Pastimes

Dining

Western Panama is unlikely ever to become an epicurean mecca, but the region does have a few upscale restaurants and many inexpensive eateries. Panamanian food tends to be a bit greasy, but the kitchens of the mountains of Chiriquí adhere to a more northern—though still fried—style of cooking. A few restaurants here specialize in food from other parts of the world. Plenty of fresh seafood is lured from the sea near Bocas del Toro, and though the local cooks aren't terribly inventive about how they prepare it, a few foreigners who are have moved into the neighborhood. In addition to the local fare, you'll also find good Chinese and Italian food on the islands. Remember that, unlike in Costa Rica, there is no service charge included in the bill at a Panamanian restaurant, so 10% gratuity is expected.

Festivals

David's Feria Internacional, a commercial exposition worthy of avoiding, takes place in late March. Boquete's extensive fairgrounds on the east bank of the Río Caldera are the site of the annual Feria de las Flores (Flower Festival). Held in mid-January, it is a colorful but noisy affair with performances of folk music and dancing and lots of loud disco music. The Feria del Mar (Festival of the Sea), on the beach north of Bocas del Toro in late September, is sort of a Caribbean version of Boquete's Flower Festival.

Lodging

Since tourism has yet to take off in Panama, a relatively small selection of accommodations is available in the western provinces. Nevertheless, Chiriquí has several of Panama's nicest hotels. The region's most charming inns are nestled in its stunning mountain valleys, and one of them is set in the middle of the forest. Although you can usually show up and find a room, reservations are necessary during Panamanian holidays (☞ When to Tour Panama, *below*). A recent tourism boom has left Bocas del Toro with an overabundance of hotel rooms and relatively low rates. The two oldest inns are in former banana-company

WITHOUT KODAK MAX
photos taken on 100 speed film

Ever see someone

waiting for the sun to come out

while trying to photograph

a charging rhino?

New!
Kodak Max film:

Now with better color,
Kodak's maximum
versatility film gives
you great pictures in
sunlight, low light,
action or still.

WITH KODAK MAX
photos taken on Kodak Max 400 film

It's all you need
to know about film.

www.kodak.com

Distinctive guides packed with up-to-date expert advice
and smart choices for every type of traveler.

Fodor's. For the world of ways you travel.

houses, which are quite charming. An even less spoiled alternative to the town of Bocas is nearby Bastimentos, just across the bay, which is just starting to get into the tourism business.

National Parks

Chiriquí's two national parks, Volcán Barú and Parque Internacional La Amistad, both lie within the binational Reserva de la Biósfera La Amistad (La Amistad Biosphere Reserve), a collection of protected areas that together cover the better part of the Cordillera de Talamanca range. Although most of Parque Internacional La Amistad—contiguous with the Costa Rican park of the same name—lies within the province of Bocas del Toro, Chiriquí offers the best access to this protected area. The two sectors of the park accessible from Cerro Punta consist of cloud forest, which is home to the emerald toucanet, resplendent quetzal, three-wattled bellbird, nearly a dozen types of hummingbirds, and several hundred other avian species. Parque Nacional Volcán Barú covers the northern slope and upper reaches of Panama's only volcano, the peak of which affords views of two oceans on those rare clear mornings. That park is home to much of the same wildlife found in La Amistad, which it borders, as well as the rare bird called volcano junco. A four-wheel-drive-vehicle-only road winds its way up to the top of the volcano from Boquete, and a footpath heads up the other side, beginning near Bambito and Volcán. There is also a footpath through the cloud forest on the volcano's northern side, which connects the tiny agricultural outposts of El Respingo and Alto Chiquero above Cerro Punta and Boquete, respectively.

Skin Diving

Whether you prefer the simplicity of snorkeling or are an experienced scuba diver itching to get back into the depths of the big blue, Bocas del Toro has what you're looking for. The islands' points, cays, and submerged reefs in this vast lagoon host an array of marine life, ranging from lugubrious sea turtles to hyperactive tropical fish. In the ocean off Panama's Caribbean coast are almost 75 different species of coral and an even greater variety of sponges, around which lurk countless vibrantly colored invertebrates, rays, lobsters, and hundreds of fish species.

White-Water Rafting

Two rambunctious rivers wind their way down out of the Chiriquí highlands, providing good conditions for white-water rafting year-round. The Río Chiriquí, which pours down from the Lago de Fortuna, to the northeast of David, is a class-III river during the dry season and recommended even if you have no rafting experience. During the wettest months, October to December, the water level rises and the river gets wilder, with some of the rapids becoming class IV. The Chiriquí Viejo, which begins in the mountains above Cerro Punta and flows through the western end of the province, provides an invigorating class-IV white-water trip really only appropriate if you have some rafting experience.

Exploring Panama

The Panamanian province of Chiriquí lies just a short trip from San Vito and Golfito, and though it's an eight-hour drive from San José, you can get there in just over an hour if you fly. It takes about four hours to reach Bocas del Toro from Cahuita or Puerto Viejo de Limón (☞ Chapter 7)—on a sequence of bus, taxi, and water taxi—and about eight hours from San José.

Numbers in the text correspond to numbers in the margin and on the Chiriquí Province and the Bocas del Toro Archipelago map.

Great Itineraries

After the long haul to get to Panama, you'll want to spend at least a couple of days in either Chiriquí or Bocas del Toro before heading back. Luckily there's plenty to keep you busy.

IF YOU HAVE 3 DAYS FOR CHIRIQUÍ

If you have three days for Chiriquí, you won't want to spend too much time in **David** ①. Head straight for the mountain air of ⊞ **Boquete** ②, which has a good selection of accommodations. Get up early the next morning, either for a bird-watching walk or the predawn drive up Volcán Barú to catch the sunrise from the summit. You can stay the second night in Boquete or make the trip to ⊞ **Cerro Punta** ⑤, which is higher and thus cooler. Whether you spend one or two nights in Cerro Punta, you'll definitely want to explore the forests of Parque Internacional La Amistad. White-water rafting trips are available out of both towns, but are more convenient out of Boquete. Other diversions include horseback riding, hiking, and mountain biking.

IF YOU HAVE 3 DAYS FOR BOCAS DEL TORO

Spend your first day wandering through the town of ⊞ **Bocas del Toro** on **Isla Colón** ⑥. Relax during the afternoon or rent a bike and ride out to Playa Bluff. On day two, wake up early and head for the long beach on ⊞ **Isla Bastimentos** ⑦, Punta Hospital, or Cayos Zapatillas, where you can dive or snorkel. On day three, enjoy either the boat trip to Isla de Pajaros and nearby Boca del Drago or a visit to an indigenous community, either on a nearby island or on the mainland.

When to Tour Panama

Since Panama's history has differed considerably from Costa Rica's, each country has its own political holidays, but the two countries share religious holidays. You'll want to make reservations well ahead of time for travel during most holidays, especially the last week of December, Holy Week (the week before Easter Sunday), and Carnival Week, which takes place approximately six weeks before Holy Week.

The massive Cordillera de Talamanca range divides western Panama into Atlantic and Pacific slopes, and the weather can differ considerably between its two provinces. Chiriquí experiences its nicest weather during the December to May dry season and enjoys some sunny days in July and August. It rains pretty much year-round in Bocas del Toro, though the province often experiences mini–dry seasons September to October and March to April. However, since most of the region's rain falls at night, it can be a pleasant place to visit just about any time of year.

Chiriquí Province

The province of Chiriquí is a land of rolling plains, green mountain valleys, raging rivers, and luxuriant forests. It is dominated by the peaks of the Cordillera de Talamanca, which extends southeast from Costa Rica into Panama and defines the province's northern edge. The range's upper slopes are covered with thick cloud forest, kept wet by the mist that the trade winds regularly push over the continental divide. That mist not only keeps the landscape green, it creates the perfect conditions for viewing rainbows and feeds countless streams and boulder-strewn rivers. Two valleys set high on either side of Volcán Barú—the country's highest peak—offer cool mountain climates and close exposure to nature, while the rolling lowlands are hot and almost completely deforested.

Much of the province is home to cowboys and Indians—vast haciendas cover the better part of the lowlands, and Indian villages are scattered along the eastern highlands—whereas such agricultural

Chiriquí Province and the Bocas del Toro Archipelago

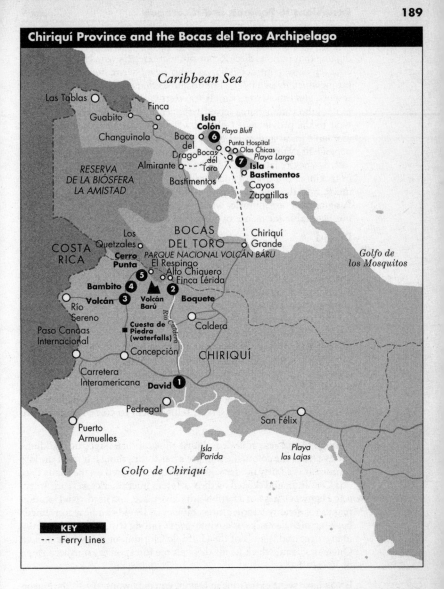

Caribbean Sea

Las Tablas
Finca
Guabito
Isla
Colón ⑥ Playa Bluff
Changuinola
Boca del Drago
Punta Hospital
Olas Chicas
Bocas del Toro ⑦ Playa Larga
Almirante
Isla
Bastimentos Bastimentos
Cayos Zapatillas

RESERVA DE LA BIÓSFERA LA AMISTAD

BOCAS DEL TORO
Chiriquí Grande

COSTA RICA
Los Quetzales
Cerro Punta
PARQUE NACIONAL VOLCÁN BÁRU
El Respingo
Alto Chiquero
Finca Lérida
Bambito ④ ⑤
Volcán ③
Volcán Barú ②
Boquete ①
Río Sereno
Cuesta de Piedra (waterfalls)
Caldera
Paso Canoas Internacional
Concepción
CHIRIQUÍ
Carretera Interamericana
David ①
Pedregal
San Félix
Puerto Armuelles
Isla Parida
Playa las Lajas
Golfo de Chiriquí

Golfo de los Mosquitos

KEY
--- Ferry Lines

communities as Boquete, Volcán, and Cerro Punta are dominated by the descendants of European immigrants. The province consequently reflects Panama's varied cultural spectrum, which includes half a dozen indigenous ethnicities, a mestizo majority, and the descendants of immigrants from all corners of the world.

During the colonial era, Chiriquí was still the realm of Indians, who belonged to dozens of ethnicities but whom the Spanish invaders collectively dubbed the Guaymí—a name that has stuck to this day. The Spaniards introduced cattle to the region, and as ranching took hold, the area's forests receded. During the last century, banana and sugar plantations were established in the lowlands, and the rich soil of the mountain valleys was dedicated to more lucrative crops, such as coffee, fruit, and vegetables. This agricultural development meant that Indian territory shrank considerably—the majority of Chiriquí's indigenous inhabitants now live in the mountains to the east—but it turned the province into a fairly affluent, independent region.

Most immigrants came to Chiriquí via the Panama Canal area, which was an important route of transit long before the U.S. government started digging that famous ditch. Some of the foreigners who ended up in the country were contract laborers who never went home, some were businessmen drawn by the opportunities that interoceanic transit represents, and others were simply travelers who got sidetracked. Though most of those immigrants stayed in the center of the country, some drifted west to the province of Chiriquí. Chiriquí's distance from the Panamanian capital and canal probably has something to do with the independent nature of the Chiricanos, as the province's inhabitants are called. They're hard-working, traditional people, with a rich heritage of folklore. You may be lucky enough to enjoy some of the local folk music and dancing, and you're almost certain to hear the popular Panamanian *típica* music, which is similar to the Colombian *cumbia* but is notable for its use of accordions and ululating vocals.

David

❶ The provincial capital of **David**, 37 km (23 mi) east of the border with Costa Rica, has little to offer travelers, but it is practically unavoidable, since it is the local transportation hub. The town is the political and economic center for a vast agricultural area, with banks, car rental companies, and a small airport. Not only do the province's scattered inhabitants head here to take care of business, Costa Ricans sometimes travel to David on shopping trips, since most imported items are considerably cheaper in Panama than in Costa Rica. The busy boulevards near town center are consequently lined with a variety of modern shops and other businesses. If you wander past some of the clothing and department stores, you may notice the peculiar habit Panamanian salesmen have of clapping and shouting about the merchandise and walking along next to passersby, telling them to come into the store and buy something.

Though David was founded almost four centuries ago, no buildings survive from the colonial era; there's hardly anything left from the last century. It is a fairly modern, grid-plan city, centered on the shady Parque Cervantes and skirted by the Carretera Interamericana (Pan-American Highway). It is not a terribly attractive place, and its lowland location makes for steamy temperatures. However, David can be a convenient base for such day trips as a white-water rafting trip, a boat tour of the mangroves and islands of the Golfo de Chiriquí, or a day hike on Los Quetzales Trail, which heads through the forest on the northern slope of Volcán Barú.

If you have some extra time in David, you may want to visit the **Museo José de Obaldía,** which has exhibits about the region's pre-Columbian cultures and colonial history. ⊠ *Avda. 8 Este and C. A Norte,* ☎ *507/775–7839.* ▨ *$1.* ☉ *Tues.–Sat. 8:30–4:30.*

DINING AND LODGING

$$–$$$ ✕ **Mar del Sur.** The best seafood in David is served at this Peruvian restaurant in a former home owned by the same people who run San José's popular Machu Picchu. It is on the north end of town, a few blocks from the bus station. The dining area has tile floors, wooden ceilings, arched doorways, and a few posters and paintings of Peru. Appetizers include seviche, *chicharón de calamar* (deep-fried squid), and *papas a la huancaina* (boiled potatoes in a cream sauce). Entrées, like the *picante de langostinos* (prawns in a spicy cream sauce) and the corvina prepared six different ways, are delicious. *Behind Fe de Doleguita supermarket,* ☎ *507/775–0856. AE, MC, V. Closed Sun. and daily 3–6.*

$–$$ ✕ **Churrascos Place.** This open-air restaurant, one block from Parque Cervantes, serves a good selection of inexpensive food and is open 24 hours a day. Plants line two sides of the restaurant, which has a red-tile floor, a high sloping roof, and a bar on one end. The menu is pretty basic, with several cuts of beef, fish fillets, rice with chicken, soups, and sandwiches. Main dishes come with a simple salad. ✉ *Avda. 2 Este and C. Central,* ☎ *507/774–0412. AE, MC, V.*

$–$$ ✕ **Pizzería Hotel Nacional.** Across the street from the venerable Hotel Nacional (☞ *below*), in the same building as the hotel's discotheque, this place serves some decent pizza and an ample selection of meat, seafood, and pasta dishes. The decor is pretty basic, but it's clean and air-conditioned, and the service is good. ✉ *Avda. Central and C. Central,* ☎ *507/775–1042. AE, MC, V.*

$$–$$$ 🏨 **Hotel Nacional.** This stately old building dates from the 1940s and
★ has regained its place as David's best hotel. Spacious guest rooms have firm beds, bright tile floors, air-conditioning, and satellite TV. Superior rooms in back are larger; most have picture windows that overlook the pool area, where there's also an open-air bar and grill. Ample facilities, which include a casino and multi-cinema, make the Nacional a relatively busy spot in this sleepy town. ✉ *Avda. Central and C. Central,* ☎ *507/775–2222,* 𝖥𝖠𝖷 *507/775–7729. 75 rooms with bath. 2 restaurants, bar, pool, casino, cinema. AE, DC, MC, V.*

$–$$ 🏨 **Hotel Alcalá.** A relatively new addition to David's lodging selection, the Alcalá stands on a busy street near the market a few blocks from Parque Cervantes. Its shiny, modern rooms offer little in the way of personality, but they come complete with telephone, cable TV, air-conditioning, and some exceptionally tacky photos on the walls. ✉ *Avda. 3 Este at C. D Norte,* ☎ *507/774–9018,* 𝖥𝖠𝖷 *507/774–9021. 57 rooms with bath. Restaurant, bar, air-conditioning. AE, MC, V.*

$ 🏨 **Hotel Iris.** Centrally set overlooking Parque Cervantes, the Hotel Iris offers basic, clean accommodations at budget rates. All rooms have tile floors, telephones, fans, decent beds, and hot-water baths; those with air-conditioning and TV cost a few dollars more. Ask for a room facing the street or all the way in back, since they have large windows that make them cooler and brighter. ✉ *C. A Norte, across from Parque Cervantes,* ☎ 𝖥𝖠𝖷 *507/775–7233. 62 rooms with bath. MC, V.*

OUTDOOR ACTIVITIES AND SPORTS

Sportfishing. The Golfo de Chiriquí, the vast gulf south of the province, features world-class sportfishing; charters can be booked through the **Marina de Pedregal** (☎ 507/721–0071) or **Marco Devilio** (☎ 507/775–3830).

Swimming. To escape the heat, head to the *balneario* (swimming hole) just north of town, across the bridge from the *cervecería* (brewery) on the road to Boquete. This simple swimming hole in the Río David has a small waterfall pouring into it and an open-air bar nearby. It's packed on weekends and holidays but is usually quiet the rest of the week.

Boquete

② **Boquete,** 38 km (24 mi) north of David, is a pleasant little town of wooden houses and colorful gardens that sits 3,878 ft above sea level in the verdant valley of the Río Caldera. For much of the year the trade winds blow over the mountains and down through that valley, often bringing a mist that keeps the area green year-round and makes rainbows a common sight. The mountains above town still have plenty of trees on them, which makes it a great place for bird-watching, and the roads and trails that head into those hills can be explored on foot, mountain bike, horseback, or four wheels.

Thanks to its rich soil, Boquete has become an important agricultural center famous for its coffee, oranges, flowers, strawberries, and apples. The combination of good farming conditions and a pleasant climate has led many Europeans and North Americans to settle here over the years, which is why you'll see plenty of fair-skinned people and architecture that differs significantly from that of the lowlands. You'll also probably see Ngwóbe, or Guaymí, Indians, who migrate here from the eastern half of Chiriquí to work the orange and coffee harvests, which together span from September to April. Tidy homes and abundant blossoms make the town of Boquete a nice place for a stroll; you can make a short loop by heading north until you come to a fork in the road, where you veer right, passing the Hotel Panamonte and crossing the Río Caldera. Turn right after crossing the river and follow it south past the flower-filled Fairgrounds to another bridge, which you cross to get back to the town square. If you drive to Boquete, be sure to stop at the Tourist Information Center, on the hill south of town for information about local sights and diversions and a splendid view of the Boquete Valley. Watch for it on the right as you climb the hill before town.

There are also a couple spots worth checking out just north of town— veering left at the sign for the Hotel Panamonte. **Mi Jardin es su Jardin** (My Garden is Your Garden) is the the private garden of an eccentric millionaire that is open to the public. Cement paths wind past flower beds ablaze with color, and all kinds of bizarre statues of animals and cartoon characters make this place a minor monument to kitsch. *½ km north of town, just south of Café Ruiz,* ☎ *no phone.* ✉ *Free.* ☉ *Daily 9–5.*

The processing plant of **Café Ruiz,** also north of town, offers a 15-minute tour of its roasting and packaging operations and a taste of its coffee. If you have a keen interest in coffee you can call ahead of time and reserve a private tour of the family farm in the mountains above town, where you can get a close look at the golden bean's cultivation, harvest, and processing. This is also the best place to purchase coffee in Boquete. *Just north of Mi Jardin es Su Jardin (☞ above),* ☎ *507/720–1392.* ✉ *Free.* ☉ *Mon.–Sat. 8–11:30 and 1:30–4.*

The biggest attraction—literally—in this area lies a bit higher than Boquete. The road to the top of **Parque Nacional Volcán Barú** (Barú Volcano National Park) begins in town. A large sign marks the route one block north of the main road. It is paved for the first 7 km (4½ mi), after which it becomes a rough and rocky dirt track that requires a four-wheel-drive vehicle for the 14 km (9 mi) to the summit. Tours to the summit are expensive, and less-expensive guided hikes include transportation to and from the end of the paved road (☞ Outdoor Activities and Sports, *below*). ✉ *$5.*

Other possible diversions include bird-watching, horseback riding, and mountain biking in the hills above town, hiking through the forest to several waterfalls, white-water rafting, or visiting the hot springs and pre-Columbian petroglyphs in the nearby village of **Caldera.**

DINING AND LODGING

$$ ✕ **La Casona Mexicana.** Run by a local woman who lived in Mexico for many years, this colorful place serves a limited selection of popular Toltec taste treats. The burritos are pretty standard, but the tacos are made with soft corn tortillas, whereas the tostadas and sopas have fried tortillas. It is set in an attractive old wooden house, the interior of which has been painted wild colors and decorated with Mexican souvenirs. It's on the left side of the main road as you enter town. ✉ *Avda. Central,* ☎ *no phone. No credit cards.*

$ ✕ **Pizzeria La Volcanica.** This simple restaurant on Boquete's busy main drag serves decent pizza at amazingly low prices. You can build your own pie since they charge according to size no matter how many different ingredients you want on it. The attraction ends there—this place has all the ambience of a prison block. ⊠ *Avda. Central, 50 m south of Parque Central,* ☎ *no phone. No credit cards. Closed Mon.*

$$$
★ 🏨 **La Montaña y el Valle.** These three charming chalets offer peace, privacy, luxurious surroundings, and the best view in Boquete. Each chalet has a bedroom and spacious sitting room with a dinner table and fully stocked kitchenette. Abundant windows and a small porch offer vistas of the valley below and of massive Barú Volcano. Footpaths wind their way through tropical gardens and forest patches—prime bird-watching territory. The friendly Canadian owners offer vacation-planning assistance and delicious dinners served by candlelight in your chalet. They also have three camping sites. This place is often full, so reserve well ahead of time. It is in hills northeast of town, near El Explorador; follow signs. ⊠ *Jaramillo Arriba,* ☎ FAX *507/720–2211. 3 chalets. Kitchenettes. MC, V.*

$$$ 🏨 **Panamonte.** You would expect to find this country inn on a quiet street near the Río Caldera in rural New England, not in Central America. The Collins family, of North American origin, have been pleasantly surprising guests since they opened the hotel in 1946. A two-story wooden building painted baby blue holds a lobby adorned with a small collection of colonial art, an elegant restaurant, and several guest rooms; a yellow house across the street has a few more rooms, and newer cement units in back are more spacious and private but not nearly as charming. The restaurant is exceptional, and a large bar in back has a fireplace and garden views. The hotel has mountain bikes, and the in-house tour company offers bird-watching on the family farm, Finca Lérida, a sunrise trip to Barú's summit, horseback riding, a coffee tour, and more. ⊠ *Avda. 11 de Abril, right at fork after town,* ☎ *507/720– 1327,* FAX *507/720–2055. 19 rooms with bath. Restaurant, bar, horseback riding, mountain bikes. AE, MC, V.*

$$–$$$ 🏨 **Villa Marita.** Spread along a ridge north of Boquete, about 5 minutes out of town, these attractive yellow *cabañas* share a gorgeous view of the valley, volcano, and nearby coffee farms. Their interiors consist of two bright rooms—a bedroom and a smaller sitting room with a couch that doubles as an extra bed. The bar and restaurant are in the second floor of a cement building that stands behind the bungalows. Hiking and horseback tours are offered, and rates drop $10 after the first night. ⊠ *Alto Lino, 5 km (3 mi) north of Boquete,* ☎ *507/720– 1309,* FAX *507/720–2164. 7 bungalows. Restaurant. AE, MC, V.*

$$ 🏨 **Hotel Rebequet.** This small hotel on a quiet corner two blocks east of the main road is a good option for people who like to cook, since it has kitchen facilities and a dining area for the use of guests. Rooms surround a small courtyard and are relatively large, with parquet floors, windows, wood ceilings, blue-tile baths, TVs, and small refrigerators. ⊠ *C. 6 Sur,* ☎ *507/720–1365. 9 rooms with bath. No credit cards.*

$–$$ 🏨 **Pensión Topas.** The rooms in this small lodge, owned by a young German couple and set in the corner of the owners' backyard, are spacious and attractive, with tile floors, big windows, firm beds, and original paintings and posters. Four of them open onto a covered terrace with a couple of tables where you can enjoy an optional German breakfast while overlooking the yard and small pool. A smaller, less-expensive room with a bathroom is in the back of the house. Turn right after the gas station, then right at the first corner. ⊠ *Behind Texaco station,* ☎ *507/720–1005. 5 rooms, 4 with bath. Pool. No credit cards.*

$ 🏨 **Pensión Marilos.** The small, clean rooms in this family-run lodge are the best deal in Boquete and perhaps the entire country. They all have tile floors and windows, and all but two have private baths. The *pensión* is on the corner of two quiet side streets, a few blocks south of the central park. ⊠ *C. 6 Sur,* ☏ *507/720–1380. 7 rooms, 5 with bath. No credit cards.*

Bird-Watching. The forested hills above Boquete are the perching grounds for abundant and varied avian life, which includes such colorful critters as collared redstarts, emerald toucanets, sulfur-winged parakeets, and about a dozen species of hummingbirds and their relatives. The area is also one of the best places in the world to see the legendary resplendent quetzal, which is most easily observed from January to May. The cattle pastures, coffee farms, and orchards that surround the town actually facilitate bird-watching, since birds are easier to see when they leave the forest and enter wide open areas. The Panamonte (☞ Dining and Lodging, *above*) has tours to **Finca Lérida,** the family farm, where you're practically guaranteed to see a quetzal during the dry season. The waterfall hike offered by Expediciones Tierras Altas (☞ *below*) also passes through prime quetzal territory. The trip to the top of **Volcán Barú** takes you to higher life zones that have bird species you won't see around Boquete.

Hiking. Plenty of hiking routes are reachable from Boquete, some of which can also be explored on horseback or mountain bike. The two paved loops above town can be hiked, but be aware that the loop reached by veering left at the fork is considerably longer and steeper. It also passes more forest and spectacular views. The **Sendero los Quetzales,** the footpath to Cerro Punta, is reached by following the road to Alto Chiquero. The trail heads through the forest along Río Caldera, crossing it several times, and then over a ridge to El Respingo in the hills above Cerro Punta. The 6-km (4-mi) hike is easier if you start in Cerro Punta, and a guided trip offered by **Expediciones Tierras Altas** (☏ 507/720–1342) includes transportation to El Respingo and pickup at Alto Chiquero. If you want to do the hike on your own, you should catch one of the first buses to David, then bus to Cerro Punta, and hire a four-wheel-drive taxi to take you to El Respingo. The trail isn't marked, and you should keep your eyes open for a left turn in a clearing about 1½ km (1 mi) into it, shortly after which you should turn right at a gate, where the trail heads back into the forest. You should arrange to have a taxi pick you up in Alto Chiquero in the evening.

The hike to the summit of **Volcán Barú** is considerably more demanding, more than twice as long, and much steeper. You'll want to leave a car or arrange to be dropped off and picked up at the entrance to the national park, 14 km (9 mi) from the summit. Bring lots of water and warm, waterproof clothing for any hike, but especially for the trek up Barú. **Expediciones Tierras Altas** (☞ *above*) offers guided hikes up Barú, as well as a much easier tour on a farm above town, where hikers visit several waterfalls hidden in the forest. **Río Monte Tours** (☏ 507/720–1327) also arranges hiking trips up Barú. If you aren't up to making the hike, you can also take a four-wheel-drive vehicle tour to watch the sunrise from the summit.

Volcán

❸ A breezy little town at a crossroads, **Volcán** (60 km/36 mi northwest of David and 16 km/10 mi south of Cerro Punta) is spread along the road on a plain to the south of Barú in an area that lost its forests long ago. The highland towns of Boquete, Bambito, and Cerro Punta are all so close to the volcano that you can't see it in its entirety from any of them. From Volcán, however, you can often admire that massive peak and the mountains beyond it, weather permitting. Like Bambito and Cerro Punta, Volcán was largely settled by immigrants from Switzerland and Yugoslavia during the early part of this century. It's a good place to stay if you intend to hike up the volcano's southern side—you'll want to get up before dawn if you're attempting that grueling trip.

A few small lakes known as Las Lagunas, several miles south of Volcán, are surrounded by some of the last bits of standing forest in the area, but they're too far to walk to, and the last stretch of road is too rough for anything but a four-wheel-drive vehicle. Though it's often windy, Volcán tends to be warmer than either nearby Bambito or Cerro Punta, which can get very chilly at night, so it's a good place to stay if you didn't pack warm clothes. If you don't hike up the volcano, you'll want to use Volcán as a base for day trips to the Cerro Punta area, which has much more to see and do.

OFF THE
BEATEN PATH
CUESTA DE PIEDRA WATERFALLS – There are several waterfalls in a valley below Cuesta de Piedra, a small community on the road to Volcán about 20 km (12 mi) north of Concepción. Since the cascades are in a restricted area belonging to the national electric institute, IHRE, you can only visit them with a guide from Cuesta de Piedra, who can be hired through the **Restaurante Porvenir** (☎ 507/770–6088); talk to Eneida or Leonel, and be prepared to haggle over the price. If you're driving, the **Mirador Alanher,** on the left side of the road shortly after Cuesta de Piedra, is a good place to stop for a *batido* (fruity milk drink)—papaya and *zarzamora* (blackberry) are the usual flavors—hot chocolate, or coffee. Be sure to climb the stairs to the *mirador* (lookout).

LODGING

$$
★
Hotel Dos Ríos. This two-story wooden building west of town houses Volcán's nicest hotel: large rooms have wood floors, walls, and ceilings and small tile baths. Two larger suites on the far end of the building have sitting areas and lots of windows and are well worth the extra $6. A large restaurant in front serves basic meat and seafood dishes, and the bar next door is a bit on the ugly side, but a large window lets you gaze at the volcano while you sip your martini. The hotel can arrange early morning transport to the foot of the volcano and a guide to the summit. ⊠ *2 km (1 mi) west of Volcán,* ☎ *507/771–4271. 14 rooms with bath, 2 suites. Restaurant, bar. AE, MC, V.*

Bambito

❹ Not really a town to speak of, **Bambito** (6 km/4 mi north of Volcán and 10 km/6 mi south of Cerro Punta) consists of a series of farms and homes scattered along the narrow valley on the western side of Volcán Barú that the Río Chiriquí Viejo winds down. Sheer rock walls, trees clinging to steep hillsides, and suspension bridges spanning the boulder-strewn river punctuate the terrain. The trade winds whip down through the valley for much of the dry season, which keeps it fairly cool, but it gets more sun than the Cerro Punta area. Small coffee and vegetable farms line much of the road, and several roadside stands sell local vegetables and fruit preserves. It's a lovely spot and is a good base for exploring the mountains around Cerro Punta or rafting on the Río Chiriquí Viejo, since it has one of the country's best hotels.

LODGING

$$$$
★
Hotel Bambito. This full-service, luxury resort has a great position at the entrance to the Bambito Valley, and all its rooms overlook a massive rock wall draped with foliage that towers over the Río Chiriquí Viejo. Rooms have hardwood floors, high ceilings, picture windows, large tile baths, and satellite TV. Junior suites feature balconies, and master suites have bedroom lofts. A small exhibit of pre-Columbian art and a fireplace are in the lobby, next to which is a spacious, plush restaurant and cocktail lounge. The large, heated pool is enclosed in a sort of

greenhouse. The hotel has motor scooters and mountain bikes, and nature guides can take you bird-watching and hiking in the nearby national parks. ✉ *Bambito*, ☎ *507/771–4265*, ⅋ᴀˣ *507/771–4207. 37 rooms with bath, 10 suites. Restaurant, bar, pool, spa, 2 tennis courts, exercise room, hiking, horseback riding, mountain bikes. AE, DC, MC, V.*

Cerro Punta

This bowl-shape valley in the shadow of the Cordillera de Talamanca holds some of the most fertile, dark volcanic soil in the country. That soil has been a mixed blessing: it is a boon for farmers, but it has also ⑤ led them to deforest most of the valley. Nevertheless, **Cerro Punta**, 78 km (48 mi) northwest of David and 16 km (10 mi) north of Volcán, offers some splendid pastoral scenery with its patchwork of vegetable farms, some clinging to steep slopes, and an extensive ranch that raises dairy cattle and thoroughbred horses. Several foliage-clad rocky formations tower over the rolling landscape, one of which gives the valley its name, which translates as "Pointy Hill." The upper slopes of the mountains that ring the valley still retain most of their forest cover, which is home for countless birds and other wildlife. Since the trade winds regularly push clouds over the continental divide and into the valley, Cerro Punta is often swathed in mist, which keeps everything green year-round and makes for frequent rainbow sightings here as well.

Cerro Punta is considerably higher than Boquete and can consequently get rather chilly when the sun goes down or gets stuck behind the clouds. It sometimes drops down near 40°F at night, which means you'll want to bring warm clothes and a waterproof jacket. The cool climate no doubt played a part in the decision of many Swiss and Yugoslavian families to settle here earlier this century. You may also see full-blooded Ngwóbe, or Guaymí, Indians in Cerro Punta, most of whom are temporary farm laborers.

The pastoral landscapes, distant mountains, colorful farmhouses, and abundant flowers of Cerro Punta are impressive enough, but if you are interested in bird-watching or hiking you have even more reason to head here. The paved road that enters the valley makes a small loop, with several dirt roads branching off it heading farther up into the mountains. These dirt roads follow small streams past farms and patches of forest, which make them ideal routes for bird-watching. There are also several footpaths into the mountains around town.

Two trails head into the forest near the park headquarters of **Parque Internacional La Amistad.** La Amistad is a 20-minute drive along a dirt track that heads into the mountains above Cerro Punta. Turn left after the Hotel Cerro Punta (☞ Dining and Lodging, *below*), and left at the next intersection, and then follow that road to the park, keeping left after you drive through the gate; the road is rough, and fit only for four-wheel-drive vehicles. You can also hire a four-wheel-drive taxi to take you to the park entrance (it should cost about $3). **Hotel Bambito** (☎ 507/771–4265, ☞ Lodging *in* Bambito, *above*) can arrange guided tours to the park.

Another way to explore that park's forest is to visit the privately managed reserve of **Los Quetzales** (☞ Dining and Lodging, *below*), which lies up a rough, four-wheel-drive-vehicle road from the neighborhood of Guadelupe. You must be accompanied by one of the reserve's guides, who charge each person $3 per hour, but they can take you to waterfalls and may help you spot quetzals. The reserve entrance is about a 30-minute hike from where the bus stops; ask for directions at the hotel.

Anyone with even the slightest interest in orchids will want to visit **Finca Dracula** (☎ 507/721–2223), which is home to one of the largest orchid collections in Latin America. Named after the Dracula orchid, one of the many rare species found here, the farm has a series of shade and green houses filled with hundreds of orchids from different parts of Panama and the world, as well as a laboratory where rare orchids are reproduced using micro-propagation methods. The farm is usually open to the public for a small fee and is on the road to the Los Quetzales reserve, which can arrange visits.

DINING AND LODGING

$ ✕ **Mama Lola.** Sandwiches, milk shakes, and homemade desserts are the specialties of this tiny restaurant down the hill from Cerro Punta's main intersection. The restaurant has lots of windows and small Formica tables and benches attached to the walls. The limited menu includes basic burgers and the *pie grande* ("big foot"), sort of a French-bread pizza. For dessert, try some *dulce de zanahoria* or *plátano* (carrot or banana cake), fresh yogurt, or one of a variety of fruit shakes. ⊠ *C. Central,* ☎ *507/771–2053. No credit cards. Closes daily at 7.*

$$–$$$ ⊞ **Los Quetzales.** The two wooden cabins in this private 600-acre re-
★ serve within Parque Nacional La Amistad stand on a ridge in the midst of the cloud forest. Each one has two floors, several beds and futons, a kitchen, wood stove, gas-heated shower, kerosene lanterns, lots of windows, and no electricity. A cement duplex at the edge of the forest, a good deal for a small group, holds two two-bedroom apartments that are similarly equipped and cheaper, but not as spectacularly situated. The best deal for single travelers and couples is the main hotel in Guadelupe, about 15 minutes from the reserve. There comfortable rooms with hardwood floors and tiled baths are surrounded by pastoral scenery; a spacious restaurant serves pizza and international cuisine, and a sauna and exercise room stand near the river. ⊠ *Altos de Guadelupe,* ☎ *507/771–2182,* ℻ *507/771–2226. 17 rooms with bath, 2 cabins, 2 apartments. Restaurant, bar, hot tub, sauna, exercise room, hiking, horseback riding. MC, V.*

$–$$ ⊞ **Hotel Cerro Punta.** This cozy lodge across from the old gas station features great views of the surrounding farms and distant peaks, simple rooms, and hearty food. Rooms are on the small side, with worn wooden floors, picture windows, and tiled baths. The restaurant serves basic Panamanian food; daily specials are the best bet. The grounds are planted with flowers, which attract an amusing cast of hummingbirds. ⊠ *C. Principal,* ☎ ℻ *507/771–2020. 10 rooms with bath. Restaurant, bar. MC, V.*

OUTDOOR ACTIVITIES AND SPORTS

Bird-Watching. Cerro Punta is surrounded by high-altitude mountain forests that are home to a large and diverse bird population. The region's varied feathered friends can be spotted all around the bowl-shape valley, especially near the streams and rivers that flow into and out of it. Several roads head off the main loop around the valley's floor, and all of them lead to prime bird-watching territory. The trails into the national parks offer access to the vast expanses of wilderness that border the valley, but the best birding area in Cerro Punta is probably the private Los Quetzales nature reserve (☞ Dining and Lodging, *above*).

Hiking. A decent selection of trails head into the mountains around Cerro Punta, ranging from short paths through the woods to the six-hour trek around the back of Volcán Barú to Boquete. Several trails also explore the cloud forests of **Parque International La Amistad,** both near the ranger station and within the private reserve of Los Quetzales. The most challenging and rewarding hike out of Cerro Punta is the 6-km (4-mi) trek over the northern slope of **Volcán Barú,** from El Respingo to Alto Chiquero, high in the hills above Boquete. The toughest part of this hike, however, may be getting back to Cerro Punta, which lies about four hours by bus from Boquete. The last buses from Boquete and David leave at 6 PM, which means it's safer to take the hike while based in David, since it gives you a couple more hours to get back to your hotel. Guides are available for this hike, as is transportation back to Cerro Punta, though it can be expensive.

Chiriquí Province A to Z

ARRIVING AND DEPARTING

By Bus. Several buses make the trip between San José and David every day, but be warned that it is a 10-hour trip. **Tracopa** (☎ 506/221–4214 in San José, ☎ 507/775–0585 in David) has daily buses from San José to David, departing San José from Calle 14 and Avenida 5 at 7:30 AM and departing David daily from the main terminal at 8:30 AM. **Tico Bus** (☎ 506/221–8954) has daily service between San José and Panama City, departing San José from next to the Iglesia de la Soledad at 10 PM and passing David around 9:30 AM the next day. Buses from Panama sometimes pick up extra passengers at the border, from where they depart at around 8 PM. **Panaline** (☎ 506/255–1205) runs the same route in newer buses for a bit more money, leaving San José at 2 PM and getting into David around midnight.

By Car. Since you can't cross an international border with a car rented in Costa Rica, the only way to drive to Panama is with a private car. The Carretera Interamericana (Pan-American Highway, CA2) enters Panama at Paso Canoas, about 15 km (9 mi) before the turnoff to Volcán and Cerro Punta and about 37 km (23 mi) before David.

By Plane. The Panamanian airline **Aeroperlas** (☎ 506/440–0093 San José, 507/721–1195 David) has five flights weekly between San José and David, with direct connections to Bocas del Toro and Panama City. Those flights depart David weekdays at 8:15 AM, returning from San José at 8:45 AM. Another quick, and less-expensive, way to travel between Chiriquí and San José is to take the daily **Sansa** (☎ 506/221–9414) flight to Coto 47 (☎ 506/783–3275), an airstrip in an oil palm plantation a 20-minute drive from the border town of Paso Canoas. If you fly to Coto 47, you'll want to call and arrange to have a taxi from **Paso Canoas** (☎ 506/732–2355) meet you at the airstrip. When traveling back to San José, try to confirm your reservation the day before. Another option is to fly either Sansa or **Travelair** (☎ 506/296–1102) to Golfito, where taxis and buses to the border abound.

GETTING AROUND

By Bus. Buses travel regularly between David and the following destinations: Paso Canoas (Costa Rican border) every 20 minutes from 5 AM to 7 PM (1-hr trip); Cerro Punta, Bambito, and Volcán every 30 minutes from 5 AM to 6 PM (2-hr trip); Boquete, every 30 to 60 minutes from 5 AM to 6 PM (90-min trip).

By Car. Renting a car is the best way to explore Chiriquí, since roads are in good repair and there are several rental companies in David. It also costs a lot less to rent a car in Panama than it does in Costa Rica. The road to Boquete heads straight north out of David, no turns required. To reach Volcán, drive west on the Pan-American Highway to the town of Concepción—a collection of modern buildings 24 km (15 mi) west of David—where you turn right. The road to Bambito and Cerro Punta, on the right in Volcán, is well marked.

By Plane. Aeroperlas (☎ 506/440–0093 San José; 507/721–1195 David) flies several times a week between David, Changuinola, and Bocas del Toro and schedules daily flights between those three towns and Panama City.

CONTACTS AND RESOURCES

Car Rentals. Car-rental companies (all of which offer four-wheel-drive vehicles) with offices in David include the following: **Hertz** (✉ Avda. 20 at C. F Sur, ☎ 507/775–6828), **Dollar** (✉ Avda. 7 Oeste at C. F Sur, ☎ 507/775–1667 or 507/774–3385), **Avis** (☎ 507/774–7075), and **National** (☎ 507/774–3462).

Emergencies. Ambulance (☎ 507/775–2161). **Fire** (☎ 103). **Hospital** (☎ 507/775–4221 David). **Police** (☎ 104).

Guided Tours. Expediciones Tierras Altas (☎ 507/720–1342), in Boquete, offers a variety of day trips in the area, including bird-watching, hiking, taking four-wheel-drive-vehicle trips up Volcán Barú, and visiting the nearby hot springs and pre-Columbian sites of Caldera. **Río Monte Tours** (☎ 507/720–1327), also in Boquete, offers bird-watching tours to Finca Lérida and four-wheel-drive-vehicle trips up Barú Volcano. **Chiriquí River Rafting** (☎ 507/720–1505, 225–8949 in Panama City, FAX 507/720–1506) is the local specialist in white-water rafting.

Telephones. International operator (☎ 106). To pay for calls in cash, go to **Cable and Wireless** office (✉ C. C Norte and Avda. Cincuentenaria).

Visitor Information. The **regional tourist office** (✉ Avda. 3 de Noviembre and C. A Norte, David, ☎ 507/775–5120), which is on the second floor of a corner building across from Parque Cervantes, is open weekdays 8:30–4:30.

Bocas del Toro Archipelago

The isolated cluster of islands known as the Archipelago of Bocas del Toro—in the northwest corner of Panama, in a province of the same name—has some spectacular scenery, a wealth of natural assets, and a laid-back, Caribbean atmosphere. The province includes a large piece of the mainland as well, but this part of mainland Panama is nothing special—it's the Chiquita Republic, an area virtually blanketed with banana plantations. The real interest for travelers lies offshore, on the islands where you'll find the capital city, also called Bocas del Toro.

The archipelago was "discovered," or at least visited, by Christopher Columbus in 1502. The islands' original inhabitants were Guaymí Indians, and they're still around in isolated villages and intermingled with African-Caribbeans and Hispanics in the larger towns. The language, too, is an interesting mix called Guari-Guari, which is a patois English with traces of Spanish and indigenous dialects. The source of the region's odd name, which translates as "Mouths of the Bull," is lost in legend. One version is that the area was named after an Indian chief called something like Bokatoro, who ruled the area when the first Europeans arrived.

Bocas del Toro is experiencing something of a tourism boom that may actually have had bureaucratic beginnings: thousands of foreigners living in Costa Rica on tourist visas have to leave the country for 72 hours every 90 days, and nearly all of them eventually make it to Bocas. Those temporary refugees quickly discovered that the islands are a very cool place: offbeat, out of the way, with great beaches, supreme diving, and mellow local people. Now the word is very much out.

Isla Colón

A look at a map of the archipelago shows what an odd piece of geog-
6 raphy **Isla Colón**, named after Cristóbal Colón, or Christopher Columbus, 21 km (13 mi) north of Chiriquí Grande, is. The town of **Bocas del Toro,** sometimes called Bocas, sits on a little head of land, connected

to the main body of the island by a narrow neck, or isthmus, that is at most a hundred yards wide. In the early part of this century, Bocas del Toro was the third-largest city in Panama. It was the hub of the banana business in those days, and elegant wooden houses belonging to the banana barons lined the town's waterfront and main streets. That prosperity was ephemeral, however, since a fungal disease began to destroy the region's banana crop during the 1930s, which led the fruit company to abandon the region for nearly two decades. Bocas consequently slipped into economic decline. Even when the banana company moved back into the province in the 1950s, it built its offices on the mainland, near the plantations.

The town's slow fade into disrepair and obscurity was hastened by several fires and the disastrous earthquake of 1991, which wrecked many of the buildings in town and left many others teetering precariously. Dozens of buildings in Bocas would be condemned anywhere in the United States, and as you ascend one of those tilting staircases, you have the feeling that you're entering an amusement-park fun house. Still, many of the older buildings in Bocas del Toro are lovely, if dilapidated, with carved porch rails, fretwork, and trim.

Only in recent years has Bocas del Toro begun to pull out of an extended period of economic depression. That renaissance has largely been the result of a tourism boom that started several years ago. Take the time to wander around town, and be sure to check out the classic, beautifully kept, circa-1926 **fire engine** in the fire-department garage. Another strange element: a couple of hundred yards offshore from the Hotel Las Brisas (☞ Dining and Lodging, *below*), a **little sunken island** slid a few feet below water during the 1991 earthquake. The entire island is underwater, but parts of it lie in water less than a foot deep. You can paddle a kayak or swim out there and walk around; there's even an underwater tennis court.

During the annual **Feria,** which is usually held in September or October, Panamanians crowd into Bocas by the hundreds. Along the right side of the isthmus road that connects Bocas with the rest of Isla Colón are dozens of simple structures housing beer shacks, restaurants, and exhibits during the Feria, which stand empty the rest of the year. Behind those shacks is the **town beach,** which is unfortunately sometimes littered. The island has much nicer beaches, though you'll want to rent a bike or hire a taxi to visit them.

If you follow the road for several miles, veering right at the fork, you'll reach **Playa Bluff,** a long swath of golden sand backed by thick foliage and washed by aquamarine waters. Four species of endangered sea turtles nest here from March to October, including the leatherback turtle, which is one of the largest reptiles in the world. Local guides take visitors to the beach at night during the nesting season to look for turtles (☞ Outdoor Activities and Sports, *below*).

If you veer left at the fork, you'll head through the middle of the island to the other side, where there's a little village called **Boca del Drago.** Between the two villages called Bocas, the island is mainly jungle. The rain forest covering much of the island is home to such animals as armadillos, pacas, several types of frogs, boa constrictors, two- and three-toed sloths, raccoons, coatis, and monkeys. Thankfully, the islands have no poisonous snakes. At the center of the island is a large grotto worth a stop—bring a flashlight! The island is pretty big, so plan on a long bike ride to cross it, or take a taxi, which should charge about $25.

Bocas is a good place to catch a boat out to the real draw of these islands: the diving in and around **Parque Nacional Marina Isla Bastimentos.**

There are dozens of great diving and snorkeling spots in the area, especially around the two **Cayos Zapatillas,** and the richness and variety of the sea life—the diversity of sponges and coral, for starters—are amazing. Panama's **Institute of Renewable Natural Resources (IN-RENARE)** had begun charging a $10 admission fee for the Cayos Zapatillas, which should be paid at their office on First Street in Bocas before leaving for the cays. Since that fee increases the cost of an excursion considerably, most of the boat drivers in Bocas are taking people to other good dive spots that lie outside the park but that hold much the same marine life as the Cayos Zapatillas, such as **Punta Hospital** (Hospital Point), **Coral Island,** and **Olas Chicas,** on Isla Bastimentos.

DINING AND LODGING

$$–$$$ ✕ **Buena Vista Deli & Bar.** The deck at the back of this wooden build-
★ ing sitting over the water is the most pleasant place in town to enjoy a meal. Ceiling fans turn above the tables, plants hang here and there, and the view out over the water is splendid. The menu consists of an interesting selection of salads, sandwiches made with imported meats and cheeses, and other unusual dishes. They always have several daily specials, which usually include fresh seafood and are the best bet for dinner. The bar is popular with the area's growing population of expatriate Americans. ⊠ *C. 1, where it splits from C. 3 (main street),* ☎ *507/757–9035. MC, V. Closed Tues.*

$$–$$$ ✕ **La Ballena.** Just behind the municipality, La Ballena—the name means "The Whale"—is a popular little place were Christmas lights brighten up the entrance at night and a colorful interior is usually complemented by good music. A few tables in front overlook one of this sleepy little town's somnambulant side streets and a garden patio next door. The Italian owners prepare some superb food, offering an ample selection of salads, pastas, and fresh seafood; dishes include pasta with a lobster sauce and steak *a la pizzaiola* (in a tomato sauce). They also rent bicycles, arrange horseback tours, rent apartments, and provide information. ⊠ *Avda. F between Cs. 3 and 2,* ☎ *507/757–9089. No credit cards.*

$$ ✕ **Baia Paradiso.** This large Italian restaurant-cum-bakery across from the town park offers everything from lasagna to lobster. Fresh bread and good coffee make it an excellent choice for breakfast, whereas the lunch and dinner menu includes fresh pastas, sandwiches, seafood, and an array of pizzas. Save room for dessert, which includes homemade cakes and Italian ice cream. ⊠ *C. 3, across from park,* ☎ *507/757–9170. No credit cards. Closed Tues.*

$–$$ ✕ **Heike's.** Heike, the German chef and owner of his small restaurant
★ on the main drag, serves a limited menu of delicious items at very reasonable prices. She happily whips up everything from chicken curry to a tasty meatless dish she's given the mysterious name "vegetarian food." The restaurant itself is a narrow affair with a colorful interior, two tables overlooking the street, and a couple more on a tiny garden patio in back. She and her Panamanian husband only serve dinner. ⊠ *C. 3, across from Municipality,* ☎ *no phone. No credit cards. No lunch.*

$–$$ ✕ **Lako's Place.** A short distance from the center of town, Lako's is
★ well worth the walk. Sitting beneath a high thatched roof on the road to the town beach, Lako's specializes in fresh seafood—be it snapper, stone crab, lobster, or octopus—prepared a variety of ways. They also barbecue chicken outside at night, which is what most of the locals head here for. ⊠ *Avda. Norte, turn left at the Hotel Las Brisas and walk four blocks,* ☎ *no phone. No credit cards.*

$ ✕ **Las Delicias.** A popular spot with the locals, Las Delicias is a great, inexpensive place to sample some of the local cuisine. The cook here prepares two or three different dishes every day around 11 AM and serves them cafeteria style, so it's best to come around noon. They usually offer some sort of soup, fish, meat, rice, and beans. ⊠ *C. 3 at Avda. B,* ☎ *507/757–9318. No credit cards.*

$$$ 🏨 **Hotel Swan's Key.** The newest, biggest, and fanciest hotel in Bocas, Swan's Key was built by an Italian family that also has an inn on the Lago di Garda. It's an extensive, two-story wooden complex with attractive interior courtyards and a bit of artwork that evokes old Italy. The furniture in the carpeted guest rooms was also brought over from the old country. Rooms all have air-conditioning, TV, and tiled, hot-water baths; the nicest ones have small balconies. A large restaurant serves international cuisine. ⊠ *C. 3 between Avdas. F and G,* ☎ *507/ 757–9090,* 🖷 *507/757–9027. 30 rooms with bath, 3 suites. Restaurant, bar, air-conditioning, pool. AE, MC, V.*

$$–$$$ 🏨 **Mangrove Inn.** A short boat trip from town takes you to this col-
   ★   lection of buildings propped over the water at the edge of a mangrove forest. Primarily a dive resort, with all the equipment and a resident dive master, the inn is just a short swim from a decent reef. Dive packages include meals and boat transportation to the province's best dive sites. It's a good spot even if you just want to snorkel, swim, and relax. Blue-and-white wooden cabins have bunks, double beds, and small baths. A large, open-air restaurant and bar serves only daily specials. Everything sits over the water and is connected by a series of docks. ⊠ *General delivery,* ☎ 🖷 *507/757–9594. 6 cabins with bath. Restaurant, bar, snorkeling, dive shop. No credit cards.*

$$ 🏨 **Cocomo on the Sea.** This small, homey place offers Bocas' only ac-
   ★   commodations on the water other than Las Brisas (☞ *below*), and the rooms here are much nicer. Four spacious rooms have hardwood floors and white walls decorated with tropical prints. They all have air-conditioning, but ceiling fans and lots of windows give the option of letting ocean breezes cool things down. The breeziest spot is the porch in back, which sits out over the water with lots of chairs and hammocks. The friendly Canadian owners serve a sumptuous, complementary breakfast on the veranda, and will arrange tours. ⊠ *Avda Norte at C. 6,* ☎ 🖷 *507/757–9259. 4 rooms with bath. Air-conditioning. MC, V.*

$$ 🏨 **Hotel Laguna.** With its carved wooden balconies and sidewalk café, the Hotel Laguna looks like it was transported from a village in the Alps and dropped into the heart of Bocas. It offers such amenities as orthopedic mattresses and air-conditioning at relatively reasonable rates. Rooms have local hardwoods, modern black fixtures, closets, and small windows. Rooms downstairs have tile floors, those upstairs wood floors. The brightest and nicest ones are the suites and the one standard room that face the street. ⊠ *C. 3 between Avdas. D and E,* ☎ *507/757–9091,* 🖷 *507/757–9092. 16 rooms with bath, 1 suite. Restaurant, bar. AE, MC, V.*

$–$$ 🏨 **Hotel Las Brisas.** Built on stilts over the water on the north end of
   ★   Calle 3, Las Brisas may look a bit shabby—it's in a ramshackle 50-year-old building—but it has a great location and friendly owner and staff. You can kayak out to the sunken island or across the channel to Carenero, or have your boatman pick you up for a ride to the national marine park or other snorkeling and diving spots. The rooms in this building and in the old wooden building across the street are pretty basic but comfortable, with private baths. If you prefer something more modern, 10 new rooms in a two-story building down the street have more comforts but less personality. ⊠ *Avda. Norte at C. 3,* ☎ 🖷 *507/ 757–9248. 37 rooms with bath. Boating, bicycles. AE, MC, V.*

$ 🏨 **Hotel Scarlet.** Actually, it's cartoon-panther pink. The interior of this cement building is much easier to look at, though it's not going to win any decorating awards. Rooms are fairly sterile boxes, with tile floors, small baths, and TV sets, but they're clean and cheap. ⊠ *C. 4, 1 block* *north of Bahía restaurant,* ☎ FAX *507/757–9290. 12 rooms with bath. No credit cards.*

$ ✉ **Pensión Delicias.** Above the restaurant of the same name, the Delicias has a collection of basic rooms, most of which have several beds packed into them. Some have private baths, whereas some share baths. More money buys privacy and hot water. They also have a collection of two-level huts on Playa Bluff with hammocks, enclosed sleeping areas up top, a communal shower, and a small restaurant; it's quite rustic but in a gorgeous setting. Cheap transportation is provided every morning. ✉ *C. 3 at Avda. B,* ☎ *507/757–9318. 8 rooms, some without bath. No credit cards.*

OUTDOOR ACTIVITIES AND SPORTS

Snorkeling and Scuba Diving. There are three dive centers on the island and at least half a dozen people who take visitors on snorkeling excursions. Though you might not encounter as many fish and big marine life here as in other parts of the world, Bocas has a great variety of corals—almost 75 different species—sponges, and small invertebrates. You're also likely to see lots of rays, colorful tropical fish, and, sometimes, sea turtles or even dolphins. The most famous spot is the reef around the **Cayos Zapatillas,** which is vast and packed with varied marine life, but the $10 parks fee makes it the most expensive place to explore. A cheaper alternative to Cayos Zapatillas is **Coral Island,** a smaller isle outside the national park. One spot not far from Bocas, which is a good option if you're short on time or money, is **Hospital Point,** where an impressive coral and sponge garden extends down a steep wall into the blue depths. **Olas Chicas,** on the northern coast of Isla Bastimentos, is another sublime spot. If you stay in Bocas, it's cheaper to bike or hike out to the reef off Paunch or, better yet, the point on the far end of Playa Bluff.

Bocas Water Sports (✉ C. 3, ☎ 507/757–9541) offers a variety of boat dives and nonscuba excursions, including trips to its Red Frog camping area on a beach on Isla Bastimentos. The **Mangrove Inn/Turtle Divers** (✉ C. 3, ☎ FAX 507/757–5954) offers a different excursion every day. It has its own hotel and dive center, the Mangrove Inn, just south of town, and offers trips to about a dozen dive spots, as well as inexpensive certification courses. **Starfleet Eco-Adventures** (✉ C. 1, ☎ FAX 507/757–9630) offers scuba and snorkeling excursions on a private catamaran and inexpensive certification courses. You can also negotiate a ride to any of the area's attractions with one of the dozens of freelance boatmen in and around town, though you might want to get a small group together to make it affordable. Dive trips usually cost about $15 per person if you go with a group.

Surfing. There are a few surfers in Bocas but no boards for rent, so you have to bring your own for the few spots. The point off Isla Colón's Playa Paunch—a meager beach on the road to Bluff—has a good left that breaks over a coral platform when the ocean gets undulant. There is also a good left that breaks over the reef on the northern tip of Isla Carenero. The first beach on Isla Bastimentos, across the island from the town of Bastimentos, has a nice beach break that is less dangerous than the other spots and is surfable when the swell is small.

Turtle-Watching. For information about turtle-watching, contact **CARIB-ARU** (C. 3, ☎ 507/757–9488), a local conservation group that has a small office in front of the town library. They run nightly guided tours to Playa Bluff during the peak nesting season (March–October) for a small donation. When turtle-watching, be as quiet as possible, don't use a flashlight once you're on the beach, and don't shine lights at or take photos of the turtles.

Isla Bastimentos

7 A large part of **Isla Bastimentos,** 24 km (15 mi) north of Chiriquí Grande, lies within the boundaries of **Parque Nacional Marina Isla Bastimentos** (Isla Bastimentos Marine National Park), which protects an important sea-turtle nesting beach and a significant expanse of rain forest that is home for plenty of birds, an abundance of colorful poison dart frogs, and various other interesting creatures. **Playa Larga,** the long beach in the park, is an important nesting area for several species of sea turtles, which arrive here at night from March to September to bury their eggs in the sand. Unfortunately, this beach is almost impossible to visit at night, which makes Playa Bluff, on Isla Colón, the best option for turtle-watching.

An easy place to visit is the little village of **Bastimentos,** also called "Old Bank," on the southwestern end of the island. It's a funky little town, with hundreds of small houses packed together on a hillside overlooking a quiet bay and friendly, Guari-Guari–speaking residents. Among other things, Bastimentos is the home of an authentic little calypso band with a not-too-original name: the Beach Boys of Bastimentos (there is actually another calypso band in Bocas, also called the Beach Boys, which is considerably better but performs much-less regularly). When the Beach Boys aren't blasting their music over the bay, Bastimentos is a tranquil, unspoiled spot, with a few small hotels that provide interesting alternatives to staying in the Bocas. Small boats regularly carry people between the towns of Bocas and Bastimentos, leaving Bocas from the dock next to the Commercial Chow Ku store and Bastimentos from the fruit company dock. The ride costs $2 each way.

Bastimentos's greatest attraction is probably the golden beach on the northern side of the island, a 30-minute hike from town on a dirt path. Known locally as the **First Beach,** that lovely strand backed by thick vegetation is a surf spot when the ocean's rough, and has decent snorkeling around the point to the left when the ocean is calm. It is just one of several sparkling beaches that line the island's northern shore, all but one of which lie outside the national park. If you take a day, and carry lots of water, you can follow that coast east to those deserted beaches. It takes almost four hours to walk to Playa Larga, which marks the beginning of the national park.

The northern coast of Bastimentos Island also has one of the best dive spots in the region: **Olas Chicas,** also known as Polo's Beach, after Polo, the friendly hermit who lives here. Boat operators in Bastimentos and Bocas offer snorkeling trips to Olas Chicas, which can even include a lunch of fresh fish prepared by Polo.

LODGING

$ 🏠 **El Pelicano.** On a tiny beach at the eastern end of town, this place consists of a couple of bungalows perched on the hillside, each of which has three rooms, and a spacious bar and restaurant built out over the water under a high, thatched roof. The beach is hardly big enough to be called that, but a short swim from shore is a small reef that offers decent snorkeling, and the owners can arrange boat trips to more distant dive spots. The restaurant serves everything from pizza to rice and beans, but it's a popular night spot, which makes this place pretty noisy Friday through Monday. ⊠ *Bastimentos,* ☎ *507/757–9008. 6 rooms with bath. Restaurant, bar, snorkeling. No credit cards.*

$ 🏠 **Pensión Bastimentos.** Housed in a wooden building over the water,
★ this small, German-owned inn has the nicest accommodations in Bastimentos, which doesn't say much. Rooms are simple but comfortable—only one has a private bath—and the deck out back has a lovely view out over the bay. Delicious meals are served on the deck. The owners

offer a variety of snorkeling and hiking trips. ✉ *Bastimentos,* ☎ *no phone. 4 rooms, 1 with bath. Restaurant. No credit cards.*

Bocas del Toro Archipelago A to Z

ARRIVING AND DEPARTING

By Boat. The most common means of transport is by water taxi between Almirante, Bocas del Toro, and Chiriquí Grande. Water taxis make the 20-minute trip between Almirante and Bocas del Toro approximately every hour from 6 AM to 6 PM. There are three companies, about 100 yards apart in Almirante, and boats leave once they fill up, so it is worthwhile to check them all and sign up at the one that has more people waiting. In Bocas, taxis leave from a cement dock near the police station on Calle 1, from the dock next to Le Pirate Restaurant and from another dock a couple blocks farther south.

There are also regular daily water taxis between Almirante and Chiriquí Grande, which stop in Bocas if three or more people want to get on or off there. Otherwise you have to take an additional taxi to and from Almirante. They are run by the same three companies that provide service between Almirante and Bocas, and the schedule varies according to demand (check ahead). A **car ferry** runs between Almirante and Bocas every Wednesday, Friday, and Sunday, but it is much slower than a water taxi, and putting a car on it is expensive.

By Bus. There's a daily, direct bus from San José, Costa Rica (☎ 506/556–1432), to Changuinola, Panama, departing at 10 AM (7-hr trip) from Calle 14 between Avenidas 5 and 7, returning from Changuinola at 10 AM. Buses depart Changuinola for the port of Almirante every 20 minutes; from here water taxis (☞ By Boat, *above*) run hourly to Bocas del Toro. Several daily buses (☎ 506/257–8129) also travel between San José and the border town of Sixaola. These buses depart San José from the Terminal Caribe (C. Central at Avda. 15) at 6 AM, 10 AM, 1:30 PM, and 3:30 PM; they pick up passengers in Cahuita 3½ hours later, and at the entrance to Puerto Viejo 20 minutes after that, and arrive at Sixaola six hours after departing San José. Buses leave Sixaola for San José at 5, 7:30, and 9:30 AM and 2:30 PM. There are also six buses a day between Puerto Limón and Sixaola, all of which stop at Cahuita and Puerto Viejo di Limón. From Sixaola, you hike across the railroad bridge into the Panamanian town of Guabito, where you can catch a bus or taxi to nearby Changuinola. The quickest way to get from Sixaola to Almirante is in a shared taxi, which should cost $5 per person.

By Plane. The Panamanian airline **Aeroperlas** (☎ 507/757–9341, 506/440–0093 in San José) has weekday flights from San José to both David and Bocas. Daily flights run between Bocas and Panama City.

GETTING AROUND

By Bike. Several places in town rent bicycles—Hotel Las Brisas, Hotel Laguna, and La Ballena Restaurant (☞ Dining and Lodging *in* Isla Colón, *above*)—a good way to reach the island's beaches.

By Boat. This is the main mode of transportation in this area. Individually chartered, motorized dugouts are the usual means of interisland travel, although there's at least one sailboat for charter in town. Boats to Bastimentos leave fairly regularly from the dock next to the Commercial Chow Ku store and charge $2 per person.

By Bus. A small bus makes the trip across Isla Colón every Monday, Wednesday, and Friday, leaving Boca del Drago at 7 AM and Bocas del Toro at 1 PM. It also sometimes makes the trip on weekends.

By Car. You won't see much in the way of auto traffic here, although there are a few cabs cruising around town. You can hire a cab to drive you from Bocas to Boca del Drago for about $25 or to take you to the closer Playa Bluff for about $5. It's possible to rent a car in Changuinola and bring it over on the car ferry, but it isn't recommended, because most spots can only be reached by boat.

CONTACTS AND RESOURCES

Bank. A branch of the **Banco Nacional de Panama** is across the street from the government office buildings by Parque Simón Bolívar in Bocas; they'll cash traveler's checks but can't give credit card advances. The currency is the American dollar, also called the balboa.

Emergencies. Fire (Corner of C. 1 and Avda. Norte, ☎ 103). **Hospitals** (Bocas ☎ 507/757–9201; Changuinola ☎ 507/758–8295; Panama City ☎ 507/263–6060). **Police** (C. 3, next to ferry-arrival dock, ☎ 104).

Guided Tours. Three dive shops and several local fishermen offer one-day excursions to the Cayos Zapatillas, Hospital Point, Olas Chicas, and other popular snorkeling spots. Day trips can be arranged through the Hotel Las Brisas or La Ballena Restaurant on Isla Colón (☞ *above*).

Temptress Adventure Cruises (351 N.W. LeJeune Rd., Penthouse 6, Miami, FL 33126, ☎ 305/643–4040, FAX 305/643–6438) sails seven-day adventure cruises that stop in Hollandaise Cayes, Portobelo, Panama Canal, Darién, and Islas Perlas; activities include national park hikes, sea-kayaking, indigenous village visits, bird-watching, and snorkeling. **Turtle Divers** (☎ FAX 507/757–9594) offers boat trips to Isla de Pajaros, Boca del Drago, a Teribe Indian village in the rain forest, and a Guaymí Indian village. **Transparente Tours** (☎ FAX 507/757–9172 or 507/757–9600) specializes in snorkeling excursions to all the local dive spots. **Starfleet Eco-Adventures** (☎ FAX 507/757–9630) features diving and snorkeling excursions on a private catamaran, as well as hiking on Isla Bastimentos. **Bocas Water Sports** (☎ 507/757–9541) offers a variety of dive trips and a day trip to their Red Frog camp on Isla Bastimentos.

Telephones. Information (☎ 507/757–9257). **International operator** (☎ 106). There are public telephones in Bocas' Parque Simón Bolívar, Hotel Bahía, and near the fire department on Calle 1.

Visitor Information. The **Immigration Office** is in the back of the Government House overlooking Parque Simón Bolívar. The **Panamanian Tourist Board (IPAT)** is a few doors down Calle 3 from the old ferry dock. **Bocas del Toro** also has a web site (www.bocas.com), which is regularly updated. For information about Parque Nacional Marina Isla Bastimentos, you can stop by **INRENARE** (✉ C. 1, ☎ 507/757–9244).

NICARAGUA

After decades of war, revolution, and political and economic struggle, Nicaragua appears at last to have achieved enough stability to merit consideration as a travel destination for pleasure and enlightenment (as opposed to the political causes that drew many idealistic Americans down here in the 1980s). For better or worse, democratic capitalism had taken hold, and both foreign investors and exiled Nicaraguans of all political persuasions are buying or reclaiming property all over the country. You will not find riots, hooligans toting machine guns, or gangs of thieves. You will find a poor but friendly country, where tourists are still rare enough to create curiosity and where few are wealthy enough to own automobiles. Roads are therefore pleasantly uncrowded, or crowded with bicycles, oxcarts, and horses rather than cars. The tourist industry, though lacking in infrastructure—and at press time grappling with the devastating effects of Hurricane Mitch on much of the country—is getting off the ground. If you have an adventurous spirit and open mind, slip across the border into Southwestern Nicaragua to discover the pristine beauty of the beach towns of Lago de Nicaragua and the dusty colonial city of Granada.

Pleasures and Pastimes

Beaches
A few miles from the Costa Rican border, San Juan del Sur is a pretty, slightly run-down beach town tucked into a perfect little bay with high headlands providing shelter to the north and south. From here, enterprising visitors can book boat or four-wheel-drive-vehicle trips to dozens of magnificent deserted beaches for great surfing, fishing, diving, turtle-watching, and sunbathing spots.

Dining
Nicaraguan food bears comparison with Costa Rican, although the tourist influx has transformed dining in Costa Rica into a more internationally rounded experience. Like Ticos, Nicaraguans favor rice and beans with meats, fish, or chicken; salads are usually made of cabbage with tomatoes and a vinaigrette-style dressing; and rice and beans usually reappear as *gallo pinto* (a mixture rice and beans) at breakfast the next day. A favorite dish that may not strike you as very appealing is *mondongo,* tripe (beef stomach) cooked with beef knuckles. Near the coast, fresh fish is abundant and relatively cheap. Fresh fruit and fruit juices are plentiful and low priced.

Lodging
The number of upscale hotels is limited to a few in the larger cities and a couple of beachfront resorts, none of which can be found in the southwestern region. A reasonable selection of medium-priced hotels and *hospedajes,* the Nicaraguan version of cabinas, can be found in the cities and small towns.

National Parks and Volcanoes
Nicaragua's southwest offers one major national park, Parque Nacional Volcán Masaya, with its own active volcano, an enormous visitor-center complex, and several hiking trails. Other area volcanoes, including Mombacha and the two on Madera, Concepción and Madera, offer prime hiking opportunities, although they have not yet achieved national park status.

Shopping
Great buys can be had all over Nicaragua, but the best shopping town is Masaya, where the scruffy, lively old market competes with a more sterile but easier-to-navigate new one. In both places, look for shoes, leather goods, pottery, and paintings—the country is full of artists making lively, colorful paintings in the style first developed in the Solentiname archipelago in Lago de Nicaragua (Lake Nicaragua), where Father Ernesto Cardenal, later the Minister of Culture in the Sandinista government, founded a commune and trained farmers and laborers to make crafts.

Exploring Nicaragua

The most populous region of Nicaragua, the Pacific lowlands territory in southwestern Nicaragua looks much like the dry country of northern Guanacaste, with rolling agricultural plains and relatively sparse vegetation. The road north from the Costa Rican border follows an unhindered, fairly straight, and level route to Managua, and there is relatively little traffic, since few can afford cars. Public transportation is easily accessed and very cheap; buses ranging from diesel-belching antique American school buses to sleek minivans connect most of the towns and cities. You can bring a privately owned car or take a bus across the border; driving a rental car across the border is not permitted, so it's best to rent a car in Managua. The primary roads are in good shape—better than Costa Rica's in many ways.

Numbers in the text correspond to numbers in the margin and on the Southwestern Nicaragua map.

Great Itineraries

This small slice of Nicaragua can be explored in four or five days—depending on how you get into the country and your in-country modes of transportation—though you could comfortably spend several weeks exploring the volcanoes, colonial towns, surf, and sun.

IF YOU HAVE 4 OR 5 DAYS

This itinerary is appropriate if you're crossing the border by private car or bus rather than flying into Managua and heading south; if flying into Managua, reverse the itinerary. Get an early morning start and negotiate the border at Peñas Blancas (Costa Rica) and Sapoa (Nicaragua) and grab a bus or taxi and head for ⛴ **San Juan del Sur** ⑧. Spend a day and a half exploring the beaches in the area, with an overnight in one of the local hotels. From here head to Rivas and take the ferry from nearby San Jorge to ⛴ **Isla Ometepe** ⑩. Tour the island and check out balmy Playa Santa Domingo. Spend a night and get an early start on an all-day hike to one of the island's two volcanic craters. Catch a late ferry, or an early one the next day, and bus up to ⛴ **Granada** ⑪, about an hour away. Spend one or two nights at the wonderful old Hotel Alhambra, with a day in Granada devoted to soaking up the colonial ambience, touring the historic buildings, and boat-cruising Las Isletas. This leaves time for a morning shopping session in ⛴ **Masaya** ⑬ and an afternoon at **Parque Nacional Volcán Masaya** ⑭. A trip up to **Catarina** ⑫ to have lunch at the spectacular mirador makes a perfect close to an intoxicating five-day trip. From here, the border is about two hours away.

When to Tour Nicaragua

The region shares the climate of northwestern Costa Rica, and so it is intensely hot at lower elevations in the dry season from late November to April. The rainiest month is usually October. It is always cooler higher up in the mountains near the volcanoes. With tourism still in its infant state in all of Nicaragua, there's no reason to avoid the height of the dry season, although the limited number of rooms at the beach might cause some crowding around the Christmas and Easter holidays.

Southwestern Nicaragua

Nicaragua's southwest, just north of Costa Rica's Guanacaste province, offers genuinely warm people, a wealth of natural beauty, dependable road and boat access to many major destinations, and one town—Granada, just north of the Lake Nicaragua—with more historic and architectural richness than all of Costa Rica put together. The oldest city in the Americas, Granada is a quiet, colorful jewel of a town and so serves as a wonderful base for exploring Nicaragua's southwest. This relatively untouristed region offers a quieter, less-expensive alternative—or accompaniment—to the pleasures of Guanacaste (☞ Chapter 4).

San Juan del Sur

 San Juan del Sur and its pretty half-moon beach are tucked in between two high headlands, offering shelter for a sweet but ramshackle little town, a small fishing fleet, and the odd pleasure craft. In the past few

Southwestern Nicaragua

years a minor influx of European backpackers has inspired the beginnings of a tourist infrastructure, centered on Marie's Bar, across the street from the beach. The beachfront boulevard is lined with open-air seafood restaurants, with a couple of small hotels across the street. This is the place to make plans for all area activities, from surfing to sportsfishing. Dozens of pristine beaches lie within a half hour by car or boat. Think of Costa Rica 20 years ago, on the brink of discovery.

DINING AND LODGING

\$\$–\$\$\$ ✕ **Marie's Bar.** This is the place to go for any and all info, tours, contacts, and gossip. Also, owners Marie and Richard and their pals from Germany and Austria serve scrumptious European-style breakfasts, great coffee, and fine fish and pasta dinners. The bar is dark and drowned in rock-and-roll at night, when you're sure to meet some interesting vagabonds or at least eccentric drunks; by day, it feels more open, with a view across the street to the sea. You'll find Marie's Bar across the street from the beach, just north of the burned-out, rambling old structure that used to be a grand railroad terminal; some day soon it will probably be transformed into a beautiful little hotel. ⊠ *Waterfront road, one block north of the bus stop,* ☎ *505/045–82555. MC, V.*

\$–\$\$\$ 🏨 **Casablanca Hotel.** We recommend the upstairs suite, overlooking the sea across the street, in this San Juan del Sur hotel. The other rooms are small but comfy and air-conditioned. It's pricey for Nicaragua, but a fine location. ⊠ *San Juan del Sur,* ☎ 🖷 *505/045–82135. 7 rooms with bath. Restaurant. AE, MC, V.*

\$–\$\$ 🏨 **Casa International Joxi.** A block off the beach, the Joxi offers eight rooms on two levels and an upstairs lounging area with hammocks and a TV. It is very small, basic, and somewhat dark, but it's clean and comfortable. Half the rooms have private baths, the other half bunk beds and shared baths. Downstairs, the three-meal restaurant is good and cheap. ⊠ *Block from beach on main street, perpendicular to the wa-*

terfront, ☎ FAX *505/045–82348. 8 rooms, 4 with bath. Restaurant, windsurfing. AE, MC, V.*

Lago de Nicaragua

❾ Lago de Nicaragua (Lake Nicaragua), one of the world's larger freshwater lakes, laps on Granada's northern shores and stretches almost to Costa Rica in the south. Once upon a time, bull sharks swam up the San Juan River from the Caribbean to live part time in the lake, although they're rarely, if ever, seen these days. A ferry from the port of San Jorge, about halfway down the lake just east of the town of Rivas, delivers people, animals, and goods to Moyogalpa on magical Ometepe, a figure-eight-shaped island in the lake with a volcano rising out of each roughly circular half.

Isla Ometepe

❿ With about 35,000 residents and 300 cars, **Isla Ometepe** is a quiet, pastoral place, worth visiting for a couple of reasons: to ascend through virgin rain forest to the tops of volcanoes Concepción and Madera; to kick back and relax at the beach of Santa Domingo; or to explore archaeological sites where ancient petroglyphs have been discovered. The ferries are small and usually crowded, and Ometepe's roads are marginally passable. With taxis and tours available at the ferry dock, we recommend leaving the car behind. There's a secure parking garage at San Jorge.

On the northern, or Concepcíon, half of the island, the two main towns are **Moyogalpa,** on the west side, and **Altagracia,** on the northeastern side. Contrary to what maps indicate, the coastal road encircling this upper half of the island no longer goes all the way around: a lava flow took out a section several years ago, and it has not been repaired. But it is relatively easy to get around regardless. Heading south and then east on the dirt road from Moyogalpa, you soon reach the turnoff for **Playa Santa Domingo,** the island's longest beach. From Playa Santa Domingo, Altagracia is just a few minutes' drive north—a drive worth taking for the petroglyphs alongside the road by Altagracia's town square. Another area with dozens of petroglyphs still in place can be found near **Balque,** the main town on the southern half of the island, dominated by Volcan Madera. Come see the volcanoes, beach, green lagoon where crocodiles live, and the little towns on this southern half of the island. The rest is pleasant country sightseeing, walking, biking, or bouncing along the bad roads with the locals.

LODGING

$–$$ 🏨 **Cari Hotel y Marina.** You can see the Cari from the ferry as you dock in Moyogalpa. Like all the hotels and hospedajes on the island, it offers small, clean rooms, some with private baths, at rock-bottom prices. The hotel rents bikes, boats, cars, and canoes and offers island tours. Or hang out in the open-air restaurant-bar and watch the island women doing their laundry on the washing platforms in the lake in front of the hotel. *Moyogalpa,* ☎ *505/045–94263. 25 rooms with bath. Restaurant, boating, bicycles. MC, V.*

$ 🏨 **Castillo Hotel.** Señor Castillo serves as tour guide emeritus, unofficial historian, and general source of all relevant info for Ometepe. His one-story hotel circling around a quiet central courtyard has clean, comfy little rooms, some with private baths, within walking distance of Altagracia's petroglyph collection. ✉ *1 block south and half a block east of Parque Central, Altagracia,* ☎ *505/055–26045. 13 rooms, 7 with bath. Restaurant. MC, V.*

$ 🏨 **Hotel Finca Santo Domingo.** This is one of two similarly priced and situated hotels on pretty, placid Playa Santo Domingo (also ☞ Villa Paraiso, *below*). The Finca Santo Domingo features a shady, open-air restaurant with an easterly view across the lake and 17 simply furnished, comfortable rooms in freestanding cabinas. Nine have private baths and the rest share them. The restaurant specializes in seafood. Try the *guapote,* or bass, caught fresh in the lake each day. ⊠ *Playa Santa Domingo, Isla de Ometepe,* ☎ *505/525–56059,* ☎ FAX *505/045– 34675. 17 rooms, 9 with bath. Restaurant, horseback riding, boating, bicycles. MC, V.*

$ ⊞ **Villa Paraiso** Like the Santo Domingo (☞ *above*), the Paraiso faces east across Lake Nicaragua from Playa Santo Domingo and offers basic, comfortable accommodations, in this case six rooms in the main building and 11 cabinas with private baths. The hotel's shady bar and restaurant overlooks the lake. They will organize volcano, petroglyph, and other island tours. *Playa Santo Domingo,* ☎ *505/244–0181,* FAX *505/045–34675. 17 cabinas, 11 with bath. Restaurant, bar, horseback riding, boating. AE, MC, V.*

OUTDOOR ACTIVITIES AND SPORTS

Hiking. Aside from visiting these pastoral little towns and beaches, the main activity on Ometepe is hiking the two volcanoes. The trail to the top of Concepción starts near Altagracia and takes about five hours each way. Another trail of similar length and difficulty begins near Moyogalpa. The trail up Madera Volcano—start at Balque—takes roughly four hours each way. For both volcano hikes the use of a guide is highly recommended, as the trails are arduous and not always easy to follow. Wildlife—monkeys, birds, and sloths—abounds, and views are remarkable from both peaks. All the hotels will arrange guides; otherwise, ask around at the dock, or contact **Ometepe Tours** (☎ 505/045–34779, 505/045–94116).

Granada

Founded in 1524, prosperous for centuries, and ravaged by the gringo maniac William Walker in the mid-19th century, **Granada** (about 102 km/63 mi north of Costa Rica border) has survived, and even prospered, through Nicaragua's troubled history. In the 1990s, the entire city was declared a museum, meaning that no tall buildings will ever be erected in or near the colonial-era downtown. Additionally, every building renovation must follow strict design guidelines intended to maintain the integrity of the existing colonial architecture. Though Nicaragua is impoverished, efforts are under way to restore Granada's finest public buildings. Today, Nicaraguans and investors from Europe, the United States, Costa Rica, and elsewhere have been buying up the city's stock of elegant 18th- and 19th-century homes, renovating them, and transforming them into restaurants, hotels, and bed-and-breakfasts, or fixing them up to live in or sell. There's a quiet little boom going on.

Surrounded by blocks of low-rise, pastel-hued colonial buildings, the city holds many charms, beginning with the **Parque Central,** or central plaza, surrounded by the **Palacio Episcopal, Palacio Municipal, Palacio de la Cultura**, and the wonderful old **Hotel Alhambra** (☞ Dining and Lodging, *below*), *the* place to stay in Granada.

The plaza is dominated, however, by the **cathedral** on its eastern side. Walker burned the original cathedral down in 1857. The rebuilding of the present structure was completed in 1910. It's a rather imposing example of neoclassical architecture, worth a visit to explore the vivid, slightly tacky examples of religious art within. *Parque Central.* ☉ *Daily 8–6.*

Two blocks east, beyond the **Plaza de los Leones,** the **Iglesia San Francisco,** dating from the 1520s, has a Baroque facade with a system of pediments and symmetrical oval windows. Next door, the old convent serves as a **museum**, with a collection of stunning carved stone artifacts dating from around AD 800 and gathered on the Ometepe and Zapatera islands in Lake Nicaragua. ⊠ *C. Arsenal and Avda. Miguel Cervantes, two blocks east of the cathedral.* ☉ *Daily 9–6.*

Stroll or take one of the ubiquitous, low-cost horse-carriage cabs (the painfully thin horses are a sorry sight, but it is a parasite and not starvation that gives them that bony look, according to local sources) down Calle la Calzada to the lakeshore, and head south to the **Centro Turístico,** a long, shady waterfront park lined with discos, restaurants, and other diversions. From here its a few miles farther south to **Puerto de Aseses,** where you can book a boat tour and while away an afternoon cruising through Granada's famed Las Isletas, the 360-odd tiny, plant-bedecked islands that lie offshore. Most are privately owned, but others protect bird reserves or feature small hotels or restaurants.

DINING AND LODGING

$–$$ ✕ **Las Colinas Sur.** The out-of-the-way location, dirt floor, and fluorescent lighting aside, Las Colinas is a find: great seafood, great prices. Wooden tables with oilcloth covers, rickety chairs, and seedy commercial signage—the usual soft drink and beer suspects—enliven the atmosphere, as does the friendly, noisy, and very efficient band of waiters and the gregarious extended families occupying many tables. The cooks have figured out a way to debone a fish and yet serve it whole, deep-fried but somehow not greasy. You can't help but wonder why the restaurant has a parking guard, but his presence is reassuring in the darkness of the neighborhood. It is only a five-minute walk (or quick taxi ride) from downtown and well worth it. *Puente Palmira, 3 C. al Lago (Sabaneta),* ☎ *505/552–3492. AE, MC, V.*

$–$$ ✕ **Mediterraneo.** Hostess-owner Enriqueta, unfailingly gracious and ★ a well-informed conversationalist, hails from Spain, Canada, Morocco, New York, and elsewhere. Her command of seven languages and worldliness shine through on the Spanish menu infused with international accents. The paellas are exceptional. The elegantly furnished, rosy terra-cotta-tone dining room flanks a lovely interior garden. A wonderfully romantic atmosphere pervades, with candlelight, plants, and quietly flowing interior fountains. This is undoubtedly the finest restaurant in Granada. ⊠ *C. El Caimito,* ☎ *505/552–6764. AE, MC, V.*

$–$$ ▥ **Hotel Alhambra.** A two-story jewel on Granada's shady Parque ★ Central, the Alhambra is slightly run-down but still highly recommended as the essential Granada spot. The columned, colonnaded, comfortably furnished lobby wraps around an interior courtyard garden with a pleasantly murmuring fountain. The rooms are filled with a hodge-podge of low-cost modern desks, lamps, and the like, matched with old carved-wooden cabinets, double beds, and atmospheric pieces. The rooms—all air-conditioned and some with hot water some of the time—vary: the second-story rooms overlooking the plaza are simply wonderful, except for the very noisy cathedral bells, which ring at the strangest times; those overlooking the pool in back are smaller but quieter. ⊠ *West of Parque Central,* ☎ *505/552–4486,* FAX *505/552–2035. 60 rooms with bath. Restaurant, café, air-conditioning, pool, laundry service, meeting rooms. AE, MC, V.*

$ ▥ **Posada Don Alfredo.** The German-run Posada, two blocks off the Parque Central, offers huge, high-ceilinged rooms with multiple beds at great prices in an exquisitely restored 165-year-old colonial building. The dining and lounging areas are invitingly comfy, and the owner serves generous breakfasts (extra). This is an appealing, lower-cost alternative to the Alhambra (☞ *above*). ⊠ *C. 14 de Septiembre,* ☎ *505/552–4455,* FAX *505/552–4455. 8 rooms without bath. Dining room, bicycles. No credit cards.*

Catarina

⑫ Watch for the turn-off to **Catarina**, 16 km (10 mi) along the road from Granada to Masaya. It takes you up to a spectacular mirador, or lookout, in the colorful little town of Catarina, overflowing with lushly attractive plant stores. On the back side of town, past the cathedral, a cluster of gaudy souvenir stands—one sells well-made paintings by the young artist manning the stand—and a row of restaurants line the edge of a cliff overlooking the crater lake called Laguna de Apoyo. The restaurants are pricey by Nicaraguan standards, but well worth the view of Laguna de Apoyo, Masaya, Granada, and Lake Nicaragua as well, stretching into the distance. A different road off the main highway—at Kilometer 38—leads to **Laguna de Apoyo** itself, where the swimming is safe and pleasant. Just across the road from Catarina lies the entrance to the village of **Niquinohomo,** birthplace of fabled Nicaraguan revolutionary Augusto Sandino.

Masaya

⑬ Twenty minutes (about 24 km/15 mi) northwest of Granada by car, the city of **Masaya** offers great shopping, pleasant strolling, and not much else. Thus a half-day trip from Granada should suffice, time-wise, to check out the two markets for hammocks, leather goods, weavings, pottery, paintings, and other crafts, and to wander the town. The original crafts market can be found within the labyrinthine confines of the main city market, five blocks east of the main plaza, known as the **Parque 17 de Octobre.** A spanking-new arts-and-crafts complex, **Nuevo Mercado,** is closer to the center of town. Remember to bring dollars or cordobas, the Nicaraguan currency, and leave your Costa Rican colones behind.

Parque Nacional Volcán Masaya

⑭ Five kilometers (3 mi) farther north along the main highway from Granada heading toward Managua is the turn-off to **Parque Nacional Volcán Masaya** (Masaya Volcano National Park; also ☞ Chapter 10). First, stop at the expansive **visitor center and museum** for an overview of regional cultural and geological history. There's a lot of fascinating information here, but, unfortunately, most material is in Spanish. Ascending into volcanic terrain, from the parking lot it's just a few feet to the edge of the smoldering **Santiago Crater,** one of four that compose the Masaya volcano. The viewpoint from which you can actually see the fire below has been closed, but the steaming, sulphurous crater is still an awesome sight. Hike up the long staircase to the overlook, where a cross—a replica of one put up in the 16th century—keeps the devil in his hole. That, at least, was the thinking of the Spanish Catholics who put up the first one, for they called this place Boca del Inferno—the "Mouth of Hell." ⊠ *Carretera Masaya–Managua, Km 23, Apdo. NI-1, Nindiri,* ☎ *505/0522–5415.* ☒ *$4.* ☉ *Daily 9–5*

Southwestern Nicaragua A to Z

ARRIVING AND DEPARTING

Getting to Nicaragua is slightly complicated by the fact that you can not take rental cars across the border from Costa Rica, but there are other means: planes, private cars, buses, boats, and taxis can all get you there.

By Car. Rental cars can not cross the border at present. You can pick up a rental cars in Managua and Granada.

By Bus. You can book a bus in San José; the **Tica** (Avda. 4 at Cs. 9 and 11, ☎ 506/221–8954 or 506/221–9229 in San José) bus line offers San José–Managua trips, and you can catch the buses in front of the Hotel Guanacaste in Liberia, providing you've either reserved a seat in advance or there's room. Ask the driver to drop you off in Rivas or Granada once across the border. The price is around $20 round-trip.

By Plane. Grupo Taca (☎ 506/296–0909 in San José) offers two flights a day from San José to Managua and back. The cost is about $200 per person plus a $20 exit tax at each end. The flights leave San José at 6:30 AM and 2 PM.

GETTING AROUND

By Boat. Ferries to Ometepe's Moyogalpa run from San Jorge, near Rivas, six days. Boats from Granada and San Jorge run three times a week. Weekend hydrofoil service operates from Granada. For ferry information call ☎ 505/055–22966.

By Bus. There are plentiful buses, ranging from low-cost locals—usually recycled American schoolbuses—to pricier air-conditioned expresses.

By Car. The numerous car rental agencies in the Managua airport and in Managua city offer a good selection of cars at rates from $25 a day and up (☞ Car Rentals, *below*), much cheaper than in Costa Rica. Getting around the country is easy. Most of the main roads in Nicaragua are in good shape, so four-wheel-drive vehicles are not necessary.

CONTACTS AND RESOURCES

Car Rentals. The following companies are among the many that offer cars at Managua's Sandino International Airport: **Budget** (☎ 505/266–6226, FAX 505/222–5567). **Hertz** (☎ 505/233–1237, FAX 505/233–1862). **Lugo** (☎ 505/263–2368, FAX 505/266–4477).

Embassies. Canada (✉ Apdo. 25, Managua, ☎ 505/268–0433). **U.K.** (✉ Plaza Churchill Reparto Los Robles, Apdo. A-169, Managua, ☎ 505/278–0014). **U.S.** (✉ Carretera Sur, km 4½, Managua, ☎ 505/266–6010).

Emergencies. Ambulance (Granada ☎ 505/055–2711; Masaya ☎ 505/052–2556). **Hospitals** (Granada, San Juan de Dios, ☎ 505/055–2719; Isla Ometepe, Moyagalpa, Del Parque, 3 C. al Sur, ☎ 505/045–94247). **Police** (Granada ☎ 505/055–2929; Masaya ☎ 505/052–2521).

Guided Tours. For those who prefer to have their arrangements made for them, **Careli Tours** (☎ 505/278–2573) and **Tours Nicaragua** (☎ 505/266–8689) both offer complete packages, with a car and bilingual driver-guide. **Ometepe Tours** (☎ 505/045–34779, 505/045–94116), near the dock in San Jorge, will set up an Ometepe island tour, with a car and driver there to greet you at the Moyogalpa end of the one-hour ferry ride. The operators will also handle any reservations you want to make on the island. Stop in and see the jaws on the office walls. They come from sharks caught in the lake. Check out the bulletin board at **Marie's Bar** (☎ 505/045–82555; ☞ *above*) in San Juan del Sur for names and numbers of every area tour operator, from sailing boats such as *Pelican Eyes* (☎ 505/458–2110) to express buses to Managua (☎ 505/453–3783).

Travel Agencies. ☞ **Careli Tours** and **Tours Nicaragua**, *above*.

Visitor Information. Granada (Next door to Hotel Alhambra; Iglesia San Francisco, C. Arsenal and Avda. Miguel Cervantes, ☎ 505/0552–6858). **Isla Ometepe** (contact Ometepe Tours, San Jorge, near dock, ☎ 505/045–34779; Moyogalpa, ☎ 505/045–94116). **Masaya** (On highway north of town, ☎ 505/052–2936).

10 NATIONAL PARKS AND BIOLOGICAL RESERVES

A selective primer to the best of Costa Rican, Panamanian, and Nicaraguan protected areas—where to find the wildlife, the spectacular flora, and the reef and volcanoes.

By David
Dudenhoefer
and Justin
Henderson

COSTA RICA AND PANAMA POSSESS an almost unfathomable wealth of natural assets. The breathtaking scenery of the two countries, for example, encompasses barren mountain peaks, lush forests, and vibrant, multihued coral reefs. Equally fantastic is the native wildlife population, more species of plants and animals than scientists have been able to count.

Moreover, the governments of both nations have had the foresight to protect a significant portion of that ecological wealth within national parks and biological preserves. There are also wildlife refuges, forest reserves, and Indian reservations where the flora and fauna benefit from some degree of protection. This conservation effort is particularly remarkable when you consider that Costa Rica and Panama are relatively poor countries with limited resources. Just three decades ago, there was hardly a protected area in either nation. Today Costa Rica's parks cover about 13% of the national territory, and Panama's national parks and reserves cover 17% of their national territory, although the Panamanian areas tend to be less protected than those in Costa Rica.

Let's hope the wheels in motion in Nicaragua prove as successful: with decades of political upheaval only recently ended, Nicaragua has had little energy or money to develop a national park system. Presently, the country's only officially designated national park is Parque Nacional Volcán Masaya (☞ *below*), established in 1979. Several other areas in the country have attained unofficial park or reserve status and will probably eventually be designated national parks.

During the first decades of Costa Rica's and Panama's park systems, conservationists raced against rampant deforestation to protect as much of the country's vital wildlands as possible. Parks were created and maps were drawn, but protecting the flora and fauna within them turned out to be a daunting task for the underfunded government agencies responsible for conservation. Thanks to the foresight of local conservationists, and ample assistance from abroad, these parks and reserves now contain examples of nearly all the ecosystems that exist in the region: mangrove estuaries, lowland rain forests, tropical dry forests, pristine beaches, coral reefs, cloud forests, caves, freshwater swamps and lagoons, active volcanic craters, transition forests, and various marine ecosystems.

The Costa Rican Ministry of the Environment and Energy (MINAE) and the Panamanian Institute of Renewable Natural Resources (INRENARE) are now concentrating on consolidating management of the parks and improving their infrastructure. Though the tropical flora and fauna they preserve is nothing short of spectacular, Panamanian and Costa Rican national parks have set in place very little infrastructure compared with protected areas in northern nations. Many of the parks require four-wheel-drive vehicles to reach them; only a few have paved roads; and some can only be visited by boat, on horseback, or on foot. Most parks still don't have visitor centers, and trails aren't always well marked.

Costa Rica is facing a new conservation challenge—controlling the crowds that flock to its most famous protected areas. Some Costa Rican parks receive so many visitors during the high season that it can be worth your while to head to less popular protected areas, where you'll be treated to a more private and natural experience. In addition to the national parks, a growing number of private nature reserves are open to the public, many of which have their own lodges. Nearly all tour companies offer trips to the national parks and reserves, although certain ones have more experience in ecological tourism.

Responsible Tourism

In Costa Rica and Panama, economic pressures still cause people to cut down trees and hunt endangered animals. Citizens of these countries are slowly coming to realize that conservation pays, and when you visit a park or reserve, you are sending a positive message to both that government and the marketplace. But your contribution to the protection of the wilderness that you visit can go well beyond the payment of entrance fees. Whether you travel on your own or with a tour group, make sure your visit benefits the people who live near the wilderness areas: use local guides or services, visit local restaurants, and buy local crafts or fruits. To ensure that these areas will be preserved for future generations, you can also make donations to local conservation groups. A few foreign environmental organizations, including Conservation International, the Nature Conservancy, and the World Wide Fund for Nature, are also aiding ecological efforts in Costa Rica and Panama.

Viewing Wildlife

Although the protected areas contain some spectacular scenery and wildlife, including such endangered species as jaguars, tapirs, and giant anteaters, don't be disappointed if you don't come face to face with one of these animals. Despite their frequent appearances in advertisements and brochures, jaguars, for example, are practically impossible to see in the wild, given their scarcity, shyness, and nocturnal schedules. Don't give up hope, though: if you take the time to explore a few protected areas, you're almost certain to spy some monkeys, iguanas, sloths, parrots, toucans, and dozens of other interesting critters.

Travelers are often surprised by how difficult it can be to spot animals in the rain forest. The low density of mammals, combined with the fact that thick vegetation often obstructs your view, means that you have to be patient and attentive to see things. River trips can provide some excellent animal observation, and because the tropical dry forest is less overgrown, it is one of the best life zones for animal observation.

Visitor Information and Admission Fees

In August 1994, Costa Rica's Environment Ministry raised the cost of entry for foreign visitors into all national parks, biological reserves, and national monuments from less than $2 to $15, a decision that infuriated many in the tourism industry. The country's environment minister claimed the high fee increase was needed to accomplish two important goals: raising the money to patrol the parks effectively and improve infrastructure and decreasing the traffic into some of the more heavily visited parks. Money was raised, and visitation decreased, but representatives from the country's tourism sector insisted the high fees were hurting that vital industry, and in 1996, the price of admission to national parks was reduced to $6 per day. The Panamanian government currently charges entrance fees ranging from $3 to $10.

For specific information on Costa Rican parks and protected areas, call the **Environment Ministry's national park information line** (☎ 192), which is attended by well-informed, bilingual operators who can quickly answer most questions. For more specific requests, such as reserving camping or cabin space, call the regional office of the conservation area in which the park in question is located. Practical information about visiting parks and limited printed material are available at the **Fundación de Parques Nacionales** (✉ 300 meters south and 300 meters east of Iglesia Sta. Teresita, San José, ☎ 506/257–2239).

In Panama, **INRENARE** is supposed to fax you written permission to visit a park provided you contact the main office in Panama City (☎

507/232–7228), but it is much easier to simply go to the park: rangers are always happy to help visitors, who are still pretty scarce.

For information on the Masaya Volcano national park and other refuges in Nicaragua, contact the **Dirección de Silvestres y Faunas** (✉ Km 12½, Carretera Norte, Apdo. 5123, Managua, ☎ 505/31112–31595, FAX 505/31112–31596).

CENTRAL VALLEY: AROUND SAN JOSÉ

Since the Central Valley was one of the first parts of Costa Rica to be settled and is now home to more than half of its burgeoning population, Mother Nature has had to retreat to the region's mountaintops and a few isolated river valleys. The parks have good access, with paved, albeit somewhat potholed, roads leading to all of them, and most are accessible for people who can't walk far. Because the floor and lower slopes of the Central Valley are covered with coffee plantations, cities, and towns, the region's parks are predominantly high-elevation, cloud-forest ecosystems—extremely luxuriant and often shrouded in thick mist (for additional information, ☞ Chapter 3).

Parque Nacional Volcán Irazú

Parque Nacional Volcán Irazú, or Irazú Volcano National Park, protects little more than the summit of Volcán Irazú (11,260 ft), Costa Rica's highest. The landscape at the top of the crater is bleak but beautiful, still scarred from the volcano's violent eruptions between 1962 and 1965, when several feet of ash covered the Central Valley. It's best to head up Irazú as early in the morning as possible, before the summit becomes enveloped in clouds, so you can catch a glimpse of its cream-of-asparagus-color crater lake and, if you're lucky, views of nearby mountains and of either the distant Pacific or Caribbean. There are no trails or visitor centers at the summit, but a paved road leads all the way to the top, through pastoral landscapes that resemble the Alps more than what you'd expect to see in Central America.

Tapantí National Wildlife Refuge

The Río Grande de Orosí flows through the middle of Tapantí National Wildlife Refuge (Refugio Nacional de Fauna Silvestre Tapantí), a protected cloud forest that covers the mountain slopes at the southern end of the Valle de Orosí. The emerald waters of that boulder-strewn river pour into some brisk but inviting swimming holes near the park's picnic area. There's a modest visitor center by the entrance, and 1½ km (1 mi) up the road is a parking area with trails that head into the woods on both sides of the street. The Sendero Oropéndola trail leads to two loops, one that passes the picnic and swimming areas and another that winds through the forest nearby. The trail across the road does a loop along a forested hillside, and La Pava trail, 2½ km (1½ mi) farther up on the right, leads down a steep hill to the riverbank. Several miles farther up the road from La Pava is a view of a long, slender cascade on the far side of the valley. Camping isn't permitted.

Monumento Nacional Guayabo

Although the ruins here don't compare with those of Guatemala and Mexico, Monumento Nacional Guayabo (Guayabo National Monument) is Costa Rica's most important archaeological site. Most of the original buildings were made of wood, so today only their bases remain. Rangers give guided tours (in Spanish) of the ruins, which include stone roads and a communal well fed by a pre-Columbian aqueduct. On your own, you can hike along a trail that loops through the surrounding rain forest, where you can do some bird-watching. Camping is permitted near the ranger station. Guayabo is closed to visitors on Monday.

NORTHERN GUANACASTE AND ALAJUELA

The several parks in the province of Guanacaste protect some of the last remnants of the Mesoamerican tropical dry forest that once covered the Pacific lowlands from Costa Rica to the Mexican state of Chiapas. Because Spanish colonists found the climate on the Pacific slope of the isthmus more hospitable than its humid Atlantic side, most of the development that followed the conquest of Central America took place at the cost of the Pacific forests, and today hardly any wilderness remains on that half of the land bridge. The protected dry forests of Guanacaste are, consequently, of extreme importance to conservationists. And the institution of new parks in Costa Rica is a work in progress: Volcán Tenorio is now protected in its own national park, but no infrastructure exists as of yet.

The daily rain deluges subside in December, and the lush landscape enters a transition: as the dry season progresses, most of the trees drop their foliage and the region resembles a desert. Many trees flower during the dry season, however, and the yellow, white, and pink blossoms of the *tabebuia* add splashes of color to the leafless landscape.

Because of the sparse foliage and partial deforestation, Costa Rica's dry-forest parks are some of the best places in the country to see wildlife. Many animals native to North America are common in Guanacaste's protected areas—white-tailed deer, coyotes, magpie jays, diamondback rattlesnakes—but they are also home to predominantly South American animals, such as collared peccaries, armadillos, parrots, and broad-beaked hawks called caracaras. Perhaps due to the wide-open spaces one encounters in the northwest, the region's parks tend to lie away from bus routes, which means you're better off visiting most of them in a rental car or on tours (for additional information, ☞ Chapter 4).

Parque Nacional Juan Castro Blanco

On the upper level of the Atlantic plain, where foothills mark the transition from the coastal lowland to the central mountains, most of the once-jungle-covered land has been cleared for cattle and dairy farming. There are, however, a number of biological preserves here, plus Parque Nacional Juan Castro Blanco. East of Ciudad Quesada, locally known as San Carlos, the 142-sq-km (55-sq-mi) park was created to protect large tracts of virgin forest around the headwaters of the Platanar, Tora, Aguas Zarcas, Tres Amigos, and La Vieja rivers. There are no facilities of any kind in the park at present.

Caño Negro National Wildlife Refuge

The river trip at Caño Negro National Wildlife Refuge (Refugio Nacional de Vida Silvestre Caño Negro) can be an interesting alternative to the Tortuguero canal trip. Another lowland rain-forest reserve, Caño Negro has suffered severe deforestation over the years, but most of the Río Frío remains lined with trees, so the boat trip up the river to the reserve provides an opportunity to see a variety of wildlife. The lagoon at the heart of the reserve also attracts numerous waterfowl from

November to January. Caño Negro is most easily accessed from the Nuevo Arenal–La Fortuna area.

Parque Nacional Rincón de la Vieja

Parque Nacional Rincón de la Vieja, or Rincón de la Vieja National Park, was created to protect the upper slopes of the volcano, with forests that stay greener than those in the drier lowland and a series of steam geysers, bubbling mud pots, hot springs, and several cascades. This extensive protected area has entrances at Hacienda Santa María and Las Pailas. There's a camping area by the old farmhouse of Santa María, and a 2-km (1-mi) hike away is Bosque Encantado, where the Río Zopilote pours over a cascade in the forest, forming an enticing pool. Three kilometers (2 mi) farther is a hot sulfur spring, and 4 km (2½ mi) beyond that are boiling mud pots and fumaroles in an area called Las Pailas. Respect the fences, and don't get too close to the mud pots; their edges are brittle, and several people have slipped in and been severely burned. The trail to the summit heads into the forest above Las Pailas, but it's a trip for serious hikers, best done in the dry season (and if you're prepared for cold weather at the top). The Rincón de la Vieja Mountain Lodge (☞ Chapter 4) offers horseback tours of the park. The lodge has its own network of trails and has turned a sulfur spring into a rock-lined, hot-water bathing pool.

A less strenuous option for visiting the park is to hike the 3-km (2-mi) loop, where you will see fumaroles, a *volcáncito* (baby volcano), and Las Pailas, a series of bubbling mud pots. Along the trail you might also see armadillos, howler monkeys, and semidomesticated, raccoonlike coatis looking for handouts (which you should ignore: a cardinal rule of wildlife encounters is not to feed the animals).

Parque Nacional Santa Rosa

Parque Nacional Santa Rosa, or Santa Rosa National Park, is one of the country's most impressive protected areas. The dry forest that covers much of the park draws biologists and nature lovers, and whereas one of the park's beaches (Nancite) is a vital nesting area for the olive ridley sea turtle, the beach next to it (Naranjo) is well known among the surfing cognoscenti for its world-class waves.

The forested slopes of Volcán Orosí, protected within Parque Nacional Guanacaste, can be seen from the Carretera Interamericana (Pan-American Highway) as you approach the entrance to Santa Rosa. A couple of miles after you enter Santa Rosa, a scenic overlook on the right offers the first good look at the park's dry forest. La Casona Hacienda, an old farmhouse and former battle site, houses a small museum with exhibits about the area's ecology and the battle between ill-equipped Costa Ricans and American mercenary William Walker. A small nature trail loops through the woods near La Casona, and a large camping area is nearby (call the Santa Rosa Park Headquarters, ☎ 695–5598). The road that passes the campground heads to Playa Naranjo, a spectacular, pristine beach with great animal watching and surfing. There is a camping area at Playa Naranjo, but no potable water, and it can only be reached in a four-wheel-drive vehicle or by a 12-km (7-mi) hike from La Casona. Be aware that Santa Rosa's campgrounds sometimes fill up during the dry season, especially in the first week of January and Holy Week (Palm Sunday–Easter Sunday).

If you don't have time to go to Playa Naranjo, there are two good animal-watching trails that head off the road before it becomes too steep for anything but four-wheel-drive vehicles. The Patos Trail, on the left a few miles after the campgrounds, heads through the forest past a water hole and several scenic overlooks. A kilometer (½ mi) farther down the road on the right is a short trail that leads to an overlook from which you can see distant Playa Naranjo, and the massive Witches Rock, which stands offshore. Nancite, to the north of Naranjo, is an important turtle-nesting beach. The *arribadas* (mass nestings) that Nancite is famous for can also be seen at the Ostional National Wildlife Refuge (Refugio Nacional de Fauna Silvestre Ostional), near Nosara.

Parque Nacional Guanacaste

East of the Carretera Interamericana but contiguous with Parque Nacional Santa Rosa and comprising a mosaic of ecologically interdependent protected areas, parks, and refuges, the Parque Nacional Guanacaste (Guanacaste National Park) stretches to the cloud forests atop Volcán Cacao. Although the park is still in fragments, the ultimate goal is to create a single, enormous Guanacaste megapark that will accommodate the natural migratory patterns of myriad creatures, from jaguars to tapirs. There are 300 different birds and more than 5,000 species of butterflies in the park. Camping is reportedly possible at the biological stations, and there are a couple of very rustic lodges; call ahead to the Santa Rosa Park Headquarters (☎ 506/695–5598).

NICOYA PENINSULA

On the sun-drenched Nicoya Peninsula, washed-up California dudes cruise the tubes along endless golden beaches while monkeys howl in the dry tropical forests, coatimundis caper, and turtles ride in on the evening high tide to deposit their eggs into the sand in one of the world's most fascinating biological epics (for additional information, ☞ Chapter 5).

Parque Nacional Palo Verde and Reserva Biológica Lomas Barbudal

Parque Nacional Palo Verde (Palo Verde National Park) and Reserva Biológica Lomas Barbudal (Lomas Barbudal Biological Reserve) protect some significant expanses of dry forest, and because both areas receive fewer visitors than Santa Rosa, they offer a more natural experience. Palo Verde's major attraction is the swampland, which becomes the temporary home for thousands of migratory birds toward the end of the rainy season. An important part of these lagoons lies near the ranger station, where a raised platform has been built for birdwatchers. From December to March you can spot dozens of species of aquatic birds in the area, including several kinds of herons, ducks, wood storks, and elegant roseate spoonbills.

Palo Verde's forests are alive with species inhabiting Santa Rosa, and the road that leads to the ranger station from the town of Bagaces passes some wooded patches where you're bound to spot birds and mammals if you drive slowly. There are also trails that head away from the ranger station—one short path into the hills behind it, and a longer one that goes to the river. The road south from Bagaces is long and rough and passes a lot of pasture before it gets to the park. An alternative route between Palo Verde and the Pan-American Highway passes through Lomas Barbudal—meaning it traverses more forest—though it's a longer haul. The ranger station in Lomas Barbudal stands by the Río Cabuya, which has a small swimming hole nearby, and the road that crosses the stream becomes a trail that winds around the forested hillside. The road that heads north from Lomas is pretty bad, but it's only 15 km (9 mi) to the highway. Camping is permitted at Palo Verde.

Parque Nacional Barra Honda

Rocky hills that contain an extensive network of caves dominate Parque Nacional Barra Honda (Barra Honda National Park), an area of protected dry forest. Local guides lower spelunkers into the caverns using ropes and a climber's ladder—a descent into darkness that is not for the fainthearted but is rewarding for the adventurous. If you're not up for the drop, you can trek into the forest-covered hills, full of wildlife and where scenic overlooks offer views of the Golfo de Nicoya and surrounding countryside. The Cascada Trail begins near the ranger's office and makes a loop near the caves that should take two or three hours to walk; serious hikers will want to continue on to the Boquete Trail, which, together with the Cascada Trail, takes the better part of a day to hike down and back. A community tourism association provides guides and climbing equipment and runs a simple restaurant and lodge, called Las Delicias, by the park entrance. Camping is permitted.

Parque Nacional Marino Las Baulas

Another important turtle nesting beach is Playa Grande, protected within Parque Nacional Marino Las Baulas (Las Baulas Marine National Park), near Tamarindo. Las Baulas, dedicated in 1991 and officially made a park in 1995, is visited by thousands of leatherback turtles—the world's largest—every year during the October to March nesting season. The adjacent Tamarindo wildlife refuge, although under some developmental pressure, protects a mangrove estuary that is an excellent bird-watching area. Just south of Tamarindo and accessible by dirt road is the Río San Francisco, with its own estuary system. Beyond this river lies Playa Langosta, added to the protected-areas list but as of yet not nearly as well organized as Las Baulas (turtle tours are less formal and less expensive). The San Francisco estuary is rich in bird life and (unlike the Tamarindo wildlife refuge) free of motorboats. Playa Langosta, like Playa Grande–Las Baulas, is a leatherback-turtle nesting site.

CENTRAL PACIFIC COSTA RICA

Thanks to its proximity to San José, the Central Pacific has two of the country's most popular protected areas, both of which receive lots of visitors. These areas are also home for plenty of wildlife, including such endangered species as the scarlet macaw and squirrel monkey. Try to get to the refuges as early in the morning as possible (for additional information, ☞ Chapter 6).

Reserva Biológica Carara

The Reserva Biológica Carara (Carara Biological Reserve), on the road between Puntarenas and Playa Jacó, protects one of the last remnants of a transition zone between the dry forests of the northern Pacific lowlands and the humid forests of the southwest. Its tall trees don't drop their foliage during the dry season, but the sylvan scenery is much less luxuriant than what you'll encounter farther south. Carara is one of two areas in the country where you can see scarlet macaws, easiest to spot in the early morning or late afternoon. The Río Tárcoles, which defines the park's northern border, is a good place to see crocodiles, and you may also encounter monkeys, coatis, and an array of birds as you explore the reserve's forests.

Carara's proximity to San José and Jacó has made it one of the country's most popular protected areas, which means tour buses arrive here on a daily basis in the high season. For independent travelers, the presence of tour buses usually means that most of the animals have been frightened deeper into the forest, but if you catch Carara when there are few visitors—very early or late in the day—you can see a lot. The trail that starts near the ranger station makes a loop through the forest that should take an hour to hike. A longer trail, a few miles to the north, is better for animal-watching, but cars parked at the trail-head have been broken into. Camping isn't permitted at Carara.

Parque Nacional Manuel Antonio

The popularity of Parque Nacional Manuel Antonio, or Manuel Antonio National Park, is not surprising when you contemplate its exuberant forests, idyllic beaches, and coral reefs. But the assets of that beautiful patch of wilderness may have made the area too popular for its own good. The road between the town of Quepos and Manuel Antonio is lined with hotels, and when their guests head to the park, its magic wanes. In an attempt to manage the crowd, the park service only allows 600 visitors to enter per day, though they almost never get that many people. It is also closed Monday.

Because it is a relatively small, protected area, Manuel Antonio isn't home to a great deal of wildlife, but it is one of only two areas of the country, together with Corcovado, where you can see squirrel monkeys. It is also a good place to see agoutis, sloths, and capuchin monkeys, which have been fed by visitors and get so close that they sometimes bite people who attempt to pet them. A tropical storm that hit Manuel Antonio several years ago toppled many of the park's largest trees. There is plenty to see in the park's coves, which hold submerged rocks, coral formations, and abundant marine life.

The park entrance is on the beach just across a little estuary (don't swim here—it's polluted) from the end of the road. A trail heads through the forest just behind the beach, but you can also walk on the sand. Another trail that does a loop on Punta Catedral, the steep point at the end of the beach, offers a good look at the rain forest. The second beach, on the other side of the point, is in a deep cove safe for swimming and has good snorkeling. From here, one trail leads to the nearby cove of Puerto Escondido and a lookout point beyond; a second, the Perezoso, heads back through the forest to the park's entrance. Camping is not permitted in the park, though it is possible just outside it.

SOUTHERN PACIFIC COSTA RICA

The southwest is a vast and wild region, where the ecosystems range from the reefs off Isla del Caño to the highland *páramo* (a landscape of shrubs and herbs) of Chirripó peak. This is one of the best regions to see wildlife such as scarlet macaws, spider monkeys, toucans, and coatis, and the forests those animals live in are equally spectacular (for additional information, ☞ Chapter 7).

Parque Nacional Chirripó

Surrounding the Parque Nacional Chirripó (Chirripó National Park) is a wild and scenic area different from what you'll find anywhere else in the country. It is also so remote that there is no easy way in; hikers usually spend one night in San Gerardo de Rivas, which has several inexpensive lodges. From San Gerardo, it's a grueling climb up to the park—6 to 10 hours, depending upon your physical condition. It's best to head out of San Gerardo with the first light of day. You first hike through pastures, then forests, and then the burnt remains of forest fires. There are extensive cabin facilities near the top, where you will want to spend at least two nights, since it is from there that you hike up to the peaks, glacier lakes, and *páramo*—a highland ecosystem common to the Andes that consists of shrubs and herbaceous plants. Trails lead to the top of Chirripó—Costa Rica's highest point—and the nearby peak of Terbi. The park's new hostel consists of small rooms with four bunks each, cold-water baths, and a cooking area. They rent camp stoves and blankets, but you will need to bring food, water for the hike up, a good sleeping bag, and plenty of warm clothes. At press time there was talk of a cafeteria opening in the park, which would mean having to pack up less food; ask when reserving space.

Camping isn't allowed at Chirripó, and though the cabin has 60 beds, it's best to reserve space well ahead of time during the dry season. Contact the Environment Ministry's San Isidro regional office (☎ 506/771–3155). If there is space available for the dates you want to visit the park, they will tell you the number of an account in the Banco Nacional into which you must deposit admissions and lodging fees to confirm your reservation. The cabin holds only 40 people, so reservations must be made well ahead of time during the dry season. Be prepared for very cold weather on top.

Parque Nacional Corcovado

A pristine expanse of wilderness covering one-third of the Osa Peninsula, Parque Nacional Corcovado (Corcovado National Park) safeguards virgin rain forest, deserted beaches, jungle-edged rivers, and a vast, inaccessible swamp. Corcovado is home to boa constrictors, jaguars, anteaters, tapirs, and if you're lucky enough to come face to face with one of these rare creatures, it is most likely to happen here. You will definitely see flocks of scarlet macaws, troops of spider monkeys, colorful poison dart frogs, toucans, and agoutis.

The easiest way to visit the remote park is on a day trip from one of the lodges in the nearby Bahía Drake (Drake Bay) area, or from the Corcovado Tent Camp, but if you have a backpack and strong legs, you can spend days deep within its wilderness. A limited number of bunks are available at the Sirena station—you'll need a good mosquito net and sheets—and meals can be arranged at all the stations if you reserve in advance. Only 35 people are allowed to camp at any given ranger station, so reserving space is essential during the peak season. The **Ministerio del Ambiente**'s Puerto Jiménez regional office (☎ 506/735–5036) starts taking reservations for each month on the first day of the preceding month, so its best to call early. Be sure to reconfirm your reservation a few days before you're due to enter the park.

There are several trails into the park, along the beach starting from La Leona or San Pedrillo ranger stations, or through the forest from Los Patos ranger station. Although hiking is always tough in the tropical heat, the forest route is easier than the beach hikes, which can be done only at low tide. The longer hike between San Pedrillo and Sirena can be undertaken only during the dry season, because the rivers become too high to cross during the rainy months. You can hire a boat in Sierpe to take you to San Pedrillo or Bahía Drake; from Drake it's a four-hour hike to San Pedrillo. You can hire a taxi in Puerto Jiménez to take you most of the way to Los Patos, and a truck leaves Puerto Jiménez every morning at 6 for Carate, which is a short hike from La Leona. It's an all-day hike between any two stations, and an especially long one between San Pedrillo and Sirena. There is potable water at every station, but don't drink stream water. Be sure to bring plenty of insect repellent, sunblock, rain gear, a pair of good boots, a first-aid kit, and either a mosquito net and sheets or a tent and sleeping bag. Finally, try to pack light.

ATLANTIC LOWLANDS AND THE CARIBBEAN COAST

The parks of the Caribbean coast—with a humid, greenhouse-like climate and lush vegetation—are the kind of wilderness one would expect to see upon hearing the word "jungle." In these Atlantic forests live South American species you won't find in the rest of Costa Rica—poison dart frogs, the crab-eating raccoon, and the great green macaw.

The Atlantic region's most popular protected areas are its coastal parks, where the rain forest meets the beach. You'll find marine wonders as well as the flora and fauna of the jungle. Aside from the surf and sand, the prime natural attractions along the southern Caribbean coast are coral reefs, whereas the northern beaches are famous for the sea turtles that come here by night to lay their eggs in the sand.

The protected areas on the Caribbean side have the added convenience of being close to good dining and lodging. And the trip here can be an adventure in its own right, since the Atlantic Highway passes through the heart of Parque Nacional Braulio Carrillo and the boat trip up the canals to Tortuguero is one of the best opportunities to see wildlife in Costa Rica (for additional information, ☞ Chapter 8).

Parque Nacional Braulio Carrillo

This amazing, accessible expanse of pristine wilderness is one of Costa Rica's largest protected areas (443 sq km/171 sq mi). Stretching from the misty mountaintops north of San José to the Atlantic lowlands, Parque Nacional Braulio Carrillo (Braulio Carrillo National Park) protects a series of ecosystems ranging from the cloud forests covering the park's upper slopes to the tropical wet forest of the Magsasay sector. The Carretera Guápiles, the main route to the Atlantic coast, cuts through one of Braulio's most precipitous areas, passing countless breathtaking views of the rugged landscape. There is a ranger station just after the Zurquí Tunnel, where a short trail loops through the cloud forest. Another trail leads into the forest to the right about 17 km (10½ mi) after the tunnel, where it follows the Quebrada González, a stream with a cascade and swimming hole, into the rain forest. The vegetation is beautiful around the highway, and you may see a few of the 350 bird species that inhabit the park. (Although Braulio is home to most of the mammals found in Costa Rica, they tend to avoid the forest near the highway.) There are no camping areas in this part of the park.

Hikers will want to explore the Volcán Barva sector of Braulio Carrillo, with its trail that leads through the cloud forest to two crater lakes. Camping is allowed at the Barva ranger station, which is far from any traffic and thus is a good area to spot birds and animals. Quetzals can be seen in the area during the dry season, which is the only time you'll want to camp here, but it's a good place for a morning hike just about any time of year. Stay on the trail when hiking anywhere in Braulio; it's easy to get lost in the cloud forest, and the rugged terrain makes wandering through the woods very dangerous.

Parque Nacional Cahuita

The near 2.6-sq-km (1-sq-mi) coral reef that surrounds Punta Cahuita is a natural treasure, and Parque Nacional Cahuita (Cahuita National Park) was set up to protect its 35 species of coral and even greater number of sponges and seaweeds, which provide food and refuge for the myriad colorful tropical fish and crustaceans. The reef alone would be ample attraction for visitors; most, however, come for Cahuita's luxuriant coastal forest and idyllic palm-lined beaches, which have stepped, seemingly, straight out of a travel poster.

The 7-km (4½-mi) path that winds in and out of the forest along the beach, from the town of Cahuita around the point to Puerto Vargas, offers a good look at the park's coastal and jungle wonders. The hike can be completed in a few hours. The forest and swamps are home to troops of monkeys, kingfishers and herons, sloths, snakes, crabs, and lizards. The beach nearest the town of Cahuita has a regular riptide, so wait to do your swimming until you're farther into the park, where the beach curves toward the point. This is also a good snorkeling area, although the best diving is off the point. Sadly, the park's coral reef is slowly being killed by sediment, run off from deforested areas such as the banana plantations in the nearby Valle de Estrella. This process was intensified by the earthquake of 1991, as many riverbank trees in the nearby jungle foothills were downed by the quake, exposing riverbank soil to the erosive effect of tropical deluges and sending trees, soil, leaves, shrubs, and everything else seaward. After the quake, local divers estimated that the reef was 80% dead, but don't despair: there is still good snorkeling to be had. Just use a local guide to find the best reefs, and don't dive for a few days after it rains, when the water is sure to be murky.

Gandoca-Manzanillo National Wildlife Refuge

Although less pristine than Parque Nacional Cahuita (☞ *above*), Gandoca-Manzanillo National Wildlife Refuge (Refugio Nacional de Vida Silvestre Gandoca-Manzanillo) stretches along the southeastern coast from the town of Manzanillo to the border of Panama, offering plenty of rain forest and many good dive spots. Because of weak laws governing the conservation of refuges and the value of coastal land in the area, Gandoca-Manzanillo has suffered steady environmental degradation over the years and continues to be developed. For now, the easiest way to explore it is by hiking along the coast south of Manzanillo, which also has some good snorkeling offshore. You can hike back out the way you came in, or arrange in Puerto Viejo to have a boat pick you up at Monkey Point (a three- to four-hour walk from Manzanillo) or Gandoca (six to eight hours). Boat trips to dive spots and beaches in the refuge can also be arranged in Puerto Viejo, Punta Uva, and Manzanillo.

Parque Nacional Tortuguero and Barra del Colorado Wildlife Refuge

Parque Nacional Tortuguero (*tortuga* means "turtle") was created to protect the sea turtles that nest by the thousands on its beach. The park comprises a variety of ecosystems, including lowland rain forest, estuaries, and swampy areas covered with *yolillo* palms. The park's palm-lined beach stretches off as far as the eye can see; you can wander here alone, but rip currents make swimming dangerous and there are rumors of sharks. This spectacular beach is even more intriguing at night, when four species of endangered sea turtles nest here. If you want to watch them, contact your hotel or the parks office to hire a certified local guide. (You won't be permitted to use a camera on the beach and flashlights must be covered with red plastic, since the lights may deter the turtles from nesting.)

The jungle-lined canals that lead to Tortuguero have been called the Amazon of Costa Rica, and the boat trip up to the park, which leaves from the docks at Moín, is an excellent opportunity to see the area's wildlife, including several species of kingfishers and herons, sloths, monkeys, and crocodiles. Hire a dugout canoe with guide to explore some of the rivers that flow into the canal; these waterways contain less boat traffic and often have more wildlife. You can also continue up the canals to the Barra del Colorado National Wildlife Refuge (Refugio Nacional de Fauna Silvestre Barra del Colorado), an immense protected area that is connected with the park via a biological corridor. Barra del Colorado is less visited, and it protects significant expanses of wilderness.

PANAMA

Panama's national park system protects an array of ecosystems as impressive as Costa Rica's, but since Panamanian tourism lags far behind that of its neighbor nation, the country's parks tend to have rather limited infrastructure. The good thing is that you don't have to share Panama's protected areas with the kinds of crowds that sometimes descend on Costa Rican parks. Panama's Renewable Resources Institute, **INRENARE** (☎ 507/232–7228), recently introduced entrance fees of between $3 and $10, depending on the park.

The Cordillera de Talamanca extends from eastern Costa Rica into western Panama, and much of that massive range is protected within a series of parks and reserves that together form Reserva de la Biósfera La Amistad (La Amistad Biosphere Reserve, ☞ *below*). Although most of the biosphere reserve covers the mountain range's Atlantic slope, its most accessible areas are found on the Pacific side, and several are in the mountains of western Panama. The trails and roads that wind into the mountains of Chiriquí, Panama's southwest province, not only pass unforgettable panoramas, they lead to luxuriant cloud forests inhabited by quetzals, toucans, tiny venomous toads, and other colorful creatures.

Most of the isolated Bocas del Toro Archipelago remains covered with jungle, and much of that jungle is protected within national parks, forest reserves, and Indian reservations, but the majority of it is barely accessible. Although adventurers with jungle gear and time to spare may want to head back into mountain refuges such as Reserva Forestal Palo Seco (Palo Seco Forest Reserve), Reserva Indígena Teribe (Teribe Indian Reservation), and the Atlantic sector of Parque Internacional La Amistad, most tourists will have to settle for the region's most accessible protected area, Isla Bastimentos (for additional information on the areas covered below, ☞ Chapter 9).

Volcán Barú

Volcán Barú (Barú Volcano), an 11,450-ft, long-extinct peak, dominates the Chiriquí countryside, inviting hiking and bird-watching enthusiasts to ascend. The upper slopes and summit of that massive volcano are protected within Parque Nacional Volcán Barú, which comprises significant patches of cloud forest and a rugged peak. The cloud forest is home to a wealth of bird life, including three-wattled bellbirds and resplendent quetzals, whereas the heights are home for the rare volcano junco. There are two routes to the summit: a footpath that winds up the western slope from near the town of Volcán, and a road (you'll need a four-wheel-drive vehicle for this) that heads up the eastern slope from Boquete. A dirt trail also leads through the forest between Cerro Punta and Boquete, along the volcano's northern slope, which makes for a good one-day hike. There are no visitor facilities at the summit, and although camping is allowed, you'll need plenty of water and warm clothes—it freezes regularly up top.

Parque Nacional Marino Isla Bastimentos

Parque Nacional Marino Isla Bastimentos (Isla Bastimentos National Marine Park), centered on Isla Bastimentos in Panama's Bocas del Toro province, is a pristine jewel of a park, comprising coral reefs, white-sand beaches, and dozens of small cays and islets. Among the things to do and see here are fantastic skin diving, beachcombing, lots of wildlife, sea-turtle nesting beaches, and an as-yet-unexplored potential for windsurfing and surfing. Although there are communities on its western and eastern ends, most of Isla Bastimentos remains covered with lush forests that are home to ospreys, iguanas, parrots, and tiny poison dart frogs. The long, palm-lined beaches of its northern coast are as beautiful as they are ecologically important, and the waters to the south and west of the island hold some extensive coral reefs.

The best area for skin diving within the park is in the waters that surround the Cayos Zapatillas—two atolls to the southeast of Isla Bastimentos. When the ocean is calm, the visibility is quite good around the Cayos, where you'll discover an impressive array of sponges and corals, including some immense brain coral formations. This colorful coral garden is home for countless tropical fish, which range from tiny angels to larger parrot and trigger fish, and a great diversity of rays. The caves at the reef's edge often hold massive snappers, drums, moray eels, and, sometimes, sleeping sharks. And if you take the time to look closer you may discover delicate starfish, shrimp, octopuses, and an array of other interesting invertebrates.

But the Cayos are beautiful enough above the water to please you even if you have no desire to don a mask and snorkel. Its pale beach, lined with lanky coconut palms and washed by aquamarine waters, belongs on postcards and travel posters and in dreams dreamt during northern winter nights. The long beach on Isla Bastimentos is equally impressive, though more difficult to visit, and from April to September it is visited by nesting sea turtles on a nightly basis. That beach is backed by thick forest, home to a wealth of wildlife, which adventurous travelers may want to take the time to explore. Isla Bastimentos and the Cayos Zapatillas can be reached by boat from the regional capitol of Bocas del Toro, a pleasant town with a small selection of lodges and a few decent restaurants.

Parque Internacional La Amistad

The single largest protected area within Reserva de la Biósfera La Amistad is Panama's Parque Internacional La Amistad, which covers more than 2007 sq km (775 sq mi), extending from cloud forests down to sultry lowland jungles. The name Amistad, which means "friendship" in Spanish, refers to its role as half of a binational park—it is contiguous with Costa Rica's Parque Nacional La Amistad, which is slightly smaller than its Panamanian twin and more difficult to visit. The ranger station at Las Nubes, in the hills above Cerro Punta, is the park's main entry point. It is a quiet spot at the edge of the forest, with a couple of houses and a grassy area where you can camp. A 2-km (1-mi) trail does a loop through the forest near the ranger station, and a second trail heads up over a ridge, which affords views of the Cerro Punta valley, to a nearby waterfall; it takes about two hours to hike there and back. If you spend a night or two here, you may be able to accompany one of the rangers up Cerro Picacho, a four- to five-hour hike deep into the forest.

NICARAGUA

Blessed with natural beauty rivaling that of its neighbors Costa Rica and Panama, Nicaragua—in the wake of decades of political turmoil—has had little resources to develop a national park system. With the recent unleashing of the fury of Hurricane Mitch on Nicaragua and Honduras, the country faces an even greater challenge to protect its wildlife, volcanoes, forests, and beaches and waters. Presently, the country's only officially designated national park is Parque Nacional Volcán Masaya, established in 1979 and encompassing approximately 20 sq km (7 sq mi), including the multiple craters of Volcán Masaya, Laguna de Masaya, and the terrain around the volcanoes and the lake. Several other areas in the country, however, have attained unofficial park or reserve status and will probably eventually be designated national parks. At present, the two volcanoes on Ometepe Island—Madera and Concepcíon—have attained unofficial park status, as has Volcán Mombacho, not far from Granada. Additionally, an officially designated wildlife refuge—the Refugio de Vida Silvestre Chococente (Chococente Wildlife Refuge)—has been established to protect a turtle nesting site on the Pacific coast north of San Juan del Sur. Tours of this refuge during turtle nesting periods can be arranged through Marie's Bar in San Juan del Sur (☞ Chapter 9). For information on this and other refuges in Nicaragua, contact the **Dirección de Silvestres y Faunas** (✉ Km 12½, Carretera Norte, Apdo. 5123, Managua, ☎ 505/31112–31595, FAX 505/31112–31596).

Parque Nacional Volcán Masaya

The evocative landscapes of Volcán Masaya, also known as Popogatepe, or "Mountain That Burns," suggest the moon with shrubbery, as the sterile lava fields slowly turn fertile and host an invasion by native vegetation, bedecked by thousands of colorful flowers, even orchids, during the dry season. Along with the plants come animals, including coyotes, skunks, raccoons, deer, iguanas, rabbits, and monkeys. Birds are plentiful as well, with flocks of parakeets gamboling within the toxic confines of the craters, where they live seemingly without ill effect. Look for them in the late afternoon, along with motmots, magpie jays, and woodpeckers. The Coyote trail offers the intrepid hiker a 5⅓-km (3½-mi) trek featuring views of petrified lava beds and bird-filled forests en route from the craters' edges to the shores of Laguna de Masaya. You shouldn't miss the San Fernando Crater, inactive for 200 years and now home to a lush forest, or the Bobadilla Cross, erected high atop a flight of 200 stairs. The cross replicates one put up by Spanish priests in the 16th century to exorcise the devil. Best of all, park your car at the Plaza de Oviedo, and stroll up to the Santiago Crater lip—fenced off, thankfully—for a look into what those Spanish priests were convinced was nothing less than the Boca de Inferno, the "Mouth of Hell." The visitor center and museum offer an insightful overview of regional cultural and geological history, with most of the documentation in Spanish. ✉ *Km 23, Carretera Masaya–Managua, Apdo. NI-1, Nindiri,* ☎ *505/0522–5415.* 🎟 *$4.* ☉ *Daily 9–5.*

11 PORTRAITS OF COSTA RICA

A Biological Superpower

Wildlife Glossary

Books and Videos

A BIOLOGICAL SUPERPOWER

COSTA RICA MAY LACK oil fields and coal deposits, but the country is not without its natural assets. Its ecological wealth includes fertile volcanic soil, sun-swathed beaches, massive trees whose thick branches support elevated gardens of orchids and bromeliads, and hundreds of colorful bird species—the kind of priceless commodities that economists have long ignored. International bankers may wonder how this tiny nation ended up with so pretentious a name as "Rich Coast," but many a barefoot Indian, grizzled biologist, and binocular-toting tourist understands where the republic's wealth lies hidden.

Costa Rica's varied forests hold a treasure trove of flora and fauna, so vast and diverse that scientists haven't even named many of the plant and insect species found within them, and of the species that have been identified, few have been thoroughly studied. Those forests are among the most diverse and productive ecosystems in the world—though tropical forests cover a mere 7 percent of the earth's surface area, they hold more than half the planet's plant and animal species—and few countries offer better exposure to the biological treasures of tropical nature than Costa Rica.

About half the size of the state of Kentucky, Costa Rica covers less than 0.03 percent of the planet's surface, yet it contains nearly 5 percent of its plant and animal species. The diversity of the country's flora and fauna can be summed up with statistics: it contains at least 9,000 plant species, more than 1,100 varieties of orchids, in excess of 2,000 different kinds of butterflies, and at least 850 bird species (more than exist in the United States *and* Canada). But such numbers don't begin to convey the awe one feels when staring up the convoluted trunk of a centennial strangler fig, listening to the roar of a howler monkey reverberate through the foliage, or watching a delicate hummingbird drink nectar from a multicolored heliconia flower.

This nation's rich and varied tropical nature is as beautiful as it is intriguing, and as complicated as it is fascinating. It may be hard to comprehend the richness and complexity of the country's forests at first glance—the overwhelming verdure of the rain forest can give the false impression of uniformity—but once you begin to examine the pieces of that great green puzzle, you come to understand why scientists have dubbed Costa Rica a "biological superpower."

That biological diversity is the result of the country's tropical location—on a slip of land connecting North and South America—its varied topography, and the many microclimates resulting from those mountains, valleys, and lowlands. But to understand why Costa Rica is such a biologically important place today, we need to look back into prehistory and envision a world that human eyes never saw but that scientists have at least partially reconstructed.

Just a Few Dozen Millennia Ago

In geological terms, Costa Rica is relatively young, which explains why precious few valuable minerals can be found beneath its soil. Five million years ago, the patch of land we now call Costa Rica didn't even exist. In those days, North and South America were separated by a canal the likes of which Teddy Roosevelt—the father of the Panama Canal—couldn't have conjured up in his wildest dreams. In the area now occupied by Panama and Costa Rica, the waters of the Pacific and Atlantic oceans flowed freely together for unfathomable millennia. Geologists have named that former canal the Straits of Bolívar, after the Venezuelan revolutionary who wrested much of South America from Spain.

Far beneath the Straits of Bolívar, the incremental movement of tectonic plates slowly completed the Central American isthmus. Geologists speculate that a chain of volcanic islands appeared in that gap around 30 million years ago. A combination of volcanic activity and plate movement caused those islands to grow and rise from the water, eventually forming a connected ridge. The land bridge was completed approximately 3 million years ago, clo' the interoceanic canal and opening a biological corridor between the Americas.

Because several tectonic plates meet beneath Central America, it has long been geologically unstable, experiencing occasional earthquakes, frequent tremors, and regular volcanic eruptions. Although being hit by one of those natural disasters can't help but seem a curse, there actually wouldn't be a Costa Rica if it weren't for such phenomena. What is today the country's best soil was once spewed from the bowels of the volcanoes that dominate the landscape, and the jarring adjustments of adjacent tectonic plates actually pushed most of the national territory up out of the sea. A recent example of this upward movement was the 7.2 earthquake of 1991, which thrust Costa Rica's southern Caribbean coastline up several feet, leaving portions of coral reefs high and dry. Shallow coral platforms that surrounded the points of Limón and Cahuita were thrust from the water, adding as much as 30 yards of land to some oceanfront property. Although that quake was a devastating natural disaster that damaged or destroyed almost half the homes along the Caribbean coast, it was but a tiny adjustment in the incremental tectonic process that created the country.

The intercontinental connection completed 3 million years ago had profound biological consequences, since it both separated the marine life of the Pacific and Atlantic oceans and simultaneously created a pathway for interchange between North and South America. Though hardly the kind of lapse that a geologist could get excited about, 3 million years is a long time by biological standards, and the region's plants and animals have changed considerably since the inter-American gap was spanned. Whereas evolution took different paths in the waters that flank the isthmus, organisms that had evolved on separate continents were able to make their way into the opposite hemisphere, and the resulting interaction determined what lives in the Americas today.

Mind-Boggling Biodiversity

Costa Rica's amazing biological diversity is in many ways the result of that intercontinental exchange, but the country's flora and fauna actually add up to more than has passed between the continents. Though it is a biological corridor, the isthmus also acts as a filter, which makes it home to many species that couldn't complete the journey from one hemisphere to the other. The rain forests of Costa Rica's Atlantic and southwest lowlands, for example, comprise the most northerly distribution of such southern species as the crab-eating raccoon and a dreaded jungle viper known as the bushmaster. The tropical dry forests of the northern Pacific slope, on the other hand, define the southern limit for such North American species as the white-throated magpie jay and the Virginia opossum. In addition to species whose range extends only as far as Costa Rica, and those whose range extends through the country into both North and South America, such as the white-tailed deer and the gray hawk, Costa Rica's many physical barriers and microclimates have fostered the development of indigenous plants and animals, such as the mangrove hummingbird and mountain salamander.

What all this biological balderdash means to visitors to Costa Rica is that they might spot a North American pale-billed woodpecker and a howler monkey—of South American descent—in the branches of a rain tree, which is native to Central America. And then there are the tourists—migrants, that is—such as the dozens of northern bird species that winter in Costa Rica, among them the Tennessee warbler, western tanager, and yellow-bellied sapsucker.

In addition to being familiar with the birds that winter in Costa Rica, you'll no doubt recognize some of the plants, such as the orchids and impatiens that grow wild in the country but cost a pretty penny at the garden shop back home. Costa Rica has plenty of oak trees, squirrels, and sparrows, but most of the country's flora and fauna looks decidedly tropical. Not only are such common plants as orchids, palms, and ficuses unmistakably tropical, but many of the country's animals are distinctly Neotropical—that which is only found in the American tropics—such as sloths, poison dart frogs, toucans, and monkeys with prehensile tails.

This varied wildlife is spread through an array of ecosystems, which biologists have divided into a dozen "life zones" but which actually consist of a biological continuum almost too diverse for classification. Though the flora and fauna found in any given life zone are determined by various physical conditions, the two most important are altitude and rainfall. Although average temperatures change very little in the tropics through the course of the year, they do change a good bit during the course of the day, especially in the mountains. The Costa Rican highlands stay consistently cooler than the lowlands, which means you can spend a morning sweating in a sultry coastal forest, then drive a couple hours into the mountains, where you will need a warm jacket.

In a more temperate area of the world, the cold weather hits the mountaintops a month or two before the lowlands, but Old Man Winter eventually gets his icy grip on everything. In the tropics, the only place where it freezes is atop the highest mountains, so high-altitude flora tends to be completely different from that in even nearby valleys. Altitude also plays a substantial role in regulating humidity, since clouds accumulate around mountains and volcanoes, providing regular precipitation as well as shade, which slows evaporation. These conditions are perfect for the luxuriant cloud forests that cover the upper slopes of many mountains. In general, the higher you climb, the more lush the vegetation will be, except for the peaks of the highest mountains, which often protrude from the cloud cover and are consequently fairly arid.

Though you may associate the tropics with rain, precipitation in Costa Rica varies considerably depending on where you are and when you're there. This is a result of its mountainous terrain and regional weather patterns. A phenomenon called rain shadow—one side of a mountain range receives much more rain than the other—plays an important ecological role in Costa Rica. Four mountain ranges combine to create an intercontinental divide that separates the country into Atlantic and Pacific slopes. Thanks to the trade winds, the Atlantic slope receives much more rain than the Pacific. The trade winds steadily pump moisture-laden clouds southwest over the isthmus, where they encounter warm air or mountains, which make them rise. As the clouds rise, they cool and become less able to hold moisture, which causes them to dump most of their liquid luggage on the country's Caribbean side.

During the rainy season, which runs from mid-May to December, the role of the trade winds is diminished, as regular storms roll off the Pacific Ocean and soak the western side of the isthmus. Though it rains all over Costa Rica during these months, it often rains more on the Pacific side of the mountains than on the Atlantic. Come December, the trade winds take over again, and hardly a drop falls on the western side until May. The dry season is most intense in the country's northwest corner, where the forests acquire a desert visage during the dry months, as most trees drop their foliage. That region, known as Guanacaste, quickly regains its verdure once the rains return in May, which marks the beginning of a springlike season that Costa Ricans nonetheless refer to as winter.

Climate variation within the country results in a mosaic of forests—from those that receive only a few feet of rain each year to those that soak up several yards of precipitation annually. The combination of humidity and temperature helps determine what grows where, but whereas some species have very restricted ranges, others seem to thrive just about anywhere. Plants such as strangler figs and bromeliads grow all over the country, and animals such as the collared peccary and coati—a long-nosed cousin of the raccoon—can live just about anywhere human beings let them. Other species have extremely limited ranges, such as the mangrove hummingbird, which is restricted to the mangrove forests of the Pacific coast, and the volcano junco, a gray sparrow that can only be found around the highest peaks of the Cordillera de Talamanca.

The Jungle Out There

The diversity of scenery found in Costa Rica is one of the things that make it such an interesting country to visit, but the landscape that visitors most want to see is the tropical rain forest. The protected areas of the Atlantic and southern Pacific lowlands hold tracts of virgin rain forest where massive tropical trees tower more than 100 ft over the forest floor. The thick branches of those jungle giants are covered with an abundance of epiphytes (plants that grow on other plants but aren't parasites) such as ferns, orchids, bromeliads, mosses, vines, and aroids. The arboreal garden of the canopy is where most of the forest's plant and animal species are found.

Although life flourishes in the canopy, the intense sunlight that quickly dries the tree-tops after downpours results in a recurrent water shortage. Plants that live there have consequently developed ways to cope with the aridity. Many orchids have thick leaves that resist evaporation and spongy roots that can quickly soak up large amounts of water when it rains. Tank bromeliads have a funnel shape that enables them to collect and hold water at the center of their leaves. Those plants act as miniature oases, attracting arboreal animals, which drink from, hunt at, or, like certain insect larvae and tree-frog tadpoles, live in their pools. In exchange for the vital water, the waste and carcasses of these animals provide the plant with valuable nutrients, which are also scarce in the canopy.

Many animals spend most or all of their time in the canopy, which can be frustrating for people who head to the jungle wanting to see wildlife. By peering through binoculars, you might glimpse the still, furry figure of a sloth or the brilliant regalia of a parrot. It's definitely hard to miss the arboreal acrobatics of monkeys, who leap from tree to tree, hang from branches, throw fruit or sticks, and generally make spectacles of themselves. For a closer look at the canopy, you may want to visit the Rain Forest Aerial Tram, near the Atlantic Highway, or spend some time in a tree platform at Hacienda Barú in Dominical, or the Corcovado Lodge Tent Camp, both in the southern Pacific.

Because little sunlight reaches the ground, the rain-forest floor is a dim, quiet place, with not nearly as much undergrowth as in those old Tarzan movies. Still, many plants—from aroids to palm trees—have adapted to this shady world. The light level inside a virgin rain forest is comparable to that found in the average North American living room or shopping mall, and some of the plants that grow there look familiar to visitors from the north, since those species have become popular houseplants. The vegetation isn't always sparse, though: whenever an old tree falls there's a riot of growth as an excess of plants fight over the newfound sunlight.

Few travelers are disappointed by the tropical forest, but some are frustrated by the difficulty of spotting wildlife. Hikers occasionally encounter such earthbound creatures as the coati or the agouti, a terrier-size rodent that resembles a giant guinea pig, and in most areas you're likely to see iridescent blue morpho butterflies, hyperactive hummingbirds, brightly colored poison dart frogs, and tiny lizards that stand guard on tree trunks. Most animals, however, spend much of their time and energy trying not to be seen, and the thick foliage aids them in that endeavor. An untrained eye can miss the details, which is why a naturalist guide is invaluable. In addition to spotting and identifying flora and fauna, a good guide can explain some of countless relationships that weave those plants and animals together in one of the planet's most complex ecosystems.

The rain forest is characterized by intense predation. Its inhabitants dedicate most of their time and energy to two essential tasks: finding their next meal and avoiding being eaten in the process. Whereas animals tend to keep from being eaten by hiding or fleeing, plants have developed defenses such as thorns, prickly hairs, and toxic substances that make their leaves less than appetizing. Because of the relative toxicity of most of the rain-forest foliage, many insects eat only a small portion of a leaf before moving on to another plant, so as not to ingest a lethal dose of any one poison. The consequence of this can be seen by staring up into the canopy—almost every leaf is full of little holes.

Camouflage is also a popular defense of animals, and there are plenty of amazing insects that have evolved to look like the leaves, bark, moss, and leaf litter that abound in the tropical forest. Some bugs have adopted the colors of certain flowers, or even the mold that grows on plants. Though they are a chore to spot, the few camouflaged critters that you discover are invariably intriguing.

Some creatures go to the opposite extreme and actually advertise with bright colors. Although some colors are meant to help animals find a mate amid the mesh of green, others serve as a warning to potential predators. Some species of caterpillars, for example, are not only immune to the toxins of the plant on which they live, they actually sequester that poison within their bodies, which makes them toxic as well. In certain areas, you may see brightly colored frogs hopping around the forest floor. Their skins are laced with such poisonous secretions that some Indian tribes use them to make their darts and arrows deadly. The typical warning pattern mixes bright colors with black, a coloration that conveys a simple message to predators: eat me and die.

A popular trick for scaring off predators is mimicry. Certain edible caterpillars look like venomous ones, and some harmless serpents have markings similar to those of the deadly coral snake. Such acts of deception often reach amazing levels of intrigue. The cocoons of certain butterflies not only resemble the head of a viper, but if disturbed, they begin to move back and forth just as a snake's head would. One large butterfly has spots on its wings that look like eyes, so when it opens them, it resembles an owl, and another butterfly species is identical to a wasp.

In addition to avoiding predators, plants and animals must compete with other species that have similar niches—the biological equivalents of jobs. This competition has fostered cooperation between noncompetitive organisms. Plants need to get their pollen and seeds distributed as far as possible, and every animal requires a steady food supply, which brings us to everybody's favorite subject: the birds and the bees.

Although butterflies and bees do most of the pollinating up north, tropical plants are pollinated by everything from fruit flies and hummingbirds to beetles and bats. The flowers of such plants are often designed so that the nectar is readily available to their pollinators but protected from freeloaders. The beautiful hibiscus flower is designed to dust a hummingbird's forehead with pollen and collect any pollen that's already there while the tiny bird drinks the nectar hidden deep in its base. That flower is too long for a butterfly, and the nectar is held too deep for a bee to reach, but no system is perfect; you may spot a bananaquit—a tiny bird with a short beak—biting holes in the bases of hibiscus flowers to drink their nectar without ever getting near their pollen.

The intense competition for limited resources that characterizes the rain forest keeps trees growing taller, roots reaching farther, and everything mobile working on some way to get more for less. The battle for light has sent most of the foliage sky high, whereas the battle for nutrients has caused the process of decay and recycling that follows every death in the forest to take place at breakneck pace. One result of this high-speed decomposition is that most of the nutrients in a rain forest are found within living things, whereas the soil beneath them retains very few essential elements. As a consequence, rain-forest soils tend to be nutrient-poor and less than ideal for farming.

Tropical Nature Works Overtime

Though the rain forest is what most people imagine when they think of the tropics, Costa Rica has other types of forests that are equally diverse and well worth visiting. The tropical dry forests of the northwest lowlands are similar to rain forests during the rainy season, but once the daily deluges subside, the dry forest undergoes a profound change. Most trees lose their leaves, and some of them simultaneously burst into full, colorful flower. Such trees as the yellow-blossomed buttercup tree and the pink tabebuia brighten up the arid landscape of northwest Costa Rica during the dry season. The dry forest contains many of the plants, animals, and exclusive relationships found in the rain forest, but it is also home to species often associated with the forests and deserts of Mexico and the southern United States, such as cacti, coyotes, and diamondback rattlesnakes. Because dry forests aren't as dense as rain forests, it can be easier to spot animals in them. This is especially true during the dry season, when the foliage is sparse, and animals often congregate around scarce water sources and trees in fruit or flower.

The upper reaches of many mountains and volcanoes are draped with cloud forests, which are even more luxuriant than rain forests. They are the epitome of lushness—so lush that it can be difficult to find the bark on a cloud-forest tree for all the growth on its trunk and branches. Plants grow on plants that grow on still other plants: vines, orchids, ferns, aroids, and bromeliads are everywhere, and mosses and liverworts cover the vines and leaves of other epiphytes. Because of the steep terrain, the trees grow on slightly different levels, and the canopy is less continuous than that of a lowland rain forest. More light reaches the ground, so there is plenty of undergrowth, including prehistoric-looking tree ferns, a wealth of flowering plants, and "poor-man's umbrellas," which consist of little more than a few giant leaves.

Cloud forests are home to a multitude of animals, ranging from delicate glass frogs, whose undersides are so transparent that you can see many of their internal organs, to the resplendent quetzal—a bird that was considered sacred by the ancient Mayas. The male quetzal has a crimson belly and iridescent green back, wings, and tail feathers, which can grow longer than 2 ft. Those tail feathers float behind the quetzal during flight, a splendid sight that no doubt inspired its ancient name: "the plumed serpent." Although the tangle of foliage and almost constant mist make it difficult to see much of the cloud forest's wildlife, you should still catch glimpses of such colorful birds as the emerald toucanet, collared redstart, and various kinds of hummingbirds.

The humidity prevents the cloud-forest canopy from facing the water shortage that often plagues a lowland rain forest. In fact, the cloud forest's canopy is usually soaking wet. During most of the year, a moisture-laden mist moves through the cloud forest, depositing condensation on the vegetation. This condensation causes a sort of secondary precipitation, with droplets forming on the epiphytic foliage and falling regularly from the branches to the forest floor. Cloud forests thus function like giant sponges, soaking up the humidity from the clouds and sending it slowly downhill to feed the streams and rivers that many regions and communities depend on for water.

Atop high ridges, and near the summits of volcanoes, the cloud forest has been transformed by the steady, strong winds that topple tall trees and regularly break off branches. The result is a collection of small, twisted trees and bushes known as an elfin forest. On the upper slopes of the Cordillera de Talamanca—the country's highest range—the cloud forest gives way to the *páramo,* a high-altitude ecosystem composed of shrubs, grasses, and hardy herbs. Most of those plants are common in the heights of South America's Andes, and the Costa Rican páramo defines their most northerly distribution.

On the other extreme, along both the country's coasts, are river mouths and estuaries that hold extensive mangrove forests. Regularly flooded, primeval-looking profusions, mangrove forests grow in tidal zones all over the tropics. Many of the trees in those inundated forests grow propped up on stilt roots, which keep their leaves out of the saltwater and help them absorb carbon dioxide when the tide is high. Those roots also provide protection for a variety of small fish and crustaceans, and they are often covered with barnacles, mussels, and other shellfish.

Mangrove forests are fairly homogeneous, with stands of one species of tree stretching off as far as the eye can see. They are also extremely productive ecosystems that play an important role as estuaries. Many marine animals, such as shrimp, spend the early stages of their lives in mangrove estuaries, whereas other species, such as certain kinds of snappers, are born and die there. Mangroves are vital to the health of the ocean beyond them and are attractive sites for animals that feed on marine life, especially fish-eating birds, such as cormorants, herons, pelicans, and ospreys.

The forests that line the Caribbean canals, along the northeast coast, are dominated by the water-resistant *yolillo* palm. This area is home to many of the same animals found in the rain forest, such as monkeys, parrots, and iguanas, as well as river dwellers, such as turtles, otters, and anhingas. A boat trip up the canals is thus an excellent opportunity to observe wildlife, as are similar excursions on such jungle rivers as the Río Frío and the Río Sarapiquí. Seasonal swamps such as Caño Negro and the *lagunas* of Palo Verde, which disappear during the dry months, are also excellent areas to see birds. There is also a vast swamp in the heart of Parque Nacional Corcovado, which never dries up but is virtually impenetrable because of the thick, thorny vegetation surrounding it.

In addition to its varied forests, Costa Rica has 1,224 km (760 mi) of coastline, which consists of beaches separated by rocky points. Although those points are home for a variety of marine life, most of the country's beaches are important nesting spots for endangered sea turtles. And submerged in the sea off both coasts are extensive coral reefs, inhabited by hundreds of species of colorful fish, crustaceans, and other interesting invertebrates. With its vertiginous biological diversity, the coral reef could well be the marine equivalent of the rain forest.

Where Have All the Jungles Gone?

Considering it is home for such remarkable biodiversity, you would expect a trip through Costa Rica to consist of natural panoramas packed with a wealth of flora and fauna. It soon becomes clear, however, that the region's predominant landscapes are not cloud and rain forests but the coffee and banana plantations that have replaced them. The country's pre-Columbian cultures may have revered the jaguar and the harpy eagle, but today's inhabitants seem to put more stock in less-illustrious beasts: the cow and the chicken.

During the past 40 years, more than two-thirds of Costa Rica's original forests have been destroyed, cut at a rate of between 362 sq km (140 sq mi) and 765 sq km (295 sq mi) per year. Forests have traditionally been considered unproductive land, and their destruction was for a long time synonymous with development. During the 1970s and 1980s, international and domestic development policies fueled the destruction of large tracts of wilderness. Fortunately, Costa Rican conservationists became alarmed by that deforestation, and in the 1970s they began creating what has since grown to become the region's best national parks system.

In addition to protecting vast expanses of wilderness—between 15 percent and 20 percent of the national territory—the Costa Rican government has made progress in curbing deforestation outside the national parks. The rate of destruction has dropped significantly, but poaching and illegal logging continue to be serious problems that, if left uncorrected, will eventually wipe out many important species and wild areas.

Deforestation not only spells disaster for the jaguar and the eagle, but it can also have grave consequences for human beings. Forests absorb the rains and release water slowly, playing an important role in regulating the flow of rivers, which is why severely deforested regions often suffer floods during the rainy season and drought during the dry months. A forest's tree cover also prevents topsoil erosion, thus keeping the land fertile and productive, and in many parts of the country, erosion has left once-productive farmland almost worthless. Finally, hidden within the country's flora and fauna are countless unknown or under-studied substances that could eventually be extracted to cure diseases and serve humankind. The destruction of Costa Rica's forests is a loss for the entire world.

Responsible Tourism

With each passing year, more and more Costa Ricans are coming to realize how valuable and endangered their country's remaining wilderness is. Costa Ricans visit their national parks in significant numbers, and they consider those protected areas vital to the national economy, both for the natural resources they preserve and their role as tourist attractions. Local conservationists, however, are still a long way from achieving their goal of involving the communities that surround the country's parks in their protection.

Costa Ricans who cut trees and hunt endangered animals usually do so out of economic necessity, and, unfortunately, the people who live near protected areas are often the last to benefit from the tourism that wilderness attracts. When you visit a park or reserve, your entrance fee helps pay for the preservation of Costa Rica's wildlife. But you can also make your visit beneficial to the people who live nearby by hiring local guides, horses, or boats; eating in local restaurants; and buying things (other than wild animal products, of course) in local shops.

You can go a few steps further by making donations to local conservation groups or to such international organizations as Conservation International, the Nature Conservancy, the Rainforest Alliance, and the World Wildlife Fund, all of which support important conservation efforts within Costa Rica. It is also good to stray from the beaten path: visit private preserves and stay at lodges that contribute to environmental efforts and nearby communities. By making your visit beneficial to grassroots conservation efforts, you can become part of the global effort to save the planet's tropical ecosystems and thus help to ensure that the treasures you traveled so far to see remain intact for future generations.

— David Dudenhoefer

WILDLIFE GLOSSARY

AN AMAZING ARRAY OF CREATURES has evolved in tiny Costa Rica, positioned between the two great American continents. Many are not terribly hard to see, thanks, in part, to the protection of the country's park and refuge system. A rundown of some of the most common and attention-grabbing mammals, birds, reptiles, amphibians, and even a few insects that you might encounter follows. Common Costa Rican names are given, so you can understand the local wildlife lingo, as are the latest scientific names.

Agouti (*guatusa*; *Dasyprocta punctata*): A 20-inch tail-less rodent with small ears and a large muzzle. It's reddish brown on Pacific side, more tawny orange on Caribbean slope. Sits on haunches to eat large seeds and fruit.

Anteater (*oso hormiguero*): Three species are found here—the giant (*Myrmecophaga tridactyla*), silky (*Cyclopes didactylus*), and collared, or vested (*Tamandua mexicana*); only the latter is commonly seen (and too often as a roadkill). This medium-size anteater (30 inches long with 18-inch tail) is seen lapping up ants and termites with long sticky tongue; has long sharp claws for ripping into insect nests.

Aracaris (*cusingo*): Slender toucans, with trademark bill, travel in groups of six or more and eat ripe fruit. Collared aracaris (*Pteroglossus torquatus*) on Caribbean has chalky upper mandible; fiery-billed (*Pteroglossus frantzii*) on southern Pacific has orange-red upper mandible.

Armadillo (*cusuco*; *Dasypus novemcinctus*): Same species as in southern U.S. and widespread in Costa Rica. Mostly nocturnal and solitary, this edentate roots in soil with long muzzle for varied diet of insects, small animals, and plant material.

Caiman (*cocodrilo*): The spectacled caiman (*Caiman crocodilus*) is a small crocodilian (to 7 ft) inhabiting freshwater, subsisting mainly on fish. It's most active at night (has bright red eyeshine) and basks by day. Distinguished from American crocodile (☞ *below*) by sloping brow and smooth back scales.

Coati (*pizote*; *Nasua narica*): A long-nosed relative of the raccoon, with long tail often held straight up. Lone males or groups of females with young are active during the day, on ground or in trees. Opportunistic and omnivorous, they feed on fruit, invertebrates, and small vertebrates.

Cougar (*puma*; *Felis concolor*): Mountain lions are the largest unspotted cats (to 5 ft, with 3½-inch tail) in Costa Rica; widespread but rare, they occur in essentially all wild habitats and feed on vertebrates ranging from snakes to deer.

Crocodile (*lagarto*; *Crocodylus acutus*): American crocodile can reach 16 ft in length and be found in most major river systems (particularly in the Tempisque and Tárcoles rivers). Despite size and appearance, it seldom attacks humans, preferring to dine on fish and birds. Distinguished from the smaller caiman (☞ *above*) by flat head, narrow snout, and spiky scales.

Ctenosaur (*garrobo*; *Ctenosaura similis*): A.k.a. black, or spiny, iguana. Large (to 18 inches long with 18-inch tail), tan lizard with four dark bands on body and a tail ringed with rows of sharp, curved spines. Terrestrial and arboreal, it sleeps in burrows or tree hollows. Though mostly vegetarian, it consumes small creatures. Seen along the coast in the dry northwest and in wetter areas farther south.

Dolphin (*delfin*): Several species, including bottlenose dolphins (*Tursiops truncatus*), frolic in Costa Rican waters. Frequently observed off Pacific shores are spotted dolphins (*Stenella attenuata*), which are small (to 6 ft), with pale spots on posterior half of body; they often travel in groups of 20 or more and play in bow wakes and around vessels.

Frigatebird (*tijereta del mar*; *Fregata magnificens*): Large, black soaring bird with slender wings and forked tail; one of the most effortless and agile fliers of the avian world. More common on Pacific coast. Doesn't dive or swim; instead swoops to pluck food from surface.

Frog (*rana*): Some 120 species of frogs exist in Costa Rica; most are nocturnal, except for brightly colored poison dart frogs (*Dendrobates* spp.), whose coloration (either red with blue or green hind legs or charcoal black with fluorescent green markings) warns potential predators of their toxicity. Red-eyed leaf frogs (*Agalychnis* spp.) are among the showiest of nocturnal species. Large brown marine toads (*Bufo marinus*) are common at night.

Howler Monkeys (*mono congo*; *Alouatta palliata*): These dark, chunky-bodied monkeys (to 22 inches long and 24-inch tail) with black faces travel in troops of up to 20. Lethargic mammals, they eat leaves, fruits, and flowers. The deep, resounding howls by males serve as communication among and between troops.

Iguana (*iguana*): Largest lizard in Costa Rica; males can grow to 10 feet, including tail. They are mostly arboreal and good swimmers. Only young green iguanas (*Iguana iguana*) are bright green; adults are much duller; females dark grayish; males olive (with orangish heads in breeding season). All have characteristic round cheek scale and smooth tails.

Jacana (*gallito de agua*; *Jacana spinosa*): These birds are sometimes referred to as "lily trotters" because their long toes allow them to walk on floating vegetation. They eat aquatic organisms and plants and are found at almost any body of water. Expose yellow wing feathers in flight. "Liberated" females lay eggs in several nests tended by different males.

Jaguar (*tigre*; *Panthera onca*): Largest New World feline (to 6 ft, with 2-ft tail), this top-of-the-line predator is exceedingly rare, but lives in a wide variety of habitats from dry forest to cloud forest. Most common in the vast La Amistad Biosphere Reserve (☞ Chapter 7 and 9).

Jesus Christ Lizard (*gallego*): Flaps of skin on long toes enable this spectacular lizard to run across water. Three species in Costa Rica: lineated basilisk (*Basiliscus basiliscus*) on Pacific side is brown with pale lateral stripe; emerald basilisk (*Basiliscus plumifrons*) in Caribbean lowlands is marked with turquoise and black on green body; striped basilisk (*Basiliscus vittatus*), also in Caribbean, resembles lineated basilisk. Adult male grows to 3 ft (mostly tail) and has crests on head, back, and base of tail.

Kinkajou (*martilla*; *Potos flavus*): A nocturnal, arboreal relative of raccoon with light brown fur (to 20 inches, with 20-inch prehensile tail). Actively and often noisily forages for fruit, insects, and some nectar. Has yellow-green eyeshine.

Leaf-Cutter Ant (*zompopas*; *Atta* spp.): Most commonly noticed neotropical ants, found in all lowland habitats. Columns sometimes extend for several hundred yards from underground nest to plants being harvested; the clipped leaves are fed to cultivated fungus that they eat.

Macaw (*lapas*): Two species in Costa Rica—scarlet macaw (*Ara macao*) on Pacific side (Osa Peninsula and Carara Biological Reserve, ☞ Chapter 6 and 7) and great green macaw (*Ara ambigua*) on Caribbean side, where population is severely threatened. Huge, raucous parrots with long tails; immense bills used to rip apart fruits to get to seeds. Nest in hollow trees. Victims of pet trade poachers and deforestation.

Magpie Jay (*urraca*; *Calocitta formosa*): This southern relative of the blue jay, with long tail and distinctive topknot (crest of forwardly curved feathers), is common resident of dry northwest, where often commensal with humans (omnivorous). Bold and inquisitive, with amazingly varied vocalizations, these birds travel in noisy groups of four or more.

Margay (*caucel*; *Felis wiedii*): Fairly small, spotted nocturnal cat (22 inches long, with 18-inch tail), similar to somewhat larger ocelot (☞ *below*) but with longer tail. It's far more arboreal: mobile ankle joints allow it to climb down trunks head first. Eats small vertebrates.

Morpho (*morfo*): Spectacular, big butterfly. Three species in Costa Rica have brilliant-blue wing upper surface, one of which (*Morpho peleides*) is common in moister areas; one has intense ultraviolet upper surface; one is white above and below; and one is brown and white. Adults feed on rotting fallen fruit (never visit flowers).

Motmot (*pajaro bobo*): Handsome bird of forest understory, most with characteristic "racquet tipped" tails, sits patiently while scanning for large insect prey or small vertebrates. Nests in burrows. Six species are found in Costa Rica.

Ocelot (*manigordo*; *Felis pardalis*): Medium-size spotted cat (33 inches long, with 16-inch tail) with shorter tail than margay (☞ *above*) is active night or day, mostly terrestrial. Feeds on rodents but also eats other vertebrates. Forepaws are rather large in relation to body, hence local name that translates as "fat hand."

Oropéndola (*oropendola*; *Psarocolius* spp.): Crow-sized bird in oriole family with bright yellow tail. Nests in colonies in isolated trees in pendulous nests (up to 6 ft long) built by females. Males make unmistakable, loud, gurgling liquid call. They are fairly omnivorous, eating much fruit, and much more numerous on Caribbean side.

Parakeet and Parrot (*pericos,* parakeets; *loros,* parrots): Prerequisites of any tropical setting. Fifteen species in Costa Rica (plus two macaws, ☞ *above*). All are clad in green (virtually disappearing upon landing in trees), and most with a splash of a primary color or two on head or wings. They travel in boisterous flocks, prey on immature seeds, and nest in cavities.

Peccary: Piglike animals with thin legs and thick necks, they travel in small groups (larger where populations still numerous); root in soil for fruit, seeds, and small creatures; and have strong musk odor. Two species in Costa Rica: collared peccary (*saíno, Tayassu tajacu*), most commonly encountered; white-lipped peccary (*chancho de monte, Tayassu pecari*), now exterminated in most areas.

Pelican (*pelícano*): Large size, big bill, and throat pouch make brown pelicans (*Pelecanus occidentalis*) unmistakable inhabitants of coastal areas (far more abundant on Pacific side). Often fly in V formations and dive for fish.

Quetzal (*quetzal*): One of the world's most exquisite birds. Resplendent quetzals (*Pharomachrus mocinno*) were revered as sacred by Mayas. Glittering green plumage and long tail coverts of male quetzals draw thousands of visitors to highland cloud forests, where most readily seen from February to April.

Roseate Spoonbill (*garza rosada*; *Ajaia ajaja*): Pink plumage and spatulate bill set this wader apart from all other wetland birds; feeds by swishing bill back and forth in water while using feet to stir up bottom-dwelling creatures. Most common in areas around Palo Verde (☞ Chapter 5) and Caño Negro (☞ Chapter 4).

Sea Turtle. *See* Close-Up: Tico Turtles, *in* Chapter 8.

Sloth (*perezoso*): Two species in Costa Rica: brown-throated, three-toed sloth (*Bradypus variegatus*) and Hoffmann's two-toed sloth (*Choloepus hoffmanni*); both grow to 2 ft, but two-toed (check forelegs) often looks bigger due to longer fur, and is only one in the highlands. Completely vegetarian; marvelously adapted to low-energy diet; well camouflaged.

Spider Monkey (*mono colorado, mono araña*; *Ateles geoffroyi*): Lanky, long-tailed, largest monkeys in Costa Rica (to 24 inches, with 32-inch tail). Hang out in groups of two to four. Diet consists of ripe fruit, leaves, and flowers. These incredible aerialists can swing effortlessly through branches using long arms and legs and prehensile tails. Caribbean and southern Pacific populations are dark reddish brown; northwestern individuals are blond.

Squirrel Monkey (*mono tití*; *Saimiri oerstedii*): Smallest of four Costa Rican monkeys (11 inches, with 15-inch tail), with distinctive facial pattern (black cap and muzzle, white mask). They travel in noisy, active groups of 20 or more and feed on fruit and insects. Tail not prehensile. Found only around Manuel Antonio National Park (☞ Chapter 6) and parts of Osa Peninsula (☞ Chapter 7), possibly introduced by humans in pre-Columbian times.

Tapir (*danta*; *Tapirus bairdii*): The largest land mammal in Costa Rica (to 6½ ft), something like a small rhinoceros without armor, has adapted to a wide range of habitats but is nocturnal and seldom seen. Completely vegetarian; prehensile snout used for harvesting vegetation. Said to defecate and sometimes sleep in water.

Toucan (*tucán, tucancillo*): Recognizable to all who've ever seen a box of Froot Loops. Costa Rica has said species, including the aracaris (☞ *above*). Keel-billed (*Ramphastos sulfuratus*) and chestnut-mandibled toucans (*Ramphastos swainsonii*) are the largest (18 inches and 22 inches, respectively), black with bright yellow "bibs" and multihued bills. The much smaller and stouter emerald toucanet (*Aulacorhynchus prasinus*) and yellow-eared toucanet (*Selenidera spectabilis*) are aptly named. All eat fruit, but also some animal matter, and nest in cavities.

Whale (*ballenas*): Humpback whale (*Megaptera novaeanglia*) most likely seen off Pacific coast between November and February; migrates from California and as far as Hawaii.

White-Faced Capuchin Monkey (*mono carablanca*; *Cebus capuchinus*): Medium-sized omnivorous monkey (to 18 inches, with 20-inch tail) with black fur and pink face surrounded by whitish fur extending to chest. Found singly or in groups of up to 20. Extremely active foragers; examines environment closely and even comes to ground.

BOOKS AND VIDEOS

Books

Costa Rica, a Traveler's Literary Companion (Consortium), edited by Barbara Ras, is a collection of short stories that lets you sample the country's best writers while providing plenty of insight into local culture. For a more factual perspective, consult *Inside Costa Rica* (Interhemispheric Resource Center), by Tom Barry and Silvia Lara. David Rains Wallace's *The Quetzal and the Macaw: The Story of Costa Rica's National Parks* (Sierra Club Books) is an entertaining and informative account of the country's exemplary efforts in conservation.

Some of the most popular books on Costa Rica are about its rich natural history. *A Guide to the Birds of Costa Rica* (Cornell University Press), by F. Gary Stiles and Alexander F. Skutch, is a first-rate field guide. Alexander Skutch has also written some entertaining chronicles that combine natural history, philosophy, and anecdote, *A Naturalist in Costa Rica* (University Press of Florida) among them.

The *Costa Rica: Eco-Traveller's Wildlife Guide* (Academic Press), by Les Beletsky, offers an overview of the most common fauna. For an in-depth look at the local ecology, read *Tropical Nature* (Macmillan), by Adrian Forsyth and Ken Miyata.

Though Costa Rica has its own rich literary tradition, few of its writers have been translated into English. Some have, but can be difficult to find in the United States: *Years Like Brief Days* (Dufour Editions) is one of the most popular novels of Fabián Dobles, famous for his humorous depiction of life in rural Costa Rica during the early part of this century. *The Lonely Men's Island* (Editorial Escritores Unidos, Mexico), the first novel of José León Sánchez, recounts his years on Isla San Lucas, the Costa Rican version of Alcatraz, where he was sent for stealing the country's patron saint, la Virgin de los Angeles (☞ Cartago *in* Chapter 3).

Videos

Jurassic Park (1993) was set on Costa Rica's isolated Cocos Island, but the film was actually shot in Hawaii. Oddly enough, much of the film version of *Congo* (1995), another Michael Crichton novel, was shot in Costa Rica. Most of Ridley Scott's *1492: Conquest of Paradise* (1992) was filmed on the country's Pacific coast. If you're more interested in the waves that break off that coast, however, check out the surf classic *The Endless Summer* (1966), both the original and remake of which have footage of Costa Rica.

INDEX

Icons and Symbols

★ Our special recommen-
  dations
✕ Restaurant
🏠 Lodging establishment
✕🏠 Lodging establishment
  whose restaurant war-
  rants a special trip
🦆 Good for kids (rubber
  duck)
☞ Sends you to another
  section of the guide for
  more information
✉ Address
☎ Telephone number
🕐 Opening and closing
  times
💲 Admission prices

Numbers in white and black
circles ③ ❸ that appear on
the maps, in the margins, and
within the tours correspond to
one another.

A

Accommodations. ☞
  Lodging
Adventure tours, *xxxiv*
Aguas termales, *143*
Air travel. ☞ Plane travel
Airports, *xiv*
Alajuela, *46–48*
Altagracia (Nicaragua), *210*
Animals. ☞ *Specific types*
Anteaters, *98, 166, 169, 182*
Apartment and villa rentals,
  xxvii–xxviii
Archaeological sites, *7–8,
  57–58*
Area Recreativa de Prusia, *53*
Armadillos, *79, 80, 124,
  182, 200*
Atenas, *122–123*
**Atlantic Lowlands and the
  Caribbean Coast,** *7, 161–
  184, 225–227*
beaches, *177*
*Braulio Carrillo National Park
  and the Northern Lowlands,
  165–169, 182*
car rentals, 183
*Coastal Talamanca, 173–182,
  183*
*dining, 162, 173, 174, 176,
  178–179, 181*
emergencies, 184
guided tours, 184
*itinerary recommendations,
  163–164*
*lodging, 162, 167, 168–169,
  171, 172, 173, 175, 176–
  177, 179–180*

*sports and outdoor activities,
  162–163, 177–178, 180–
  181*
timing the visit, 165
*Tortuguero and Barra del
  Colorado, 169–173, 183*
transportation, 182–183
visitor information, 184
ATMs, *xxix–xxx*
Australian travelers, *xx,
  xxxiii*

B

Bahía Drake, *154–156*
Bahía Salinas, *83–84*
Balque (Nicaragua), *210*
Bambito (Panama), *195–196*
Banco Central, *19*
Barra del Colorado, *172–
  173*
**Barra del Colorado Wildlife
  Refuge,** *172, 226–227*
Barra Honda Peak, *100*
Bars. ☞ Nightlife *under
  specific cities*
Barva de Heredia, *43, 45*
**Basílica de Nuestra Señora
  de Los Angeles,** *52*
Bastimentos (Panama), *204*
Beaches
*Atlantic Lowlands and the
  Caribbean Coast, 177*
*Central Pacific Costa Rica,
  126, 128, 130, 133*
Nicaragua, 210
*Nicoya Peninsula, 88–89, 98,
  101–103, 105–116*
*Northern Guanacaste and
  Alajuela, 80–81, 83*
Panama, 200, 204
*Southern Pacific Costa Rica,
  145–146, 148, 150, 151*
Bed-and-breakfasts, *xxviii*
Bicycling, *xiv, xxxi*
*Atlantic Lowlands and the
  Caribbean Coast, 177*
*Northern Guanacaste and
  Alajuela, 74, 84*
Bird-watching, *xxxi*
*Atlantic Lowlands and the
  Caribbean Coast, 165, 166,
  167, 171, 182*
*Central Pacific Costa Rica,
  124, 125, 134*
Central Valley, 47, 55, 56, 58
*Nicoya Peninsula, 96, 98, 99,
  109, 114*
*Northern Guanacaste and
  Alajuela, 71, 74–75, 77, 79,
  83*
Panama, 194, 197, 204
*Southern Pacific Costa Rica,
  141, 142, 152, 153, 196,
  204*
Boat travel. ☞ *Also* Boat
  trips; Cruises; Ferry

travel; White-water
  rafting
*Atlantic Lowlands and the
  Caribbean Coast, 183*
Costa Rica, xiv–xv
Nicaragua, xv, 214
Nicoya Peninsula, 117–118
Panama, xv, 205
*Southern Pacific Costa Rica,
  156, 157*
Boat trips, *114, 125, 162*
Boca del Drago, *200*
Bocas del Toro (Panama),
  199–200
Boquete (Panama), *191–194*
Brasilito, *110*
Bus travel, *xv–xvi*
*Atlantic Lowlands and the
  Caribbean Coast, 182, 183*
*Central Pacific Costa Rica,
  134, 135*
Central Valley, 58–59, 60
Nicaragua, xvi, 213, 214
*Nicoya Peninsula, 116–117,
  118*
*Northern Guanacaste and
  Alajuela, 84, 85*
Panama, xvi, 198, 205
San José, 34
*Southern Pacific Costa Rica,
  156, 157*
Business hours, *xv*
Butterfly farms, *47*
Butterfly gardens, *22–23, 76*

C

**Cabo Blanco Strict Nature
  Reserve,** *98*
Cabo Matapalo, *153–154*
Cahuita, *175–177*
Caldera (Costa Rica), *94*
Caldera (Panama), *192*
**Cámara de Turismo de
  Montezuma** (CATUMA),
  97
Cameras and photography,
  xvi–xvii
**Canadian Organization for
  Tropical Education and
  Rainforest Conservation,**
  169
Canadian travelers, *xxxiii*
Caño Negro Wildlife Refuge,
  71, 219–220
Canopy tours, *75, 79*
Camping, *xxviii*
Car rentals, *xvii–xviii*
Car travel, *xviii–xix*
*Atlantic Lowlands and the
  Caribbean Coast, 182, 183*
Central Pacific Costa Rica, 135
Central Valley, 59
Nicaragua, 213, 214
Nicoya Peninsula, 117, 118
*Northern Guanacaste and
  Alajuela, 84–85*

Panama, 198, 205–206
San José, 34, 35
Southern Pacific Costa Rica, 157–158
Caribbean Conservation Corporation (CCC), 171
Carrillo ranger station, 166
Cartago, 52
Casa de la Cultura (Liberia), 105
Casa de la Cultura (Puntarenas), 94
Casa Orquiedas, 148
Casa Verde Green Turtle Research Station, 171
Cash machines, xxix–xxx
Casinos, 32, 130, 133
Cataratas de Nauyaca, 144
Catarina (Nicaragua), 213
Catedral Metropolitana, 19
CATIE (Centro Agronómico Tropical de Investigación y Enseñanza), 56
Caves, 68, 70, 99–100
Cayos Zapatillas, 201
Central Pacific Costa Rica, 6, 121–136, 222–223
beaches, 126, 128, 130, 133
car rentals, 136
Central Pacific Hinterlands, 122–126, 134, 135
children, attractions for, 126, 129
Coast near San José, 126–134, 135
dining, 121, 126–127, 129, 130–131
emergencies, 136
guided tours, 136
itinerary recommendations, 122
lodging, 121, 123, 124, 125, 127, 128, 129, 131–133
nightlife and the arts, 127, 129–130, 133
shopping, 134
sports and outdoor activities, 121, 126, 127, 128, 130, 133
timing the visit, 121
transportation, 134–135
visitor information, 136
Central Valley, 5–6, 38–60, 218–219
car rentals, 60
children, attractions for, 47, 49
dining, 38, 41–42, 48, 54
Eastern Central Valley, 51–53, 58, 59, 60
emergencies, 60
festivals, 38
guided tours, 60
itinerary recommendations, 39–40
lodging, 38–39, 42, 45, 46, 47–48, 49, 50, 51, 55, 56–57
Orosí Valley, 53–55, 59, 60

shopping, 49, 50–51, 53, 54
sports and outdoor activities, 46, 49, 57
timing the visit, 40
transportation, 58–60
Turrialba and the Guayabo National Monument, 55–58, 59, 60
visitor information, 60
volcanoes, 39
Western Central Valley, 41–51, 58, 59, 60
Centro Biológico Las Quebradas, 142
Centro Comercial El Pueblo (San José), 22
Cerro de la Muerte, 142
Cerro Punta (Panama), 196–198
Children, traveling with, xix
Chinese cemetery (Puerto Limón), 174
Churches, 19, 43, 47, 49, 50, 51, 52, 54, 100, 211
Ciudad Neily, 146
Ciudad Quesada, 67
Climate, xxxviii
Clothing for the trip, xxxi–xxxii
Cloud forests, 55, 74–76, 77, 86, 141. ☞ Also Rain forests
Coastal canals, 171
Coatis, 79, 80, 100, 124, 169, 200
Coffee industry, 44, 60
Coffee plantations, 43, 192
Computers, travel with, xix
Correos (Central Post Office), 19
Coto Brus Indian Reservation, 146
Cougars, 98
Credit cards, xxx
Crocodiles, 125, 126, 169, 181
Cruises, xix, 149, 154
Cuajiniquil, 81
Cuesta de Piedra Waterfalls (Panama), 195
Currency exchange, xxx–xxxi
Curú National Wildlife refuge, 96
Customs and duties, xx–xxi

D
David (Panama), 190–191
Dining, xxi, 8. ☞ Also under specific areas and regions
Disabilities and accessibility, xxii
Discos, 32
Dolphins, 153
Dominical, 143–145
Drake, 154
Drug stores. ☞ Emergencies

Duties. ☞ Customs and duties

E
EARTH (Escuela de Agricultura de le Region Tropical Humeda), 174
Ecotourism, xxii–xxiii, 8–9, 145, 149, 180–181, 217–218
Electricity, xxiii
Embassies, xxiii
Emergencies, xxiii
Atlantic Lowlands and the Caribbean Coast, 184
Central Pacific Costa Rica, 136
Central Valley, 60
Nicaragua, 214
Nicoya Peninsula, 118
Northern Guanacaste and Alajuela, 85
Panama, 199, 206
San José, 35
Southern Pacific Costa Rica, 158
English language media, xxiii–xxiv
Escazú, 41–42
Etiquette, xxiv

F
Ferry travel, xiv–xv, 201–202
Festivals and seasonal events. ☞ Under countries and regions
Film, 31
Finca de Mariposas (Butterfly Farm), 47
Fire engine, 200
Fishing, 9–10
Atlantic Lowlands and the Caribbean Coast, 162
Central Pacific Costa Rica, 130
Nicoya Peninsula, 114
Northern Guanacaste and Alajuela, 70, 83–84
Panama, 191
Southern Pacific Costa Rica, 145, 150, 154
Frogs, 75, 152, 167, 200, 204

G
Gandoca-Manzanillo National Wildlife Refuge, 181, 226
Gardens, 22–23, 53, 72, 146, 192
Gay and lesbian travelers, xxiv
Golfito, xxxviii, 147–150
Golfito National Wildlife Refuge, 148
Golfo de Santa Elena, 81

Granada (Nicaragua), *211–213*

Grecia, *49–50*

Guaitil, *100*

Guanacaste Province. ☞ Northern Guanacaste and Alajuela

Guápiles, *173*

Gymnasiums, *32*

H

Health clubs. ☞ Gymnasiums

Health concerns, *xxiv–xxvi.* ☞ *Also* Emergencies

Heredia, *43, 45*

Hermosa, *106–107*

Hiking

Atlantic Lowlands and the Caribbean Coast, 162, 178

Central Valley, 46, 49

Nicaragua, 211

Northern Guanacaste and Alajuela, 70, 78

Panama, 194, 197–198

Southern Pacific Costa Rica, 142, 152, 153

Holidays, *xxvi.* ☞ *Also* Festivals and seasonal events *under countries and regions*

Horseback riding, *9*

Central Pacific Costa Rica, 128, 130, 133

Central Valley, 46, 49

Northern Guanacaste and Alajuela, 70, 74, 78, 84

San José, 32–33

Southern Pacific Costa Rica, 154

Hostels, *xxviii*

Hotels, *xxviii.* ☞ *Also* Lodging *under specific regions*

I

Iguanas, *22–23, 100, 124, 134*

Inner tubing, *145*

Insect collection, *49*

Instituto Costarricense de Turism (ICT), *19*

Institute of Renewable Natural Resources (INRENARE), *201*

Internet cafés, *xix*

Insurance, *xxvi, xxxii*

Isla Bastimentos (Panama), *204–205*

Isla Bolaños (bird refuge), *83*

Isla Cabo Blanco, *98*

Isla Colón (Panama), *199–203*

Isla del Caño, *156*

Isla Mogote, *134*

Isla Ometepe, *210*

Isla Pajaros, *99*

Isla Santa Catalina, *109*

Isla Tortuga, *94*

J

Jacó, *126–128*

Jaguars, *79, 98, 165, 169, 182*

Jail (Alajuela), *47*

Jardín Botánico Arenal, *72*

Jardin de Mariposas Spyrogyra (butterfly garden), *22–23*

Jardín Gaia, *129*

Jardín Lankester, *53*

Jardín Mariposa (butterfly garden), *76*

Jogging. ☞ Running and jogging

Joyas del Bosque Húmedo (Jewels of the Rainforest), *49*

Jungle boating, *162, 171*

K

Kayaking

Atlantic Lowlands and the Caribbean Coast, 181

Central Pacific Costa Rica, 133

Central Valley, 57

Nicoya Peninsula, 114

Southern Pacific Costa Rica, 152, 154

L

La Casona Hacienda, *80–81*

La Cruz, *82–83*

La Fortuna, *68–70*

La Fortuna Waterfall, *68, 70*

La Gamba, *148*

La Selva Biological Station, *167*

Lago de Nicaragua, *210*

Language, *xxvi–xxvii*

Las Hornillas, *79*

Las Horquetas, *166–167*

Liberia, *104–105*

Lizards, *22–23, 124, 182*

Llano de Los Indios, *81*

Lodging, *xxvii–xxix, 9.* ☞ *Also under specific regions*

children and, xix

travelers with disabilities, xxii

Los Quetzales (private nature reserve, Panama), *196*

Luggage, *xxxii*

M

Mail and shipping, *xxix*

Manatees, *169*

Manantial de Agua Viva, *125*

Manuel Antonio, *130–134*

Margays, *166*

Maritza Station, *81*

Masaya (Nicaragua), *213*

Mengo Biological Station, *81*

Mercado Central, *19*

Miniature golf, *126*

Moín, *175*

Money, *xxix–xxxi*

Monkeys

Atlantic Lowlands and the Caribbean Coast, 165, 166, 167, 169, 171

Central Pacific Costa Rica, 124, 134

Nicoya Peninsula, 96, 100, 114

Northern Guanacaste and Alajuela, 80

Panama, 200

Southern Pacific Costa Rica, 152

Montezuma, *97*

Monumento Nacional Guayabo, *57–58, 218–219*

Moyogalpa (Nicaragua), *210*

Mundo de las Serpientas (World of Snakes), *49*

Museo de Arte y Diseño Contemporáneo, *20*

Museo de Cultura Popular, *43*

Museo de Jade, *19–20*

Museo de Oro, *20*

Museo del Niño, *23*

Museo José de Obaldia, *190*

Museo Juan Santamaria, *47*

Museo Nacional, *20*

Museums

Atlantic Lowlands and the Caribbean Coast, 171

business hours, xv

Central Valley, 43, 47, 54

Nicaragua, 213

Nicoya Peninsula, 105

Northern Guanacaste and Alajuela, 80

Panama, 190

San José, 19, 20

Music, *31, 94, 175*

N

National Parks Service, *142, 151–152*

Nature lodges, *xxviii–xxix*

New Zealand, tips for travelers from, *xx, xxxiii*

Nicaragua, *7, 206–214, 228–229*

beaches, 207, 208–209, 210

car rentals, 214

dining, 207, 209, 212

embassies, 214

emergencies, 214

guided tours, 214

itinerary recommendations, 208

lodging, 207, 209, 210–211, 212

shopping, 207

sports and outdoor activities, 211

timing the visit, 208

transportation, 213–214

visitor information, 214

Nicoya, *100*
Nicoya Peninsula, *6, 88–119, 221–222*
beaches, 88–89, 98, 101–103, 105–116
car rentals, 118
Central Nicoya Beaches: Punta Islita to Nosara, 101–104, 117, 118
dining, 89, 94, 101, 103, 105, 106, 109–110, 112
emergencies, 118
festivals, 89, 105
guided tours, 118–119
itinerary recommendations, 91–93
Liberia and the Northern Nicoya Beaches, 104–116, 117, 118
lodging, 89, 94–95, 96, 97, 100, 101, 102, 103, 104, 105, 106, 107, 108, 109, 110, 111, 112–113, 114, 115–116
Nicoya and the Tempisque River Delta region, 98–101, 117, 118
Puntarenas to Cabo Blanco, 93–98, 116, 117, 118
sports and outdoor activities, 89–90, 95, 99, 107–108, 114
timing the visit, 93
transportation, 116–118
visitor information, 119
Niquinohomo (Nicaragua), *213*
Northern Guanacaste and Alajuela, *6, 62–86, 219–221*
Arenal and the Cordillera de Tilarán, 66–78, 84, 85
car rentals, 85
children, attractions for, 76
dining, 63, 68–69, 76, 82
emergencies, 85
Far Northern Guanacaste, 78–84, 85
guided tours, 86
itinerary recommendations, 64, 66
lodging, 63, 67, 69–70, 72, 73–74, 76, 78, 79, 81, 82–83
shopping, 67, 73, 78
sports and outdoor activities, 63, 70, 74, 78, 79, 83–84
timing the visit, 66
transportation, 84–85
visitor information, 86
volcanoes, 63
Nosara, *103–104*
Nuevo Arenal, *71–73*

O

Ocelots, *80, 169*
Olas Chicas (Panama), *201, 204*
Orchids, *148, 153, 166*

Organization for Tropical Research, *99*
Organization for Tropical Studies (OTS), *167*
Orosí, *54–55*
Orosí Valley, *53–55*
Orotina, *124*
Ostional National Wildlife Refuge, *104*
Otters, *169*

P

Packing for Costa Rica, *xxxi–xxxii*
Panama, *7, 186–206, 227–228*
banks, 206
beaches, 200, 204
Bocas del Toro Archipelago, 199–203
car rentals, 199
Chiriquí Province, 188–199
dining, 186, 190–191, 192–193, 197, 201–202
emergencies, 199, 206
festivals, 186, 200
guided tours, 199, 206
itinerary recommendations, 188
lodging, 186–187, 191, 193–194, 195, 197, 202–203, 204–205
sports and outdoor activities, 187, 192, 194, 197–198, 203
telephones, 199, 206
timing the visit, 188
transportation, 198, 205–206
visitor information, 199, 206
Parks, local
Alajuela, 47
Granada, 211
Heredia, 43
Puerto Limón, 174
San José, 21–22
Parks, national, *216–229*
Atlantic Lowlands and the Caribbean Coast, 165–166, 169, 177–178, 225–227
Central Pacific Costa Rica, 134, 222–223
Central Valley, 48, 218–219
Nicaragua, 207, 213, 228–229
Nicoya Peninsula, 98–100, 111, 221–222
Northern Guanacaste and Alajuela, 79–82, 219–221
Panama, 187, 192, 196, 197, 200–201, 227–228
San José, 21
Southern Pacific Costa Rica, 143, 145–146, 148, 152–153, 223–224
Parque Central (Alajuela), *47*
Parque Central (Granada), *211*
Parque Central (Heredia), *43*

Parque Central (San José), *20*
Parque España (San José), *20–21*
Parque Internacional La Amistad (Panama), *196, 197, 228*
Parque Morazán (San José), *21*
Parque Nacional (San José), *21*
Parque Nacional Barra Honda, *99–100, 222*
Parque Nacional Braulio Carrillo, *45, 165–166, 225*
Parque Nacional Cahuita, *177–178, 225–226*
Parque Nacional Chirripó, *143, 223–224*
Parque Nacional Corcovado, *152–153, 224*
Parque Nacional Guanacaste, *81–82, 221*
Parque Nacional Juan Castro Blanco, *67, 219*
Parque Nacional La Amistad, *147*
Parque Nacional Manuel Antonio, *134, 223*
Parque Nacional Marina Isla Bastimentos (Panama), *200–201, 204, 227–228*
Parque Nacional Marino Ballena, *141, 145–146*
Parque Nacional Marino Las Baulas, *111, 222*
Parque Nacional Palo Verde, *98–99, 221*
Parque Nacional Piedras Biancas, *148*
Parque Nacional Rincón de la Vieja, *79, 220*
Parque Nacional Santa Rosa, *80–81, 220–221*
Parque Nacional Tapantí, *55, 218*
Parque Nacional Tortuguero, *169, 226–227*
Parque Nacional Volcán Barú, *192, 227*
Parque Nacional Volcán Irazú, *218*
Parque Nacional Volcán Masaya, *213, 229*
Parque Nacional Volcán Poás, *48*
Parque Vargas (Puerto Limón), *174*
Parque Zoológico Simón Bolivar, *23*
Parrita, *128*
Passports and visas, *xxxii–xxxiii*
Peccaries, *169, 182*
Pharmacies. ☞ Emergencies
Pico Blanco, *41*
Pitilla Station, *81*
Plane travel, *xii–xiv*

Atlantic Lowlands and the
  Caribbean Coast, 183
Cental Pacific Costa Rica, 135
Central Valley, 59
  with children, xix
Nicaragua, 214
Nicoya Peninsula, 117
Northern Guanacaste and
  Alajuela, 85
Panama, 198, 205
San José, 34
Southern Pacific Costa Rica,
  157, 158
Playa Avellanes, 115–116
Playa Ballena, 146
Playa Blanca, 81
Playa Bluff (Panama), 200
Playa Cabo Blanco, 98
Playa Cacao, 148
Playa Carrillo, 102
Playa Conchal, 110–111
Playa del Coco, 105–106
Playa Escondido, 134
Playa Espadilla, 130
Playa Espadilla Sur, 134
Playa Flamingo, 109–110
Playa Garza, 102–103
Playa Grande, 111
Playa Hermosa, 128
Playa Jacó, 126
Playa Junquillal, 115–116
Playa Langosta, 114
Playa Larga (Panama), 204
Playa Manuel Antonio, 134
Playa Nancite, 80–81
Playa Naranjo, 80, 95
Playa Negra, 115–116
Playa Ocotal, 108
Playa Paco Seco, 128
Playa Pan de Azúcar, 108–
  109
Playa Pavones, 151
Playa Pinuelas, 146
Playa Portrero, 109
Playa Rajada, 83
Playa Santo Domingo, 210
Playa Uvita, 146
Playa Ventanas, 146
Playa Zancudo, 150
Plaza de la Cultura (San
  José), 21
Plaza de la Democracia (San
  José), 21
Porcupines, 98, 166, 182
Pozo Azul, 144
Price charts, xxi, xxvii
Private nature preserves,
  139, 166–167, 196
Puerto Jiménez, 151–152
Puerto Limón, 174–175
Puerto Soley, 83
Puerto Viejo de Limón, 178–
  181
Puerto Viejo de Sarapiqui,
  168–169
Punta Catedral, 134
Punta Hospital, 201
Punta Islita, 101–102
Puntarenas, 94–95

Q
Quepos, 129–130
Quetzal (bird), 48, 55, 74–
  75, 141, 166, 194, 196

R
Raccoons, 79, 165–166,
  169, 200
Rafting. ☞ White-water
  rafting
Rain Forest Aerial Tram, 166
Rain forests
Atlantic Coast, 165–167, 177,
  225–227
Central Valley, 56, 57–58,
  218–219
Northern Guanacaste and
  Alajuela, 74–76, 219–221
Panama, 200, 204, 227–228
Southern Pacific Costa Rica,
  141, 223–224
Rara Avis (wildlife
  preserve), 166–167
Refugio Nacional de Vida
  Silvestre Caño Negro, 71,
  219–220
Reptile exhibit, 75
Reserva Biológica Bosque
  Nuboso Monteverde, 74–
  76. 78
Reserva Biológica Carara,
  124–125, 222–223
Reserva Biológica Hitoy
  Cerere, 182
Reserva Biológica Lomas
  Barbudal, 98–99, 221
Reserva La Biósfera La
  Amistad, 146, 147
Reserva Santa Elena, 75
Reserva Sendero Tranquilo,
  76
Rio Pacuare, 57
Rio Reventazón, 57
Running and jogging, 33

S
Safety, xxxiii–xxxiv
Sámara, 102
San Antonio de Escazú, 41
San Gerardo de Dota, 141–
  142
San Gerardo de Rivas, 143
San Isidro, 142–143
San José, 5, 14–36
arts, 31
car rentals, 35
children, attractions for, 21–
  22, 23
climate, xxxviii
day tripping, 14
dining, 14–15, 23, 25–28
doctors and dentists, xxiv, 35
embassies, 35
emergencies, 35
English-language bookstores,
  xxviii–xxiv, 33–34
exploring, 15–17, 19–23
festivals, 15
guided tours, 35–36
itinerary recommendations,
  16–17
lodging, 15, 28–31
nightlife, 31–32
pharmacies, 36
shopping, 33–34
sports and outdoor activities,
  32–33
transportation, 34–35
travel agencies, 36
visitor information, 36
walking tours, 17, 19, 22
San Juan del Sur
  (Nicaragua), 208–209
San Rafael, 43
San Ramón, 51
San Vito, 146–147
Santa Cruz, 100–101
Santa Elena hills, 81
Santa Maria peak, 79
Santo Domingo, 43
Sarchi, 50–51
Scuba diving, xxxi, 9, 107–
  108, 133, 156, 162, 181
Panama, 187, 201, 203
Sendero los Quetzales
  (Panama), 194
Senior citizens, tips for,
  xxxiv
Serpentario Monteverde, 75
Serpentarium, 21–22
Shopping, xxxv
  business hours, xv
Sirena ranger station, 151–
  152
Skunks, 98, 100, 169
Sloths, 79, 134, 165, 166,
  171, 200
Smithsonian Institution's
  Observatory, 71
Snakes, 21–22, 49, 171,
  200
Snorkeling, 9
Atlantic Lowlands and the
  Caribbean Coast, 162, 178,
  181
Northern Guanacaste and
  Alajuela, 83
Panama, 187, 201, 203
Southern Pacific Costa Rica,
  156
Soccer, 33
Southern Pacific Costa Rica,
  6–7, 138–159, 223–224
beaches, 145–146, 148, 150,
  151
car rentals, 158
dining, 138, 144, 147, 152
emergencies, 158
General Valley, 141–151, 156,
  157
guided tours, 158–159
itinerary recommendations,
  139–140
lodging, 138, 141, 142, 143,
  144–145, 146, 147, 148–
  149, 150, 151, 152, 153,
  154–156

Osa Peninsula, 151–156, 157
private nature preserves, 139
shopping, 147, 150
sports and outdoor activities,
138–139, 142, 143, 145,
150, 152, 153, 154
timing the visit, 140
transportation, 156–158
visitor information, 159
Spelunking, 70, 89
Sports and outdoor activites,
xxxi. ☞ Also under
specific types
Student travel, xxxiv
Surfing, 10. ☞ Also
Windsurfing
Atlantic Lowlands and the
Caribbean Coast, 162–163,
181
Central Pacific Costa Rica,
127, 128
Nicoya Peninsula, 90, 114
Panama, 203
Southern Pacific Costa Rica,
145, 154
Swimming. ☞ Beaches

T

Tabacón Resort, 68
Taller Eloy Alfaro e Hijos
(ox-cart factory), 50
Tamarindo, 111–114
Tambor, 96–97
Tapirs, 79, 80, 165, 166,
169, 182
Tárcoles, 125–126
Taxes, xxxv
Taxis, 35, 60
Teatro Nacional, 22
Telephones, xxxv–xxxvi
Tercipelo Cave, 99–100
Theater, 22, 31, 94
Thermal pools, 54
Tilarán, 73–74
Time, xxxvi
Timing the visit, xxxvii–
xxxviii
Tipping, xxxvi
Tortuguero, 169, 171–172
Train travel, xxxvi
Transportation, xxxvi
Travel agencies, xxxvi
Traveler's checks, xxxi
Turrialba, 56–57

Turtles
Atlantic Lowlands and the
Caribbean Coast, 163, 169,
170, 171, 181
Nicoya Peninsula, 90–91, 104,
111, 114
Northern Guanacasta and
Alajuela, 80–81
Panama, 200, 203

U

Ujarrás, 54
U.K. travelers, xxi, xxxiii

V

Venado Caves, 68, 70
Villa rentals, xxvii–xxviii
Visas. ☞ Passports and
visas
Visitor information, xxxvi–
xxxvii
Volcán (Panama), 194–195
Volcán Arenal, 71
Volcán Barú (Panama), 194,
227
Volcán Barva, 45–46, 166
Volcán Cacao, 81
Volcán Irazú, 52–53
Volcán Orosí, 81
Volcán Poás, 48–49
Volcán Rincón de la Vieja, 79
Volcanoes, 10, 39. ☞ Also
specific volcanoes
**Volunteer and educational
travel,** xxxvii

W

Waterfalls
Atlantic Lowlands and the
Caribbean Coast, 182
Central Pacific Costa Rica,
125
Northern Guanacasta and
Alajuela, 68, 70, 79
Nicoya Peninsula, 97
Panama, 191, 195
Southern Pacific Costa Rica,
141, 144, 145
Waterskiing, 83–84
Water sports, xxxi, 83–84,
154, 181–182, 191
Weather information, xxxviii
Web sites, xix, xxxvii
Whales, 153

White-water rafting, xxxi,
10–11
Central Pacific Costa Rica,
130
Central Valley, 57
Northern Guanacaste and
Alajuela, 70
Panama, 187
San José, 33
Southern Pacific Costa Rica,
143, 152
Wildlife refuges
Barra del Colorado Wildlife
Refuge, 172–173, 226–227
Cabo Blanco Strict Nature
Reserve, 98
Caño Negro Wildlife Refuge,
71, 219–220
Centro Biológico Las
Quebradas, 142
Curú National Wildlife
Refuge, 96
Gandoca-Manzanillo National
Wildlife Refuge, 181–182,
226
Golfito National Wildlllife
Refuge, 148
Isla Bolaños, 83
La Selva Biological Station,
167
Los Quetzales, 196
Ostional National Wildlife
Refuge, 104
private nature preserves, 139,
166–167, 196
Rara Avis, 166–167
Reserva Biológica Carara,
124–125, 222–223
Reserva Biológica Hitoy
Cerere, 182
Reserva Biológica Lomas
Barbudal, 98–99, 221
Reserva La Biósfera La
Amistad, 146, 147
Wilson Botanical Gardens,
146
Windsurfing, xxxi, 11, 63,
74, 83

Z

Zarcero, 66–67
Zoo Ave (bird zoo), 47
Zoos, 22–23, 47, 129
Zurqui ranger station, 165

NOTES

Looking for a different kind of vacation?

Fodor's makes it easy with a full line of specialty guidebooks to suit a variety of interests—from adventure to romance to language help.

L@@king
© FOR A
great place to go?

We know just the place. In fact, it attracts more than 125,000 visitors a day, making it one of the world's most popular travel destinations. It's previewtravel.com, the Web's comprehensive resource for travelers. It gives you access to over 500 airlines, 25,000 hotels, rental cars, cruises, vacation packages and support from travel experts 24 hours a day. Plus great information from Fodor's travel guides and travelers just like you. All of which makes previewtravel.com quite a find.

Preview Travel has everything you need to plan & book your next trip.

air, car & hotel reservations

vacation packages & cruises

destination planning & travel tips

24-hour customer service

previewtravel.com

preview travel℠

aol keyword: previewtravel
www.previewtravel.com